The Romance of Transgression in Canada

THE ROMANCE OF TRANSGRESSION IN CANADA

Queering
Sexualities
Nations
Cinemas

THOMAS WAUGH

Foreword by Bruce LaBruce

McGILL-QUEEN'S UNIVERSITY PRESS
Montreal & Kingston · London · Ithaca

ISBN-13: 978-0-7735-3069-0   ISBN-10: 0-7735-3069-X (cloth)
ISBN-13: 978-0-7735-3146-8   ISBN-10: 0-7735-3146-7 (paper)

Legal deposit third quarter 2006
Bibliothèque nationale du Québec

Printed in Canada on acid-free paper.

This book has been published with the help of a grant from the
Canadian Federation for the Humanities and Social Sciences,
through the Aid to Scholarly Publications Programme, using funds
provided by the Social Sciences and Humanities Research Council
of Canada. Funding has also been received from Concordia
University, Faculty of Fine Arts and Office of the President.

McGill-Queen's University Press acknowledges the support of the
Canada Council for the Arts for our publishing program. We also
acknowledge the financial support of the Government of Canada
through the Book Publishing Industry Development Program
(BPIDP) for our publishing activities.

Library and Archives Canada Cataloguing in Publication

Waugh, Thomas, 1948–
The romance of transgression in Canada : queering sexualities,
nations, cinemas / Thomas Waugh.

Includes bibliographical references and index.
ISBN-13: 978-0-7735-3069-0   ISBN-10: 0-7735-3069-X (bnd)
ISBN-13: 978-0-7735-3146-8   ISBN-10: 0-7735-3146-7 (pbk)

1. Homosexuality in motion pictures. 2. Gays–In motion pictures.
3. Motion pictures–Canada–History and criticism. I. Title.

PN1995.9.H55W39 2006   791.43'653   C2006-900852-3

This book was designed and typeset by studio oneonone
in Sabon 10/12.8

For John, with love
Hoist it like a flag for all to see

Contents

Illustrations

Foreword

When Tom Waugh asked me to write a foreword to his new book, *The Romance of Transgression in Canada: Queering Sexualities, Nations, Cinemas*, my first response was, who, me? After all, as his book amply points out, I am an outsider in a band of outsiders, a character on the margins of the marginalized, an ancillary fairy. What insight could I possibly contribute from the drama of my exile? But once I dove into this remarkably deep and thorough work, I began to realize that in some ways I could be its poster child. For you see, Tom's tome is not merely a bold step toward redressing the historical neglect of a disenfranchised cinematic minority. It's about a whole spectrum of minorities that have been marginalized within a realm that is itself marginal: Canada. That is something I can certainly relate to. For as I've learned on my extensive international Gulliverian travels (bondage imagery intended), to be gay (or lesbian or transgendered or intersexed or intertextual or any of the other vast array of peregrinations from the ho hum, humdrum orthodoxy of heterosexuality) and Canadian is to be doubly queered. In fact, I can easily argue, and frequently do, that Canada is itself a queer state, not only as the fey, red-headed stepchild of our lumbering, macho-patriarchal neighbour to the south but as the repository of all things sissified: our socialized medicine and strong history of socialist policies in general (always a sign of weakness, if not downright limp-wristedness), our various attempts to decriminalize marijuana and legalize gay marriage (reliable political signifiers of the soft and the swishy – let's not even get into softwood lumber!); our image as international "peacekeepers" as opposed to unilateralist

war-mongers (surely only the boast of a milquetoast), our dependence on
government institutions and funding (beware of those smothering mothers!), even, or perhaps especially, our predilection for figureskaters, curling
(men with brooms indeed!), kilts, quilts, and a suspicious dedication to
the House of Windsor.

(Please don't take it personally. I wrote a similar piece for a French
academic journal, arguing that France is, by definition, queer. In fact, as
a character in one of my highly marginalized movies says, "The whole
goddamn world's a fag. Don't you realize it even yet?")

While I was overcoming my initial hesitation, another one popped up.
As a recovering academic, would I even be able to negotiate the sometimes
choppy waters of such a diligently researched, intellectually vigorous, and
staunchly theoretical work? Once I hopped on board, however, my faggoty
fears were allayed. As Mr Waugh himself points out, the style of his book,
which he refers to as "mock-pedantic" and which is borrowed from the
tone of narration archly used in a 1952 NFB documentary called *The
Romance of Transportation in Canada*, somehow drew me into the maelstrom without drowning me, allowing me to float giddily through the
more difficult passages on a raft of gentle irony. God knows that a return
to a more intellectual agenda within the GLBTLMNOP community is long
overdue (I never thought I'd wax nostalgic for *The Body Politic!*), and
Mr Waugh, not unlike his antecedent Evelyn, manages it with a nimble
wit and a good dose of personal style.

And, at the risk of extending a metaphor, what a cruise down the river
of cinematic queerness it is! Mr Waugh deftly slaloms from one abstruse
subject to the next: from a cluster of Quebecois male hunting features to
a survey of regional and national subtextually homosexual hockey movies
to the iconography of toilet sex in queer Canadian works over the last
twenty-five years ... One could almost get seasick if not for the steady
hand of the captain at the helm. It doesn't hurt that the author was born
and raised in Ontario but has spent half his life living in Quebec, providing
him with the unique opportunity to paddle assuredly across the often
turbulent and unforgiving white waters between Anglo- and francophone
Canadian cinemas.

Okay, enough with the nautical imagery already. Let me conclude,
before I dry off, by reiterating how impressed I am by the encyclopedic
breadth and investigative depth of Mr Waugh's book. From psychoanalytic
theory to regional and national politics to issues of colonial and postcolonial identity to personal anecdotes and rants against the lumbering
institutions that sometimes clumsily manhandle the delicate sensibilities
of "queered" artists and film-makers (are you listening NFB and Telefilm?),

this heartfelt work literally says all that needs to be said about, as Rodgers and Hart would have it, the "queer romance" of cinematic transgression. And I'm not saying that just because he calls a sex scene from my first feature film, *No Skin off My Ass*, "the hottest scene in world film history." How can one resist an author with such manifestly impeccable taste?

BRUCE LABRUCE
Toronto, 2005

Acknowledgments

Like many books about community and culture, especially in the nonprofit Canadian network, *The Romance of Transgression in Canada* would not have been possible without the support and contributions of hundreds of scholars, artists, arts professionals, institutions and agencies, and other accomplices. To the following individuals and institutions, I offer my heartfelt thanks.

For intellectual comradeship, consultation, and collaboration: José Arroyo, Peter Dickinson, Richard Dyer, Evergon, Jane Gaines, Louis Goyette, Marcus Skidley Greatheart, Jason Garrison, Matthew Hays, Ross Higgins, Magnus Isacsson, Saleem Kidwai, Steve Kokker, Brenda Longfellow, Chantal Nadeau, R. Raj Rao, and Eric Savoy. For research assistance: Jean-Martin Casséus, Stevie Dam, Jon Davies, Alison Davis, Neil Dideles, Marie-Pier Gendron, Timothy Lawrence, Friedrich Mayr, Christine Harkness, Randal Rogers, Leanne Ashworth, Ronald Rose-Antoinette, and Aidan St Martin, and with gratitude for her exceptional commitment and knack, Lisa Fotheringham.

To the following film and video people for their generous help: Hana Abdul, Norma Bailey, Tanya Ballantyne Tree, Maureen Bradley, Richard Comeau, Jeanne Crépeau, Emily Cummins, Thirza Cuthand, Shawna Dempsey, Martin Duckworth, Jeff Erbach, Andy Fabo, Richard Fung, Anne Golden, Noam Gonick, John Greyson, Mike Hoolboom, Rodrigue Jean, Patricia Kearns, Kevin Kelly, Peter Kingstone, Kathryn Klassen, Bruce LaBruce, Yves Lafontaine, Jean-Denis Lapointe, Steve Lawson and Aaron Pollard, Patrick Loubert, Liz MacDougall, James MacSwain,

Barbara Mainguy, David McIntosh, Ormond McKague, Wrik Mead, Roy Mitchell, Michelle Mohabeer, Jean-François Monette, Moze Mossanen, Terre Nash, Joan Nicks, Angela Phong, Pam Pike, Phillip Pike, Éric Rancourt, Cynthia Roberts and Greg Klymkiw, Gerry Rogers, Mirha-Soleil Ross, Bernard Rousseau, Shawn Selway and James Aquila, Bashar Shbib, Nik Sheehan, Atif Siddiqi, Kim Simard, Moira Simpson, Liz Singer, Scott Smith, Nico Stagias, Lisa Steele and Kim Tomczak, Harry Sutherland, Shannon Taylor, José Torrealba, Ziad Touma, Deb VanSlet, Ann Verrall, Clement Virgo, Margaret Wescott, and many, many others to whom I apologize for overlooking their indispensable support.

To the following festival organizers, distribution and research people, and festivals and production and research institutions for their generous assistance: Chris Adkins, Michael Barrett, Anne Golden, Kathleen Mullen, Katharine Setzer and Charlie Boudreau, Sylvia Jonescu Lisitza of Moving Images, Cazzo Films, Lauren Howes of Video In, Daniel Cockburn and Wanda Vanderstoop of Vtape, Jeff Crawford and Deirdre Logue of CFMDC, Anne Golden of Groupe intervention vidéo, Annie Tellier and Denis Vaillancourt of Vidéographe, Lorraine Leblanc and Pierre Jutras of the Cinémathèque québécoise, Richard Bradley and Marcel Raymond of the Archives gaies du Québec, the Toronto Film Reference Library, James Quandt of Cinematheque Ontario, Alethea Lahofer of Video Pool, reelout queer film + video festival (Kingston); Sally Bochner, Peter Kallianiotis, Bernard Lutz, Germaine Wong, Claude Lord, and Moira Keigher of the National Film Board of Canada, and the National Archives of Canada.

For early support for the publication of portions of this book, Janick Aubergers, Robert Ballantyne, Colette St-Hilaire, Richard Cavell, Bruno Cornellier, Terry Gold, Helen Lee, Christie Milliken, Richard Morrison, Jean Antonin Billard, William Wees, Jerry White, Wyndham Wise, and Patty Zimmermann. For immeasurable support in the last lap of publication, Ron Curtis, Jonathan Crago, Peter Dickinson, David LeBlanc, Brenda Longfellow, Susanne McAdam, Joan McGilvray, and Aurèle Parisien. And to the following publishers for authorization to revise and update embryonic portions of this book that first appeared under their imprint: Arsenal Pulp Press, Canadian Journal of Film Studies, *Conjonctures Nouvelles vues sur le cinéma québécois*, *The Spectator*, *Take One*, the University of Alberta Press, the University of Toronto Press, and *Wide Angle*.

For research and publication funding, to the Social Sciences and Humanities Research Council of Canada, and the Canada Council, and Fonds pour la formation de chercheurs et l'aide à la recherche (Québec), and to Concordia University, above all to the Mel Hoppenheim School of Cinema, the Faculty of Fine Arts (thanks to Deans Christopher Jackson and Catherine Wild, and Associate Deans Brian Foss, Ana Cappelluto and Liselyn Adams), and Presidents Frederick Lowy and Claude Lajeunesse.

Reader's Guide

Names of artists and entities featured in part 2 appear in small capital letters at their first appearance and and periodically thereafter. A title of film
or videotape is followed at its first appearance by its date, as well as its
running time, if available (rounded off, in minutes). This space is too limited and the film and video data to complex to provide distributor information or precise original format. Fortunately, the catalogues of the principal
distributors of nonfeature films and videos are easily accessible online:
CFMDC (Toronto); Centre for Art Tapes (Halifax); Group intervention
vidéo (Montreal); Moving Images Distribution (Vancouver); National Film
Board of Canada (Montreal); Video Out (Vancouver); Video Pool (Winnipeg); Vidéographe (Montreal); VTape (Toronto). Citations from French-
language sources are translations of the author unless otherwise indicated.

ACRONYMS AND ABBREVIATIONS

CBC | Canadian Broadcasting Corporation
CFC | Canadian Film Centre (Toronto)
CFDC | Canadian Film Development Corporation
CFMDC | Canadian Filmmakers Distribution Centre (Toronto)
cr | "Consciousness raising" (documentary film genre)
DIY | "do it yourself" (filmmaking practice)
DLGQ | Diffusions lesbiennes et gaies du Québec
ECIAD | Emily Carr Institue of Art and Design (Vancouver)
GIV | Groupe intervention vidéo (Montreal)

Image + Nation | Festival international de cinéma lesbien, gay,
   bisexuel, transexuel & travesti de Montréal
Inside Out | Lesbian and Gay Film and Video Festival of Toronto
LIFT | Liaison of Independent Filmmakers of Toronto
MTF | male-to-female [transsexual], cf. FTM
NTS | National Theatre School
NFB | National Film Board of Canada
NSCAD | Nova Scotia College of Art and Design (Halifax)
OCAD | Ontario College of Art and Design
OISE | Ontario Institute for Studies in Education (Toronto)
Out on Screen | Vancouver Queer Film and Video Festival
PFLAG | Parents and Friends of Lesbians and gays (organization)
PQ | Parti québécois (sovereigntist political party)
PSA | public service announcement
PWA | person living with HIV/AIDS
pure laine | Québécois individuals descended from original French settlers
   of New France (literally, "pure wool")
ROC | rest of Canada (jocular Quebec-centric expression)
SFU | Simon Fraser University (Vancouver)
SODEC | Société pour le développement des entreprises culturelles
   (Quebec arts funding agency)
TBP | *The Body Politic* (Toronto newspaper, 1971–87)
TIFF | Toronto International Film Festival
TVO | TV Ontario
U. de M. | Université de Montréal
U. of T. | University of Toronto
UBC | University of British Columbia (Vancouver)
UNB | University of New Brunswick
UQAM | Université du Québec à Montréal
UWO | University of Western Ontario

PART ONE

Ten Episodes

1

How to Queer Sexualities, Nations, and Cinemas, or The Romance (and Paradoxes) of Transgression in Canada and Elsewhere

OF CITIES AND AMBASSADORS

The Romance of Transgression in Canada is a book about queer Canadian film and video – its texts, contexts, makers, and audience. But as I write this introduction at the end, rather than the beginning, of this epic process, I am far from Canada, holed up in the Indian Ocean megalopolis of Chennai. This is an odd place, one might think, from which to reflect on the relativities and peripeteias of transgression and romance in general and Canadian queer cinemas in particular. Yet it seems right, and not only because the maitre d' at the South Indian fast-food palace Saravanbhavan last night invited me to their new branch, just opened in Mississauga. Yes, the planet is shrinking, and globalized markets and diasporas are competing with the anchored senses of national place that (allegedly) once defined national cultures. And there's no better place than an Indian metropolis to think about sexualities, national feelings, and cinemas.

Even here, in the mosaic of this sweltering Tamil port city, there is something that reminds me of the three Canadian port metropoles that take up the lion's share of the critical energy of this book. I am thinking not only of the cities' omnipresent vestiges of a recognizable Victorian colonial past and transformed toponymy (Chennai used to be Madras, of course, and Canada is not immune from tinkering with colonial traces – witness Pile of Bones, Saskatchewan; Berlin, Ontario; and Dorchester Boulevard, Quebec).[1] The reminders come also from the electric humidity and mystical potentiality swept in from the great bodies of water that brood alongside the cultural crossroads and harbour hinterlands of Chennai, Montreal, Toronto, and Vancouver. All resound (each in its own distinct way of course) with the undercurrents of transgression that traffic with the sea or the great lakes and rivers has traditionally fostered. Much of the electricity for me is erotic, of course, and the heat somehow accents the sensuous beauty of the Tamil men, with their fastidious pompadours, compulsory mustaches, graceful lungis (the long wrap-around skirts, whether half hoisted or in full sail – losing out to polyester slacks, sadly …), and the unself-conscious delicacy with which they dangle their fingers among those of their best friends as they wait for the bus or stroll along the waterfront. But my hotel seems to be the centre of the local wedding reception industry, and this is a vivid reminder of the commodified fabric of heteroconjugality that cannot be escaped – here or in Toronto.

Tamil movies, like other South Indian cinemas, as well as the Northern Hindi-language Bollywood, hinge on an idolatrous star system that is profoundly homosocial in its energies. The disproportionately male audiences fixate on (and often vote for, come election day) the male stars with a volatile mixture of identification and erotic fascination. No matter how much the films harp endlessly on the institution of marriage, this same-sex audience dynamic dominates (and I daresay a similar pattern prevails for female fans as well, though there is predictably less research on this).[2] On the screen, even the biggest, burliest and hairiest of Tamil screen heroes are light on their feet and are followed everywhere by a lineup of sweating chorus boys (on whom the camera never rests sufficiently for my taste) ready to gyrate at the drop of a cue. The movies' on-screen homosocial queerness matches the gender-segregated public space and cultures of Indian cities: intermale choreographies of friendship, tenderness, enmity, and combat, hanging out in public space, as well as, literally, of dance (the latter is an element sadly absent from the Canadian corpus soon to be engaged in this book, with isolated works by CAFFERY, GREYSON, MCLAREN and MOOTOO[3] providing some exceptions that prove the rule).

All of this came through yesterday at a screening of *Lord of the Rings: The Return of the King* I attended at an upscale multilingual multiplex that could almost have been in Montreal (except that I was with my pal Nagarajan, and here imports make up only a tiny fraction of the 95 percent market share they make up at home). I could not fail to notice how much the audience reception made the whole thing seem like just another Tamil movie, all those Oscars from halfway around the globe notwithstanding. Exultant whistles from the stalls greet the cuddly, childlike and asexual Frodo and Sam when the Hobbits are finally and tearfully reunited after so many ordeals and misunderstandings (here and there throughout the film, there was also a charged response to the perfunctory idealization of women, stuck in roles that have been minimized to almost irrelevant cameos). I could also not fail to notice a warm response from the almost all-male crowd to the proto-fascist political sentiments of the film (from the title on down to the *Triumph of the Will* crowd configurations of the climactic scenes) and remembered again how film fan cultures are intermixed with political cultures here, especially in these southernmost states. An election campaign is under way here, and the three-storey-high effigies of Jayalitha, the former screen starlet and now iron-willed chief minister, are everywhere. This redoubtable figure incidentally got her start in politics as the mistress of an earlier movie star populist chief minister, making the world outside the theatre oddly continuous with the coronation going on inside.

Yet somehow the even more radical discontinuity between the imaginary world of the air-conditioned theatre and the fetid and loud city outside overwhelmed me and brought me back to this book, which was waiting to be introduced, a book about a corpus of moving images that are also somehow cut off from their host culture and context. Obviously, the divergence between my Canadian corpus and the passionate and prolific Indian cinemas I reacquainted myself with on this trip couldn't be more blatant. For all the unspoken queernesses of this populist entertainment industry, it is a different kind of queerness from the identity-defined queerness that predominates in the works I am about to explore, so much so that comparisons seem futile, above all because the Indian cinemas are commercially viable and popular to their core. Our subsidized and perennially crisis-ridden film efforts are virtually defined by the absence of a commercially grounded and interactive audience that might guarantee their spontaneity, confidence, and accountability, but that commerciality and popularity paradoxically could both foster and brake their transgressiveness, as in India. Our Canadian cinemas (and videos) are defined, rather, by their artists, audiences, and stakeholders, by their longing *search* for some kind of impact and pop pertinence. At the same time, untrammelled by the conservative effect of box office so palpable in Hollywood and Bollywood, Canadian cinemas have been defined in the generations since World War II by a spiralling flirtation with the romantic possibilities of transgression.

Earlier on this trip to India, I had presented the work of a Canadian video artist, RICHARD FUNG, whom I judged to be a good ambassador of Canadian transgression to the South Asian cultural sphere. The Canadian studies conference in the North Indian desert capital of Jaipur, where I was speaking, was another kind of crossroads (funded by Ottawa, as is this book) where the traffic, this time in ideas and cross-cultural capital, was considerably more subdued. Here the conference's official theme of diversity scarcely touched on the themes of sexual diversity that back home seemed to constitute one of the decade's major themes. Only two papers out of dozens (other than my own plenary paper) touched on queer themes, and these considerations of lesbian writing were safely stowed in a feminist sidebar session. Both the Indians and the Canadians in attendance seemed to be oblivious to this. I had chosen Fung's *Sea in the Blood* as the focus of my talk (see chapter 9), knowing that however cosmopolitan this assemblage of middle-class intelligentsia would be, the Indian audience would respond well to Fung's melodramatic narrative of rupture and loss within a star-crossed, diasporic nuclear family – the formulaic theme, after all, of the hit Hindi film cycle of the last decade.

I also hoped the Jaipur crowd would be unsettled by the matter-of-factness of Fung's narrative of same-sex conjugality, which (as Fung could not even have imagined when he made the tape five years ago) was echoing the big news stories of 2003 and 2004: the legalization of same-sex marriage in Ontario and British Columbia and, finally, as I wind up my stay in Chennai, in my home province of Quebec. I was right. The response to Fung was lively, and yet although everyone was aware of the continuous headlines from Canada about same-sex marriage, something still didn't compute. The Indian academics had no trouble whatsoever dissecting the themes of Canadian writers from A to Z and relating them to their own cultural contexts, but this theme was gently excised from the landscape, as much by the Indian scholars as the foreign participants. A foreign English-speaking traveller over here often encounters representatives of the Indian middle classes who

Richard Fung exhales as he swims through partner Tim's legs in *Sea in the Blood* (2000): rosy-bubbled same-sex conjugality as ambassador of Canadian transgression. Frame grab. VTape

can be smug about the superiority of their own institution of marriage as a primarily endogamous social and economic alliance. Even the most pointed of my "coming-out" rituals in a crowded train compartment or a graduate-student tea break will still usually lead to anxious questions about my own marital status and children, as if marriage has nothing to do with sexuality. Which it doesn't ... and does ... all at the same time. Still, my experiment of presenting a taste of this book and the Canadian queer corpus to a nonimplicated trial audience was crucial. If nothing else, it reinforced for me the necessity of purging my own insider smugness, of regarding from the outside not only Fung but the entire body of lively and diverse work, passionate, fierce, and lucid, both hesitant and impetuous, brash and serene, whose encounter has sparked this book.

OF MARRIAGES AND QUEERNESSES

This book is about sexualities, nations, and cinemas, all three terms judiciously in the plural that befits the pluralism of our times and places. It is also about queer Canadian film and video, about queerness in Canadian film and video, about the queer compulsions towards transgression and its romance that have gripped Canadian cinemas and video corpuses since they emerged from the foundational decades of the 1950s and 1960s – ultimately it is about *queering* Canadian cinemas. Wrapping it up in India has helped me to interrogate at a distance my assumptions and axioms, methods and boundaries, to reexamine the premises of sexual and national identities and visual cultures – ours and others' – that underlie this book. Those charming, conniving Chennai drivers, with their honking rickshaws, movie star heroes, and unquestioned codes of familial allegiance have kept me alert to the relativity of the cultural priorities inhering in films and videotapes, artists and audiences and have reminded me to factor in the oddities, volatilities, and blockages in their cross-cultural transmigration. Recovering from the writing of this book over here, where it is cricket that is the compulsory rite of male socialization, and not what Indians call *ice* hockey (see chapter 7), has given me the delicious distance to put into relief the interconnected corpuses of easily two thousand films and tapes I viewed for the writing of this book. Rickshaws and cricket have tuned me into the distinctiveness and coherence of their negotiation of sexual identities and national belongings – or lack thereof.

In this culture, where marriage is enthroned as the denouement of every narrative, Western-style queerness is all but invisible (except in some pockets in this and a half dozen other metropoles and of course in cyberspace, where it is out of control ...). Yet other queernesses, that is, instances of "incoherences in the allegedly stable relations between chromosomal sex, gender and sexual desire," to borrow Annamarie Jagose's fine definition, are everywhere (1996, 3). As just one example, one of the features of this otherwise depressing ongoing election here is that *hijras*, that cult-like minority community of sex/gender outlaws often called "eunuchs" (a very unsatisfactory Indian English moniker), are for the first time getting on the very electoral rolls that had previously banned all gender ambiguity. This breakthrough is thanks in part to high court decision making that seems eerily similar to the decisions back home that brought Canadians same-sex marriage last year.

Transgression seems to travel well, and I will never forget my surprise at the Mumbai Film Festival two years earlier when ATIF SIDDIQI had presented what I thought to be his very masculinity-subversive *M! Mom, Madonna and Me* (2001), only to be swarmed afterwards by adoring male fans. Accordingly, the Siddiqi revelation and the Fung experiment have also, paradoxically, reinforced my sense of these queer Canadian works' universality, as implied in my evasive and over-generalized subtitle, *Queering Sexualities, Nations, Cinemas*. Our respective national traffics in transgression connect on many levels, and the parallels between those burly male chorus lines bucking across the screens of Chennai and Fung's sober yet sensuous underwater choreography in Ontario remain an open issue.

SEXUALITIES

My subtitle says much but does not say it all. *Canadian Queer Cinemas and Videos*, my unspoken sub-subtitle, had been used as a working title, perfect shorthand to explain to collaborators and subjects what I was *really* doing. But I passed over this shorthand title for the final format, with its fashionable notion of *queering*, because I had hesitations about the ghettoized feel of "queer." I wanted to refuse any admission or implication that a book about Canadian queer moving images was not above all by definition about *all* Canadian moving images across the board. It may be a truism that the peripheries define the centre, but in this case, as I will try to demonstrate, it couldn't be truer. With this in mind, the prevailing sense of "queer" I have used throughout the book, as inconsistently as Jagose's definition allows, is as a continuum, a spectrum encompassing both a fixed sense of queerness as a grid – a network of discrete sexual identities, social constituencies, and strategic political agendas with a cultural canon belonging to them through historical accident and active construction – and a fluid sense of queerness as a "zone of possibilities" troubling the traditional configuration of gender and sexual identities (Jagose 1996, 3). This latter queer fluidity is inextricable from, as Eve Kosofsky Sedgwick once put it (1990, 2), a "long crisis of modern sexual definition," that is, "the potent incoherences of homo/heterosexual definition [that have left] no space in the culture exempt" and "the centrality of this nominally marginal, conceptually intractable set of definitional issues to the important knowledges and understandings of twentieth-century Western culture as a whole."

Peter Dickinson's sense of queer is also useful (1999, 4, 5), doing masterfully for literary corpuses in Canada what I hope to be able to accomplish for our cinemas, encountering a "textual *superabundance* of a destabilizing and counter-normative sexuality" that traditional criticism had refused to "come to grips with." Shifting perspective slightly, my sense of queer sets up a spectrum of cinemas encompassing, on the one extreme, homoerotic work defined by explicit vantage points of sexual minorities and marginalities and then, not far off, a group of works that have been appropriated as queer through rereadings and recirculations, thanks to their textual or contextual status as utterances from within the individual or collective closet. Further along the continuum there follow gradations of homosocial narratives embodying increasing entanglements with the sex in same-sex relations – either affirmations or symptomatic repudiations or both. For example, a cluster of Québécois male hunting features discussed in chapters 7 and 8 belong more or less to what I call the getting-away-from-it-all "boys in the bush" genre, namely, *La bête lumineuse* (Pierre Perrault, 1982) and *Un zoo la nuit* (Jean-Claude Lauzon, 1987) – and *Les mâles* (Gilles Carle, 1971) and *Visage pâle* (Claude Gagnon, 1985) could serve just as well. These films are impeccably heterosexual in provenance and no doubt in intent but are all similarly and resolutely queer in the intensity of their obsessive denials of, and confrontations with, the spectrum between homosociality and homosexuality, as very queer as they are very incoherent. In this sense, I push my sense of queer beyond Dickinson's notion of "counter-normativity," since for all their "queerness," these Quebec features and a dozen other films of their ilk hardly go against the grain of heteronormativity. In other words, if my basic premise of "Canadian queer cinemas and videos" seems to stem from my first sense of "queer," feeling like a minoritizing conception and practice of sexual identity that Sedgwick goes on to evoke (1990, 82–6), I am also holding on to her "universalizing" conception of queer at the same time. I am sort of having my cake and eating it too. This second, universalizing sense of queerness as a zone of trouble and definitional crisis is applied by Dickinson (1999, 5): "queer as a literary-critical category of an almost inevitable definitional elasticity, one whose inventory of sexual meanings has yet to be exhausted, challenges and upsets certain received national orthodoxies of writing in Canada." As such it potentially sheds light on cultural corpuses far beyond any restricted sense of a queer cinema shaped by the first minoritizing sense of queerness.

In maintaining this double sense of queer, I shall not only be trying to upset orthodoxies, queering all inherited canons. I shall also be tackling the down-to-earth task of reinvigorating the queer canon, however minoritizing it is, that is, the gated cultural enclave often defined de facto by the queer community festivals from coast to coast and strategically constructed by this book as well. This canonical universe has its own internal coherence and boundaries to which an artist and a work either do or don't belong. This is the canon that has sustained community through several decades of Anita Bryants, Clause 28s, Butler Decisions, Julian Fantinos, sex panics, and a pandemic to boot and that continues to be refreshed each festival season. It's all very relative and relativist, yes, but difficult as the task is, this book's mandate is to weigh the specificities of the self-defining identity microconstituencies, political and cultural, that have attached themselves to the 1970s proto-queer moniker "lesbian and gay." The letters continue to proliferate in the alphabet soup in the drive towards the ultimate inclusivity in the new century. In fact, why not consider BLLAGTITTISQQ as an at last pronounceable acronym: bisexual, lesbian, leather, asexual/celibate, gay, transsexual, intersex, transgendered, two-spirited, intergenerational, sex-worker, questioning, queer ... Have I left you out? Each of the letters in the soup has its long and distinctive history both before and after Omnibus/Stonewall, both on-screen and off.[4] Our festivals and media are fervent and unequivocal about the mandate to enfranchise these micro-constituencies, and this book is in many ways about their artistic articulations. Accordingly, "queer" finally and inevitably ends up being used in this book, as elsewhere, as a convenient shorthand umbrella term to gracefully bypass tongue-twisting acronyms and promote strategic coalition and affiliative affinities at the same time.

Transgender voices are sometimes the most articulate in challenging the invisibility abetted by such coalitional shorthand, as demonstrated by the research and publications of Viviane Namaste (2000, 2005) in relation in particular to the history of cinematic and other cultural representations of transsexual and transgendered bodies and identities, particularly in Quebec. Toronto's shortlived transgendered film and video festival, active for as many as five years beginning in 1998 (see COUNTING PAST TWO), and numerous curating efforts at the larger Canadian GLBT festivals are equally eloquent of this particular assertion of community and do not necessarily always aspire to a place under the larger BLLAGTITTISQQ umbrella. The continuity and historical roots of this assertion in relation to moving images is clearly a subject for further research, as evidenced by anonymous fragments of the past that occasionally surface. For example, a fifteen-minute anonymous video document of a trans meeting and survival stories from 1972 entitled *Trans-sexual Lifestyle* was rediscovered by Vancouver's Out on Screen festival in 2003 (see also HALLIS).

If sexworker can also be considered a queer identity and if festivals, even when short-lived, are a reliable gage of community and identity aspirations, one might consider the global sprinkling of sexwork media festivals, which has included Toronto at least once in its trajectory, as another case in point. As for bisexuality as an identity, this may be the category that historically has come up short in this book and in the community festival network, as well as in explicit community claims. Whether this short shrift in terms of artistic voice is a function of lingering stigma attached to bisexuality by both queer and straight cultures or simply a reflection of social practice and community formation or the personal places of artists, it cannot be denied that bisexuality as a pragmatic or erotic practice or de facto life path is everywhere – in this book as it is in life – gender-inflected like everything else, from CLAUDE JUTRA's *À tout prendre* (1963) to PATRICIA ROZEMA's *When Night is Falling* (1995).

Any pressure to recognize a symmetrical or parallel identity constituency and cultural canon for transsexuals or sexworkers or bisexuals or for certain other groups defined by a letter in BLLAGTITTISQQ would be precarious from the outset: minority communities and cultures are all unique and constituted differently in every case – all the more so when incarnated on the screen. That said, it is tempting to add a P to the alphabet acronym for the fringe of remaining perversions, what Gayle Rubin calls "outer limits" sexual identities and practices, whose voices emerge either on-screen or behind the camera in the spectrum of works confronted in this book, from HIV infection to bug-chasing to pornography to toilet sex and "john" identities, plus the numerous fetishes around which micro-identities have been constituted partially and unevenly. The constitution of queer communities has fluctuated over the years, reflecting the volatility of the ideological regimes that decide from one era to the next where the line is drawn, to use Rubin's formulation, between "good ... Normal, Natural, Healthy, Holy" sex and "Bad ... Abnormal, Unnatural, Sick Sinful, 'Way Out'" sex ([1982], 1993). Such communities can never by definition be stable or fixed. The censorship of mere *discussion* of the more outer of these "outer limits," especially of intergenerational sexuality – whether applied structurally through self-policing mechanisms developed by publishers, academics like myself, and community festivals, or enshrined in the Criminal Code (as may well happen as we go to press) – does not, as they say, contribute to either knowledge or community.

NATIONS

In laying out the framework of national identities and communities that are implied in both my title and my subtitle, I also follow Dickinson (1999). His scope of "the affiliative spaces of Canadian, Québécois, and First Nations literatures" allows an exemplary model of political neutrality, as well as scholarly accuracy in relation to fairly autonomous corpuses within the political entity we live in north of the forty-ninth parallel. A renegade Westmounter educated in Toronto and settled in Vancouver, Dickinson's strategic deployment of multiple senses of a three-sectored "Canada" and "Canadian" subverts the centralizing and totalizing presumption, anglocentric or even Toronto-centric, that has plagued so much cultural criticism here. And this negative presumption ranges from the book *Mondo Canuck: A Canadian Pop Culture Odyssey* (Pevere and Dymond, 1996) to the magazine *Take One: Film and Television in Canada* to the so-called Academy of Canadian Cinema and Television (the "Genies").

As a Québécois by adoption for what has now been more than half my life and as the survivor of two referenda, I can hardly do otherwise than to follow Dickinson's (1999) example. A regional and cultural neutrality – and passionately partisan local commitment – is all the more apt since moving images are different from literature in their industrial infrastructure and funding apparatus. Thus, an even stronger sense of multiple regional/cultural centres emerges in this book than in Dickinson's. In fact there is much to be said for a view of Canadian cinemas as a matrix of three metropolitan sub-cinemas situated in Montreal, Toronto, and Vancouver, without denying the lights of the regional arts hinterlands of Atlantic Canada and the Prairies flickering on and off in their shadow. I make the argument in chapter 4 that the founding energies of Canadian cinemas in the sixties and seventies were resolutely urban reflections of the two metropolitan cultural crucibles of the day, Montreal and Toronto, a factor underappreciated in Canadian film historiographies. I have also insisted in this book on a balanced apprehension of the English- and French-language cinemas in these two "founding" centres, profiting from my advantage as a bilingual Anglo-Quebecker and developing what I hope my readers will find is a rich and detailed insider canvas of both, separately and in (sometimes unidirectional) relation to each other.

This balance may well be unprecedented in Canadian film studies, a discipline that has hitherto been shaped by the two solitudes that seldom speak to each other. Here I take the opportunity to pay full respect to the undeniable distinctiveness of the Quebec cinematic imaginary, a distinctiveness that has been consistently downplayed by Torontonian critics, curators, and scholars for generations (but that, paradoxically, federal institutions such as

Camille deserting her male fiancé in *When Night is Falling* (Patricia Rozema, 1995): bisexuality less as a cinematic identity than as a life path. Production still, VOS Productions Ltd.

Telefilm Canada, the NFB and the CBC/Radio-Canada all assume unquestioningly). Approximately one-third of my entries in the Portrait Gallery in part two of this book are devoted to Quebeckers, and the remaining two-thirds to the ROC (depending on how the cohorts of queer migrants are counted ...). I have at the same time attempted to reflect the "other" regional cinematic cultures that have emerged, whether with the (intermittent) support of provincial funding bodies or of National Film Board branchplants or thanks to lively local arts scenes bolstered by funding from the Canada Council for the Arts, most conspicuously in Winnipeg and Halifax.

By the same token, First Nations queer moving-image work does not seem to have the discreteness that there arguably is with its literary cousins, as is so evident in Dickinson's book: although my portrait gallery includes listings for EVAN ADAMS, CLINT ALBERTA, MARJORIE BEAUCAGE, THIRZA CUTHAND, ADAM GARNET JONES, ZACHERY LONGBOY, GAIL MAURICE, KENT MONKMAN, and no doubt others, I don't come away from this research with a strong sense of a coherent two-spirited or aboriginal queer corpus (though the fact that there's a Prairie connection with almost every one of these folks, however dispersed they ended up, hints that there might be a topic here for further research). Similarly, I did not see fit to include a separate chapter or chapters on moving-image production by or about people of colour, despite Dickinson's challengingly rationalized and excellent chapter that does exactly that for literature. I ultimately decided that works shaped by a politics and culture of racial/ethno-cultural difference must be integrated into my chronological essays, rather than airlifted out of them, while my portrait gallery would endeavour to do justice to makers and works belonging to black, Asian, Latino, or other traditions, cultures or iconographies. This decision implies some criticism of "multicultural" approaches to factoring in diversity through separate parcels, rather than integrated dialogue, and the criticism that my policy is certain, in turn, to engage is welcome. It is delicate work, this special handling of alterity in a book about alterity. In short, Canadian cultures, queer or queered, cinematic or otherwise, are agglomerations of "differences," of ethno-cultural and regional cultural practices, or "micro-cinemas," as Lee Parpart has put it in a slightly different context (2001, 174). These micro-cinemas have been inflected, as it will be repeatedly stressed, not only by cultural, creative, and textual realities, but also by everything from funding protocols to local educational resources (who could deny the indispensable role Nova Scotia College of Art and Design has played in developing regional Maritime moving image culture?), from local censorship practices to exhibition and broadcast patterns, even to climate. And I have done my best not only to reflect this diversity but to engage it.

CINEMAS

I am using the third term of my subtitle, "cinemas" (with apologies to video nationalists), as an umbrella terms for "moving images," standard shorthand within film, media, and visual studies disciplines and institutions, in Canada as elsewhere. Following the insistence of my publisher, I hope "cinemas" will connote both a vision and a mandate that encompasses cinema, video, and television, this in an digitalized era when the three once distinct and autonomous formats and cultures are increasingly integrated – artistically, infrastructurally, and above all technically. The term "cinemas" admittedly bandages over lingering gulfs between the three universes constituted around these traditional formats, universes whose discourses traditionally have viewed each other with obliviousness, if not disdain, but that are becoming increasingly difficult for lay audiences to tell apart. This is especially true at the community queer festivals where *Queer as Folk* episodes, video wizard STEVE REINKE, and celluloid-centred films like ANNE WHEELER's *Better than Chocolate* can sometimes appear in the same theatre on the same day. Almost no one in the audience apparently worries about the difference, even if they are aware of it, and I suspect many are not. Historically things were different, and I have tried to reflect the autonomy of the three media as they evolved beginning in the 1950s and 1960s until this autonomy was gradually attenuated in subsequent decades.

It has been especially critical for me to bring the once-distinct worlds of art video and cinema together in the same volume (as they are not only in queer festivals but also increasingly in institutional setups from the Canada Council for the Arts on down the cultural ladder). Both universes were traditionally endogamous, and video art, in particular beginning in the 1970s, tended to be hermetic in its claims to separate infrastructures and electronic aesthetics – low-budget but high-cultural capital – identifying more with the rarefied gallery circuit than with the rabble at the cineplexes and film festivals. More than macho film culture, the video world tended to be resolutely queer queer queer: of the twelve winners of the Bell Canada Award for Outstanding Achievement in Video Art from the award's launch in 1991 to 2003, fully half the individuals or teams have been outspoken queer artists featured prominently in this book, while two other winners of the heterosexual persuasion are also featured for their commitment to queer thematics. If this book can be considered a critique of the insularities of both film and video networks, the once insurmountable chasm between them is still reflected in some institutional configurations and personal sensibilities (PAUL WONG and ANNE WHEELER may have worked in the same city, but never in the same solar system; Toronto, like many other centres, has separate film and video distribution outfits; and at my home institution of Concordia University's Faculty of Fine Arts, the film and video programs are bewilderingly still separate, long after the technological base for either has stopped being distinct). But the chasm is something no one can afford anymore: JOHN GREYSON, in his flitting back and forth between no-budget film-pumped art video, video-inflected 35mm celluloid features, and hybrid television documentaries, has long since served as an exemplary model, with artists as diverse as RODRIGUE JEAN and MIDI ONODERA following in his footsteps. Early on in the project I threw up my hands in exasperation and abandoned any consistent policy of rigorously specifying original formats for works (the majority of which I screened on video) as I attempted to provide scholarly references for them.

All this said, I have not been able to do full justice to the third universe, television, for want of resources and energy, not to mention support (the CBC archives are apparently so underfunded and oblivious to academia that staff cannot even answer or return telephone calls or email). Television is included in *The Romance of Transgression* only by the occasional factoring in of a K.D. LANG music video or a hockey movie-of-the-week in the essays in the body of the book. Although the portrait gallery takes up some of the slack with its encounters with figures from SCOTT THOMPSON to ANDRÉ MONTMORENCY, the short shrift I give television is admittedly an example of another personal bias, as well as a recognition of the impossibility of doing everything. I leave the development of an integrated history and analysis of queer television and televised queers in Canada as a challenge for a future researcher.

These gestures towards diversity and balance do not reveal the whole madness in my method. The plurals in my subtitle and working title also connote inclusion, thoroughness, and comprehensiveness. My insistence on inclusion may seem to imply a methodology that is ecstatically eclectic, catholic, and on-the-fence. Readers will note a frequent abstinence from evaluative judgment and a positivist pleasure in every work and category of work, often simply because it is there, despite everything. If my writing thus seems like a concatenation of descriptions of texts, this is because recognition and description are a necessary first step. Certainly close description is a legacy of film studies in the 1970s, which emphasized above all the materiality of the film text (in retrospect, those were the days before video archives did it for us). Now in a postmodern, "post-cinematic" context of lazy and sloppy image saturation and amnesia, cultural studies has perhaps moved too far away from textual analysis, and we need to come back to a concentration on the denseness of the work, not as an example or an illustration of broader social or cultural currents, but as a *player* in them. And dense description is all the more urgent in the present Canadian context of the invisibility of our moving-image cultures. In the here and now, my sometimes exhaustive focus on films and tapes, at the risk of overwhelming the reader, is a reparative, therapeutic tactic as well. If it seems like a contradiction to apprehend typographically this wealth of audiovisual works (I am contractually limited to about one hundred film stills and video frames, for reasons of cost), so be it – pending the CD-Rom version of the book that I have been fantasizing about.

One exhaustiveness requires another. Here I also bring together the whole spectrum of image regimes, all the layers of the cultural hierarchy from popular narrative (to the extent that popular visual culture is permitted in English Canada) to auteur-based art cinema to the minimalist avant-garde, from radical documentary to pornography. I respect and even *like* everything. I really really do. (With some exceptions.) Lest this be mistaken for an approach that disdains or avoids theory, on the contrary it is rigorously thus, defiantly materialist in its anchor in the text, in the diverse Canadian context of moving-image culture and politics, and in the primacy of the reader as potential consumer and negotiator of moving-image texts that are both here and queer.

Although my secret passions are not so secret and shine through at every turn, I try otherwise to be scrupulously neutral in finding merit and interest in the entire landscape of cultural production – from the complicitly populist blockbuster to pretentious or ascetic esoterica. There is as much to be gained in establishing a conversation among different formats and textual and demographic worlds as there is in setting up metaphysical grids. Let copulation thrive! While respecting the range of aesthetic and cultural baggage of every format and subculture and rung on the cultural hierarchy, I insist on a certain irreverence at the same time, never hesitating to call works to task for blind spots, ideological or otherwise. This may all seem like positivist fence-sitting and indiscriminately eclectic packrat collecting, but it may be the teacher in me that wants to let a hundred flowers bloom, an affirmation and apprehension of the rainbow spectrum of what has been and is being done here.

This strategy of rainbow inclusiveness is connected, of course, to the notion of "reinvigorating the canon" that I proposed earlier in this chapter. One radical art historian friend who read an earlier draft of this introduction was quite alarmed at the notion that anyone would want to do anything positive with a canon, let alone reinvigorate it. Inevitably canons have tended to coagulate on the queer Canadian scene over the years, particularly at the community festivals. But those same festivals, with their diversity initiatives and their youth support programs, have by and large taken the most steps at challenging and enriching the spectrum of works and artists that we get to know and want to return to repeatedly. Inevitably, in this book my own interests and biases have also enshrined certain works or tendencies over others. Yet in the present context of the overwhelming inaccessibility of queer Canadian work, there is little danger that my choices or the perennial favorites of the festivals are going to stultify and stagnate into the kind of canon in Canadian queer cinemas and videos that both art historians and film scholars have struggled against. We hardly have any Monets or Hitchcocks that cast their chilling shadow over the development of fluidity and diversity. Although some of the pioneers, such as COLIN CAMPBELL, are beginning to get their due, others, like HARRY SUTHERLAND, remain virtually unknown to the generations of the 1990s and 2000s. A book as comprehensive and encyclopedic as this will hopefully provide those generations with the choices and options to develop canons of their own – or to refuse them. My inclusive packrat practice – some might say exhaustive and exhausting – is a necessary first step, and a political one at that. Indeed, for me all the words in my titles, subtitles, and working title imply politics, and this book would be a failure if it was read as canon formation and not read and applied as a political manifesto around works, artists, images, and histories that demand our attention.

STRUCTURES

This book on queer Canadian cinema and videos *has* a structure and design, believe it or not (after this most subjective of introits about copulation and eclecticism). For my title I have appropriated the title of a legendary (to me at least) Canadian cartoon *The Romance of Transportation in Canada* (1952) by Colin Low, one of the straightest of our canon of filmmakers. I have appropriated as well that title's campy, mock-pedantic tone, which was given to it by Low's queer collaborator GUY GLOVER. Even back in 1952, the National Film Board (which turns out to be a major player in this book) was determined to move beyond its reputation as the producer of dry and sober didactic materials and implanted a rather campy spirit in its animated riff on the epic subject matter of portage canoes, corduroy roads, steamships, continental railways, and bush pilots. In this title choice, my intention is to honour the irreverence of this wonderful cartoon, as well as the absolute sobriety with which the NFB produced a work that was going to impart to generations of schoolchildren the absolute necessity of the topic of transportation for Canadians once and future (an appropriate topic for the year of Harold Innis's death). The cartoon starts with blasé First Nations communities greeting their rather foppish French guests and moves chronologically through four centuries and a coast-to-coast tapestry of landscapes to end in a Toronto traffic jam caused by a flying saucer.

I have more or less preserved the cartoon's sober historiographical mission – this book in your hands is a history after all, a didactic analysis of objects (films and videos) and players (makers, audiences) and their interconnections in their unfolding context of material sociocultural forces. I have also produced a book that is an assemblage of ten semiautonomous essays on this subject arranged, like the cartoon, in more or less chronological fashion and eager to take inspired liberties wherever possible – even envisioning queer equivalents of flying saucers wherever possible. No cultural history can be pursued in a tight teleological trajectory, and even less this history of queer Canadian films and videos, with its dynamics of one step forward and three steps sideways, of wheels invented and reinvented, of connections and echoes but also chasms among regions and languages, of discontinuities as overwhelming as the vertical wall of the Rockies that the animators had suddenly loom up in front of their transcontinental wayfarers, of cabals of artists as hermetic and awe-struck and self-important as the little clusters of paddlers dwarfed by the enormities of the Canadian Shield, of gaps between works and artists and above all between works and audiences.

My chronology, then, is sometimes more, sometimes less. Following the present introductory chapter, the essay "Monkey on the Back" covers queer glimmers and symptomatic denials alongside the betrayed revolutions, retrenchments, and silences of the first decade and a half following World War II. Then chapters 3 and 4 cover the subsequent sexual ferment and revolutionary outbursts of the sixties and seventies, those that followed the early stages of the Cold War, as if in counterreaction. Thereafter is a loose sense of macrochronology that allows us to arrive into the nineties and the new century without too much disorientation by the final chapters; all the while the micro-chronologies of the individual essays that constitute chapters 5 to 10 defer to a more substantive sense of thematic evolution and coherence. Chapter 5, "Passages," broods on profoundly gender-inflected queer narrative mythologies about movements from the country to the city (and back again) and from youth to adulthood (er … and back again), focusing on a broad spectrum of regional cultural contexts. With chapter 6, devoted to the queering of the National Film Board, chronology returns, though overwhelmed by a sense of an institutional subculture trying to keep pace with rapid social and sexual changes outside its walls. Chapter 7, "Boys and the Beast," has perhaps the most universalizing thrust of all my essays, scrutinizing – and queering – masculinity itself through an analysis of sports films in both French and English settings, based on a transhistorical scan from 1960 to the present. Chapter 8, "Sex, Money, and Sobriety," is the longest essay in the book, not surprisingly, since the three terms in the title are the favourite subjects of visual media artists, queer and not-so-queer. Here I focus on the explicit sexual discourses of pornography and meta-pornography, mostly from the eighties and nineties, as well as on male and female iconographies of sexual fantasy, politics, and subversion. The all-too-contemporary topic of cultural struggle around AIDS is the focus of chapter 9, scanning both the general two-decades-long trajectory of queer media work about the HIV crisis and three exemplary artists of the nineties. Chapter 10, a final-wrap up conclusion, returns to the related but much more transhistorical problematic of shame, considering moving images as the artistic encounter with and management of that primal emotion.

But this conclusion ties up few strings, for I had the feeling that, end as I must, I was cutting the work short. Initially envisaged chapters on television; on the coherent tradition of queer documentary activism; on the intersections of Québécois nationalism and sexual identity politics, of racial difference with sexual identity politics, and of theatre and film through the framework of adaptation; and, finally, on the evolving culture of queer community festivals – a kind of microcosm of the entire book – all fell by the wayside, victim to length and time restraints. Hopefully, much of the initial research and questions around these topics have been integrated into the existing chapters and especially into part 2 and will also find their way into future books – by others!

PORTRAITS

As the reader has already been alerted, the historian in me was not satisfied with these ten essay-chapters, and the impulse to include, to be comprehensive, to be fair and complete in acknowledging the incredible wealth that had been accumulating before my eyes for a quarter of a century compelled

The Romance of Transportation in Canada (Colin Low and Guy Glover, 1952): as with this book and this country, the tone is epic, campy, and self-reflexive, and clusters of railroaders are dwarfed by the immensities of the landscape. Frame enlargement, used with permission of the National Film Board of Canada

me to add the encyclopedic portrait gallery in part 2. This gallery no doubt reflects the hoarding compulsions I developed as I came of age in proto-queer academia and film cultures during the famine of the 1970s. But these short articles will hopefully increase this volume's value as a reference work, not only on queer culture and history but also on Canadian moving images across the board. As a ravenous consumer of reference resources on Canadian cinema, both books and websites, I know how important use-value is to the study of a collection of national cinemas notable for their absence from the screens. *I* wanted to use these appendices. If I didn't provide them, who would?

My portrait gallery is perhaps overambitious, a listing, a kind of dramatis personae of the careers of individuals – and in a score of cases, of entities and institutions – who participated in the construction of the masses of moving images that have inspired my ten essays. Here, not only film directors and video makers proceed past, but also producers, scriptwriters, actors, critics, authors of original sources – in short, as many of the players in the cultural constituency as possible. In this I felt a strong sense of accountability to the communities and microcultures that cumulatively have fostered the rich, brilliant, and diverse corpus that is the subject of this book, all the more anxious because the corpus has struggled with invisibility and denial from its earliest glimmers and has never been assembled all together, all at once. Although my first plan was to accompany this gallery with a "desert island list" of one hundred key *works*, this option immediately careened out of control in the face of a database that lists more than fifteen hundred queer films and videos, and I finally decided to limit myself to individuals rather than works.

The portrait gallery posed daunting challenges and was in itself a major research project, and to encounter dozens of new friends by means of the telephone, the internet, and email from sea to sea to sea, most of them eager and supportive collaborators, was one of most exciting aspects of writing this book. This rush of rediscovery of community is palpable, I know, in this gigantic document.

From the very beginning of the project I understood that I must face the task of identifying makers according to their sexual orientation or identity. From the time of choosing the title of my first published article, a "coming out" manifesto entitled "Films by Gays for Gays" (written in 1976 and published in 1977), I have insisted that authorship is an intrinsic to the understanding and negotiation of a politics of sexuality and representation – the much-vaunted "death of the author" notwithstanding. This insistence was in tune with the ideological emphasis on "coming out" in the gay seventies, especially during the increasing ideological backlash of those Anita Bryant–tainted years. If the queer 2000s require less dogmatism around who is and who isn't what, with a more mature and confident political sense of contingency and coalition, I was all the same not willing to allow my necessary and strategic deployment of ambiguity to be founded on avoidance or misplaced discretion, to let the closet creak closed on this historical who's who of makers and shakers. When heterosexual film or video people would miss the point of the entire exercise, I knew I was doing the right thing. Take, for example, a heterosexual Studio D veteran who, as I was trying to decipher the intricate negotiations of sexual sensibilities within the institution that made *Forbidden Love,* recommended that I should not use my euphemistic phrase "lesbian energies" but, rather, the "more inclusive" one "feminist energies" and thereby immediately reinforced my label-dogmatism.

This determination was heightened all the more when I found myself caught up in a traumatizing ordeal around research ethics upon receiving three-year research funding from the Social Sciences and Humanities Research Council of Canada, administered through my university, in 1998. Within a research culture increasingly dominated by engineering and the natural and social sciences, I was required to submit an ethics protocol to a Concordia review committee as soon as I acknowledged that I might be interviewing and discussing real live artists. With not a single representative from the humanities – let alone queer studies – and chaired by an expert in "exercise science," this committee decided the whole research project was a cut-and-dried issue of "outing" or not "outing." They presumed that the indication of an artist or other public figure as nonheterosexual was automatically both defamatory and a betrayal of confidential personal information. It mattered little that the author's work might be thoroughly saturated with queerness and that the last anti-outing litigation anyone remembers was Liberace's in the fifties. Discussing authorial queerness is a violation and not at all equivalent to discussing Mordecai Richler's Jewishness or Margaret Atwood's femaleness (to mention two Canadian cultural figures a few of the committee members had heard of). The committee did not understand and would not listen to issues about the complexity of voice in autobiographical work, the volatility of sexual identity in a postqueer universe inflected by gender, class, generation, and culture, or the gradations of "outness" in the world of K.D. LANG. Instead, the exercise scientist and her henchpersons could focus only on the eight-page consent protocols dancing in their literal-minded brains – one that would scare off most artists worthy of the name – and refused to release my money until I had signed a reductive and simplistic promise not to out anyone without their consent. I am complying with this nonsensical contractual obligation to the exercise scientists in as creative and subversive a way as possible. The vast majority of the individuals included in the essay chapters of this book, as well as in the portrait gallery, are proudly and publicly identified/unidentifiable as one or more letters in BLLAGTITTISQQ, on the record either through their work or their media presence, and this is the default option necessary for reading this appendix. If they're here, they're queer.

With some exceptions. I have also included individuals who have not publicly identified as one of those initials but who have made a major contribution to the field, or have at least turned over a few furrows. In my opinion, queer cultures need not fear the risk of cultural appropriation that native artists were debating in the 1990s. Accordingly, this furrow-turning group, primarily heterosexuals – and I do not use this term pejoratively, since some of my best friends belong to this endangered group – are more than welcome to *The Romance of Transgression in Canada*. In a dozen or so cases I designate with "queer-friendly" living artists with substantive queer oeuvres whose sexual identification as BLLAGTITTISQQ or heterosexual is neither a matter of consent nor of public record, or who have declined or not responded to my request for clarification. But they, for once, are the ones who have to suffer labels, and are identified as friends of friends of Dorothy – if friendly is what they are. Here I was inspired by LYNNE FERNIE'S and AERLYN WEISSMAN'S disclaimer at the start of *Forbidden Love*: "Unless otherwise stated the people who appear in this film should not be presumed to be homosexual ... [pause ... next frame] or heterosexual." In public screenings, this disclaimer, which wittily turned the tables on all lawyers, social and exercise scientists, and ethics bureaucrats, was always greeted with uproarious approval by queer audiences, who got the whole point immediately. This component nevertheless provoked a certain amount of delicacy, as I ended up asking sexual orientation information from several heterosexual individuals who had clearly never been asked such things before. In fact, if any evidence of the fluctuations of identity is required and if maker ex-trick oral histories and industry/festival scuttlebutt are to be believed, let me reveal that the "queer-friendly" entries include a share of de facto serial bisexuals (you know who you are), as well as a share of closet cases. I apologize in advance for any ethical offense given in mistakenly identifying queers as "queer-friendly."

The question of identity and identification is clearly not academic, all the more so since, as the reader has already discovered, this work of historiography and criticism starts from an autobiographical premise and investment on the part of myself, the author. I've been around for most of this history, and I enter many of the chapters in terms of my own personal experience with the corpus, then or now – even to the extent of sharing my personal erotic response to some of the works described in chapter 8, "Sex, Money, and Sobriety," and elsewhere. Even more important, my friendship with many of the makers is an indispensable element of my critical methodology. As I've argued before (1996), desire is an indispensable part of the impulse to knowledge, and I am happy to declare this upfront, ethics or no ethics. There are limits of course to the role of subjectivity in research, as the reader will gather from reading between the lines of the same chapter's segment on "toilet sex," a practice that has for some reason consistently eluded me. The biographical premise of my research is of course most visibly invested in the portrait gallery articles, built painstakingly on the conviction that individuals' lives and life experiences are inextricable from this history of moving images.

The portrait gallery was conceived of at some early point as a modest compendium of major movers and shakers, divided into two lists of men and women respectively. Gender segregation was the first naive plan to go out the window (and I have proudly resisted for the rest of the project any temptation to a chromosomal tally, not only because of the ambiguity around the emergence of a dozen or so transgendered individuals in the register [Toronto's trans festival is called, after all, "COUNTING PAST TWO!"]). The second naive idea was my hope and that of my original collaborator, Chantal Nadeau, way back in 1998 that such a listing could be limited to fifty or perhaps even one hundred. Wanting to include a representative diversity among groups and regions – linguistic, artistic, cultural, and sexual, as well as geographical – I found my selection criteria becoming increasingly unwieldy and impossibly difficult. Before I knew it the compendium had become an encyclopedia with one entry for almost every day of the year. At the end of this process, I find myself reeling and energized from the apprehension of this cultural community, undertaken in innocence and completed in amazement – in fact never terminable, a work in progress.

Obviously, not everyone who has made any kind of contribution to the corpus could be included in this queer who's who, but most makers and shakers, voices and ventriloquists, who have signed a couple or more long or short works over to the queer cultural milieu can be found somewhere in this alphabetical listing. In some cases, collaborative works that incorporated major queer contributions are listed under the queer contributor's name, even if he or she is not the director. I apologize to anyone whose role I have unintentionally understated or ignored altogether. I have tried to be rigorously historical in providing dates and origins and places of work for the listees and their works (the cut-off criterion for works to be mentioned in *The Romance of Transgression*, chronologically speaking, is a release date of 31 December 2003 or earlier). Given my vocation as educator, I have tried to mention major educational influences as part of the biographical information provided, alongside short descriptions of exemplary or representative works. Unfortunately, full filmographies could not be provided without them taking over the entire book; fortunately, with distribution catalogues from the major alternative distributors and from commercial video outlets freely available on the internet, this is less of a problem than it might once have been.

Obviously, other biases will immediately be recognized by the alert reader, both in the portrait gallery and throughout the essay chapters. My own training in film studies may have resulted, despite my best inclinations, in my following the mainstream culture in privileging feature films over shorter works and videotapes. Furthermore, my own setting in the Toronto-resentful metropolis on the St Lawrence may also lead to rumblings about short shrift from other regions, as well as from Toronto itself. Moreover, women and transgendered people may also be tempted to join the rumblings about biological male bias (most evident perhaps in the absence of a chapter about women's sport films). People of colour may also grumble about white presumption, although I have done my best to be fair and objective, as well as true to the materialities of a historical setting that traditionally privileged white male metropolitan voices and visions – like my own – and inarguably still does.

It is thrilling to recognize the diversity of the community that I have convoked, not only linguistic, cultural, gender, and sexual but also generational. Born in 1948, I get all teary-eyed at the vast spectrum of generations that became reflected in the portrait gallery once I started compiling birth dates for the subjects. Ranging over eight decades, the queer cohort's largest group is constituted by those born the decade of Stonewall/Omnibus, the sixties. My own generation, born in the forties and coming of age just as we were being decriminalized, bring up the rear in approximately the same proportion as the generations born in the fifties and seventies respectively. At the same time, I am riveted by the decisive showing by those born in the eighties, who don't remember when Pierre Elliott Trudeau was in power, let

alone when he decriminalized sodomy or brought forth the Charter of
Rights and Freedoms, and who obviously don't remember a time before
AIDS. "La relève," as we say in Montreal – the relief – is clearly in full view
and they won't take any shit from anyone, least of all Stonewall-sentimen-
talists like myself. We baby boomers can coast creakily into retirement,
fully confident of a queer future in moving images.

There is one further bias from my status as a Stonewaller, however, that I
am happy to declare and defend. As a historian belonging to that generation,
it has been essential for me to give proper due to the pioneers of queer cinema and video, who took risks in the sixties and seventies and even early
eighties that many of those then being born – too often an amnesiac generation, to be frank – sometimes scarcely acknowledge. In a way my portrait
gallery is a work of historiographical reparation and includes especially long
entries for artists like AUDY, CAMPBELL, COLE and Dale, HAIG, JUTRA,
MCLAREN and GLOVER, MOORES and Travassos, SECTER, SUTHERLAND,
WESCOTT, WONG, and others, that may seem disproportionate to some.
This catch-up work is not meant to instal these groundbreakers in a hall of
fame, to construct heroes whom it will be necessary later to demystify. We
can hopefully learn from the feminist film history movement, which has to
move beyond an early impulse to discover and rediscover ancestresses as
exceptional heroines and idols. The cultivation of heroine-worship blinded
us to their context, networks, communities, and all-too-human stature.
Canadian queer cultural history presents a somewhat different challenge.
This history has been shaped by gender and sexual marginalities, with their
range of attendant isolation and closets, censorships and self-censorships;
shaped also by colonial, regional, and class dynamics and the overwhelming
interface of governmentality and economic ostracism within all cultural production in Canada; and shaped most palpably by the fundamental linguistic
divide, which meant that Secter had never heard of Audy or Jutra of Moores.
In this tribe there's not much room for idolatry.

Birth dates are one thing, but death dates are another matter entirely,
and it would be a serious oversight if I did not mention anywhere the terri-
ble loss of a whole cohort to AIDS, including MICHAEL BALSER, RICHARD
BENNER, ANDREW BRITTON, WILLIAM DOUGLAS, WILLIAM DUFFAULT,
PETER JEPSON-YOUNG, MICHAEL MCGARRY, Feliz Partz and Jorge Zontal
(GENERAL IDEA), CRAIG RUSSELL, JAY SCOTT, Tommy Sexton (CODCO),
DAVID TUFF, ESTHER VALIQUETTE, and surely others I am unaware of.
The silence of these voices is compounded by that of others, mourned in
their premature succumbing to accidents or their own hands or cancer, cut-
ting short careers of such promise, including CLINT ALBERTA, AMY BURT,
COLIN CAMPBELL, GLORIA DEMERS, BILLY HILL, CLAUDE JUTRA, ALAN
LAMBERT, and TANYA TRÉPANIER.

Reclaiming pioneers for an amnesiac generation: Norman McLaren, Queen of Canada. NFB portrait, c. 1980, used with permission of the National Film Board of Canada

Dead or alive, the works of most of the elders and "pioneers," except for NFB-ers such as McLaren and Wescott, of course, are more or less inaccessible. If any benefit can come from what may seem like my positively archeological emphasis on founders, I hope that it will give a push to any efforts underway to make the works of these innovators available on DVD and in festivals, hopefully with subtitle options in the other language. This idea may seem utopian, especially in view of the inertia in public institutions about keeping canonical works alive, let alone getting them subtitled, but it is desperately urgent for us as a network of communities to resonate with the brave visions of the past. This is all the more true since they were the generations whose careers were hampered by a virulent censorship that the Generation x-ers cannot imagine, whether institutional or born of crude political violence. Fortunately, the video sector is much more active on this preservation front than the film sector, thanks to the stunning work of such queer-friendly production/distribution outfits as Toronto's Vtape, Vancouver's Video In/Out, and Montreal's Vidéographe. Accordingly, the works of 1970s pioneers like Campbell, Wong, and PARADIS are readily available – if not on DVD, at least on VHS.

I started this introduction amid a blazing Tamil summer in Chennai and finish in a cool Montreal spring abuzz with marriages in the air, the few that have happened since the historic ruling and the others lining up, and with a country abuzz not with the Indian election but with our own on the horizon. What are its ramifications for a kiddie porn law being rammed through Parliament that will criminalize dozens of works and artists represented in the book you have started to read or for a hate crimes amendment stalled by Senate homophobes and the Christian right? Yet the law is not always an ass, and as I write, another brave bookstore, Toronto's Glad Day this time, has seized a breath of freedom in a court judgment throwing out the censorship function of Ontario's film surveillance board, a body that has been the bane of queer moving images since 1912 and our active persecutor since the early 1980s. It is a reminder, both negative and positive, that this book, this compendium of moving images and histories, of voices and faces and bodies, of desires and fears and denunciations and meditations, has never been, can never be, far from love, freedom, and politics.

2

Monkey on the Back: Canadian Cinema, Conflicted Masculinities, and Queer Silences in Canada's Cold War

PRELUDE

The prehistoric stirrings of Canadian queer cinematic cultures are indelibly stamped by war, but in this chapter I will argue that it was not so much the Hot War of 1939–45 that had the formative impact but rather, the Cold War of 1945–60. Yes, the National Film Board's patriotic propaganda efforts during World War II inevitably reflected the gender crises sparked by the great dislocations of the war effort and laid out a suggestive canvas of homosocial relations, both male and female, that were fortified by the epochal moment. Yes, these films inevitably recorded glimpses of transgender eroticisms that surfaced within the homosocial military institutions around the world. Yes, MCLAREN and GLOVER were at the helm, and a pioneering cadre of women filmmakers was present in the corridors of the studio and in the field, in the munitions factories, and at the CWAC recruitment and training sites, and the excitement of new frontiers was palpable. I have even gone on record, perhaps prematurely (Waugh 1999, 11–13), suggesting that two examples of wartime NFB films might be appropriated as part of "an alternative queer Canadian canon of voices, visions, and images of alternative male sexuality:"

Soldiers All, "Canada Carries On," NFB, 1941
A show mounted by Canadian soldiers stationed in England to entertain their host community.

NARRATOR
And in return for their hospitality, Canada presents "The Sultan's Saturday Night," a dire drama of the Middle East.

A Canadian soldier, dressed provocatively as a harem dancer, enters and gyrates across the stage. The spectators are agog: a 12-year-old boy gleams wide-eyed in excitement, a bespectacled middle-aged male is in hysterics, a young man in uniform tweaks his male companion's nose ...
Future for Fighters, "Canada Communiqué no. 10," NFB, 1944.
Demobilizing servicemen and their wives benefit from government assistance. Two beaming ex-sailors who will set up as a fishing partnership are shown meeting the government grant committee and trying out a new boat.

NARRATOR
Fishing was the trade of these seamen, and they want to get back into it as partners. Can they get a loan to set themselves up? Better than that. As the farmer gets his farm and the city worker buys a property, a fisherman gets $1,200 toward a boat and net and fishing gear. As partners these two receive a $2,400 grant as well as assistance in buying their own home.

Several queer Canadian filmmakers have come back to such suggestive evidentiary fragments to probe the emergence of queer cultures and lives during the war, most notably MARILYN BURGESS and JOSÉ TORREALBA in 1989 and 2003. But as exciting as such paleontological digs always are, there's no sense that they will lead to the excavation of a sustained body of filmic queer texts that establish this period as a formative one for Canadian queer cinemas. Rather, as the rest of this chapter demonstrates, it was the next generation, that of the Cold War, an era of division and indulgence rather than consensus and sacrifice, who went on to congeal the first solid body of queer cinematic triggers and dreams.

GENDER INSECURITIES

Don't you like girls, Arthur?
Sure I like girls, but do I have to marry one? I like you, Harry, but I don't want to marry you.
~ *Is It a Woman's World?*, NFB 1956

I was born the year of the Berlin Blockade, and hence my memory of the Cold War, at least of the 1950s phase that I would like to address in this chapter, is fairly unreliable. I do remember hearing about Sputnik on the way to church one morning in Brantford, Ontario, and I remember even more concretely hearing about the DEW Line, the Suez crisis, and the For-mosa bombardment in Miss Davies's current affairs class. Miss Davies, an elderly spinster with rouge-red cheeks, was the best teacher I ever had. My anxiety of the time was focused less on nuclear annihilation than on her strap, though it would never be used on me of course, the perfect four-eyed anti-athlete poet pet who loved her slides of her summer trip to Switzerland in the company of her "roommate," another unmarried schoolteacher. I also remember the projectionist from the Brantford Board of Education, who would show up every once in a while and show us 16mm NFB programs of nature films and Norman McLaren cartoons, a tall thin man in a suit, bow tie, and red moustache whom I reconstruct retroactively as a slightly eccen-tric bachelor.

The point of these reminiscences is to suggest how public education, mar-ital status, and the National Film Board of Canada interface with geopolitics in a cultural analysis of the Canadian Cold War. This analysis builds not only on the work done in Canada by social scientists such as Reg Whitaker and Gary Marcuse (1994) and Gary Kinsman (1996), literary historians such as Robert Martin (1991) and Peter Dickinson (1999), and communica-tions experts such as Michael Dorland (1998) and Andrew Dowler (1996) who have scrutinized the development of Canadian cultural policy during the postwar period. It is indebted also to the work of American queer and feminist cultural and sociopolitical historians such as Allen Bérubé (1990), Steve Cohan (1997), Robert Corber (1993, 1997), John D'Emilio (1983), Barbara Ehrenreich (1983), and Amy Villarejo (1999), whose work is usual-ly assumed to be applicable to the Canadian context, but in ways still to be pinned down.[1] My analysis scrutinizes a more elusive and amorphous trace than the typographic archives of courts, cabinets, and print media that have been examined thus far, namely, the cinematic imaginary of the Canadian Cold War in the period that begins with the end of World War II and lasts approximately to the late fifties of Suez, Sputnik, and Formosa.

There is a consensus about this period in North America among these social and cultural historians, albeit a contradictory one, and it might be summarized as follows. Both Canada and the United States saw a certain osmosis of geopolitical insecurity and gender insecurity, although, predictably, Canadians seemed to experience a muted or sometimes delayed version of U.S. sexual panics, paranoia, purges, and scapegoating, a kind of branch-plant tagalong version. Nevertheless, the reign of terror in both countries was inseparable from what Corber, following postwar sociologist C. Wright Mills, has called the postwar gender settlement, or consensus, a negotiated truce brought on by postwar economic displacements. It enshrined the organization man as the hegemonic model of masculinity, replacing the cow-boy and the entrepreneur in cultural imaginary and socioeonomic organization alike and shifting the predominant ethos from production to consumption. This settlement, however, did not prevent what Corber calls "the crisis in masculinity," which was resonant with conflicting models of masculinity, cultural resistances, and what Ehrenreich has called flights from commitment on the part of men resisting domestication as heteroconjugal consumers. Canadians seem in this period to have imitated only halfheartedly the emerging American modes of resistance to the white middle-class regime of gender and political conformity, from beat culture and the artistic avant-garde to the civil rights movements, the embryonic youth revolt and the Sexual Revolution.[2]

On the other hand, Canadians by and large seem to have taken a back seat to no one in the institutionalization of psychiatry, judging from Kinsman's chilling study of this insidious medico-scientific infrastructure of the new settlement as implemented in Canada (1996, 109–16, 124–5, 129–33). Bolstering Kinsman's study is the primary evidence of the National Film Board of Canada itself, whose series on mental health, *Mental Mechanisms*, appeared immediately after the war in 1947, to great international success. Produced in collaboration with Montreal's Allan Memorial Institute (notorious with Cold War historians for its CIA-sponsored research on LSD somewhat later), the series went on to the sequels *Mental Symptoms* and *Mental Health* and kept proliferating in various guises throughout the fifties. *Mental Mechanisms,* to which I shall return, was at first produced for professionals but struck a popular chord with lay audiences. As such it may be seen as symbolically cementing the discursive shift in the public sphere from the collective politics of the Popular Front and the War Effort toward the individual regulation of private life, from the villainy of fascism to the villainy of controlling or distant mothers (Setliff 1999). If security was the bogeyword of Cold War geopolitical ideology in Canada, as Whitaker has established with his witty subtitle, *The Making of a National Insecurity State*, Dowler and others have confirmed that security was also the key to emerging Canadian cultural policy in the 1950s. But it was American mass culture, not the commies and perverts, that provoked Canadian cultural insecurity and our embrace of the quickly consolidating model of governmentality in the cultural sphere. Dowler (1996, 338) has described this model as aimed at "secur[ing] the internal, 'metaphysical' frontier of culture" and "repairing economic dependency in the realm of the material," in short, as "the use of culture as a disciplinary regime to ensure the development of a distinctive and therefore defensible character of the Canadian state." I am not challenging this consensus in this chapter but, rather, showing how the Canadian cinematic imaginary engaged with, mediated, and merged these anxieties, discourses, and issues, sometimes explicitly, often obliquely, throughout the postwar period.

In cinematic terms this period, 1945 to approximately the end of the fifties, might be called the last premodern phase of Canadian film history, dominated almost entirely by the activities of the National Film Board. Traditionally viewed as a kind of dark ages – in my mind to a large extent because film noir seems to have been the presiding stylistic influence over this chilly phase when Canadians seemed to wear winter clothes all year round and performed in morbidly didactic docudramas – this gloomy Ottawa interregnum stretched between John Grierson's originary inspiration in the heat of the antifascist conflict and the moment when the scarred but modernized board emerged blinking from its pupa in the sunny Montreal suburbs after its move down here in 1956.

It is especially fitting symbolically that the National Film Board should be the focus of this reflection on cinematic traces of the Canadian Cold War in its first decade. After all, founder Grierson and the board had been among the first Canadian sacrificial victims, individual and institutional respectively, of the postGouzenko versions of Cold War fear, desire, and indeed censorship between 1945 and 1951, as Whitaker and Evans have recounted (Whitaker and Marcus 1994, 227–60; Evans 1991, 6–17). Indeed, the uneven and intermittent cinematic output that explicitly addressed the geopolitics of that period hardly merits attention otherwise. In contrast to the pioneering "World in Action" films of World War II that had cemented the institution's world reputation for its cutting-edge discourse on international issues, the half-hearted postwar series of commissions for the various armed forces, the Mounties, and NATO, and a few dutiful works on such subjects as the nonmilitary uses of nuclear energy and democracy in the developing world, are hardly worth a second look. Although the NFB received a large and secret special subsidy from the Psychological Warfare Committee to produce a "Freedom Speaks" audio-visual program for international audiences during the early fifties, as recounted by Evans (1991, 20–6), the NFB apparently diverted most of these funds towards its own traditional hobbyhorses and dexterously avoided the assigned subject throughout the whole period. With a well-timed film about the Mounties or Berlin being periodically tossed as a bone to the wolves, the work of governmental liberalism went on unperturbed, either because the rank and file and producers alike had profoundly learned their lesson from the earlier blows dealt their charismatic founder and colleagues or because of some deep-seated resistance by artists to bureaucratic control.

One prominent exception that proves this rule is an all-but-explicit allegory of the Korean War, and more generally of the arms race, released in 1952, one of the most popular films ever made in Canada and an entrenched staple both of the Canadian film canon and of my old Brantford projectionist's package, no doubt, though I don't remember it: Norman McLaren's *Neighbours*. In subsequent interviews, McLaren (1978) confirmed the starting point of the famous parable about fatally pugnacious neighbours as an impartial reflection on the Korean conflict between two civilizations he identified with. He also expressed amazement that he had got away with it at a time when "peace" was a dirty word – not to mention impartial views of anticommunist conflict. It is all the more amazing when we consider that the film, unbeknownst to McLaren, was purportedly funded through the "Freedom Speaks" program (Evans 1991, 23–5). These ironies may have accrued to the film because Canadians, as usual, hardly noticed it until it received an Oscar or because politicians and bureaucrats of the time were as little gifted in film exegesis as their successors fifty years later, especially exegesis of a film as deceptively light and inconsequential as a cartoon. There may have been the additional factor that McLaren was the board's most prestigious in-house artist – despite being tainted by his sympathy with China and a "fellow traveller" background and despite having the particular personality bent highlighted in this book – and as such was untouchable, all the more so since he successfully played the grand naïf.

Whatever the explanation, *Neighbours* is as interesting fifty years later for its treatment of Cold War gender insecurity as it is for its brave discourse on Cold War missile envy. Indeed the film seems to be a textbook articulation of the regimes of masculinity that arose in the aftermath of the war. Here laid out upon the screen is what has been called the "feminist folk myth" of the postwar gender settlement (Wilson and Weir 1992, 97): women evicted from the factories into the domestic space of the nursery, crouching and hiding, and "organization men" esconced in the suburban public space of the front lawn, comfortable in their domesticated masculinity and corporate suits, pipe-smoking providers for the nuclear family. They are providers, it is clear, not the producers or individualist entrepreneurs of yore, and are seen only as passive consumers, conformist subjects of the white-collar, middle-class suburban dream. But the dream is precarious and insecure, as flowers and fences start appearing and conflicts about territoriality and commodity acquisition explode in the escalating savagery of neighbourly violence. McLaren's parabolic logic ironically maintains the Cold War slippage between private affinities and political loyalty, but it also acknowledges the intense ideological struggle over masculinity within the postwar settlement. The settlement's exclusions and disenfranchised others are also here – if only in the form of the war-painted primitives whose guise the men take on – as well as its release valves, all funneled into and at the same time disguised by McLaren's allegorical combat, abstracted by his hyperbolic and hysterical slapstick pixillation.

Neighbours (Norman McLaren, 1952): Domesticated Cold War husbands about to explode in a paroxysm of missile envy and commodity fetishism over a flower. Production still, used with permission of the National Film Board of Canada

MODELS OF MASCULINITY

Deciphered in this way, *Neighbours* allows us to see with fresh eyes the NFB Cold War catalogue and identify a contradictory but rich body of work similarly concerned with gender and sexuality, specifically with masculinity. How else, for example, can we look at *Corral* (Colin Low, 1954), another of the most canonized Canadian works of this period, a romantic portrait of an Alberta cowboy taming mustangs and a macho cameraman taming a handheld 35mm camera, except as a nostalgic fantasy – the organization man in denial – of a model of masculinity now increasingly outmoded by proliferating suburban conformity and consumption Down East? A whole body of several dozen less canonical films (more in fiction or docudrama than in conventional documentary) comes into view, films that specifically address either through denial or celebration those congealing new models of masculinity. Some explicitly riff on the new Millsian social science filtering in from the United States, offering surprisingly explicit and insightful critiques of the new regime. Take, for example, *The Cage* (Fergus McDonell, 1956, 27), a kind of Canadian *Death of the Salesman* in which, to quote the official description, "a capable business man [is] caught on the treadmill of our competitive society." This organization man in a split-level house has an existential crisis and discovers he's a "big phony nothing."

Other films from this obsessive cluster of works are narrativized as inter-generational conflicts or as conflicts quite literally between older and emerging models of masculinity. Among this group my sentimental favourite is *A Musician in the Family* (GUDRUN PARKER, 1953, 17), a short fiction that apparently borrows without acknowledgment from Sinclair Ross's story "Cornet at Night" ([1939] 1968; the board later adapted the story under its original title in 1963 [see chapter 5]).[3] In the film, a prairie farm boy, Andrew, is forced to choose between his agricultural heritage, figured by the gruff father who expects him to follow in his footsteps, and his musical talents, figured by his effusive new young, blonde male school teacher Mr Phallup, who is mentoring him on the trombone and has no spouse in sight. This film, directed by one of the board's small network of female creative people and producers, heads a subcategory of these masculinity films that can be called protofeminist. These films insist on an alternative model of masculinity that is neither old-fashioned entrepreneurial or contemporary corporate but that is sensitive, expressive, creative, tender, nonconformist – in short, sissy. The most dazzling film along these lines came from one of Parker's scripts that she had scarcely remembered when I interviewed her and about which I have already written elsewhere (1999, 24–5, 39–40). Like *Musician*, the film *Being Different*, released four years later, shows a boy about twelve struggling between the pressures of his jock paperboy peers and his desire to chase butterflies with new naturalist friends, and he is encouraged to do so by the bespectacled Miss Davies clone who mentors him in his gender rebellion. The "discussion trigger" format leaves the sober and stressed boy caught between hockey and butterflies and mercifully allows the ending to be unresolved – we all know what the possible endings are, and none was very nice in 1957.[4]

Parker's performing-arts documentaries, many A-list prestige productions such as *Opera School* (1952, 35) and the Oscar-nominated *Stratford Adventure* (1954, 39), can also be seen in this light. The latter contains, in addition to a delicious queer subtextual moment I have discussed elsewhere, yet another vision of masculinity as artistic expressiveness (1999, 23–4, 35–7; see also FINDLEY). But it is also a key text in the symbolization of cultural governmentality, with its walk-on performance by Vincent Massey, then governor general and recently prophet and advocate (in the 1951 Massey Report) of high cultural governmentality itself. Cultural policy and alternative masculinity thus came together, though ineffectually; a certain grass roots preference for *Gunsmoke* and American mass culture over the effete Canadian high culture enshrined by the new postwar institutions – the Canada Council, the Stratford Festival, the new National Ballet and

Caught between butterflies and hockey, George (foreground) struggling with the peer pressure of his jock paperboy friend in *Being Different* (1957). Production still, used with permission of the National Film Board of Canada

Opera companies, and the CBC (which, incidentally, was repeatedly queer-baited in tabloids in both Montreal and Toronto) – was the overwhelming dynamic (Setliff 1999; Higgins and Chamberland 1992). (The first thing that appeared on our brand new TV screen back in Brantford in the mid-fifties was the World Series.) Further research may gauge the extent to which governmentality absorbed artistic resistance, forestalling, for example, the development of an effectual Canadian artistic avant-garde, just as it had a hand in diverting and determining the development of a bona fide indigenous cinema industry (as Dorland (1998) and his counterparts in the private sector have traditionally argued).

Another prophetic film, *Howard* (Donald Haldane, 1957, 30), was a cornerstone of the board's growing youth film genre that would come to dominate in the next decade. *Howard*, the story of a high-school graduate torn among the various future options as they are embodied by those around him – organization man, family founder, cynic, dropout – was the NFB's closest echo of the Beat-inspired "road movie" mythology then resonating south of the border. The film sets up specific equations between the domesticated organization man and heterosexual familial entrapment and maps resistance to this hegemonic configuration in terms of homosocial opting out. Howard's temptation is a summer hitchhiking jaunt from sea to sea, sleeping out under the stars, with his best friend, the loner George, who doesn't flirt or dance at parties and actively parodies the rituals of female heterosexual socialization. Not surprisingly, similar fantasies of male homosociality are recurring preoccupations of the masculinity films, whether evoked with nostalgic longing for an all-male public sphere, with the psychologizing discourse of "phases" and "immaturity" that the new psychiatrization would specialize in, or with the sympathetic identification and crypto-eroticism that energize *Howard*.

The issue of homosociality brings us back to *Neighbours*, which calls out in this light to be read as a version of the homosocial triangulation that structures *Howard*, each man killing first the thing his buddy loves before finally killing the thing he loves in that film's orgiastic ballet. The homosocial reading, ironically, is all the more apt when one looks at the truncated version of *Neighbours* that circulated in the fifties and sixties after complaints that the shocking segment showing violence against wives and babies made the film unsuitable for young audiences. The censored version became a parable about rivalry over a flower between apparent bachelors, which must have looked very queer indeed. In either version, the two men end up in adjacent graves, as if homosocial camaraderie had replaced heterosexual genealogy as the main principle of cemetery organization.

Loner George tempts Howard (foreground) with his fantasy of homosocial sea-to-sea "dropping out" in *Howard* (1957). Production still, used with permission of the National Film Board of Canada

CELIBACY ANXIETY

A large number of films spoke of bachelorhood during this period, oddly enough, contrary to our mythologies of Cold War compulsory heterofamiliality, and they didn't need to be censored to do so. Indeed, bachelorhood is the most stressed and least coherent trope of the whole corpus and one that spreads across the gender line. In the most anomalous film of them all, *Is It a Woman's World?* (Donald Haldane, 1957, 30), a dream fable purportedly about misogamy, Fred Davis, decked in three tubes of Brylcreem, plays a suave bachelor lawyer fighting off potential matchmakers and suitors: he must have seemed like Hugh Hefner's ideal constituency for his new magazine.⁵ Davis's misogynist playboy conveniently has a nightmare of matriarchal persecution and workplace gender role reversal (where male clerical staff are sexually harassed by cigar-smoking female bosses) and naturally ends up succumbing in the end, like his contemporaneous Hollywood marriage resisters, to the tender trap. *Is It a Woman's World?* was rediscovered and recycled by the women's Studio D in 1977 and repackaged for latter-day feminist audiences as the "conventional myth that women indirectly exercise power through their ability to manipulate men through sex and marriage."⁶ But this disturbingly limited and literal reading of an unusually witty and acute protofeminist narrative seems in denial of everything really going on on the screen, including a discreet queer joke or two that surfaces in the gender-role-reversal dream skit and elsewhere, as in the deceptively blithe repartee Davis lets drop, which I quote in the epigraph to this section. Here is a film that needs an updated reading through a postmillennium, postJudith Butler filter; despite the playful and energized female performances and the unprecedented feminist camp humour of the script, its real energies articulate male anxieties about marital status, gender performance, and sexual identity.

A similar film with a different generic sensibility is *None but the Lonely* (1957, 30), a docu-melodrama set in Toronto that purports to be about modern urban anomie ("I'm just a number!") but ends up expressing the same anxieties about marital status and masculinity. Sad, shy Henry Smith is a twenty-something unmarried male office worker stuck in a rooming house with a nagging landlady ("I can't go back to that room ... Maybe I should join the Y, I might meet someone") and an alienating white-collar job with invasive but unfriendly coworkers. Unable to chat up the waitress at lunch or engage in meaningful homosocial intercourse with a fellow "lonely" drunk in the local tavern, Henry's worst humiliation is the moment he tries playing ball on the street with a little girl. The latter is rescued by a mother who shrieks, "How often I have told you not to speak to strangers?" and effectively sums up the antipervert paranoia of the whole decade. The

Marital-status anxiety in *None but the Lonely* (1957, 30): sad, shy bachelor Henry's worst humiliation comes when he offers to play ball on the street with a little girl and is rejected by her mother in a panic of antipervert paranoia. VHS frame grab, used with permission of the National Film Board of Canada

final moments show Henry sitting alone in his room, his milk on the hotplate boiled over, along with his tears; if Canadian bachelors and spinsters were already feeling suicidal when this strange and chilling work was broadcast, they no doubt were pushed closer to the edge.

Many of the board's psychosocial-issue films from the period are immersed in this trauma of the married/unmarried binary. The pregnant heroine of *Woman Alone* (Julian Biggs, 1956, 30) sums it all up when she blurts out histrionically, "I'm not married!" as if this was not already fully evident to the kindly Salvation Army matron who is welcoming her to her "home." The ghost of Miss Davies hovers over these films' procession of singles: frustrated, hostile, rejected, and altruistic spinsters, lonely and frustrated bachelors, fey arts performers, benevolent mentors and homosocial couples – and none quite so well lubricated and oblivious as Fred Davis. Marital status becomes a determining slant of an entire discourse on marginality. Even the two pioneering and prize-winning films about drug addiction, *Drug Addict* (Robert Anderson, 1948, 34) and *Monkey on the Back* (Julian Biggs, 1956, 29), depict substance abuse in the context of conjugal and extraconjugal relations. Here homosociality is the conduit for infection, and conjugal relations are its principal casualty, whether through pimping, prostitution, and "promiscuity" in 1948 or marital betrayal and breakup in 1956.[7]

Symptomatically, the first two of the "Mental Mechanisms" films, *Feeling of Rejection* (Robert Anderson, 1947, 21) and *Feeling of Hostility* (Robert Anderson, 1948, 31) depict the eponymous feelings in two unmarried female characters. Both films posit happy marriage as the prophylactic against emotional maladjustment and position distant or smothering mothers presiding over crippling nuclear families (with weak or absent fathers, of course) as the cause of all trauma. The two lead characters, while not literally lesbians, do go to movies alone and have "complex sexual inhibitions."[8] Fortunately, after therapy the rejected dowdy mouse develops the skill to fend off salesmen trying to sell her unfeminine apparel (she proudly declares that she wants to see "gayer" shoes than the practical ones first shown). The hostile one

Mädchen in Ottawa. A hostile schoolgirl develops an unreciprocated crush on her female schoolteacher in *Feeling of Hostility* (1948). Production still, used with permission of the National Film Board of Canada

manages a vestimentary triumph as well: progressing beyond her unreciprocated schoolgirl crush on her female schoolteacher and compensating for her own mother's distance à la *Mädchen in Ottawa*, she later acquires a smartly severe wardrobe that complements her chilly intellectual demeanour and man-hating frigidity. The narrator keeps spelling it out for us: "These are the subtle, disguised ways in which her repressed hostility for men has expressed itself. Love is fascinating but very dangerous. The danger of being deserted, the experience with her father and her failure with her mother following her second marriage, have damaged too much her capacity for love. She cannot trust men. She is also envious of them."

Not all the unmarried are damaged goods however. On the male side the wonderfully expressive Mr Phallup is one of the most appealing and lively characters in the whole Cold War catalogue, as well as just one degree this side of swishy. On the female side there is a whole roster of luminously sentimentalized portraits of unmarried female school teachers, including a "kindly" older professor cameo'd in *Hostility*.[9]

The nicest spinster of them all shows up in another film about sexual marginality called *The Street* (Fergus McDonell, 1957, 30). Here, working-class prostitutes who hang out in a Yonge St cocktail lounge and talk Hollywood slang are led back to the pink collar workforce and proper English by one Miss Walker, of the Elizabeth Fry Society. The knowing smile of this middle-aged and portly social worker, her patient support, jaunty perm, little beanie, and efficient chauffeuring to job interviews would convert the whore of Babylon to the straight and narrow. Needless to say, by the end of the film the hooker heroine Kathy is well on her way back from the brink of marginality thanks to the male attentions in her new workplace. Both office mentorship and heterosexual courtship have come to the rescue as Miss Walker fades into the background, her work done.

I don't mean to parody these films about social and sexual marginality too viciously. I have been genuinely amazed in the course of this research at how, as the Cold War progressed, liberal social dramaturgy became bolder and more acute in its perceptions of the exclusions and margins of the postwar settlement, including those of a sexual, racial, class, generational, and social character. No wonder censorship brouhahas erupted so predictably around these films: *Drug Addict* was too compassionate for Americans; *Neighbours* and *The Street* were too frank about violence and sex, respectively, for children.[10] Of course, as Studio D was so quick to accuse, the films are ultimately complicit in the "settlement," for all their critical entanglement with it; nevertheless, the films resist facile generalizations about the conformity and homogeneity of Cold War culture.

THE REAL MONKEY

That said, it must be noted that one kind of marginality remains unmentionable and off-screen in these films and that paradoxically that marginality, namely queerness, is at the very centre of the corpus, the real monkey on the back of the postwar NFB. This monkey clings not only to all these mysterious bachelor and spinster films and other works on sexual marginality, and not only to the troubled films about masculinity and homosociality but also to the entire corpus of psychosocial issue films that constitute, I would argue, the Canadian cinematic imaginary of the Cold War period. This is a large claim about a silence, but silences in cultural imaginaries are a familiar problem, as Michel Foucault has compellingly argued ([1976] 1990, 27): "Silence itself – the things one declines to say, or is forbidden to name, the discretion that is required between different speakers – is less the absolute limit of discourse, the other side from which it is separated by a strict boundary, than an element that functions alongside the things said, with them and in relation to them within overall strategies. There is not division

The Street (1967). The nicest spinster of them all, social worker Miss Walker (right) with hooker heroine Kathy. VHS frame grab, used with permission of the National Film Board of Canada

to be made between what one says and what one does not say; we must try to determine the different ways of not saying such things."

This is not the place to ponder at length the historical reasons for what Corber calls the "gay male expulsion from representation" (Corber 1997, 101), or its continuation at the board right up into the 1980s. It is hardly surprising that a governmental institution could not have sheltered the minitempests and tentative probings that Martin and Dickinson have documented within modernist literary subcultures in both English and French Canada or the avant-garde visual and literary experimentation increasingly visible within the United States in the postwar period or, of course, the constant discourse that Eric Setliff and Ross Higgins have dissected in the lively tabloid press of English and French Canada respectively (Higgins and Chamberland 1992; Setliff 1999). Looking at the board's way of *not* saying queerness has already proven to be interesting itself, but this culture of silence has further faultlines that I have deliberately left out of my analysis until now. I can't finish without probing further these underground registrations of same-sex sexualities that are lurking within the NFB corpus. It is not the first time I have done so, for from the beginning my auteurist fallacy discovered in discreet and tiny closet networks more than one phallic auteur. Witness my almost facetious account of McLaren's *A Chairy Tale* (1957, 10), a collaboration with his acolyte CLAUDE JUTRA, another of the closeted queer artists at the Board (2000, 195; see also the portrait gallery). *Tale* is another pixillated relationship fable, but one that is very pronoun-

Neighbours (1952): does the pixillated male-male combat operate less as an allegorical sparring match than as an orgiastic pas de deux? Photo, used with permission of the National Film Board of Canada

avoidant and gender-ambiguous, in contrast to the gender-extremist *Neigh-bours*. Relationship roles between the handsome young male intellectual and the chair that doesn't want to be bottom until s/he's been top, the question of who gets the tail and who loses the cherry, all must be negotiated on-screen, and the film, rather than being about geopolitics, seems to be exactly about what it seems to be about, the couple, *all* couples.

These observations prompt another look at *Neighbours*, for like all silences, its silence is less overwhelming than is immediately apparent. In the thrall of my subtextual impulses, it is not too difficult to imagine for starters the discreet zeal with which McLaren must have manipulated his two performers into ripping their shirts off. Somewhat more significant than the beefcake, however, is the way the male-male combat in pixillated form operates in fact less as a sparring match than as a modernist same-sex *pas de deux*, which would be repeated in *Chairy Tale*, albeit between man and ungendered chair. This *pas de deux* would be repeated yet again with a man and a woman in McLaren's two great ballet films of the late sixties and early seventies, *Pas de deux* (1968, 13) and *Ballet Adagio* (1971, 10), in which other types of image-processing dissect and lyricize the ritualized heterosexual mating that is the core of classical ballet. The trope is repeated for

Norman McLaren and Claude Jutra's *A Chairy Tale* (1957), a gender-ambiguous relationship fable. The chair that doesn't want to be bottom until s/he's been top shifts the theme away from Cold War geopolitics to the couple, *all* couples. Frame enlargement, used with permission of the National Film Board of Canada

the last time in McLaren's testamentary film, *Narcissus* (1983, 22), in which two stunning male-male *pas de deux* conclude the career of an artist most commonly and erroneously seen as an abstractionist. In this film only one of the all-male duets is the result of a special effect; the other is performed in the pro-filmic flesh. The special effects of pixillation and, later, optical printing had perhaps been the postproduction distancing mechanisms that allowed McLaren to confront his actors' torsos in *Neighbours* and real bodies and real desire in general over the next decades. His strategy of dispensing with them at last in *Narcissus* and filming in real space and time a seminude male duet gives a teleological shape to his career, that of a fifty-year coming-out process.

The *pas de deux* is not the only link between *Neighbours* and *Narcissus*: both narratives of homosocial interaction revolve around a flower, of course. I won't belabour the stereotype of men who feel strongly about flowers, though this and many other stereotypes are absolutely pertinent, but I would like to dwell on the particular nature of *Neighbours*' flower itself. The flower, a 3D puppet creation, gets a little choreography of its own, flaunting its leaves and stem in a way that looks like a parodic per-

Norman McLaren's *Narcissus* (1983): the final rendition of the animator's same-sex *pas de deux*, performed not through special effects but in the pro-filmic flesh, giving a fifty-year coming-out shape to the career of the NFB's most famous artist. Frame enlargement, used with permission of the National Film Board of Canada

formance of a mating dance (similar to Ann Miller's performance in Hollywood's *Kiss Me Kate* the following year). In other words, this is a very queer flower, rather camp at the very least. Indeed, at least one observer of the time, Adolfas Mekas, called it in print, and did so admiringly, a "fairy flower."[11] In the light of American queer art historians' explorations of the ways configurations of camp and silences operated as an expression of resistance and criticism during the Cold War, this little flower in its own context of silence can be seen as a full-blown icon of Cold War desire, alongside Jasper John's flags, Robert Rauschenberg's erasures, Andy Warhol's shoes, and John Cage's conceptual silences (Katz forthcoming).

In the past (and in chapter 1) my auteurist outing methodology has not spared McLaren's lover of forty years, Guy Glover, with whom he shared a muralled Ottawa apartment that had nothing to do with suburban territoriality and whose role as top-ranking bureaucrat and producer at the board is otherwise well known. Was it their collaboration and the conviviality of their legendary Saturday night parties, so public according to board insiders that the term "closet" is hardly appropriate, that made them the object of an anonymous denunciation to the Mounties in the late forties? As Whitaker notes, the denunciation "incorporated what could only be called malicious gossip about 'gay private parties' given by members of the 'clique' at which [targeted NFB commissioner] McLean was usually in attendance, and even a suggestion that McLean was being blackmailed. Some of these innu-endoes came from private film makers whose veracity was questioned by the Mounties themselves" (Whitaker and Marcuse 1994, 461 n7). It is not anachronistic to focus on the word "gay" in Whitaker's note, as the term was in use as subcultural argot in the postwar era with very much its current meaning, in anglo Montreal as elsewhere.[12] Whitaker's note, together with its citation, offers the standard slippage in Cold War discourse between con-ceptions of communist and homosexual subcultures. It becomes fairly con-clusive in its implication that both queer networks and queerbaiting were part of an overall picture that is further fleshed out by the combination of "malicious" and "gossip" with the original terms "clique," "private party," and "blackmail."

Leaving behind the silences that have grown up around this "gossip," let us return in conclusion to textual evidence, beginning with anecdotal data on yet another film's production history. McLaren's one-person floral arti-sanal model of animation was not to remain forever the only one in the age of Fordism – even at the board. Some of the younger artists of the embryon-ic Studio B, heterosexuals all, started working on a more industrial model of production, cel animation, around the turn of the decade. Their second effort was the spry cartoon on the history of transportation in Canada; the industrial cartoon tradition was an appropriate medium for adding parody and punch to such a deadly topic. The cartoon became *The Romance of Transportation in Canada* (1952, 11; see chapter 1), but as Colin Low, the director, explained to me, there was uncertainty about how to complete the final package (telephone, 25 February 2001). The traditional NFB stentori-an voice-over would normally be necessary to rescue the Hollywood-style apparent fluff for the NFB's national-security mission, but what Low calls "a straight narration" [*sic*], commissioned from their usually reliable com-mentary expert, was clearly not working with the new format and sensibil-ity. Producer Glover, who kept his tactful distance from McLaren's work but who sometimes seems to have been involved in everything else that was going on at the board, was in the studio that day. Glover joined in the brain-storming and came up with a new commentary, and his spontaneous read-ing of the text was so obviously right that it was immediately attached to a film that was to become another canonical text of the Cold War. Over a rel-atively slow moment in navigation history, for example, Glover's mock-pedantic voice intones, "By the eighteenth century, fleets of bateaux (as they were called after the French *bateau*) plied an extensive lake and river system made more navigable by the construction of canals and locks," with the affectedly obvious etymological parenthesis sending up the entire self-seri-ous trope. This text and its eccentric voice-over constitute the perfect wry gloss on this strictly homosocial history of flouncing and pompous white men carving a capitalist empire out of a so-called wilderness; they are also clearly camp, and in fact downright sissy. Indeed, how else could the film articulate so concisely and so flippantly the insecurities that clouded discourses both of nationhood and of masculinity – not to mention those of the governmental documentary – all at the same time? When one learns that the Liberal minister and hatchetman Robert Winters saw *Romance* and barked, "Who authorized that?" (Evans 1991, 26), one wonders whether the question exemplifies the befuddlement of yet another Canadian politician confronted by arm's-length cultural activity or whether the question reveals some more fundamental phobia.

Many of the titles I have mentioned in this chapter were produced for a new communications medium that was to become an even stronger instrument of cultural governmentality, gender hegemony, and queer exclusion than the NFB's celluloid, namely, television. *Howard, The Street, Monkey on the Back, Is It a Woman's World? The Cage,* and *Woman Alone* were all part of the "Perspective" series produced by the board for the CBC between 1956 and 1958. (Interestingly, many of these films were scripted by Charles Israel, who departed from an apparently successful screenwriting career in the Los Angeles television milieu in 1953 for the backwoods of Toronto/Montreal, for reasons never fully explained, in order to pursue his interest in writing on social issues.)[13] It was the CBC that panicked at the appearance of prostitutes for the first time on the screens of the nation and ominously yanked *The Street* from the airwaves. Indeed, television was the Cold War medium par excellence, as Senator McCarthy himself found out, and it installed its own silences.

The NFB would eventually lose the turf war with the CBC that it pursued throughout the fifties, but its precarious relationship with TV became a permanent one all the same. Television did not have the same opening, or the same kind of opening, for the entangled tropes of social marginality, male crisis, and national insecurity that had become so prominent in the NFB imaginary. Thus, television may well have been one of the factors extending the long silence around the monkey on the board's back. Ironically, the fresh new regime that gradually took over the NFB in Montreal after 1956, including the new French studio, would do little to disturb that silence. Its new technologies and new aesthetics of direct cinema, *la vie à l'improviste*, preferred the surfaces of experience rather than its faultlines and undercurrents, the centres of society rather than its margins, thus relegating the docudrama style of "Perspective" to the archives and its spinsters and bachelors along with it. The new silence, even deadlier than the fractured silence of the first Cold War era that has been analyzed in this chapter, was unfortunately to last several more decades (see chapter 6).

3

Sexual Revolution, Canadian Cinemas, and Other Queer Paradoxes

The fact that so many things were able to change in the sexual behavior of Western societies without any of the promises or political conditions predicted by [pioneer sex therapist/theorist Wilhelm] Reich being realized is sufficient proof that this whole sexual "revolution," this whole "anti-repressive" struggle, represented nothing more, but nothing less ... than a tactical shift and reversal in the great deployment of sexuality.
~ Michel Foucault, 1976

"Go join your love-in, but leave me alone!"
~ Guy, 13, in *Don't Let the Angels Fall*, 1969.

This whole sexual revolution, now a decade or two or five safely behind us, is increasingly stirring up struggles and shifts in the great deployment of scholarship and won't leave us alone. I would like to do two things in this chapter: first, fine-tune and evaluate the concept of the sexual revolution as a way of defining a certain moment in international film history. Second, I would like to apply the concept to a selected corpus within Canadian cinema of the sixties. Probing sexual representations within that corpus – and discourses of queerness unexpectedly discovered therein – may help us in understanding the overall trajectory of the sexual revolution in the cinema internationally and in the Canadian cinema in particular, not to mention the construction of sexuality – indeed homo- and heterosexuality – within that historical moment.

WAS IT REALLY SEXUAL, WAS IT REALLY REVOLUTIONARY, AND WHEN WAS IT?

However we might want to define it, there is no doubt that something sexual happened in Western industrialized societies in the three or four decades following the Second World War. However we might share Foucault's hesitation as to the revolutionary character of that something, there can be no dispute about the momentousness of the shifts in social attitudes, behaviours, and social organization during that time and the central role played by sexuality in those shifts.

Periodizing amorphous objects like attitude shifts isn't easy. Historian David Allyn dates the sexual revolution (henceforth, the SR) between the "early sixties" and the "late seventies" (2001). Others have started the SR with the launch in 1953 of *Playboy*, or in 1960 of the Pill, or more whimsically at some point in 1963 – "[b]etween the end of the *Chatterley* ban, And the Beatles' first LP (Larkin 1988, 167)." The following January, *Time* magazine's discovery of the "Second Sexual Revolution" made it official: "all America is one big Orgone Box" (24 January 1964).¹ The magazine put on its uncharacteristic cover a painting of a postcoital heterosexual couple situated rear view in the lush draperies of a bedroom, presumably having enjoyed illicit sex *without* the consequences that Hitchcock had reserved for Marion Crane five years earlier after a similar scene in *Psycho*. As for the SR's closure, this has been identified with greater evasiveness and less hyperbole, usually at various points in the late seventies or early eighties (*Time* pronounced it over in 1984). I like to date the SR symbolically, perhaps too symbolically, as inaugurated by the first Kinsey Report in 1948 and wrapped up in the early 1980s with the advent of Reagan and HIV and the defeat of the American Equal Rights Amendment. But for the purpose of this chapter I will focus on the late sixties, the high point of what might be called the prefeminist phase of the SR, and specifically, I will zero in first on the documentary culture of the first half of the sixties and then on four feature art films undertaken in 1968 – the iconic year of revolution, sexual, cinematic, and otherwise.

Foucault wasn't interested, of course, in such historiographical nitpicking, and on the rare occasions he acknowledged the SR, he situated it as a mere continuation of the discursive explosion around sexuality that he had traced from the late seventeenth century. Within this framework, the period of so-called Victorian prohibitions, the "great repression" from which the SR hypothetically liberated us after the war, had lasted perhaps just over a century and was a mere blip on the screen of the larger discursive pattern. This larger dynamic, encompassing most of modern European history,

Foucault famously characterized as an intensification, a multiplication, an incitement to discourse, a dissemination of polymorphous sexualities, a perverse implantation, and so on. For Foucault, a twenty-two-year-old middleclass queer intellectual the year of the Kinsey Report and thus a major stakeholder in its revolutionary potential, the SR was at most a question of the prohibitions' "loosening of their grip," "less a rupture than an inflexion of the curve" of the macrohistorical intensification (1990, 119). Writing in 1976, just before the end of the periodization I have set up, Foucault, as we saw in the epigraph to this chapter, was already quite lucid that it was a question, not of the revolutionary dismantling of the deployment of sexuality, but of some ultimately less paradigm-shifting tactical accommodation.

Nevertheless, such ardent Foucauldians as Jeffrey Weeks have no doubt that this "tactical shift and reversal" was of considerable consequence (1985, 19–20). Weeks characterizes the shift as the "permissive moment" and the "explosion of speech around sex ... a decisive, *qualitative* escalation of the volume" (my emphasis), and he identifies four sets of changes that took place:

- the commercialization and commodification of sex,
- the shift in relations between men and women,
- changes in the mode of regulation of sexuality, the emergence of new, or re-ordering of old social antagonisms and the appearance of new political movements.

With the first of these diagnoses, Marxist film historians such as David James have no quarrel whatsoever. James's *Allegories of Cinema: American Film in the Sixties*, published in 1989, was one of the most focused studies of the SR *in* and *of* the cinema – at least in the American cinema of the sixties – since Amos Vogel wrote *Film as a Subversive Art,* just as the momentum of the "antirepressive struggle" in the cinema was beginning to wane in 1974. James's model of the industrialization of sexuality and of the central role of the cinema in this process is far in spirit from Vogel's utopian celebration of subversive image-making. Rather, James's pessimism evokes other voices belonging to the late sixties and early seventies, voices as distinct as Herbert Marcuse and Pier Paolo Pasolini – and thirteen-year-old Guy in one of this chapter's epigraphs – echoing their denunciation of false liberation, "repressive desublimation," and the hope of negation pre-empted by the permissive consumer society. Though Foucault seems also to have been able to speak in terms that echo Marcuse (1964), speaking of a control by stimulation that replaced a control by repression, Foucault would surely have qualified, if not disavowed James's ultimately materialist analysis of the invasion of capitalism into the private realms of intimacy and fantasy through the commodification of sexual representation. He was on record as disputing the Marxist notion of recuperation and as seeing, rather, a negotiation process (1980, 56), the "strategic development of a struggle," *power and the body "answering" each other back.*

Not that the discourse-centred and materialist perspectives are necessarily incompatible in their applicability to sexual representation, as Linda Williams has shown (1999). She has combined them most fruitfully, albeit in relation to the hard-core theatrical pornography of the seventies. But of course pornography was not the only cinematic sector working discursively at what Williams calls the problematization of sexuality occasioned by the SR. Other sectors of the cinema were engaged no less in this work on their own terms, in dialogue with pornography, and constituted, no less than the skinflicks, that *something* that was the SR in the cinema, either in their emergence, in their proliferation, or in their own strategic shifts. Each sector had a particular stake in the SR and embodied a distinctive relationship between the sexual marketplace and the discursive arena, whether we are thinking of the underground and avant-garde cinema; the narrative art cinema (aka the "foreign film" back then, film whose audience typically disguised its sexual fascination with cross-cultural pseudoethnographic respectability); the sex education/documentary cinema; or the mainstream commercial entertainment industry, at either level, mainstream A or disreputable "exploitation" B (the latter subsector overlapping with all other categories). Some of these sectors have been receiving recent attention as sexual discursive problemsolvers and material economies thanks to scholars such as Steve Cohan (1997), Lauren Rabinovitz (1991), and Eric Schaefer (1999). But a *global* perspective on the volatile relationship in the sexual cinema between commodity, discourse, and context in a multisectorial, cross-cultural grid remains a high priority. Providing this perspective will not be easy, for the accelerated sexualization of the cinema is difficult to extract from the other material and cultural dynamics of postwar cinematic history, such as the fragmentation of its markets, the proliferation of parallel and subcinematic production sites, and the disintegration of the studio system and its Production Code (the Code era now looks itself also like a Foucauldian repressive hypothesis, a mere blip lasting barely more than three decades beginning in the early thirties, as little as one-quarter of the sexual cinema's century-long trajectory).

In short, each sector enacts on its own terms the cinema's modernization, and in each this process is inextricable from its sexualization. One reason for the murkiness of the historical object is the historical tendency of sexual discourses to disguise themselves as something else. In the late sixties, for example, the eroticism of two of the era's most notorious sex films, the highbrow Swedish *I Am Curious (Yellow)* (Vilgot Sjöman, 1967) and the lowbrow American *Vixen* (Russ Meyer, 1968), bleeds into, absorbs, or camouflages itself as radical or antiwar political discourse. The reverse is often also true, in films from *Medium Cool* (Haskell Wexler, United States, 1969) to *Terre em transe* (Glauber Rocha, Brazil, 1967) (and, a bit later, *Coming Home* [Hal Ashby, United States, 1978]). Both Vogel and James echo this process by interweaving sexual and political (and formal) subversion in their accounts of the period's film history. Sexual revolution often also figures itself as discourses of youth revolt and counterculture and even, as in Quebec and elsewhere in the decolonizing world, as discourses of nationalism and national liberation.

Sorting this mosaic out is no doubt easier in relation to the modestly proportioned Canadian cinema than to the Babylonian behemoth south of the border. This is especially true of the 1960s, when the cupboards were relatively bare. We had no porno industry except as an import sector and no underground cinema except in exile, and we also were restricted to only ominous murmurs of a commercial entertainment industry, especially before the foundation of the Canadian Film Development Corporation in 1968 (mandated by the profligate federal government to pull a film industry out of the hat). The sixties, however, were the golden age of our documentary cinema and the baptism by fire of our art cinema. Both sectors were largely funded by a benevolent and philistine state bureaucracy and implicated in the commodities markets of international cultural prestige and domestic policy, as well as in the research-and-development economy of branchplant industrial development (indeed, all filmmakers discussed in this chapter moved at some point from the public sector to the private film industry, and in some cases back and forth). With such a simple grid, we can distil the process of sexualization within these two hothouse sectors of the Canadian cinema without too much interference. First, I will tackle the Canadian documentary and its evasive implication in the SR – from its animated lessons in STDs and cautionary parables of teenage pregnancy to its "direct cinema" celebrations of a permissive lifestyle and pop culture. Then looking at the narrative art cinema, manageable in scale, will allow us to see succinctly some of the discursive and material dynamics at work in the "sexualization" of this sector.

DOCUMENTARY: DIRECT CINEMA, DIRECT SEX, 1956–1970

ANN LANDERS: Sex belongs in marriage, this is what it's for.
ALBERT ELLIS: I would recommend that teenagers be encouraged to pet to climax.
MARY WINSPEAR: And I've been trying to say look my dear if you don't have to, don't.
ANN LANDERS: Sex without a good spiritual and emotional relationship is just

like sneezing, it's just something that you get over with, but it doesn't
mean anything.
~ Tanya Ballantyne Tree, *Merry-Go-Round*[2] (NFB, 1966)

Canadian film aficionados are a remarkably amnesiac crowd. The sixties
are progressively disappearing from our "best" lists, pruned of all but those
one or two most familiar feature films that still haunt our short-term memory. When I mention *Merry-Go-Round* as one of my favourite Canadian films
from the sixties and salaciously describe its remarkable scene of teenaged
boys attending a strip club and salivating over a statuesque dancer taking it
all off, followed by a graphic scene of one of the boys masturbating to a
Playboy centerfold, I am stared at in disbelief, especially when I reveal the
work's NFB provenance. If one of my goals in this book is to uncover the
hidden secrets of Canadian film history, then I nominate *Merry-Go-Round*
as one of dozens of prime candidates, not only because of its intrinsic merits
as bold and fresh film art, not only because it might sum up even better than
Nobody Waved Good-bye where I personally was at as a pressured and
horny seventeen-year-old egghead stuck in Guelph, and not only because
of director Tanya Ballantyne Tree's and cinematographer Martin Duckworth's later emergence as household names of our Canadian documentary
film heritage (born 1944 and 1933 respectively). *Merry-Go-Round* deserves
rediscovery also because it hooks up with one of the largely unexamined
issues of Canadian film history, our national cinemas' fateful encounter with
the SR on its path to the present. Not a queer film in the narrow sense, it
nonetheless is part of the queering of Canadian cinemas that is the subject
of this book.

As with many national cinemas, Canadian movies emerged into artistic
modernity at the same time as they embraced *sexual* modernity – simultaneously, interactively, irreversibly – during the successive generations after World
War II. The context of the SR is indispensable for understanding our cinemas of the sixties. The SR is the backdrop for the first stirrings of a commercial theatrical industry, for example in Larry Kent's great and recently
restored sexploitation epic *High* (1967); for all those sobre youth alienation
and coming-of-age docudramas (both on the Anglo and the Québécois side
of the divide) by emerging baby boomer auteurs Don Owen, CLAUDE
JUTRA, Gilles Groulx, Jacques Godbout, George Kaczender, Robin Spry,
and so on, most getting their start at the National Film Board; for the
embryonic queer cinema detectable in David Secter's *Winter Kept Us Warm*
(1965) and Claude Jutra's *À tout prendre* (1963), both most decidedly *not*
at the NFB (see the following chapter).

If, as Foucault has argued, the SR was only the inflexion of a curve, let
us not forget at the same time the perceptions of filmmakers, audiences and

critics who lived during the baby boomer era and who experienced what felt like a monumental dislocation, both in the social and in the cinematic field. As Albert Ellis's expert voice-over booms in *Merry-Go-Round*, "there's been a profound sex revolution among the attitudes and the behaviour of the young people." Like other film historians following Barbara Ehrenreich's germinal analysis of the "male flight from commitment" in North America after the War, I would identify a first *Playboy* phase of the SR, one of male entitlement and consumption, which the cinema and the documentary cinema in particular – as we shall see – played out and problematized in the 1960s.[3] Thereafter, a second phase that has been called "the women's Sexual Revolution" would be played out off-screen and on-screen in the 1970s, laying the groundwork for queer and other extensions of that momentum in the eighties and ever since.

Coming back to documentary, let us first note the uncanny historical convergence of breakthroughs in medical technology and in representational technology during that first *Playboy* phase: on the one hand, the Pill and on the other hand, the legendary tape recorder the Nagra or, in general, the 16mm sync-sound portable documentary technology that made possible the new documentary aesthetic of direct cinema (or *cinéma vérité*, as North American anglophones usually called it, thinking they were being hip and French). Thus, a new art form extended the field of public representation and visual commodification into previously untapped areas of private life, and *at exactly the same time* we have global shifts in social organization, identities, and attitudes around sexuality, gender, reproduction, and the family. These shifts have been conceptualized also precisely in terms of their bearing on private life, namely, the "blurring of the distinction between private and public," according to historians John D'Emilio and Estelle Freedman (1988, 277). Boundaries that had once seemed stable and clear were redrawn, escalating the war over the sexualization of the public sphere, the intrusion of the state and the marketplace into the private realms of fantasy, relationships, and the body.

There's another NFB documentary from the same period, *Ladies and Gentlemen ... Mr. Leonard Cohen* (1965), where the young poet lets a camera crew follow him around and comments, naked and wry from his on-screen bathtub, about a man allowing strangers into his bathroom to observe him cleaning his body. The comment is pertinent but somewhat disingenuous, for the new situation is not about public surveillance of private hygiene (although that is also an issue within the SR of course). Rather, to put it more aptly, it is about a group of straight male white middle-class intellectual filmmakers, including codirectors Don Owen and Donald Brittain, planting themselves in the private space of a male public figure, using the alibi of homosociality and the aesthetic of the everyday to look at the male

The intrusion of the camera into the bath is less about public surveillance of private hygiene than the cult of sexualized celebrity flesh: *Ladies and Gentlemen ... Mr Leonard Cohen* (1965). VHS frame grab, used with permission of the National Film Board of Canada

body but disavowing this desire, using the mystique of the ordinary to camouflage the cult of sexualized celebrity flesh.

This entry of the camera into Leonard Cohen's bathroom – which may be the first such intrusion by filmmakers not involved in law enforcement, incidentally – posits on a more general level the naked, private, individual body as receptacle of the self. If this film and other films of the sixties began to see the gendered sexual body as the site of identity, as the locus of cinematic and social discourse, it was a clear departure from earlier documentary discourses that largely attached such meanings to *groups* of bodies in social or economic formations and contexts.

This interface of documentary technology/aesthetics with the SR had not exactly leapt off the screen during the first years of the new documentary of the late fifties and early sixties. It seems that the indexical realist form par excellence was cautious and even prudish, entrenched in what Bill Nichols has called the "discourses of sobriety." There were admittedly a few important pockets of unabashed doxploitation around, such as *Mondo Cane* (Gualtieri Jacopetti, Italy, 1962). But these sex-and-violence voyeurism docs reflected the revolutionary societal shifts less vividly and later than every other sector of the cinema, documentary bringing up the rear, well behind the underground cinema, the art cinema, the erotic and exploitation cinemas, naturally, and even the still heavily censored commercial-entertainment cinema.

Still, beginning about the time of the two documentaries I am discussing in this section, from 1964 to 1966, and certainly by the end of the sixties, the direct cinema escalated its effort to testify to, understand, and sometimes deflect the major shifts in sexual regimes going on in the world outside. This happened first in literal terms of subject matter, with the sudden flood of films coming out of the NFB on teenage sexuality and abortion and so on, slightly in advance of Euro-American documentary as a whole. It also happened in the more tangential areas, whose connections to sexuality were often disavowed, from baby boomer youth culture to science and education. This work took root in both of direct cinema's emerging branches, the observational (the American Frederic Wiseman, the Canadian Allan King) and the interactive (the American Emile de Antonio, the Québécois Denys Arcand), as well as in the lingering expository mainstream (the heirs of Lorne Greene and Walter Cronkite). All three branches come together in *Leonard Cohen* and *Merry-Go-Round* in the distinctive ironic or self-reflexive manner characteristic of so many NFB products of the decade.

Now let's get down to dissecting *Merry-Go-Round*, released the year after *Leonard Cohen* by Ballantyne Tree, a director a generation younger than the established male directors of the Cohen film, a work that I rediscovered at the casual suggestion of its cinematographer Martin Duckworth (to whom I will come back shortly). As I've said, the film was anomalous: it isn't every twenty-one-year-old McGill Philosophy and History grad who gets complete artistic control over her first film, then or especially now, nor every SR film that is more playful than sober about all those traumatic changes underway. But despite its exceptional status *Merry-Go-Round* is still symptomatic of the filmic impulses at play in the SR wave, of their roots and subsequent outgrowths, of the range of sexual iconographies, problems, and solutions they offer, and specifically of the dialectic of public-private that shapes them.

At first it might seem odd to select a largely dramatized work to launch this discussion of the interface of direct cinema and SR, partly because Ballantyne Tree's dramatizations seem to hark back to an earlier generation of NFB social-problem films of the late forties and fifties, those dark earnest docudramas glimpsed in the previous chapter that have been banished as far from the canon as you can get. These earlier films use scripts and acting to tackle then daring subjects like labour conflict (*Strike in Town*, 1955), prostitution (*The Street*, 1957), mental illness (*The Feeling of Hostility*, 1948), unmarried pregnancy (*Woman Alone*, 1956), and drug addiction (*Monkey on the Back*, 1956). All these films show individual private conduct and identities impinging upon the public sphere as a "problem." They thus set in motion cultural assumptions about ethics, privacy, and tact – in short, about stigma. Along the way they also confronted the limitations of classical sound-documentary technology in capturing the human dimensions of these issues: the NFB was not about to go out interviewing hookers on Yonge Street in 1956 even if the right mikes had existed, which they didn't ... not quite yet. So the docudrama recipe of dramatization, scripts, and actors was the solution to the aesthetic problems, but it maintained its marginal characters within the framework of social stigma and victimization.

Clearly, by 1966 the sensitivity of the topic of adolescent sexuality, especially in the government and educational production sector, was still high enough to maintain the assumptions of the earlier decade about documentary ethics. But the dramatization was now rendered in the new improvisational sync sound direct style using real social actors in real social space. (Interestingly, Ballantyne Tree would get into ethical hot water the following year with her more famous film, *The Things I Cannot Change*, where she abandoned the tactful dramatisation she imposed on middle-class sexuality and assaulted the working-class-bound cycle of poverty with no-holds-barred direct observation, inadvertently humiliating her family subjects publicly; this film would become an object lesson in problematical ethics for generations to come.) In *Merry-Go-Round*, docudrama performances are shaped by Ballantyne Tree's finely tuned peer-group complicity; the protagonists and the target audience are spared the victim construction of the earlier films. We no longer have the tragic sexworker of *The Street* as victim (as my schoolteacher mother would have put it back then in Guelph, Kathy drops her "ing's" and smokes and drinks – no wonder she's on the street!). Instead we now have the sympathetic and horny heterosexual teenage couple, not as problem Other, but as self, as subject.

Ballantyne Tree's incipient feminism notwithstanding, in *Merry-Go-Round* it is primarily the male body, as in *Leonard Cohen*, that embodies the subjectivity of the film. The camera just can't stay away from the bathroom, but now the childlike homosocial bathing body and the athlete's body are in play, unlike the depiction of Cohen, the charismatic poet exhibitionist. (It was Duckworth's memory of shooting the astonishing group shower scene featuring seventeen-year-old Eric and his high-school classmates that triggered my sudden queer interest in this film.) "The male body was considered public territory," recalled Ballantyne Tree twenty-five years later, but it was a body whose sexuality was mostly carefully deflected by hygiene, homosociality, and sports (telephone interview, 10/98). The *desiring* body does come up later, but as consumer rather than as object, when we see Eric in the coded masturbation scene tossing aside the well-thumbed *Playboy* magazine and its opened centrefold and when we see Eric and his buddies visit a (heterosexual) strip club (Rockhead's, the famous black Montreal jazz club, which by the mid-sixties was clearly using strip acts to keep the doors open).

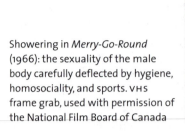

Showering in *Merry-Go-Round* (1966): the sexuality of the male body carefully deflected by hygiene, homosociality, and sports. VHS frame grab, used with permission of the National Film Board of Canada

No doubt because of its alibis and codes, the male body has not been sufficiently acknowledged as an icon of the sixties documentary canon, especially the American canon. The flurry of sports and pop celebrity films at the start of the decade ended up with the youth revolt and social-marginality films of the end. Canadian films never really developed the extreme voyeuristic attachment to the male body, principally marginalized, evinced in their US counterparts, where naked or all-but-naked child molesters and psychotics, drag queens, surfers, soldiers, tribals, and rock fans suddenly became common currency (in *Titicut Follies*, *The Queen*, *The Endless Summer*, *In the Year of the Pig*, *Dead Birds*, and *Woodstock*, respectively). Allan King's voyeuristic *A Married Couple* (1970) would be the Canadian exception that proves the rule, though his yuppie patriarchal advertising executive in his bikini briefs is hardly marginal. All that documentary beef-cake – or rather crypto-beefcake – conveyed with the luminous physicality that the new technology encouraged, together with the surprising invisibility of cheesecake (a pattern that was obviously reversed in the erotic sector of the mainstream cinema proper), simply confirmed the sensibility of male entitlement, taken-for-granted male subjectivity that was the underpinning of the *Playboy* phase.

In *Merry-Go-Round*, the female body gets a different treatment indeed. Although Jennie's performance is authentic and nuanced, the revelation of both her body and her subjectivity is restricted (she even keeps her coat on during the prelude to the surrender of her virginity). In terms of her sexuality, she is more compliant with the desire of her boyfriend than acting on her own desire, but admittedly Masters and Johnson, the American gurus of the clitoral orgasm (their pioneering *Human Sexual Response* was first published the year after the film's release), had not been absorbed by either the protective Ballantyne Tree or the still patriarchal NFB. Elsewhere in *Merry-Go-Round*, the female body retains much of its traditional otherness, female authorship and female expert commentary notwithstanding. This is due to

Ballantyne Tree's protofeminist discourse of the female body as public territory, not as desexualized homosocial subject but as commodity object of representation that is explicitly sexual, rather than disavowed (alongside the centerfold, we see a hard-hitting barrage of lipstick and other sexist ads in the consumerist visual environment of rue Ste-Catherine). Ballantyne Tree's refusal of the camera voyeur with regard to her heroine is entirely set aside in the sequence presenting the stripper watched by the boys, who as an African-Canadian is all the more "other." She is performed by a real-life social actor, conveyed as spectacle through the boys' eyes, but with her sensuous glamour and dignity is surprisingly uninflected by Ballantyne Tree's earlier reticence or by any hints of the feminist moralism that would come to the surface a decade later in Studio D.

The final image of the film shows the couple silhouetted against a window after they have finally, by implication, "gone all the way." This lyrical but ambiguous freeze-frame establishes the couple itself as the centre of the film and avoids the sexual morality and victim sympathy of earlier work. The image offers a very sixties projection of feelings and relationships, pleasures and bodies as ultimate gauges of morality, not rules and prohibitions. In short, what they used to warn us about in Guelph Sunday school as the New Morality was being promulgated by our very own government film studio!

Apart from the conventionally sentimental aestheticism around the heterosexual couple, the film's approach to the social-issue docudrama format is decidedly irreverent. The chorus of three contradictory experts – the advice columnist, the permissive psychotherapist, and the tolerant motherly educator – are gently satirized in the scenes of floor hockey that precede the famous shower passage (myths of working off all those hormones!). This send-up is taken even further later when Ann Landers's admonition to teenage daters to avoid temptation by "do[ing] something" is mocked by accelerated shots of skiing, swimming, and movie going. The film is topped off by a virtuoso machine-gun montage where the three expert voices, both interdictory and sympathetic, literally cancel each other out. This demolition of the NFB voice-of-God expert voice-over – at long last – is the final signal not only of a new sexual morality but also of a shift in documentary modes. Rather than the closure of the earlier expository conventions entrenched by John Grierson, this open ending ushers in the age of modernist ambiguity and interactivity. Imagine the scene in the NFB mixing studio when the pretty young McGill upstart must have had to cajole the technicians into having the three voice-overs drown each out!

Cinematographer Martin Duckworth, eleven years older than Ballantyne Tree, is known now as *the* cinematographer of the English Canadian New

Left both inside and outside the NFB. In 1970 he might rather have been identified with the youth film and the SR, and not only because of his appearance in what must be the only film in world history where the entire crew appears nude (the 1970 NFB-Swedish coproduction *Pure and Untouched*)! Duckworth's camera virtuosity belongs already to a second English Canadian generation of direct cinema, a moment less of discovery than of perfected fluidity, bringing the spectator not only into the showers, the gym, and the dim strip club, but also into elevators, bedrooms, smoky folk clubs, and the interior of a car parked on the midnight make-out spot on Mount Royal, peering over the shoulders of the necking couple. Duckworth's camera confronts whatever barriers between public and private space remain, between private experience and public roles.

Duckworth's technical virtuosity, almost taken for granted by 1966, masks an aesthetic and an ethic that become explicit in his archetypal youth movie, *Christopher's Movie Matinee*, shot for NFB director Mort Ransen in 1968. One of the teenage protagonists is visibly distressed about having been filmed in a "terribly personal" moment of kissing her boyfriend the previous day. "You broke into something personal and that upset me," she complains. Duckworth's voice responds, "It's only the personal things that are worth filming," followed by an unrepentent zoom in on her tears. In a nutshell, this transformation of sex into cinematic discourse, as St Michel would say, enacts the new aesthetic of the sexual private as public and the SR ethic of sexuality as the core of personal identity.

Duckworth, along with Ransen, Derek May, Robin Spry, and others formed a kind of straight male auteur network in the English studios at the board in the late sixties, a network specializing in the youth and sexuality genres. In keeping with Duckworth's maxim, they veered towards personal documentary, often autobiographical and confessional in sensibility, interrogating the sexual subjecthood, as well as the parenthood and husbandhood, that accrue to male heterosexual identity. Duckworth, as cameraman in May's 1970 autobiographical *Film for Max,* for example, intimately and tenderly interviews the director about his fears of losing his wife, Patricia Nolin, whom, incidentally, he has just shown topless. This patriarchal confessional moment in direct cinema history has not been sufficiently explored by film historians, if at all. Aside from anticipating Foucault with their enactment of both surveillance and confession, such films articulate both the male entitlement and homosocial intimacy, the male anxiety and crisis, that epitomize the *Playboy* phase of the SR in other cinematic sectors as well.

In direct cinema, paradoxically, this *Playboy* moment also points ahead to the second *women's* phase of the SR and of the sexual documentary. In this second phase those invited into private space are not strangers but sisters, and the invitation would be not so much into the bathroom as into the kitchen, the bedroom, the nursery, the laundryroom, and onto the consciousness-raising sofa, one day even onto the mattress. The NFB didn't touch queer, of course, for a very long time, until it went all the way in the 1990s, but that's a merry-go-round for chapter 6.

ART CINEMA: YOUTH, SEX AND POLITICS, MONTREAL, 1968

Now, as promised, I will analyze four feature films, two in English and two in French (to allow cross-cultural comparison), from my adopted hometown of Montreal, films that I, like many English Canadians, first encountered during the sexy Expo 67 celebrations of that same decade. All four were produced by the National Film Board in that critical year of 1968 as part of their investment in developing a Canadian feature cinema in the absence of a commercial base (and not, incidentally, as a means of keeping nationalist Québécois auteurs out of trouble with the radical *indépendantiste* movement). The films I have selected are currently outside the Canadian or Québécois national canons but were received as important, though commercially insignificant, at the time (the two English-language films had uneventful New York openings). Finally, though I decipher queer goings-on in all of them, the films are equally outside currently solidifying queer canons as well: *Don't Let the Angels Fall*, George Kaczender (b. 1933), 1968; *Jusqu'au coeur*, Jean-Pierre Lefebvre (b. 1941), 1968; *Prologue*, Robin Spry (1931–2005), 1969; and *Wow!*, Claude Jutra (1930–86), 1969. Jutra and Lefebvre are of course major figures within the Canadian/Québécois canons, but the two films selected here are generally passed over as "minor." Kaczender and Spry are both familiar directors from this period and the seventies but doomed to the status of "minor" auteurs. Their works here fall into the category of respectable festival entrants (Cannes and Venice, respectively) and thereafter would have been quietly, unjustly shuffled out of history were it not for the diligence (until recently) of the NFB in maintaining its celluloid library in circulation.

All four features belong more or less to the "youth film." This genre has been generally agreed to be *the* characteristic one of the first modern generation of Canadian cinemas in both English and French – and as we shall see in chapter 6, one of the back doors for the queering of the NFB. These four directors were among the genre's masters. The youth film celebrated, anguished over, and pruriently spied on the generation that was the first to grow into the SR, the by then postpubescent baby boomers. The youth genre also defined baby boomers as its intended constituency, as well as its object, either through didactic uplift or pandering condescension, thus extending our Griersonian cinematic traditions of documentary aesthetics and social intervention.

All four films, which I have marked as symptomatic enactments of the SR on our provincial screens, were produced, as I have stated, in Montreal. This location is significant, for Montreal was then the largest city and the commercial capital of the nation and our international showcase during Expo 67. It was also throughout the decade our cinematic capital – thanks to the institutionalization of state film production and broadcasting there – and our sexual capital. (As a measure of its status in both these regards Montreal had managed by middecade to lure Larry Kent, the most risqué of our tiny sprinkling of independent art cinema directors, away from the quiet anglophile outpost of Vancouver into its cosmopolitan vortex.) Montreal also boasted the most liberal regime by far of cinematic censorship in Canada and was the site of the liveliest hetero red-light and nightlife scene, the most brazen gay entertainment ghetto, the most rambunctious student, left, and labour movements, and the most turbulent eruptions of public struggles over the shifts in sexual culture (for example, vice cleanups).

Not surprisingly, all four films, all undertaken by male directors in their twenties and thirties the year after the 1967 Summer of Love (and released either that year or in 1969), capitalize on their host city's sexual and cultural aura. All four films are jam-packed with the iconography of the SR as it was implanted in this distinctive urban geography. This iconography is flaunted self-seriously as a badge of hip sexual modernity: from centrefolds on every wall to go-go dancers in the corner of every frame; from the requisite female and male nudity (skinny-dipping in *Prologue*, psychedelic nude trampoline acrobatics in *Wow!* immortalized on the film's poster, vanilla hetero lovemaking in bed in *Angels*, also posterized) to a plethora of the various markers of the youth revolt – sartorial, tonsorial, musical and pharmacological. Furthermore, all four directors tackle thematically and narratively the requisite "issues" of the day (which had already turned up, less obliquely, as documentary subjects) such as premarital sex, adultery, drugs, the generation gap, abortion, the male flight from commitment, and even, prophetically, the female claim to autonomy and pleasure.

If we come back and assent to D'Emilio's and Freedman's contention that the SR involved fundamental redrawings of the boundaries between private and public, we can read all four films as participating intradiegetically in these redrawings. This is most dramatic in tropes of the public flaunting of private or sexual behaviours (for example, the nude street exhibitionism of *Wow!* to be discussed below), which is set up alongside the more conventional sixties street theatre of public demonstrations, also running through all four films. Both sexual and political, individual and collective demonstrations occupy, almost jingoistically, the familiar metropolitan public space of our city. Finally, the four films all offer, like Montreal itself, a tentative acknowledgment of nonheterosexual bodies, sensibilities, and desire.

Monique's autoerotic fantasy of psychedelic trampolining bespoke both corporal narcissism and social enfranchisement, but also made a groovy poster for Claude Jutra's *Wow!* (1969). Film poster, used with permission of the National Film Board of Canada

STRAIGHT COUPLES AND QUEER OTHERS

All four films deploy one of the major narrative conventions of the youth genre, the construction of the young heterosexual couple as allegory, not only of their baby boomer generation but also of the nation itself (whether that might be defined as Quebec or Canada), of Western civilization, or indeed of humanity. This allegorical tenor of the couple is vividly shown on the publicity image for *Jusqu'au coeur*. The films are not the unqualified celebrations of heterosexuality that this poster might imply, however. Rather, heterosexuality is troubled, the couple disturbed, masculinity anxious. How could it be otherwise when the couple is at the centre of both narrative momentum and political discourse and filtered through the various earmarks of modernist ambiguity needed to access the international festival and arthouse circuit, from Lefebvre's Godardian collage to Kaczender's black and white asceticism à la Resnais-Antonioni-Bergman to the experimental docufiction hybridity of both Spry and Jutra? Even aside from the modernist packaging, there is a fundamental problematization of the heterosexual couple in these films.

In one passage from *Jusqu'au coeur*, this problematization seems most symptomatically violent. It starts with the hero, Garou, coming home from a hard day out in the city, surfing the ideological winds of a society driven by war, to be greeted with beer by his supportive girlfriend (the two characters are both played by pop stars of the period, Robert Charlebois and Mouffe, respectively, if any further indicator of allegorical status is required). Garou reads the paper, Mouffe hovers, Garou then proposes to his consort with a beercan ring, asks if they should have babies, and then announces that he really has to get a job. This tender and whimsical conjugal scene, rendered in black and white and self-conscious location sync sound, is suddenly interrupted by a full-colour vignette set in Mount Royal's woodland park, wherein a white hunter figure guns down a black man with a rifle. Then follows an extended interior shot, also in full color, of two nattily attired young men on a sofa sheepishly necking with each other; then the conclusion to the racial vignette set now in a dilapidated *ruelle*, where the apparently resurrected black man ambushes the white hunter with a stranglehold and leaves him for dead; and finally an interior shot matching the earlier one, this time of two short-haired young women in slacks necking on the same sofa in turn (the shot is slightly longer, the behaviour somewhat more explicitly sexual than with the women's male counterparts). Both racial and queer vignettes are silent, and unlike the surrounding images, the shots of the two queer couples are constructed in documentary mode, clearly presenting social actors performing, albeit somewhat self-consciously, their sociosexual identity. The subsequent sequence moves on with Lefebvre's plot of the hero's psychiatric and political subjugation by war-driven society.

The filmmaker's sudden interruption of the heteroromantic moment with a collage of racist violence, subaltern revenge, and transgressive eroticism is anomalous, to put it mildly. Assaultive in its abrupt silence and switch of stock, it is as unmotivated and cryptic as it seems, not related in any obvious way to any other thread of the film. As for the gay and lesbian content, it certainly goes beyond the standard queer-disavowal scenes, which from the midsixties on, became virtually omnipresent throughout Hollywood and Europe, especially in the homosocial genres. Logically, it might stand as a vague positioning of the romantic couple in relation to the 1968 environment of racial upheavals and increasingly visualized sexual marginality, which no doubt many Canadian audiences of the day would have associated with U.S. media culture.[4] But as the author's intentions revealed, as explained in an interview with the Montreal daily *La Presse* (1 February 1969, 33), it is also Lefebvre's comment on the couple's parenting fantasy and mandate to go forth and multiply, an opposition of sterile nonprocreative sexuality to the couple who hold the future of the planet in their hands. Not that this intent transmits to many viewers, for in my mind the

un film de jean pierre lefebvre
jusqu'au coeur

faire la guerre
c'est trop facile

et si par hasard l'homme
pouvait disparaître
sans que l'univers
en soit affecté...!

la vie est belle

c'est peut-être un film
qu'on voudrait tuer,
comme la guerre

je mourrai dans
mon champignon
atomique

dites-moi
à quoi rêvent
les enfants avortés?

tu crois
aux martiens,
mouffe?

robert charlebois et mouffe

paul berval
denis drouin

pierre dufresne
luc granger

gaétan labrèche
claudette robitaille

producteur:
clément perron

une production de
l'office national du film du canada

image: thomas vamos
son: claude hazanavicius
montage: marguerite duparc
musique: robert charlebois

The heterosexual couple as allegory of nation and humanity in *Jusqu'au coeur* (1968). Ads promised that rock star Charlebois "has lost the sense of the war" but that his consort Mouffe "has kept the sense of life." Film poster, used with permission of the National Film Board of Canada

Jusqu'au coeur (1968): lesbian transgression interrupts the art cinema's allegorical hetero-romantic conjugality. VHS frame grab, used with permission of the National Film Board of Canada

assaultiveness of the edit signals no more than the license of the art cinema to flout clarity and taboos and enunciates the author's profound and phobic personal disturbance at same-sex identities and kisses. Like the standard disavowal tropes, the passage also serves to define, through the visual echo and the semiotic opposition (as if a perverse parody of the lead couple's romance), the "naturalness" and normativity of the protagonists' relationship. The shots of the two queer couples necking shocked a lot of people it seems,[5] no doubt because the digression refused to perform the reassuring disavowal conventions of either the fag joke or the queer bash. The interviewer disguised *his* disturbance at the sexual and social iconoclasm by focusing on the ethical and aesthetic affront, asking if the shots might not exemplify the "limits of direct cinema" (it is likely that the journalist's invocation of this popular topic in sixties Quebec film culture was a reference more to an offense to the "normal" spectator than to the ethics of voyeurist abuse and Lefebvre's possibly fraudulent enlistment of the social actors, both of which sprang to my mind almost four decades later). Regardless of the shots' indisputable value as among the first unambiguous documentary images of lesbian and gay couples in our national cinemas (and as rarissimo documentation of queer kissing and affection from any period), homosexuality gets lumped in with racial conflict, war, aggression, and federalism in the complex of external factors that besiege and martyr our heterosexual representatives of humanity.

Spry's images of homosexuals in *Prologue* are also documentary and "elsewhere." Anticipating *Medium Cool,* Montreal radical activist Jesse (shown in the film's poster) makes a documentary visit to the demonstrations at the 1968 Democratic Convention in Chicago that is woven into a fictional heteroconjugal narrative. His relationship with Elaine, who, as a go-go dancer-waitress, has been supporting his activism is faltering, and she has declined the pilgrimage to Chicago to try out another consort. This option is a laid-back Yankee draft dodger, another model of heterosexual masculinity and another form of radical politics, who takes her to a country commune where the aforementioned skinny-dipping takes place. Meanwhile, Jesse encounters *the* three most famous living homosexual writers in the Western world – William Burroughs, Jean Genet, and, most prolongedly, Allen Ginsberg – with whom he even participates in a sunrise group yoga session on the Lake Michigan shore. Spry does not name the three writers as homosexuals of course (it's still 1968, after all, and Spry's soft-pedalling of sexual identity may be consistent with the New Left blend of coolness, complacency, and obliviousness, rather than necessarily sharing Lefebvre's phobia). But the three writers' function as speakers at the Chicago rallies is not quite the conventionally political role of intellectual fellow travellers in the Old Left either – the freaky yoga sessions make sure of that. The queer triumvirate seem monk-like in their asceticism, especially in comparison to guest cameo star Abby Hoffman, also represented in the film and played up in the publicity, who comes across as aggressively deviant in his heterosexual rapaciousness.

All four documentary stars are part of the intense and transgressive otherness of the conflictual social and political atmosphere in which Jesse has immersed himself in the belly of the beast south of the border, but it is the queer ones that he most emulates in his own deadpan asceticism and serenely aggrieved righteousness. Against the symbolic meaning that Chicago thus acquires are countered the calm, repressed Montreal civility to which Jesse returns to carry on his work on the street and his orderly conjugal relationship. This relationship is ultimately vindicated when Elaine discovers what a chauvinist creep the hippy draft dodger is, for all his pantheistic narcissism and golden facial hair, and returns to patient Jesse and normative coupledom. Is she also returning to less exciting sex? the spectator wonders. Regardless, Jesse and the film are resolutely respectful of the autonomy of her choice, which is more than can be said for most 1968 films. Spry's relation to the other, the world outside and down there, a world of violence, deviance, and radical sainthood, is attraction, rather than Lefebvre's revulsion. But he resembles Lefebvre in that this other world is still the defining framework of normative allegorical heterosexuality, and politics is still the narrative motor of the sexual scene, albeit this time the politics of radical street mobilization, rather than abstract antiwar sentimentality.

QUEERNESS AS AUTHORIAL SUBJECTIVITY

Queerness enters the other two films in my selection as authorial subjectivity, rather than as narrative hinge or as definitional otherness: I am speaking of gay scriptwriter TIMOTHY FINDLEY in *Angels* and gay director Claude Jutra in *Wow!* both negotiating the SR from within the semiprivate space of eve-of-Stonewall ambiguity.

Don't Let the Angels Fall, as one of the posters makes dramatically clear, figures not one heterosexual couple nor *Prologue*'s heterosexual triangle, but two heterosexual couples, both crumbling in the face of social alienation and change. The bourgeois paterfamilias protagonist has three women revolving around him emotionally and sexually but cannot commit or respond to either his terrified wife, his supportive French Canadian secretary, or his nurturing and serene young blonde mistress, the ingenue appearing as the main publicity attraction. His twenty-two-year-old son, who crystallizes the radical revolt element in this film with his faddish participation in public student protest and premarital sex, is no better than his father at performing "masculinity" (as it was increasingly defined in the post–Masters and Johnson sixties in terms of the cool, sensitive lover solicitous of his partner's pleasure). He takes his sensuous French Canadian girlfriend for granted – she is shown symptomatically prone in the poster, as her boy friend kisses her back – and he is oblivious to either her career or her sexual needs. If Lefebvre's nuclear family bore the weight of an oppressive world, the nuclear family in *Angels* implodes under its own inertia, repression, and obsolescence.

The most intriguing character in the film, however, is the thirteen-year old son, Guy, who frightens everyone with his catatonic rejection of both bourgeois institutions and his brother's empty libertinism and radicalism. His defiant critique and opting out, shouted to his brother, we have already heard at the start of this chapter: "Go join your love-in, but leave me alone!" It is as if Guy had just read Marcuse and is diagnosing and rejecting, a decade before Foucault, the compulsory nature of the sexual society. As the film draws to an end, Guy slowly becomes its moral centre, as the designer for one of the film posters for once perceptively understands in the use of Guy's silhouette to enclose the other plots. Guy's refusal of family and society, as well as of revolution, sexual and political, is a gesture of true revolt and authenticity: in the Findley scenario he is the only one who is not "buggered up," and in Kaczender's more Bergmanesque words to a Montreal *Gazette* interviewer, he is the only one who can be saved (3 May 1969). Guy escapes from the upper middle-class neighbourhood of Westmount in the middle of the night, wandering exultantly near the Vieux Port, and finally ends the film by exuberantly and confidently climbing the geo-

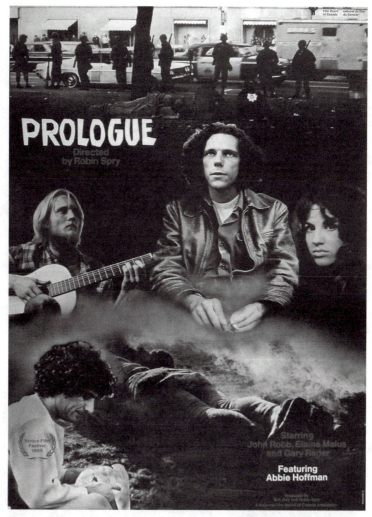

Prologue (1969): radical activism as a model of hetero-masculinity, but blond American draft dodger guitarists seem sexier. The NFB pushed Abbie Hoffman (lower left), but the three most famous homosexual writers in the world are also on-screen. Film poster, used with permission of the National Film Board of Canada

desic dome from the previous year's American pavilion at Expo, a symbolic moment as cryptic and fraught as art cinema conventions allowed.

I like to decipher Guy as Findley's embryonic gay hero. I know that Findley's work would never express the reductively "positive heroes" that the following year's Stonewall would eventually usher in, but asexual (self-sexual? presexual? – the talented young actor Jonathan Michaelson's voice is not changed) Guy is so other to the crumbling heterobourgeois universe around him, so enamoured of the night through which he strides, buoyant

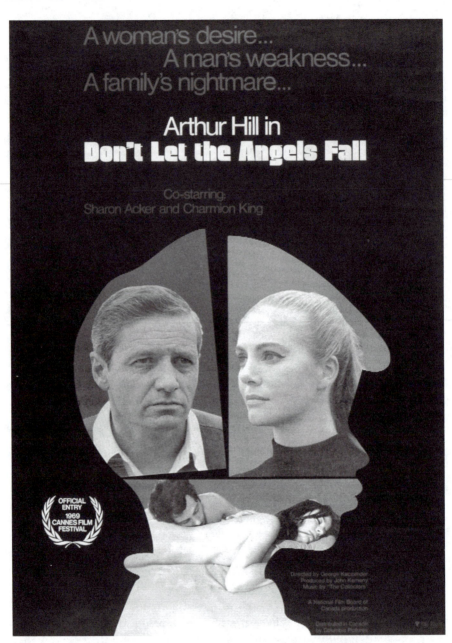

Don't Let the Angels Fall (1969). This poster shows disintegrating heterosexual coupledom but understands that protoqueer thirteen-year-old Sexual Revolution–dropout Guy (silhouetted) is the moral centre of the film. Film poster, used with permission of the National Film Board of Canada

Thirteen-year-old Guy refuses family, society, and sexual revolution, climbing cryptic symbolic structures instead, in *Don't Let the Angels Fall*. VHS frame grab, used with permission of the National Film Board of Canada

and glowing, that I can't resist. Apart from his mother's intuition that his problem is "sexual" (she pauses dramatically and cocks her eyebrow as she says this word in her futile attempt to open him up), there may be scant textual justification for this reading (all the more so since heterosexual director Kaczender [b. 1933] adds his own disavowal to Findley's script, the visual touch of Guy looking up a woman's skirt on the Metro escalator). Still, his character concentrates the most hope of both negation and affirmation in the entire corpus, and as we have already seen in the foregoing chapter, subtextual negotiation was often all we had to go by in pre-Stonewall Canada.

Wow! is the furthest among the four films from the conventional-couple movie format and thus reveals most about that format's arbitrariness and discursive construction. Jutra selected a group of teenagers as his documentary subjects, three girls and six boys, drawing out from them their opinions and attitudes about sex, politics, drugs, friends, parents, and the future. In true Foucauldian confessor fashion, he also draws out their intimate desires and fantasies, which he dramatizes with his typically lavish NFB budget and the characters' performances. Significantly, only three of the fantasies involve heterosexual coupling, two male and one female, and these are the most static and conventional of the entire anthology. And surprisingly, only one of the six male fantasizers could be described as stereotypically macho in his dream of being a rock star who motorcycles toward the horizon, bare-chested, naturally, with his long-haired chick holding on tight.

The others' fantasies, all nonspecific, erotically speaking, can be characterized in two ways. First, several are self-satisfying expressions of auto-eroticism and exhibitionism. Monique's trampolining, like the other two girls' fantasies, enunciates a fantasy of both corporal narcissism and social enfranchisement. Of similar orientation is Flis's public flaunting of his comely body as he runs nude down the city's main artery, rue Ste-Catherine, shocking shoppers and a Mrs Grundy–type clown in drag. One need not attach anachronistic meaning to the giant pink and blue ribbons around Flis's neck to infer a strong homoerotic overtone to Jutra's mise-en-scène of this fantasy, regardless of the rather skittish reliance on rear projection for the documentary setting (and rear nudity, alas, as well). Homoeroticism aside, these characters' self-sufficiency is not far from that of Findley's Guy in *Angels*: all are significantly expressed through the open-ended symbols of both the art cinema and the historical closet, rather than in concrete socio-political options. Whereas Garou's public exhibitions in *Jusqu'au coeur* were tropes of humiliation and submission (wheeled on a float down the same rue Ste-Catherine on the way to his lobotomy), Jutra's and Kaczender/Findley's performances of solitary corporal pleasuring and display are tropes of revolt and risk. Autoeroticism may on one level seem like an alibi for the homoeroticism that dared not quite yet speak its name. But on another level it seems like an instinctual cinematic analogue of Pasolini's affirmations that the body is the only preserved reality, vulnerable and doomed, in the face of compulsory, commodified sexual consumerism ([1973] 1994; [1975] 1982) or of Foucault's repeated affirmations of the body as the ultimate site of resistance, an answer to power.

Homosociality is the other predominant fantasy dynamic of *Wow!* The majority of the participants are male (a trace of the NFB's pre-feminist androcentrism, as well as of Jutra's erotic taste to be sure), two of the males are discursively constructed as buddies, and two of the fantasies are male homosocial. Also, the relationship of male subjects with confessor-mentor Jutra constantly flickers on the continuum between social solidarity and erotic complicity. For example, at the conclusion Pierre enacts a marijuana scene with a buddy, bare-chested and spaced out, the two of them sprawled on his mattress, inches from the lens. The scene aches with longing and tenderness, its voyeurism both sensuous and respectful at the same time, scarcely camouflaged by the Griersonian social worker pretext of the youth film that no doubt got *Wow!* funded. The rare apparent serenity of this authorial flickering between identification and desire in *Wow!* does not seem threatened by these instabilities in the continuum of homosociality. To what extent was Jutra aware that the cinema was still, after all, an overwhelmingly male cinematic institution confronting serious challenges to its

Wow! (1969): Flis's public flaunting as he runs nude through Montreal adds a homoerotic overtone to Claude Jutra's fantasy of youth empowerment but also celebrates the way in which power and the body answer each other back. VHS frame grab, used with permission of the National Film Board of Canada

legitimacy? In the three other films, and throughout the culture at large, the consequence of such flickering is violence.

Elsewhere in *Wow!* as in the other three films discussed here, youth revolt is figured through radical politics. A fantasy bomb explosion shatters Westmount bourgeois order at the start of the film, equal parts Front de libération du Québec[6] and flash forward to *Zabriskie Point*. Later, in Jutra's own version of the requisite south-of-the-border episode, the director parachutes his participants into Resurrection City, the Washington tent city protest that was confronting LBJ's record on poverty. But the young Montrealers come away with a sense of powerlessness, in contrast to Jesse's empowerment in *Prologue*. Jutra's political interludes and excursions are much more of a momentary deflection of his major agenda than a structural core of the film, as Spry's were. Contemporary commentators noted how ultimately conservative Jutra's teenagers were, bombs, nudity, and pot notwithstanding. What interests them and Jutra alike are not so much upheaval, sexual or otherwise, but comfort, intimacy, self-pleasure, and security in the context of a sex-gender system in flux, not so much transformation but freedom and trust unrestrained by rigid expectations and scripts.

CAUTIOUS AMBIVALENCE

In conclusion, these films' modest accumulation of self-consciously hip sexual discourse may admittedly not rival in their sexual radicalism the contemporaneous 1968 European and American art films *Teorema, If..., Weekend, Belle de jour,* or *Lonesome Cowboys*. After all, we *are* Canadians, this is the NFB, and, politeness aside, colonial cultures usually emulate metropolitan revolutions with some restraint. Still, all four 1968 youth/couple films, produced within the context of the embryonic Canadian art cinema, are graphically caught up, like the turbulent metropolis whose imprint they bear, in the "antirepressive struggle" of the SR. They welcome the extension of cinematic language and the reinvention of audience and social implication that the SR inspires. They articulate a fierce attraction to the risks of sexual freedom, couching them as much in the safe exoticism of American iconography[7] as in the stakes of domestic struggle, and yet they figure them politically in terms of radical oppositionality and youth revolt. All four Montreal filmmakers recognize the failures of traditional patriarchal masculinity, albeit with great tenderness and complicity for the wounded phallus, but are implicitly critical of the inherited sex-gender system, which the SR in its first *Playboy* phase had jolted but maintained intact. Furthermore, if one looks carefully, all except Lefebvre offer an incipient problematization of women's relationship to the SR, of the question of women's sexual enfranchisement, autonomy, and pleasure – or, in other words, a glimpse of what Ehrenreich, Jacobs, and Hess would later call a second phase (1987), the *"women's* Sexual Revolution." Finally, all four offer explicit flashes or subtextual hints of the sexual diversity then acquiring increasing visibility in the public and cinematic spheres. Yet instead of the defensive hyperbole of pornography, the euphoria of the avant-garde, or the blinkered opportunism and hesitation stampede of the commercial popular cinema, we find in this art cinema a cautious ambivalence.

In view of the filmmakers' historical positioning as young male members of the middle-class male intelligentsia in the West in the sixties, the SR's and the sexualized cinema's principal beneficiaries to date, this ambivalence about the promise of sexual liberation might seem remarkable. Instead of the mythologies of community, conversion, and salvation that one would find later in a second cinematic phase beginning in the seventies, a phase in which first women and soon openly queer artists would be more positive in recognizing the emancipatory potential of the "antirepressive struggle," the male filmmakers of 1968 are surprisingly restrained, just as concerned about the altered regulatory regimes that are accompanying the sexual shifts. They are caught, as a group, vacillating between utopian and dystopian visions, between the normalization and destabilization of the hegemonic heterosexual couple, between a self-critical awareness of the cinema's centrality in the deployment of sexuality within modernity and a blinkered complicity in it. Dehistoricized and allegorized, the heterosexual couple is nostalgically lamented by Lefebvre, tentatively, pragmatically restored by Spry, interrogated and dissected by Kaczender/Findley, and indulged but ultimately bypassed by Jutra.

Finally, as I have affirmed with an admittedly essentialist nuance, the queer authorial input in *Angels* and *Wow!* sets those films apart. In *Jusqu'au coeur* and *Prologue*, cameo queer tropes position and define the heterosexual couple and act as decoy for its trouble at ground zero of the SR. In *Angels* and *Wow!* a discreet queer subjectivity is much more direct in probing that trouble and in envisioning the space or spaces it opens for alternatives. The latter two films are too prudent to name the queerness of those alternatives, for the colonial context and state funding scarcely provided the avant-garde haven for queer artistic practice afforded Allen Ginsberg in New York and San Francisco and Jean Genet in Paris. Still, the resilient bodies of Guy climbing the dome and beribboned Flis defying rue Ste-Catherine seem to crystallize a measured hope on the part of Findley/Kaczender and Jutra, a slate as open as their enigmatic art film endings.

Those climbing and running bodies echo Tanya Ballantyne Tree's proto-feminist claim of sexual empowerment and autonomy for teenagers and the entire direct cinema's fumbling and tentative exploration of new bodies, new desires, new moralities, new cultures. Together these Canadian films of the sixties encapsulate a cinematic confidence that the Sexual Revolution is an ongoing, perhaps asymptotic process, rather than a static fait accompli, an *incomplete* perverse implantation, a curve with inflection still being formed, a process where power and the body will continue to answer each other back.

4

Fairy Tales of Two Cities, or, Queer Nations(s)/Urban Cinemas

It was the best of times, it was the worst of times ... we had everything before us, we had nothing before us ... There were ... a queen with a plain face on the throne of England ... and a queen with a fair face on the throne of France.

CLAUDE (voice off): In this way has escaped the secret that I've kept inside me even longer than I can remember. Johanne ... has lifted the heaviest part of my burden. She has made me confess the unconfessable and I had no shame, I had no hurt. And now everything is changed, for that driving desire that was never satisfied, that torment, has taken the form of a ray of hope.
~ *À tout prendre* (1963)[1]

BEV : Why Doug you'd almost think that you guys were –
DOUG : Oh come on cut it out, Bev."
~ *Winter Kept Us Warm* (1965)

SANDRA: Hormones! isn't life exciting on the Main!
MAURICE, club owner, to "protégé": If [the Chez Sandra Club] didn't pay so much, I would have got rid of this fucking rabble long ago ... You don't know if they're men or if they're women ... And they spend their lives making dumb jokes about it ... That's all they talk about, try to get them talking about anything else! Goddamm gang of lunatics. Give me straight people anyday, who go to straight clubs, see straight shows. To look at cunt, dammit, real cunt, not imitation rubber ones ... When you come here, dammit, the men smell like cunt

and the girls are built like trucks. But what can you do? It pays...
~ *Il était une fois dans l'Est* (1973)

SOCIAL WORKER : Have you been sleeping with this roommate?
LIZA: Oh no, Robin and I sleep in different worlds.
~ *Outrageous!* (1977)

FOUR FILMS

Claude, Bev, Doug, Liza, the Social Worker, Sandra, and Maurice are all talking about identities and desires, but only Maurice is talking about the bottom line, the economics of sexual marginality.

This chapter continues the previous chapter's focus on the 1960s but pursues that decade's queer cinematic élan into the following formative decade. Here I also move beyond exploring embryonic queer subtexts within the revolutions in sexuality and filmic language to confront for the first time in this book unabashed, upfront, and articulate queer voices, namely four pioneering gay-authored feature films of the sixties and seventies whose dialogue I have offered for tasting above. In doing so, like Maurice I would like to talk about the bottom line, to explore materialist methods for sorting out the interface of these momentous queer cultural texts and a certain "habitation/nation system" within the legal borders of the precarious political entity called Canada. I will attempt to factor in the "sex/gender system,"[2] or certain overdetermined queer corners of it, in an attempt to flesh out, as it were, Maurice's analysis. Furthermore, my endeavour is to historicize this interface within our so-called national cinemas. No one would deny that these two decades were key to the transformation of national feelings, sexualities, and cinemas within the state called Canada. Looking at these representative cinematic texts from this period of invisibility and transformation will render them less invisible, more material ...

To do so representatively is of course to straddle borders, both geographical and chronological, as well as political. It means keeping one foot in both of the bicultural camps of private-sector[3] Canadian film production of those decades, Montreal and Toronto, and one foot as well both before and after the chronological watershed of the late sixties, the historical divide around 1968–69 that partitions the period. (Perhaps as an Anglo-Montrealer by adoption I am especially qualified to do so, a straddler by history, geography, culture and choice.) This somewhat artificial time-and-space border straddling requires a grid, no doubt too neat, for highlighting the symmetries and oppositions through which our four films partook of and can illuminate retroactively the material constructs of nation, sexuality, and cinema in that formative historical period that began with the Quiet Revolution and ended with the first referendum of 1980. The dividing line of 1968–69 marks both the founding of the Canadian Film Development Corporation and the Omnibus Bill. These two acts of state symbolize, respectively, the official transition from an artisanal cinema to an industrial one (and from sober black and white to glitzy colour) and from underground sexual subcultures to decriminalized sexual constituencies, a "gay and lesbian" political minority. Geographically speaking, though the sixties formed the age of the Trans-Canada Highway and the St Lawrence Seaway, these east-west vectors scarcely spanned at all the huge chasm between the two metropoles of French and English Canada or between the two "national" cinemas and the two sexual and political cultures they (coyly?) embraced.[4]

Our corpus of four feature fiction films – two from Toronto and two from Montreal, two from the sixties and two from the seventies: (*À tout prendre* [1963], *Winter Kept Us Warm* [1965], *Il était une fois dans l'Est* [1973], and *Outrageous!* [1977]) – are stuck schematically but symptomatically within the four quadrants of this grid. These texts are particularly – and materially – fraught with the queer, national, and cinematic identities

Table 1: The Grid

being constructed within the borders of this federal state and of this formative period. The four films, their respective careers, and the symptomatic critiques I have selected resonate with echoes and divergences in every direction, across both geographical and chronological borders. They allow us to trace tandem trajectories of queer identities and desires through a cinematic sifting of class, economic, geographical, cultural, linguistic, and sexual variables, on-screen and off, in the two urban locales in the era of Expo 67 and the Spadina Expressway. The films are representative of the queer-authored fiction features that emerged from these spatial and chronological quadrants: they *had* to be, they were virtually the only ones,[5] and they thus acquire a disproportionate historical weight, dialoguing with each other like an epochal chorus.

À tout prendre (Take It All, CLAUDE JUTRA, Montreal, 1963, Best Canadian Feature Film Award). This semiautobiographical experimental narrative shows a privileged young filmmaker named Claude who is passionately involved with a black model named Johanne, who suddenly guesses that he likes boys. He strolls with Johanne up the Mountain, the famous gay cruising area,[6] where he fantasizes that the couple is attacked by a leatherman biker. Johanne gets pregnant, Claude dumps her, and the relationship dissolves in narcissism, rejection, and bitterness.

Winter Kept Us Warm (DAVID SECTER, Toronto, 1965; Semaine de la critique, Cannes). This University of Toronto student production, a realist social melodrama, impressed international critics at Cannes in 1966: Doug, big man on campus, meets Peter, a shy young Finnish-Canadian theatre major from Capreol, and discovers that his friendship is more than male bonding and more even than frolicking in the snow within the University of Toronto residences compound. Doug is jealous of Peter's girlfriend, and Doug's girlfriend is jealous of Peter; Peter loses his virginity to his girlfriend, Doug suddenly can't get it up with his, and their friendship dissolves in narcissism, rejection and bitterness.

Passing the watershed, *Il était une fois dans l'Est* (Once upon a Time in the East, André Brassard, Montreal, 1973; Official Canadian Representative, Cannes) is a downbeat melodrama based on characters from the plays of the brilliant young stage sensation MICHEL TREMBLAY. Hosanna, the Queen of the Main, is planning the greatest transformation of history as Elizabeth Taylor, Queen of the Nile, but her rival, Sandra, hostess of a club modelled after the landmark *Club Cléopâtre* – still in existence as of this writing – plots to steal both Hosanna's thunder and her boyfriend, Cuirette, in the same big night of revenge on the Main. This story and the other plots woven in and around the universe of the Duchesse de Langeais, drag queens, waitresses, lesbians, housewives, and drunks of the "East" dissolve in rejection, bitterness, and rage.[7]

In the shadow of the new Toronto Dominion Centre, meanwhile, *Outra-geous!* (RICHARD BENNER, Toronto, 1977; Silver Bear, Berlin Film Festival), an upbeat hybrid of backstage musical and melodrama, narrates a hairdresser named Robin, a refugee from a closety salon, and his roommate Liza, a refugee from schizophrenia and psychiatry. Robin is the best female impersonator in town but can make it only as a diva impressionist in New York. Robin's triumph is qualified because Liza's baby is stillborn, but hey, everyone has "a healthy case of craziness" and let's dance.

THREE FRAMEWORKS

The films must first be situated within three intersecting discursive and material frameworks.

Cinema/Culture

Along with the passage from artisanal feature fiction to industrial state-financed cinema is the parallel passage from the gay subtext – not so much the voice of the *other* as the voice *from under* – to the gay spectacle, from innuendo to performance, from acting to acting out. The cinematic cultures of the two regions are diametrically opposed: in the sixties Rouch, Cocteau, and Truffaut, plus Hitchcock and Anger, are the presiding geniuses of cinephilic Montreal, but in Toronto they're all still colonial English and drama majors fixated on Ibsen, Eliot ... and Harry Belafonte.[8] In the seventies, Montreal cross-fertilizes Genet and Bergman, but Toronto counters with erratic dreams of vintage Hollywood and contemporary Greenwich Village. Despite different genres and cultures, all four films embody a cinema of alienation and despair, the sublimated desire and self-directed violence that struggling New Wave cinemas by thirty-year-old male would-be auteurs have embodied in many national cultures. In Montreal this means Jutra's three surrogate suicide fantasies and Brassard's heavy theatrical screaming in rainy nocturnal streetscapes. In Toronto, Secter's recourse is to fistfights and poetry, and Benner's to a climactic disco dance party that can scarcely disavow the traumatic stillbirth. Enlivened by their autobiographical authenticity (both *À tout prendre and Outrageous!* star their real-life protagonists, and the other two films are also strongly, though obliquely, self-referential), all four films are nonetheless fragile butterflies. Anomalous even within the self-financed auteur movie making of the sixties and the erratic early years of CFDC financing of the seventies, none were ever really part of a continuum of film culture, despite their respectable critical and commercial success. Even *Outrageous!* which the CFDC seemingly couldn't believe was a hit, despite raves from *Variety*, Rex Reed, Judith Crist, and the rest and despite sellouts in New York, was a flash in the pan

Craig Russell as Judy in *Outrageous!* (1977). Toronto counters seventies ideals of activism in the streets with dreams of vintage Hollywood. Production still, Cinémathèque québécoise

(notwithstanding an uneven sequel a decade later produced shortly before the AIDS-related deaths of star CRAIG RUSSELL and director Benner [*Too Outrageous!* 1987]; Waugh 1988b). Their lonely marginality and intense sincerity makes all four films seem so vital and enduring today.

Sex/Gender

Heterosex abounds in these queer films. But Claude's passion leads to a pay-off for an implied abortion and Doug's to impotence. Tremblay/Brassard's characters are too stressed or drunk or mad to fuck, except in flashback, and in any case fucking would lead, in the story's prelegalization period setting (allegedly c.1965, though the art design belongs more or less consistently to 1973), to the devastating botched abortion of the film's dénouement. Liza's male one-night stand just doesn't understand anything – women, queer roommates, or schizophrenia and their bad sex leads to the corpus's third fruitless pregnancy! Do these images of sterility cast a displaced metaphoric shadow over the films' same-sex fucking? Perhaps, for queer love happens only in the loose sense, in surrogate, oblique, and off-screen forms. *Outrageous!* is the exception, but even there Robin has to pay for its begrudging enactment by "trade." Both of the sixties films displace the homoerotic onto the erotic exoticism of ethnicity, onto otherness as a space of sexual liberation (Claude's deluded Haitian fantasies of Johanne and their sensuous dalliance at the famous black jazz club Rockhead's; Doug's delectation of Peter's Finnish pastries, folksongs and – wink, wink – sauna). The breezy homosociality of Jutra's café-terrasses and Secter's university residence clearly masks the fissures of taboo desire and sadistic initiation.[9] In the seventies films, images of erotic expression may be more outspoken and upfront, but they are also no less disturbed, banished to the idyllic country of the past by Brassard's stylized flashbacks or restricted to the glittery artifice of masks and performance in both films.

In general, between the sixties and the seventies the transitions are telling: from closeted isolation to a collectivity (for better or worse); from conflictual triangles of girlfriends and boy friends (in which the girlfriends get the short end, it goes without saying) to supportive circles of gay male-female solidarity that transcend biological gender; from the surrogate intimacy of homosocial bathing, drinking, and sports to the heterosocial claustrophobia of the dysfunctional family kitchen, workplace, and play space. Above all, the shift is from intense moments of private confession to spectacular outbursts of public acting out. In other words, all four films are animated by the overwhelming momentum of "coming out" as a performative political ritual and narrative trope with, as Sedgwick discusses it (1990, 76–7), "immense potency," the trigger of the "flow of power." Claude's moment of truth, prompted by Johanne's intuitive enquiry (repeated with a haunting echo chamber accent), is not only articulated by the momentous and poetic voice-over declaration excerpted in an epigraph to this chapter but also accompanied by the clash of percussion and frenetic zooms into facial closeups (according to Martin Knelman, when the CBC cut this passage out of A tout prendre for its broadcast of the film, this caused an "excruciating ordeal" for the director [Knelman 1977, 60]). Doug, in the face of a parallel enquiry from his girlfriend in another epigraph at this chapter, cuts it off and out, but the entire film is shaped by the emerging shame of his realization that he is what you'd almost think he is, a realization that finally explodes in violence. In short, in the sixties the dream of bursting through the shells of repression animates the films, provides the potential for harnessing what Claude calls the burden of his shame and hurt and what Sedgwick calls the "powerfully productive and powerfully social metaphoric possibilities" of shame.

But even in the seventies, when everyone is already "out," the act of coming out requires its daily update of "shame consciousness and shame creativity" (Sedgwick 1993a). Ex-waitress Hélène strolls through the Plateau back alley, arm in arm with her butch girlfriend Bec-de-lièvre (hare lip), to the sound of the Belle-soeurs' intolerant and voyeuristic catcalls from their

Bev, Doug, and Peter (standing) in *Winter Kept Us Warm* (1965). The film epitomizes 1960s conflictual triangles of girlfriends and boyfriends ... and ambiguous looks. Production still, provided by the Canadian Filmmakers Distribution Centre

galeries; Hélène's tense supper *en ex-famille* follows and Bec-de-lièvre eats in dignity on the back *galerie*, from which she is not allowed to enter the inner sanctum of the familial kitchen – surely one of most powerful sequences of coming out and reinscribed shame in queer cinema of any decade. Even Robin, the most "flaming" and "out" of queens, must have his scene of confrontational truth with his closety hair salon boss, who wants him to butch it up. Yet for all the transformative animus of these coming out narrative dynamics, the identity utopias of the seventies are deferred, and the sex is still unaccountably bad. It is the decade of Hosanna's betrayals, the Duchesse's delusions, Robin's humiliations, and Liza's hallucinated bone crunchers, where everyone knows how little salvation can be found in the flesh and keeps looking for it anyway.

À tout prendre (1963). Girlfriend Johanne's question "Est-ce tu aimes les garçons?" triggers Claude's coming-out moment, the sixties dream of bursting through the shells of repression and productively harnessing the burden of his shame and hurt. Production still, Cinémathèque québécoise

Space, or Habitation/Nation System

All four films claim the urban geography of their cities, undertaking the pleasurable bricolage of fictional worlds through on-location shooting and community-recruited extras, materialist strategies that seduce audiences through the boosterish recognition of naming and familiarity. The pairs of films from Montreal and Toronto follow surprisingly similar trajectories through this space. For one thing, they follow instinctively the political agendas of gay politics of their respective periods.[10] Jutra's and Secter's narratives prophetically inhabit the anxious bedrooms where, according to one Pierre Elliott Trudeau, author of the Omnibus Bill, the state has no business. Yet in the private space of Claude's ground floor bachelor pad and Doug's dormitory room, privacy doesn't really exist: even when beer bud-

Il était une fois dans l'Est (1973): the post-Stonewall's decade's slogan was "Out of the closets and into the streets," and Brassard literally has his queen Sandra stop the traffic at the intersection of rue Ste-Catherine and the Main. Production still, photo by Attila Dory from the Cinémathèque Québécoise Collection, ©Les Productions Pierre Lamy

dies aren't crowding through the doors and windows, hidden looks and hovering innuendos can erupt at any moment into the violence of flouted desire. Claude's masochistic fantasy of street urchins shoots through his apartment windows at him; Doug beats up Peter in his dorm room because he can't fuck him. On the other side of Stonewall, Brassard and Benner, in tune with their decade's slogan of "Out of the closets and into the streets," literally have their queens stop the traffic on rue Ste-Catherine and Yonge Street, respectively. Urban public nightlife and streetlife are the settings for tumultuous climaxes of both seventies films, as well as the refuges from all that bad bedroom sex.

The sixties camera also explores the ambiguous haunts of the middle-class intelligentsia as they play out their high-cultural alibis on the Radio-Canada film set (where Claude directs and cruises a sexy actor with more hyperkinetic zooms) or at the University of Toronto drama club rehearsal space (where Peter plays Ibsen and seduces a sexy actress with his faux-naïf Finnish hayseed act); the seventies see a shift to rawer subaltern regions, the working-class bathroom and kitchen, the vocational ghettos of hair salons, snack bars, and liquor stores, tacky in Montreal, more sanitized in Toronto. The sixties are also charged with the furtive eroticism of the unorganized sexual undergrounds of Mount Royal (the cruising area to which Claude

À tout prendre: Claude (with clapboard) directs and cruises a sexy actor (with cigarette) at Radio-Canada, an ambiguous haunt of closeted middle-class intelligentsia playing out high-cultural alibis. Hyperkinetic zooms and sound effects follow. Production still, Cinémathèque québécoise

climbs with Johanne) and the Hart House shower room (where Peter – flir-tatiously? sadistically? – commands Doug to scrub his back!).[11] Both films seem to have one spatial mythology strategized for "national" audiences, and another for private recognition by queer audiences knowing surveys of *our* undergrounds, *our* ghettos and *our* liminal spaces.[12]

In the seventies, this territory is replaced by organized public visibility and commodification, the profit and spectacle of the Main's *Club Cléopâtre* and the gleaming Manatee Club at the centre of Toronto's emerging Welles-ley–Church St gay ghetto. (As Maurice says, it pays.)[13] The two seventies films brazenly and defiantly proclaim gay public geography, but the prob-lematical and provisional status of this declaration remains discernible, whether in Brassard/Tremblay's garish misanthropism or in Benner's over-stated cheerfulness and escapes to elsewhere. If Claude had seemed unac-countably at home in Montreal's toney Anglo West End downtown (which incidentally housed the embryonic gay ghetto of the sixties), a decade later

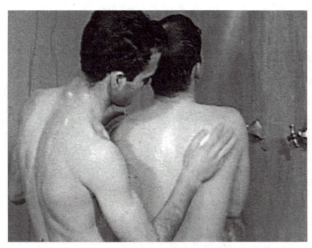

Winter Kept Us Warm (165) reflects furtive eroticism of unorganized sexual undergrounds such as the University of Toronto Hart House shower room (where Peter – flirtatiously? sadistically? – commands Doug to scrub his back). VHS frame grab, still provided by the Canadian Filmmakers Distribution Centre

Brassard embraced the red-light district and *balconvilles* further east,[14] the at once tolerant and intolerant crucibles of marginalities of every kind (where housewives may scream "bibite" [loosely, "creepy-crawly"] at the "butch" [lesbian] in the "ruelle" [alley], despite there being an outcast in every family). The Torontonians are more into urban renewal than slumming, moving up from Secter's seedy beverage rooms of the Yonge Street hetero tenderloin towards the domesticated and gay-friendly strip that Benner frequents in the seventies (skating at City Hall rink, anyone?). In short, all four films are shaped by the volatile urban dialectic of private and public intrinsic to the metropoles of the sixties and seventies, the cyclical tunnelling and emancipation, taming and merchandising of the zones of the forbidden.[15]

TWO NATIONS

Despite or perhaps because of?? – their inextricable centrality to collective discourses and material frames of cinema/culture, sex/gender, and habitation/nation, the four films are seldom revived and have resisted canonization, maintaining their invisibility within the official boundaries of the "national" cinemas of both Quebec and English Canada. Only the name brand auteur label of *À tout prendre* merits an occasional flash out of oblivion.[16] Yet all four films were situated as "national" texts by heterosexual critics upon their initial release, a legitimation withdrawn by subsequent taste makers in each case.

Of *À tout prendre*, Denys Arcand, in his film critic hat, was quick to draw connections between film, sexuality, and (French Canadian) nation (1964):

Why can Claude have a valid relationship only with this foreign Johanne whom he wants to make even stranger? There are after all "everyday" Québécois women all around him … both on-screen and psychologically. *À tout prendre* doesn't succeed in getting close in tenderness and satisfaction to real everyday women. And in that, the hero is like lots of 30-year-old French Canadians, sensitive and cultivated, who have to have women who are black, yellow or red, in any case "foreign," in order to have their intoxicating affairs. There is here, it seems, an unconscious refusal to coincide with his collective self, at the same time as an unquenchable thirst to perfect oneself in *a mythic exteriority* that arises from the global situation of our people …

… Nothing very surprising that at that point the film seems to claim the right to homosexuality … Nothing very new or very immoral in that. The only question is to know to what extent homosexuality is a solid form of sexual activity and in what manner it has a special state of self-affirmation, given our global context of existence in relation to artistic expression.

Of *Winter Kept Us Warm*, a more sympathetic French critic Louis Marcorelles started with a comparison of this "very very beautiful film" to Salinger's *Catcher in the Rye* (1964). Hinting at, rather than sermonizing, sexual marginality, he was no less ready and sweeping than Arcand with ethnic and national sexual stereotypes, matching them perceptively to Secter's cinematic style. Marcorelles then went on prophetically to decipher the rivalry across the linguistic divide to which the Winnipeg-born Jew Secter couldn't have been more oblivious:

A literature of the heart in the best sense: emotions, Anglo-Saxon style, without infinite nuances, but with strong feelings, an unconscious cruelty. The joy of living, of loving, of hurting … frantic egoism. The little beast in you and me.

Winter Kept Us Warm has above all the quality of being Anglo-Saxon to the extreme: its little dose of humour, skin-deep, *its tenderness that doesn't dare declare itself*, of unconscious cruelty …

Winter Kept Us Warm is beyond everything else a Canadian film: Canadian as one breathes, according to the strange mixture which has created a nation that is comparable to no other, a misaligned door opening on the edge of history. David Secter knows nothing of the NFB, has vaguely heard the name of Michel Brault, is unaware of Groulx and Perrault and Macartney-Filgate. Who cares as long as the Canadian "grace" … remains. This freedom of tone, this camera as tall as a man, stopping on a whim to follow a squirrel, frolicking in the snow among the flakes.

Il était une fois dans l'Est had beat out *The Apprenticeship of Duddy Kravitz* (Ted Kotcheff, 1974), as well as other films, to represent Canada at

Outrageous! ends with overstated cheerfulness and escapes elsewhere, in this case to a Greenwich Village club where postmiscarriage Liza dances with Robin/Peggy Lee. Everyone has "a healthy case of craziness" and let's dance. Production still, Film Reference Library

Cannes in 1974. In response, in Jean Leduc's review in *Cinéma Québec* the phobic political undercurrents beneath Arcand's feigned sophistication came out into the open (1974). Leduc began out with a valid question but then lined up drag queens, intellectuals, and Tremblay himself (marginalized to the point of the "infinitesimal") for the firing squad for their "inability" to understand and belong:

In what sense can a work of fiction really represent a national reality with its network of socio-economic-cultural implications … Did the criterion of representativeness ever play a role at any level? Is the milieu of drag queens on the Main strongly representative of the reality of Canada, of Quebec, of Montreal? What infinitesimal proportion of this reality does it represent? In any case is the image *Il était une fois dans l'Est* offers faithful to this supermicroscopic reality? (I am told that it is not.) And does the reality of drag queens on the Main differ noticeably from the reality of drag queens in London, Hamburg, Berlin, and Rome? *Il était une fois dans l'Est* gives the impression of being focused principally on this reality even if other elements dredged up from other Tremblay theatre play a part. There remains the general feeling from the whole of the film of great despair.

Is this a true image of Quebec reality or would it be an image equivalent to those favoured by certain intellectuals who need this security in order to disguise their inability to really grasp Quebec reality.

Outrageous! the Canadian sleeper success story of the 1970s, merited three pieces in *Cinema Canada*, a rave, a pan, and a production story. John Locke's rave (1977) began with an anecdote about a New York moviegoer's praise for its non-national generic spectacle value and then led in to a dissection of its un-Canadian Canadianness:

"It's the best show you've ever seen." This is not a typical reaction to Canadian films ... *Outrageous!* ... is the best Canadian narrative film I have seen, and forgetting about nationalism for a moment, it is a very good film indeed in 1977 international terms ...

The acting is so uniformly excellent that it is positively "un-Canadian" ... *Outrageous!* is un-Canadian in this specific sense: all the performers say their lines in a believeable fashion ... Canadian films often seem to disguise their nationality. Actors and actresses never say "aye." Canadian artifacts like money and license plates never appear ... *Outrageous!* breaks these conventions usually followed by Canadian films looking for United States distribution, and it makes the broken conventions work in its favour...

Thank you Richard Benner whoever you are, I have been waiting for years to see a really good Canadian narrative film.

These national linkages to our four "really good Canadian narrative" films call for several observations. The fact that the two Quebec films were marked negatively national by nationalist critics, that is, as nationally unrepresentative, indicates two things: the ways problematical questions of sexuality and class were postponed or papered over by the nationalist consensus of the intelligentsia and the and the ways cinema was assumed to be a privileged medium of national expression in the sixties and pre-PQ seventies.[17] The struggle to end film censorship during the Quiet Revolution had been in every way a "national" struggle,[18] yet Quebec filmmakers were called into line when they diverged from some undefined but sentimentally monolithic fantasy of the young *pure laine* heterosexual couple. (Paradoxically, Arcand's ideal couple rarely appeared in Quebec narrative of the period, other than in the softcore hetero stampeders *Valérie* [Denis Héroux, 1968] and *Deux femmes en or* [Claude Fournier, 1970] – certainly not in his own films!). On the other side, signficantly, both *Winter* and *Outrageous!* were tagged as essentially and positively Canadian through the objective outside eyes, respectively, of a French champion of Québécois nationalist cinema and an American expatriate critic who saw the film in New York.

Il était une fois dans l'Est (1973). Club hostess Sandra shamelessly tries to steal Hosanna's leather biker boyfriend Cuirette (centre). But does she represent "a true image of Quebec reality?" wondered the new breed of nationalist film critics. Production still, photo by Attila Dory from the Cinémathèque Québécoise Collection, ©Les Productions Pierre Lamy

Interestingly, of the four films, only *Outrageous!* directed by an American expatriate and resolved intradiegetically in New York, explicitly claims in on-screen textual terms the national as boldly as it does the queer. I am referring not only to the jingoistic flaunting of Toronto's cosmopolitan urban monuments in the very decade when Toronto was bypassing Montreal in size and representative aspirations – alongside the TD Centre and Nathan Phillips Square on-screen are the CN Tower, Union Station, and the streetcars. I am referring also to the famous and all too symptomatic jokes about the Canada Council and "making it in New York" (whose absorption by audiences effectively inoculated them against a film about a Canadian impersonating American divas and brain draining to New York). *Outrageous!* was thus participating in the simultaneous and interconnected awakening of nationalism and cinephilia in English Canada (later crystallized, beginning in 1983, at the Perspective Canada series at the Festival of Festivals) – a full generation after Quebec had seen the same phenomenon. In comparison with the queer Montrealers' unexamined assumption of national belonging, was Benner protesting a bit too much?

NAMING SEX

Naming the nation is one thing, but what about naming sex? How do the thematics of sexual marginality that retroactively seem so central enter the critical discourse? As we have seen, the practice and politics of naming in criticism is as tortuous as in the films themselves. Arcand's racist and homophobic slur on *À tout prendre*'s "claim" to the "non-solid" activity of homosexuality is as disingenuous as Claude's coming out is courageous, and it is as obscured by Arcand's irrational panic logic as Claude's claim is by narrative intricacy. Marcorelles' Wildean euphemism about tenderness is as graceful as *Winter*'s oblique sincerity. (One Canadian review of Secter's film explicitly named the "homosexual" thematic only to declare it "not really necessary" (Medjuck 1966), just as the *New York Times* was opining that Jutra was throwing in homosexuality simply to be avant-garde [26 April 1966].) Leduc's pseudosociological scapegoating exceeds even Tremblay's characters' gutter vilification – sampled in my epigraph above – of women and queers, and, most significantly, of themselves. In *Cinema Canada* Locke (1977) hiply avoids commenting directly on the queer thematics, and though *Outrageous!* is actually the first of the four films to use the g-word, the critic prefers "raunchy," "leather," and "unique" to "gay." (But the magazine's accompanying pan makes up for this delicacy with the by now very unhip "homosexual" and decries the addition of all the "lamentable" drag stuff to the source story [Fox 1977]). It goes without saying that none of the four critics identified the films as queer, gay, or homosexual cinema, and it would be anachronistic to expect otherwise, even in the seventies, all the more so with the avoidance and innuendo that traditionally invested criticism as much as it did the cinema itself. In sum, all reviews referred to the sexual marginalization of the film's diegetic world, either naming to disavow or avoiding to tolerate. But only the Québécois reviewers connected sexuality with the collectivity – negatively in both cases, as we have seen – even if the filmmakers conspicuously didn't dare. Needless to say, Benner's grafting of gay pride onto English Canadian nationalism was rather unique for 1977[19] – something that perhaps only an immigrant director would have dared in the days when the "national" gay newspaper *The Body Politic* was spending more time in court than in the pressroom,[20] and something no native critic, gay or straight, dared to do in any way whatsoever.

By 1977, however, we can finally speak properly of the existence of gay criticism and its engagement with our corpus. One discreetly gay critic, the late Jean Basile, had warmly welcomed *À tout prendre* in *Le devoir* (12 August 1963),[21] and the late festival impresario Richard Roud (1966), also discreetly gay, had provided one of *Winter*'s most glowing raves, a coy but retroactively lucid recognition of a "something": "a [stunning] moment when all of a sudden one realises that one has got it all wrong, that something quite different is happening up there on the screen, but that that something is nevertheless completely convincing and right." But only *Outrageous!* a dozen years later, was received and assessed – and in fact hotly debated – by a gay critical constituency, both in Toronto and abroad. Interestingly, *The Body Politic* hated it, printing a long denunciation of the film by Michael Riordan (1977). The piece acknowledged only indirectly, by virtue of its generous three-page length and photo spread, the film's momentous historical place as the first explicitly gay Toronto feature. Riordan's grounds for his savagery were political:

Will one heterosexual, even one heterosexual parent, march with us because of it, fight on our side, vote us into power, grant us custody, let us teach her/his children what it is to be gay? Will one heterosexual be changed by it – not comforted but changed, challenged, moved to original thought … What is there in its images for us? Will it make us stronger in any way? What does it contribute to our view of ourselves or of the world? Does it challenge any of the learned misconceptions that weigh us down? Most important, does it move us closer to a fresh non-heterosexist way of dealing with each other?

This eloquent invocation of the conventional "positive image" problematic and its instrumentalist conception of social effect reflects a common – and no doubt mobilizing – slant in early feminist- and gay-liberation criticism. Riordan's failure to recognize other politics of representation was offset by his forceful statement of a political contextualization that is decidedly local: his fury against the enthusiastic embrace of *Outrageous!* by the local tabloid, the *Toronto Sun*, which more than any other medium had actively led the campaign against both the beleaguered *Body Politic* and the inclusion of sexual orientation in Ontario's human rights code. Gay criticism was even more deluded then than now about the ideological coherence of right-wing media and even more conspiratorial about the one-dimensional performativity of media images. Riordan's only reference to the "national" stature of the film was indirect, an acknowledgment of the director's New York roots and the film's boffo reception in the American media and in *Variety*. He also pointedly referred to a gushy notice in an "American" gay paper, not naming Boston's *Gay Community News* as the source of the rave.

GCN, the most prominent American gay and lesbian community paper and the paper closest in spirit to *The Body Politic*, had indeed run a review that was both positive and uncharacteristically superficial (Holland 1977): "From the gay liberation point of view, the film is far ahead of almost anything that has come before … four star rating. [One wants Benner to give us] even more of his vision, now that he has furthered the image of gays as human beings on film ... In *Outrageous!*, gayness is a normal ordinary feature of life and neither the characters nor director Benner give it a second thought ... It's a bravissimo accomplishment." GCN had followed up a few months later with a long, glowing interview with Russell featuring the star's pouting observations that straight audiences were receiving the film more positively than gay audiences (1 April 1978). However, judging from Russell's reference to a pan in the *Chicago Gay News* that had particularly stung him, it seems that Riordan's views were not isolated and that the gay reception of *Outrageous!* was at least mixed. The GCN coverage, like most American notices then, as now, mentioned the Canadian label only in passing, if at all, and this omission clearly signified a "non-Hollywood" sensibility, rather than an expression of a national culture. The queer critical debates about *Outrageous!* then, all assumed its utmost pertinence to their constituency but the relevance of its "national" origins never entered the picture, regardless of how overstated its "Canadianness" was on the screen. Preoccupied with the pan-national constituency for the emergent gay and lesbian cinema, late seventies gay criticism overlooked other political contexts and frameworks for the new films, local and national, regardless of the fact that the local and the national were the arenas where the politics of sexuality were being hammered out.[22]

TWO URBAN CINEMAS

In conclusion, I have shown how these four muffled but haunting voices of the sexual other in the Montreals and Torontos of the sixties and seventies offer symmetrically parallel stories probing the intersection of sexual identity and collective space before and after the critical 1969 watershed of gay urban histories in the West. Queer nation? Perhaps. But do the important synchronicities between the two pairs of films add up to Canadian nation, our national cinema? Perhaps only in one sense, in their combined "otherness" in the face of the now canonized American models rooted in their respective decades. The queer-friendly film avant-gardes of sixties New York (*Flaming Creatures*, Jack Smith, 1962–63) and California (*Scorpio Rising*, Kenneth Anger, 1963) had celebrated figures of defiant marginality as the prophets of the impending gay revolution, but the flaming creatures of Toronto and Montreal of the sixties are the worried young men in conservative suits and narrow ties learning folk songs and dating girlfriends. Interestingly, a ghost from Anger's *Scorpio Rising*[23] makes an appearance in *À tout prendre* as the motorcycle leatherman who attacks the heterosexual couple, but this is Claude's masochistic fantasy, not a "real" character. In the seventies, American models of post-Stonewall "positive image" realism

Il était une fois dans l'Est (1973): Hosanna, Tremblay's proletarian transvestite hairdresser and politically incorrect flaming creature of the 1970s, upsets her boyfriend Cuirette as she plots her transformation into the Queen of the Nile. Production still, photo by Attila Dory from the Cinémathèque Québécoise Collection, ©Les Productions Pierre Lamy

proliferated in both documentary (*Word Is Out*, 1977) and fiction (*A Very Natural Thing*, 1974);[24] Riordan had referred to the latter. Both also went virtually unseconded north of the border. The Toronto and Montreal equivalents now seem to have been our very own politically incorrect flaming creatures, Hosanna and Robin. These two proletarian transvestite hairdressers I posited in an earlier publication (1993) as spectacular dual emblems of interfacing queer nationality and schizophrenic "Canadian" cultural identities in the post-Stonewall decade. Acting up and acting out, screaming and singing, Hosanna and Robin were performing delayed-reaction multiple-identitied marginalities on Yonge Street and the Main, while their American cousins were aspiring to a respectable aesthetic of national belonging and centrality. It may only seem that the sixties took a decade to reach north of the border, but it is doubtful that the felicitous synchronicity of this parallel "otherness" of the Montreal and Toronto myths and icons constitutes a "national" consensus, queer or Canadian.

What is visible, rather, in these two sets of magnificently anomalous and uncanonizable films, these four fairy tales of two cities, so full of everything before us and nothing before us and queens both plain and fair, is neither one nation nor two nations nor two solitudes nor four auteurs. Instead, alive on the screen are two queer metropoles and two distinctly lived and felt inhabitations of those metropolitan spaces, two cultural geographies, two geographical cultures of desire. The four films' respective mythologies and materialities of desire and identity are distinct, overdetermined by their distinct authorial sensibilities and cinematic heritages and their two distinct sociopolitical, cultural, and historicospatial environments. Among other things, they are legible in retrospect also as the origins of two peripatetic historical trajectories in which Montreal's queer cinema would one day most characteristically explore the perils of private intimacy (*À corps perdu* [LÉA POOL, 1988], *Quand l'amour est gai* [LAURENT GAGLIARDI, 1994], *L'Escorte* [DENIS LANGLOIS, 1996]) and Toronto's would explore the assertion of public rights (*Urinal* [JOHN GREYSON, 1988], *Out: Stories of Lesbian and Gay Youth* [DAVID ADKIN, 1993], *Skin Deep* [MIDI ONODERA, 1995]). (And what better way to view the delirious incoherence of Greyson's *Lilies* (1996), that Torontonian's English-language film of a Montreal French-language play within a play within a play celebrating a shared queer past in an imagined rural hinterland, except as the merger of these two trajectories?)

The grid of *À tout prendre* and *Il était une fois dans l'Est*, *Winter Kept Us Warm*, and *Outrageous!* reminds us squarely of how cities – their communities, both imagined and demographic, their crowds and their outcasts, their infrastructures and their networks, their cultures, their economies, their geographies – have been the motors, crucibles, and canvases of our cinemas. These fairy tales of two cities urge us to refocus not so much on the national but on the metropolitan and the material, both the subnational and the supranational, the transnational and the postnational, the local and the global – in short, to reclaim the urban.

5

Passages: Going to Town, Coming of Age

While I may know where I come from I'm not quite sure where I'm going.
~ Dennis Day, *Auto Biography*, 1994.

Once I left the big queer city, my urban arrogance exploded and I realized
that these names we call ourselves are strategic.
~ Maureen Bradley, *Queer Across Canada*, 1993

OTHER PLACES

If the previous chapter was deeply rooted in the stable urban pavement of
the two leading metropoles of English and French Canada of the sixties and
seventies, this chapter offers much more of a spatial and temporal flux. "Passages," organized thematically rather than by region or period, offers an
exploration of queer narrative mythologies about passages from the country
to the city (and back again) and from youth to adulthood. It may seem like a
catch-all, but in fact these two distinct mythologies involving the movement,
potential movement or thwarted movement, of the individual – either
chronologically or spatially – so often overlap or converge within queer
Canadian cinemas that it makes sense to treat them in relation to each other.

As I argued in "Fairy Tales" (chapter 4), the queer imaginary within
Canadian cinemas has historically been resolutely urban, from *À tout prendre* to *Outrageous!* and onwards to *Better than Chocolate*, *Touch*, and
Take-Out. This argument could not have been surprising, considering that
metropolitan settings were the privileged crucibles for the emergence of

queer communities, cultures, and politics over the last half century. Since the key decade of the 1960s, when the cinematic queer imaginary first began to show its face unveiled, the demographic and economic determinants of Canadian queer cinemas have reflected the social history of the city as queer refuge, diaspora, mecca, ghetto, garrison, and utopia.

Nevertheless, looking more closely, we recognize the importance, albeit secondary, of nonurban structures and sites also for queer stories and sensibilities on our screens. Michel Foucault proposed that the "other place" has always been an important concept and organizational principle for societies, serving social functions that evolve historically as a society changes, and he suggested "heterotopia," the literal Greek translation, as a term for designating the "other place" (1986, 22–7). Whether we rely exclusively on Foucault's examples of boarding schools, prison camps, psychiatric hospitals, cemeteries, gardens, museums, festivals, fairgrounds, bathhouses, brothels, colonies, and ships or propose an updated list applicable to our current theme, the notion of "other place" is, I think, most relevant to the history and practice of a cinema that addresses the experience and desire of "other people." (The term "heterotopia" has of course potentially misleading and unfortunate nuances for a book about the cultures of homosexuality, but our vigilance together as writer and reader can forestall any confusion about the Greek prefix meaning "other," and most definitively not "straight.") Nonmetropolitan spaces have indeed functioned in a crucial way as heterotopias for our audiovisual corpus of Canadian queer cultures. This chapter explores this functioning and scouts out the parameters of these nonurban heterotopias in the ensemble of queer imaginaries in panCanadian cinema and video in a variety of regions, languages, genres, and periods. Along the way, the intersections of these "other places" with stories and images of *chronological* otherness will also come to the surface.

Testing these waters, and the general hypothesis of this chapter, let's consider at the outset as almost arbitrary examples the two queer features of PATRICIA ROZEMA, English Canada's most commercially successful lesbian director: the breakthrough smash hit *I've Heard the Mermaids Singing* (1987, 81) and *When Night is Falling* (1995, 94), both whimsical, Toronto-centric coming-out narratives incarnated as flip sides of the generic coin, comedy and melodrama respectively. Here, Rozema unabashedly delineates the patterns of spatial and chronological otherness as almost unconscious, underlying structures for her contemporary urban queer narratives. Despite their differences, both films have fantasy currents that unfold as pastoral heterotopic interludes and play essential structural roles in the films.

Polly, of *Mermaids*, the lonely and alienated heroine, escapes from her anomic urban reality through her voyeuristic stalking of heteroconjugal spooners in Toronto's parklands, living vicariously through their sylvan dalliance.

At the end of *I've Heard the Mermaids Singing* (1987), city girl Polly sees her fantasy of lesbian sociality evaporate and retreats into a sylvan "other place" through her apartment door – like Dorothy in *The Wizard of Oz*? VHS frame grab, *I've Heard the Mermaids Singing*; Cylla Von Tuedeman, VOS Productions Ltd.

More satisfying, however, are her black and white fantasies, not only of scaling those gleaming, inhuman skyscrapers and flying like a caped super-heroine among the steel and glass canyons of the financial district but also of Victorian-lady picnics in the leafy landscapes of the Don Valley ravines, where art and philosophy are discussed and tea is sipped in intense and behatted homosocial communion. When Polly's deluded narrative of lesbian voyeurism and projection ends in humiliation and abjection, she retreats into a psychic other place, a sylvan paradise accessed simply by opening her cramped apartment door in the last scene of the film. That she is accompanied into this heterotopic escape space by the lesbian couple that has been the focus of her fantasy projection may be either a tantalizingly open ending or a screenwriter's desperate copout, but it is the only way for this sad fable of samesex in the city to go.

In *When Night is Falling* the verdant heterotopias become the wintry universe of the Scarborough Bluffs, where the courting lovers escape from the repression and regulation of urban academia for a bout of frosty hang gliding. High above the snowy woods and cliffs and frozen lake, Camille and Petra consolidate their erotic bond riding the winds, clinging to each other in half elation, half terror before returning to the pavement-bound narrative crises still to be resolved. It is also in the snowy forest that Camille is rescued from near death by her new lover, also where she has buried her dead pet dog. But it is in that forest too where the animal comes to life in a miraculous, post-credits resurrection – straight out of that other Calvinist Carl Dreyer's *Ordet* (1955), via Monty Python – shaking the snow off its cute silvery fur as it arises to figure the happy-ever-after, born-again ending for the lovers as they once and for all escape the city with its spying fiancés and repression, not hang gliding this time but in a van with a road map. Rozema's sense of *chronological* otherness is less developed, though it is clear that her heroines are among the most child-like adults in the canon, stalking their inamoratae with bows and arrows, as well as cameras. For Rozema likewise, since coming out is so close to coming of age as to be almost indistinguishable, it thus removes any need for the characters to have a past life, psychological or chronological.

Having sampled Rozema's blueprint for the nonurban imaginary and tentatively verified thereby our hypothesis of heterotopia as a recurring underpinning of queer narrative in Canadian cinemas, let us proceed to flesh it out, starting with a preliminary generic breakdown of our corpus. Let's identify several nonurban spatial genres within Canadian queer cinematic imaginaries, spanning fiction, documentary, and experimental film and video. I shall then organize this chapter around these genres.

First, a broad range of works posit rural areas and small towns as places where one comes from or momentarily goes back to or through. These are works, at times nostalgic or idyllic, at times gothic, about memory, initiation, and socialization, in short about "coming of age in the sticks." A large proportion of these works are literary adaptations, at least on the male side – not surprisingly, since Canadian literature and drama in both English and French, queer and nonqueer, has been traditionally much more interested in the rural as the crucible of contemporary identities than the urban-fixated cinema.

Related but distinct are the "boys/girls-in-the-bush" genres that posit nonurban spaces as a place of refuge, self-discovery, catharsis, escape, and "getting away from it all" through homosocial bonding amid nature. Both these genres seem most often to be told from the point of view of the implied urban present, constituting mythologies of the nostalgic nonurban as spatial Other, the heterotopic elsewhere. Since many of the boys-in-the-bush narratives are included under the larger generic umbrellas of sports films or erotic films – hunting in the woods seems to be generically close in many respects to fucking in the woods – this particular group of films will be taken up in chapters 7 and 8, respectively, and I shall focus here only on girls-in-the-bush, or as my poetic side prefers, "chicks in the sticks."

Second, I will engage with what I might call the "return-of-the-native" genre. These films are about adult queers returning to the scene of rural or hinterland childhood socialization and discovering, as the cliché goes, that you can never come home again. Since many of these films come from Atlantic Canada, they may seem to constitute a kind of regional subgenre whose implications I will consider briefly.

Another corpus of films and videos assumes the nonurban as the place of here and now, the site of the self, rather than of the other, anchored in the everyday texture of rural or small-town life without the normalizing urban referent. (This place of here and now I might have wanted to call the "homotopia" but will desist to avoid confusion. This Greek formulation is what Foucault might have had to call the "same" place, had he pursued the matter as a parallel to his "heterotopia": "the space in which we live, which draws us out of ourselves, in which the erosion of our lives, our time and our history occurs, the space that claws and gnaws at us," to which the "other place" is other). Again not surprisingly, this nonurban corpus is far less significant than the other genres: MICHEL AUDY, the Trois-Rivières auteur, is the most insistently rural of queer Québécois filmmakers, and his artisanal oeuvre persisted over two decades between the sixties and eighties, producing several admirable present-day narratives of country longing. But even Audy moved in his most important work, *Luc ou la part des choses* (Luc, or His Share of Things, 1982, 90), to the implication that for Luc coming out means not sailing out with the buddy he has always loved down the wide St Lawrence but moving upstream to noisy and cramped Montreal. Nevertheless, much-admired queer documentaries from the Ontario hinterlands of Sudbury and Sault Ste Marie (as well as Crystal Beach, the Lake Erie resort town near Niagara Falls, which I will touch on again in chapter 9, on AIDS cinemas), as well as an interesting film or two in French from the Acadian Maritimes, may be well be shifting this nonurban here-and-now pattern towards a greater significance.

Fourth, since women's experience of both coming of age and urban-rural migration are distinctive, shaped irremediably by gender determinants of both geography and biography, I will devote a section to films and videos within the chicks-in-the-sticks and girls-into-women genre together.

All of these genre/gender narratives can be told in either utopian or dystopian terms and can be situated anywhere along the continuum of queer cinemas, from the explicitly queer-centred to the appropriated queer-referential to the ambiguously, openly, or defensively homosocial. But wherever on the grid these films and videos are located, the mythologies seem surprisingly similar. A final cautionary note: in case my examples would suggest that patterns are coherently continuous across our linguistic cleavage, I maintain and will hopefully demonstrate in passing that our cinemas in English and in French inhabit these genres in the distinctive and autonomous ways that we are discovering elsewhere in this book. (Yet, the fact

Michel Audy's claustrophobic hinterland coming-out tale, *Luc ou la part des choses* (1982), did not allow Luc (right) to sail out with his buddy down the St Lawrence in the boat they have just built but sent him upstream to noisy, cramped Montreal. Production still, Cinémathèque québécoise

that several of the works in this chapter, most obviously *Lilies*, can be considered French-English syncretisms may give pause on this question ...)

COMING OF AGE IN THE STICKS

Having established this overall terrain, then, and my conceptual apparatus, I would like to look in this section at a cluster of five fiction films spanning over forty years, two features and a trilogy of shorts, that belong to the male coming-of-age-in-the-sticks genre. These five works illustrate various gradations of queerness across the above linguistic cleavages and along the above continuum. First I'll examine three shorts, from the fifties, sixties, and eighties respectively, all adapting short fiction of Depression boyhood on the prairies by our literary ancestor SINCLAIR ROSS (1908–96), who came out as an elder literary lion in the years before his death and helpfully suggested rereadings of his writings from decades earlier: GUDRUN PARKER'S NFB film *A Musician in the Family* (1953), apparently inspired unacknowledged, if not stolen outright, from "Cornet at Night"; two instances of the real thing, Stanley Jackson's *Cornet at Night* itself (1963) and ANNE WHEELER'S adaptation for Atlantis of the canonical Ross story *One's a Heifer* (NFB, 1984). Next, my two longer works, CLAUDE JUTRA's 1976 CBC "For the Record" production of Anne Cameron's teleplay *Dreamspeaker*, and finally,

Lilies, JOHN GREYSON's 1996 adaptation of MICHEL MARC BOUCHARD's stage play *Les Feluettes* (1987). The eclecticism of this selection is not to suggest that the coming-of-age-in-the-sticks genre expresses some pan-national mythology in any essentializing manner but rather to suggest how what is no doubt a transcultural, transhistorical queer genre has taken root in different regional, historical, and authorial soil here and absorbed its energies from these respective contexts.

Capsule descriptions of the five works are in order before proceeding:

1   Parker's *A Musician in the Family* is the sunniest of the five. Andrew, a Saskatchewan farmboy, discovers the trombone through the encouragement and inspiration of a young blonde male music teacher in town, defying paternal castration and maternal smothering. The natural and barnyard universes vibrate pantheistically to his excited discovery of creativity, beauty, and a possible self beyond the grim farmer that his father is intent on moulding; of course it's the fifties, the patriarch smiles, and all ends happily.

2   A decade later, with *Cornet at Night,* Ross had still not yet been canonized by McClelland and Stewart – much less come out as a geriatric "gay lib" figurehead. But Peter Jones, the prairie producer then working on *Drylanders* (1962), was evidently an aficionado and delivered a much more faithful adaptation of Ross, properly credited this time. The mentor, still blond, still playing a masculine brass instrument, is now a soft-handed, soft-skinned (probably tubercular) urban band player who fails miserably both at Tom's father's hay-stooking test and Tom's own fantasy that he will join the farm family and stay in the adjoining bunkhouse forever. Too bad, for the cornet player embodied an alternative both to the model of workaholic masculinity represented by his father and to the maternal repression enforced by his mother through sabbath hymn-playing on the feminized parlour piano. Again, a pantheistic rural universe hums along to the uncanny melody of this alternative (it's an opera tune, wink, wink), and the boy grows up to redeem this failure as a lesson learned and memory savoured, a bittersweet adult narrator who talks and protests a bit too much.

3   *One's a Heifer,* in contast, is anti-idyllic, antinostalgic. Peter is an orphan, not a cherished son, and the story is set not in golden August but brutal winter. Tom sets out after his famous lost heifer (a young *female* cow ...) and instead discovers a "queer fellow" on a snowbound homestead. Chequers and shared chow are the closest this mentor comes to the life of cornet-style creativity and feeling, and in fact he becomes a negative mentor, associated with the violence that seems to be the birthright of bachelors on the frontier. He is not gently let down like the

cornet player but ostracized by both nature and society, and especially by Peter who kicks him (possibly in the groin) and lashes him with leather in return for his hospitality. The suspicion that an unsolicited bride lies murdered in the famous mystery box stall, victim of the queer bachelor's panic at the enforcement of homestead heterosexuality, may well be the red herring that Ross claimed it was, though Wheeler doesn't treat it as such. Whatever the case, in both story and film the eccentric gothic homesteader is still, however scary and ambivalent, the boy's alternative to the harsh familial model embodied by his bedridden uncle and worn-out but benevolent aunt.

4   *Dreamspeaker* is a Vancouver Island yarn about Peter, an emotionally disturbed orphan, who escapes his juvenile "facility" to spend a north-woods idyl with a native elder and his twenty-something adopted son, a friendly, mute muscleman. This mentor pair is an idealized alternative all-male family that also has creative leanings, not as a brass band, but as a dancer/storyteller and woodcarver team who feed and clothe the boy, pump up his self-worth, teach him native lore, and take him skinny-dipping. Of course it can't last, the trio are denounced by an urban handicraft dealer, and the Mounties burst in to puncture their rhapsody. While the justice system may well recognize the men as Peter's "natural parent" equivalents for visiting privileges in the "facility," everyone dies anyway, the elder peacefully of a broken heart after the boy is taken away, the two younger ones violently by their own hands.

5   In *Lilies*, the queer adolescent triangle is the primary unit, two teenagers in love in turn-of-the-century Lac-St-Jean region, Simon and Vallier, plus a jealous third boy, Bilodeau, who destroys them. The artsy bachelor mentor has been reduced to a slightly comic Quebec stereotype: the parish priest as lecher/aesthete. More important is the mentorship of the feminine principle, the deluded Countess and the exotic foreigner Lydie-Anne, literally landing by balloon from who knows where, who affirm authenticity and feeling, like Ross's resigned mothers, but who have more intensity and agency – and let's not forget that on-stage/on-screen they're drag queens. As with *Dreamspeaker*, the end is martyrdom, with the destroyer role played not by Jutra's benign government bureaucracy or by Ross's castrating father (though Simon's father whips his son to shreds at the first sign of sexual noncomformity) but by the Church, another Quebec nuance. The jealous and repressed future bishop Bilodeau spies on and destroys with murderous fire the pastoral idyl and his own hopes of love and redemption along with it. Unlike in *Dreamspeaker*, there is a survivor, a surpassor, to reenact the tale in the urban homosocial present and exact vengeance, derive knowledge, and perform absolution.

The five works thus display certain generic commonalities. First, the hero's situation is pervaded with stigma: Andrew's stern father says he will turn the milk sour and nags him about gallivanting off, fiddling around, and blowing his brains out; Tommy's father snorts at the vocation of the trumpet player, berates the "nonsense" of maternal piano lessons, and need say nothing more about the cornet player than "look at his hands"; in *Heifer*, Peter's uncle swears at the boy's carelessness and poisons the household with his complaints about him not pulling his weight; *Dreamspeaker*'s Peter is branded a fairy by his fellow inmates and with the labels "emotional disturbance" and "learning disability" by the medical and institutional authorities, while his sylvan mentors have their own physical disabilities that stigmatize them as loony and half crazy – not to mention their native identity, which bonds with Peter's delinquency in the backwoods fellowship of alterity; *Lilies*' brave lovers are *feluettes*, "lily-whites," or sissies, branded with both medical and religious stigma by the future bishop, and their ritualized humiliations are both public (their defiant reenactment of the St Sebastian play at the hotel reception) and private (the wordless paternal flogging is so shameful that Simon tries to cover up his wounds).

A second generic thread has the heroes of all five films discovering the world beyond the outpost, a sympathetic natural or agrarian universe (even in *Heifer*, whose windy, icy foothills offer in their own way a distinctive natural space that looks as sublime as it does freezing cold), set in implied opposition to an unnamed urban present, whether Ross's Winnipeg, Cameron's Victoria, the NFB's Ottawa,[1] or Bouchard's Paris. Greyson's pomo intertextual take on his Lac St-Jean landscape, rear projections and all (shot in the Montreal region and the Laurentians), adds to, rather than takes away from, the breathtaking lyricism of the four earlier, more realist works. The pantheistic quality of the natural universe hardly has any of the terror attached to it in the traditional readings of the Canadian literary canon à la Northrop Frye. In fact the garrison-landscape relation is overturned – and one wonders whether the American queer pulp frontier mythology of *Song of the Loon* (Richard Amory, 1966), the proto–New Age eroticization of horny, hung, and hairy cowboys and their lithe Indian guides, might be more akin to these queer pastoral tales of wilderness than the nineteenth-century homosocial forest romance *Wacousta* (R. Richardson, 1832) that is conventionally associated with the origins of English Canadian wilderness mythology (McGregor 1985). For queer Canadian boys coming of age in the sticks, timidly holding on to their place within Frye's garrison, it is not fear of nature that animates their narratives but, rather, fear of violence within the garrison. In short, these five narratives of nonurban coming of age that I have focused on, whether utopian or dystopian, demonstrate how the classical grid of garrison and nature assumed within classical Canadian studies may well be reversed within queer marginalities of Canadian cinemas: violence *inside* rather than *outside*. But both variants ultimately have analogous structures: both the straight nightmare of terrifying forest and the queer dream of refuge outside play political/therapeutic roles as the vital "heterotopias," a "simultaneously mythic and real contestation of the space in which we live" (Foucault 1986, 24).

Third, this rustic "beyond" universe is inhabited or visited or presided over by an elder-bachelor mentor figure. The hero discovers in the mentor figure a hitherto unarticulated alternative model for the masculine self, a redeemer of stigma, and this intergenerational socialization process has a more or less explicit eroticized gloss. This mentor figure echoes the historical reality of the mentor role in sexual subcultures promulgated through socialization rather than kinship, as Ross Higgins (1997) and other historians have described them. But he would seem to constitute an inverse variation of the "third-body" generic pattern that I have analyzed elsewhere as a predominant transcultural pattern of gay male narrative cinema for most of the twentieth-century, that is, the figure of the gay artist/intellectual as narrative subject looking at and mediating his objects of desire (Waugh 1993). In this corpus the boys coming of age in the bush are clearly fulfilling this function all by themselves, as once and future queer discursive agents, and the mentor figure is supporting cast, although with a hinge function. In any case, through this mentoring process in these coming-of-age films, the initiate is enabled to escape, even if only temporarily, the brands and constraints – paternal, familial, or institutional – of homestead, "facility," seminary, small town, or, in short, of what Frye might have called the garrison. This

The coming-of-age-in-the-sticks genre usually offers male mentor figures, and in *Dreamspeaker* (1976) Peter is blessed with two kindly native backwoodsmen who enable him to temporarily escape the "facility." Production still, Cinémathèque québécoise. Courtesy CBC

escape may be through affirmation, reconciliation, or inoculation, as in the first two defanged Ross adaptations; through martyrdom and sacrifice, as in *Dreamspeaker* and *Lilies*; or simply through the open-ended gothic panic and enigma of *Heifer*.

Next, the five films recount to various degrees of intensity the threat and enactment of violence – in fact, it escalates progressively, if not teleologically, through the five films, launched by Andrew's father's single-minded sharpening of his reaper blades and Tom's father's expulsion of the soft-handed idol from paradise, to the literal violence of the final three works, culminating in fisticuffs and whipping in *Heifer* and the veritable massacres of *Dreamspeaker* and *Lilies*. In fact, the violence in these latter three films especially is so incommensurate with the narrative premises of the coming-of-age tradition that they clearly point to the narrative mythologies of abuse touched on elsewhere in this book, amythologies that which, were there space, would merit separate treatment.

A final generic trope shared by these five tales comes out of the manner or structure of telling. These five films are all *coming-of-age* stories, far from, but close to, exact cinematic equivalents of the *coming-out* story that Kenneth Plummer has defined as the essential narrative of modern sexual cultures and politics. According to Plummer, the teller of the coming-out story redeems the stigma of the past through learning and surpassing, declares his sexual identity, and thereby performatively embraces community rather than isolation (1995, 49–50). Narration thus assumes transformational functions. Only *Lilies* fully takes on the post-Stonewall cast, or what Plummer calls modernist ramifications, of this narrative mode, but all five films share its basic dynamic to some degree in the structure of retroactive narration. This structure is literally present in the first person voice-over of *Cornet* and structurally present in the editorial construction of heterotopic flashbacks in all the other films, on sound track or image track or both. Even in *Dreamspeaker* – which includes what must be the most brutal film ending in the Canadian canon, unique among my five coming-of-age works for its body count and rivalled only by the notorious Quebec abused-child melodrama *La petite Aurore enfant martyre* (Jean-Yves Bigras, 1951) in its desolation – the voiceless editor assumes the role of omniscient narrator and infuses posthumous memory and learning onto the final cataclysm, retroactive wisdom and absolution. The triple deaths are followed by a flashback of – what else? – the sacramental skinny-dipping scene, the last two shots of the film showing the cavorting youths in the shimmering water and the applauding elder on the bank. On the soundtrack is his homespun homily about death not being the finish, a transcendant denial of the earthly violence we have just been mercilessly assaulted with. This vocal flashback effects a surpassing, a transformation of the stigma and alterity that have been the core of the story (glossed with scriptwriter Cam Hubert's sentimental filter of seventies-style New Age–appropriated native spiritualism).

Lilies has the most developed flashback structure in both play and film: in short, its famous central narrational device, a contemporary reenactment of the tale by the surviving protagonist's peer community in a prison, the classic Foucauldian "other place," set in the present time of the work, the 1950s. Bouchard sensed how stigma can be processed and community embraced only retroactively in the present-day retelling within the microcosm of homosocial urban solidarity represented by the prison (which Greyson has updated through diversity casting from Bouchard's "pure laine" monoculture into a multicultural utopia). Although this embrace of the fellowship of peers in the modern day prison narrative echoes the formula that all the buddy films of our two linguistic heritages, from *Goin' Down the Road* (Don Shebib, 1970) to *Les Boys* (Louis Saïa, 1997), take for granted, this one is different in its "outness," as opposed to the covert or repressed contradictory intimacy of the buddy movies. This explicit conjugality, I think, is what makes the explosion of violence inevitable in the period story.

Another aspect of Greyson's adaptation of *Lilies* is worthy of mention as well. For Kenneth Plummer, the first-person narration of the coming-out tale performs not only survival but also "surpassing," a function that is essential to the contemporary political affirmations of community and public agency – surpassing the stigma inherent in the initiates' alternative masculinities, surpassing the violence that emerges out of it. If the play was thus attuned more to the pre-Stonewall martyrdom sensibility of *Dreamspeaker*, Greyson's imposition of a *mitigated* martyrdom in effect constituted the modernization of the story in Plummer's terms. For the original play belonged only incompletely to Plummer's coming-out tradition, ending as it did in an attempted joint suicide by the teenaged lovers Simon and Vallier, rather than in their attempted murder by Bilodeau, which happens in the film. In both versions Simon is rescued by the vacillating Bilodeau and only Vallier joins St Sebastian in heaven. But the change from failed suicide pact to attempted double murder is a significant ideological adjustment, an "anti-dead-queer" modernization that must have felt to Bouchard like the p.c. imposition of a Torontonian "positive image" residue on his own updating of Gabriele D'Annunzio's symbolist mysticism. Still, both the play *Les Feluettes* and the film *Lilies* were "out" queer renditions of "out" queer material, with the flashback tale's open conjugality between Simon and Vallier performing in both play and film the fusion of the coming-of-age genre with the coming-out mode. Significantly, the two boys from Lac St-Jean are the only postpubescent initiates in this section's corpus (which Greyson's fastidious attention to the secondary sexual characteristics of his actors doesn't allow us to forget – though they don't always *act* grown-up) and thus the only ones to actually

The teenaged lovers' defiant reenactment of the St Sebastian legend in *Lilies* becomes a ritualized public humiliation, a generic element of the queer coming-of-age-in-the-sticks film. Production still, courtesy of Triptych Media Inc. and Gala Film Inc.

get it on. The effrontery of the sexual bond no doubt also allows for both the downscaling of the mentor function from narrative motor to observer status and the foregrounding of the present-day narrational and transformational frame: no wonder commercial producers without any stake in queer culture or politics wanted to film the play without the present-day transgender frame and no wonder Bouchard always refused.

Lilies thus obviously stands apart from the four earlier, more ambiguous works, which rely on various levels of subtextual decipherment and authorial outing (in either source or adaptation) for their affinities of sexual identity with Greyson's film. Yet their generic affinities with *Lilies*, as I hope I have demonstrated, are very strong indeed, effectively queering the Sinclair Ross and Claude Jutra films, reclaiming them as sexual, as well as, genre ancestors to post-Stonewall *Lilies*. As I have argued in several other contexts (1999), digging around in texts and cleaning out closets thus must remain basic methodologies of Canadian film history – adapting genre and auteur perspectives in a national cinema complex that has marginalized and allegedly outpaced both. This closet-auteurist, retro-generic methodology seems essential to our national cinemas and literatures both, whose past

Lilies gives an explicit conjugality to the male coming-of-age-in-the-sticks genre, as indicated in this delirious bathtub scene, which director Greyson retained from Bouchard but amplified, making the explosion of violence seem inevitable. Production still, courtesy of Triptych Media Inc. and Gala Film Inc. Photographed by Jonathan Wenk

and present are so marginalized. (Furthermore, I feel impelled to dogmatically assert, retroactive reclamations of Ross and Jutra as the subtextually queer ancestors of English Canadian literature and Québécois cinema, respectively, disallow any subsequent readings of these oeuvres that do not acknowledge them, recent film and critical studies of Jutra notwithstanding.)[2] Such retro methodologies will be a means of outing contemporary queer cultures' roots in and links to narratives and geographies of both urban and nonurban heterotopias and societies. Coming out in the sticks, whether utopian or dystopian, remains a vital memory, story, and fantasy for boys in the burbs and the urbs.

RETURN OF THE NATIVE: ATLANTIC CANADA

The urban gay man in what I call the "return-of-the-native" narrative – at least the male branch of the genre – returns to the rural small-town site of his childhood, works on or works out the traumas he thought he'd left behind, and finally returns to ambivalent exile in the urban diaspora. All the boys-in-the-sticks films discussed in the previous section have an element of retroactivity, implicit or explicit, but in the return-of-the-native narrative the boy is replaced by the man who revisits the scenes of his socialization and coming [out] of age. Various regions have been the setting for these "return" mythologies: a more resonant Quebec myth usually involves *departures* from the hinterland, without ever looking back, rather than *returns*, as in two momentous films from the 1980s, *Luc et la part des choses*, mentioned above, and *Sortie 234* (MICHEL LANGLOIS, 1988), where queer exodus is tinged with both painful loss and the sense of open horizons. I will, however, concentrate on two other regions, Atlantic Canada and Northern Ontario, both of which have produced distinctive genre configurations of the return-of-the-native myth that, interestingly, posit distant metropolitan zones as *their* heterotopias.

First, Atlantic Canada seems to be a custom-made locus for this mythology of the return, not surprisingly in the light of the way that region's economic decline and diasporic migration have already contributed so substantively to other vectors of Canadian cinematic culture (from the NFB's epic community activist Newfoundland Project, part of "Challenge for Change" [1966–80], and brimming with iconographies of abandonment and economic migration, to the canonical narrative of Pete 'n' Joey headin' for Toronto in *Goin' Down the Road* [1970]). (Sadly, of the score or more of Atlantic queer film and video makers mentioned in the portrait gallery in this book, the number who continue to work in the region as of this writing can be counted on one hand.) If this regional underdevelopment is symptomatised by the iconography of what Lee Parpart calls "colonial masculinity" (1999), we might expect to also encounter an unevenly developed logos of queer cultural development, always within the framework of masculinity, of course, and we would be right. Focusing on variations of the return-of-the-native myth from three of that region's distinctive provincial cultures, we will discover uneven or interrupted mythologies of queer migration and return.

Auto Biography (Dennis Day, Toronto/Newfoundland, 1993, 15). *Auto Biography* is from Newfoundland, but it resembles in no way the earnest black and white "Challenge for Change" documentaries. This is a short and funny experimental video is set in the clichéd locales of an outport clapboard house, a cramped but homey kitchen/living room, rocky shorescapes, and unctuous ecclesiastical interiors. Rather than a narrative, what unfolds is an unconnected series of delirious stand-up performance tableaus by an amiable actor functioning as Day's alter ego. Metropolitan gay-male lifestyle activities are made to clash ironically with these spatial evocations of the enforced familial and religious values that surround growing up on the Rock. "Dennis" offers a first-person narration that is jocular but hints at the trauma: "I lived here seventeen years until I was old enough to leave …

This is the window I stared out of for one-third of my childhood." When "Dennis" announces his sexual orientation to the camera, even the local dogs, seen in cutaway reaction shot, are heard to growl menacingly! But the rest of the video articulates the fantasy of what it would all have been like if the outport had been magically transformed into a gay-inclusive environment. "Dennis" openly reads *Torso* in the family kitchen, and his lesbian parents serve him and his boyfriend refreshments while they're watching *Married with No Children*. Then he finds a job in fashion without even leaving, and the wharf becomes a runway for a campy parade of typically Newfoundland queer fashions, the latest in matching sou'westers and oil-skins over plaid briefs. The incongruity of gay "lifestyle" displays parachuted into outport settings and the impossibility of this utopian fantasy are underlined by the artist's resort to chroma-key backdrops for the scenes, with the performers eerily suspended over, rather than placed within, the settings. The adult man is retroactively transposed over the child, who in fact is never seen, and the gay ghetto has transformed the outport into Church Street.

If Day's sprightly, even gimmicky, humour thus seems to make light of the pain of ostracism and exile, another work, a short documentary from the previous decade, from Nova Scotia this time, indulges in it all the way: James MacSwain's *Amherst* (1984) is a simple essay, originally in Super 8, about the author's eponymous birthplace, a small industrial town in decline. Twenty years after MacSwain's departure, his viewpoint, as riveting as it is, still includes almost none of Day's redemptive humour: his jittery tour of street scenes and architectural monuments from the Baptist church to the Ford dealership is overlaid with a voice-over that some might describe as shrill: "This is the town of Amherst. My name is James MacSwain and I was born here in 1945. I lived in Amherst until I was 19 years old in 1964 … When I left Amherst I felt I was escaping from a cage … The Post Office. I began to receive letters from friends who had already left Amherst far behind. The Bus Station. Freedom is only a ticket away. The train station: if you move out you might just save yourself … a dying town within a colonized nation." Can the difference be ascribed to the cultural difference between Day's Catholic large-family heritage and MacSwain's puritanical Baptist upbringing or, rather, to a fifteen-year generational difference between a fey youngish baby boomer (born at the cusp in 1960) and an artist who knew the 1950s and 1960s, as well as the more strident politics of post-Stonewall "gay lib" politics?

The two features I analyze next confront and orchestrate emotion head-on as well but are mediated and partially absolved through the feature melodrama genre, and with precious few laughs between them.

The Hanging Garden (Thom Fitzgerald, Halifax, 1997). *The Hanging Garden* was one of the most-honoured first features in English Canadian film history. *Garden*, along with *Full Blast*, a French-language feature from New Brunswick's Acadian coast (which I shall come to next), are the strongest nonmetropolitan queer features of the late nineties.

In *Garden*, Sweet William, a twentyish gay waiter-cum-[underemployed]-actor returns from an unnamed metropolis (that feels like Toronto but might be in the States) to his dysfunctional family household on Nova Scotia's South Shore for his sister's wedding to his boyhood buddy Fletcher. In this ramshackle white frame house and its lush flower garden, William rediscovers and finally puts to rest the pain of a childhood in which sympathetic mother and alcoholic father participated in complementary impositions of abuse. The native's return this time unexpectedly sparks the final meltdown of his parental family but reconstitutes an alternative family of his own (returning to Toronto with the rebel baby-butch daughter he never knew he had). In what all the critics called a "magical realist" structure, Fitzgerald layers the story over with a palimpsestic mosaic of memory shards and botanical symbology (the characters are named after flowers of the titular garden, in which tormented adolescent Sweet William may or may not hang himself until the present-day William cuts him down once and for all). This allows the Fitzgerald narrator, like Day and to a lesser extent like the narrators of the boys-in-the-sticks films, to oppose a conflicted child to an adult who is the agent of memory, serene but with evident scars nonetheless. Throughout, Fitzgerald maintains the strong, direct narrative of the obese pubescent boy who undergoes all at once rejection by the flirtatious Fletcher, corporal and psychological violence by his drunk father, and coercive sexual initiation by his panicky mother (who sets him up with the local hooker when confronted with the evidence that her son might not be a straight arrow). No doubt the strength of this coming-of-age-narrative owes much to what the *Advocate*'s Jan Stuart called a "heroic peformance" by Fitzgerald's round teenage actor Troy Veinotte (12 May 1998, 90), who performs the role as much by his corporal presence as by histrionics, padding impassively to the phone to hear Fletcher's betrayal, for example ("I don't want to talk about it, OK?"); paradoxically, the implausibly huge physical discrepancy between William the teenager and the svelte, self-possessed clone he becomes ten years later is the basis of its impact.

Like Day, Fitzgerald is ultimately ambivalent about the relative values and charms of past and present, of here and there. The rural community left behind is the site of torment, rejection, and an apparent suicide, after all, but also the site of paradisal rustic beauty, with not only the bountiful garden bathed in fiddle music but also the sun-dappled dock where the shared pas-

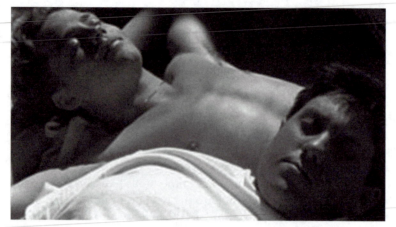

William, the obese teenaged hero of Thom Fitzgerald's *The Hanging Garden* (1997), cuddling with flirtatious Fletcher in a seaside moment of paradisal beauty ... before the grandmother starts screaming. VHS frame grab, production still, courtesy of Triptych Media Inc. and Gala Film Inc.

sion with Fletcher plays out, as intensely sweet in its promise as its imminent denouement is intensely bitter. After all, we never see the city that has provided William with a gay adult identity or learn anything about the partner he claims to have there (just as Day and MacSwain never show us Toronto or Halifax). The emphasis is, rather, on the catalytic effect the native's return has on the home, as well as on himself. Fitzgerald offers several inspired twists within a closure full of the hope of redemption and change: a kind of corporal reconciliation between father and son accompanies the departures of both matriarch and proto-dyke [grand]daughter, both echoing William's original migration. The family may be reconstituted in queer alternative form, but the cycle of migration continues with the daughter and mother – sympathetic for all her bungling, now disappeared – and the future of the new family in the distant, metropolitan "other" space is uncertain.

Xtra!'s resident Maritimer-in-exile critic R.M. Vaughan (see ACHTMAN) balked somewhat at Fitzgerald's auteur mannerisms but otherwise found recognition and emotion in the film (6 November 1997):

Fitzgerald's landscape is cluttered with walking ghosts – an entire family of misfits who are unable to realize the beauty inherent in their otherness. This mass psychological block is the film's most convincing Atlantic Canadian trait, more so than its setting or the (sometimes badly mangled) down home accents. For me, the film's gayness is secondary; its success is rooted in geo-political ideas. The story of the prodigal gay son parallels, and is fueled by, the double bind of Atlantic experience: You can't go home again, but you'll never really fit in anywhere else. Last month I did go home again. *The Hanging Garden* resonates with that same phantom limb feeling my family can create – the feeling of knowing the exact shape of one's difference.

Full Blast (RODRIGUE JEAN, Acadia, 1999). *Full Blast* offers a direct melo-drama version of the same tale with none of Fitzgerald's postmodern layer-ing of whimsical magic over its gritty, intense realism. Charles, the adult gay prodigal son, comes back into the surroundings of his childhood and com-ing of age – in a red sports car seemingly borrowed from Fitzgerald! His dysfunctional family is not of the consanguineous kind but, rather, a tight friendship circle of two other young men, Piston who is straight and Steph who is an "unlabelled" of the apparently bisexual variety. Also part of the circle are Marie-Lou, Piston's harried ex-wife, and Rose, a wise but resigned matriarchal bar owner who is Steph's on-again-off-again lover. The setting is not Fitzgerald's shabby but idyllic household but a small pulp-and-paper town riven by labour conflict, economic deprivation, and the generalized desperate boredom that a returned native (like director Jean himself, who lived in London for a decade) attributes sometimes too hastily to the hinter-land. Migration is constantly on the characters' minds: Piston keeps saying things like "All I want is to make some cash and get out of this place," and Marie-Lou's bravura rock song is "I think of leaving now and then / Don't know where, don't know when." She used to be lead singer in the gang's rock band, and their efforts to revive it and recapture old times – futile, of course, since the men all have too much baggage – helps give the narrative its shape. The film as a whole shares precious little of these characters' deluded nostalgia – for it is a loose adaptation of a taut and bitter novel of rural and generational alienation, the prizewinning *L'ennemi que je connais* (Martin Pître, 1995), in which nostalgia is notably absent.

Full Blast is a significant transformation of the novel, not the least in the aging of the characters from numb teenaged Pink Floyd fans into resigned twenty-somethings and in the construction of the women characters virtual-ly out of thin air. Jean plays down the fierce antiglobalization theme (the characters are locked out by the mill's American owners, whose local henchman is the never-seen father to Charles) at the same time as he plays up the theme of sexual marginality. He builds up Charles from an unsympa-thetic minor gay character, a sexual predator and arsonist (in addition to being the spoiled son of the boss), into the sympathetic native who comes back home and whose class status is more neutral than a marker of shame.

The novel's narrator is Steph, an impassive and suggestible character who is considerably less interesting than his on-screen incarnation, the stat-uesque blond lead played by David La Haye, the Quebec star who in this film, as in most of his others, can't keep his clothes on his graceful lean body (he plays a queer character in *Nelligan* [1991], as well). Steph can't seem to love anyone but puts out for Charles (who is still carrying a torch for him) in two very hot scenes, public/vertical and private/horizontal, as well as for Rose and for Marie-Lou, just enough to keep them – and us – panting.

Everyone, male and female, loves or lusts after Steph, and he's one of those beauteous creatures who emotionally craves the attention from everyone who comes close but is too dysfunctional to return the love responsibly. Jean's eroticized visual treatment of Steph, as well as of the other male actors (all get their nude scenes), is the core of the film's homoerotic element: Jean, a former choreographer, knows how to heighten the grace of his actors' bodies, especially La Haye's, no matter how alienated, deluded, and stoned they are. As he explained in an interview (Castiel 2000), Jean skimmed off the novel's homophobia, removing what he called the novel's "hierarchy in terms of sexual orientation and sexual practices" (at the novel's shocking climax, in a seemingly unmotivated explosion of violence, Steph shoots and kills a beautiful young blond gay scab his own age whom he has lured into the woods). Jean thereby legitimized Charles's vain desire to rekindle things with Steph: in a beautiful scene not in the novel, Charles is reassured by wise and benevolent Rose that he can find someone else better, someone who is worthy of and who will return his love. "This town is too small for you. Forget about it … Charles, the world comes to those who don't chase it … A handsome guy like you, I'm sure you'll find someone who will really love you." For her and for the film, the impulse to leave and Charles's sexuality are thus intertwined.

One strikingly evident contradiction on-screen is that all these characters are bigger-than-life in their tragic existence (this sparked *Xtra!*'s literal-minded complaint that they are "the swankiest, hippest, sexiest backwoods 20-somethings you'll ever see" [6 April 2000, 39]). Both Rose and Marie-Lou are played by Montreal music industry divas (Louise Portal and Marie-Jo Thério), and the five lead men and women may well be stuck in the banal kitchens, truckstop parking lots, bars, and factories of dead-end Bathurst, but they are also set against the magnificent natural settings of the region, especially the brutally breathtaking shorescapes. Jean explained his intentions in portraying this contradiction (Castiel 2000, 34): "The first space is that of the infinite: the sea, the forests, nature. But there are also interior spaces where people are confined and thrown against each other. In *Full Blast*, I tried to establish the interior/exterior dichotomy in terms of space, even if it most often creates conflicts … Some have reproached me for not having exploited poetry in my vision of space. But, in fact, I wanted to make a raw film, without concessions, almost animal, natural." In fact, the rawness of hinterland space is undeniably poetic, or rather cinematic, and I wonder on one level why Charles the native should leave such a dramatic arena. But leave he must, returning like Sweet William to the safety of the metropolis that remains as unseen in this film as it is in the others I have discussed. Jean's dramatic ending is perhaps as open and tentative as Fitzgerald's: he has hinted at of the possibility of reconciliation between the

Mutual handjob between Steph (left) and Charles (right), in *Full Blast*, (1999): director Jean knows how to heighten the homoerotic grace of his hinterland characters' bodies, no matter how alienated, deluded, and stoned. Production stills, courtesy Les Films de l'île

impossibly dysfunctional heterosexual couple Piston and Marie-Lou and has shown resolve and caring among the other characters.

The queer plot is thus one of several, the others having to do with Jean's strong and resourceful heterosexual women characters, with Steph as the common denominator. Jean's amplifications restore complexity and ambiguity to the relationship of sexual underdevelopment to economic colonization that Pître had set at the reductive level of class and sexual scapegoating. Charles's woodland cottage has been the setting for the two men's stunning hearthside lovemaking, and his final act before leaving is to set the place on fire, a gesture of rejecting both his heritage as boss's son in this exploitative economic arena and his sexual marginality in this town that is too small. Jean is sensitive to the contradiction in Charles's escape to the freedom of the very metropolitan centre that keeps his native society in economic thrall, but he softens it in the dramatic, night-time, rain-swept moment of the native's departure. As the red sports car takes off and Steph ambles back towards the still-idle smokestacks, queer politics is maintained in its contingency against a landscape fraught with all the other political tensions of economics and gender, as well as of sexuality. Ultimately, this ending and its poetry offer less redemption than the humour we found in *Auto Biography* or the provisional restoration of queer family in *Garden* – only its possibility elsewhere. The wild geese repeatedly seen flapping over the sublime Baie des chaleurs seem to be migrating all year round and never landing.

RETURN OF THE NATIVE: CANADIAN SHIELD

Northern Ontario is an economically underdeveloped resource-based hinterland also, but even more *cinematically* underdeveloped than the Atlantic provinces, with only Sudbury having intermittently served as a production centre for NFB regional French-language production over the years. It is not surprising, then, that in the queer-cinema department, the region has spawned not two full-blown star-studded Telefilm Canada melodramas but, rather, two low-budget Canada Council documentaries (both from 1998) much more akin to Day's *Auto Biography* in their comic spirit and experimental aspirations. Both Roy Mitchell's *I Know a Place* and *The Pinco Triangle* (Chris Patrick Crowe and Ruthe Whiston) are lively documentary portraits of regional industrial hubs, Sault Ste Marie and Sudbury, respectively. Both use hybrid strategies not dissimilar to Day's to capture a sense of queer life and coming of age in the two metallurgical (steel and nickel) company towns, deploying intertextual, comic, and performance tropes. Both qualify for the return-of-the-native genre, since both have one eye centred in Toronto, way down the TransCanada. Their perspectives, very personal in the case of *I Know a Place*'s author Roy Mitchell and collective in the case of *The Pinco Triangle,* both incorporate the look back – this time the indulgently nostalgic longing – of the queer exile. Mitchell is in fact based in Toronto, to which he once escaped to study theatre, his voice-over tells us, while Crowe and Whiston carry out interviewing in the Queen City and benefit from the production largesse of the cosmopolitan Banff Centre. A third Northern Ontario documentary, straight this time – in fact, *hyper-straight* – *Project Grizzly* (Peter Lynch, NFB, 1996), has been rightfully criticized by Brenda Longfellow for the way it frames its [working-class, masculine] hinterland culture with a "metropolitan and ironic perspective" that positions its subject as "a perpetual ethnographic 'other'"(1999, 93). In contrast, the two non-NFB queer docs, however imbued they are with the return-of-the-native mythology, do not impose an ironic, outsider layer over their subjects but rather embrace them with the palpable generous identification of insider humour and shared marginalization.

I Know a Place is the more effective of the two films, perhaps because of this very first-person quality. "I don't live here anymore but this is where I grew up and came out" are among artist ROY MITCHELL's first understated but affectionate words in his narration, and this double perspective of identification and distance informs the film, as with most of the heterotopic works in this chapter. But rather than the suffering subject of fiction, he is the jubilant agent of real-life experience. Emotion inflects his voice as he remembers growing up and coming out and finally meeting the documentary's star, "Mother" Bob Goderre, during his two years at the Algoma Steel Mill. Goderre's jocular oral history of being the host, mentor, and impresario for the entire queer social life of the community for almost three decades is at the core of the film, and Mitchell attends to him with eagerness and even awe as he hears the same old stories he has obviously heard before.

Hinterland cultures and communities in *I Know a Place* (1998): filmmaker Roy Mitchell (left) and mentor "Mother" Bob Godderre, posing in front of the Sault Ste Marie steel mill where they both worked. Production still, courtesy Roy Mitchell

Weekly or monthly parties in Bob's private basement rec room, attended by scores of men and women from all over the region, were apparently not a resource that the queer denizens of Bathurst or the South Shore had at their disposal, so Roy's socialization was much less traumatic than Sweet William's or even Charles's. Mitchell "knew there were others like me but not here. From what I could understand from TV, movies and magazines, people like me lived in big cities and got careers in the arts, hairdressing and theatre. Love and sex were things that I could only dream about. I knew nothing of any gay community. I was alone ... And so [via amateur theatre], I was immediately recruited into the gay underground of Sault Ste. Marie," which for him and countless others was "a pride laboratory."

Goderre's role as "den mother" or mentor to this semiclandestine community in formation, as affirmed by Goderre himself ("We looked after the gays in this city"), corresponds to a dominant pattern in premodern urban communities, and Mitchell makes further connections: "Mother Goderre was the unofficial wacky scientist, leader, archivist and court jester. When I was coming out over twenty years ago, small town queers felt isolated from the queer urban centers. But that isolation created people like Mother Goderre, unofficial leaders of the gay and lesbian movement. In Sudbury there was Mother Brown and after him there was Popeye and across the river in Michigan it was D.D." In the video, this analytic framework of the returned native, part mythological and part an affirmative ideological search for ancestors, vies for dominance with the chief witness's lively stories of parties and networks, and of workplace indiscretions that are devoid of the overtones of violence and contempt located in the Atlantic features (Goderre remembers losing his earring on the Algoma shower room floor and being helped by other naked crouching steelworkers in the hunt).

The only poignant notes in *I Know a Place* concern, first, Goderre's ex-wife, an invisible and abandoned player in the narrative of this *peterfamilias* (*sic*). Gender politics is not altogether avoided, however, since the role of supportive sisters is mentioned, and a rare lesbian couple is cheerfully encountered in a fine scene. It is just that Mitchell's discourse is openly and self-reflectively a cinematic vision of primarily male subcultures and communities. A second poignant note is hit by the off-screen character of Jean-Guy, Goderre's partner of twenty-nine years, lost to AIDS the year before the production of the documentary and indulgently memorialized. Snapshots are the common currency of this life retold, although the gestural and verbal performances of first-person history are perhaps more vivid. Mitchell intermittently attempts to liven up the proceedings with intertextual embellishments (vintage industrial documentary from Algoma Steel) and even a slapstick redramatization of the revellers' flight from the only police raid that tarnished the history of the milieu. He also tries to vary his interviewing strategy from time to time, trying for example a word association game as Bob whips up one of his legendary meals; although this strategy fails abysmally to bring out the texture of Bob's sensibility, it certainly accents the dynamic of generational difference between clever artist and hard-of-hearing subject. Such variations are charming and don't distract from the narrative cores, the filmmaker's homage to his mentor and his transmission of the telling of his life back then and there. As with the two Atlantic melodramas, much of Mitchell's encounter with the past is spatial, but the settings are not the generic cinematic set pieces of shorescape or symbolic garden; rather, they are the prosaic everyday decors of fake wood-panelled rec room and vinyl kitchen, of barbershop and working-class neighbourhood street, imbued with the overtones not so much of loss but of rediscovery and of kitsch (but heartfelt) celebration.

Pinco Triangle retains a modicum of autobiographical material in introducing the work's two gender-equitable co-authors Chris and Ruthe and their inauspicious childhood gender identities as revealed in the predictable family snapshots ("Ruthe was a typical boy in every way except her parents encouraged her to wear a dress"). Otherwise this sprawling thirty-eight-minute work has much more of a collective, anonymous feel to it. A procession of cheery young adult gays and lesbians revisits the vintage corporate newspaper the *Inco Triangle* and its quaint formats for promoting its workers' heterofamilial normality. The paper's campaign of sexual and social uniformity within its blue-collar constituency from generation to generation is easily and jubilantly subverted by the constituency's queer scions and their caption-subtexting skills: "Biff is a pretty good advertisement for gymnastics at bat. Here you see him with the old biceps bulging. And, in this second picture as Biff does a handstand, look at the way those back and shoulder muscles are sticking out like the stops on an organ. Just a little exercising now and then is Biff's casual explanation of how Biff got that way."

The native returns not only chronologically but also spatially: many of the witnesses speak with the implied perspective of the metropolitan Sudbury diaspora, and at times the city seems as bleak as MacSwain's Amherst: "Sudbury is kind of like the Canadian version of the Gulag. People say that if you do something wrong in another life, this is where you get sent." One witness recapitulates MacSwain's emphasis on the role of the bus station, remembering the shuttling back and forth down Highway 69 to Toronto as a milestone dynamic of coming of age in the North. Interviews and other footage shot during Toronto's Gay Pride festivities bolster the normativity of the metropolitan viewpoint. One high point of the tape is in fact a parodic dramatization of the return of the native: the co-authors get off the bus from Toronto, discover the regreening of their hometown thanks to pollution controls in their absence, and rush into the verdure, arms outstretched, beginning to "look at their hometown with new eyes. Then they began to search for other things that had been hidden beneath the surface, out of sight when they were children." Day's use of comic sketches is extended here, to mixed effect, as well as his use of keyed-in backdrops of the city, to which, I suspect, many of the witnesses are returning only in virtual terms for the shoot. One leather-harnessed daddy bear gives the return-of-the-native theme an anatomical thrust, opining to the camera that the cocks get smaller the further south you get and thus reinforcing an unspoken mythology about hinterland sexual potency that has been glimpsed also in Atlantic Canada.

There may be several reasons for this documentary's relative lack of success in comparison to *I Know a Place*, the pressures of nineties identity activism perhaps being one of them. I am certainly not one to flail political correctness, but the strict gender equity of this cinematic initiative seems to flatten the distinct dynamics of gender difference in the histories of coming of age in the native place. Two women witnesses offer experience that seems to contradict the men's, one coming to Sudbury *as* the metropolitan hub itself and another trying out Toronto and then returning for good to a place where she could see the sun setting among the buildings and go fishing and swimming in the lakes. (The NFB portrait from the previous decade of a close-knit circle of older francophone lesbians, *Maman et Ève* [1996, see chapter 6], suggests that this may be a fruitful issue for further research.) It may be that the filmmakers found the gender issue too complicated or divisive or didn't trust enough in the power of direct address oral history or couldn't find or didn't look for the historical informants like Mother Brown and Popeye (the Sudbury den mothers identified by Mitchell from the other side of Lake Huron). There are inklings of early underground community formations, especially in the somewhat contradictory interviews with the men about sex in the mines and with certain miners in the Carlton and Frontenac Hotel bars, but these are not elaborated or reconciled with the women's memories above. Whatever the reason, the artists applied their apparently luxurious Banff Centre budget to introduce an ambitious layer of discursive clutter, assembling material that still remains to be processed. Not that the climactic finale, a huge production number featuring never-returned native rock star Lorraine Segato and her out-of-control backup singers, against the backdrop of the Big Nickel no less, is unsuccessful on its own terms. It's just that – as if to compensate for the slightly raggle-taggle quality of the Toronto-style Pride demonstration that precedes it – the finale is protesting a little too much and is hip to the extreme of self-congratulation.

Still, *The Pinco Triangle* is unique in queer cinema and Canadian documentary, and not even *Project Grizzly* can match its ebullient excess. It is ironic, as well as a symptomatic contradiction of the cultural processing of experience, that, compared to the tragic weightiness of the two dramatic features by Fitzgerald and Jean, this documentary, as well as Mitchell's and Day's experimental shorts, is so resilient in its portrait of the place to which the native exile has returned. Nevertheless, the uneasy gender problematic of *Pinco Triangle* and *I Know a Place* is a reminder that we are now due to turn from these primarily male-authored and andro-centred visions of coming of age in the sticks and the return of the native, towards a focused look at women's treatment of the same generic dynamics.

CHICKS IN THE STICKS: COMING OF AGE AND RETURN OF THE NATIVE

As women's movements have been telling us for two hundred years, the social dynamics of geographical mobility and socialization are overdetermined by gender in our society. The generic patterns of lesbians' and bisexual women's cinemas may well be analogous to this chapter's patterns of coming of age in the sticks and the return of the native, as well as to the pattern of boys in the bush (which will be addressed through the sports framework of chapter 7). However, everything from the female homosocial continuum to the historical materialism of housework has dictated that women's renditions of the patterns are quite distinctive. In this section I would like to look at an eclectic assortment of women's films, mostly from the 1990s and the 2000s, films that engage or skirt or reinvent these generic patterns (including a 1970s ancestor and a more recent work, neither of which really fits perfectly, because of its male authorship).

I list these works here at the outset because they cross-pollinate each other persistently and do not break down into neat clusters:

- the Québécois narrative feature films *Revoir Julie* (*Julie and Me*, JEANNE CRÉPEAU, 1998, 92), *Les muses orphelines* (*The Orphan Muses*, ROBERT FAVREAU, 1999, 107), *Emporte-moi* (*Set Me Free*, 1998, 95), and *Lost and Delirious* (2001, 103), the latter two both by LÉA POOL;
- two semidocumentary, improvised English-language narratives *August and July* (MURRAY MARKOWITZ, 1973, 93), and *The Company of Strangers* (Cynthia Scott, NFB, 1990, 101), as well as a slew of other NFB films, including the medium-length documentary *Maman et Ève* (Paul Carrière, 1996, 53) and the feature documentaries *Forbidden Love* (LYNNE FERNIE and AERLYN WEISSMAN, 1992, 85) and *Stolen Moments* (MARGARET WESCOTT, 1997, 92);
- a cluster of Caribbean-diasporic first-person films: *Coconut, Cane and Cutlass* (MICHELLE MOHABEER, 1994, 30), *Listening for Something ... Adrienne Rich and Dionne Brand in Conversation* (DIONNE BRAND, Studio D, 1996, 56), and *Sadomasochism* (DEANNA BOWEN, 1998, 14); LÉA POOL's canonic feature *Anne Trister* (1986), a diasporic melodrama referencing the desert landscapes of Israel, rather than Caribbean beaches, bears comparison with this group; and finally,
- three clusters of short comic and experimental films and videos, respectively by the Torontonians MARGARET MOORES and Almerinda Travassos (*Labyris Rising* [1980, 14] and *Dog Days* [1999, 40]), by the Winnipeggers SHAWNA DEMPSEY and Lorri Millan (*Medusa Raw* [1992, 9], *Calamity* [2001, 5], and *Lesbian National Parks and Services: A Force of Nature* [2002, 23]), and by Montrealer Anne Golden (*Big Girl Town* [1998, 25], *Site* [2002, 2], and *Somme* [2003, 12]).

The relatively scattered nature of this corpus and the erratic construction of these heterotopic energies testify of course to the continued marginality of lesbian filmmaking within the Canadian landscape, even after the important breakthroughs of the 1990s, but even worse perhaps, they testify also to what my colleague/co-conspirator CHANTAL NADEAU criticizes as our failure of imagination (2000), wherein "the lesbian body doesn't exist outside of its urban materiality."

Curiously, of the three generic patterns the coming-of-age-in-the-sticks narrative is apparently not an object of sustained focus on the part of lesbian makers in either French or English. Women-loving women would seem to be as resolutely urban as their brothers but perhaps without us boys' accumulated literary heritage of rural childhood mythologies to sustain cinematic investment. Are we to be satisfied with a hypothesis about lesbians springing into life as fully formed urban adults – "lesbian orphans," to use Lorri Millan's smart moniker from *Day in the Life of a Bull Dyke* (1995) – rather than assigning them the richly mentored, formative nonurban childhoods of so many gay men? There are fortunately some interesting exceptions, enough to constitute a proto-subgenre that we might be forgiven for calling the "chicks-in-the-sticks" genre. Within this group, the most salient is k.d. lang's intervention in the continental pop culture of mainstream country music in the late 1980s.

To have to pin an entire mythology on lang and a few other exceptional textual traces might be symptomatic of this mythic silence around lesbian socialization, but it might also be construed as a potential richness as yet untapped. In any case, lang's enigmatic 1989 music video for the mournful country ballad "Trail of Broken Hearts" (director Ethan Russel, from lang's *Absolute Torch and Twang* album of that year) is a case in point. The video is explicit in its evocation of the windswept prairie grassland through which the sun-spangled adult lang walks singing in her loose blue shirt. The video belongs principally to the "return" genre, since the singer is plaintively conjuring up her past, to which she is returning robust and serene. But the coming-of-age narrative seems implied in her vision of an earlier version of her adult self on a hot, windy, hazy day in a heavy brown jacket and broad-brimmed hat, wandering up the eponymous trail to a farmhouse perched on a desolate horizon, complete with windmill and rail fences, witnessing what may be a foreclosure. The enigmatic flashback also includes a child covering her face with her hands (perhaps lang in an even earlier version of herself ?), who is then fleetingly glimpsed rushing through the grass with a little boy who is no doubt her brother. Then finally the hatted lang encounters much more concretely an anxious looking, not-so-old Ukrainian "babushka" figure (the children's mother?) seated on a sofa on a large farm wagon that passes by, stoically facing in closeup the grassland that she presumably finds less imbued with picturesque nostalgia than we. The narrative clearly involves not only broken hearts but also migration in both time and place, plus just an inkling of a trauma touching the singer persona's own coming of age on the prairies.

A slightly different glimpse of lang the child is provided in the singer's prizewinning CBC variety special "k.d. lang's Buffalo Café" (written by, as well as starring, the hometown girl), from the same prolific 1989. In this program, the song "Big Boned Gal [from Southern Alberta]" is an upbeat but nostalgic evocation of a large woman in a loose blue dress whose self-absorbed, self-pleasuring dancing at the small-town Legion Hall Saturday-night social is the object of the townsfolk's admiration, despite her physical and social incongruity (a stand-in for *sexual* marginality?). The child k.d., maybe ten years old, an androgynous sprite whose hairdo is pretty close to that of the adult entertainer, is seen shyly gazing with awe at the evening's star performer. These glimpses of familial and community socialization – one traumatic, the other full of the magic of childhood discovery of another possible world and possible female roles and bodies – are overwhelmed by the main energy of the video and the program. "Buffalo Café" offers a return-of-the-native dynamic, whether in the toned-down getup of the melancholy grassland *flâneuse* or in the over-the-top sequined and tassled masquerades of the star exile returning triumphantly back home where she belongs, on Saturday night no less. If lang's co-authored lyrics in "Trail" *suggest* a return of the exile to a site of earlier experience, the script and mise-en-scène of "Buffalo Café" make it *explicit*, even hyperbolic. She flamboyantly makes her entrance in the dazzling cowboy outfit, moving on a float down the main street of Red Deer toward the café, fiercely strumming away and belting out "Big, Big Love" as the announcer solicits a "big Alberta welcome" to the superstar coming back to her roots. The musical performances are framed by a couple of comic sketches wherein lang interacts (flirts?) with a couple of big-haired femmes (old flames?) who just happen to be leading lives of local melodrama right there in Stockwell-Day Land.

Of course all of this is laid out with a measure of ambiguity at this stage in lang's career, for the country music scene and Alberta culture were still nervously but proudly bedazzled by the star who had arisen from their midst, and in full denial, considered her simply "outrageous" (as guest star Stompin' Tom Connor's homage to her on the program puts it), rather than a radical transgressor of the heterosexual and carnivore order. Three years later, when her music veered off course from "country" on its long road towards Tony Bennett and she finally spoke the L word they all knew in their hearts buried in the sand, this kind of return might no longer have been possible. But for now all the ominous cracks are papered over, thanks to the conciliatory mediation of the national public broadcaster. For the CBC, the overstated mythologization of small-town communal harmony is part of its traditional vocation (at the same time as the institution's modern history is punctuated by the foreclosure of local outlets and services), and the gentle celebration of undeclared gender outlaws, whether big-haired, big-boned, big-loved, or big-voiced, is part of its regionalist mandate. As with Mitchell and to a lesser extent the Sudbury duo of the previous section, there are glimpses of rebel bravado, underground circuits, and premodern eccentricity, all embraced, or at least tolerated, by the agrarian world the native had abandoned. But audiences are inoculated from too much too soon through sanitized and oblique staging and the lens of variety programming.

Another national cultural institution, the National Film Board, provided shortly thereafter another rare glimpse of the rural coming-of-age, or chicks-in-the-sticks, narratives, coincidentally also in the West, this time with a stronger grounding in documentary discourse. In the epochal *Forbidden Love: The Unashamed Stories of Lesbian Lives* (1992), two of the film's witnesses to lesbian cultural life of the 1950s and 1960s, Amanda White, the educator and former Vancouver street-person of First Nations heritage, and Kelley Moll, the rancher dyke from the British Columbia interior, both recount their rural upbringing and position it in relation to the urban sub-cultures they would discover and appropriate as adults. White, seated in front of huge traditional wooden sculptural panels evoking the natural universe, talks of her Haida values and the shift they faced with her migration from the Queen Charlottes to the mean streets of Vancouver, caught between irreconcilable cultures. Meanwhile, Moll, riding through her Marlboro Man landscape in cowboy hat and denim, then leaning butchly against her log dwelling, is no less anecdotal about her upbringing on the Northern Alberta frontier (daughter of Eastern European homesteaders), recalling her ill-fated romance as a teenager with a nineteen-year-old school teacher that set in motion its own dynamic of expulsion, migration, and exile for both parties. These isolated narrative fragments are echoed by other narrators' reminiscences of their obsessive drive to get to the city, above all to Greenwich Village. All are given their significatory thrust by the overall fictional framing narrative of the film, the story of Laura, a country lass who has been abandoned by her inamorata in favour of a man and who takes the CNR into town and into the urban lesbian utopia of jukeboxes, cigarettes, pulp novels, butches, and anonymity. The tongue-in-cheek, pulp-patinated opening sequence shows the ex-girlfriend, brought by her anxious fiancé in a red pickup truck, moving through the desolate and scrubby farmland to the vintage village train station to bestow a glinting farewell locket on tearful Laura – all under a torchy fifties pop song. "Come with me!" Laura pleads, but the tragic logic of solitary big-city exile cannot be altered, and the dubious security of rural roots must cede to the glamorous and more hopeful discourse of the urban (whether that be the three Canadian metropoles discussed in the film or, even better, Manhattan!). Thus unfolds the overwhelmingly urban history that this film and most other film efforts at history presume. Abandoned homes and families and heterotopic shadows are seen as the sacrificial price of sexual modernity.

The Caribbean-diasporic cluster of first-person films offers another case in point. These films, of course, tend to be about other things in addition to memories of coming of age, namely economic exile and [post-]colonial and gendered power relations. But memories of socialization and growing up in a nonurban heterotopia, crystallised in tropical waterfront landscapes that have an almost hyperbolically lyrical beauty, still haunt these films. Mohabeer's *Coconut/Cane and Cutlass* is a lush and complex first-person essay on lesbian desire and genealogy in the context of postcolonial exile and a return to "what used to be my homeland," Guyana. The film is structured around a visual refrain of present-day women strolling along the edge of oceans, backwaters, and wetlands alive with sensuous leaves and flowers (when they are not making love in the privacy of exotically decorated studio sets that seem required by the repressive context described by one local witness). Both personal and cultural memory are evoked as the poetic voice-over addresses first the tropical land where the artist persona grew up and then her "coolie woman" ancestor. The effort to remember and reconstruct is sometimes distilled in close-ups of the lovers' feet, adorned with anklets, sensuously immersed in the shallow waters or rubbed with sand, images of childlike tactility.

For Brand in *Listening for Something,* the conversation and poetic exchange with American poet Adrienne Rich bring back the memories of a Trinidad childhood that are often the subject of her poetry. From her privileged middle-class urban roots, Rich also "fix[es] on the land" associated with her Southern U.S. upbringing, but for Brand the rustic tropical setting is doubly evocative on a strong gut level: the history of slavery and racism at the centre of her political consciousness but also more-primal images of her mother carrying her on her hip through rivers that are too deep for little girls. The Caribbean beachfront interludes also remind her of her old longing for escape, the "taste of leaving already on my tongue," and paradoxically display the lush pastoral quality that only a big-budget NFB crew can conjure up, overgrown ruins and all. The beachfront settings, often unpeopled, are anchored in recurring shots of the poet reclining against a picturesquely peeling wall, reading her adult work and looking up out over the palm-dotted sites of childhood – echoing lang the returning native minstrel in an incongruous way.

Even in Bowen's *Sadomasochism*, the most disturbing film in this group and no doubt in the canon, the brutal black-and-white North American urban imagery and texts are woven into a serene web of repeated colour shots of the artist's unshod feet firmly imprinting on the sand of an island beach. It is as if a childhood and cultural memory is sustaining her in her negotiation of the other harsh voices and feelings in the work. There are other footprints already in this allegorical sand – perhaps the ancestors that the narrator says she is both indebted to and moving beyond? For this network of Toronto artists, the islands of their childhood serve a psychic and social function similar to that of lang's mythic grasslands or Fernie's scrubby backwoods, but for the exile the landscape of memory also holds additional weight, and this weight is often carried by all three works' dense and poetic voice tracks.

Léa Pool's *Anne Trister*, as I mentioned, is similar to this cluster of diasporic films in its nostalgic referencing of an other geographical space, in this case, the Israeli desert. But Pool's Swiss-Jewish, bisexual artist heroine follows a personal and artistic trajectory very distinct from that of the above economic exiles. A "psychic" refugee, she has after all migrated to Montreal to escape mysterious parental and heteroconjugal pressures, rather than leaving behind the space of economic and sexual "underdevelopment." Moreover, it is significant that in the end, after grappling with a maternal lover (the middle-aged psychiatrist), a nasty bisexual triangle, and, literally, an artistic collapse, Anne returns to the desert, her conflicts and crises of identity, vocation and lineage, somehow resolving each other. Indeed, the desert interludes become framing passages at the beginning and end of the film, the first showing a funeral and the second the serenity of homecoming and artistic rebirth symbolized by the glittering packet of sand Anne airlifts back to her Montreal psychiatrist mother/lover surrogate. They have a cultural and psychic operation in relation to the Canadian urban here and now, completely different from the Caribbean beaches remembered by Mohabeer, Brand, and Bowen.

Pool's two much-later coming-of-age features, *Emporte-moi* (1998) and *Lost and Delirious* (2001), respectively a French-language hit and an English-language failure, are more ambitious and richer developments of the heterotopia structure than the 1986 trial run. In both cases it is the merging of other spaces with other times, namely the world of adolescence, that yields a return. *Emporte-moi* is a thinly veiled autobiographical narrative that reworks many of the issues of *Anne Trister* – indisputably with more success – and *Lost* is an uneven but rich adaptation of an English Canadian novel dealing with a WASP girls' private-school world, of which the immi-

In Deanna Bowen's *Sadomasochism* (1998) disturbing North American urban imagery of racial and sexual violence are anchored in images of the artist's unshod feet firmly imprinting the sand of an Caribbean beach. Video frame grab, used with permission of Deanna Bowen

grant director personally could have known nothing. Both deal with the traumas of adolescent girls coming of age and both integrate more or less prominently an urban-rural migratory dynamic with a coming-of-age-narrative.

Emporte-moi narrates the decidedly urban coming of age of thirteen-year-old Hannah, trying to assert her identity in 1960s Montreal while buffeted on all sides. The pressures are firstly interpersonal. Like Anne's, her protolesbian search is primarily in the direction of the maternal, shaped by quasierotic attachments to three females: her distraught but sensuous French-Canadian mother who is caving in to even more unbearable pressures than her daughter; a luminously supportive mentor in the form of a schoolteacher who just happens to look like her sexworker idol, Godard's Nana from *Vivra sa vie* (Pool's cinematic reference is more clearly New Wave art-film than experimental Barbara Hammer!); and finally, an exotic classmate who is also her first love. But the paternal presence is also felt in the form of her abusive father, alienated by his stymied writing aspirations and his Jewish Polish culture in a French Canadian Catholic society, and her complicit and flirtatious older brother, who enacts his incestuous attraction by sharing, indeed stealing, her first love, in a typically Poolian triangle configuration. The pressures are also environmental, which is more important for my perspective in this chapter, and her emerging identity is ineradicably marked by the working-class neighbourhood in which she is brought up and its proximity to hostile neighbours, sexually harassing tradesmen, her mother's fur-industry sweatshop workplace, cinemas, lively street life, and, above all, the red-light district.

Hannah's urban trajectory of awakening, suffering, and discovery is framed at the start and end by countryside visits, not to the Israeli desert but to the riverside grandmaternal home, for nourishment and restoration, as well as for linking up with her female genealogical roots. Water functions as a complementary attribute of this rural "other place," a symbolic site for bathing in a natural setting of corporal well-being and sensual affirmation. Water offers self-discovery, as well, both her biological maturing (she discovers her menarche while swimming) and her sexual awakening (her brother's kiss). The main urban section of the film is punctuated a few times by an effort to return to the water, but these episodes at beach and swimming pool stop short of full access to the primal rural immersion. Significantly, the final return to the country coincides with a return to the maternal bosom, where both mother and daughter will be healed – there's even a kind of iconic overlap between mature daughter and young mother, aided by the casting as the mother of leading lady Pascale Bussières (who at the age of thirty was not exactly over the hill and on the brink of maternal-role type-casting). The migration to the country coincides also with Hannah

taking up the movie camera that her mentor has given her. Indeed, the journey back to the country is seen largely through this lens, including the
soothing glimpse of the St Lawrence as the bus travels along its shore and of
her mother who comes to welcome her. This supplementary trope of the
identity-forming and therapeutic potential of art-making, though it has here
the added nuance of reference to her father's artistic impulse (and to that of
Hannah's ancestor Anne), echoes any number of similar insights in queer
works about coming of age, from several of the male coming-of-age films
treated in the first section of this chapter (*A Musician in the Family, Cornet
at Night, Lilies*) to *rollercoaster* (SCOTT SMITH, 1999, 90).

Pool returned to the triangle in *Lost*, but this time it's tragic, all-girl, and
sweet sixteen in the sylvan surroundings of a posh private school (it was
shot on the manicured Bishop's University campus of Quebec's Eastern
Townships). In this rendition of the coming of age of three roommates, the
meek heterosexual narrator Mouse gives us the prevailing point of view of
the protofeminist lesbian rebel Paulie and the fluctuating Tory who abandons Paulie for the boys. If *Emporte* had been considered by many Pool's best
film, *Lost and Delirious*, her first film in English, was roundly trounced by
all critics except the kind who gets off on girl-girl scenes ("The movie would
be dishonest if it didn't provide us with visuals to match the libidos of its
two young lovers," said Roger Ebert, virtually the only name-brand critic
who offered a rave [2001]). No doubt the film would have done better had
it been in French with subtitles, for the anonymous writer online at the
Canadian Guide to the Movies got it right in pointing at the reason why this
hyerbolic art film melodrama didn't catch on (2003): "In a country where
Art House filmmakers indulge in icy, aloof films, one about out-of-control
passion is refreshing, and it could've been – should've been – truly great, but
isn't." (By "country," the writer obviously does not include Quebec or else
has never seen a film by Léa Pool, who couldn't be farther from icy, aloof
Atom Egoyan in her trance-like orchestration of emotion.)

Pool had come onto the project relatively late in its development, but all
the same she brought her distinctive melodramatic mark, as well as an
authoritative nuance to several strong scenes. These include the ones where
all three upper-class roommates reveal they have just as heavy maternal
issues as working-class Hannah in the previous film and deliver impassioned
imaginary letters to their absent mothers and where the sympathetic but
ineffectual mentor/headmistress Faye Vaughan vainly tries to intervene in
Paulie's mad course towards implosion by hinting at her own coming out as
a means of support. Pool was clearly not responsible for scriptwriter Judith
Thompson's ill-advised decision to update the repressed 1960s climate of
Susan Swan's original source novel, *The Wives of Bath* (1993), to the "twenty-first century" (as one of the girls mentions by way of challenging a homo-

Hannah's return to the country at the end of *Emporte-moi* (1998), coincides with her artistic inspiration as she takes up her new camera for a glimpse of the redemptive countryside, reflected here in the bus window. DVD frame grab, photographer: Jan Thijs

phobic discourse). On this issue of the attitudes among the student body, American lesbian critic Cynthia Fuchs expressed surprise at this "particularly time-warped all-girls school": "somehow, lesbianism (even girl-girl crushes or experimental sexual activities) is completely unheard of and so, much feared and mocked ... Everyone ... on campus is ignorant, mean, or outright phobic" (2003). I have no trouble believing that spoiled, rich younger sisters can be vicious, and for me the more significant issue was how a coming-of-age narrative that ends in suicide for the lesbian/tomboy character might recuperatively be framed in 2001, all the more so since it cannot be reclaimed and mediated through *The Hanging Garden*'s return-of-the-native narrative.

Thompson had Swan's consent to set up the suicide as a metaphorical one à la *Garden*, where Paulie is transformed into a falcon (according to the literal unfolding of what's on the screen). This scene replaced the novelist's original device of incorporating a real-life 1970s Toronto crime, the castration/murder of a randomly chosen man by the same disturbed character Paulie, who pins the victim's genitals on her own body to legitimize her claim to her girlfriend. In either case, it is important to note that in both novel and film it is not the voice of the sexual other who presides but the "normalcy" of the narrator's voice. With the changes, *Lost* became, not Canada's *Boys Don't Cry* (United States, 1999), but our belated entry into the hoary seventy-five-year-old lesbian girls' school film genre, in which all films have had somber, if not tragic, endings (even those where lesbianism is only a subtext, as in *Picnic at Hanging Rock* [Australia, 1975]: some have ended in suicide (*Olivia* [France, 1950] and *The Children's Hour* [United States, 1961]), some in "almost suicide" (*Mädchen in Uniform* [Germany 1931]) and some only in separation (*Thérèse and Isabelle* [United States/ West Germany, 1968]). And all except *The Children's Hour* are period pieces, interestingly enough. Yet 2001 is still 2001, and despite Pool's blithe European denial of the politics of sexual identity, the decision to cut short the lesbian character's coming of age through madness and self-destruction has an inevitable ideological edge. By the very fact of resorting to the pre-Stonewall trope of figuring such destruction as a lesson for the heterosexual characters' own uninterrupted coming of age, Pool loses her nerve, backtracking into an oddly incongruous and anachronistic othering of Paulie's gender and sexual identities.

The question of suicide is tied in not only to the present-day updating of story and genre but also to the urban-rural migratory dynamic that is also intrinsic to this film, in a way unlike what happens in the other coming-of-age and mentorship films in this chapter. The girls' school is not "the sticks," nor is it a city, of course, but a microsociety apart from society at large to which the girls' wealthy families have banished them. In feminist novelist Swan's terms it is a "fiefdom in the kingdom of men," a place where women "lack real power or authority" but are allowed to "live by their own rules" (2001). But we can also see it as yet another Foucauldian heterotopia, one of society's "other places," in fact an "other place" of the kind where traditional societies send members in a state of "crisis" such as adolescence, in this case where coming of age or initiation is sanctioned to take place. No wonder the boarding school is the site of so much melodramatic crisis, revolt, and suppression within film history! This heterotopia, however, is surrounded by its own "other place," the luxurious forest so suggestively photographed day and night by Pool's team. There is a constant back and forth motion between the oppressed social microcosm of the school and the zone of freedom in the verdant and shadowy other space. The inmates continuously resort to this space, either to jog or for romantic liaisons (perfidious Tory meets her boyfriend there),[3] and there they discover the wounded male falcon that Paulie nurses back to flight and with which she increasingly identifies as her gender revolt becomes more and more acute. "You wouldn't just lie there and take it like a girl," she says to the falcon as she increasingly rejects the "weakness" inherent in her gender identity. The forest, then, is not only a zone of freedom, discovery, and healing but also a contradictory zone of revolt and refusal, on the one hand, and of danger and suicidal madness, on the other.

Elsewhere in Quebec a tomboy lesbian character who is the mirror opposite of Paulie in every way shows up unexpectedly in another literary adaptation, the successful 1999 rural melodrama *Les muses orphelines*. Here, as I mentioned in the previous section, the coming-of-age trope is almost entirely subsumed, as with k.d. lang, under the present-day return-of-the-native framework as a supporting character in MICHEL MARC BOUCHARD's narrative about the futile reconstitution of the dysfunctional heterosexual family. As in *Hanging Garden*, adult siblings are reunited at the family homestead to renegotiate consanguinity and individual identities, but in this case the mother has long since fled the coop, rather than taking advantage of the confusion of a "coming home" crisis to suddenly go while the getting was good, as Sweet William's mother did. The lesbian middle sister Martine is a supporting character, and in fact the most well-adjusted of the bunch, a serene and butch soldier adept at the firearms necessary for warding off village vigilantes, wisely trying to detach herself from the familial vortex around her. That Martine is so matter-of-fact about her sexual identity and the girlfriend she's left holding the fort (literally) in the far Arctic and to whom she will return at film's end, the only "together" character in a messy ensemble of hysterical siblings, reflects of course the queer provenance of this otherwise relatively nonqueer source play by a gay man. This story is already a quite unique variation of the urban-rural dynamic, but there is a further, interesting complication: this native is returning to the (literal) sticks of the sawmill/hydroelectric centre St-Ludger from an even more remote ultra-sticks, a Canadian forces base at Alert Bay that no doubt has something in common with Pool's heterotopic private school but is unfortunately never shown – in contrast to the chaotic East End Montreal from which her heterosexual brother, a violent and disturbed failed writer, has come.

CHICKS IN THE STICKS: COUNTRY GETAWAYS

The fragmentary and hybrid nature of the foregoing coming-of-age and return-of-the-native permutations suggests that the generic chicks-in-the-sticks impulse may turn out by default to be the most important in this female corpus, and such is indeed the case. For this assortment of film and video texts, the forest, country, garden, or village signifies a kind of heterotopia, to come back to Foucault's phrase. But its crisis function as "other space" is not restricted to adolescent initiation; rather, it serves more generally as a refuge of utopian resonance that mediates a range of either personal or collective crises within patriarchal or heterosexist urban society. This rural utopian ideal is distinct to many lesbian feminist discourses, whether it symbolizes a return to archetypal wellsprings of the feminine or of the goddess or to more materialist or ecological constructs of alternative social organization. BONNIE DICKIE's prairie lesbian-feminist documentary, *Sandra's Garden* (Studio D, 1990), sets up the eponymous country garden as a bucolic therapeutic space for the urban characters to construct community and overcome the trauma of sexual abuse. Dionne Brand in *Long Time Comin'* (1992, 57) offers a resolutely urban setting for two exemplary portraits of a black lesbian painter and a singer, Grace Channer and Faith Nolan respectively, but the film is framed in Muskoka interludes where black lesbians are building a forest house or walking through the woods, harmonica in action, in a retreat and a "safe place" away from the urban patriarchy where "sisters are destroyed." These two very different pastoral heterotopias function in similar ways as aestheticized articulations of both archetypal and social options. (We shall see in chapter 7 that a related mythology on the male side, as articulated within hunting narratives within Quebec cinema in particular, signifies differently: as a primal release from the rat race, whether of heterofamilial obligation or corporate/consumerist entrapment.)

As a kind of problematical founding text of the lesbian bush genre in its Canadian manifestation, let us let us start with the seventies and the earliest "lesbian" film in the Canadian corpus, *August and July*, the 1973 cinéma-vérité feature of a lesbian couple spending a summer on an Ontario farm. This idyl of long-haired and long-skirted Alexa and Sharon long-windedly talking through their relationship while picking pears, chopping wood, going for long walks in beautiful meadows, skinny-dipping, and cuddling and groping and sulking was unique for its time within Canadian cinemas.

This film's immediate historic context of post-Stonewall mobilization, coinciding with the winding down of countercultural energies, ties it in chronologically, as Chantal Nadeau points out in her critique of a later chicks-in-the-sticks film *Revoir Julie*, with what might be called the "ur-source" of this rural mythology, the "lesbian cultural feminist film" originating in that same period ([2000] 2004). Within lesbian cultural feminist film, as Richard Dyer describes the loose 1970s movement/network of avant-garde, documentary, and short fiction works, which were primarily American in origin, major iconographic impulses connected lesbian identity, bodies, and sexuality to natural and pastoral iconography, from fruits, flowers, and seashells to caves, meadows, and the ocean surf ([1990] 2003, 169–200). The migration of the urban radical-lesbian political sensibility to its real or imagined rustic roots, whether in pursuit of utopian political community or spiritual renewal or escapist fantasy, was another major energy of this cultural movement. Interestingly, Sharon shares her recollection of childhood abuse at one point in the film, anticipating *Sandra's Garden*'s theme of the pastoral healing of abuse trauma two decades later, but

Markowitz did not know how to develop this theme in *August and July*. In fact, he could not have been aware that his film was made the same year as the debut of the prototypical filmmaker of American cultural feminism, Barbara Hammer, but the coincidence has symbolic value. For Markowitz's two subjects, caught up in the late-hippie fantasy of rural communalism, are evidently on the same wavelength as the West Coast New Age ethos of Hammer's and other kindred works, such as the Hindu-influenced vulva-as-fruits manifesto *Near the Big Chakra* (Anne Severson, United States,1972).

Be that as it may, *August and July* never struck a chord (except with the Yonge Street voyeurs who caught it in its theatrical run): it was spurned both by mainstream critics (unanimously) and by the emerging sprinkling of queer critics (see MARKOWITZ) despite the obvious breakthrough status of the subject matter. Perhaps its outsider (male) voyeurism was the problem, along with the filmmaker's interested, if not conflicted, attitude to Alexa, as my radical lesbian friends of the day thought and Markowitz interviews confirm (1973). But the more serious problem was likely the insistence and obsessiveness of the heterotopic pastoral mythology without any hookup with a social, geographical, dramatic, or chronological "homotopia." The spectator apparently felt as much in a rut as the women themselves.

There are contrasting invocations of the pastoral heterotopia in *La vie rêvée* (1972), a Québécois feminist dramatic feature that is contemporaneous with *August and July*. This legendary but little-seen film is not a "lesbian film" in terms of authorship or explicit theme, as director MIREILLE DANSEREAU keeps reminding her latter-day audiences, but a homosocial narrative that has been appropriated by lesbian film culture. However much Dansereau's two Plateau-based heroines are fed up with the patriarchy and periodically resort to sylvan greenery for its therapeutic or fantasy operation, they ineradicably come back to "where they live" – jobs, bosses, apartments, and neighbourhoods, here and now.

A slightly later Toronto work, this time of bona fide lesbian authorship, *Labyris Rising* (MARGARET MOORES, 1980), testifies at least to the authenticity of the chicks-in-the-sticks tendency. The Michigan Women's Music Festival, which by the end of the 1970s had begun to institutionalize in the U.S. Midwest the more spontaneous pastoral impulse of earlier West Coast lesbian culture, is constructed by Moores as nostalgic flashbacks intercut with the decidedly urban present of motorbike maintenance and pool halls, as well as with movement dances and marches in city boots. Moores's film offers a recognizable embrace of rural carnival as heterotopia, but the fact that her pastoral imagery was caught in still images, images from south of the border to boot, might suggest that the chicks-in-the-sticks narrative lacked resonance with any of the Canadian contexts I have been exploring. Whether this is true or whether the mythology was simply percolating

Two young women in love...with each other

AUGUST
& JULY

A film by MURRAY MARKOWITZ
Starring ALEXA DE WIEL & SHARON SMITH
Executive Producer: F.R. CRAWLEY
Produced & Directed by Murray Markowitz Film Editor: Andre Herman
Director of Photography: James Lewis Associate Producer: Findlay Quinn
Produced & Distributed by Crawley Films in Eastman Colour

The earliest Canadian "lesbian" film *August and July* (1973): pretty, pastoral, and prob-lematical. Film poster, used with permission of Murray Markowitz

below the surface throughout the eighties (cropping up in Rozema's Victorian ladies' picnics, for example), the fact remains that the bush narrative
does reemerge in the 1990s with several new and distinct energies. By the
time Wescott's transhistorical, transurban sapphic (literally) epic *Stolen
Moments* (1997) returns to the Michigan Women's Festival, the pastoral
blowout has become even more institutionalized as heterotopia – if not Tay-
lorized – almost like a humungous carnivalesque penal colony (to use others
of Foucault's examples of traditional heterotopias). There's now a kitchen
serving ten thousand vegetarian meals and mobs of topless women pulsating through work detail, as well as consuming well packaged musical acts in
the sun, thereby injecting some ambiguity into the film's theme of alternative lesbian community through overdoing it a tad. Closer to home, Wescott

delivers two Canadianized aquatic versions of the mass camp-out with, first, her rather implausible fantasy of "a rural dyke community outside of Montreal" (as opposed to "A wood near Athens" for this midwinter dream) where tobogganing and skating constitute the principal activities and, second, with a more abstract, archetypal version in her recurrent motif of waves softly crashing on an isolated shore.

But this imagery of mass campground logistics, snowy recreational outings, and maritime metaphors is not the only vestige of the heritage of *August and July*'s countercultural mindspace and Hammer's "cultural feminist" poetics. Studio D's big hit of the start of the nineties, *A Company of Strangers*, the tale of a sexually and ethnically balanced "bomber crew"[4] of seniors marooned in the bucolic countryside of the Laurentians, had more than a little in common with its ancestors. Certainly no one could deny the lingering attraction of the 1960s and 1970s for the women's studio right until its demise in 1996. And the cultural ethos of the 1970s "lesbian continuum," which was expressed by this film perhaps more than any other, had certainly been a part of Studio politics from its origin (at the expense of lesbian visibility, it has been argued [see chapter 6], but that was about to change in the 1990s). Otherwise the chicks-in-the-sticks mythology was updated by [heterosexual] director Cynthia Scott and [lesbian] scriptwriter GLORIA DEMERS in the application of the heterotopic pretext to current social issues: aging, historical dimensions of native-born and immigrant women's roles and aspirations in Canadian society (crystallized in the characters' individual documentary biographies), and, finally, multiculturalism as embodied in its casting panorama. Not surprisingly the "out" lesbian inserted within this panorama handles the country better than some of the others: "out" writer MARY MEIGS has not only dry humour, calmness, and charisma but also birdwatching and wildlife-watercolour hobbies, along with her other more practical skills. As for the butch nun Catherine Roche, this resourceful character was clearly to the country born, not only as a mechanic and hiker but also as a kind of Amazon bush-pilot-ex-machina who rescues the whole party on her pontoons and presumably triggers their return to the urban tenements. The idyllic lakeside meadow thus functions with a glimmer of lesbian hetero/utopia but also much more concretely as a social laboratory, both real and metaphorical, for the celebration of gender community, as well as for the understanding and transformation of society (in contrast to the utter denial of society à la *August and July*).

In comparison to the Quebec men heading for the woods with their rifles and bows in *La bête lumineuse* (see chapter 7), who discovered in that crucible for defining and testing gender community what Eve Sedgwick called the disjunctiveness of the male homosocial continuum (1985, 2), the lady seniors of *Company* discovered the continuousness and fluidity of the female homosocial continuum. If the contrast between the gals who reluctantly kill frogs for a shared mealtime ritual of survival and the guys who want to shoot a moose but can't even find one, so instead beat up on each other, is telling, that's the whole point.

One other NFB film from the decade comes from a completely different cultural and demographic space. *Maman et Ève*, produced by a man, is about francophone lesbians in the same Sudbury that in the previous section was the epitome of the resource-based hinterland. While the homosocial group of four mature women who came out relatively late in life is in some ways the equivalent of *Company*'s lifeboat community of elders or the alternative families of the Sault Ste Marie party underground, the familial dimension engaged in does not involve parents and siblings but, rather, offspring, and sometimes recalcitrant ones at that. And for the Sudbury *mamans*, the heterotopic elsewhere is not a retreat for renewal to the boreal forest and certainly not to Toronto (though some of the women do show up at Toronto Pride, just like their younger queer co-citizens in *Pinco Triangle*). They migrate much further afield to the Bahamas, the tropical paradise not of spiritual or feminist counterculture but of consumerist cooptation and commodified leisure, a pina-colada bacchanalian heterotopia linked more solidly to Foucault's carnival than to the pear-picking and frog-eating asceticism of the earlier films from Toronto and Montreal.

Despite the contribution of the foregoing films, the NFB no longer dominated women's cinema in Canada in the 1990s, thanks in no small part to Tory cutbacks. Outside the NFB lesbian heterotopias were surfacing just as strongly as inside but in ways that seemed a little more in touch with the skeptical, postmodern spirit of the age. Take JEANNE CRÉPEAU's gentle postmodern romance *Revoir Julie* (1998) as a prime example. Here the heroine Juliet retreats from her stressed Plateau–Mont Royal surroundings to lick her postbreakup wounds in the bucolic DisneyWorld splendour of the Eastern Townships and there jump-starts a childhood friendship with Julie, remolding it into a same-sex romance that Nadeau chastises for being far too chaste (2000). Crépeau's work has always been resolutely urban, as the memory of *Usure* (1986) testifies with its not dissimilar narrative of a burnt-out couple rekindling the fire, all the while standing on the pavement in the middle of a bleak Montreal street. This time there's a kind of self-conscious bracketing of this urbanity, summoning it only as a framing device at beginning and end (somewhat the reverse of Pool's structure in *Anne Trister* and *Emporte-moi*). As if the singing of birds and cutaway reaction shots of placid cows were not enough to accent the self-conscious and no doubt impossible heterotopia of this world, which is somewhat akin to Polly's absurd black and white fantasies in *Mermaids*, Crépeau brings intertextuality to the rescue. Her richly allusive mosaic serves not only to compensate

Jeanne Crépeau's *L'Usure* (1986) is resolutely urban, with its burnt-out couple rekindling the fire standing on the pavement in the middle of a bleak Montreal street. Production still, photo: Jeanne Crépeau

for the lost complexity of her script (sacrificed when the funders lowered her budget and imposed restraint) but also to contextualize, comment on, and undermine the interrelated dialectics of city and country, of heterosexuality and homosexuality, and also – given it's Quebec – of French and English. Crépeau's simple story (city girl loses city girl, meets country girl instead) becomes a web for weaving texts that pertain to all three dialectics, from naive early French-language documentaries mystifying the wildflower-bedecked and maple-sweet heartland to a traditional English heterosexual folk ballad ("John Riley," sung by Juliet with a decided nuance of gender transgression) and a collage of veiled and not so veiled homoerotic European oil paintings, deftly animated to wink at the viewer.

The weave of the linguistic text is especially complex. Juliet is a perfect-ly bilingual anglophone, having been educated in French at convent school with her chum Julie (Juliet is played by STEPHANIE MORGENSTERN, the naive country girl heroine of *Forbidden Love*), while Julie is a *pure laine* francophone whose presence ensures that French is the dominant but far from overwhelming language of the scintillating Rohmerian script. Nadeau sees this configuration confronting linguistic and sexual identity with geography as a *péquiste* plot:

There is much question of language(s) in the film, even if we don't really see a lot of it. A pity, but true. The repartee flies, but seduction is first and foremost a

With her first feature *Revoir Julie* twelve years later the Montreal director would go pastoral, but in a self-conscious, postmodern way. Production still, courtesy Jeanne Crépeau

matter of wit. Language becomes here the through-route of identity geographies: from homoeroticism to the rural … Julie, in order to keep her holy *pure laine* long johns intact as a barricade, persistently communicates in French: don't forget Bill 101! … Sexual identity gets reconciled in Juliet's movement towards Julie, in the confusion of city and countryside. In the commonality of words, in speeches in French, Crépeau claims I believe an identity boundary that is both francophone and – dare I say it – *nationaliste*.

Admittedly, Juliet's "to do" list has only one entry in French, and that is to see Julie again, but I prefer to read the narrative not as a clash but as a harmonious encounter among the various sets of identity zones – linguistic, geographical, and sexual. This is a process of osmosis rather than "boundaries," not osmosis between the reductive terms of urban and rural but between the cosmopolitan multilingual and multisexual metropolis and the heartland off the autoroute, full of maple syrup and wildflowers but also of funky dance music and open to the world. Julie's mother, after all, buys American ice cream and remembers to put it in the freezer even when she shows up unexpectedly after a grocery run and accidentally discovers her daughter *in flagrante delicto*. I am more troubled by the disparity between the two women's jobs: Juliet is busy without having a livelihood (a morning talk show about doing nothing, not a common occupation in Montreal's yuppie bohemia), while Julie equally implausibly does geological surveys, and this interface of metropolitan and rural economies doesn't ring true, especially in the vacuum of social contexts other than the snooping Maman. Otherwise, how many *péquiste* tracts have we seen in which a bravado recitation of Coleridge's "Kubla Khan" is an epiphany and the performance of an English folk song is not only shaped to the contour of lesbian romance but also provides the dénouement?

Crépeau was no doubt aware of the Anglo-Saxon cultural-lesbian model for any North American dream of sapphic pastoral heterotopia but chose to bracket her story with her idyllic probing of specifically maple-syrup analogies. ANNE GOLDEN (positioned within a concretely bicultural women's video milieu in Montreal), the Moores-Travassos team in Toronto, and the Dempsey-Millan team in Winnipeg have also been aware of this ancestor and have sometimes given it a cursory nod. But they have done so principally as a citation among a plethora of other local and global referents for the well-acculturated young urban lesbo, not as a valid sociocultural option. If the urban positioning of lesbian cinematic culture and society is in fact the kind of impasse Nadeau has pointed to, it is not surprising that the experimental video sector, rather than the Telefilm Canada commercial sector or the NFB public sector, has best met the challenge of that impasse. The video *girlz* have done so with their ethos of grass-roots subsistence and artistic independence and their aesthetic, not of romantic or melodramatic narrative as highlighted above, but, rather, of the subversively satiric or parodistic versions of the chicks-in-the-sticks genres. It is surely this proudly subversive subculture, of which Vancouver examples could no doubt be substituted for my Winnipeg, Toronto, and Montreal examples, that favours what Nadeau would call "the lesbian subject's regimes of recognition and dissonance" and that "blows up the normative border" of sexuality and of sexual identity (2000).

For example, Golden's *Site*, a two-minute, minimalist example of her characteristic, exceedingly dry humour, assembles constructions of *faux* documents to evoke three different stages in a teleological trajectory of lesbian culture. The three stages are seemingly based literally on Foucault's heterotopia theory, evident in her focus on his prototypical "other places": respectively, the clinic of the pre-Stonewall era, the commune of the post-Stonewall era, and the "Lesbian Amusement Park" (or LAP) of the posthistorical, identity-consumerist present. If the clinic, with its gloomy pastiche of investigative direct cinema, connotes the dark ages of psychiatric stigmatization and the enforced regimentation of aversion therapy and if the LAP, with its glitzy promotional kinetics of midway rides, connotes the day of commoditized sexualities (the title reads "Dykeland thrills and chills!"), the hilarious middle panel evokes a third intermediary heterotopia, the rural "commune" of the intervening decades' identity essentialism. Purporting to be from a 1987 documentary, *I Will Sing You a Lesbian Song*, by "Rose Croswell," the degenerate images, replete with a water motif that would do both Hammer and Pool proud, show a row of scraggly seeming refugees from an early California-type country dyke film hoeing a nondescript garden, followed by the title "These are lesbians proudly working their land." Even their equipment, shown in closeup, has a sexual identity – "This is a lesbian wheelbarrow."

Golden's irreverence for the rigid dogmas of sexual identity, including both their heterotopic textuality and their co-optation by larger sociocultural systems, is diffused through all of her work. *Big Girl Town* sends up the spaghetti western as a mythology of masculinity on the presocial wilderness frontier and transforms it here into a postmodern fable of fat vs thin that ends with an all-girl square dance – not in k.d. lang's agrarian utopia but in a postindustrial wasteland. In *Somme*, Golden's most accomplished work in many ways, the pastoral heterotopia recedes even further into the zone of impossibility. This work is organized around the mock-scientific syntax of a sleep research project, in alternation with the subjective voice of a sleep-deprived narrator (Golden), who is increasingly disoriented between her urban reality and the natural parkland images that keep popping up – a dream or hallucination? a somnambulatory trajectory? She tells her girlfriend that she was sure she went to sleep in Montreal last night, but here she is now in a verdant woodland garden. The pastoral, though it is vividly portrayed and crunching under the sleeper's bedroom slippers, loses its dimension as social heterotopia and is overtaken by its constitution as psychic space, as dreamworld. Or is it simply a nonreferential representational space?

Moores and Travassos are no less irreverent in *Dog Days* (1999), but the ambitious characterization in this whimsical narrative of a bomber crew of four trendy young Toronto intellectuals homesteading in bucolic August-and-July country gives their film much more of a social character than Golden's postmodern dreamscapes. Not that *Days* doesn't have its whimsical, magic-realist character, what with love potions, talking dogs, magic carpets, and ghostly gender rebels from dyke herstory wandering around the farm. The video is based on real nineteenth-century letters discovered by the artists, and the question of invisible queer history in rural Ontario gives all the serendipity a serious edge.

Golden's fascinated appropriation of benighted, inherited forms, from the spaghetti Western to the trash documentary, is shared by Dempsey and Millan – not surprisingly, for the latter is her frequent collaborator. In *Medusa Raw*, *Calamity*, and *Lesbian National Parks and Services: A Force of Nature* (henceforth LNPAFON), they range wildly from, respectively,

Lesbian National Parks and Services: A Force of Nature (2002): a hyperbolically Canadian exercise in roving the wilderness bush garden as a national vocation, as well as the setting for serious uniform-wearing. Production still, Dan Lee, BANFF Centre for the Arts

gynephobic Greek mythology through the Hollywood western (done more authentically than *Big Girl Town*, not surprisingly, considering Winnipeg's geographical advantages) to the Discovery Channel expository wildlife documentary cross-pollinated with the NFB regional landscape dithyramb and the youth recruitment genres. If *Medusa* blends prairie kitsch à la W.O. Mitchell (a quaint white prairie church on a broad horizon with a jilted rubber-snake-headed harpie left on its doorstep or else ecstatically waltzing with a more conventional bride amid the grassland), *Calamity* follows, in more sober black-and-white style, an ageless and archetypally transhistorical cowgirl and her horse meandering over the range, in what much surely be a remake of the NFB's canonical *Corral* (Colin Low, 1954). *LNPAFON* offers not just a lesbian wheelbarrow and an amusement park but also a hyperbolically Canadian exercise in roving the wilderness bush garden as a national vocation, as well as the setting for fantasy myths of eco-intervention, socialization, serious uniform-wearing, and the policing of hetero male reprobates (the scene where deadpan Dempsey tickets a too-glib guy for wearing an "inappropriate T-shirt" rivals any highlight of forty years of Canadian satiric TV comedy). There are also just enough overtones of regimentation in the rangers' recruitment and training segments – showing lockstep drilling of obviously inner-city baby dykes who spout the party line for the camera – to gently interrogate the economy of enforced identity diversity throughout the culture. And the haunting and sublime moment in the tape's ringing peroration, where the two artists, in their wetsuits, dive into the surf in perfect, graceful tandem, like a combination of porpoises and *Baywatch* lifeguard extras, has a zany magic beyond description. For Dempsey and Millan, as for Golden, the nonurban heterotopia may sometimes be just a textual one, from the postmodern world of representation rather than the world of social experience, but further signifying levels recognize and question bodies, desires, identities, and communities positioned within the historical and geographical "space in which we live."

CONCLUSION

It has thus far been possible to identify the various crosscurrents of three narrative patterns in this chapter – coming of age in the sticks, return of the native, and boys in the bush/chicks in the sticks through a wide range of narrative, documentary, and experimental works. Gender determinations have shaped these patterns on both sides of the XX/XY divide: for example, most obviously the coming-of-age trope has relatively greater importance and focus for the boys than for the girls and, conversely, the in-the-bush trope prevails for the girls (that is, the bush is more important for the girls than the *gay* boys: *straight* boys have it as one of their central existential dogmas, as we shall see in chapter 7).

It would be remiss, however, to conclude without analyzing somewhat more carefully the various kinds of bushes and sticks on view. No sociologist would accept the monolithic lumping together of various kinds of non-metropolitan social and geographic spaces envisioned in this chapter: from the primeval rain forest and seashore of *Dreamspeaker* to a slightly more domesticated boreal version traversed by jogging paths in *Lost and Delirious*; from the abandoned farmland of *August and July* to the actively cultivated agricultural farmland populated by interested cows in *Revoir Julie* or its golden prairie variant in the Sinclair Ross adaptations; from the symbolic aquatic spaces of *Lilies* and *Emporte-moi* to the symbolic gardens of *Hanging Garden* and the therapeutic territories in *Sandra's Garden* and *Company of Strangers*; from the part nostalgic, part ironic, distinctly postmodern textual heterotopias of *Forbidden Love*, LNPAFON, and the work of Moores/Travassos and Golden; from the oppressively nosy but organic small-community garrisons of Sinclair Ross, k.d. lang, and Michel Marc Bouchard to the stressed hinterland resource-extracting hubs of Sudbury, Sault Ste Marie, and Bathurst; from the historical Caribbean and Levantine homelands of Brand, Mohabeer, Bowen, and Pool to Rozema's psychic and symbolic other spaces; from the other countries of the past and the elsewhere found everywhere, conjured up either as ideal or inferno, to the gritty materialism of the present, here, now, fiction version in *Full Blast*, documentary version in *The Pinco Triangle*. It would be misleading also to elide the many distinct cultural functions served by these heterotopias, from crisis treatment to therapy to socialization to "pride laboratory" (to quote Roy Mitchell), functions inflected with the experience and the memory of difference, trauma, and stigma but also of discovery, jouissance, and growth. No doubt it would be supreme metropolitan arrogance to lump together the rich diversity of Canadian spaces as seen through queer urban eyes, to claim that Sudbury is an imaginary space equivalent to a Sinclair Ross wheat farm. Even more so, as my chapter epigraph taken from Maureen Bradley's epochal video *Queer across Canada* suggests, it would be no less arrogant to apply urban grids of knowing upon pan-national spatial experience and identity formations across the board. My point has not been that the Canadian queer imaginary constructs in any unifocal way the opposition of the metropolis and the rural hinterland but, rather, that male and female artists are in sync in constructing one urban space of safety, community, diversity, and desire with a myriad of nonurban heterotopias in its orbit. Regardless of geographical or demographic character or social function, all these heterotopias are situated through the imagination of film and video makers in dialectical relation to that metropolitan zone, all intertangled with spatial narratives of migration back and forth and chronological narratives of coming of age and growing up, understanding the self, and finding community. We may be living in an impasse and crisis of urban shortsightedness, "an identity essentialism ordained by geographical confinement" (Nadeau 2000), but it is not for a lack of artists imagining other places.

6

Forbidden Love, or Queering the National Film Board of Canada

to interpret Canada to Canadians.
~ Mandate of the National Film Board of Canada

BURSTING SUITCASE, OR THE ELEPHANT AS AUTEUR

As all the foregoing chapters have shown, no institution has had more impact on shaping Canadian cinematic cultures historically, whether in English or in French, than the National Film Board of Canada. Even more than other excluded and silenced constituencies, GLBTQ Canadians have had a rollercoaster love-hate relationship with John Grierson's studio, founded in 1939 to construct our national imaginary, as per my oft-invoked epigraph above. Many of us have watched very carefully the innovative documentary and animation studio of the forties, fifties, and sixties as it became the stodgy old uncle of later decades. Today the board is a minia-ture version of the behemoth it became during the Trudeau era, having barely survived the ferocious downsizing imposed by the Mulroney regime and the attrition perpetuated by the Chrétien regime. It is perennially in urgent need of renewal, most recently, as I write in 2003, having fired all of its in-house directors and placed itself in the hands of freelance indies from coast to coast, desperately searching for an expanded vision and an extend-ed mandate in the cyber-digital era. Regardless of the instability of the last decades, few would deny that the board's queer documentary cycle of the 1980s, 1990s, and, 2000s, a corpus of almost fifty documentary films (depending on how you count) has had a major impact on queer cultures and on larger political cultures in both English- and French-speaking Canada and, moreover, that it constitutes an important repository of queer voices and visions by queer artists, one recognized around the world.

This chapter is devoted to this bursting suitcase of films, sprawling, contradictory, and uneven, often inspired and brilliant, often infuriatingly outdated and beside the point, full of holes. (For example, not a single film on the AIDS crisis in relation to its domestic gay-male epidemiology emerged from the English programs – perhaps the most shocking betrayal in a sea of small betrayals.) This suitcase can be opened and unpacked through several methodological frameworks. The films constitute a pan-national documentary tradition and invite a perspective in terms of Canadian cultural themes, landscapes, and iconographies, with the usual gulf between anglophone and francophone constituents and the usual regional mosaic. But at the same time they form a genre cycle determined by its dialogue with a political constituency that overflows national boundaries, what we could call the international "sexual diversity" or queer-documentary genre cycle; the corpus contains within its margins, often within the same film, both "affirmation" and "postaffirmation" energies and stages (to use Dyer's terms for the initial waves of post-Stonewall "positive image" community-building, and the subsequent post-AIDS tide of self-reflection and diversification [(1990) 2003, 215–64]). At the same time, the NFB queer corpus is work produced within a single production studio (and its regional branchplants) and thus calls for analysis from a "studio as auteur" perspective. In this light, the work reflects the personalities who came and went through the cavernous labyrinth in suburban Montreal and its regional garrisons, from persistent staff directors like MARGARET WESCOTT and powerful producers like DON HAIG to young independents like ATIF SIDDIQI. But the work is also stamped by one of the weirdest bureaucratic subcultures in the world, combining both the idealism and the inertia, the profligacy and the tokenism, of any civil service – but especially ours. This chapter will intermingle all three of these angles upon the elephant, commencing with an overview of the studio as auteur and building a chronology of the quarter century in which the queer corpus emerged. I shall then offer a generic breakdown of the films, exploring the cultural and political ramifications of the various narratives and formats in play. Finally, I will summarize the basic themes that have emerged in terms of national discourses of art, politics, economics, and sexuality.

Two or three of the films nurtured within this microclimate have received wide international attention (i.e., from Americans), especially *The Company of Strangers* (aka *Strangers in Good Company* in the United States, 1990) and *Forbidden Love: The Unashamed Story of Lesbian Lives* (1992). Such films are canonized by chapters in anthologies from American university presses, by entries on U.S. queer websites, and by their inclusion in a whole critical literature; the foreigners are not likely to situate the films within the historical frameworks I am trying to scan, but they sometimes see things insiders can't.

Dozens of the other films and videos make the domestic rounds of the proverbial church basements, school AV centres, and community library loan shelves, flow out through cassette and DVD merchandising online and over the counter, occasionally make it onto cablecast, and even stream down from increasingly common cyber servers. This everyday product is unrecognized by cultural arbiters but reaches huge numbers of people efficiently and quietly, providing invaluable resources for isolated individuals and grass roots groups. My study attempts to redress both the oversights and the taken-for-grantedness, as well as to go beyond the prototypical Canadian carping, whether born of low self-esteem and envy or my NDP-ish idealism or the cultural arrogance of arts avant-gardes, to come up with a coherent analysis and overview of this critically important collection of our images. But it begins with a personal story.

J'ACCUSE

On 10 November 1986, in one of my more militant moments I wrote an angry letter to the government film commissioner, François Macerola, John Grierson's successor at the helm of the NFB and figurehead of one of the most prestigious documentary studios in the world. The state film studio was then getting set to celebrate, in 1989, the fiftieth anniversary of its founding, but I wasn't in a celebratory mood. What sparked my *J'accuse* was *Passiflora* (1985), an ambitious, bold, and expensive French-language NFB feature documentary about the simultaneous visits of the pope and Michael Jackson to Montreal's Olympic stadium in 1984. The visits were the backdrop against which a Breughelian foreground of dramatized sex/gender transgressors, including gay men, transgendered characters, abortion seekers, refugees from psychiatry and from domestic violence, and alienated young people with great haircuts were all teeming. All these people were excluded from the visits but integrated into the postmodern urban landscape of dissent/consent depicted in the film. Highlights included the celebration of queer street theatre (a procession of "papettes" mocking the liturgical drag at hand)[1] and queer desire (the public performance of homoerotic exchange and transgender transgression in public space). As if this were not enough to frighten the horses, the filmmakers Fernand Bélanger and Dagmar Teufel – respectively an experienced and out gay documentarist with anarchist and pro-youth sympathies and a feminist who had championed disempowered rural women in several documentaries – were

Passiflora (1985). Which was scarier for NFB brass, same-sex kisses, transvestites, and teenaged abortions or this video pope booming "bow down and obey" over the field of cardboard seats abandoned by faithful bums? Production still, used with permission of the National Film Board of Canada

perhaps the first to puncture the realist sobriety of the NFB documentary ethos with their irreverent graffiti-ization of real-life voices and bodies, overlaying image tracks and sound tracks alike with mischievous doodles (the pope's "re-mixed voice" booming out "bow down and obey!" from his giant video screens). It was probably this irreverence for "reality," in combination with the film's more literal dissidence around sexual identity and reproductive rights, that was guaranteed to raise eyebrows.

Even before *Passiflora* was released, Bélanger and Teufel sensed that there was funny business afoot from the studio brass around the sensitive issues of ecclesiastical show business, queer sexualities, and reproductive rights that the film had tackled. They were furious that the board had without precedent declined to subtitle the film for its prestige invitation to the 1986 Toronto International Film Festival and that the board's strategy of damage control was being abetted by its internal festival and release bureaus (little pockets of absurdly unaccountable and refractory bureaucracy, which seemed this time to be taking orders from on high). Bélanger and Teufel blew the whistle. Recognizing an ambitious, experimental work that, moreover, was clearly the first unabashed gay lib work from the old uncle, I rushed to champion the film, programed it in its original French version at the 1987 Grierson Documentary Seminar in Toronto, and got onto the CBC's *Journal* denouncing the suppression of the film. The board denied everything and said festivals around the world had rejected the film, and we all watched the noses grow on their faces. My partner at the time, José Arroyo, championed the film in *Cinema Canada* as a film "in concept and form much more daring than any other Québécois film I've seen recently … [and one that will] continue to be talked about long after the awards being given to some other films have turned to dust" (1986). And the Scotsman Ian Lockerbie (not my partner and not even gay) proved him right a few years later, claiming that with *Passiflora* and an earlier Bélanger work, the documentary "has acquired a complexity of language and a richness of texture and meaning of which there are hardly other examples in all its history" and that the films "should endure, and become reference points for measuring many works to come" (1994).

Since I had been smarting under the NFB silence for a decade, the ham-fisted suppression of this artistically innovative, bravely anarchist, and prophetically queer film by the NFB was the last straw. So I wrote my letter, indicting the institution for failing to fulfil its mandate with regard to Canadian lesbians and gays and just happened to "cc" the letter to not-yet-out MP Svend Robinson and a few others. I did not mince words and could be accused of slight exaggeration (10 November 1986):

I have frequently criticized the National Film Board for failing to fulfil its mandate with regard to two million lesbian and gay Canadians (a conservative estimate), a criticism that is bitter and widespread in the gay media throughout both Quebec and English Canada. Throughout its history the NFB has represented every conceivable Canadian minority in its films, from the Inuits to the Hutterites to the handicapped, with the glaring exception of this large stigmatized minority still struggling for its rights.

The NFB's unacceptable record of contemptuous silence has been broken on only two exceptional occasions: a passage in *Some American Feminists* (1978) that deals with *American* lesbians and an inept short *New Romance* (1975) riddled with derisive stereotypes, a film fortunately now absent from the catalogue. I suppose we should be grateful that the independent short film *Michael a Gay Son* is distributed through the NFB, that a few recent NFB co-productions in Quebec theatrical fiction have included sympathetic gay characters (*Anne Trister*, *Pouvoir intime*, *Déclin de l'empire américain*), or that regional NFB offices occasionally contribute small amounts to independent gay and lesbian productions. However, this is clearly less than we are entitled to according to the NFB's mandate, and in view of our investment as taxpayers in the world's leading producer of documentaries of social conscience.[2]

I urged the commissioner to "expedite the preparation of an English version of *Passiflora* ... and to furthermore implement immediate plans for affirmative action in fulfilling the NFB's mandate to gay and lesbian Canadians."

Svend complained to Flora MacDonald, the Tory minister of communications in charge of the NFB, who responded with the usual "arm's length" line but passed on the complaint to Macerola (27 January 1987). Two months after my letter, the commissioner replied timidly that no, the New York queer film festival had refused *Passiflora* on the grounds that it was irrelevant to the event and would not be of interest to gays and lesbians, and that no, "unquestionably, no one had deliberately obstructed the production of films for this minority group. As you know, film proposals are generated through filmmakers and producers – it may well be that good ideas on the subject have simply not emerged. However, I am told that Studio D has identified the need for such films, and is currently investigating the possibility of a one-hour documentary looking at the heterosexual institution and the history of lesbianism throughout the ages" (8 January 1987).

Government cultural institutions specialize in this kind of feeble self-justification and damage control. Who had they expected to come up with "good ideas"? Bonnie Klein, who had actively suppressed queer identities from *Not a Love Story: A Film About Pornography* (1981)? Michael Rubbo and Giles Walker, who were throwing away huge NFB budgets on, respectively, "sensitive" documentaries about women and plastic surgery and on idiotic male backlash comedies like *The Masculine Mystique* (1984) and *90 Days* (1985)? Or any of the rest of the blinkered male fraternity who were having trouble dealing even with mild liberal feminism in their Town of Mount Royal bungalows and Outremont duplexes, let alone gay liberation and AIDS downtown? What kind of documentary filmmaker could have looked at thousands of angry queers surging through the streets of Toronto after the bathhouse raids in 1981 or rallying there in the very month that I was writing my letter (pushing the new provincial Liberal government for protection from discrimination in the provincial human rights legislation), or more recently at the "waves of dying friends" precipitated by the HIV pandemic,[3] and not said immediately, "Wow, there are some films there!"? And the particular thrust of the self-justification – passing the buck to the women in the convenient feminist Studio D, founded in 1974 – further inflamed me.

I therefore continued the tirade into a new instalment, which I happened to run as an open letter in four film and gay magazines and which I sent to a dozen well-located NFB people:

I am glad to be informed that "no one has deliberately obstructed the production of films for this minority group." However I am not reassured by your conjecture that "good ideas on the subject have simply not emerged." This of course is the crux of the matter: the silencing of minorities through omission and institutional inertia is perhaps the most insidious kind of censorship because no one can point to "deliberate obstruction." Over the years NFB filmmakers have come to understand this problem and remedied it through affirmative action with regard to almost every Canadian minority or disenfranchised group – whether determined by gender, class, race, age, language, religion, handicap or ethnic or regional identity – every group in fact *except* homosexuals. If NFB filmmakers have avoided coming up with "good ideas on the subject," then it is the institution's responsibility to initiate affirmative action. Gay Canadian taxpayers are no longer willing to accept this silence. (1987)

I continued, spelling out three demands: consultative meetings between studio brass and producers and gay community representatives across the country, the distribution of eight independent films through NFB channels as a stopgap measure, and the publication of an audiovisual resource guide for gay and lesbian film users. For good measure I appended a list of "good ideas," including films on AIDS, the history of gay-rights struggles, a history of Toronto's *The Body Politic* (the legendary gay lib magazine had just given up the ghost after fifteen years of battles with the Ontario police and court system), a Canadian *Before Stonewall* and a Canadian *Times of Harvey Milk* (evoking the major American queer historical-documentary features of the decade, both from 1984, the latter an Oscar winner), a male *Firewords* (referring to Studio D's just completed feature by Dorothy Todd Hénaut on three Québécois lesbian writers), and finally, topical treatments of parents/teenagers/seniors/couples/ghettos, of freedom of speech/civil rights issues, and of public sex and policing. Finally, I presented Macerola with proof that either his festival office had lied to him about the New York queer festival refusal (or that my friend, festival director Peter Lowy, was lying to me), and repeated my demand for the subtitling of *Passiflora*, since I was about to show the film in Winnipeg in April. The letter ran in gay magazines but, most importantly, filled a whole page of *Cinema Canada*, and the egg hit the fan.4

Macerola responded on the same page, but did not add anything new to the discussion, continuing to pass the buck to women. For instead of the two male program branch directors, Georges Dufaux and Peter Katadotis, who he promised in his letter would contact me, the latter's first lieutenant, Isobel Marks, programing director for English production, soon showed up fairly nervously at my office. Marks tried to convince me that ongoing projects were just what the doctor ordered:

1 The forthcoming Puberty Package was surely exactly what I was looking for, since it included a brief reference to AIDS and a nonjudgmental treatment of homosexuality (this project apparently ended up as the *Growing Up Series*, 1989). In this connection she also mentioned West Coast producer JENNIFER TORRANCE, a youth and women specialist, who, in addition to the "Growing Up" series in 1985, had co-produced then heterosexual MOIRA SIMPSON's *Lorri: The Recovery Series* (1985). This instalment in a Vancouver substance abuse series profiled a recovering alcoholic who happened to be a lesbian depicted in conversation with her therapist for fifteen minutes, and everyone was going on about it as if this brave and articulate woman absolved the NFB in perpetuity from developing programs on queers. (Torrance would end up having her name on the NFB lesbian and gay and diversity packages of 1994 and 2003, respectively.)

2 Marks was also thinking about short dramas on teen issues, perhaps even homophobia, to follow up on existing pregnancy films (what turned out to be the 1994 Teen Pregnancy Package, one of which bore Torrance's mark as well).

3 The good news from Edmonton was that there was an "investigate" (the studio's quirky noun) underway on masculinity, which apparently was to end up as the homophobic *Life after Hockey* (1989; see chapter 7).

4 She also had on her mind some programs on families in transition (which would become a major theme of late-1990s productions).

5 And finally, don't forget good old Studio D and Margaret Wescott (who, as Macerola had intimated, had just undertaken her "history of lesbianism since Sappho" project, which was not to emerge for another decade, in 1997, as *Stolen Moments*, but I'm getting ahead of myself), who were going to let the male directors off the hook and bear the entire weight of the institution's responsibility to both gender and sexual minorities and everything else.

6 And oh yes, there's already plenty of factual material available on AIDS (!!!) that shouldn't be duplicated, but she'd met with Margaret Somerville in Medical Ethics at McGill (an early champion of the rights of people with HIV), and perhaps something to help teenagers with the issues might be appropriate.5

Marks was acting and speaking in better faith than her boss, and in fact the momentum of educational materials aimed at children and teenagers turned out to be a creditable one as far as it went in its isolation and however isolated it was. However, I couldn't believe her utter obliviousness to the political problematics of sexual minorities and wouldn't have any of the pathetic crumbs that she was tossing my way – or rather, at straight teenagers. When I threatened to initiate a lesbian and gay boycott of board products, she looked at me as if I had just started speaking Klingon.

Though the institution clearly was not budging on *Passiflora*, it was, admittedly, like all liberal sociocultural microcosms, capable of yielding slightly to guilt. Soon after, they briefly entertained a film proposal, developed in response to the controversy, by Montreal indie gay producer Hugh Campbell in cahoots with my friend, Toronto video bad boy John Greyson. Their film would be called *Flaunting It!* and would treat the *The Body Politic* as a symbol of the trajectory of the gay and lesbian movement in Canada over the previous fifteen years. The proposal was brilliant, strategically savvy ("to both gay and straight audiences"), and sensitive to the emerging political agenda of community diversity, and it tied the pandemic into a concluding wrap-up of the work: "*Flaunting It!* will present and challenge *The Body Politic*'s very engaged version of the history of the movement. It will capture from within those turbulent decades when TBP was the very subjective eyes and ears of the community. Just as TBP did in its day, *Flaunting It!* will acknowledge a wealth of contradictory opinions and voices. Each in itself is incomplete. Together they present a richer, fuller version."[6] (The topic of *The Body Politic* was in the air, for the legendary magazine had just issued its farewell issue in February 1987, and Challenge for Change veteran Harry Sutherland also had a proposal for a never-realized documentary called *Our Body Politic*, which was circulating at the same time).[7]

Three opinions about the proposal were solicited by John Taylor, of the Toronto office, one positive and two negative evaluations apparently from conservative, older gays hostile to *The Body Politic* or to Greyson's style. One of these offered a very chip-on-the-shoulder assessment, e.g., "I would like to see less emphasis on the reminiscences of those involved with TBP," and "While *Flaunting It!* may only be a first or working title it reflects a flamboyant male homosexual 'queen' image. If the gay community wants a serious and honest examination of its history represented then it's going to have to straighten up a little ... (On a very personal note, I was not a supporter of TBP's "Men Loving Boys Loving Men" article. I didn't then and I don't now think that we are struggling for the recognition of sexual orientation so that men can fuck little boys.)"[8]

Well, the consultant's last parenthetical segue seems to have frightened the horses. These lukewarm and contradictory assessments from three homosexuals selected in heterosexual Taylor's wisdom who knows how and assigned full representativity in relation to the "gay community" became the pretext for closing down discussion – and the project. Immobilized by the apparent assumption that a single film about homos could cover the whole issue, the brass gradually stopped jerking and quietly dropped the whole baton. After all there *was* already *Lorri: The Recovery Series* (which Taylor and Torrance had produced together). The world was never to know what an unrealized project directed by Canada's most important queer filmmaker and produced by the NFB might have looked like. Taylor moved on within the next couple of years to act as executive co-producer of two films on AIDS – but certainly not AIDS in Canada – of which one, *Karate Kids* (1990), was one of the most hateful and homophobic works ever to have shamed the institution (see chapter 9).

Nineteen eighty-seven was otherwise a key year in NFB history, or, rather, in the history of Studio D, then in its twelfth year of sales surges, Oscars, and international acclaim and the source of such causes célèbres as *Not a Love Story* (1981) and *If You Love This Planet* (1982). The studio was in the process of passing the reins of power to an outsider, Rina Fraticelli, an imaginative cultural administrator and activist with no background in film. Fraticelli immediately embarked on a project of shaking things up through various inclusiveness programs (as well as through edging out into the male studios their established stable of white middle-class directors like the heterosexual *Firewords* director Dorothy Hénaut and Wescott, the resident lesbian director, until then relatively discreet). To celebrate the studio's fifteenth anniversary Fraticelli commissioned a feature-length package of five-minute films selected from proposals from independent female practitioners across the country, which was to appear in 1990 as *Five Feminist Minutes*. The result was electrifying on several scores, a triumph of rainbow representativity that recharged the aesthetic batteries that the now tired baby boomers at the studio had let run low. The package also, from our point of view, revealed a groundswell of lesbian cinematic energy that had previously been untapped. Of the seventeen selected projects, one was an explicit programmatic manifesto by lesbians of colour: *Exposure*, by Toronto first-time director MICHELLE MOHABEER, stands as *the* first NFB lesbian documentary in terms of both public authorial identity and explicit subject matter. Fully six others of the shorts in the package were of varying degrees of queer – crypto, quasi, partly, implicitly, or authorially.

The momentum continued: Fraticelli went on to commission another independent project from two freelancers, LYNNE FERNIE and AERLYN WEISSMAN, who had been around at the start of the Wescott epic and were itching to get out. The new project would be fully explicit and unabashedly hip in its identity discourse, no pussy footing around this time: a monumental epic of community and history. *Forbidden Love: The Unashamed Stories of Lesbian Lives* (1992) went on to standing ovations at the new breed of viable community queer festivals around the world and even had successful theatrical runs in such places as New York and London as one of the most internationally canonized and award-winning feminist or queer documentaries of the 1990s. And its commercial success did no harm either. *Forbidden* almost single-handedly restored the credibility of the NFB in the eyes of anglophone queer constituents and, I would conjecture, was the impetus that maintained the NFB on its queer boom over the next decade.

A corpus of about almost fifty documentaries accumulated, long and short, almost a quarter from the French studios and the rest from the English-language studios. Almost none is by old-guard or staff directors, for the new boom was bolstered by the increasing reliance of the savagely defunded institution on freelance-initiated projects and increasingly rooted regional bases. The changing political tide did not hurt either. The studio might seem to have treaded cautiously during the last years of the budget-slashing Mulroney regime, but the floodgates were wide open starting in 1993 after the Tories' cataclysmic defeat at the hands of Jean Chrétien's Liberals. This party, traditionally more favourable to multiculturalism and diversity, had decriminalized sodomy in the first days of Trudeau's leadership back in 1969 and traditionally favoured public funding of the arts, so, at the very least, it did not continue the Tories' homocidal sabotage of the studio.

Thus, on a roll after the surprise commercial success of *Company of Strangers* (1990, see chapter 5), the pastoral idyl of geriatric homosociality, and especially of *Forbidden Love*, the board had the brazenness in 1994 to put together retroactively a Lesbian and Gay Film Package, bringing together ten films of full or partial interest to the queer audience. Alongside the mega hit *Company* (1990), in which one of eight characters briefly comes out to another, were assembled and marketed together the following films (listed in chronological order of their release date): *Lorri: The Recovery Series* (1985, Vancouver); *Sandra's Garden* (1990, Winnipeg); *Forbidden Love* (1992, Montreal); *Father and Son* (1992, Vancouver); *A Kind of Family* (1992, Winnipeg); *Toward Intimacy* (1992, Montreal/Atlantic); *Long Time Comin'* (1993, Toronto); *Out: Stories of Lesbian and Gay Youth* (1993, Toronto); and *When Shirley Met Florence* (1994, Montreal). Unfortunately, Her Majesty's Loyal Opposition, already harping on *Forbidden Love*, discovered the package and behaved in its best imported Jesse Helms mode on the floor of the House of Commons. Then Reform Party cultural critic Monte Solberg (Medicine Hat), who was typically confused, having as usual not seen the materials addressed, announced to the House that the "unaccountable" NFB had produced "a series of videos ... on lesbian love. They were restricted videos, ones that contained very explicit scenes." He called for guidelines to prevent the expenditure of "taxpayers' dollars" on "anything that is pornographic in nature or is x-rated" (1 November 1994). Ottawa, unlike Washington, is used to weathering such tempests within our long history of arm's-length state-funded cultural products, knowing that the attention span of Alberta philistines is as limited as it is erratic, so aside

Epic docufiction *Forbidden Love: The Unashamed Stories of Lesbian Lives* (1992) was the hit of the festivals and even had theatrical runs. Above, the heroine in the arms of her new big-city butch girlfriend in one of the pulp-inspired dramatic segments. Production still, used with permission of the National Film Board of Canada

from whatever behind-the-scenes pressures might have been brought to bear, no serious consequences ensued.

In fact, the package was not quite as dangerous as the Reform Party contended, as an analysis of its contents reveals. The fact that the package was cobbled together post facto is immediately evident: only two of the films could boast applied focus on the issue of sexual identity, *Forbidden* and *Out*, but four others involved queer authorship (director or scriptwriter), discreetly including sexual-identity politics within the scope of another or related issue, whether racial identity (*Long Time Comin'*), aging (*Company*), female homosocial friendship/post-Holocaust Jewish diaspora (*Shirley/Florence*), or abuse (*Sandra's Garden*). The other four belonged only by the narrowest and most incidental of threads, neither through authorial identity (at the time, to my knowledge) nor by concentrated focus, all more or less clinging to the package through the "who happen to be" connection: *Lorri* (the eponymous lesbian is one portrait alongside four heterosexual women recovering from substance abuse); *Father and Son* (an effective first-person essay on masculinity based on the testimony of six male witnesses, of which three are constructed as gay with varying degrees of up-frontness); *Toward Intimacy* (in this serial exemplary portrait of four disabled women and their sexuality, the ratio of one to three wasn't bad); and *A Kind of Family* (this straight-authored, warm-hearted portrait of a gay adoptive father, future Winnipeg mayor Glen Murray, is the best of the four in this category, thanks to a central subject who is proud and "matter-of-fact" [which is different from "who happens to be"], and a magnetic portrait of his adopted HIV+, sometime hustler, prodigal son Michael Curtis).

Though the ten films represented a vivid spectrum of regional representation, two huge gaps were immediately apparent. First, French-language films from Quebec and elsewhere were conspicuously absent. And although the French studios lagged behind the English studios in waking up to queer politics, their absence from the package was not because there were no obvious candidates: the two arts biopics *Firewords* and *Les Trois Montréal de Michel Tremblay* (Michel Moreau, 1989), as well as the anomalous and beautiful Sudbury film *Lettre à Tom* (Paul Crépeau, 1987, about gay fatherhood), would have been obvious inclusions. Apparently, several conditions were lacking for a bicultural queer package. Extra investment would have been required for versioning, that is, money where the mouth was – though that does not explain why *Firewords*, whose original version was English, was not included. Were certain films not included because the packagers actually ended up believing their own bowdlerized descriptions for the films and did not realize how flaming many of them actually were? ("Controversial" is, hilariously, the code substitute for the l-word in the NFB catalogue descriptions in both English and French for this forthright, richly coloured tapestry of lesbian culture and writing from a queer-friendly hetero-feminist point of view.) The other condition lacking was simply the vision necessary to look over the high walls between the two distrustful linguistic solitudes that had existed at the board since the implantation of Québécois nationalism there in the 1960s (which was probably an important factor in the anglophone blinkers about *Passiflora* in the first place). The second gap was around gender representation: it's hard to believe that of the ten films, only two pertain to gay men, and one, *Out*, by the only gay male author, examines the only mixed-gender thematic in the whole package. Where were the men? Apparently as assiduously passing the buck as moguls Macerola, Katadotis, and Dufaux. The residue of passive homophobia that tainted the male New Left (the familiar tune of "sexuality is not a class issue") was clearly still at play within the progressive male cadres outside of Studio D at the board, presumably including the branch directors that Macerola had promised would contact me; sexual identity politics had clearly not even entered the radar screen as a political issue on the testosterone side.

Nevertheless, the NFB got away unscathed with their queer collection, and their queer roll continued, churning out two extremely strong films by gay men in 1995 in the Montreal English and French studios respectively (*Anatomy of Desire*, by freelance couple team JEAN-FRANÇOIS MONETTE and PETER BOULLATA-TYLER; and *Quand l'amour est gai*, by NFB veteran LAURENT GAGLIARDI). An eclectic array of other films reflecting the divergent interests of independents in various regions gradually lined up, including everything from a large number of low-cost trigger films about youth, family diversity, and homophobia for use in schools to Wescott's long-awaited *Stolen Moments* (1997, 92). The latter must be the largest-budget lesbian-history film in the world if one calculates the director's full salary over the film's decade-long gestation. Unfortunately, this particular film's commercial record, despite some rave reviews, was embarrassing and must have broken the hearts of the producers, who were hoping for another *Forbidden Love* or *Strangers*. By this time budgetary stress had led to the closing of Studio D in 1996, but the queer productions continued elsewhere within the institution with no sign of abating to this day, reflecting evolving political priorities within both the NFB and the queer cultural environment.

The inevitable transgender film appeared from the Toronto office in 2000, *In the Flesh* (Gordon McLennan, 47), an uneven and erratic serial portrait (two MTF and one FTM), buoyed mostly by the effervescent energy of star MIRHA-SOLEIL ROSS. Two later, more promising additions reflected the NFB's "diversity" agenda: both Atif Siddiqi's *Solo* (2003, 54) and JOSÉ TORREALBA's *Open Secrets* (2003, 52) were born from the studio's Reel Diversity competitions, whereby winning "visible minority" filmmakers had their proposals produced in-house at the standard budgets (and with the producer-director relationships so entailed), which the erstwhile indie video artists Siddiqi and Torrealba, born in Karachi and Caracas respectively, could never have dreamed of in the real world. That invisible minorities and visible minorities come together in these two films is a sign of the new maturity of the institutional politics. And that Torrealba's project, an archival/interview, historical/topical essay moved beyond the burden of ethno-cultural representation in the narrow sense (his documentary addresses the issue of gay soldiers within the Canadian Forces during World War II, and

Margaret Wescott's long-awaited *Stolen Moments* (1997) dramatized "lesbianism from Sappho to Dikes on Bikes" (including the Paris Left Bank, above), and toured urban dyke "refuges" across centuries and continents. Production still, used with permission of the National Film Board of Canada

the entire handful of survivors encountered belong to the then hegemonic white caste) may be a hopeful and healthy sign of the open-endedness of queer problematics and positions *chez* the old uncle during the new decade.

Perhaps an even more hopeful sign was the sudden appearance in 2002 of another "package," the "Celebrating Diversity" collection, six films yoked together retroactively again and intended to "equip you to deal constructively with a broad spectrum of issues in the lives of today's young people." Aside from such euphemistic and bowdlerized copyspeak one more time, the package is a strong assortment of queer perspectives and voices, formats and genres, with a valid focus on youth and educational contexts that makes more sense than the encyclopedic "catch-up" compendium invoked the first time around. The new package nevertheless perpetuates some of the same contradictions that were evident a decade earlier: only one male author was squeezed in among the six, and he was David Adkins, whose *Out* was recycled from last time. One "adult" film was also a most welcome addition to the NFB repertory but was not specifically part of the youth/educational focus: WEISSMAN's *Little Sister's vs Big Brother* is an outside production brought within the fold and represents, thirty-three years after Stonewall, the old uncle finally sticking his neck out on a contemporary politico-legal struggle, indicting another finger of the federal hand that feeds it, Customs Canada. As far as "adult" films go, however, another absence is much more striking: the board had mysteriously withdrawn *Forbidden Love* from circulation, still burningly relevant a decade after its release, without even informing the filmmakers that their labour of love was now itself *really* forbidden. The other four items, all with lesbian creative input, are "trigger" shorts geared specifically for elementary or secondary classroom use (the short, open-ended format is designed to spark discussion), and with their constructive focus on bigotry, bullying, and name-calling, they shift the onus away from earlier identity essentialism that activists and intellectuals were themselves calling increasingly into question: *In Other Words* (JAN PADGETT, [2001, 27], a "consciousness-raising" forum about name-calling); *One of Them* (Elise Swerhone, scenario Nancy Trites Botkin, Winnipeg [2000, 25], dramatization of a high school antibigotry initiative that leads to a coming out in an unexpected place); *Apples and Oranges* (Lynne Fernie [2003, 15], a fresh classroom consciousness-raising exercise with younger participants than in the Padgett film, bountifully interpolated with didactic cartoon narratives); and *Sticks and Stones* (Jan Padgett, 2001, 17). The last named, another trigger work for elementary school children, was a matter-of-fact excursion into the fraught territory of lesbian and gay-male parents for its discussion of familial diversity, and it thus unexpectedly became one of the only NFB films to date to have chanced upon in a fleeting way the urgent problematic issue that equally unexpectedly became a political front-burner of the first decade of this century, the queer-family/same-sex-marriage issue.

I make no assumption that my letter had had anything to do with this proliferation of the NFB queer corpus over the last fifteen years as I have described it. Rather, it can be attributed to aspects of the institution's production system and apparatus as they evolved in the new era of tight budgets, low overhead, and proliferating cable outlets and to the increasing importance of TV window financing – in combination with alterations in the Canadian political environment conducive to the emergence of "new ideas" from both personalities entrenched within the institution and the new generation of independents that increasingly found a foothold there.

The new abundance of films must also be connected to the genres that were available to these filmmakers as vessels for the "ideas" that were emerging, the funding opportunities that were on hand, and the audience/market niches that were identified. My look at the NFB corpus in this chapter will now proceed to examine those genre slots and categories, which shaped the corpus both individually and as a whole. The corpus is extremely

Sticks and Stones (2001), a trigger doc for school children, was a matter-of-fact but rare and prophetic excursion into the fraught territory of lesbian and gay male parenting. Production still, used with permission of the National Film Board of Canada

diverse, including many different modes and styles of documentary film production, reflecting different regional and cultural differences and coincidentally incorporating all but the scariest of the topics suggested in my original letter.

GENRES AND GENDERS

What all these modes and styles and topics have in common, however, aside from their NFB logo and their public financing (often "commissioned" by various federal ministries), is of course their pedagogical mandate or their didactic premise, what Bill Nichols might call their "kinship" to the

nonfictional systems that together make up what we may call the discourses of sobriety. Science, economics, politics, foreign policy, education, religion, welfare – these systems assume they have instrumental power; they can and should alter the world itself, they can effect action and entail consequences. Their discourse has an air of sobriety since it is seldom receptive to "make-believe" characters, events, or entire worlds ... Discourses of sobriety are sobering because they regard their relation to the real as direct, immediate, transparent. Through them power exerts itself. Through them, things are made to happen. They are the vehicles of domination and conscience, power and knowledge, desire and will. (1991, 3–4)

Paradoxically, despite this instrumentalist modality and this mandate of sobriety, all these film frames, furthermore, exhibit a general tendency toward narrative, all the while remaining for the most part within the documentary format. They indulge wholeheartedly in the pleasure of the story, rather than being stuck in the expository or analytic structure that one might have expected to prevail after the board's first decades. The narrative thrust is no doubt a populist acknowledgment of the NFB's non-specialist constituency, the studio's track record of reaching their audience through clarity and directness rather than enigma, ambiguity, and challenge, their potential to win hearts, if not minds, through entertainment and identification (as well as the obsession of certain executive producers, I am told). This narrative thrust is reflected twice in the films' subtitles alone – *Stories of Lesbian and Gay Youth* and *Unashamed Stories of Lesbian Lives* – and is otherwise evoked in the narrative desire solicited by others of the more pulpy titles, from *When Shirley Met Florence* to *Stolen Moments* and *Open Secrets*.

Within this overreaching mandate of sobriety and interwoven with this extensive (though not universal) narrative fabric lies the following range of generic structures that tend to give shape and continuity to the corpus across its two-decade-long trajectory and vast regional/cultural/linguistic disparity. The range of genres represented is somewhat more orderly and manageable than the risqué topics – even predictable – and most films cross-pollinate two or more of the genres. It makes sense, then, to inventory the films according to a generic grid, starting with the five variations of what is by far the most significant, numerically speaking, of the genres, the exemplary portrait.

The Exemplary Portrait (Solo)

The queer exemplary portrait-genres have certain easily identifiable and discrete ancestors in film history. NFB queer filmmakers were not the first to implicitly connect the narrative of a "typical" individual's life to the collective experience of the whole, reflecting the rampant individualism of postmodern, postindustrial cultures. Not surprisingly, the queer portraits echoed recent patterns within Studio D's output, most famously the "Working Mother" portrait series that inaugurated the feminist studio in 1974–75 (e.g., *Tiger on a Tight Leash* [Kathleen Shannon, 1974, 8] or the later elaborations of the formula, such as *Patricia's Moving Picture* (Bonnie Sherr Klein, 1978, 26). In such work, the diversity and commonalities of women's lives across Canada were explored, usually incorporating the before-and-after dynamic of conversion ("I once was lost, but now am found, was blind, but now I see").

Studio D itself had in turn reinvented similar generic structures that shaped the board's first ventures into peacetime nation-building with an entirely different political agenda after the war. This chest of representative regional profiles was called "Faces of Canada," of which *Paul Tomkowicz: Street-Railway Switchman* (Roman Kroitor, Winnipeg, 1953, 12) is the best-known. In these often folkloric portraits, stability was the emphasis, rather than change. This series itself had in turn built on earlier "personalizing" experiments at the dawn of the international expository social-issue documentary in the 1930s, experiments that were reactions against the impersonal "voice of God" convention that had quickly become entrenched after the introduction of sound (for example, Joris Ivens introduced an exemplary Republican soldier, Julian, in his *Spanish Earth* [1937] to counter the booming voice of God in the implicitly profascist *March of Time* newsreels). Thus, the board responded to the cutting-edge challenge of sexual diversity by reviving one of documentary's most reliable formal traditions, the exemplary-portrait genre family, of which the solo profile is its most rudimentary and efficient varation. The two most outstanding examples both come from Winnipeg. First, *Sandra's Garden* (BONNIE DICKIE, 1990, 34, 1994 Lesbian & Gay Collection) is as decorative and sentimental as its prototype *Lorri* was plain, raw, and confessional. This documentary focuses on a lesbian abuse survivor who has sought healing in nature and community, both floridly brought to life (see chapter 5). Second, *A Kind of Family* (Andrew Koster, 1992, 53, 1994 Lesbian & Gay Collection) is a strong narrative in which a gay municipal politician, himself once an adopted child, discovers family through adopting an HIV+ teenaged street hustler, for better and worse.

Exemplary Portrait (Serial)

An extrapolation of the solo category, the serial portrait has the added ideological benefit of "bomber crew" representativeness within an official national culture of regional, ethnocultural, and gender diversity. For queer cultures, an additional asset is that this is one of the few genres where gay men and lesbians come together.

Out: Stories of Lesbian and Gay Youth (David Adkin, 1992, 79 , 1994 Lesbian & Gay Collection) is a relatively early film in this saga and the first (openly) gay-male-authored work. The serial format, introducing a spectrum of personae from the effeminate Native kid from a Manitoba reserve to a hip white Toronto gal with a proud PFLAG mother at her side, gracefully accommodates the stressful and ultimately impossible mandate of covering an encyclopedic range of identities, issues, options, and spaces.

Other works in this category include *Toward Intimacy* (Debbie McGee [1992, 62], on sexuality and the disabled); *Variations sur un thème familier*

Kristyn confronts Queen's Park in *Out: Stories of Lesbian and Gay Youth* (1992), which broke through the NFB silence with its series of exemplary portraits. A decade later the work was still the sole gay male voice in the studio's second queer package. Production still, used with permission of the National Film Board of Canada

(*Variations on a Familiar Theme*, German Gutierrez and Carmen Garcia [1994, 57]; this survey of contemporary models of family structure is prophetic, but why it took queer-friendly Latino filmmakers to introduce diversity into the French-language program is anyone's guess); *In the Flesh* (Gordon McLennan [2000, 47], on transgender); and *Seuls, ensemble* (*Alone, Together*, Paul Émile d'Entremont [2000, 25], an Acadian take on the interface between national identity and queer identity).

Exemplary Portrait (Group)
These films push the portrait format up one notch, and access the merit of fleshing out not a series of individuals but *relationships* and *communities*. Along with the superb *Médecins de coeur* (see "consciousness-raising," below), three films stand out in this category.

In *Company of Strangers* (Cynthia Scott, 1990, Montreal, 101 [see chapter 5], 1994 Lesbian & Gay Collection), the strategy of bringing together diverse players actually worked, and the alchemy of improvised interdynamics among the marooned seniors – cranky, euphoric, or practical – is palpable on the screen. Other excellent examples include *When Shirley Met Florence* (RONIT BEZALEL [1994, Montreal, 27], an intimate study of lesbian-straight homosocial friendship) and *Maman et Éve* (*Mum's the Word*, Paul Carrière [1996, Sudbury, 53], a study of another friendship circle, this time of middle-aged, late-blooming hinterland lesbians, for whom the filmmaking is a catalytic opportunity to strengthen bonds; see chapter 5).

Exemplary Portrait (of the Artist as an Old Queer)
The "arts biopic" subgenre of the exemplary portrait has the most ideological leeway, since it is the most oblique, and is thus common to most discursive regimes shaped by censorship, from the darkest days of Socialist Realism under Stalin to 2000s Hollywood. Its popularity at the board (eight entries) is due not only to the institution's cultural mandate but also to the easy recourse to either the "this is not about homosexuality" disavowal mechanism – the standard NFB liberal kneejerk reaction – or its inverse, the "artist as doomed martyr to excess" mythology (predictably, not so common in NFB treatments of living artists). Interestingly the living portraits are better than the posthumous ones: only the board could somehow overturn the traditional minefield of the biopic documentary and produce timid and conservative documentaries about dead queer artists (MCLAREN, JUTRA), but four relatively fresh and risk-taking portraits of living ones (FINDLEY, TREMBLAY, BRAND and her subjects, and Hénaut's triptych). *Tommy: A Family Portrait* (Mary Sexton and Nigel Markham, 2001, Montreal/Halifax, 71), a moving elegy to "Codco" star Tommy Sexton may be the best of the lot, perhaps because of the dazzling Codco raw material, and the minimum of filmmaker intervention it required to string it together. That the filmmaker is the subject's sister rather than his former partner Greg Malone (who is mysteriously absent), with the resultant emphasis on consanguinity rather than erotic filiation, which no doubt suited the board's agenda perfectly, is not a gnawing defect.

Other notable examples are *Firewords: Louky Bersianik, Jovette Marchessault, Nicole Brossard* (Dorothy Todd Hénaut, 1986, 85), a lavish Studio D serial arts biopic reflecting the Women's Studio's eagerness to rush in where the men's studios feared to tread; *Les Trois Montréal de Michel Tremblay ou Promenade dans l'imaginaire d'un écrivain* (The three Montreals of Michel Tremblay, or walking through a writer's imagination, Michel Moreau, 1989, Montreal, 58), a frank encounter with Tremblay's queer characters, spaces, and sensibility, falling only slightly into the trap of excessive rever-

Dionne Brand reads her poetry in *Listening for Something* (1996), her second embodiment of the board's safest queer genre, the artist biopic – in this case *auto*biopic. Video frame grab, used with permission of the National Film Board of Canada

entiality (that this expensive movie from the French studio was never taken up by the English versioners is one more of many NFB mind-bogglers); *Norman McLaren: The Creative Process* (Donald McWilliams, 1990, 116), bursting with fastidious queenery, an otherwise dutiful film falling within the "not about homosexuality" disavowal category; *Timothy Findley: Anatomy of a Writer* (Terence Macartney-Filgate, 1992, 57), refreshingly candid, including the subject's longstanding conjugal and creative relationship with Bill Whitehead; *Long Time Comin'* (Dionne Brand, 1993, 53), the first of the Caribbean Canadian poet's collaborations with Studio D, nonchalantly mediating the highly combustible interface of race and sexual identity through safe profiles of an artist and a singer respectively; *Fiction and Other Truths: A Film About Jane Rule* (Lynne Fernie and Aerlynn Weissman, 1995, 58), a lavish, Genie-winning outside production, unflinching towards – in fact, celebrating – the element of sexuality that usually constitutes the genre's first ballast thrown overboard (see also the same authors' more digestible shorter version *Jane Rule: Writing*, 26); *Claude Jutra portrait sur film* (*Claude Jutra: An Unfinished Story*, PAULE BAILLARGEON, Montreal, 2002, 82), dutiful but timid portrait by the late filmmaker's neighbour and friend.

The Self-Portrait

Autobiographical discourses constitute one of the most fundamental energies of independent film and video documentary in the postmodern age –

nowhere more so than in Canada. But the self-portrait genre is the least encouraged in the studio that has perhaps never recovered from its founder John Grierson's enforced Calvinist cult of collective anonymity in the credits department. The NFB's legendary budgets allowed for the incorporation of performance elements in all four examples of this rare genre, the wave of the future for the Studio if its future dependence on freelancers allows it to absorb the strong confessional energy out there in the real world. Alongside Brand's *Listening for Something* and Siddiqi's *Solo* (see chapters 5 and 10 respectively), two works by white male authors, heterosexual and gay respectively, stand out:

Father and Son (Colin Browne, 1992, 88 min; 1994 Lesbian & Gay Collection) is a long and indulgent but rewarding meditation by the author, a father and writing professor, on his relationship with his own silent and repressive naval-officer father. It abstracts from his own pain and his determination to rise above his genetic legacy. Building on the wisdom and experience of six interlocutors who become less "expert witnesses" than characters (from intellectuals and artists to hockey dad) and who share the artist's strong feelings and, sometimes, tears, this interrogation of masculinity puts to shame the other, earlier homophobic NFB efforts in this direction, such as *The Masculine Mystique* (1984). Highlights include British filmmaker Terence Davies elaborating on the tortured relationship with his sadistic father (his sexuality not acknowledged), outspoken American gay-feminist John Stoltenberg coming on strong in favour of the full jettison of the "complete manhood sham," and the haunting final image of the nude author, literally up to his neck in the Pacific, having stripped off the symbolically potent military uniform of his father and setting it adrift in flames.

Le fil cassé (*The Broken Thread*, MICHEL LANGLOIS, 2002, Montreal, 50) is a vindication of the French studio's frequently *auteur*-driven aesthetic. This prizewinning genealogical investigation takes as a departure point the childless gay filmmaker's sadness at interrupting his family's lineage, which has spanned over the generations both in his ancestral France and in Quebec. He makes many discoveries along the way about himself and his relationship with his parents and his family, including his maternal uncle Louis, handsome and seductive, who bore his queer identity with less equanimity than his nephew.

Docufiction

Though dramatization requires a hefty budget, the NFB has often thrown the necessary money at their staff directors' pet projects, especially when the topics are ethically delicate or the subjects underage, or else when the work covers the invisible, inaccessible corners of social history that are the queer legacy, e.g., in the case of *Forbidden Love*. Dramatized elements are usually part of larger hybrid texts at the NFB and help to maintain their overall mode of "sobriety" or "didacticism" – the combination in general gives the NFB corpus a distinctive stamp, especially in films from the 1980s, since independent U.S. works usually couldn't afford them. I have already listed the dramatized *Company of Strangers* under the group portrait rubric, and most of the other bigger-budget arts biopics contain dramatized elements as well, not to mention Lynne Fernie's most recent gem, *Apples and Oranges*, mentioned below under "Consciousness-Raising Film." Otherwise, at least seven other films depend importantly on dramatized tropes and reflect their in-house favour. In inverse proportion to the NFB's institution-wide taste for dramatization, pure observational cinema has never been its in-house style, contrary to some film-historical assertions. Its mandate for instructional sobriety and clarity dictated that a few in-house directors with clout may have experimented with cinéma-vérité ambiguity. But the majority of the others' works were constructed through more controllable modes, and the queer corpus pushed this tendency even further in its arena of great delicacy. Ironically, as the prototype film *Passiflora* sadly revealed, it is the dramatized films that have led most to the spectre of censorship and public scandal, affecting or threatening the circulation of several of the following works, as if the mix of sobriety and fantasy are so destabilizing that silence is the only solution. The Reform Party notwithstanding, *Forbidden Love* was too big to run into trouble until the studio "forgot" to renew its purchase rights a decade after release, but the first gay male production on the French side frightened more than a few horses when it hit the lightning rod test of broadcast.

Quand l'amour est gai (LAURENT GAGLIARDI, 1995, Montreal, 48), understandably tried to cover everything from the gay elderly to AIDS, but the interview-compilation format could not handle sexuality, which Gagliardi had the political courage to confront head-on. Dramatization came to the rescue and involved more than the very dramatic performance in the strip club Taboo where a dancer corporally addresses the camera. Two dramatized scenes with professional actors offered the uninitiated, first, a rather daring display of "sixty-nine," no doubt with the NFB instructional mandate in mind, and then a locker room scene, frontal nudes and all, intended to demonstrate the gay cult of eroticized machismo. After the broadcast of the film, some spectators were outraged by most of the scenes where sexuality was even discussed, but the sixty-nine scene was unaccountably not mentioned by the complainant to the Canadian Broadcast Standards Council, perhaps because of the exquisite lighting and the lack of "explicit display of genitals."[9]

Lettre à Tom (Paul Crépeau, Sudbury, 1987, 28) avoided the attention of the censors but, unfortunately, most other attention as well. In this case dramatization supports the portrait genre, sparking a cinematic rendition of the real-life emotions and stock-taking of the protagonist Raymond, a gay man in his late thirties writing to the man he loves, who has helped him come out. This type of dramatization, the reenactment of the subject's "everyday," is closer to standard observational documentary than scripted narrative enhanced by professional actors. The artifice is still palpable and essential to the way Crépeau captures the loneliness and marginalization of his subject (an activist engaged with his community, but who, once married, has just lost custody of his daughter) as he rediscovers his complex relations with his family at the same time as he affirms his identity.

Stolen Moments (MARGARET WESCOTT, 1997, Montreal, 92) was distinctive for its frank sexual representation as well as its record-breaking production span (see the section, "J'accuse," above). As with Fernie and Weissman, the dearth of documents of lesbian history, ancient or modern, led Wescott to dramatize large chunks of her "lesbianism from Sappho to Dikes on Bikes" epic. Her tour of urban dyke "refuges" across centuries and continents builds on varying degrees of artifice, imaging everything from 1950s Manhattan butch-femme bar culture (Wescott started earlier than her Studio D rivals and finished later) to 1930s Weimar cabaret life and then back to seventeenth century Amsterdam trials of "passing women." Even present-day scenes unfold with a high degree of authorial control and subject collaboration.

Also belonging to this genre are *Safety for You* (Louise Ford, 1998, Ottawa, 23), incorporating dramatized illustrations of an abusive relationship between two hearing-impaired women for the purpose of informing hearing-impaired spectators of available recourse from family violence, using dramatization as a response to ethical contingencies (It is so unavailable for all but its targeted audience, that it is the only film in the corpus that I had to finally give up trying to see). *One of Them* (Elise Swerhone, 2000, Prairies, 25), a high school narrative about homophobia and an unexpected "coming out" is the closest to standard fiction of the corpus.

"Interactive" Topical Essay (Archival Compilation/Interview Mode)
The nonnarrative conventional assemblage of talking heads intercut and interacting with illustrative stock shots has been familiar and even prevalent since the late 1960s, especially on the U.S. independent scene. With the NFB, surprisingly, what Nichols has branded the "interactive mode" is relatively rare, perhaps because of the board's hesitation to relinquish the expository mode and the voice of God in its mission of clarity, accessibility, and sobriety. The purest examples in the queer trunk tend to reflect budgetary restrictions, as with the two examples below: the first is an "adopted" indie project, and the second was developed from a proposal by a "novi-

Quand l'amour est gai (1995), a first from the French studio, tried to cover everything from the gay elderly to AIDS, including a frontal performance in Montreal's legendary strip club Taboo. Television viewers complained. VHS frame grab, used with permission of the National Film Board of Canada

tiate" adopted through a diversity competition at the convent. Interactive films more lavishly supplemented with dramatized passages are the expensive in-house productions *Forbidden Love*, *Quand l'amour est gai*, and *Stolen Moments*, which I have already discussed under the rubric of docufiction (this may be a distinctively Canadian contribution to the international interactive genre).

Anatomy of Desire (JEAN-FRANÇOIS MONETTE and Peter Tyler Boullata, 1995, Montreal, 48), which offers queer-slanted history of the science and theory of sexual identity (nature vs nurture), deploys the classical-formula assemblage of heads and footage and had the virtue of recruiting queer experts who were up-front about their personal stake in the history. In addition, its approach to the archival compilation has a campy originality and humour (an illustrative clip from Paul Morrissey's *Heat*, 1972, to comment on reductive notions of lesbian identity?) that Monette would develop even further in *Where Lies the Homo* (1998). In-house pressure led Monette to maintain a voice-over narration (the "forceful ways" of a "bully producer" brought in to "rein the production in" and "to steer the film into a more standard and palatable direction" [email, 5 January 2004]), rather than the reliance on internal voices that is the trademark of the interactive mode in its purest and most innovative form.

Open Secrets (JOSÉ TORREALBA, 2003, Montreal, 52) is a moving tribute to gay men who had fought in the Canadian Forces in World War II and survived institutional homophobia. The surviving elderly interlocutors are set off against all-too-rare documents, milked for all they are worth, including some subtle "homosocial" period paintings by a queer soldier that speak eloquently but discreetly about barracks and shipboard camaraderie. *Open Secrets* reflects a countertendency to the "expert talking head" syndrome of many mainstream works within the interactive mode, giving ordinary people a platform to talk about their everyday lives, making them the "experts" and trusting them to speak with authority about what counts.

Consciousness Raising Film

The feminist realist documentary of the early seventies borrowed the "consciousness" format (hereafter "CR") from the real-life women's movement, and to a lesser extent from the New Left, and developed a format based on the discursive exchange of individual experience as a path towards synergy and the collective realization of wisdom and strategy. Studio D handily built on this format as it had been developed especially by its direct forebear, the "Challenge for Change" program (1967–80), which had relied on CR as a cinematic forum for community needs assessment and action plans and as a structure especially suited to the bulky new Port-a-pak three-quarter-inch video toy/tool it was pioneering for this purpose. It is not surprising that this ethic and aesthetic showed up in the queer corpus, given how many of its practitioners had been trained within Studio D and given the fact that the initial gay and lesbian movement had itself appropriated CR from the women's movement as a major organizational tactic. *Médecins de coeur (Doctors with Heart*, 1994, Montreal, 112), Tahani Rached's underrated AIDS film, is no doubt the most ambitious and accomplished of the CR films. Otherwise, in addition to the already listed *Sandra's Garden, Company of Strangers,* and *Quand l'amour est gai*, as well as the "triggers" *Apples and Oranges* and *Sticks and Stones*, the following films from the queer trunk are among the CR standouts.

Exposure (Michelle Mohabeer, 1990, Toronto 5, included within *Five Feminist Minutes*), the first up-front lesbian film from the NFB, happened also to be one of the first works by a lesbian artist of colour in the Canadian canon, as well as Mohabeer's first film. Not surprisingly this groundbreaking but simple five-minute CR work displays the awkwardness perhaps intrinsic to such weighty historical "firsts." Mono Oikawa and Lalti Tamu are depicted in a formulaic gab-sharing session, validating their experience as lesbians of colour ("We share colonization, imperialism, appropriation, oppression"), but without a synthesizing energy that will push them on to a new "consciousness" they don't already have.

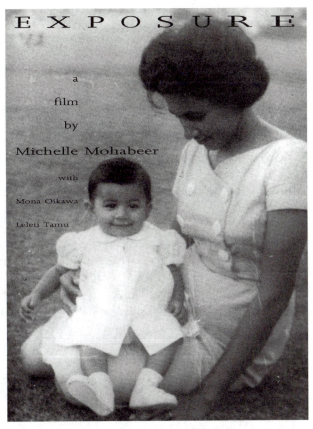

EXPOSURE

a
film
by
Michelle Mohabeer

with

Mona Oikawa

Leleti Tamu

The ad for *Exposure* (1990, *Five Feminist Minutes*) was discreet about its many firsts – first up-front NFB lesbian film, first Canadian film by a lesbian of colour, first film by Michelle Mohabeer – as well as about its consciousness-raising format. Film poster, courtesy M. Mohabeer

Another three CR films worth noting are all understandably aimed at youth: *Taking Charge* (Claudette Jaiko, 1996, Toronto, 26), a dynamic swan song from Studio D using animation, media backdrops, and music, along with gab offered by participants from four different Toronto high schools on the topic of sexual/gender/racial bias, violence, and harassment in the corridors and classroom; *School's Out* (Lynne Fernie, 1996, Toronto, 24), a spinoff from Fernie's indie-produced Jane Rule biopic, showing a high-school queer focus group in conversation with the elderly lesbian writer, set within a forty-year historical context and attaining breakthrough communication between generations who have never listened to each other; and *In Other Words* (Jan Padgett, 2001, West Coast, 27), again with teens and queer-specific.

Trigger Film

Harking back to its first appearance at the board in the 1950s (e.g., *Being Different*, 1957, see chapter 2), the trigger-film genre, a short, discursive, open-ended format designed to ask questions and spark discussion rather than provide answers, overlaps with other categories. In general, the trigger film is the ultimate, most direct expression of the board's mandate of instrumentalist sobriety, the work of art as catalyst of social process. In addition to *In Other Words* and *Taking Charge*, this category includes yet another fresh and original contribution by Fernie (*Applies and Oranges*, Toronto, 2003, 17), this time with young children animated by a dynamic elementary teacher (twice counter-stereotype as a black male)

Two other noteworthy entries are, first, *Multiple Choices* (Alison Burns, 1995, Montreal, series), a five-volume, thirteen-episode series by a queer-friendly feminist freelancer that had a mandate that is a masterpiece of vagueness: "open the lines of communications between the sexes, generations and cultures as participants express their opinions on a variety of life issues and values." Burns relies on the simple structure of assigning an in-studio, diversely constituted focus group a certain topic to hash out, and the compact edited version leaves a discursive cliff-hanger for the putative audience to take up and resolve. The *Families* episode offers a lively debate about evolving variations of the family, with a dynamic young lesbian mother challenging preconceptions, while *The Agony and the Ecstasy* is specifically about parenting and includes another older lesbian mother of four within the spectrum. Disappointingly in the "sex episode" *Who, What, Where, When?* the same younger mother becomes pronoun-ambiguous, and hetero-sexism-by-default takes over. After all that water under the bridge, the NFB was still capable of making a film about sexuality where what they really meant was heterosexuality.

In *Sticks and Stones* (Jan Padgett, 2001, West Coast, 27), Vancouver and Toronto elementary classroom discussions touch on variations in family patterns as the crux of bullying and teasing in this fresh and articulate, though longer than usual, trigger item. Same-sex parents are centre-stage in the discussion, and though they seem to preside mostly over beach barbecues (dads) and Hanukkah candles (moms), the treatment is fresher in the gender stereotype department than this might imply.

PACKAGES AND BULGING ASSUMPTIONS

Towards the end of the nineties, the agglomeration of these short works in both the CR and the trigger genres generally targeted the next generation of (English) Canadian citizens, and this was indeed a hopeful sign of the board's fulfilment of its mandate around sexual diversity in a shifting climate. Regardless of whether this youth orientation signifies a write-off of the adult majority as beyond learning about "other words" and a write-off of the adult queer minority as too challenging to address through the mission of sobriety, the body of work aimed at children and teens – and the concomitant progress in enlisting racial, cultural, and social diversity – is by any measure laudable.

At the same time, it is hard not to notice that the overwhelming majority of the films in the corpus continued to be directed and produced by women, both straight and gay, and that heterosexual male authors by and large continued their boycott of queer issues on the screen. Other sections of this book, with their attention to non-NFB, non-gay male filmmakers from EGOYAN and SIMONEAU to ERBACH and MADDIN, suggest that this boycott was specific to liberal documentary culture in general and somehow endemic to the NFB microclimates in particular. The phenomenon of heteropatriarchal buck-passing was not the only cultural miasma underlying the NFB queer corpus, and in conclusion, I would like to revisit several other cultural and political assumptions that percolated over the fifteen years of this period, assumptions evident in the discourse around those films (as well as in my original letters to Macerola) and deserving to be scrutinized and situated.

Sex and Nation

The assumption of sex and nation holds that cultural texts about sexual identity and diversity have a more or less specific relation to national citizenship. We wanted a Canadian *Harvey Milk*, not just access to the American original. Many of the films are concretely "grass roots" in their feel, whether *A Kind of Family*, a textured Winnipeg documentary on a gay politician and his adopted teenage son, or the evocatively landscaped capsules from pastoral Acadia and rustbelt Sudbury. There may have been little agreement about exactly what constituted the Nation, especially from the Québécois and the makers of colour, but everyone agreed that films should be about people and the places they're in. The regional energy is very strong in the corpus, in constant dialectic with the NFB's elusive centralizing imperative (as I've tried to draw out by insisting on the regional provenance of the films, from Vancouver to Moncton. But remember, regional roots notwithstanding, the *Toward Intimacy* star Amethya attended a congress in *Ottawa*!).

The international dialectic may be even stronger. At the same time as being fervent nationalists in the sense of the prosaic "where is here?" makers were just as eager exporters, out of a sense both of shared communities and economic realpolitik. The North American audience could not be discounted in the decade of budgetary rationalism and would always be kept in mind in interpreting the grass roots Canadian voices and places. *Forbidden Love* was so full of imported U.S. pulp novel covers that Americans didn't even notice its interlocutors were talking about cities north of the border; and *Stolen Moments* provided film-stealing performances by New York lesbian stars Audre Lorde, Joan Nestle, and Leslie Fineberg, with perfunctory nods to Vancouver volleyball coaches and Québécois novelists – overlooking Toronto entirely! Still, in the dialectic between the here and the there in these and many of the other films, this corpus eloquently embodies the interface of national- and sexual-identity discourses. It acknowledges not just the market realities of the NAFTA era but also the dynamics of Canadian cultures and identities – including those diasporas that are both sexual and cultural/linguistic. And one forgets at one's peril that this multicultural and multinational political entity is separated, often arbitrarily, by an imaginary latitudinal delimitation from not only the new world economic order but also from the most confident, wealthy, and film-consuming queer community in the world.

Form and Politics

My initial premise was that *Passiflora* was indeed an exemplary aesthetic and political model, however slow audiences and NFB bureaucrats were to appreciate it. And the low-budget work of the independents that I suggested for the NFB to distribute had their share of aesthetic innovations but in fact paled in comparison.[10] In the discussions there was also an unspoken tone of resignation – in my letter to Macerola and even in Greyson's cranked-up proposal to the board – that, yes, we wanted the NFB to make gay and lesbian films, even if they were not cutting-edge formally or politically queer (to use the nomenclature that was coming back into vogue in the late 1980s). Which is exactly what happened.

Yes, there were flashes by Fernie and Siddiqi (whose presence alone reminds us that the funk and spunk of the independent video art movement documented elsewhere in this book somehow failed to make more than a few inroads into the bastion of sobriety), several but not all of the indie contributors to *Five Feminist Minutes* showed aesthetic verve, and Monette's editing flourishes were campy and insightful. But on the whole, a sedate body of work emerged. The queer corpus basically domesticated for the NFB's traditionally conservative parallel audience of school librarians and church basement community groups the rough aesthetic and political edge of the 1970s and 1980s. The films seldom moved beyond the affirmation era discourse of *Word is Out*'s positive images (1978) into the postmodern political energy of such video artists as Greyson and Dempsey/Millan. Yes, *Stolen Moments* would present some evocative glimpses of experimental dyke theatre, as well as a surprisingly bold cunnilingus climax for a state production, but its eclectic mix was cobbled together with a redundant voice-of-goddess commentary that referred to lesbians in the third person – as KATHLEEN ADAMS complained (1998) – and evoked the darkest days of

Lorne Greene, Grierson's chosen narrator of the 1940s. Voice-overs aside, the predominance of portraits – solo, serial, or group in the queer package – confirmed the recourse among filmmakers and producers alike to the most familiar and comfortable formats when entering uncharted waters, their tendency to extol exemplary individual lives rather than unsettle collective politics. No doubt the TV-window financing increasingly imposed on virtually all documentarists by Telefilm Canada and other funders (no broadcast or cable investment? no funding, period) consolidated the inherent formal conservatism of the queer NFB stable and hangers-on. At the same time, few would disagree that cutting-edge Canadian queer cinema/video could not exist did it not lean on a discursive infrastructure and staging ground of populist conventionality and instrumentalist sobriety.

Love and Money

Another underlying assumption concerned the entitlement to state funding for cultural expression. This entitlement was couched in terms of many decades of discourse around public cultural infrastructure and protectionism, which originated even before Grierson himself but which gained its contemporary momentum in the 1950s, a discourse that Michael Dorland has called, after Foucault, governmentality (1998). Dorland developed his concept in relation to the commercial sector during the years of clamour for a publicly supported funding infrastructure, but its applicability to the parapublic sector of the board and the CBC is a promising subject for further analysis. As my letter to Macerola indicated, the discourse of governmentality ran steady in queer media-watchdog circles, especially during the bleak regime of our own Thatcher-Reagan-style axe man named Mulroney, which would come to an end just as *Forbidden Love* was knocking them flat in the early nineties. This Liberal discourse contained both NDP-ish and Red Tory impulses: don't forget that the minister of communications who had replied to NDP-er Svend Robinson when he forwarded my complaint about the NFB, fully respecting the "prerogative" of the agency and its "carefully selected, responsible board and ... experienced management," was a Tory of the "Red" persuasion, descended from conservatives who supported arts funding as a kind of protection against U.S. mass culture. The queer assumption of governmentality entailed publicly defending the state studio at all cost, however much in public and private our favourite pastime was railing against their stupidity, bureaucracy, wastefulness, and homophobia. My own use of the term "taxpayers" in 1986 still makes me grimace, however knowingly I was appropriating the vocabulary of the culture slashers and queer bashers in the hope that it would have more currency with the bureaucrats. Being queer and culturally minded requires a certain grace around contradiction and inconsistency.

Sex and Politics

A final assumption can be called political, even more so than the other three assumptions, since it is political in the conventional sense. A double-pronged, contradictory strategy was at play here as well: in my letter I was capable of championing the gay lib-flavoured subversion of *Passiflora* out of one corner of my mouth and speaking out of the other the increasingly state-oriented rights discourse of the 1980s and 1990s, the drive for minority inclusion within the national citizenship that was the NFB's mandate. One thing I did not mention in my letter, though it was on everyone's minds, was the effect of Trudeau's new Charter of Rights and Freedoms, passed in 1982 but coming into force only the previous year in 1985. As the last half of the 1980s unfolded, its effect was already beginning to be felt, with the courts already beginning their gradual addition of sexual orientation into the prohibited grounds of discrimination in the Charter (made official in 1992).

A whole new political culture of often publicly funded litigation and state-centered, rights-based ideology for queer social movements in Canada was emerging. At the same time and in concert with the increased litigious activity was the escalation of political agitation by the "lesbian and gay" lobby, especially in Ontario, where they seized the opportunity of the provincial Liberals' accession to power in 1985 to step up the ante. In fact it was in the same tense November 1986, as I had fingers to keyboard, that the extremely bitter struggle to add sexual orientation to the Ontario charter was finally won. The series of dominoes continued to teeter one by one over the next decade: 1992 was a kind of midpoint, with new protection for forbidden love in British Columbia and New Brunswick greeting the premiere of the film of that title, and 1995–96, when Ottawa's jurisdiction joined the swell, was the peak moment for the queer corpus, with fully nine films released, from *Quand l'amour est gai* to *School's Out*; Fortress Alberta was the last to fall in 1999, a year, paradoxically, with nary a queer release.

While there is no space here to go into the ongoing debates by legal and political theorists about this shift of objectives from social transformation to legal equality, this general context overshadowed the NFB queer corpus as a whole as it would develop. As one commentator claims, "sexual orientation cases generally privilege a certain representation of homosexuality, a stable couple that mimics the heterosexual nuclear family, and ... the claim for equality on the basis of sexual orientation is shaped by human rights codes that have created boxes of discrimination into which litigants must fit." (Smith, 1999, 19). In tune with the political tide, the NFB queer corpus is in fact focused very little on the politics of sexuality: the challengingly frank sex scenes of *Forbidden, Stolen, Quand l'amour est gai,* and *In the Flesh* were the exceptions that proved the rule. As a whole the corpus is focused predominantly on the politics of family, the crux of the new post-Charter rights litigation strategy. And this focus on family was selective, symptomatically spotlighting almost entirely not conjugality but the issue of parenting and homosociality. The brave dad of *A Kind of Family* was followed by parallel pairs of same-sex parents in *Sticks and Stones* and similar inclusiveness in other trigger films. Meanwhile, no one has been holding their breath for films on same-sex pornography, swinging, intergenerational sexuality, prostitution, and other sexual problematics in which queer communities have stakes. It was as if the traditional NFB avoidance was still in operation on a fundamental level.

As I write this under the commissionership of Jacques Bensimon, a francophone Moroccan-born Jew, who may be the first in a line of leaders to replace political appointees like Macerola at the helm of Grierson's great creaking ship, attention is being refocused on the board's mandate of instrumentalist sobriety, and social development schemes are being reinvented. There's even a web forum up and running called parole citoyenne [roughly, citizens take the floor] in which social issues of the day like same-sex marriage are being debated online as if in some virtual-arena variation of CR in the old trigger format. Still, history exerts a powerful force even on a studio forever in search of renewing itself. The old patterns of labyrinthine bureaucracy linger, and the two linguistic solitudes seem as entrenched and irrational as ever (*Seuls, ensemble* got versioned in English, but francophone lesbians had to know English to appreciate *Forbidden Love* and *Stolen Moments*, two films that feature Montreal in a significant way). And in the new decade "new ideas emerge" with the same haphazard retroactiveness and opportunistic arbitrariness that gave indies Bezalel and Monette their big chance in the 1990s but always allowed the board to sleep at the switch throughout the seventies and eighties. But I write this at the end of 2003, the year of both the Siddiqi and Torrealba releases, and it seems that the corpus has continued to proliferate in spite of everything, acquiring its own post-affirmation and idiosyncratic queer sensibility, fostered by a combination of the sixty-five-year-old reflex to represent people and places in the here and now, however queer they've turned out to be, the reflex to fall back on familiar genres, narratives, conventions, and modes to move those cassettes and reach those audiences, and the twin parents of arts governmentality and rights governmentality. No wonder, with those two mummies, that Heather may well be a very queer child, but also a very strange and contradictory one.

7

Boys and the Beast

Back in 1961 of course, any Canadian kid who wasn't subject to perverse influences was a fan of one of the two Canadian [hockey] teams.
~ *Life after Hockey*, NFB, 1989

PERVERSE INFLUENCES

As a queer boychild coming of age in Southern Ontario as the Cold War and the sexual revolution were both raging hotly around me, I discovered that one fundamental element of my socialization left me very cold, namely, team sports in general and hockey in particular. This was a serious transgression, and only at great cost was I able to reject the enforced socialization that team sports and hockey represented, whether as collective ritual of television spectatorship or as even more frightening initiation on the rink, the court, or the playing field. As the glib narrator-protagonist of the 1989 NFB documentary cited in my epigraph insinuates, deleterious influences were clearly at work on me. I remember one occasion, probably around that very year, when my Sunday school teacher, a well-meaning veterinarian, invited us boys, perhaps a dozen of us on the cusp of puberty, over to his home for spaghetti and "the game" – not "the hockey game" or "a hockey game" or "the hockey game between X and Y" but "the game." But this initiation of the future film studies expert into the rituals of male bonding through media spectatorship was a stultifying and baffling failure. What on earth was of interest in those frenzied movements on that small black and white screen and in that excitable male voice, and why do I even remember such a banal moment?

With regard to the rink itself, I had earlier been a miserable failure in the peewee league I was pressured to join, small and unmotivated with ankles painfully turned in, and I could not have been more relieved when I was rescued through a scheduling conflict with the junior choir at church. This polarity between hockey and "creative" pursuits was in fact acknowledged several times by the NFB in that very decade: George, the protagonist of the 1957 discussion trigger film *Being Different* (1957), is forced by an anxious peer to choose between hockey and chasing butterflies, as we have already seen in chapter 2. In the 1954 TV reportage *Police Club for Boys* (NFB, 1954), which is about youth sports clubs organized by the Montreal police as a campaign to curb juvenile delinquency, the host has the temerity to ask about boys who won't play sports. This potential crisis is quickly resolved through a glimpse of the police *music* clubs, where sports dissidents are taught very masculine brass instruments, rather than junior choir anthems, narrowly escaping the perverse influences that had entrapped me and that are what this book is all about.

As an adult, having lived half my life in Guy Lafleur Land, hockey especially has followed me like a curse, from the preemption every spring of my CBC-National addiction for months at a time by Stanley Cup finals, semifinals, and semi-semifinals to the major assault of being implicated as a stakeholder in some "national" crisis every time Ron McLean renegotiates his contract or some Lindros gets another concussion. Not to mention the obnoxious presumption of goals scored against the Soviet hockey players in 1972 or 1984 being enshrined as founding moments in my cultural identity by every authority from *Life after Hockey* to the Royal Canadian Mint. And all this without even any compensatory erotic pleasure in watching those robocop exoskeletons on the ice (unlike for soccer or gymnastics or figure skating, for example, where bodies are sexy, graceful, and bare)!

Still, like any self-respecting gay man of my generation, I appropriated as an adult the ideal of strength and health and the athletic body – but as a participant, not as a spectator, at least in the standard sense. The gym is indeed one of the few sites of so-called masculinity that I do frequent, despite the risk of having to endure conversations about "those Habs" every day in the sauna. The YMCA pool, not the court or the playing field, is where I have been able to perform my own sense of physical worth and reconstructed masculinity – individually, never as part of a team. Splashy, sluggish, and inefficient swimmer that I am, the therapeutic thrill of exertion and of cool water sliding along naked skin, not to mention the fantasy of the tank-topped lifeguard perhaps awaiting me at the end of the lane, have more than compensated for the identity damage of my youth, and the endorphin by-product is not unwelcome. It is at the Y also, not by accident, that I have been able to realize my spectatorial, not to say voyeuristic, potential, observing not only the athletic male body, lustfully and obsessively I confess, but also the very rites of masculinity themselves. I have done so methodically over the decades, never as a true insider of course, but at very close ethnographic distance all the same: from the rites of territorial aggression, hazing, and rivalry to those of collective urination, grooming, weighing, accoutrement, depletion, and bathing. My relationship with the corpus of the Canadian cinema of male bonding that I would like to explore in this chapter, specifically of male sports narratives, is one that extrapolates from my metamorphosis from the failed peewee to the supreme pool queen of the Montreal Y and affiliated pools around the world. In this chapter I have already reopened childhood trauma and adult alienation, but adult redemption and pleasure are also at stake as I examine the corpus of male bonding sports films, both English Canadian and Québécois, launched at the time of my childhood and maintained to this day. Through a genre perspective I will try to make sense of these texts and tap into cultural anxieties about masculinity and sexuality as crystallized in the cinema, probing some of the queer fissures opened by those anxieties. No pain, no gain, they say.

As I was first discovering my conflicted relationship with male sociality and socialization through sports, Canadian cinemas were traversing the modernizing phases of Cold War sex-gender retrenchment, discovery, and "revolution" outlined in chapters 2 and 3 and heading towards the new frontier of the feature film. Filmmakers and functionaries were laying out the genres of male bonding, establishing sports as as a privileged preoccupation, first in documentary, and then in the embryonic feature film sector that would come into its own with the governmental financing framework in 1969. I begin with a fresh look at some of the classic NFB sports documentaries of the early sixties, continually keeping in view the cultural dialectic of the distinctive francophone and anglophone cultures of Canada. I will move through sports motifs and iconography in some of the classic features of the seventies and eighties before coming to rest on some of the key texts of the 1990s and the present decade.

I draw a theoretical framework from three interlocking sets of literature:

1 Recent bountiful work on Quebec and Canadian national cinemas, most specifically Bill Marshall's analysis of the coming to the fore of comedy as the principal generic manifestation of Quebec popular cinema of the 1990s (2001), and Christopher Gittings's (2002) study of alterity within the trajectory of Canadian cinemas as a whole,

2 The genre-focused analysis of sports films in general, including, for example, Vivian Sobchack's (1997) analysis of the various cycles of baseball films within American cinemas and their cultural and ideological significance,

3 Queer-theory-influenced, interdisciplinary cultural studies of masculinity,

sexuality, representation, and sports, bringing together Leo Bersani (1987), Varda Burstyn (1999), Allen Guttmann (1996), Brian Pronger (1990), Mark Simpson (1994), and others.

ÉQUIPE QUÉBEC

Male bonding and camaraderie in domestic, workplace, and leisure sites have been among the most recurring cinematic preoccupations within both the popular and parallel cinemas in Quebec, both fiction and documentary. So much so that Chantal Nadeau (1999) and other commentators have repeatedly indicted an unquestioning equation of the masculine with the national in discourse around national identities and cultures within Quebec cinema. Many films within this tradition channel their homosocial preoccupations through sporting mythologies. Hockey and hunting, especially, are the two activities most commonly associated with the Quebec national character in popular media and scholarly literature alike. But combat sports also hold a perennial fascination for Quebec filmmakers, and a major new boxing documentary seems to appear every five years. These sports have surfaced repeatedly in Quebec cinemas: sports were explicit subjects for analysis in the documentary essays that marked the first cinematic surge of the Quiet Revolution (Gilles Groulx covers boxing and hockey in *Golden Gloves* [1964], and *Un jeu si simple* [1964] respectively, while Hubert Aquin's *Le Sport et les Hommes* [1961] includes hockey in its cross-cultural survey of five sports and the collective *La Lutte* [1961] treats wrestling). Sports also animate narrative works as thematic motifs, as in *Un zoo la nuit* (Jean-Claude Lauzon, 1987, hunting, see chapter 9) or as major narrative foci and self-contained cultural universes, as in *Le temps d'une chasse* (Francis Mankiewicz, 1972, hunting) or in the long-running 1980s television series *Lance et compte* (Jean-Claude Lord, 1986–89, hockey), a veritable national epic. The breakthrough recipe of the Quebec hockey megahit *Les Boys* (1997) and its two hardly less popular sequels *II & III* (all directed by Louis Saïa and co-scripted by star Marc Messier, 1998, 2001) is the alignment of two overlapping cultural worlds, hockey and cinematic low comedy. The cultural iconography of the so-called national sport is wed to that of the snowballing low comedy phenomenon of the nineties, populist and masculinist. This alignment, deploying the full force of Quebec's TV-anchored star system, almost single-handedly sustained the Quebec film industry until the start of the new decade. In English Canada, in contrast, where cinematic traditions are less directly plugged into a cohesive and continuous popular cultural energy, as we shall see, the cinematic tradition of sports homosociality is more discontinuous and tentative but equally obsessive.

I will first focus on Quebec, disproportionately perhaps, and situate the hockey hit *Les Boys* in relation, somewhat incongruously, to two more respectable earlier documentaries. Neither is about slamming warm-bodied brothers against the boards but rather about, respectively, damaging those brothers' faces and bodies with padded punches in *Golden Gloves* (Gilles Groulx, NFB, 1961) and about killing larger warm-blooded mammals in *La Bête lumineuse* (*The Shimmering Beast*, NFB, 1982), the now canonical 1982 documentary on moose hunting in the Quebec north woods by nationalist filmmaker laureate Pierre Perrault. All three films are more or less typical of the diverse international corpus of sports films in the way they crystallize the crisis in masculinity, in the way the films explore more or less self-consciously the eruptions of violence and desire along the axis of maleness. Indeed the *Boys'* navigation through the murky border zone of the homosocial and homoerotic on the rink so precisely traces that of the earlier boxing and hunting documentaries that it feels like a kind of uncanny remake across boundaries of film genre, sport iconography, and box office, as well as across an almost forty-year historical divide. Deeply Rooted Dynamics must be at stake!

First, here is a summary and description of these three films. *Golden Gloves* was the masterpiece of the early cycle of "direct cinema" essays that emerged from the NFB's new *équipe française* in the first years after the opening of the new Montreal headquarters in 1957. This film by Groulx (1931–94), the fierce genius of the group, encounters a network of aspiring young boxers within the emerging urban working-class culture of Montreal, chiefly a black anglophone, Ronald Jones, and a white francophone tavern waiter, Georges Thibault, and follows them towards their first major challenges in the ring. Twenty years later the next film, *La Bête lumineuse* was widely seen to be launching a new direction in Perrault's career, shifting from the nationalist cycles on rural Québécois and aboriginal cultures to an explicit focus on gender, on contemporary rituals of male socialization within a younger, more urban, less proletarian generation. The two-hour film follows a group of moose hunters in a Maniwaki forest camp over a two-week pursuit of the elusive "shimmering beast." Perrault as usual introduces catalytic elements into the profilmic world, namely, the poet-intellectual and novice hunter Stéphane-Albert, whose tormented initiation within the world of the hunt and whose up-and-down relationship not only with the elusive moose but also with his friend, the seasoned hunter Bernard, becomes the narrative core. Finally, *Les Boys* broke all Quebec box office records with its narrative of a garage-league hockey team Les Boys, a mix of *pure laine* white-male Quebeckers ranging demographically from a heart surgeon to a welfare recipient and a cokehead rocker. The team, sponsored by the eponymous neighbourhood brasserie owned by their avuncular coach Stan, struggles against the machinations of the gangster Méo to take over the business and eventually prevails against his team of goons in a climactic playoff. (In the sequels, the Boys' playoff opponents include those other "others" of the Quebec imaginary, blacks, women, and Frenchmen.)

Let's reflect first on the narrative action of the three films, then on the discursive apparatus around that action. This is an artificial separation to be sure, since talk doesn't always match action, but one that will allow me better to trace the films' parallel generic patterns of eruptions and containment of violence, abjection, and desire. Traditional psychoanalytic interpretations of sport, whether of the eroticized body of the athlete or the libidinal economies of contact and combat, accoutrements and uniforms, territorial penetration and scoring – as sublimation or denial or outright jouissance – have been absorbed so unquestioningly within popular culture that filmmakers' all but explicit fleshing out of these insights, along the lines of *Raging Bull*'s penis fist (1980), hardly attract critical debate. In the current films, the phallicization of group sporting activities goes without saying: boxing, hunting, and hockey respectively are so tightly interwoven with sensuous physicality and with sexual conquest, scapegoating, and sublimation, class-inflected punishment and hand-wringing, that they are inextricable.

Golden Gloves is the most unself-conscious of the three films, a gauge, no doubt, of more innocent times, but who could have been oblivious even in 1961 to the physical intimacy of the camera's relationship with the strong but tender young boxers and hangers-on? In the virtuoso opening sequence, almost five minutes long, the hand-held camera wanders down a long line of bare-chested young boxing aspirants in their underwear looking unabashedly into their vulnerable eyes and then descends into the gym where a small group of boxers are training, engaging kinetically and spontaneously in the action. As the athletes spar, skip, stretch, and jump, the camera interacts with the movements at close quarters, and as the partner of the athlete luminously captures his proffered torso, his limbs outstretched, his crotch is often at centre screen. The camera performs the analogy between fighting, dancing, and sexual flirtation, joining the intimate circuit from the athlete to his opponent to his camp followers. The opening choreography ends, not surprisingly, with depletion, with the boxer seen from above, supine on the floor, arms outstretched in a "take me" posture of total accessibility.

In the two movements that follow, Groulx cultivates a relationship first with Jones and then with Thibault, and this intimacy is extended through both interviews and direct cinema observation. The question of authorial subjectivity is relevant in these patterns but is perhaps too complicated to adjudicate. Were some of the above elements of eroticization somehow connected to Claude Jutra, the closet queer lurking behind one of five credited cameras in this film (and part of the collective author of *La lutte*, with its landscapes of fleshy, heavy bodies in mock-coital body locks, echoing

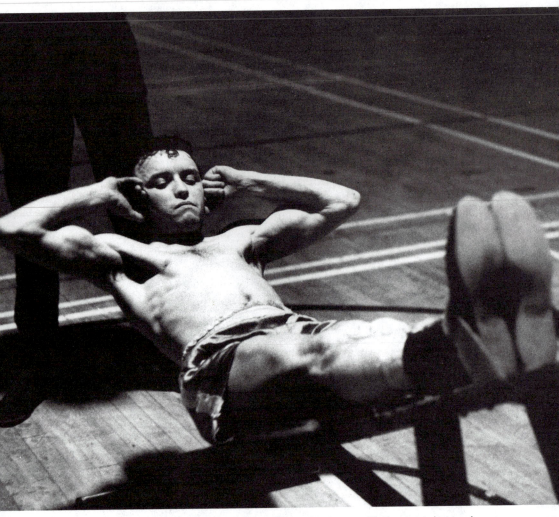

Golden Gloves (1961) is unself-conscious in its physical intimacy with the strong but tender young boxers. Who could have been oblivious even in 1961 to Groulx's camera and the analogy it enacts between fighting, dancing, and sexual flirtation? Production still, used with permission of the National Film Board of Canada

uncannily a major softcore gay erotic genre of the day)?[1] Not that Groulx would have needed Jutra's special pleading to register the sensuality of the male body and its combative engagements, despite his apparently unproblematical heterosexual identity, for he was demonstrably open to looking and appreciating and after all did not shrink, as it were, from providing the Canadian cinemas with their first prolonged full frontal male nudity in *Entre tu et vous* (1969). In any case, queer authorial sensibilities are not necessary within the sporting genres for undermining smug monolithic masculinity, as I shall confirm as I proceed.

In *La Bête lumineuse* it is the moose hunt that is continuously phalli-cized by the documentary mise-en-scène, whether through the suggestive fetishization of objects such as the rifles, the bows and arrows, and the fun-nel-shaped moose caller or through the penetrative relationship of camera with forest, wherein lurks the putative target (sometimes an inebriated man named Bernard, rather than a moose, as Perrault gradually makes clear). Often the pattern is literal, as where the men luridly stroke the fur of a slaughtered bear (and then, to make sure subjects and spectators have got the point, it is said that once you touch that you never want to touch a woman again). Throughout, the starkly phallic embodiment of hunting is both acknowledged and disavowed through a coarse humour that would seem to belong more comfortably in *Les Boys* and its ilk: at least one drunk-en pantomime of anal coitus by the supporting cast enacts the obsessive sex-ualization of the hunt.

In *Boys* the analogy between sex and the game is equally explicit: the players watch each other's romantic scoring as closely as they do their scor-ing on the ice (and conversely, their female sexual partners cheer on the men in their assault on the net – incidentally the most hackneyed editing trope of heterosexual sports cinema, one that falsifies the predominantly male demo-graphics of sports audiences). Mark Simpson refers to the dynamics of fan-ship and spectatorship in soccer, which also comes alive on the screen, especially with the boxing and hockey films. He speaks of the "failure ... to effect a complete distinction between identification and desire in the man-ner in which they are expected ... Men do not merely wish to *be* the foot-ballers but they also wish to *have* them." (1994, 78). In both *Bête* and *Boys*, the display of prowess to male comrades is inextricably part of the sporting activity, and each of the boxers in *Gloves* is surrounded by a coterie of fren-zied male fans.

Queer theorists and latter-day feminists have pushed these interpreta-tions even further into an exploration of anal and masochistic dynamics within male sports cultures. While Allen Guttmann (1996, 152) and others touch on the "perverse pleasure" of the bodybuilder in his/her physical pun-ishment, there is an analogous masochism in group sports, as recognized by Simpson, that jumps out from the screen with all three of the Quebec films:

It is "the goal" that is the ultimate symbol of this desire. The tremendous displays of physical affection and ecstasy of male for male ... that [a goal] can provoke is either absurdly grotesque or a beautiful momentary vision of utopia according to whichever perspective you prefer. Hugging, kissing, jumping on top of one another, delirious with pleasure, young men and old, express for a moment, within the sacred walls of the football ground, a love that is as exuberant and irrepressible as it is inconceivable outside those walls. The imagery that footballers like to employ to describe that moment is well-known as sexualized ... In fact the pleasure associated by the hetero male with goals can go far beyond that associated with mere sex. For it is in the "goal-fuck" that the player achieves both his goal of manhood – "a fucker" – *and* the (semi)fulfilment of his homoerotic desire – "a fucked."

... goals are valued for what they buy the scorer in terms of masculine adoration: a few moments of being at the centre of the male gaze and on the receiving end of his body ...

... A *passive* enjoyment of "sex" and male intimacy ...

But all this joy is predicated on "pain"; the team scored against and their fans are a study in dejection and humiliation, eyes cast down ... They have all become, in a symbolic sense at least, merely "a fucked," the shame of which isolates them as much as scoring a goal unites: the terrible private secret of the *anus*, the vulnerability of the male to penetration, has been made public. The goal mouths of each team are the acceptable representation of the male orifices that must remain hidden and guarded, admitting no entry. "Whereas the phallus is essentially social, the anus is essentially private." This is the script of masculinity acted out by football, where goals are publicly celebrated as phallic victories and defeats as private shames." (1994, 79)

I am not so sure that the shame of defeat is as private as Simpson and his cited authority Guy Hocquenghem contend, based on the evidence of the films, where the humiliation of defeat is savoured collectively as public spectacle, and it is this pleasure of defeat that I would like to analyze further. Even as superficial a comparative survey of hockey films as Stephen Cole's (1995) observes that "In American films, the hero beats the odds. In Canadian films the odds beat the hero to a bloody pulp." What Cole should have added (in addition to a little nuance in his cross-national comparison and a modicum of sensitivity to the class-based determinations of the construction and images of sports heroes) is that the Canadian heroes *enjoy* being beaten to a bloody pulp – *collectively and in public*. One does not have to subscribe to Robert Fothergill's thesis of Canadian masculinity as colonized loser-dom to take further the masochistic pleasure of collective bloody pulp ([1973] 1977).

In the boxing film, the bloody humiliation of defeat in the ring is especially palpable and is always set within a montage trope of escalating collective dejection. Although Groulx's two heros emerge relatively unscathed, the unconscious stupor of Ronald's KO'd opponent Clément, once cocky and surrounded by confident camp followers, is aestheticized, and Georges's defeat through a technicality, the especially painful loss of rapidly reversed fortunes, leads to a concluding tone of group chaos. (The later two Quebec documentaries about lightweight boxer Gaétan Hart, *Métier boxeur* [1981] and *Le Steak* [1992], as well as the most recent instalment in the fighter-doc tradition, *Le Ring intérieur* [2002], which is most similar to *Golden Gloves* in its eroticized relationship of camera and fighter, all fetishize the bloody pulp into which their tragic working-class protagonists' faces are pummelled as public spectacle.) In *Bête*, Stéphane-Albert is the prime butt, as it were, and several observers commented on the scene where the real-life intellectual and would-be hunter is flaked out at the base of a tree, passively submitting to his peers literally walking over him. In one interior camp scene Stéphane-Albert, Bernard, and a third hunter, Michel, all bare-chested and stumblingly drunk, engage in an orgy of submission and humiliation, both feigned and deliberate, including the smearing of marmalade, mustard, and syrup on Stéphane-Albert's baby-like, round, hairless abdomen and culminating in a ritual slap of the poet's face. This seems to have the effect of eliciting a poetic serenade by Albert to the sadistic Bernard's hair, face, and lips, now indifferent as he has simply passed out.

The Boys team, it is frequently commented, are a "gang de losers," and much cinematic energy is invested in excessive depictions of them in the masochistic delectation of losing. There are perfunctory wrap-ups of final victory in all three episodes, where submission has led somewhat implausibly to redemption – a rote dynamic in sports films in every culture, from *Field of Dreams* (United States, 1989) to *Lagaan* (India, 2001). But masochistic excess is usually prioritized over the feel-good coda, and one example in *Boys* is the visual mise-en-scène of the body checks to which the players repeatedly submit throughout the trilogy, often taken from the other side of the plexiglass barrier, so that the character's mangled face is splayed across the screen, with the goon opponent positioned behind him in the position of anal assaulter. Stan the oedipal coach gets his own shot of utter corporal humiliation: submitting to Méo and his goons for loan default, he perversely and repetitively fantasizes about the broken legs he is going to receive and then accepts a highly theatricalized mise-en-scène of the punishment, reclining on his back, eyes closed – a scene meant to be hilarious no doubt but one that reminded me of *La petite Aurore enfant martyre* in its aestheticization of torture. This is not to mention the punishment and abjection the characters dole out to each other, physical as well as verbal, a continuous texture of pratfalls and betrayals throughout. Sports and low comedy are indeed, as I said, the perfect recipe blend, not only for the male-dominated box office but also for drawing out masochistic desire.

The drunkenness that seems to be a necessary condition for the enactment of this desire is not irrelevant to this theme. In all three films, alcohol is a fundamental sacrament of debasement. In *Golden Gloves*, the tavern scene is a classic cinematic representation of Quebec working-class male culture, playing up the conviviality of the group of boxing fans and their idol, now the tavern waiter at his day job. The plentiful draft beer lubricates the homosocial community in its precombat stress and leads, first, to a ritual of phallic humiliation (poor Thibeault spills his trayful of beer on his crotch, to the hysterical elation of all present) and, next, literally to a trial by anal tribulation (the "operation hot seat" practical joke, where a buddy is selected as victim and a fire built literally under his ass) and then to an even escalated display of infantile merriment involving generalized dousing and a few drunken fisticuffs. In the later two films especially, the characters drink each other towards states of utter incapacitation, matching their humiliation in the forest and on the rink with their abjection around the drinking table, orgies of vomit, piss, and dissolution. (It is no surprise that Saïa's and Messier's career-setting hit was the forever-running stage play *La Broue* [i.e., Brew., 1979]). It is not only that drunkenness gives licence to enact without accountability the erotic undercurrents of homosocial relations and sports (a hoary cliché of sports films from *Slapshot* [1977] to *Personal Best* [1982]). Drunkenness also becomes an end in itself, a chemical means of acceding to the dissolution inherent also in athletic defeat (being creamed), low comedy (being cream-pied), and anal sexual submission (well, you get it ...).

Leo Bersani's comments on the appeal of powerlessness and loss of control for men seem custom-made for these films: "Phallocentrism is exactly that: not primarily the denial of power to women (although it has obviously also led to that, everywhere and at all times), but above all the denial of the *value* of powerlessness in both men and women. I don't mean the value of gentleness, or nonaggressiveness, or even of passivity, but rather of a more radical disintegration and humiliation of the self." Bersani looks to Freud for corroboration, linking this disintegration to sexuality, paraphrasing as follows: "sexual pleasure occurs whenever a certain threshold of intensity is reached, when the organization of the self is momentarily disturbed by sensations or affective processes ... the sexual emerges as the *jouissance* of exploded limits, as the ecstatic suffering into which the human organism momentarily plunges when it is 'pressed' beyond a certain threshold of endurance. Sexuality ... may be a tautology for masochism." And Bataille gives him a hand as well, "reformulat[ing] this self-shattering into the sexual as a kind of nonanecdotal self-debasement, as a masochism ... in which, so to speak, the self is exuberantly discarded." Bersani continues (1987, 217–20), linking masochism to the politics of sexuality within the context of the pandemic, coming to assert along the same lines that the sexual act of being penetrated "has the terrifying appeal of a loss of the ego, of a self-debasement." Can this fundamental core of male sexual desire not help explain the powerful synthesis of sports, low comedy, and narrative identification that these films enact?

Golden Gloves, *La Bête lumineuse*, and *Les Boys* are not only fraught with such phallic and anal resonances, they also can't stop talking about them. These and other films like them are filled not only with the gruff, taciturn rituals of masculinity channelled through the structures of sport, stalking prey, and being scored on through inter- and intra-group violence and drunkenness but also with nonstop orality. The oral discursive fabric has the function of embroidering, justifying, masking, or displacing the fundamental social dynamics of group sport, whether it is violence or desire. Training for the ring, the hunting expedition, and hockey season all engage what Pierre Perrault calls "a festival ... of speech and game of truth under the tent ... the great tournament of speech where the soul doesn't hide ... a joust." Through the intricate verbal texture within the film the participants, says Perrault, show an "extreme childlike tenderness that they hide badly and which they can't shed" (1982, 10–11).

The interview-based confessionality of direct cinema in *Gloves* evolves into the refined rendition of the same structure twenty years later in *Bête*, where Perrault's *cinéma vécu* process not only records but also incites the characters speech, endlessly drawing out the violence and sexuality inherent in everything from archery practice (the bow gets a "hard-on") and driving to the camp (the convoy of vehicles moving north, one driver tells the one ahead by CB radio to step on it or else he'll fuck him up the ass) to skinning a rabbit (which includes banter about Stéphane's cock, allowed by the French language by using the word "tail" [*queue*] as slang for "cock") and luring the elusive moose into the range of the bullets. In *Boys* the combined art of scriptwriter and standup improv comic produces a no less graphic, though perhaps less poetic, run-on texture of speech. Ironically, while certain codes of decorum still dictated the speech of Groulx's participants in 1961, the two subsequent films are variations on the theatre of cruelty: explicit homophobic abuse permeates the fiction film from start to end but is rare in *Bête*, perhaps having been edited out by Perrault; contradictorily, the range of crude, abusive, and eroticized interactions are much less censored in the documentary than in the relatively tame *Boys*, which has the compunction to be relatively politically correct in its vulgarity.

By emphasizing the elements of phallic, anal, and oral desire in these films, I am not necessarily making use of Freud's classical but somehow facile theory of phases of childhood sexuality, though there is something about the infantilism of male-bonding film genres in many cultures that implies a fundamental dynamic. I don't have space here to elaborate fully on the rich texture of, as Foucault would put it, the transformation of sexuality into discourse in these three films, the interface of action and speech. But I would like to comment on what Perrault has perceptively called, in relation to his own film, "the games of truth," a climactic eruption of performative recognition of desire, performed and contained or rebuffed – in short moments of cinematic "outing." In *Bête*, the gradual escalation of tension culminates in a long, drunken, late-night confrontation wherein Stéphane-Albert (a man incidentally with wife and offspring already encountered in the film) reads a love poem he has written to Bernard. This ritual paean that metaphorizes its object as the wind, the rain, a goat, a tuber of orgasms, and the blue of the autumn sky is no sooner offered than it is rejected by Bernard, who concisely tells him what to do with it by means of another interesting metaphor, namely, to stick it up his ass. Perrault, who realized how unacceptable Stéphane-Albert's gesture was, how unconfessable his confession (1982, 10), sets it up as the climax of the film but legitimizes and dissipates his shame in the editorial dénouement that follows, backing off from the moment of truth that, all the same, cannot be forgotten. Whereas in the early fictional classic *Le temps d'une chasse*, the mixture of hunting, [hetero]sexuality, and homosocial initiation led to an explosion of fatal violence, documentarist Perrault peters out with a final quarter hour of talk.

Boys has its own spectacular coming-out scene, occasioned by a climactic tie-breaking penalty shot. The sole (to our knowledge) gay character on the team, a closeted lawyer, Jean-Charles, who, we have discovered, is partnered with a temperamental and effeminate man jealous of his participation in the team, is given the opportunity to score the winning goal (there is a wry intertextual resonance around this character, since the actor Yvan Ponton had a major role in the previous decade as the castrating NHL coach in *Lance et compte*, a series that incidentally didn't get its gay character until the final season, and then not a Québécois character, only an American coach and blackmail victim). At the moment of highest tension, Jean-Charles's lover arrives at the rink, having got over his jealous sulk at his husband's devotion to his teammates, and publicly declares his love with a huge placard held against the plexiglass and a loud cry in his shrill deviant voice. This brings the entire proceedings to a halt before the lover spurs on his boyfriend to successfully score in dramatic slow motion. This unexpected outing through speech and naming is a complete surprise for his rather dense teammates, who hadn't had a clue, a moment of crisis that provokes first a cringe and then a rally round their teammate's side. The Boys have suddenly become implausibly cool, and it doesn't hurt that their team and masculinity have been spectacularly redeemed by the outcast within, a clean and up-front way of narratively expunging all the stress that has been accumulating around sexuality and gender in the film. The lover characterization grates badly, and the whole thing is not done very well, but certainly no worse than the heterosexual players' sexual relations. For Saïa's and

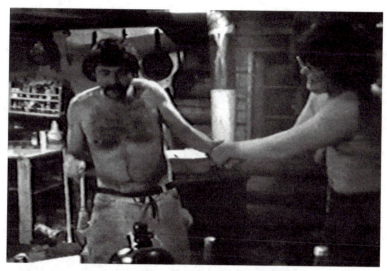

In *La Bête lumineuse* (1982), failed moose hunter Stéphane-Albert's long drunken late-night confrontation with his homosocial beloved Bernard (left) includes a poetic serenade and abject masochistic humiliation. VHS frame grab, used with permission of the National Film Board of Canada

Messier's specialty is clearly homosociality, not conjugality, whether hetero or homo.

In *Gloves*, this dynamic is lower-key and even anticlimactic and low on the 1961 radar screen, defused through editorial structure. The triumph of Jones against his overconfident opponent seemingly leads into a parallel triumph by Thibault, the great white *pure laine* hope, but this final victory is immediately deflated by the castrating referee who announces his disqualification. Thibault leaves the ring in humiliation and confusion, without even the ceremonial trauma of defeat, a whimper not a knockout. At that point we cut away to two of his frenzied male fans in the arena who are so carried away in their elation that they kiss each other on the lips. This shot is inserted incongruously as a strange distraction in the moment of despondency. Is this a temporal and logical mismatch (since Thibault's pals would scarcely be celebrating so playfully at the moment of humiliation) seized by editor-director Groulx who is desperate for a cutaway, or is it some unconscious or even conscious recognition of undercurrents in this carefully regulated all-male universe (after a preponderance of clichéd reaction shots featuring attractive but statistically insignificant female onlookers)? A fluke, a taunt, or ... a wink? Oblivious, benign, or ... conspiratorial?

These three passages provide single moments of direct discursive confrontation with the dynamics of desire in their respective films, situated by editor and scriptwriter as narrative climaxes or in *Gloves* as a stealth denouement, moments that break through the texture of verbal dissimulation. Within the *Boys'* highly dramatized and contrived genre narrative of popular cinema, the public declaration of love performs a stigmatized social identity on the part of speaker and also automatically of addressee, but it is no sooner enacted than it is recuperated and denied. This "gang de losers" may be crude and sexist, but they're no homophobes, and they immediately jump, silence, and ostracize their sole teammate who speaks for possibly all of them in remarking that that explains why Jean-Charles wouldn't go to the strip club after the game and to think they'd all been showering with this guy for years! In fact the homophobe is the coward who has extricated himself out of the action of every single game, and the outing paradoxically redeems not only their game but also their masculinity. The dexterity of this ideological acrobatics is matched only by that of the scriptwriter, who thereupon transforms his cowardly lawyer not only into winning goalscorer and MVP but also into a tough who in turn shames and punishes the gangster through a phallic dousing and anal chokehold and his own setup of masochistic comeuppance, in the toilets no less. Thereafter, in the two sequels, the scriptwriters all but lose interest in the queer hockey player who stood out in many ways as the hero of part 1. Having thus exorcised and tamed the terror of sexual diversity, the plots can continue in their pursuit of oedipal reconcilation and masculine self-flagellation.

Interestingly, the game of truth is turned upside down in the second sequel three years later in a scene I found hilarious, despite having my ideological guard up. Guy the fast-talking real estate salesman and bungling ladies' man is caught up in a coming-out lunch with his sympathetic mother, who says she knows he's gay and it's OK and she likes a nice bum too and it's time to come out and she loves him anyway, deaf to his protestations (maybe she saw *Les Boys I*!). It all leads to Guy's agitated and increasingly loud affirmations of his heterosexuality, which finally interrupt the crowded restaurant with a loud, cringe-inducing affirmation of heterosexuality that echoes the earlier scene. (Here, too, an element of intertextuality is inextricable, for the actor Patrick Huard, a popular stand-up comedian with notorious ladies'-man credentials, has made a career out of pretending to be gay, at least in an earlier box office sensation *J'en suis* [I'm One of Them, Claude Fournier, 1997], in which Huard and his buddy, the heartthrob Roy Dupuis, have to pretend to be gay in order to get a job. This nasty piece of business, which according to the critical consensus was "*imbuvable*,"[2] stitched together by an inexecrable director who has made a fortune peddling offensive and, worse, incompetent queer jokes for three decades, was pitched at gay audiences. With this idea the film incorporated as its opening sequence a long and very sexy wrestling sequence between Huard and Dupuis, fol-

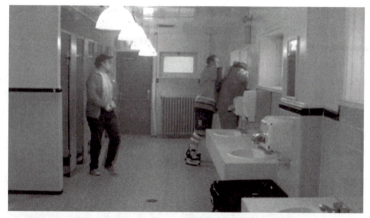

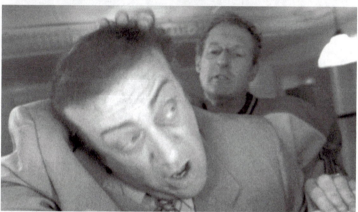

Les Boys (1997): script contortions transform the cowardly gay lawyer into a winning goal-scorer who deflects his own anal shame by punishing the gangster villain with a phallic dousing and anal chokehold in the arena toilets. DVD frame grab strip

lowed by an even sexier full-frontal shower scene of the two straight boys setting up their pathetic plot). In other words, *Boys* was not the first film in which queer sexuality, in combination with sports cultures and the movie marketplace, led to narrative contortions even more acrobatic than the ideological ones: in *Les Boys* the spectre of anal abjection is enacted and named throughout but finally exorcised in its spectacularly comic, politically correct denouement, this sudden parachuting in of the redemptive queer hero and the implausibly affirmed homosocial community that results. Female critics generally hated the operation, but that hardly kept the hordes away.[3]

Containing the fissures within masculinity is just as hard in nonfiction. In *Gloves* – not only prequeer but even prefeminist – the spectre of desire as enacted in the opening choreography and final kiss was ultimately absorbed in the whirlpool of other discourses, from the energized nationalist claim to the high spirited sense of cine-technological discovery to the populist melancholy arising out of Groulx's class solidarity. *Bête*'s declaration of ambiguous but presumably homosocial love within the catalysed profilmic world provokes discomfort on the part of the community and verbal violence on the part of the beloved, as well as, ultimately, shame and repentance on the part of the poet. *Bête* is no comedy, despite the slapstick pratfalls throughout, for the verbal jousting penetrates far too deeply, the laceration of desire and shame transforms this text of male entitlement into a disturbing melodrama of masculinist abjection, but one without the cathartic resolution of drama.

TEAM CANADA

Hockey and other sports films were common on the English side of the industry since the very beginnings of Canadian filmmaking but lacked the continuity and centrality of Quebec popular film and television. *Face-Off* (George McCowan, 1971) inaugurated the Canadian Film Development Corporation (CFDC) with one of the few commercial feature success stories of the seventies, a typical interweaving of homosocial action and conjugal pressures, in this case the downbeat romance of an NHL rookie sensation and a drugged-out rocker written by sports writer Scott Young. The artier *Paperback Hero* (Peter Pearson, 1973) offered an even grimmer canvas of amateur hockey leagues in small-town Saskatchewan, the locus of infantile homosocial acting out, self-punishment, violence, and alienation as the team, the last sign of community life as the rural economy closes down, forfeits its last game – not exactly something to convert either hockey fans or hosers to the nascent English Canadian feature industry. Imported American hunk Keir Dullea was much more convincing as the broken-toothed, demented loser clinging drunkenly to his friendship with his buddy who went and got married on him than as the ladies' man who bares all for sex with his long-suffering girlfriend in the team shower room (the privileged site of male-male physical intimacy being a rather telling choice for heterosexual consummation …). In 1980 *The Hounds of Notre Dame* offered another variant of the prairie hockey narrative, stressing coming of age and coach-team mentorship. And then in the 1990s there was *Perfectly Normal* (Yves Simoneau, 1990), a gentle comedy that shifted Pearson's down east metropolitan view of rednecks to a more introspective urban immersion into soft, fluid, and quirky masculinity, integrating hockey with male bonding, assembly-line alienation, real estate, ethnicity, opera, yes, heterosexual romance, and did I say male bonding? Hockey is not the major element, except perhaps to stabilize this volatile mix, an effective antidote for the opera and other suspect deviant behaviours like drag and refusing to go to strip clubs with the boys. (We know what *that* meant for Jean-Charles in *Les Boys*.) Here hero Renzo is a goalie, and keeping pucks out of the orificial symbol of desire is certainly a very important job in a tightrope queer-straight movie like this one.

Yes there have been English Canadian hockey features, but never the equivalent of Quebec's *Boys* cycle or *Lance et compte*. The English version of the latter 1980s megahit miniseries, *He Shoots, He Scores*, had been an embarrassing failure. But that did not prevent the CBC from giving Atom Egoyan the plum TV-movie project, *Gross Misconduct* (1993), which is an NHL bad boy, as we shall see, nor CTV and Alliance Atlantis from trying an Ontario equivalent to *Lance et compte* at the end of the decade, namely, *Power Play* (1998–2000), a creditable but short-lived effort about keeping

Perfectly Normal (1990) gently probes a soft, fluid, and quirky masculinity, integrating hockey with male bonding, assembly-line alienation, real estate, ethnicity, opera, and, yes, heterosexual romance, plus other suspect behaviours as well – like drag. Production still, Film Reference Library

the struggling Hamilton NHL franchise from going south (as the Winnipeg and Quebec City franchises had just done) in the face of high-finance wheeler-dealing and various romantic and familial crises. Other than *Hockey Night in Canada* – which, pace Neil Earle (2002, 327–32), is less "play as idyll ... collective mythmaking ... bardic television ... electronic Aeschylus" than a humungous target-broadcast commercial for beer and cars – hockey and sports mythologies in general functioned for filmmakers less as a national epic than as a vehicle for probing other themes. Such themes were the regional/class alienation and dysfunctional masculinity that Pearson tackled so vividly or male-male sexual abuse, which Norma Bailey examined through the CTV biopic movie *The Sheldon Kennedy Story* (1999), as timid a rehashing of prairie social-mobility myths as you would expect on CTV and one less skeptical about prevalent mythologies of ephebophile abuse than one would hope.

Perhaps the entire English Canadian mythology of hockey, its claims and contradictions, is condensed most compactly not into a feature but into the medium-length docudrama I have already mentioned at the outset of this chapter: the 1989 NFB-Northwest (Edmonton) production *Life After Hockey*, an adaptation of an autobiographical stage play by Kenneth Brown, who plays the lead and on-camera narrator. The Brown persona, a thirty-something commitment-phobic adult who, like many sports figures in the generic cinematic landscape, has never grown up, offers dramatized reminiscences of coming of age into hockey as an all-encompassing adult universe. He focuses with a modicum of self-awareness on the role of hockey in the socialization of gender roles and on the hetero- vs homosociality polarity that is standard to all male-sports narratives. "We have to get away from our Almas sometimes," he says of the homosocial drive that hockey fulfils, referring to the name he gives his mother, wife, and daughter in the story. The enforced masculinist conformism of hockey socialization is touched on in a scene where the child hockey fanatic encounters a male figure skater working out gracefully and alone on ye olde prairie rink one early winter morning. The narrator passes on some wisdom about how it wasn't at all "strange that a guy should be wearing a girl's skates instead of playing hockey," namely, the reassuring fabrication that in fact NHL players practise "fancy skating" all the time. The figure skater, played by the then international star Kurt Browning, of convenient Alberta roots and appropriate sexual orientation (Browning came out as straight in his 1991 autobiography), befriends the boy and even sparks feelings of exclusion when he coaches his girlfriend in "fancy skating." But from this fleeting confrontation with lies and contradictions around gender diversity, the persona and the filmmakers back off so quickly and completely that the spectator is left dizzy. We are then led in the next breath into a rhapsodization of the Canadian NHL teams of the day, including the idiotic and slanderous statement used as the epigraph to this chapter and the memory that in comparison to his idolized Canadiens, the Maple Leafs were "upright and *straight* and Protestant!" (my emphasis). This glib transmission of not only heterocentric but also androcentric presumption, this violation of my own remembered personal sense of place and self in 1961, perversely influenced or not, leads on to further discourses involving hockey idols, putative national cultures centred on anti-Soviet games, and heteroconjugal resolution. I have tried to keep Alberta-bashing to a minimum in this queer Canadian book, but this apologia for hatred and violence almost pushes me over the edge.

In a way the CBC came to the rescue three years later with similar geographical premises but more solid source material and a more self-critical result. Egoyan's *Gross Misconduct*, the biography of tormented and violent 1970s NHL star Brian Spencer, is based on Martin O'Malley's biography and scripted by future *Due South* and *Brooms* wunderkind Paul Gross. For a TV movie, Egoyan was apparently given unusually full rein, and he responded with an uncompromising Brechtian parable of hockey as a cruel form of upbringing by a tyrannical father, a disingenuously violent form of popular spectacle, a familiar mythology of social mobility, especially in rural hinterlands, and a surprisingly adult view of the historic player's childlike persona and tragic fate. The paternal topos anticipated another real-life source that materialized a few years later in Bailey's *Sheldon Kennedy* and, according to Debra Shogun (2002–3), constitutes an important social and mythic undercurrent of male hockey culture that the media and mainstream popular culture are in serious denial about.

Structuring the narrative by intercutting the trajectories of both father and son towards their respective violent deaths, Egoyan and Gross also inserted an over-the-top array of intertitles, as well as on-camera retroactive narration by Spencer the boy. Egoyan, the slight child of Armenian immigrants, is clearly and mercifully no captive of sentimental national mythologies of hockey and masculinity, and he is especially unrelenting and agile in exploring the linkage between the character's obsessively driven hockey identity and his knee-jerk careening in and out of heterosexual marriages, fornication, and paternity. (Interestingly, with regard to the middle term, Joan Nicks has blown the whistle on the CBC's decision to censor an unusually frank and important sex scene from the film for its second broadcast [1995].) It may be significant that with regard to Spencer's sexuality, his first explosion of uncontrollable violence within the world of adult hockey comes in the weight room when teammates haze him with queer jokes (for some unimaginable reason – perhaps because they are part of this shirtless hick's ritual initiation?). But Egoyan never pushes further the inextricable relationship of hockey machismo and homophobia until the last scene of his character's life when Spencer is summing up his conflicted attachment to hockey with an idolatrous anecdote about Bobby Orr, who had once praised his pugnacious playing style: "Don't get me wrong, I'm no fag but he was beautiful ... Bobby Orr talked to me." Moments earlier, as the tragedy is beginning to move in, another moment of summing up unfolds: he and the camera admire his naked Brillo-pad torso in the mirror, especially his strong right pectoral in close-up, and then his distorted, grimacing face, as if to assess both body, identity, and masculine ideal one last time.

Fellow Torontonian John Greyson had developed similar insights two years earlier in *The Making of Monsters* (1993). My favourite English Canadian hockey film and the only one from an outright queer perspective, to my knowledge, *Making* resembles so many others of the corpus in using sport as a vehicle rather than as a subject in itself – not a single actor laces up his skates! (Greyson's apotheosis of male synchronized swimming and nude calisthetics in *Zero Patience* demands further research as a key to his dialectical understanding of male sports.) A Brechtian musical essay about queer-bashing and public sex, based on the 1985 murder of a Toronto gay teacher in a public park by a gang of teenagers, *Making* offers as a refrain an abstract choreography of four adolescent hockey players clad only in jock straps, running shoes, and rather terrifying hockey masks. The dancers perform a ritualized condensation of hockey, bringing out its role as socializing force of violence, group bonding, and ambiguously displaced eroticism. It's disturbing and very sexy at the same time and brings out the intense ambivalence within both the sports spectacle and sports participation. While Greyson doesn't probe the element of masochistic abjection that Egoyan and Perrault and many of the other narratives engage, all the tenderness of *Golden Gloves* is there, especially in the brief monologues of the shirtless young actors, their masks removed. These short scenes transmit Greyson's characteristic generation-based sympathy – as opposed to the class-based sympathies of the Québécois filmmakers or the regional identifications in the Rest of Canada – and offer a note of pathos around the enforced masculinist socialization to which we submit boys in our culture.

MYTHOLOGIES: LOVE HATE LOVE HATE

Hockey, of course, is not the only sports mythology within Canadian cinematic cultures. With regard to other sports, from the beginning of the sixties English Canadian documentarists had been much less preoccupied with jockdom than their francophone peers, who saw wrestling, hockey, and boxing as key social rituals of the Quiet Revolution and Quebec modernization. One interesting exception, however, is from Quebec but in English: *I Was a Ninety Pound Weakling* (Georges Dufaux and Wolf Koenig, 1960),

John Greyson's *The Making of Monsters* (1993), a musical about queerbashing and public sex, offers a choreography of four adolescent hockey players, in order to bring out the sport's socialization of violence, group bonding, and displaced eroticism. Production still

in which two pioneers of NFB direct cinema focus on the first modern fitness craze. Much of the film is tongue-in-cheek, especially its cheap shots at overweight female slimming and yoga clients. The portrait of the Montreal YMCA as an all-male homosocial community, as well as a sports institution, is somewhat more observant and profound. The wrestling scenes, carnal mountains of heaving and gasping flesh, are an evocative image of the naked physicality of the male body at play but lack the tenderness and sensuality of *Golden Gloves*. Most striking in retrospect is the film's unwitting excursion into the border zone between homosociality and homoeroticism, between male corporal exertion and erotic display.

In fact, the film's encounter with bodybuilding is a rare early document of Montreal's emerging crypto-gay "physique" scene. Joe Wieder, the Montreal barbell tycoon who blinked at his huge gay market (Waugh 1998), pitches his products and of course physical health and strength with the usual interface of image and merchandising and introduces BILLY HILL, former Mr Montreal and Mr Canada. (Wieder glibly introduces him also as Mr America and Mr Universe, but is not corroborated by the historical record.) Hill stiffly twitches his magnificent muscles for himself in the mirror and for the camera (Dyer has often reflected on traditional stereotypical associations between queerness and narcissism, and this scene is a capsule seminar on the topic [Dyer (1990) 2003, 79–80]). There follows a rather static tour of the Billy Hill Gym in what is now the heart of Montreal's Village gai. Of course the filmmakers could not have foreseen the quirks of future subcultural geography. But they were likely oblivious to Hill's stature as a gay beefcake icon even in 1960. The self-promoting star of his own posing photo and film series, Hill's gyms, like several others, functioned, as Montreal's postwar gay subcultures proliferated, as a covert nexus of gay community networks fed by the ambiguities and alibis of sports and physical culture in particular. The subculture is fully evident on the screen, however (at least to the informed viewer), in an unconscious eroticism combined with the slightly tongue-in-cheek subjectivity characteristic of the entire post–Candid Eye momentum of the early sixties (the cycle that gave us, after all, Paul Anka in his underwear in *Lonely Boy* [1962], as well as Leonard Cohen in his bathtub [1965; see chapter 3]), but this film is queerest of all.

The NFB English studio tongue found its cheek again twenty-five years later with Peter Lynch's *Project Grizzly* (1996), a documentary update on English Canadian hunting mythologies that is a hybrid of *Bête lumineuse*, *Paperback Hero*, and, yes, *RoboCop* (United States, 1987). *Grizzly* is an indulgent full-length portrait of a wacko hinterland "research" scheme to develop an armour suit for protecting a man against a grizzly bear, a scheme hatched at a Country Style donut shop and carried out in the wrecking yards, pool halls, welding shops, trailer camps, and remote forests of the Canadian Shield and the Rockies – in other words, the true terrain of hyperbolic hoser masculinity. Lynch's portrait of the Don Quixote of North Bay, Troy Hurtubise, retains many of the elements of the hunting and hockey films, the gospel of the same-sex group and the hero, this time literally with a hard shell and vulnerability underneath. There's not much queer about this film except its over-the-top performative masculinism, an intensity that is truly beyond camp, and the double consciousness that Brenda Longfellow (1999) has explored in relation to audience responses (metropolitan irony vs hinterland insiderness, smug detachment vs narcissistic identification).

This is the cinematic context, then, in which Paul Gross and Atlantis Alliance tycoon Robert Lantos developed another Northern Ontario narrative of masculinity, *Men with Brooms* (2002). Although media interviews usually mentioned their desire to make a Canadian *Full Monty* (United Kingdom, 1997), it is impossible that they did not have their eye also on a product closer to home, *Les Boys*, and not only on its staggering box office but also on its popular tie-in with resonant sports mythologies (Quebec reviewers of *Men* immediately picked up on this kinship, though no one noted that the Anglos had promoted the boys to manhood ...). But there was one problem: Gross and his producer Robert Lantos were missing the foundation that Saïa and Messier were building on, a solid tradition of sports narratives within a coherent and continuous popular-film culture dating back half a century, the discursive processing of the crises of masculinity through stories of goals and teams. But rather than following the first impulse to make this deliberately conceived popular English Canadian film about hockey – the first since *Face-Off* thirty years earlier – they opted for curling, since it was "unpolluted" (McKay 2002). Lantos came up with a relatively large budget ($7.5 million) and an unprecedented $2 million promotional budget, riding on the post-Olympics fever of 2002, for a 175-screen release. The *Boys* formula was seemingly followed to the letter: the underdog team of thirty-something amateurs; the homosocial narrative whose peripatetic humiliations are mediated through sympathetic and familiar stars (well, as many "stars" as English Canada can muster, namely Gross himself as the straightissimo Mountie, alongside Leslie Nielsen, Peter Outerbridge, and Molly Parker, whose screen personas all carry varying degrees of recognition plus nuances of perversity); the motif of drunkenness, mostly displaced onto the increasingly typecast Parker character; victory against the evil empire (the curling team from Butte, Montana, one of the string of predictable anal jokes); an upbeat feel-good ending involving gender redemption and conjugal string-tying for all; and finally, a strong sense of place that is in many ways the most appealing aspect of the film (it's called Long Bay, but we know it's Sudbury because of the dramatic molten slag backdrops taken right out of the NFB's *Helicopter Canada* [1966] and two hundred national anthem trailers).

Les Boys and *Full Monty* had been at least partially forthcoming about the homoeroticism intrinsic to their pretexts, and each had its token gay character (hard to avoid with a film about male strippers, after all). Gross and Lantos, however, were caught up in playing off an arch self-consciousness about "Canadianness" (with a populist nationalist Canadian discourse suddenly fashionable in the aftermath of the Molson "I am a Canadian" TV-commercial phenomenon of 2000) against a thereby diluted self-consciousness about the mythologies of masculinity. There is the requisite texture of male bonding imagery, including a team skinny-dip jump off a cliff replete with erection and shrunken scrotum jokes (cold water, you see ...), a sweat lodge pregame ritual (curlers apparently don't have team shower rooms) interpolating the interminable rink climaxes conveyed by intense close-up eyeline communications. Gross also includes the generic interfaces between sexual performance and performance on the ice (in fact, our didactic workshop on curling is drawn in lipstick on one girlfriend's abdomen), and there is the usual conflict between conjugal duties and homosocial desire, especially for one of the rink, the wimpy undertaker. But the self-laceration of the genre is diluted or displaced by the cool hoser affirmation. At the same time, surprisingly, Gross seems to have adopted the strategy of steering completely and implausibly clear of queer (queer disavowal, queer jokes, queer characters, queer subtext, queer fissures, queer anything), presumably to spare the untapped curling crowd audience anything more risky than the four-way midair bum shot. Or was it just that a curling rink is smaller than a hockey team or stripper lineup, so with the bomber crew of henpecked husband, dysfunctional husband, promiscuous dopehead, and sympathetic wounded bachelor (all types recognizable from *Les Boys*), there's no room left for token gay demographics, which don't apply to the hinterland in any case, and certainly have nothing to do with [English] Canadian identity? (The only possible inference of queerness on the screen is a lightning-fast same-sex kiss between the female town constable and the waitress bookie at the moment they've won all their bets.) But no doubt the same pressures, part neo-Canadian hipness, part politically correct caution, and part conservative audience pandering, led to the relative downplaying of the homosocial sharing of women (these are "relationship guys," and the serial promiscuity is restricted to the ditzy girlfriend who flits from one stamen to another). They also led to the emergence of stronger female characters than in the average hockey flick, even to the extent of the first female astronaut character in Canadian film history (though she sure doesn't look like Roberta Bondar!). I want to like *Men with Brooms*, since it's very close to the button, but I can't but lament Gross's backpedalling away from the

Men with Brooms (2002),
Toronto's answer to *Les Boys*, has
much male bonding, including
a nude team jump off a cliff,
but the self-laceration around
masculinity is diluted by too
cool hoser affirmation, and
queer is nowhere on the rink.
DVD frame grab strip, Serendiity
Point Films

articulate recognition of male crisis that infused his script for *Gross Misconduct* and even his campy self-consciousness of *Due South* (1994–99) before he arrived at the slick but evacuated remake of a Molson "I am Canadian" commercial with brooms.

The meandering trajectory of sports narratives shows no sign of slowing down, either in English Canada or in Quebec in the new decade. Major new documentaries on combat sports have suddenly appeared and got major play from both the French and English programs at the NFB. *Le Ring intérieur* (*The Ring Within*, Dan Bigras, 2002), on "ultimate combat," and *The Last Round* (Joseph Blasioli, 2003), on boxing, confirm the enduring chord that sports narratives strike among both the heterosexual-male producing community and the corresponding audience. *Ring* makes certain strides in terms of reflecting Quebec's increasing cultural diversity (most of the fighters are of Haitian descent) and in pushing point-of-view documentary aesthetics towards increased versatility (and budgets). A first-person encounter between the white singer-filmmaker and his fighter subjects, in particular, Charles Ali Nestor, a champion of one of the emerging fusion-combat sports, the film veers wildly among its various discourses, part homosocial love story between filmmaker and subject, part social analysis of Nestor's biographical trajectory as juvenile delinquent redeemed through sport, part journalistic presentation of the growing circuit, and part aestheticization – if not eroticization – of the body, movement, and conflict. Still, the film feels disturbing, swallowed up in a kind of uncritical masculinist mystification of violence and anger. Bigras's brooding first person voice-over, addressing Nestor, sums it up:

after we fight our hearts open up ... you entered my real life ...
I don't consider fighting indecent.
I've seen greater indecency in the violence of silence, the silence that engenders
    sadness, the sadness that engenders anger.
Do we have the right to our own anger?
What do we do with it?
I know my anger well, I use it often.
Everything I've done, I've done with a lot of anger, but is there a clearly defined
    line between healthy anger and destructive anger?
Love hate love hate
Can we live with one and get rid of the other?

Bigras's film shares the tragic populism that is intrinsic to all the Quebec sporting films, with the heightened class consciousness, nationalist-flavoured, that sets them apart from their English Canadian equivalents – not to men-

Le Ring intérieur (2002): part love story between filmmaker and fighter subject, part analysis of juvenile-delinquent-turned athlete, and part aestheticization of the body and conflict – in all an uncritical masculinist mystification of violence and anger. DVD frame grab, used with permission of the National Film Board of Canada

tion Hollywood parallels like *Fight Club* (1999). But its complicit indulgence in a world of hyberbolic machismo, where a gospel of same-sex intimacy, seemingly adopted from the white middle-class men's lib backlash movement of the 1980s (epitomized by Robert Bly's American bestseller *Iron John,* 1990), is predicated on a denial of gender politics and sexual diversity and, at the same time, on an uncritical idealization of violence. This is very scary indeed.

The Last Round is a big-budget but routine interview/stock shot history that parallels the career of Toronto heavyweight George Chuvalo with that of Muhammed Ali and then focuses on their allegedly legendary match at Maple Leaf Stadium in 1966. This film, issuing from Toronto's CBC/sports journalism subculture, is also very disturbing, not so much for the unimaginative blandness that fails to grasp the interest of the bountiful archival material, but for its totally uncritical absorption in masculinist sports ideologies in general and in the murderous sport it promotes in particular. It is no surprise that that subculture is oblivious to and untouched by the momentous last thirty-five years of the women's movement, but does the reminder have to come fully financed from the NFB? Furthermore, like *Men with Brooms, Round* is caught up in fanciful and facile neo-Canadian mythologies, setting up Chuvalo as a persistent and solitary Canadian underdog who "didn't win but neither did he lose." The only time my ears perked up was when Ali calls his Canadian opponent a "sissy" who fights like a "washerwoman," and the screen is suddenly taken over by the Toronto hulk publicly confronting Clay in a strange drag interpretation of a washerwoman costume, taunting him with a squeaky falsetto – for once upstaging the suddenly speechless Louisville Lip, who acts as if he's seen a ghost. But the filmmakers seem equally at a loss and don't probe Chuvalo's accidentally revealed potential for gender performativity or develop the theme of colonial emasculation or even the levels of subjectivity that Bigras was able to solicit from his fighters.

There couldn't be a greater contrast between these two complacent combat documentaries and CLEMENT VIRGO's first feature, *Rude* (1995), a film much more explicit about the racial dynamics of boxing. The protagonist of one of its four interwoven inner-city narratives is Jordan, a gay boxer pushing himself to assert his identity and integrity against the homophobic pressures of his jock buddies. No token character, Jordan's tender locker-room kiss with his sparring partner and his penitential reconciliation with the "batty boy" he and his pals have bashed in the park are two of the most astonishing scenes in the Canadian queer canon and perhaps the most successful of Virgo's four efforts to orchestrate redemption within his rough and disempowered Toronto-Caribbean settings. Other heterosexual poets of male action and anxiety through sports iconographies would do well to emulate Virgo's courage.

Before I come to some concluding comments on the corpus of sports films that I have been examining in this chapter, a reminder is needed that only male sports narratives are the object of this study thus far. Female sports fictions and documentaries come out of a different world, of course, given the marginalized context of underfunding, low status, and blatant sexism that shapes women's sports, and are thus articulated in distinct cinematic genres, since they run by definition against the grain and are queer even when they are not implicitly or explicitly Queer. Manon Briand's two features are a case in point: *2 Secondes* (1998), a drama of a washed-up bicycle racer who establishes a new life and purpose as a bicycle courier, heterosocial pal, and homosexual lover, and the CTV film *Heart: The Marilyn Bell Story* (2001), a narrative of the legendary swimmer's 1954 Lake Ontario crossing. Both are narratives of individual drive and strength: the former is the more explicitly queer and in fact a successful programmer in queer festivals, while the latter is content to be covertly subtextual in its 1950s way, winkingly throwing in a subplot about Marilyn's teammate who is available for lots of hugs and leaps into Lake Ontario in her bra and panties to swim alongside the champion when the going gets rough. In comparison, Brenda Longfellow's *Our Marilyn*, an avant-garde essay on the same material as *Heart*, is more about historical context and sensual corporal experience, as well as codes of gender and nation. As for the more conventional documentary field, Justine Pimlott and Maya Gallus's *Punch like a Girl*, a TV series on women boxers (2003), is also distinct from the similar

Clement Virgo's *Rude* (1995) follows Jordan, a gay boxer standing up to homophobic jocks. This post-sparring deliberation leads to a sweet locker-room same-sex kiss, the bravest moment by any heterosexual poet of male anxiety in sports. Production still, courtesy The Feature Film Project, Executive Producer "Rude"

male subjects treated in this chapter: the fact that most of the subjects are up-front lesbians already forces the undercurrents of the male films to the surface. While perverse pleasure and pain are certainly still part of the dynamic in the female films, the homosocial element that is so determining of the male mythologies is, perhaps surprisingly, quite minor and unproblematized chez les femmes.

In conclusion, setting aside the very interesting autonomous chapter on women's queer-sports mythologies that will someday be written by someone other than me, I need to come back and sort out or at least recognize some of the dichotomies or polarities that are continuously being negotiated within the corpus of Canadian male sports:

First, Québécois sports mythologies vs English Canadian sports mythologies. This dichotomy points to a world of cultural difference, the tragic class-based populism that is a continuous foundation of popular cultural forms in Quebec opposed to regional identifications, nostalgias and sentimentalities on the "Rest of Canada" (ROC) side. There, lacking a tradition other than "Hockey Night in Canada," the erratic efforts to substitute and reinvent national sports mythologies are at the expense of authentic confrontations with the contradictory stresses, traumas, and desires within masculinities. My formulation reflects, of course, my idealizations as an English Canadian of Québécois popular culture and of Québécois (working-class) male bodies and iconographies, but there is no doubt that it captures distinctive materialities of culture and society.

Second, populist and popular cultural mythologies vs the various marginalities of feminist and queer ideological critique, documentary and experimental analyses, and auteurist/art cinema subjectivities. All these marginalities are of course in constant dialogue with popular cultures, and I want to carefully avoid the trap of setting up auteur art films in privileged comparisons with popular star-driven genres and cinemas. It is true that I feel exhausted by often futile efforts to find shreds of new cultural understandings of masculinity on the popular screen, and it is undeniable that the Egoyans, Greysons, and Perraults, sheltered by the CBC, the Canada Council, and the NFB, have come closest to my own personal sense as an elitist queer metropolitan academic of the core of male sports cultures. The struggle to maintain and increase public funding for this work is absolutely necessary, but at the same time, what aspect of *Men with Brooms* is an equally essential part of the Cinema We Need (to reprise the polemical slogan from the eighties)?

Regardless of my disdain for the neoliberal marketplace, one has to acknowledge the good faith of the initiative engaged by Gross and Lantos and others in pushing a commercially viable popular cinema in English Canada, even to the enviable but still precarious and contradictory level of the Quebec box office. We have the right to this popular film culture in this country, both in the metropoles and in the curling hinterland, as messy and contradictory as that can be, but a popular film culture that escapes being mired in the cynical and commodified masculinism of beer commercials or stuck in the bankruptcy of violence, backlash, displaced desire, and enforced conformity. This popular film culture will respect the pain and anxiety within the crises of masculinity, the traumas that I experiencd in the face of male socialization in Gretzky-land. But it will also search out pleasure, community, and growth beyond the self-laceration, finding in contradictions a space for collective healing and empowerment. (And while we're at it, let's not forget to reconfigure the institutional cultures and economies of sports themselves in this country!)

One sign of hope may be on the small screen, where CTV offered in the 2003 season of LINDA SCHUYLER and Aaron Martin's *Degrassi: The Next*

Generation an out high school hockey star as love interest for its evolving gay protagonist and hockey itself as the crucible where its teenaged boy characters act out in a progressive way their anxieties over masculinity.

If there is otherwise more hope in Quebec for a popular cinema capable of all these things, breaking through the masculinist cults of sports and violence and discovering cinematic narratives true to the fluidity of gender and sexuality, as well as to the beast in the boys and to the queerness of homosociality, let's not give up in Toronto ... or in Fort St James. As Brian Spencer's doomed father in *Gross Misconduct* shouts out moments before being gunned down by the Mounties, in a cry of desperation that could apply not only to the public broadcaster but also to the entire cinematic infrastructure and industry in this country, "I've got a serious disagreement with CBC programming, and there's going to be a revolution unless something changes."

Aside from the work of Brenda Longfellow and John Greyson, there has been little evidence of experimental cinema in this chapter (although I may have overlooked some key films and videos that tie in with my argument). This absence, of course, is symptomatic of the cultures of elitism that I have just decried, but it is also an opportunity for addressing the challenge of masculinism within sports mythologies (as a few heterosexual artists such as Bruce Elder have demonstrated with regard to nonsports imageries). As I write, my former student Brett Kashmere is finishing a short experimental documentary film decorticating the infamous deliberate foul by Canadian hockey player Bobby Clarke that broke the ankle of key Soviet offenseman Valery Kharlamov, thus ensuring the 1972 Summit Series victory – and its spurious key moment in the formation of national identities in this country. While there is unlikely to be a Queer energy to this film, using the avant-garde apparatus to shift the artistic mythology from Paul Henderson's overdone orificial penetration to this moment of violence and shame may well give momentum (and integrity) to the discourses of sports, masculinity, and nationalism in Canadian cinemas.

Queer vs straight is the third polarity. If this chapter has been trying to tease out the "perverse influences" that distance me from mainstream masculine sports mythologies, I have been trying neither to discover a Queer Cinema under the rink nor to set up rigid boundaries between that cinema and our cinema. Coming from a place both outside of and belonging to masculinity, this chapter has sought the commonality and the continuities between so-called queer masculinity and so-called straight masculinity, its borderzones like the Montreal Y and the moose-hunting lodge, the shimmering beasts we share. This is not a longing for acceptance by the curlers, hunters, and defensemen, on-screen or off, but a claiming of our place. We're here, we're queer, so are you.

8

Sex, Money, and Sobriety

trying to find a "positive" or "normal" image of sexual coupling
in Canadian film is very difficult – but not impossible.
~ Katherine Monk, *Weird Sex and Snowshoes*

First of all *Bubbles Galore* is not a pornographic film. It's a very interesting
experimental filmmaker looking at the situation of a woman in a man's world,
trying to make a buck, if you wish, on the production of pornographic films.
There's a high level of irony and satire in the film. Cynthia Roberts has an excellent reputation in the film world. She has won awards throughout the world for
her films ... We have confidence in her, by placing money in her grants so that –
who knows – in five years' time, she produces a film worthy of international
reputation, along the lines of François Girard with *The Red Violin* or Atom Egoyan and any of his films. You're raising the question of whether or not the state
should fund the arts. Arts have always needed funding, whether it has been
from royalty, king, princes, aristocrats, the Vatican – I'm thinking particularly of
the time of the Counter Reformation, the sixteenth and seventeenth centuries,
with the great blossoming of baroque architecture and baroque painting – or
whether it is the current state funding for the arts in Germany, France and Italy.
The artists themselves I believe have an average income of about $13,000 a
year. That is not enough to buy materials – and this is particularly grievous in
the visual arts field – and produce their arts.
~ Shirley Thomson, director, Canada Council, parliamentary hearing,
Heritage Canada, 2000

Sexuality is always notoriously close to the surface in the talk around cinemas in Canada – not only around queer cinemas but around cinemas in general, on-screen and off-screen – and though Katherine Monk may not acknowledge this, where sex rears its head, money always seems to be trailing not far behind, inextricably connected. In this chapter I would like to consider an eclectic cluster of queer films of different genres and contexts that frankly display sexuality – coupled, solo, or group, funded or nonfunded, positive or normal or otherwise – and think about them in material terms. This whole book is about sex, you could say, but this chapter focuses specifically on the nitty-gritty, putting the sex back in (homo)sexuality. First I would like to stretch a bit more the bubble around *Bubbles Galore*, the 1996 Toronto "lesbian porn/feminist fantasy" by CYNTHIA ROBERTS that sparked that characteristic English Canadian mix of sex panic and adulation within the right-wing media and Parliament in 1999. Next I will consider the four feature films of director Roberts's fellow Torontonian BRUCE LABRUCE, whose work also titillated repeatedly throughout the 1990s. His films share with *Bubbles Galore* a number of important qualities: the shared head-on collision with fornication intrinsic to their hybrid vocation of porn and art cinema; their shared propensity towards, not so much metaphorical *money* shots, but rather shots self-consciously showing the transfer of real cash in close-up; an intertextual debt to queer American trash cinema icons Andy Warhol and John Waters (and to nonqueer Russ Meyers, as one reviewer noted with regard to *Bubbles*);[1] and finally a dedication to folks who exchange sex for money, namely sexworkers (*Bubbles* is "dedicated with love to working girls everywhere" and LaBruce's No *Skin off My Ass* "to the Ho").

I will then move beyond this preliminary auteur/art cinema framework, wielded strategically by Canada Council head Shirley Thompson in my epigraph above, invoking no less daunting authorities than the Vatican and Atom Egoyan to defend *Bubbles* from the encircling philistines, in order to discuss a roundup of images and themes from a motley assortment of the queer-friendly Roberts's and the ultra-queer LaBruce's contemporaries and forebears in both English Canada and Quebec. In two sections I will skip about the cultural hierarchy, first considering a spectrum of high-art avant-garde practices that situate themselves in relation to porn – a practice one might call meta-porn – and then the full monty itself, the low down *real* "lesbian [and gay male] porn." In so doing I will explore these films' overlapping interest with the foregoing Toronto "auteurs," that is, the interface of sexual with monetary exchange. I will posit this interface as a recurring determinant of queer sexual cinemas within our national frameworks (all the while keeping in view the range of different sensibilities and contexts, as well as the range of different relationships to the commodification of sexual representation, from complete immersion to critical distance). My fifth and final section will deal not so much with individual films but will corral a particular species of queer sexual *iconography*, visual thematics that are outside of, or in defiance of, the monetary nexus, the diametrical opposition to the "normal and positive coupling" so ardently but vainly championed by Monk in *her* epigraph – namely, "T-room trade," or public/toilet sex.

Overall, one of the major themes to emerge is national (though I hope I will not be as reductive as Monk): surprisingly and not surprisingly the dynamics of our economic dependence on our southern neighbour, whose government would never fund sex films in the "exciting and different" way ours does (as Nina Hartley put it so charmingly),[2] are most vividly played out in the realm of explicit sexual representation. A corollary discovery will be that, paradoxically, it is in the same realm of sexual representation that our queer cinemas assert most vividly some of those stereotypical traits of [English] Canadian identity of which Northrop Frye might have been proud. My selection for this chapter, those cinematic works whose explicit depiction of sexual exchange is most likely to "give you a rod like you would not believe" (whether intentionally or un-),[3] are those most caught up in the Anglo-Calvinist conception of public morality and citizenship: instrumentalism, public service, delayed gratification, and survival. They are most caught up also in the exercise of sobriety, or rather the "discourses of sobriety," to use once again Nichols's shorthand for the vocation of documentary film. It may well be a slightly outdated cliché that Canadian cultures are infected with a documentary sensibility as well as an ineradicable documentary heritage. But looking at these distinct corpuses of sex films, one would be remiss in not identifying something of the sober mission of public education and uplift. Would John Grierson be turning over in his NFB cenotaph? Or would he be even more fascinated than the Reform/Alliance demagogues of 1999 to whom Thompson so eloquently replied?

BUBBLES, BUNNIES, AND BEAVERS

I was in for a surprise when I finally got my hands on a copy of *Bubbles Galore*, one of the most famous, least seen, and least accessible of Canadian feature films (never made available on video), finally screening it a few years after the brouhaha had died down. Somehow I had been conned by yet another critical "consensus" into expecting a *bad* film – I, the epitome of the skeptical Canadian film consumer, taught time and time again not to trust any critic or festival programmer other than my own eyes. With the incestuous suggestibility of the English Canadian media and PR cartel for whom a wire service pull-quote immediately becomes a received opinion and with the fatal combination of all the vested interests and "centricities" (Toronto-, middle-class-, hetero-, and andro-) at play in the critical fraternity, should I not have expected that a cinematic masterpiece was waiting to be discovered? All the more so since the pans from the straight male critics – the very constituency sent up once and for all by the film – were unanimous? To be fair, one *female* critic from the *Toronto Sun*, Claire Bickley, joined the chorus of straight male poopooers, who ranged from the *Globe's* tony John Allemang to the brash new breed of amateur online reviewers, all of whom showed how superior they were to the idea of a feminist porn satire/fantasy and declared, sagely or frothingly, that this was neither effective hard-core heterosexist pornography nor many other things *Bubbles* did not claim to be.[4] ("A film so shockingly bad ... it makes Fran Dresher seem like Katherine Hebpurn ... a piece of crap ... cheesy beyond compare" went one of the frothing online notices.)[5]

Whatever the case, *Bubbles Galore* is indeed, contrary to expectations, a mission accomplished, a very effective exercise in both of those objectives identified by the creators, fantasy and "a high level of irony and satire," both technically competent and aesthetically inventive, an over-the-top contribution to that most rarefied of Canadian genres – arty trash. "Satire" and "fantasy" are not totally accurate labels for the aesthetics of trash but passable common-denominator labels for arts bureaucrats and demagogues alike, serviceable for the difficult task of describing for the uninitiated this volatile mix of postmodern pastiche, high-camp subversion, and ideological critique and appropriation. "Garbage" is not exactly "trash" in terms of cinematic taxonomy, of course, but Canadian Alliance demagogue Monte Solberg was relatively close to the truth for once in denouncing *Bubbles* in the House of Commons as "garbage" and, what is more, the very garbage that makes Canadians pay the highest taxes in their history.

The plot has everything to offer the porn connoisseur who savours hokey narrative pretexts almost as much as hard-core action numbers: a vaguely plausible boardroom/bedroom potboiler where Bubbles (Nina Hartley), a pornstar-turned-director/entrepreneur, must defend her new market niche against her rabidly vengeful displaced competitor and ex-lover, Godfrey Montana (DANIEL MACIVOR). Bubbles has a serious deadline for her next production and for the lead role must train a new starlet, Dory Drawers, despite her virginal inexperience; the latter, unbeknownst to all, is a reincarnated murdered hooker sent back to earth to "make it a safer place for all sex workers, porn actors, strippers, prostitutes everywhere." Further plot twists involve Bubbles's former leading man, Buck, down-and-out and substance-dependent, who can't get his two-foot prosthesis up, and her loyal assistant Vivian Klitorsky, who's been carrying a torch for her boss all these years and finally, after a few plot meanders, gets to realize her desire. The villain and his two sneering rapist henchmen get their comeuppance at the end, but this is not surprising, since all the proceedings are orchestrated by God or, rather, by a neo-feminist pro-sex pagan deity in the person of feminist sex activist Annie Sprinkle. When the interiors need air, *Bubbles* even offers a very Toronto sense of place for the down-to-earth, realist-minded Canadian spectator, from the phallic jokiness around the CN Tower to the wintry chase scene on Toronto Island and the Yonge Street cutaways – even a Canadian flag insert to remind one and all of its Heritage Canada sponsorship. All the spatial referents, not to mention the uncharacteristically recognizable *Canadian* one-hundred-dollar bills bandied about, compound the delicious weirdness of the conceit of a *Canadian* porn industry! (More on the reality of that industry later).

Variety complained about the film's low production values (21 October 1996) – a standard displaced lament by deflated straight male reviewers about a film that upsets them – but in fact for a low-budget Canadian feature with minimal Telefilm support, the film's cinematography, art design, and mise-en-scène are all impressively resourceful. Its look is dominated by gels, golden glows, and rosy auras, a "wash of pink" to express Roberts's "divine, orgasmic energy that we don't normally see [in porn]"[6] (in one high camp self-reflexive moment Bubbles examines and chooses gels for her porno within the porno, with all the seriousness of a Tippi Hedren). The editing is also clearly a labour of love, from the efficient, climactic intercutting of narrative threads to the great blossoming of baroque special effects of the layered divine dimension and her decoratively overlaid, sperm-like angel dust. As for the film's status as porn, the straight male reviewers got at least this part right: there's no hard-core at all, but the softcore girl-girl action is plentiful between Bubbles and Dory, between Bubbles and Vivian, and between Bubbles's legs in the shower and elsewhere, not to mention the walk-on go-go girl gyraters regularly decorating the corners of the screen. And from what I could tell as a nonimplicated viewer, the "steamorama" (to use the generic *Variety* term) is as effective and celebratory as it is felt. Roberts herself confesses in one interview to being especially fond of "the love scene where Nina sort of flips her leg back, and one of her stiletto pumps gently touches her own buttock" (Alioff 1997). The blatant artifice of the prostheses attached to the MacIvor character, as well as to the superannuated Buck, admittedly undercuts the sustained erotic effect. In fact, the whole film solicits a double consciousness on the part of the viewer – a positioning that, come to think of it, porn shares with most English Canadian feature filmmaking – the pleasure of the flesh and the look and, at the same time, the pleasure of distancing through the layers of irony, stylization, didacticism, self-consciousness, or discomfort. And to complete both the porno discourse and the Canadian aura, the credits offer a whole gamut of pseudonymous craft credits (e.g., "Sound – Mindy Melons; Assistant Art Director – Selina Stroker") ironically bringing together the economic realpolitik of a nonunion "poverty row" Canadian production with the career stigma of porno.

Many of the critics' complaints dwell on the acting with literal-minded reductiveness, as is usual with both porn and Canadian cinema. But as is often the case with English Canadian features, the film offers a connoisseur's delight in comparative national thespiantics/histrionics. The U.S. star leads reign with authority and confidence, the California porn diva Hartley offering a performance as the glamorous but put upon porn impresario Bubbles that is uncannily similar to that of Lana Turner in *Imitation of Life*, emoting the same kind of wooden authenticity (and, as with Lana, not a hair or trace of lip liner is out of place); Sprinkle's God, in what was clearly a half day quickie shoot (on a Long Island Beach, according to the credits), does what the neofeminist sexual activist always does, perform interactively and winkingly for the lens in a kind of burlesque queen complicity, and her performance is woven editorially into the film as a presiding fairy godmother muse for the proceedings. Meanwhile, the supporting Canadian cast have a different style and have to do all the "real" acting, whether that is the sniggering grand guignol of Toronto queer theatre stalwarts Daniel MacIvor and SKY GILBERT, clearly relishing the respective roles of archvillain porn tycoon and his right-hand goon or of Tracy Wright, like the men a distinguished Toronto theatre actor playing the long-suffering Vivian, got up just fetchingly butch enough to ensure a role-playing erotic frisson in her climactic copulation with the autopilot Hartley. And then there's the genuinely Hamilton-bred "Penthouse Pet" Shauny Sexton, who plays the reincarnated ingenue porn nymphet Dory as if everything depended on how sincerely she's memorized her lines rather than on how radiantly platinum and bosomy physicality.

Much debate within the sympathetic cultural community attempted to analyze what had triggered the brouhaha. In introducing the film for its momentous post-brouhaha *Showcase* broadcast in 1999, Cameron Bailey hypothesized:

You know I think the reason the editorialists and politicians got so hot and bothered about it isn't just the sex. Canadian filmmakers excel at putting sex on the screen. That's what we do. I think it's more the feminism. It's the idea of a woman choosing to produce sex films, choosing to take control inside the sex industry. I don't know why exactly it scares some people but it does. So does the way Cynthia Roberts smears those borders between straight and gay, between art and erotica, between politics and comedy. Cynthia Roberts never gives you sex straight up, there's always a twist, and as Martha Stewart says, that's a good thing.

Aside from the relevance of bringing yet another American blonde tycoon into the discussion, Bailey is onto an issue with the "smeared borders," but as we see repeatedly in this book, anxiety over such queerly smeared borders is not confined to sexist prairie demagogues and in fact infects queer audiences themselves. Otherwise, I think Bailey underestimates the self-reinforcing populist resentment against elite groups to which both artists and queers allegedly belong and gives the demagogues too much credit in attributing any identifiable conscious logic to the response at all – even in the unlikely event that they actually ever saw the film! Roberts herself may also be onto something about talk as an inchoate psychic avoidance, about what Foucault would call the transformation of sexuality into discourse ([1976] 1990, 15ff.): "My movie has given members of the Reform party a chance to talk about sex without having to admit that they like talking about it – and without having to admit that they actually enjoy having sex like everyone else."7 And I would not discount Chantal Nadeau's interpretation that an anti-American reaction also fed the flames (the beavers threatened by the bunnies, as she puts it), a hinterland presumption that Canadians do not and should not make such things as porn or trash or even art and entertainment (2000). I insist, however, that the knee-jerk reaction could also be traced (insofar as censorship panics in their opportunism and arbitrariness are ever about *anything*) to the L-word, a word that historically has proven to have an uncanny ballistic potential in Alberta (Gilbert 1999). All are compounded, of course, by the very scary combination of sex and money and the inherited Calvinist double standard about both.

What struck me as among the most interesting aspects of the film, however, beyond the scandal it caused, is linked to Bailey's perception that Roberts always delivers sex with a twist. To my mind, its *didactic* twist constitutes perhaps its queerest and most Canadian aspect. Beyond the amplitude and self-indulgence of its girl-girl cheesecake element, it is most striking for its pedagogical fervour, the integration of learning with pleasure in the whorey, er ... hoary old Brechtian formula. Hartley and Sprinkle both have had missionary vocations in their U.S.-based porno careers for almost twenty years now, and Roberts clearly recruited them with this in mind. Their bountiful sermons are as trashy, as tongue-in-cheek – and as deadly serious – as the sex. Object lessons and pedagogical props are everywhere, from the large satin cunt and condom on a crystalline demonstration dildo for Dory's orientation workshop to the didactic dialogue delivered straight up on at least two occasions in the slightly reworked 1999 *Showcase* version of the film. (This must be the element *Variety* found clunky and sentimental, I believe.) A whole scene is set up with a journalist patently in order to allow Bubbles to make an explicit reference to the obscenity of the

Bubbles Galore (1996), Cynthia Roberts's "lesbian porn" "garbage:" Will the bunny from Hamilton (centre) come between the lonely Canadian butch (left) and her voluptuous American boss (porno matriarch Nina Hartley, right)? Production still, Greg Klymkiw and Cynthia Roberts, Horsy Productions 1996

1992 Butler decision, which transformed Canadian obscenity jurisprudence and stepped up homophobic censorship with its pseudofeminist criterion of "degradation":[8] "I don't think pornography is inherently degrading. No, what is wrong is denying women executives creative and managerial control in an industry wherein its greatest commodity and its greatest number of workers are women." Aside from this literalism, the entire project of recuperating the tawdry pseudo-lesbian formulae of *Penthouse* and Meyer parallels the 1980s initiatives in the United States of Hartley and Sprinkle, along with Candida Royalle and others, initiatives that were originally aimed at politicizing and feminizing porn. Roberts adapts those initiatives for feminist and Canadian politics with rosy-gelled romanticism, updating them this time with a queer-positive plot, a positive role-model narrative complete with happy ending, and, in the spirit of NAFTA, the reunion of the lonely Canadian butch, together at last, with her voluptuous blonde American boss.

Interestingly, a Quebec film was being hatched just as the *Bubbles Galore* scandal was being played out across the Ottawa River, a film that was in many ways its documentary version: the grafting of pleasure onto the traditional medium of sobriety, in order to counter the earlier cross-fertilization of didacticism onto the medium of pleasure. Marielle Nitoslawska's hour-long TV documentary *Bad Girl* (2001) features the same message of women's empowerment through sexual images, as well as the same stars, Sprinkle and Hartley, and in one memorable scene shows the latter efficiently but distractedly jerking a man off as she delivers to the camera a version of the same sermon as in *Bubbles*. Elsewhere, Hartley is revealed as a real-life version of the Bubbles character, shown striding efficiently about her San Fernando Valley porn factory-warehouse in her neat business suit, the mistress of her market. Nitoslawska includes California and Las Vegas as primary stops in her investigation, fascinated with the runaway commercialization and glitzy hucksterism of the industry, and she also interviews Berkeley porn expert Linda Williams and several grotesque male luminaries of the scene. But *Bad Girl*, in a reflection of its Télé-Québec financing, by and large substitutes a European-flavoured intellectualism for the American glitz, injecting French art films and philosophers (feminist theorist/den mother Luce Irigaray!) into the mix (*sans* substantial Canadian content, oddly enough). At the same time *Bad Girl* offers much more hard-core imagery than *Bubbles*, and, not surprisingly, it got caught up in its own dynamics of censorship. Though it sparked no parliamentary shenanigans despite having been financed by largely the same government bodies (or their Quebec equivalents) as *Bubbles*, the frequent recourse to male genital action clearly panicked the public broadcaster as the original broadcast date approached. Nitoslawska defied the pressure to soften up her film, and the network eventually rescheduled the broadcast six months later in a late-night time slot. An apparent internal self-censorship dynamic also led to exclusion of the lesbian branch of the women's erotica movement from her survey, though heterosexuals Nitoslawska and her producers would prefer to cast the decision as a focusing process rather than an exclusion. Nevertheless the final shots of the film are a deliciously aestheticized extreme closeup of rosy girl-girl kissing (Nitoslawska is a virtuoso camerawoman) that resonated as an unspoken overtone and afterimage.

BRUCE

If any Canadian filmmaker laid the ground for their straight country-woman's bubbly fun with trash, arousal, and didacticism, it was Bruce LaBruce. Was the washed-up porno star character in *Bubbles Galore* an echo of that earlier immortal characterization by LaBruce himself as the porno star has-been in *Super 8½* Regardless, unlike Roberts and many other sex film producers in Canada, and much to the regret of the Opposition, no doubt, LaBruce's work has never been financed by public agencies (aside from a few Ottawa-funded trips to foreign film festivals once LaBruce became a Canadian cultural icon). And he's proud of it. It all adds up to his multiple and contradictory persona: one of the few commercially viable queer feature filmmakers in Canada, perhaps the only one not plugged into the Telefilm trough, and at the same time the one most obsessed with the sex-money nexus in his work and the most contemptuous of the new world order of commodified relationships, desires, and identities. It's paradoxical too that LaBruce is also the unabashed author of the most romantic views of coupledom (and the sexiest films) in the Canadian corpus. Is this contradictory elusiveness a contributing factor to LaBruce's status of prophet without honour in his own country – as with a small elite of artists in this book – more successful in foreign markets than at home? Often touted as a key player in the so-called international New Queer Cinema of the 1990s, LaBruce has not a single one of his four or five video features (depending on how you count) available from Canadian distributors.

Prolific, complex, elusive, and volatile, LaBruce's oeuvre is sometimes difficult to distinguish from his prolific, complex, elusive and volatile persona as lead performer at centre stage in the three first features, *No Skin off My Ass* (1991), *Super 8½* (1994), and *Hustler White* (1996). These films are thus not only notable for their explicit erotic episodes but self-reflexive as treatises on movie-making and a moviemaker – as such they are also self-criticizing. LaBruce thus makes the job of the critic especially hard, if not superfluous. In comparison, John Greyson, Toronto's other queer pomo narrative essayist most commonly connected to the international New Queer Cinema, is a critic's dream: discreetly self-effacing behind the camera rather than heart-on-screen self-obsessed star persona; sweet-tempered and tripod-steady rather than self-indulgent steadi-cam rollercoaster; communitarian coalitionist rather than rampant iconoclast/individualist; subversively risqué rather than confrontationally hard-core; a romantic hiding behind modernist analysis rather than a romantic hiding behind antisentimental iconoclasm. No wonder that Greyson's work has attracted an orderly and growing accumulation of scholarly articles, while LaBruce is banned from the respectable reference works,[9] the object of an erratic and cultish attention at best. Despite his household-word status, few Canadian critics have even begun to do him justice (other than MATTHEW HAYS and DAVID MCINTOSH, programmer for "Perspective Canada"), and it's his New York, London, and Paris critics who have come to the rescue.[10] (LaBruce himself is a prolific and engaging writer whose output nicely complements his on-screen work, one of many things he has in common with Greyson.) This book cannot remedy the neglect, but nevertheless, in keeping with the theme of this chapter, I would like to start the process by offering a focused reading of the three films in terms of their queer explorations of the sex-money nexus and ending up once more, believe it or not, finding a very Canadian sensibility of documentary authenticity and public education. The three feature-length narrative essays form a kind of gradually escalating, unintended trilogy that justify a *vue d'ensemble,* and I shall save my look at LaBruce's later softcore/hard-core feature combo *Skin Flick/Skin Gang* (1999) for a little bit later.

Fresh from making his mark as "homocore" 'zine activist and Super 8 rabble-rouser (and a Dr Jekyll-esque career as irreverent but academic film critic under the name of Bryan Bruce in the Toronto magazine *Cineaction!*), LaBruce developed No *Skin off My Ass* ostensibly as a remake of Robert Altman's kinky 1969 melodrama with Sandy Dennis, *That Cold Day in the Park*. In that film a repressed upper-middle-class "spinster" finds a hunky drifter in the park, shelters him in her posh apartment, develops an erotic obsession with her mute house guest, and goes to extremes to keep him. With LaBruce it's a petit bourgeois hairdresser and his indigent skinhead protégé, played by then boyfriend Klaus von Brucker (pseudonym for NICHOLAS DAVIES), whose encounter ultimately turns into a sensuous and reciprocal romance (quite unlike Altman's downbeat film, which slides into a denouement of murderous psychosis and surrender). In *Skin* this relationship is interwoven with a subplot about the skinhead's sister (played by Bruce's former fanzine collaborator G.B. JONES) who is making a film *Women of the SLA* and who spends valuable screen test/audition time discussing revolutionary politics with her female cast and interfering in her brother's life with a controlling, even incestuous, attitude.

The economic dynamics of both narratives are played out in discourses of class and work. The women's glib rhetoric about antibourgeois violence intersects with the skin's life-style revolt against capitalist conformity, which in turn must measure up against the sister's summation of the class differential between gay men and skins – "Being a fag is a definite plus, better than being a skin" – and his de facto status as a kept boy bounces off the women's pseudofeminist ideology. The film's zero-production-value aesthetic (for example, flouting the basic standards of sync sound) and that of the film within the film, whose shoot is finally stopped for funding reasons, matches the skin's poverty-inflected social status and personal style. And the whole matrix comes out in the LaBruce character's voice-over commentary on the crisis around his livelihood: "I'm a hairdresser. I have a very loyal clientele. I make a pretty good living at it, I guess. But I've been having some problems. Since I discovered skinheads, my heart's just not in it anymore … Now, a shaved head is the only haircut that makes sense any more. I feel like throwing away all my brushes, combs, scissors, shampoos – everything but my electric clippers."

The workplace scenes of Bruce attending to his trendy customers distractedly and with increasing hostility in his "subcultural chic" skull-etched T-shirt and leather accoutrements, show this vocational crisis and lead into an extremely powerful long sequence that is in many ways the centrepiece of the film. The shots of haircutting as workplace alienation are intercut with shots of haircutting as fetish eroticism, with shirtless Bruce fastidiously clipping and caressing towel-wrapped Klaus, with the ritual of erotic grooming displaying increasing tenderness. The minimalist aesthetic of these shots, lovingly extended (the whole sequence lasts almost eight minutes) is yet another Warhol homage (to *Haircut*, 1963) in an oeuvre already overflowing with Warhol-winking. On the soundtrack, meanwhile, is Bruce's voice-over reading of a semischolarly ethnographic account of skinhead politics, culture, and style. Over seven hundred words in length and clocking in at almost eight minutes, the unexpurgated text has an aesthetics that is also very Warholian (if not Straubian) but also has an undeniable and vivid expository operation:

The skinhead cut is a smart clean and tight one which proclaims identity. The young people who developed this style rejected the finery and the slightly effeminate characteristics of the art college kids and the hippies for clothes that were more related to their working-class background ... Fathers liked the style because it was neat and workmanlike. Unlike the families of middle-class dropouts, skinhead families were generally supportive, helping with money and acting as some sort of barrier against school and the police. A skin would normally live at home.

There are periodic cutaways to shots of Bruce reading the magazine that is the source of this account, first in the hair parlour, neglecting his clients under the dryers, and then in his apartment. Meanwhile, as the text unfolds, the interwoven scenes of professional haircutting and fetish haircutting yield to another grooming scene, namely the film's second bathtub set piece: Klaus and Bruce share a bubble bath together (with Bruce periodically absenting himself to attend to the tripod). There inevitably follows an explicit scene of kissing, sucking, and jerking to climax, one also of ineffable tenderness but matter-of-fact at the same time, and, to this jaded old shower queen's taste, the hottest scene in world film history – despite the maintenance of the surprisingly sober documentary voice-over all the while! *The Village Voice*'s Amy Taubin (12 November 1991) incongruously called NSOMA "more aesthetic than sexual" (this from the critic who once called *Haircut* the most erotic film ever made? [December 1990]), but the aesthetics compound the sexual and vice versa (as Taubin's colleague James Hannaham perceptively

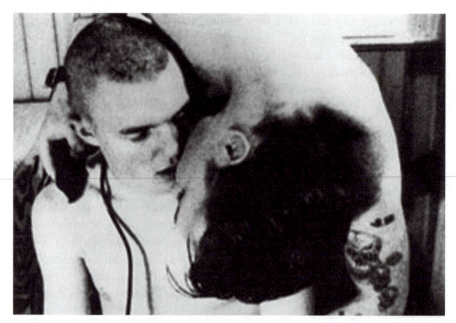

The didactic haircut scene from *No Skin off My Ass* (1991): haircutting shown as workplace alienation, fetish eroticism, and skinhead ethnography, with shirtless Bruce (foreground) fastidiously clipping and caressing towel-wrapped Klaus. Production still, courtesy Bruce LaBruce

put it with regard to *Super 8½*, "art that jerks off *with* you, not at you" [14 March 1995]). The soundtrack's excursus into ethnographic documentary mode, as the whole sequence comes to closure, is matched on the image track by an excursus into sexual documentary, with the explicit images of response and jouissance offering their own didactic meaning of real bodies, real response, and real interaction. This of course is a feature of all hardcore, with the nudity, hard-on, and money shots always attesting to the "reality effect/truth value" of the scene. But this effect is heightened here with the film's additional layer of autobiographical resonance, together with LaBruce's orchestration of real-world-identity performance by his nonprofessional cast, outside of porno conventions.

No Skin off My Ass is in retrospect, for all its complexity, the simplest and most romantic of LaBruce's three narratives. Its elements of sexual representation, materialist analysis, and documentary orientation are heightened in the subsequent two features. *Super 8½*, subtitled *A Cautionary Biopic*, is ostensibly a remake of *Play It As It Lays* (1972), but in fact it mimics every Hollywood backstage epic of celebrity decline from *Citizen Kane* to *Valley of the Dolls* to *The Rose*. The plot is straightforward: washed-up porno star Bruce agrees to appear in up-and-coming Warhol-type filmmaker Googie's latest film, his last chance at a comeback. But she's only exploiting him in order to finance her film *Submit to My Finger* with the far-out lesbian Friday Sisters, and Bruce's descent into breakdown and madness continues. This narrative line is the base for an extravagant intertextual web of films within films (hers and his), edgy and explicit sexual segues and performances, and self-reflexive discursive digressions of every other kind as well, in short, what is variously referred to hyperbolically by critics as a "deconstructionist's wet dream," (Hannaham 1995) or "a map of the collective homo unconscious" (McIntosh 1997, 149). This dream/map "crazy quilt" is stuffed with transactions and transgressions, both sexual and economic, from rape to shoplifting. But the prevailing metaphor is sexwork, set up as an analogy to filmmaking and pornography. One of many set pieces is the Friday Sisters' screen test for Googie, which the Bruce character has agreed to direct: these two naughty and bewigged women improvise for the camera, talking mostly about their work as prostitutes and strippers, going on about such vocational hazards as VD, and offering burlesque performances of shimmies and gyrations as illustrations of their (p)lay-for-pay techniques. The cash nexus is explicit: "As long as [straight male customers] pay, the money's the same colour. Sometimes if you just sit there they pay you hundreds of dollars to just sit there." The Bruce character's attitude towards pornography is similarly articulate and mercenary: "A French critic once called my work 'pornology' because it was like a study of pornography. After throwing up neatly, I said no, I make 'pornology,' because I want to have a monopoly on pornography so I can make some money. You see, I've been called a cult director with a nose for commerce." The attitude applies equally to legitimate film, with added jibes about Canadian governmentality "I knew she was only making a movie about me so she could get some financial backing. I mean, anything with a fag in it was getting money that year" and a diatribe to his sleepy hustler partner about the work ethic and low-budget arts funding reminiscent of Divine's assumption of a thrifty housewife persona in *Female Trouble* (1974): "And look at you! Wasting your time with this petty nickel and dime hustling when you could be out there parlaying your slightly conventional and classical yet idiosyncratic and modern good looks into money in the bank! Somebody has to pay those bills, but it won't be me. Not with roles in underground art films like this." The sex scenes, not surprisingly, all involve performances with this same aura of cynical sexuality for hire.

The film's most virtuoso and inspired sequence is the comic sex scene with scrappy hustler Johnny Eczema. In this accidentally recorded out-take from *Super 8½* (the film within the film), the tropes of sex, money, film, and pornography all come together. It starts with a Brechtian clapper insert, then a close-up revelation of Johnny and Bruce kissing, with the former shown twisting his neck to push his mugging face into the lens, then a zoom-out to a classically composed lateral long-shot tableau in a glistening white backdrop. The whole moment is interrupted when Bruce accuses Johnny of trying to upstage him – rightfully, as we have seen. An escalation follows as the two performers trade accusations and insults related mostly to porn industry status, all the while dressing partially and dodging the hovering boom mike; Bruce fires and hurls a drink at Johnny, who lashes back with a blow to the face, provoking a melodramatic nosebleed and then a nasty kick, which leads to more retaliation by the aggrieved hustler costar.

At that point the camera rolls out in a Warholian flash whiteout, and when the image returns we are straight in the midst of a close-up blowjob, with the incorrigible Johnny, at the receiving end, still concentrating more on the camera lens than his fellater. The sequence of events is not clear (a reconcilation sequel? an alternative syntagm?), and the style is completely different. A graceful and intimate hand-held camera now captures the hardcore interaction, masterfully racking focus throughout to register the interactivity at very close range – intense reciprocated sucking and kissing – and finally returns to the original sofa tableau, with an "authentic" anal-penetration scene this time establishing a kind of symmetry to a sequence that at this point has lasted almost eight minutes. The montage includes ample meat shots, as Bruce manipulates himself into ejaculation with Johnny deep inside him, followed, not by the conventional first-you-now-me turn of the penetrator for a money shot, but by more postcoital kissing and hugging. The scene is fluid and beautifully shot and edited (and, incidentally, a shimmering black and white reminder of what we lost aesthetically when porn switched to colour in the late sixties). But just in case this intense and inventive lyricism goes too far, LaBruce typically undercuts the whole scene with an apparently looped reprise of the synthetic and kitschy score from the sixties porn film *Sweden Heaven or Hell*, no doubt stolen, and in the last minute with Googie's snide voice-over about the meaning of the title *Super 8½*, juxtaposing cinephilic reference to Fellini with a denigration (by all evidence, unjustly) of Bruce's cock size.

The sequence encapsulates concisely the entire sex-money matrix of LaBruce's work, as McIntosh summarizes: "In exploiting himself as the central image in his exposé of the lurid workings of desire's circulation system in the porn realm, LaBruce succeeded in eroticizing the endlessly reproduceable sex-self-fame-money equation itself" (1997, 152).

The key is that, as LaBruce's terse découpage of the film in *Ride Queer Ride* matter-of-factly mentions, the sex in this scene is "unsimulated," but this is more important than he lets on. The performance not only continues LaBruce's campaign to shatter art film conventions but also steps up the terms of the documentary element within this convergence of discourses:

after the play with simulated nonfiction conventions throughout the film, in, say, the Friday Sisters' clever improvisation on-camera or the contrived randomness of the cinematography during the fight, the sequence has climaxed in the real thing, in a self-reflexive, indexical record of desire, response, and performance. Or as McIntosh put it, "but his most important signifier of authenticity by far is pornography – hard-core representations of cocksucking, ass fucking, piss drinking, fisting. Without the regular hardcore porn intervals, *Super 8½* would just be another embarrassing fashion and attitude exercise. Of all our industrially exploitable selves, the eroticized meat self is the most authentic, the most renewable and the most liberating" (1997, 151).

Bruce LaBruce (right) as dubious sex researcher Jurgen Anger in *Hustler White* (1996), his pseudo-ethnographic homage to the L.A. strip. The celebrity frissons of boy toy Tony Ward's performance (left) add to the "sex-self-fame-money equation." Production still, courtesy Bruce LaBruce

Hustler White, LaBruce's pseudo-ethnographic narrative essay on Santa Monica Boulevard's hustler strip, released two years later in 1996, develops further this sex-self-fame-money equation through a documentary discourse, the most explicit yet. This film is another romance featuring the author himself as star (Jurgen Anger, a composite of his German producer's first name with the surname of an earlier Los Angeles queer rebel), this time with much-touted celebrity Madonna-protégé Tony Ward as Monty, his hustler love interest. The intertextual mosaic is consecrated this time, not to the porn/film milieu as metaphor of prostitution, but to prostitution itself in the literal sense. *Hustler White* doesn't compete with the earlier two features in the hard-core sexual-representation department (it's preponderantly soft, with no money shots and only a few long-shot hand jobs). It makes up for this restraint with the authenticity of diversity rather than intensity, with the trope of the "outer limit"spectrum of marginal sexuality: the notorious stump-fucking of the amputation fetishist (in lateral long shot, so maybe …) and other SM moments, notably the application of cigarette burns on an all-too-eager, strung-up elderly Englishman (something mainstream reviewers found no less strong than the relatively "inner limits" vanilla meat shots of the two earlier films).

Perhaps even more important is the vivid participation on-screen and off-screen of the hardworking denizens of Hollywood's hustler strip themselves, recruited by LaBruce's participant observer co-director, photographer Rick Castro – a guarantee of an equivalent resonance of social veracity and ethical accountability. The frissons arising from the explicit sexual performance of the brave celebrity star Ward – no stranger to similar discourses in his collaborations with Herself – also contribute to this sex-truth resonance. Furthermore, as befits the subject of sexwork, the money connection is the most explicit of that of the three features. There are no fewer than four insert shots of cash being exchanged within sexual-exchange scenes, usually close-ups of bills being piled on a bedsheet. The last one is under Ward's voice-over explanation of the fluctuations and devaluations in sex-work rates, and the dialogue elsewhere is no less concrete. Not that the materialist analysis doesn't have its own romantic curve in Monty's trajectory from john-rolling to freebies ("You know now that we're collaborators you can do anything you like – on me, no charge," he announces to his newfound love Jurgen as the dénouement impends).

Meanwhile, *Hustler White*'s fictional documentary pretext is winkingly set up and fleshed out as part of the intertextual fabric. If in *Skin* the films within the film were underground Warholian screen tests and if in *Super 8½* they were porno and art film shorts, in *Hustler White* the camouflaged sexual research documentaries of the sexual revolution are referenced. In answer to a street prospector's assertion that Jurgen knows why he's really here, the latter replies with queenly condescension, "I assure you I am here strictly for anthropological reasons. I'm conducting research for a book I'm writing," a homage to all the suspect documentary subterfuges of LaBruce's favourite period, the fifties and sixties, where the censorship regime required the cloak of documentary pretension over sexual representations from *Glen or Glenda* (1953) to *Mondo Bizarro* (1966). But for all this trash-flavoured disavowal of sexual interest, the documentary layer of the film is at the same time very straight, sober, and thick indeed, and not only at the level of the on-camera bodies and performances of the native informants. Significant swatches of the film function effectively as authentic exposition, for example, the repeated evocative landscape tropes of lyrical low-angle travelling processions down the Boulevard, past its legendary hustler hangouts and the Stupid Light gay bookstore and all those rainbow flags (both of which denote the anathema of "gay community" for LaBruce and his fictional mouthpiece Monty) or of the sunny street corners and curbside telephone boxes that serve as backdrops to the scenes of public interaction of hustlers with customers or each other. If *Skin* and *Super* were grey Toronto city films, *Hustler White* is an LA city symphony sun-drenched with colour. Meanwhile raw expository data are delivered on the soundtrack by Jurgen (into his tacky tape recorder) or by his insider informant Monty or else inscribed on the screened surface of his laptop. Even the comic tropes have their expository function, as in the gang bang sequence, an excursus on race within the Hollywood hustler subculture. The sequence also becomes a footnote on network communication logistics when all seven or eight bangers simultaneously halt their banging to check their pagers. LaBruce has tirelessly railed against the New Queer Cinema and may well make the claim, "You see, I don't feel I have a lot in common with a bunch of rich kids who have degrees in semiotic theory, who make dry, academic films with overdetermined AIDS metaphors and *Advocate* men in them." (1997, 15). His films are not dry, but he shares more than he admits with the overdetermined metaphors and didactic discourses of his peers. Certainly, in what crystallizes with the final film *Hustler White* as a trilogy of sex, money, and sobriety, LaBruce is unsurpassed for an instructional orientation mixed à la Brecht with pleasure – and with the queer-core ingredient of unbridled taboo lust mixed in for good measure.

PORN AND META-PORN

Regardless of the existential questions you may encounter, all that is really important is that you will need a towel.
~ "Lodger," Filethirteen[11]

Imported American film, video, and magazine pornographies have constituted, without a doubt, the overwhelming common cultural reference for gay male artists and audiences north of the forty-ninth parallel, arguably since the beginning of the seventies. In this section I will start by exploring an assortment of film and videomakers who sometimes probed the newly expanded horizons of explicit sexual representation but more often and more importantly produced a kind of "meta-porn," encompassing a spectrum of avant-garde practices but all referencing explicit imported erotic film or video in their work, starting in the mid-1980s. I will then examine a few of the home-grown porno products designed to compete with the import market, both gay male and lesbian. This section will keep in view throughout the individual quirks within my eclectic assortment of queer artists, but overall it will demonstrate that queer Canadian meta-porn and porn anticipate or echo Roberts's and LaBruce's preoccupation with sexual and monetary exchange as a shared theme of Canadian queer cinemas, together with their orientation toward a documentary mission of public didacticism.

Before the 1969 Omnibus Bill, to my knowledge any serious erotic filmmaking in Canada was soft-core and belonged to the "physique" network (Waugh 1996, 176–283; 1998, 53–80). Montrealer ALAN B. STONE's quirky 8mm posers of his populist hunk champions strutting and flexing awkwardly on the St Lawrence waterfront may be the only extant examples. The first public/theatrical exhibition of imported hard-core gay porn in Toronto reportedly took place in 1973 at Rochdale College, the high-rise fortress of the rebel University of Toronto student union, in the context of a defiant series of porno screenings organized by Reg Hartt over that and the following year. *The Body Politic*'s Robert Trow found the Wakefield Poole classics *Boys in the Sand* (1971) and *Bijou* (1972) boring and, oddly enough, preferred the hetero hit *Devil in Miss Jones* (1972) because of the "authenticity" of its lesbian sex scenes. Later that same year, the Club Baths is reported to have been showing the same films in weekly programs, but it is hard to imagine they got away with that for very long in Toronto. No doubt other similar fly-by-night screenings were taking place in Montreal, Vancouver, and elsewhere in Toronto during the seventies, but because of the tight regulatory climate, regular public exhibition of porno in Canada was limited to heterosexual materials – and mostly softcore at that. Otherwise, throughout the seventies the circulation of hard-core gay porno was by and large an irregular and private affair, principally on Super 8, which in its last decade as a commercial medium had acquired sound and adapted easily to the new hard-core commercial reality in the United States. Most of these materials were illicit, acquired by tourists in the States and through "special" arrangements by local sex shops as well, especially in Montreal. One mail order firm, Cinerex, advertised thirty-two Super 8 titles in Montreal as late as 1981, apparently taking advantage of the increasingly tolerant atmosphere to unload stock that would soon be going the way of the dodo. Another major supplier, an East End sex shop, gave up on their Super 8 trade much earlier than this, not because of technical obsolescence or because the vice squad could find their cache carefully hidden under a floor (it tried but couldn't) but because it was no longer worth the effort and harassment.[12]

All that changed at the start of the 1980s, when the VCR home video revolution transformed the audio-visual cultural environment and shifted porno from the public arena to the living room as a privately consumed commodity. The new Beta and VHS cassettes were still technically illegal in the early eighties, but they began to circulate all the same more or less freely across the porous border. Starting around 1982, illicitly duplicated porno cassettes became freely available from at least one Montreal dealer, and no doubt licit copies from the Vancouver mail order firms Stallion and After Dark. As the decade came to an end, the trade was completely regularized, rights and all, but the Montreal up-front merchandising was still an anomaly in Canada as the bug-eyed tourists from Toronto kept exclaiming. (Toronto didn't join the brave new world of over-the-counter hard-core video until around 1991.) Montreal also saw a whole decade of theatrical exhibition of gay porn in Priape's legendary Cinéma du Village between 1984 and 1994, at a time when the public exhibition of gay porno was quickly dying out south of the border. Regardless of the quirks and fluctuations in the gradual implantation of marketplace legitimacy, the new imported iconography left a permanent imprint on the gay male visual imaginary across Canada.

Several rather brave artists began to explore the newly permitted iconography of explicit representation. In Toronto, COLIN CAMPBELL's *White Money* (1983) was probably the first Toronto work to splash – or rather sprinkle – hard-core same-sex humping and sucking on the small screen, but the effect was more timorous and coy than focused and bold. This diffuse send-up of carnality and storytelling in Florida offers mostly Campbell's characteristic run-on monologues by deadpan artworld trash (male and female, one in Spanish), but staged tableaus of female-on-female SM (soft-core wax-dripping and high-fashion bondage) flesh out the assemblage, and there are a half dozen flashes of male-on-male hard-core humping and sucking inserted as additional spice or punctuation. The latter effect is tentative and even apologetic, but at least it tested the water. Two years later JOHN GREYSON's third instalment of the Kipling trilogy, *Kipling Meets the Cowboys* (1985), unfolds in large part on the set of a Toronto multiracial gay porno shoot in which nude cowboys dangle, diddle, cuddle, and lipsync to Roy Rogers western songs – an unlikely fantasy world where porno production is normalized, politically correct, and luscious fun, if lamentably soft-core.

Perhaps the most concentrated experiment with hard-core sexual representation in Toronto came two years later with MICHAEL BALSER's *Pogo Stick Porno Romp* (co-signed by Balser's lover, visual artist Andy Fabo). This essay on nature, culture, and sexuality, while reflecting tendencies of the Ontario College of Art and Design (OCAD) video school towards a not always successful intellectualization, vividly deploys sexualized animal images both in a playground and on Fabo's superimposed fantasy graphics of phallic stallions and the like. It culminates in strong and sustained images of the lovers having vigorous oral sex and otherwise rubbing and juxtapositioning their impressively snake-like penises. The effect is heightened as usual by extratextual knowledge of the autobiographical nature of the sexual performances. The same is true of *In the Dark* (1986), the previous year's autobiographical opposite-sex fuck peformance by the Toronto video scene's first couple, LISA STEELE and Kim Tomzcak, but this latter tape (since withdrawn from circulation), which has to be the queerest heterosexual work in the canon, is much more explicitly a political intervention in the porn wars than Balser's playful and abstract meditation.

While Vancouver artist JOE SARAHAN has a nervous and perfunctory flash montage of rather confrontational gay SM imagery (original footage, not "recycled") in his *Holy Joe* (1987), it was in Montreal, not surprisingly, that the most sustained effort to integrate explicit sexual representation within the artistic vocabulary of queer video production occurred, due entirely to the efforts of one man, MARC PARADIS. Paradis's vision of gay male sexuality is much more caught up in the angst of shame, loss, hurt, and betrayal than that of his ebullient Torontonian counterparts, and his sense of politics is invested more in interpersonal power dynamics than the Toronto debates about pornography, censorship, and public-identity claims. Nevertheless, his work broke important ground in its unflinching portrayal of gay sex and surfaced earlier than anywhere else. His background in theatre, as well as in visual arts, is reflected in his skill in recruiting handsome young amateur collaborators to perform improvised speech and genital acts before the camera, especially in his unsettling first two works *Le Voyage de l'ogre* (1981), where the ogre is gay serial-killer John Gacy and his incarnation of sexual excess, risk, and predation, and *La Cage* (1983), where the titular metaphorical cage connotes both artistic impasse and sexual resentment. Later works, like his triptych on "la relation amoureuse," comprised of *L'incident Jones* (1986), *Délivre-nous du mal* (1987), and *Lettre à un amant* (1988), extend this project, but on an even more personal scale, with the sexual performances, languid and sensual, usually carried out by brunette

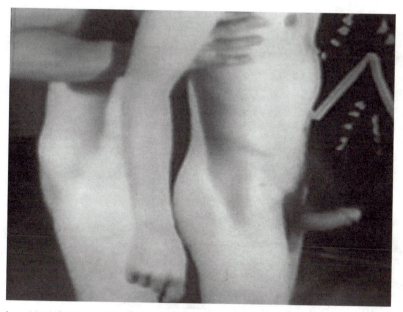

Insert in Colin Campbell's *White Money* (1983), the first Toronto "meta-porn" initiative. A timorous sendup of carnality and storytelling that at least tested the water. vhs frame grab, VTape

Simon Robert, the artist's striking, handsome then-lover. For all the evident tenderness in these images of masturbation and ejaculation, hauntingly aestheticized, the overall tone of bitterness and reproach remains, and one wonders what cultural or psychic baggage incited a post–Quiet Revolution Quebec artist to fixatedly attach such negative emotions to frank queer sexual iconography, all the while denying by implication its political import.

In general, however, artists positioned themselves in relation to the new porn commodity flow less through original explicit imagery than through the meta-porn current going on at the same time, a more fertile direction than the often hung-up efforts to re-create "the real thing" with skittish local actors, etc. John Greyson was predictably the first in Toronto's queer art video community to lay claim to this iconographic stake, in 1985. In *Jungle Boy*, the second of Greyson's "[Rudyard] Kipling trilogy," hard-core porno inserts embroidered his appropriation of Zoltan Korda's 1942 over-the-top adaptation of the Mowgli parable, combined with an essay on toilet-sex surveillance and a coming-out melodrama. The vcr revolution had laid the way for the decade's predominant "scratch" style, exemplified both by the lurid Korda citations and the five no-less lurid, boldly thrusting meat shots jumping off the screen during the tape (the political context of the Toronto anticensorship wars and anti-antiporn wars also explains the

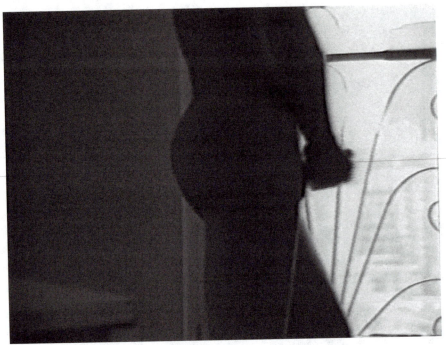

Marc Paradis's *Délivre-nous du mal* (1987): a vision of sexuality more caught up in the angst of shame, loss, hurt, and betrayal than that of his ebullient Toronto counterparts, more caught up in private power dynamics than public sexual politics. Video frame grab, Marc Paradis, 1987, Distribution Vidéographe

ardently political, in-your-face quality of this material). Sabu, the star of the Korda epic, has a campy swim with a monster python that gets punctuated with two of the porno inserts, a blatant but amusing riff on the phallic [not-so-]subtexts of the film. Then three more inserts punctuate the concluding apotheosis, in which Korda's crane-mounted bombast, the melo resolution sustained by Colin Campbell's superbly restrained acting, and assorted zoo iconography are all cobbled together with the crescendo of the Mexican pop song "Perdone me" that has dominated the video soundtrack throughout (which Greyson himself, in one of his rare on-screen performances, shamelessly lip-syncs at one point in a seminude jungle dance). Inspired editing matches the thrusts of buggery with the steady footsteps of the flamingos and lions under the strong beat of the song and thus amplifies Greyson's metaphorical association of outlaw gay desire and untamed tropical fauna, its still undomesticated opposition to the normalized world of sexual commodification.

Greyson tried a more developed version of the device the following year with *Moscow Doesn't Believe in Queers*, a longer and even more ambitious work that doesn't quite have the force of *Jungle Boy* in retrospect but is a rich example of vintage scratch aesthetics tackling the politics of fucking all the same. A self-styled "docudiary" of the artist's effort to raise gay politics at an international Soviet "youth" congress, *Moscow* is dramatized through two nude fuckbuddies lounging about in bed talking sex and politics, together with an intertextual essay on the Rock Hudson/AIDS story that had broken at the same time as the Soviet trip (crystallized in lengthy borrowings from the 1968 *Ice Station Zebra* [the Cold War thriller starring Hudson], whose homosocial eyeline encounters with submarine sailors and Soviet spies provide much fodder for Greyson's frantic editorial winking). The other interpolated text is an interview with feminist Bolshevik Alexandra Kollontai strolling through a Toronto greenhouse and pronouncing on the tragic trajectory of sexual-reform politics in Soviet history. The Charles St Video editing suite seems to have been upgraded since the previous year, for the tape is punctuated with hyperactively multiplied frames within screens, which outline the bountiful porno inserts (meat shots) throughout the tape. The porno inserts function loosely as a refrain, a reminder of what sexual politics is ultimately all about as the anodyne discourses unfold before or after or elsewhere on the screen. The effect is bold, and I heard a report later, no doubt apocryphal, that subsequent to my programming the tape at the 1987 Grierson Documentary Film Seminar in Toronto, the negative response of some of the librarians in attendance was one of the straws that broke the back of the entire seminar organization.

Such a world is far from the meta-porn universe of RICHARD FUNG's *Chinese Characters*, made the same year as *Moscow*. Here porn inserts are not a rhythmic punctuation device, a defiant political midfinger to the state, in-your-face shock rhetoric for librarians, or a dirty joke but, rather, part of an anguished but whimsical reflection on culture, sexual identity, and belonging. *Characters* is an intertextual essay on Chinese Canadian gay male subjectivity in relation to the "mainstream community" – that is, gay anglophone and white male (GWM) – articulated through its imported iconography of commodified video fantasy and framed by Fung's personal search for Chinese cultural roots in another form of narrative: traditional legend. Fung's anxious and solitary cruisers, masturbators, and life-narrators recount a conflicted relationship to porn. All their monologues are lip-synced by Fung himself in various guises in distancing pseudointerview setups – information that, for insiders, heightens the video's personal quality. The first witness reminisces about the acquisition of porno products as a relationship ritual with his partner, talking of the benefits of the sex-positive imagery in terms of the ability to fantasize, overcome guilt, "become more free," and "reinforc[e] my self-image" – in short, in terms of "making a difference in my life." The next respondents are more ambivalent, stressing the

Chinese Characters (1986), Richard Fung's reflection on culture, sexual identity, and belonging, keys in late-seventies American porno to set up the gap between GWM commodified fantasy and real-life Chinese Canadian gay male subjectivity. Video frame grab, VTape

videos' and magazines' role – paradoxically both acculturative and exclusionary – seeing them as a GWM image being *sold*, denying "Asianness," and cultivating a feeling of not belonging. One introspective interviewee describes how in sexual encounters he reverts to an unaccented "dirty talk" English idiom markedly different from his everyday accented English, an index of his alienated sexuality. The discussion is disembodied – one assumes for reasons of anonymity – and laid over not only the shots of Fung the *faux* interviewee but also over video monitors showing the tape's familiar bespectacled subject performing, hyperbolically and in close-up, various fetishistic and masturbatory activities.

Most importantly for my discussion here, Fung also interlaces the interview and monitor material with appropriated excerpts from the late-seventies American porno films that were by now circulating in Canada on video format – as if to accentuate the gap between commodified fantasy and real-life erotic experience. Under the positive discussion a bare-chested Chinese man is seen editorially/intertextually interacting with shots from Joe Gage's *Kansas City Trucking Company* (1976), which provides shaggy "bear" star Richard Locke as his virtual partner. They undress in tandem in a rugged natural landscape, and then thanks to the Chroma-key interface, the man caresses his chest and beckons to Locke, who responds and approaches him and reaches for his genitals. This romantic tryst is cut short, and another encounter is less satisfying. The Chinese man has suddenly donned a conical "coolie" hat, while "his" voice is replaced on the sound track by dramatized voices of objectification and stereotype that "he" encounters in GWM bars (e.g., "You're so gentle ... "). Now he is keyed in front of generic blond-surfer-orgy footage, this time staying aloof from the fantasy, rather than romantically interacting.[13] Soon the same figure is keyed into a scene of passersby on a busy street in Toronto's Chinatown, but the feeling of outsiderness continues, with the figure literally caught in the middle between GWM commodity and ethnic/racial public community.

Compared to this complex iconographic juxtaposition and layering, Marc Paradis's citation of commodity porn in his work seems strangely abstract. As we have seen, throughout the 1980s this Montrealer's work had preceded and surpassed the tendency of several Torontonians like Campbell and Balser to explore the possibilities of homegrown explicit sexual imagery, but in his 1989 *Réminiscences carnivores*, Paradis shifts from re-creating porn to its appropriation. This meditative essay, shot in Colombia (on a Vidéographe exchange program), continues Paradis's perennial themes of love, rupture, and memory, showing various male social or erotic interactions, solo and duo, in exteriors and around windows and exotic courtyards. The dreamy, tropical imagery is overlaid by recurring excerpts from the early 1980s porno film, *Tall Timber,* mostly close-up shots of a head tossing back and forth in *jouissance*, or bobbing up and down in intent sucking, all slowed down or otherwise processed and layered over the primary images in long, slow dissolves and subtle, sometimes barely discernible, superimpositions. The effect is languorous and aestheticized, somehow matching the elegiac or otherwise melancholic tone of the imagery and especially of the poetic voice-over, and intermittently the superimposition is so abstract that just a hint of the sexual content of the image is perceptible. Paradis certainly makes no reference to the image's status as commodity porn and offers no critical re-looking at the imagery as representative of other discourses more blatant elsewhere.

The year 1989 was perhaps more significant in the meta-porn current for the launch of STEVE REINKE's legendary *One Hundred Videos*, the ambitious epic project consisting of one hundred short videos produced over the next seven or eight years. Postmodern scratch-appropriation is one of the principal strategies in this massive, five-volume, four-hour- and fourteen-minute agglomeration of miniature works ranging in length from fifteen seconds to eleven minutes. Despite the sometimes mechanical feeling of the scratch technique, the videos cumulatively transmit a very personal sensibility, due in no small part to the regular surfacing of Reinke's characteristic voice-over, laconic but whimsical, ordinary but decidedly kinky. The voice is not autobiographical in the literal sense, but the artist's wryly, lustfully, campily, introspectively, speculatively, fetishistically queer sensibility presides in a recognizable and increasingly familiar way over this miraculous and self-reflexive encyclopaedia about the artistic process and the image-bank unconscious of civilization; about the body, the self, and identity; about childhood and regression; about narrative and humour; and about same-sex desire, obsession, transgression, fetishism, and, above all, voyeurism.

From the very beginning Reinke's videos were addressing sexuality explicitly (for example, the 1989 *Family Tree* started with a "fairly substantial" list of the narrator's sexual partners), and between 1991 and 1994 four of the tapes, all staples of the queer community festival circuit, quoted gay video pornography (a later 1996 work referenced heterosexual pornography). Reinke specialized, like Fung, in the seventies, though by now seventies porno had acquired a distinctively retro aura, not only because of the ephemerality of hairstyles (above and below the waist) and ideal body types but also because of the major impact of AIDS devastation on erotic fantasy. Each of the four tapes is distinct, but all are engaged in the clash of fantasy commodity with other more respectable and conventional forms of representation. The artist's apperception of the porno universe fluctuates, sometimes evoking a surreal magic in these intense bodies, almost as if from another planet, and at other times constructing them through a kind of intense documentary gaze upon distinct down-to-earth subjects frenetically engaged in the mundane, even banal, production of ecstasy.

Why I Stopped Going to Foreign Films (1991) and *Barely Human* (1992) come early in volume 1, almost back to back. The backbone of *Why I Stopped* is a series of action shots from a range of run-of-the-mill porno films, each processed in an orangish hue; these are intercut with excerpts from five canonical works from the 1960s-era, black and white art cinema marketplace, including Bergman, Bunuel, Fellini, and Ozu. While one possible reading of this alternating structure is a probe of cinephilia as a kind of queer sensibility (which I think the whole international range of distinctively queer uses of found footage within experimental film and video exemplifies), the work is also more complicated than that: each excerpt is overlain with a personal meditation that is a variation on "I have never done this (the action in the 'foreign' film), but I have done this (the porno action) and … " Each of the five setups leads to ever more complex mental states, from the acquisition of a photographic memory to narcolepsy to a dizziness culminating in an out-of-body experience of floating high above the city streets watching the populace. The final narration, sparked by the hypnosis scene from Fellini's *Nights of Cabiria* (1957), in which the spunky heroine is publicly humiliated by the on-stage revelation of her sexual history as a gullible "loser," is much more banal. The narrator remembers a date, an abuse survivor who dumped him after several months because he experienced his ejaculations in the face as abusive (rhyming with the porno excerpt then unfolding on the screen); he then concludes on the banal hope that they'll bump into each other some day and be able to go out for coffee. The narrator obviously has a film-reading disability, having blocked response to the "foreign films" because he doesn't recognize the action as belonging to his own field of experience. At the same time he responds to the porno excerpts, conventionally considered less rich, in terms of intense subjective experience, than so-called "art cinema" and in the last case of interpersonal experience much more complex than his offhand voice-over acknowledges, a dysfunctional and botched application of porno conventions to the intimate relationship with the abuse survivor. As such, the tape becomes an essay on individual cinematic response, on the complex relations between representation, commodity, psychic states, fantasy, and the everyday world of experience and sociality.

The next year's *Barely Human* completely eschews meat and money shots and concentrates on almost fifty decontextualized close-up cutaways of orgasmic male faces in rapid succession, only a few seconds each, increasingly abstracted and aestheticized as the montage progresses, so that by the end all colour and texture are eventually removed and only movement and minimal outline remain. The narration, a fine example of Reinke's quirkily improvised extrapolations, starts with a riff on the localization of sexual pleasure in these faces – feverish panting, lips parted, eyes closed – taking up Bataille's well-known exploration of parallels of carnal ecstasy with both spiritual ecstasy and mortality ([1957] 1986) and describing the silenced aestheticized faces as verging on the "angelic … barely human." This leads into an obsessive catalogue of erogenous body parts off-screen (such as "the erectile tissue of the nipples"), as well as their positioning within an endless chain of mankind, which itself leads into the voyeur's fantasy of manipulating the models' genitals all the while scrutinizing their faces. This necessitates a refashioned, more functional octupus-like "new physiology" with several flexible trunks for caressing and penetrating every orifice and finally a return to the overriding concept of voyeurism: "One of these trunks would end in a single large rectangular eye." The artist as a voyeur octopus is certainly a curious update of the utopian modernist conceits of the twentieth-century artist as techno-visionary, but perhaps one more apt in the postmodern era of the subsumption of art within commodity fantasy.

Of the four Reinke meta-porn works, the best-known is the 1993 *Lonely Boy*. Excerpts from 1970s nubile superstar Kip Noll's 1980 solo masturbiece *Roomates* are collaged together with the NFB's classic docuportrait of crooner Paul Anka, *Lonely Boy* (Wolf Koenig and Roman Kroitor, 1962), made almost two decades earlier. Reinke, the devilish editor, sets up prehistoric, black and white, New Jersey teenyboppers to scream hysterically at the triumphant sight of Kip's processed-colour ejaculation. Jane Gaines has fully excavated this wonderful work in terms of assumed discourses about the truth of documentary and the truth of sexuality (1999), but the piece also points to interesting connections to the commodification of desire. The crass discussion of the marketing of Anka's "personality" and "sex appeal" by his handlers in this amusement-park setting gets repositioned and reread in the context of the hyperactive colour masturbator, and the whole accelerating editorial frenzy of sexual performance and spectatorial response is whipped into an accelerating frenzy of expenditure and consumption (both libidinal and material).

By the time Reinke arrived at the 1994 *Windy Morning in April*, the whole project of meta-porn was perhaps running out of steam, and this work about dream, narrative, and auto-fellatio, less processed visually and editorially than the others, may be of most interest to those not yet acquainted with the "come-blow-your-horn" sub-subgenre of gay male porn. Regardless, all four of these works acquire a documentary aura in their reflection on the porno raw materials, whether observing the interface of spectatorship and erotic experience, its states of affect and visual stimulation, or the commercial construction of sexual hunger. At times romantic and mystical, Reinke is incontrovertibly at the same time postmodern and materialist, the 1990s video scene's most original scribe of desire.

On the women's side of the universe, meta-porn took on an entirely different perspective, reflecting lingering caution on the part of lesbian circuits after the porn wars about moving into the full embrace of film and video eroticism. For example, Vancouver video veteran LORNA BOSCHMAN's 1992 *Drawing the Line*, an account of the touring interactive photo exhibition from the artists group 'Kiss and Tell,' is restricted to the issue of eroticism vs pornography, dedicatedly undermining this facile and unproductive polarity through the creation of a continuum. As such, the provocative still images of the exhibition are given second priority to the debates around

Steve Reinke's best-known meta-porn work, *Lonely Boy* (1993), sets up a colour-processed 1970s superstar Kip Noll alongside his black-and-white 1960s predecessor Paul Anka in a frenzied editorial crescendo of commodification. VHS frame grab, courtesy Steve Reinke

them, pondering issues from audience to penetration. The video is not so much about desire as about representation, response, and politics.

The answer to why meta-porn was such a core genre of independent queer Canadian film and video throughout the 1980s and 1990s is peculiarly Canadian (and applies as well to the larger question of why so much Canadian narrative in general from *My American Cousin* [Sandy Wilson, 1985] to *I Love a Man in Uniform* [David Wellington, 1993] to *Project Grizzly* has as its reference self-consciously American genres of popular culture). JOSÉ ARROYO has written eloquently about the Canadian experience of viewing American (i.e., Hollywood) movies (1992):

Canadians looking at American films see them both differently and the same as Americans. That is to say we not only know the meaning that Americans are supposed to create, and share it with them, but we can also create a different meaning that may or may not be shared nationally ... Most Canadians of my generation would have a frame of reference they could share with Americans of my generation, which is not to say we have the same frame of reference ... Canadians confronted with American movies make a different meaning and make meaning differently because of our knowledge of America and our knowledge that we are not American ... I think cultural mobility seems to be a distinguishing feature of colonial subjectivity in *its* cultural construction. We comprehend as if we were the intended audience but realize we are not directly addressed ... When watching American films we too have to put on a masquerade, re-align our cultural identity so that that gap, which is the result of being Canadian watching films as if we were Americans, can be bridged ... [Ours was] a consciousness that the movies were of a world that was not ours and an unconscious message that movies didn't come from our world.

This process of colonial subjectivity and spectatorship, I would argue, was (and still is) doubly acute in relation to imported American porn films for queer audiences, heightened by the additional aura of alienation buoyed up by the apparatuses of contraband, illegitimacy, importation, censorship, and customs. Canadian queer spectators already consciously experience the alienation experienced by Fung's Asian subjects – with examples ranging from uncut Quebeckers' bemusement at the universally circumcised Californians to the down-home-accented dirty talk – thus rendering the Asians' alienation triply acute. In particular, Greyson (in *Moscow*) and Reinke (in *Lonely Boy*) bring together within their works both the general apprehension of American pop culture and that specific application of it with regard to imported American porn. That is why Rock Hudson and the New Jersey amusement park fit so well into the same tapes with the naughty glossy porno-thrust excerpts. But in general what all the meta-porn works of Greyson, Fung, Paradis, and Reinke have in common, I think, is their reflection of Arroyo's layers of self-consciousness, cultural mobility, and making meaning differently, layers applied to the particular experience of porno consumption.

PORN

> There is no pornography industry in Canada – I mean essentially, I'm it.
> ~ Bruce LaBruce

If these fruitful experiments with explicit sexual representation and meta-porn in such respectable realms as the art video sectors of Montreal, Toronto, and Vancouver had been the only initiatives in explicitly sexual imagery, Bruce LaBruce's 1997 statement, epigraphed above, that there is no pornography industry in Canada other than himself would still have been largely true. However, as we have seen, the industry of porno distribution and consumption dates from the 1960s, and the inevitable trial effort of porno-video production dates back to 1992. By that year, Wega Video had emerged on the other side of rue Ste-Catherine as major competition for the thriving

Montreal sex shop Priape in the porno-video distribution business. It was Wega that was first off the block with a full-fledged porno feature produced in Montreal. Mostly a not very imaginative Québécois inflection of the California model (with such local flavours as natural pine décor and a country setting), *French Erection/Au maximum* (WILLIAM DUFFAULT, 1992) hinted with the bilingualism of its title at the film's major claim to fame, namely, a series of extremely silly bilingual dialogue scenes among its mullet-haired stars that makes the whole thing feel like a diabolical parody of the Ottawa civil service. No doubt conceived of as a reasonable pitch for both the local francophone and the anglophone/American markets all at once, the plot pretext is the reunion of old friends from the two cultures and leads to absurd "Bonsoir/Goodnight" exchanges among the horny lads. Two other related epiphanies are forthcoming in the tape, together seeming to ominously preview in allegorical fashion the referendum coming up three years in the future:

1   a voice-over line by the insatiable twinky lead just as he gets the phone call announcing the anglos' imminent arrival: "on ne parle pas tous la même langue mais on est vite devenu de bons amis ... seulement des amis malheureusement. J'aurais facilement baisé avec l'un ou l'autre." (We don't speak the same language but we quickly became good friends ... only friends unfortunately. I could easily have had sex with one or the other.") and

2   a sex scene flimsily set up in a "disco cruising bar" (involving sex with the barman who flubs his big opportunity, the witty line "Last call!" after getting royally ploughed by his customer). Most interestingly the sex is innovatively matched with what might be a muddy audio collage from the blazing TV nearby (apparently being channel-zapped by a bored production assistant?) but punctuated midscene by the phrase "Toronto fascist state," repeated loud and clear at least four times.

Wega customers apparently did not respond to this work's documentary vocation, or to its Confederation allegory of bilingual friendship or its referendum rhetoric, for *French Erection/Au maximum* seems to have been a one-off effort for the firm. That did not stop the pseudonymous Duffault, however, for he went on to several more Quebec-based or Quebec-flavoured porno video features in the decade, all pursuing the mercenary dream of capturing pan-Canadian bilingualism within the universe of fantasy. *Northern Exposure* (1993) is another pastoral exercise, this time involving country campers and felonious hitchhikers. One plot highlight offers the most perfunctory political conversion in film history: after a lively threesome between two Greenpeace-type treehugger eco-activists in green T-shirts and a rather desultory lumberjack, the latter abandons his chainsaw without a second thought for the cause of the environment. But the linguistic imperative rears its head without fail, and two other characters, no doubt driven mad with lust, actually have the following conversation:

"You know it's really too bad that [new arrival] can't speak in English. I mean you must be getting dizzy going back and forth to both languages all day long." "No not at all, it's like a queer United Nations! I grew up in Montreal and speaking lots of languages is great!"

Duffault's next film, *Sure Shot*, made the following year, continues more of the same, but set within the universe of hockey, shamelessly lifting situations (and subtexts about major league scouts and casting couches) from *Lance et compte* and fetishizing hockey pads throughout (see chapter 7). At least on the linguistic front, the bold new innovation of subtitles in several scenes, such as the special moment where, to help him relax, the coach ends up rimming a stressed and bellicose player with a maple leaf tattoo on his chest, at least brings porn back to more conventional linguistic protocols. Duffault's 1995 death after his next production, *Les hommes au naturel*, brought this production cycle to an end.

Quebec porn auteur William Duffault's *Sure Shot* (1994) substituted selective subtitles for pan-Canadian bilingualism, fetishizing hockey pads and a strategic maple leaf tattoo on a stressed player who is learning pre-game relaxation. DVD frame grab

Towards the end of the decade, the potentially rich francophone porno market niche again tempted local producers. Of two Priape feature productions, *Alex et Bruno* (1999) and *Fuck Friends* (2000), the first, directed by "André Tardif" (a transplanted Québécois Vancouverite), showed definite room for improvement on both the technical and directing side. The eponymous duo indeed had their perky charms: Alex is a Montreal voyeur escaping to the countryside when the cops close in on his prowling and spying through Plateau alleys and balconies, and Bruno is his easily distracted new boss on the farm and eventual sex partner. A few other redeeming features include a greater range of male types than are found in Falcon Studios (in a bucolic skinny-dipping orgy scene that degenerates into a very sculptural tableau vivant, one ephebe is even wearing eyeliner), a pastoral lyricism that was already becoming a Quebec porno formula, and a funny post-credits complement of out-takes in which the director complains about the lack of a fluffing budget. *Alex et Bruno* turned out to be a huge hit, both in Quebec and abroad (distributed in France by local porn legend Jean-Daniel Cadinot), and paved the way for a follow-up film.

Its title notwithstanding, the greatly improved *Fuck Friends* (STANLÉ LUBRIK, 2000) is entirely in French and in fact has lots of dialogue, using improvised conversation and storytelling among the amiable cast of three roommates (one allegedly straight ... at the start) as a central part of the erotic formula (going far beyond the "Ah c'est bon!" that was the limit of the sex talk in the previous production). With *Fuck Friends*, Stanlé Lubrik moved from scripting and art direction to directing and delivered a creditable package with a strong flavour of everyday populism and a distinct Quebec sensibility. The evocative locations – the roommates' Plateau apartment and the nearby Parc Lafontaine skating rink, the snowy Carnaval celebrations in Quebec City, a tavern, and the now *de rigueur* interlude in a country farmhouse complete with fireplace – push the film precariously close to the feel of Quebec tourism promotion. Even the casting of amiable nontwinky types with unshaven faces and unshaven balls tumbling out of long johns (*pure laine*, no doubt!) contributes to the "national" discourse niche that this production was obviously aiming for. Director Lubrik was quite explicit in describing his original goals as being to show his foreign audiences (in particular the French) "our way of talking sexuality" (interview, 20 October 2003), hence the long scenes of improvised dialogue among his performers, as well as the development of particular local fantasies (firemen!) and anatomies. Some spectators criticized him for casting relatively ordinary bodies instead of Jeff Stryker types (the friendly hairy redheaded "straight" roommate is in fact a courier delivery guy, and one of the firemen went on to be a champion wrestler at the Sydney Games). However, the populist anatomy is in my mind a merit of the film (the emphasis on uncut performers was another of Lubrik's strategies for cultural specificity). Only the ambitious "suspense/supernatural" episode developing themes of voyeurism and bondage seems to end up moving beyond the search for *pure laine* Québécois erotic mythologies. But in fact, other than getting perilously close to a Priape accoutrements ad, the scene acquires the nuance of political intent: the ominous and omnipotent voyeur/dominator turns out to be a policeman, injecting an element of denunciation common to the genre as a whole (namely, the anticop motifs in many of the films in this corpus). One might be tempted to mutter that only in Quebec do explicit queer videos become less a pornotopia than a product placement site for "the nation." But to complete the paradox, *Fuck Friends*, while less successful than *Alex et Bruno*, reportedly sold one thousand DVDs in the United States!

Meanwhile, women were not sitting idly on their hands and leaving all initiative to the boys for the development of indigenous erotic fantasy on video. Somewhat surprisingly, the 1980s had not been totally hung up by the aftermath of the porn wars. In Montreal in 1988, Diane Heffernan, a mainstay of the perennial community video group Réseau vidé-elles, took the leap with *Orgasmes à la crème fouettée* (Whipped Cream Orgasms), representing herself and her partner engaged in the eponymous activity for lesbian spectators. Her strictly nonprofit intent was to turn around a culture in which "lesbian sexual practice still remained a bit of a mystery – even to the women involved" (Troster 1999). The tape was also a deliberately conceived riposte to the SM imagery that the Amazones network perceived to be diffusing into *pure laine* lesbian culture but that didn't resonate with them. Nevertheless, *Orgasmes* reportedly "raised eyebrows" in Montreal and Paris, and the artist would later withdraw it from circulation because of its "tremendous emotional impact" on her life. Some of that very SM imagery that the Réseau was resisting shows up in Boschman's 1992 *Drawing the Line*, as we have already seen. Whether or not the Kiss and Tell imagery confirmed that the dominoes had already fallen beyond the Rockies, it was safely couched and framed in metacommentary, unlike Heffernan's erratic and soon regretted gesture. In any case, both tapes reflected a steady cultural momentum, undermining, rather than still harping on, the semantic polarity "pornography vs eroticism" that had been the dead end of the 1980s porn wars.

The censorship jolts of the 1990s may have further loosened up the logjam in lesbian sexual representation: both the ongoing Little Sisters bookstore fiasco, in which even nonerotic lesbian works were being desecrated by the state and the momentous legal lynching of Toronto's Glad Day Bookstore for selling the U.S. "bad girl" magazine *Bad Attitude* immediately after the Butler obscenity decision of 1992 (Cossman et al. 1997). Whatever the reasons, the decade saw the growing normalization of the subject of lesbian porn within Canadian communities.

Once again, on the eve of the millennium Montreal set the scene for the breakthrough: the 1999 production *Classy Cunts*, by a then anonymous, mostly anglo network of Concordia and McGill students (identified by a dizzying array of pseudonyms: LIVE PEACH PRODUCTIONS, by Poison Ivy and Eden, also known as Jane M. [Jane Meikle, b. 1976] and Emily M. [Emily Cummins, b. 1977]). A forty-five-minute anthology of three episodes, *Classy* offers a menu of, first, a communal meal (no doubt a potluck) with an orgy for dessert, then a comeuppance delivered in an SM den to a "haughty little princess," and finally, a hands-off initiation by a pagan priestess of her dildo-worshipping acolyte. Of these narrative nuggets, the second may be the most successful, with its felt atmosphere and taut dramatic structure. But most important is the transmission, amid all the heavy humping and shuddering, of an aura of community initiative, a feeling of zero-budget creative excitement located universes apart from the cynically mercenary Priape production going on the same year across town (well in fact, perhaps not *across*, since *Classy* was shot in a fetish club in the *Village gai* just around the corner from Priape). Such an ambience is deliberate, for the authors' political objectives are explicit but it's a different sort of politics from *Bubbles Galore*'s brassy if-you-can't-beat-em-join-'em recuperation of the marketplace.

"We wanted to go with the two r's: raunch and respect," said Cummins in a media interview.[14] "We're aiming for similar goals [to Annie Sprinkle's]. To make sex products that are also educational." Ethnic diversity, for one thing (something that had yet to occur to the male producers, despite an embarrassingly clumsy decision to introduce an African Québécois janitor in *Sure Shot*) is a sine qua non, sex is archi-safe, and bodies are usually distinctively "everyday" – on the chubby, femmy side in general – rather than the anorexic/silicone-implanted standard of the commercial model. Noncommodity fetishism and technical amateurism become ideological virtues. Well before the final title assurance to the viewer that all the foregoing activities were "consensual and enjoyed," it is clear that everyone is having fun and the orgasms and orgies are real. As with the men, the out-takes postscript offer a moment of significant revelation: one amateur actress announces how dehydrated she feels, and the all-round feeling of fluid depletion is evident. Audiences at queer community festivals and even at the queer-friendly Edmonton bookstore Orlando seem to have agreed. Not that *Classy,* co-sponsored by the Toronto sex shop Good for Her, is any less a showcase for merchandise and gadgets than the boys' tapes; it just has a greater ambience of complicity and intimacy amid all those dildos and

Erotic pedagogy and community responsibility underlie the sex in *Pornograflics* (2003), by Dirty Pillows. "Billie's New Toy," the butch-femme motorcycle episode (above), shows that "A horny femme is an angry femme!" Production still, Dirty Pillows Inc.

harnesses (despite the masks resorted to by several performers). Efforts to recoup costs were made but were so halfhearted that the California lesbian grapevine fielded complaints about how hard it was to access the new item.

Four years later, another collective production, this time from Toronto, had in comparison to *Classy* become the epitome of even classier production values, while maintaining that distinctive feeling of erotic pedagogy and community responsibility alongside the horny fun. *Pornograflics*, a collaboration by DIRTY PILLOWS, a pseudonymous team composed of Angela Phong, Mishann Lau, and "Miss Bea" and relying on deft screenwriting rather than improvisation (e.g., "A horny femme is an angry femme!"), was a hit once more at the major Canadian queer video festivals. Each of the three women got a chance to direct, and seven episodes all came together smartly in the loosely knitted composite: "Billie's New Toy," a butch-femme motorcycle action; "Five-Finger Discount," a moral tale in which a defiant white shoplifter gets punished by a butch black security guard; "BMX-O," a more politically correct ten-speed romance among babydykes along the bike path; "Clothes Are Better Off," a roughhouse rivalry between two butches over a femme in a clothing boutique; "Bitch-slap," a roommate squabble that ends in high in-bed acrobatics; "Peek a boo," a moody voyeurism narrative that would seem a little incongruous in its black and white soft-core restraint were it not Lau's big chance to perform and were the package not already deliberately eclectic; and, finally, "Housewifey," ye olde plumber-fix-my-leak narrative that was already hoary when *Boys in the Sand* (Wakefield Poole, 1971) tried it out thirty years earlier and absolutely geriatric when *Bound* (A. Wachowski and L. Wachowski, 1996) and *Skin Flick* gave it a new lease on life in 1996, and 1999 respectively. All are mortared together by burlesque performance interludes featuring a corpulent blonde twirling pasties and grinding heavy attitude. In other words, the ninety-minute tape is a rich repository of narrative mythologies, both classical and fresh, embracing the role play that Heffernan eschewed and Live Peach nervously tried out. My favourite may be the shoplifting drama, not just because it's shot ironically in the historic battlefield of Glad Day Bookstore and has male beefcake as a backdrop but also because this tale of theft and punishment is most fraught with both deliriously earnest pleasure and the textures of commodity compromise and political stress. As we have seen, this pleasure, this compromise, and this stress had increasingly shaped queer sexual representation over the previous decade.

GHOST SHIT ON YOUR TONGUE

> And goo, strong on smell,
> has the power of ammunition
> to trigger off memories of a long forgotten lover ...
> Underground is where you belong.
> While the city buzzes overhead,
> ghost shit on your tongue.
> You undress underground
> and find your garden of Eden ...
> ~ R. Raj Rao, "Underground"

The monetary nexus has presided over the corpus of sex films discussed thus far in this chapter. *Bubbles Galore* broadly satirized it, *Bad Girl* analyzed it, Bruce LaBruce decried it while cynically manipulating it, Steve Reinke, Richard Fung, and John Greyson appropriated and critiqued it, while Priape and Dirty Pillows enacted and domesticated it. All the works have in common an utter fascination with the interface between monetary exchange and sexual exchange, whether negative or positive. In this final section, I offer a parallel roundup of queer sexual iconography *outside* of, or in defiance of, both that monetary nexus and the "normal coupling" that is all too often interwoven with it in public discourse (interwoven as well on centre stage of the Canadian political arena as I write this in 2003, surrounded by headlines about same-sex marriage and betrayal by married Liberal bankbenchers). The films in this section show and are about public sex, sex in public toilets.

Toilet sex, whether a utopian fantasy of sexual liberation, an incontrovertible historical fact of sexual organization over the last two centuries of advanced capitalism and urbanization, or a crux of queer political resistance in the political arena of this place at this time, is here and queer. The films discussed in this section are on the soft side of soft-core – at least in comparison to Bubbles, No Skin off My Ass, Lonely Boy, Fuck Friends, and Classy Cunts – but depict sexual exchange frankly and directly all the same (despite the challenges that toilet cubicles present to the average camera crew). They constitute a coherent body of alternative work with which to tie up this chapter on sex and money. Somewhat unexpectedly, toilet sex films comprise the corpus that not only most explicitly enshrines the ethos of documentary sobriety but also reflects most truly the real space of where we are in urban undergrounds and abovegrounds in Canada, most liberated from the dependent relationship on U.S. performers, iconography, and markets that inflect all the other works in this chapter's repertory.

There is a spectrum of opinions on John Greyson's first feature film, Urinal (Toronto, 1988). The Berlin Festival awarded it the Teddy (Best Gay Feature) recognition in 1989, a mainstream Toronto daily praised its "style," and American film theoretician John Champagne dedicated twenty-five densely argued pages to its exegesis, evoking Bataille, Nietsche, and Foucault. Yet I was surprised that a coterie of my gay male students found it fatally clogged with 1980s art video gadgetry and that the Toronto gay political magazine Rites had originally panned it upon its release as both "heavy-handed" and even soft on fascism (October 1988)! Regardless of where one stands within this spectrum, one must concede that Urinal is unique, perhaps the most anomalous film in a national cinema known for one-off meteor showers. Of Greyson's four feature-length film essays (the others are Zero Patience [1993], After the Bath [1995], and Uncut [1997]), Urinal is the most uncompromising and most complex, brilliant in the way it channels the issue of toilet sex through a labyrinth of narrative paths and refracts it into an intertextual documentary of thematic investigations and political manifestos. (In fact, two earlier Greyson works can be considered trial balloons for Urinal: Jungle Boy, with its off-screen narrative of a married man fatally caught in flagrante, and You Taste American, 1986, a succeeding essay narrative on the Orillia Opera House toilet busts of the 1980s, itself based on an earlier performance of the same title. Each successive version became more and more ambitious, until with Urinal Greyson can be said to finally have got it out of his system).

The narrative pretext of the film brings together a typically Greysonian cast of characters through some kind of throwaway Mission Impossible time travel (at first they and we think it's Toronto, 1937, but it's Pride Day, 1987): a multicultural assortment of reincarnated queer artists from the first part of the twentieth century plus Oscar Wilde's fictional character Dorian Gray, incarnated as a dreamy Asian beefcake star. They are assigned the task of researching the issue of toilet sex, which had embodied a major political "crisis" for Ontario queer communities throughout the decade. Frida Kahlo, Sergei Eisenstein, Langston Hughes, Yukio Mishima, plus their Toronto lesbian hostesses, the sculptors Florence Wyle and Frances Loring (even more than *Bubbles Galore*, Greyson has always been faithful to the principle of Canadian content) all present, as instructed, a research presentation on a particular angle on the subject. Their semiautonomous minidocumentaries are entitled "A Selective Social History of the Public Washroom" (Loring), "A Dramatic Reading of Toilet Texts" (Mishima), "A Guided Tour of Toronto's Hottest Tearooms" (Eisenstein), "A Survey of Small-Town Washroom Busts in Ontario" (Hughes), "The Policing of Washroom Sex in Toronto" (Wyle), and "The Policing of Sexuality in Society" (Kahlo) and are interwoven with essayistic inserts and narrative episodes among the six characters. Finally, another obscure plot mechanism, involving the unveiling of Dorian as a Mountie double agent (I think), wraps up the film, mission accomplished.

The relevance of this film on toilet sex to a chapter on films that give rods, however, might be seen as ambiguous, since the film shows no explicit sex, despite its racy subject, and its cerebral business has never been described as erotic. The flirtations among the characters are mostly discreet and consummated off-screen (the sculptors are a monogamous unit and more or less resist Frida's Latina-spitfire overtures, but the men go a bit further, connecting all three sides of their Tokyo-Moscow-Harlem axis). The only full-frontal nudity belongs to Eisenstein, who is rather over-the-hill for a character forty years old, historically, in 1937, and there's little anatomical interest demonstrated in his scene in the shower with horny adolescent Mishima who wants to soap his back. However, Mishima, and Eisenstein do come to the rescue of the film's peter meter content with their respective minidocumentaries: Mishima's Foucauldian collage of texts on toilet sex assembles a wide range of disciplinary discourses, including fiction (his own), tabloid journalism, sociology, and law enforcement/criminology. The voice-over excerpt of a toilet adventure from Mishima's *Forbidden Colours* is "illustrated" by a typically Greysonian interlude featuring plastic mercenary "GI Joe–type" figurines in a miniature orgy scene with little square wipe effects emphasizing their fully clothed genitals as they sixty-nine and everything else. This nonindexical figuration of explicit sex is escalated shortly by the voice-over discourse of pornography in the form of a first-person toilet-orgy narrative from a Boyd McDonald collection of "real-life sex experiences," injecting a gritty sexual explicitness into the collage ("all I did was sink to my knees, open my mouth, and eat one and then the other"). Finally, a translated Argentine poem sums up the montage with a utopian manifesto ("The walls shout of love and liberty. / We toss out the dirty paper. / Long live the stinking washrooms!").

In his guide to the Toronto toilet network, the less romantic, hyperintellectual Eisenstein has at first a more cerebral, sanitized approach to explicit sex, for example, with his inventory of sexual activities observed in order of frequency, followed by step-by-step instructions for engaging in toilet sex, as if in an NFB documentary. But his documentary monologues by two "expert witnesses" restore the level of affect, immediacy, and frankness. A young man of Chinese descent offers a firsthand, vernacular description of the culture and logistics of toilet sex, paradoxically buoyed up by the hilarious disguises he wears (a send-up of conventional confidentiality measures à la CBC, potted palms, Hallowe'en eyeglasses, etc.).[15] Second, an older white male victim of an Oakville, Ontario, raid courageously, if nervously, abjures all disguise, telling about his ordeal straight on in a conventional head-and-shoulder setup. For all their matter-of-factness, a quieter utopian ring is also present in these two monologues, both in the Asian man's affirmation of the nondiscriminatory community he experiences within the vividly described

Sergei Eisenstein, the time-travelled queer filmmaker, conducts his on-site research of glory holes in *Urinal* (1988). Greyson's first feature celebrated toilet sex as "nonproductive expenditure" but interwove a very Canadian didactic sobriety. VHS frame grab

underground and in the Oakville victim's statement of his response to seeing the videotape that destroyed his career and permanently altered his life: "I didn't expect to see myself behaving sexually on tape. It was a very self-affirming experience. I was rather surprised by how good I felt, even given the anxiety-provoking experience and the anxiety-provoking circumstances, even given that, it was a very self-affirming experience to have to watch yourself behaving sexually on tape. I was delighted by how human and how physical and how sexual and how beautiful I was, and I was surprised" (Greyson 1993, 78).

This key moment deserves comment. First, the testimonies may have absurd, even implausible rings. But I think of the impact that the only genuine surveillance footage that I have seen had for me when I first saw it, 16mm shots made in Mansfield, Ohio, in 1962 of soon-to-be-jailed toilet participants. What I felt was the combination of shock at the combined brutality and violation of this secret intrusion, as if seeing Holocaust images from another time and universe, and elation at the everyday banal dignity of the players and their activities. In this context, then, the Oakville man's epiphany becomes meaningful. A second comparison, to the only other similar moment in Canadian cinemas, the testimony of Marc Paradis's nubile young performer in his disturbing tape about the extreme limits of desire, *Le Voyage de l'ogre*, is also telling (although the testimony is probably semidocumentary improvisation): Sylvain tells directly to the camera about getting started on a hustling career through hanging about the public toilets at Eaton's. Although the artist's complicity in this exposure of his beautiful subjects leaves an uneasiness, there is, despite ambivalence about his response and his older eventual customers, a similar flash of a social, psychic, and existential self-recognition in the act and place. Greyson/Eisenstein's testimony from the Oakville man, although more euphemistic than that of the second interwoven account from the Asian man, stands apart from the rest of the film's clever postmodern surfaces and allusive density – and indeed from the entire corpus of this chapter – for the unique directness of its affect and the brave authenticity of its voice but also for its insight into the nature of toilet sex.

It is this utopian theoretical and political resonance that no doubt attracted Champagne to *Urinal*. Champagne applies a model of socioeconomic organization derived from French philosopher/pornographer Georges Bataille both to gay pornography and to Greyson's film. Bataille divides "human consumption" into "productive" activity and "non-productive expenditure." The former is measured in money and is "the basis of social homogeneity," his descriptor for the capitalist social organization that measures human worth in terms of productivity and reduces everything to a commodity form. We have seen how *Bubbles Galore* and many of this chapter's films observe or embody or satirize – and sometimes even go so far as to denounce – the way in which desire and sexual relations become absorbed within the productive economy, and all of Nina Hartley's cultivatedly sincere orgasmic moaning or empowerment sermons cannot convince us otherwise. This insidiously totalizing and rapacious encroachment of productivity into the realm of desire and affect – especially since the sexual and Stonewall revolutions – accounts in part for the ferocity of Bruce LaBruce's skinheads, especially in his fourth feature *Skin Flick/Skin Gang* (1999), which I have left to this section to integrate into my discussion. The futile, self-destructive, and misplaced revolt of these skin characters is, as we shall see, an extension of the high-powered satire LaBruce brings to bear on his guppie couple. With their briefcase jobs, immaculate river-view condo, hip sushi meals, gay art coffee table books, and dinnertime conversations about commodities, this couple performs an excessive conjugality that mimics heterosexual marriage and constitutes the ideal productive and consumptive unit.

In contrast, Bataille's second category, "nonproductive expenditure," "moves toward loss, waste, and often violent pleasures" such as "luxury, mourning, spectacle, the arts, and so-called perverse sexual activity." Nonproductive expenditure is accompanied by a "high degree of affect," and its transgressive manifestations, including perverse sexuality, belong to the heterogeneous world of the Other. Such transgressions threaten productive, homogeneous society and must be suppressed. Champagne identifies the transgressive, nonproductive pleasures of toilet sex, as explored in *Urinal*, as the epitome of a resistance to the constraints of "productive" society – as well as to those accommodationist elements within queer communities who want to join. Champagne is, interestingly, critical of Greyson's vision of the state, personified by violent and stupid cops, as a reductive and simplistic top-down image of how power operates within contemporary society (as embodied by Frida Kahlo's final report).

This criticism might be qualified in the light of the context of the work, however. We must think further through Greyson's artistic, formal intervention in the context of his track record of strategic street-level, everyday-image activism in the face of symptomatic acts of violence – from arts censorship to police scapegoating to official AIDS denial – that informed Ontario sexual politics throughout the 1980s. It then becomes clear that this context of strategic activism is compatible with Champagne's macrocosmic, more theoretical Foucauldian notion of a diffused power embodied beyond and outside state hegemony. Greyson's political conception of power through bodies, desire, culture and community, and coalition and disruption is as much a mosaic of contradiction as his aesthetics, micro and macro – as his oeuvre and accompanying activism as a whole make clear in the postmodern, postcolonial context of NAFTA. Whether or not we expect artists to deliver cogent political and theoretical platforms, Champagne is right in identifying the nonproductive and resistant energy invested in toilet undergrounds by Greyson both as symbol and as site of struggle. And not only by Greyson, but also – little does the American know – by a whole tradition of Canadian queer filmmakers.

For Greyson's work is not unique in its serious concern with the topic of toilet sex. On the contrary, if we trace the iconography of toilet sex in queer Canadian works over the last twenty-five years, one notes many filmmakers, and not only men, who anticipate and echo Greyson's interest in the ghost-shit zone. Like him in *You Taste American* and *Urinal*, they understand the toilet as an abject and liminal zone whose nonproductive energy confronts the mainstream political and economic regulation of sexuality with a transgressive politics of sexuality as pleasure and excess, waste and contestation. Canada's first gay feature, in 1963, Claude Jutra's autobiographical *À tout prendre* was called a "toilet film" by its straight cameraman – though toilets in that film are strictly for grooming and bathing – and ever since it's as if queer filmmakers have been intent on embracing and transforming this stigma. Love has indeed kept pitching its mansion in the place of excrement, and not only love but also art, politics, and community. I am not saying that some propensity for toilet transgression is a national characteristic, translated into our cinema as a full-blown thematic, but rather that there is a gently persistent artistic interest in this setting and issue. The evolution in the formulations of this iconography articulates the trajectory of crises in queer politics in Canada since the 1970s especially – mostly male but also two female voices confirm the queer centrality of the subject. In other words, the toilet images negotiate through resistance or appropriation the imposition of productive economics and normalized conjugality that have also been the consolidating pattern within mainstream queer cultures over those years. This iconography occupies a range of artistic and audience practices across avant-garde, documentary, and narrative feature formats. It reflects many voices across the interface of individual authorship, collective identity, and cultural infrastructure that is characteristic of Canadian cinemas as a whole. I will discuss eight key films or film clusters in this trajectory of toilet desire:

In Black and White, MICHAEL MCGARRY (1979). Emerging seemingly out of nowhere in perhaps the darkest hour of Canadian cinemas (the capital[ist] cost allowance period), this ten-minute experimental short from Vancouver is an uncanny, miniature anticipation of *Urinal*, both thematically and aesthetically. Like *Urinal*, McGarry's narrative has a basis in fact, in this case sixty toilet arrests carried out through video surveillance in suburban Richmond, British Columbia, in 1978. Two young men, one married and the other an "out" seventies clone, meet in a public toilet and have hot sex, but they're caught through video surveillance and arrested by brutish policemen – the married one is traumatized, his partner is defiant. The crisp black and white images of the meeting and sex are interpolated with surveillance-screen images of the same, all underscored by an additional documentary layer on the soundtrack, a "consciousness-raising" chorus of self-reflexive male and female voices discussing the politics of toilet sex. McGarry's emphasis is on victimization (the shaken, sweating closeted man) and on resistance (the clone character, a mustachioed McGarry himself, physically resisting the arrest – in vain, of course). McGarry also highlights the not-so-veiled voyeuristic erotics within this audiovisual technology of entrapment: the clone brands the cop as a closet case getting off on the surveillance images, and indeed the haunting video images we have seen could not be more erotic, with their alternating, sensuous points of view of furtive but hungry looks and caressed torsos. Nor could they be less plausible, logistically, as the static viewpoint of a surveillance camera: the only toilet surveillance imagery I have seen, those haunting Ohio images from the 1960s, mentioned earlier, were indeed capable of panning thanks to a live cameraman behind the mirror, but even these did not offer the selected insert close-ups that McGarry's artistic licence imagines. The trope of police violation is, not surprisingly, more intense in the 1962 film – and indeed in Greyson's documentary excursus in *Urinal* – than in McGarry's dramatized version.

Ten Cents a Dance (Parallax), MIDI ONODERA (Toronto, 1985, 31). Onodera's debut film, this experimental narrative triptych was perhaps the most notorious Canadian queer film of the eighties. Shown at the San Francisco International Lesbian and Gay Film Festival in 1986 as part of a program of lesbian shorts, *Ten Cents* offers three semicomic narrative panels. The central panel, an eight-minute, static long-take showing a high-angle view of two frisky, taciturn, and efficient young men having sex in a public toilet, provoked the never-forgotten riot at the Roxy Theatre, in which lesbian spectators shouted at the screen, stomped out of the auditorium, and, legend has it, even stormed the projection booth (Rich 1999, 80). This is not the place to analyze the American audience's stereotypically bad manners and chauvinism towards an invited young Asian Canadian artist. Nor should we wonder here whether their closed-mindedness baulked most at the nonlinear narrative or at male sexuality or at their combination, nor delve into the way the crisis led, according to the official history of the festival, to a heightened community process in festival programming.

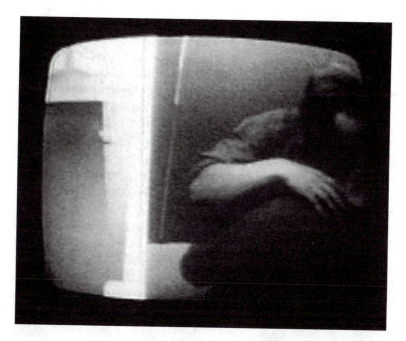

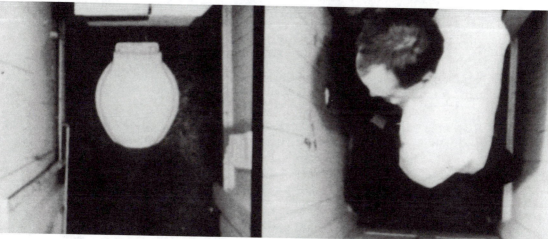

Top
Michael McGarry's 1979 *In Black and White* was an uncanny, miniature anticipation of *Urinal*, a masterful manifesto about public sex, surveillance/voyeurism, and the politics of desire. Video frame grab from the film *In Black and White*, by Michael McGarry (1979), courtesy Moving Images Distribution

Bottom
In Midi Onodera's widescreen, double-framed *Ten Cents a Dance (Parallax)* (1985), an overhead view shows a head in a public toilet. San Francisco was not amused by the childlike sexual exchange unburdened by monetary relations. Production still provided by the Canadian Filmmakers Distribution Centre

Rather, it is interesting to dissect Onodera's contextualization of toilet sex within her three-part narrative and her brilliant insight into sexuality in general. The offending middle panel's deceptively frivolous choreography of the two-cubicle encounter is not genitally explicit, for all the vigorous gestural mise-en-scène on screen, and it is positioned between two other wry, satiric, and equally discreet vignettes. The first shows a romantic courtship in a Japanese restaurant involving an interracial lesbian couple framed in profile on either side of a single red rose, talking a lot and just barely touching hands, and consuming much saki and nicotine: the butch Asian partner, played by Onodera, is coyly putting the make on her chic blonde companion, a purportedly heterosexual femme who is playing equally coy and extremely curious. The third and final panel shows heterosexual telephone sexwork. This panel finally reveals an explicit narrative function for the double-framed setup referred to by the title, with horizontally adjacent frames slightly overlapping (the two "lovers" of the third panel are not in the same geographical space, so the parallax setup literally matches the telephone encounter and, not surprisingly, resembles the split screens that delivered Doris Day and Rock Hudson's widescreen telephone conversations of yore). The lubricious female sexworker occupies frame right, distractedly doing her nails while whipping her young male customer in frame left into a frenzy with her false, customized descriptions of her lingerie and wet pussy, etc. This third couple are by far the most talkative of the three, since talk is the currency of the man's masturbatory fantasy and the monetary transaction.

The exact intent of Onodera's parallel among the three conjugal transactions, none fully sanctioned by mainstream sexual ideology, is never made clear, and it may be this ambiguity that so infuriated its San Francisco audience. Does her juxtaposition satirize mythologies of lesbian romance and heterosexual desire, with the cash nexus so explicit in the latter and implicit in the former (as it is in the entire tradition of companionate marriage in Western society, where questions of who is paying for the saki and in exchange for what never surface until divorce proceedings)? The title, *Ten Cents a Dance*, the traditional lyrical summation of the monetary contract between dance-hall sexworker partners of the first part of the twentieth century, would seem to bolster this reading of Onodera's interest in the material terms of the first and third of the transactions shown. According to this reading, Onodera would seem to be privileging the middle panel with its image of nonproductive sexual exchange unburdened by money and carried out with a childlike playfulness that could certainly be interpreted according to the utopian mode we have already discussed. Along the same lines, the order of the three-part construction would be significant in itself, with the transgressive "no fuss, no muss" sexuality of the middle episode bridging the gap between the heavily coded repression of the lesbian panel and the up-front mercenary sleaze of the phone sex episode (up-front within the bounds of its own mutually understood codes of course). Is Onodera perhaps even articulating a subtle gendered envy vis-à-vis the unaccountable sexual fun permitted men by patriarchal privilege (discernible also in the mock-disapproving discourse by the lesbians in *Urinal*)? Is she challenging in this way the antisex, antiporn feminist "consensus"of the sex wars era that was only just beginning to wane in 1985? Or, on the other hand, is Onodera simply showing an ethnographer's neutrality concerning the three instances of stigmatized sexual coupling, all belonging to "outer limit" sexualities (queer interracial romance, public sex, sex for money) – if we can come back to Rubin's categories ([1982] 1993, 11ff.)? Such an astute, nonjudgmental eye for the cultural codes and textures of the games that horny perverts play would imply a neutrality that, within its charged antisex context of Toronto 1985, is in itself ideological. Probably all the above interpretive options are in play, with all the ambiguities encouraged within the avant-garde system of criticism and reception. Regardless, Onodera could clearly not be less interested in the police apparatus of the repressive state, a disinterest she shares with two heterosexual male contemporaries from Montreal from whom she could not otherwise be more different.

Pouvoir Intime, YVES SIMONEAU (1986). Quebec genre director Yves Simoneau is not gay, but he delivered two accomplished gender- and genre-bending features, first in French and then in English, before moving down to Los Angeles in the early 1990s, both works injecting fresh air into the Canadian feature film milieus. The first, known in English as *Intimate Power*, is a hybrid heist film with a decidedly queer tint. A a gang of underworld losers hatch a plot to hijack a Brinks truck; the group includes Roxane, a woman who changes her look for the project and ends up seriously butch. The toilet scene is very interesting. As the plot unfolds, Roxane goes into the men's washroom in a restaurant near the proposed holdup site, perhaps to test her new look, ensconces herself in a cubicle, and almost immediately hears someone else come in: Martial, a stocky armoured-truck guard whose colleague is in on the caper. As Roxane continues to watch, in comes the diminutive and cute blond waiter Janvier, whom Martial suddenly lunges for from behind and unexpectedly hugs. A counterstereotypical surprise revelation has suddenly transpired – they're lovers, and the closety Martial has lain in wait in the secrecy of the toilet to give his boyfriend a sign of outside-world conjugality, a rather inauspicious first-anniversary present of an engraved knife. A warm embrace and kisses follow (the kisses are off-screen, with Roxane seen watching in cutaway through the crack in the cubicle partition). The lovers

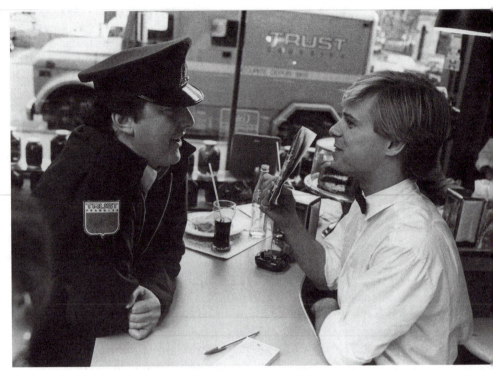

Discreet gay conjugality in the greasy spoon in *Pouvoir intime* (1986), just before
the lovers meet for their secret transgression in the public toilet. Production still,
Cinémathèque québécoise

confirm their date for that night, and leave, first one then the other – but not
without Janvier discovering that the gender transgressor has seen all and that
she's complicit in their secret transgression.

Several elements of the toilet sex formula are present: tropes of
voyeurism and surveillance (first with the ceiling vantage point of the mise-
en-scène and then the spying through the crack), plus the elements of
shame, risk, illicit sexuality, and secrecy – and defiance. The only differences
are that the repressive state is absent from the scenario (too busy guarding
its money to care about morality) and that the element of working-class
conjugal romance standing in for genital exchange, sanitized tenderness
that is, however, not without tension, provides an innovative, if ominous,
twist. Needless to say, the heist goes wrong, and a bloodbath ensues – a logical outcome of the contradictory sentimentalization of the productive conjugality of Simoneau's couple(s)? Only the butch Roxane and the cute
widower Janvier survive, and even better, the two get away into the sunset
with all the booty in their pockets, forming a new, triumphant social coalition among the sex/gender outlaws. The toilet has been the oasis in which
difference and transgression are first identified and performed in a *noir*

desert of disempowerment and violence, but the money only slightly contaminates the high spirits of the end.

Un zoo la nuit (*Night Zoo*), Jean-Claude Lauzon (1987). Another equally significant but very troubling toilet sex scene from the same years in Quebec feature filmmaking can be found in this more canonical, mega-prizewinning feature by that decade's hotshot auteur. We first see Marcel, the sympathetic protagonist of this violent and neomacho urban *film noir*, being brutally raped in jail by a goon sent by his former drug gang, who want the stash he hid before serving his sentence. Once out of jail, he ends up at a grungy poolroom-restaurant to hook up with his old girlfriend but instead encounters George, a sleazy Anglo cop in cahoots with the old gang, who clumsily hits on him. Marcel lures him into the toilet, sordid and dark, and lets him go down on him. (For some reason Lauzon has George pull out a bottle of Johnson's Baby Oil in preparation for the act, as he announces "I'm going to make you a big big boy," but my several hours of intense semiotic analysis in collaboration with a jury of qualified experts cannot decipher the exact intended function of this lubricant, given the setup, other than to allow the director to inject one additional element of inscrutable slime into Marcel's already greasy hairdo and the encounter itself.) The conventional ceiling viewpoint shows the blow job in progress, before the scene erupts into one of the most disturbing scenes of homophobic violence in Canadian film, presumably justified by Marcel's revenge for his rape. He throat-rams his fellator, throws him out of the cubicle, bashes him against the wall, then does up his fly and kicks him while he's down, grabs his gun, and imposes an extended ritual of oral humiliation on him, telling him to say "ah," and, the gun at his mouth, accuses the cop, now blubbering hysterically, of buying sex from teenage boys. He shoots the gun twice to whip up even more hysteria, before calmly walking away.[16]

This is a far cry, of course, from toilet sex as nonproductive expenditure, underground resistance, innocent fun, or secret romance. For Lauzon the toilet condenses the productive relations of the outside world, as well as being the site for restoring ravished manhood and for paying the debts of the world. The toilet is the zone of violence, hatred, trickery, scapegoating, and anger, of the filth and greed from which the hero must be absolved. In contrast to Simoneau's sense of curiosity and the pleasure of experimentation, Lauzon's scene expresses an intense anxiety over the threat posed to traditional masculinity both by queerness (the pleasures and the terrors of the anus, the orifice for which the cubicle is home) and, more generally, by the homogeneous order of productivity (to paraphrase Bataille again), incarnated now by the narco-mob, rather than by advanced capitalism. The anxiety is maintained throughout the film by the hypermasculine iconography of motorcycles, sunglasses, leather jackets, weapons, and hunting. Finally, at one of the climaxes of the film the anxiety is released in the volley of bullets Marcel pumps into George's naked body just as he's having sex in a sleazy prostitution hotel, lured there by Marcel's prison inamorato for that purpose. That the bait is another queer Anglo, this time a handsome blond-highlighted "American" who developed an unrequited crush on the self-important little hood hero in jail and will do anything for him, is of course rather interesting. Is Lauzon simply displacing queer desire onto the anglo-phone world as a reflex of Péquiste *ressentiment*, or is it a version of Frantz Fanon's displacement of black queer desire onto the white imperialist ... or both?[17] I can't explain why, of all the Canadian examples of toilet sex scenes that I have assembled, *Zoo* is the only one to feature the trope of goon violence that is a recurring part of the international generic trope of toilet sex, from *Fireworks* (Kenneth Anger, United States, 1947) to *Midnight Cowboy* (John Schlesinger, United States, 1969) and *Bomgay* (Riyad Wadia, India, 1996),[18] but no doubt it is symptomatic of something deeper and troubled about Lauzon that the goon basher is the sympathetic protagonist. No wonder an American queer review found the film "mean-spirited."[19] Stay out of toilets with Marcel.

Skin Flick/Skin Gang, BRUCE LABRUCE (1999). LaBruce's only head-on hard-core feature takes place in a composite metropolis and interweaves two narratives: an attractive young interracial gay couple, Karl and Leroy, go about their daily activities of domesticity, livelihood, and extramural sexual dalliance, and a rambunctious gang of teutonic skinheads, including one Wolfgang, prowl around the same city causing trouble. The narratives come together first in a toilet sex scene involving the breadwinner Karl and Wolfgang and finally when the gang invades the couple's domestic abode, where an eruption of sexual assault and revenge, all racially inflected, provides the climax to the film.

As we have already seen, the scandalous Toronto queercore sex director of the nineties was partaking of a completely different sensibility and context both from the politicized Vancouver/Toronto experimenters of the seventies and eighties and from the two Quebec "enfant terrible" auteurs of the eighties, advancing an international gay-male erotics, rather than mythologies of resistance or national masculinity. Yet LaBruce's sex scenes, in both the soft-core version developed to meet British censorship conventions and distributed in North America and the hard-core version circulating within the porno circuits of Germany and the United States, belong to the same basic iconographic trajectory as those of his precursors, albeit cross-fertilized with the cultural iconography of commercial gay porno. Karl, the guppie hero of *Skin Flick/Gang*, gymbag and umbrella in perfect condition, is

Un zoo la nuit (1987): Marcel getting roughed up by George, the corrupt gay anglophone narc who doesn't know the homophobic savagery that awaits him in the public toilet, the zone of hatred and filth from which the hero must be absolved. Production still, Cinémathèque québécoise

first attracted by the skin Wolfgang's purse-snatching in the hybrid London-Berlin park he just happens to be wandering through on his way home from work. This Genet-esque erotics of thievery is already implanted as a kind of rebellion against productive society (to use Champagne's terms). Eye contact having been established, Wolfgang follows Karl towards a public toilet that has the look of a bucolic English country cottage, rather than a scene of abject transgression. The two men stare at each other side by side at the urinals, jerk off a little in tandem, pretend to spar a bit, and then at the sinks, pretending to wash up, they jettison all decorum, knock heads, kiss ferociously, and next, equitably trade vigorous oral service. The inevitable culmination has Wolfgang fucking Karl long and hard against the sinks, first doggy-style and then "missionary position," narcissistically watching himself in the mirror scowling and thrusting. Inside the toilet, departing from the gritty black and white punk aesthetics and the documentary energy of much of the film, the toilet acquires the aestheticized abstraction of a commodity fantasy, a full-colour, high-production-value fantasy set, with little of the grunge or grime one might have expected from the narrative pretext. For one thing the lighting is too bright and efficient for an on-location sensibility, and for another the graffiti is just a little too felicitously "art designed" in its variously pro-skin, queer-baiting, or antifascist rhetoric to be any more than a perfunctory reminder of the politics of the place. More importantly, the furtiveness and spontaneity of toilet sex, signalled by half-opened or hastily lowered clothes or awkward choreography, is missing, replaced not only by the fully nude, perfect bodies but also by efficiently disclosed acrobatics of porno: instead of the awkward high views down into a tight cubicle, the standard porno angle of perineal scrutiny from a studio-based, floor-level camera is substituted. Only the witty line thrown into the midst of the soft-core version of the toilet encounter, a line alluding to the contradictory politics of celebrity cottaging ("Do I look like George Michael to you?"), momentarily brings back the LaBruce piss and vinegar of yore.[20]

Interestingly, the hard-core version undermines the class-based role-play in the soft-core version, given the enthusiasm with which Wolfgang engages in sucking. In both versions the toilet sex scene is mounted through the typical LaBruce mechanism of intercutting a parallel narrative thread (Karl's spouse Leroy's dalliance with the plumber in the kitchen of their condo), setting up an opposition between the simultaneous adulterous encounters at home and in the wild, respectively, and then throwing it off with the addition of a third narrative line of skinhead street roughhouse near the end of the sequence. The hard-core version attenuates the vigorous rhythm and structure of the intercutting, however, weakening the opposition by imposing the porno conventions of climactic buildup and close-up meat fixation. In both versions, the toilet becomes less a specific site of disruption than a vague zone of neutral fantasy and of one-on-one sexual display and exchange, as if free of economic dynamics and social conflict. With both guppy spouses simultaneously indulging in rough, interclass extracurricular activity, their complacent conjugality remains unchallenged and the potential frisson of abjection is dissolved.

The real explosion comes later, not in the place of excrement and the zone of abjection but in the guppie living room, not through "coupling" but through gang rape and not through a celebration of nonproductive free sexuality but through LaBruce's assault on the smug utopianism of earlier ideals of sexual liberation and identity politics.

rollercoaster, SCOTT SMITH (1999). Perhaps the most enigmatic toilet scene in the whole selection happens at the off-season midway where a group of teenagers are on a lark. Ben, a handsome, bland young security guard is recklessly allowing the kids' presence in the park. While the hypermacho kid Stick is in the men's room cubicle taking a pause from the gang's drunken and raucous antics, Ben, who is scarcely a decade older than Stick, is drawn to him at that particular moment, and it's unclear why. It is also unclear whether the sexual act in the cubicle between Ben and Stick constitutes a rape, as one of my students characterized it, or an encounter with a contradictory mix of resistance and consent. What is clear is that the guard penetrates Stick's mouth, that the tough kid doesn't put up any fight, and that the encounter is both a trauma for Stick and his moment of self-knowledge. The toilet, the most abject place in this utopian wonderland of whirling lights, is the place of truth. Stick later refuses a suggestion by his friend's younger brother to kill the guard because "he's a fag," replying, "No he's not, I'm a fag. He just fucks kids. Pull yourself together, you're so screwed up." Having thus bonded through truth, Stick and the boy, at film's end, light out for the territories.

Hey Happy! NOAM GONICK (2000). LaBruce's biggest fan and frequent collaborator, Noam Gonick not surprisingly shares a certain cynical sensibility with his queercore mentor, but perhaps allows sexual utopianism another chance. Gonick's first feature is set in a ruinously sublime wide-screen landscape (the film's irrepressible documentary lens, for all its fantasy excess, pinpoints the vulnerable flood plain of the Winnipeg outskirts), part apocalyptic, part carnivalesque. Here the scarred and substance-dependent young heroes, Sabu and Happy, wander on their vision quest in search of fulfilment and each other, dogged and continuously separated by Spanky, the queen of all evil hairdressers, who is stalking Happy, killing dogs, and spitting venom. The toxic landscape is not only postindustrial, postsexual revolution, and postmodern but also postgay, populated almost entirely by the sexually disempowered and marginalized. Sabu's boss at his open-air used-porno shop scolds him for mixing business and pleasure when he starts kissing hottie customers. But this doesn't seem to be a serious taboo for a rather irrelevant productive system wherein the main activity involves the relatively nonproductive activities of getting one's hair done, raving, and riding around on motorbikes.

The public toilet that serves Gonick's denizens is situated in a huge gas station and provides a kind of sanitized refuge from all those flood warnings and from screaming and dissonant soundtrack pieces. Here, characters of all genders and sexualities can make out and do drugs and occasionally even urinate, and in its amyl nitrate–misted atmosphere, all documentary energy, hitherto concentrated in the film's landscapes and bodies, dissipates. Gonick offers not one but two toilet scenes, each involving literally over-the-top Spanky intruding on the peace of the toilet's inner sanctums, competing with Sabu to be the despoiler of Happy's virginity. In the first toilet scene, Spanky disturbs sensitive Happy's solo ablutions, shriekingly invading the sanctuary of the cubicle he has fled to, penetrating the glory hole with protruding eye and thrusting tongue, and sliding under and above the partition with animalistic snarls. Then later, when Happy and Sabu retreat to the cubicle for some romantic kissing (Happy's preference is for low-intensity courtship because he hasn't really done much fucking before), Spanky is perched right up at ceiling level, shrieking sexual assault at the two, leaping down into the space, and driving the terrorized Happy out into the night. In a nightmare postgay universe where sex and gender are the least problematic of a hundred fluid categories, the public toilet is no longer a political zone, and not even excrement is restricted to this obsolete vestigial corner of refuge. As a neutralized zone, as it is in *Skin Flick/Gang,* the toilet in *Hey Happy!* is robbed of its social function as a site of abjection and subversion of the productive world. In a surely significant footnote, David McIntosh, the credited story editor on *Happy* and the most committed queer programmer at "Perspective Canada," played one of the frisky cubicle Lotharios a generation earlier for Midi Onodera, but clearly a lot of water has flushed under the bridge since then.

Better than Chocolate, ANNE WHEELER (1999). Released the previous year but developed simultaneously with *Happy,* Wheeler's urban baby-dyke romance follows Greyson and McGarry's (and even Gonick's) inspiration in current events: the harassment and censorship of Vancouver's Little Sisters bookstore since the 1980s by Customs Canada. She thus revives the issue of real-world political reference and documentary energy that was evacuated from the lowly toilet stall by LaBruce and Gonick. Wheeler is not the first female director in this section about toilet sex, but she is the first to depict lesbian sexual exchange within a public toilet in her film. Onodera had of course depicted only men in action and had explicitly ordained gender difference as its determining framework through juxtaposing the male-male toilet action with female-female courtship and female-male telephone sex. In fact, lesbian toilet sex – or the fear thereof – has a respectable history, and it touched a nerve in pre-Stonewall queer tenderloins, as Joan Nestle recalled in Margaret Wescott's *Stolen Moments* (see chapter 6): "all kinds of bargains had to be worked out with the vice squads and with the police to even allow these bars to exist, and one of the compromises was that we were not to be allowed in the bathroom more than one at a time because we couldn't be trusted not to make love in the bathroom." Nevertheless, toilet scenes in lesbian films before Wheeler's had been more about homosociality than subversive sexuality (although it could be argued that in such a film as Holly Dale and JANIS COLE's *P4W: Prison for Women* (1982) all the intimately shared trying on of makeup before the semipublic jailhouse-toilet mirrors between the soon-to-be separated lovers Debbie and Janis, lipstick

Better than Chocolate (1999) shows domesticated toilet sex: 1985 anti-sex has dissipated in favour of a pro-sex consensus within lesbian-feminist politics and sex commodity culture alike, and everyone applauds. VHS frame grab, Rave Film

lesbians before their time, is surrogate coding for the sexual exchange that neither the social actors, the prison officials, nor documentary ethics would allow us to see).

Wheeler's toilet scene unfolds when the baby dyke heroines-in-love, Maggie and Kim, go out on the town to a trendy girls' club, in part to escape Lila, Maggie's in-the-dark heterosexual mother who is unexpectedly lodging with the couple. The two agree that it's very hard to make love when your mother's in the next room and doesn't know about you, so they repair to the ladies' room cubicle and get it on, opening the pent-up flood-gates. The predictable ceiling viewpoint is soon supplanted by the camera getting right in the booth with them, and the oral scene that follows is one of the most intimate in the film. In fact, the sex is so noisy that the growing lineup outside the stall start listening and giggling supportively. Not only do lesbians not fight in the toilets, but the crowd even applauds when the sated, red-faced couple emerge, and another couple rushes in to follow their example. The private/public dichotomy becomes tangled and reversed: the closeted couple can escape detection only within the semipublic commercial space of the queer nightlife ghetto, and the descent into the place of excrement paradoxically cements respectable "inner limits" relationship-sex, rather than the transgressively anonymous jouissance that the guys have. By 1999 the stressful antisex response of 1985 has so dissipated and the pro-sex consensus within lesbian-feminist politics and sex-commodity culture alike is so entrenched that the applause is built into the film, and heterosexual feminist directors and their heterosexual actors are leading the parade.

But Wheeler and her scriptwriter Peggy Thompson are not finished. Maggie and Kim return to the romantic glitz of the dance floor, and their transsexual friend Judy is suddenly on stage, performing the show-stopping cabaret song "Don't Fuck with My Tender, Trans-Gender Heart," whereafter she makes a romantic assignation with repressed bookstore clerk Frances, and before they are to leave together she herself repairs to the ladies' room. There, as Judy fixes her lip-liner, she is insulted and physically assaulted by a 1980-style gender fundamentalist who orders her to go to the men's room, before being restrained by Maggie and Kim, who come running to the rescue (regardless of the veracity of the trope of lesbians fighting in the toilet after all, the scene has a probable real-world reference, namely, to a successful British Columbia human rights complaint by a transgendered woman against a notorious rape crisis centre that would allow only women-born women to counsel female rape survivors, a case that was still ongoing in the appeals tribunals as of this writing in 2003). In fact, Wheeler has kept one step ahead of her audience: having gently satirized the consensus and merchandising of relationship [same-]sex, she has immediately re-problematized the politics of gender and localized it also in the place of sit-down urination.

In the next scene it's back to the bedroom where Lila discovers the girls' huge Y-dildo toys under the bed, as if Creatures from the Black Lagoon, but Lila quickly tames them and embarks on her own initiation into the commodification of sexual pleasure. Before catching her breath, Wheeler has re-opened one more time the politics of sex, not for lesbians or for the transgendered, but for another marginalized group, the postmenopausal, a demographic that Wheeler (born in 1946) can be said to know personally rather well (after all, the personal is political, as she learned at Studio D). Still, for all Wheeler's ideologically deft extension of the film's horizons and for all the film's denunciation of hatred, bias, and silencing, the climactic political struggle unfolds, not in the toilet and not in or under the bed, but in full public view in the bookstore display window where the naked Maggie claims her social identity as a lesbian reader rather than her lesbian identity as a sexual subject (though she is naked, admittedly) and defies social violence rather than state suppression.

In conclusion, while I don't want to overstate the allegorical discursive apt-
ness of the shifting trajectory of toilet sex over the quarter century in question, it is possible to make several pithy comments on how toilet sex in these
films and videos mirrors the larger cosmic universe and the smaller Canadian cultural reflection of it. First, however, we must remember that toilets are
not necessarily bathrooms, and a whole other segue could be developed on
bathrooms and bathing in Canadian cinemas, which I am capable of but will
restrain myself from doing. But if only to accent the specificity of toilet sex
imagery by comparison, I might mention that bathing scenes are much more
plentiful and prolific than toilet sex (and more evenly distributed between
the male and female, queer and straight sides – even David Suzuki has shown
straight young men comparing penises in the shower), and they are less risk-
taking, due to their reference to classic iconography, their shared belonging
to heterosexual iconography, and their association with a whole gamut of
alibis among both queers and nonqueers, from sports to hygiene. Furthermore, they have a longer genealogy and a wider range of functions, from the
early closety exploration of the nude male body and almost sacramental
homosocial/homoerotic intimacy of the sixties (*Winter Kept Us Warm*, just to
cite one shower scene that I have never recovered from; see chapter 4) to the
later up-front explorations of self-eroticism and identity (those steamy mirrors!), such as are found in the works of filmmakers like LÉA POOL (*Anne
Trister*), or of initiation, as in the high-school shower-room scene of JEAN-
FRANÇOIS MONETTE's *Take Out*.

The comparison can bring out an interesting Toronto-Montreal dialectic
as well. With Montreal's long-standing tradition dating back to the sixties
of queer visibility on the arts stage, which leaked into the cinema, the crys-
tallization of queer discourses within bathing or toilet scenes engendered
less of an overt political function than those in Toronto. We have already
seen this in the toilet as an affirmation space for conjugality in Yves
Simoneau, and we might see it elsewhere, from the masturbatory intensity
of Marc Paradis's very private bathroom scene in *Délivre-nous du mal* to
the full-blown romanticism of bathtub scenes in two features that won foreign queer-festival audience prizes in 1989 and 1997, respectively *The Heart
Exposed* and *Lilies*. Generalizations are treacherous, however, for surely
the most erotic, tender, and romantic bathtub scenes in the entire cinematic
repertory come from the hard-boiled LaBruce in *No Skin off My Ass* and
Hustler White. Interestingly, Greyson's early eponymous bathing scenes in
After the Bath offered his more usual confrontational politics/aesthetics. On
the women's side as well, the features *Anne Trister* and *2 Secondes*, international queer-festival hits in 1987 and 1999 respectively, are also notable for
the intimate autoeroticism and corporeal expression of their bathtub scenes,

rather than for defiant "in your face" political statements. In contrast to Montreal queer cinema's characteristic exploration of the perils of private intimacy through the sensuous rituals of water and soap, Toronto's tradition seems more rooted in the assertion of public rights: even *Prison for Women*'s melodrama of homosocial makeup workshops in the pen toilets is contestatory in its own closety way. With my segue about clean and sacramental uses of bathing images now over, the distinctive raw filth of toilet sex iconography and its closeness to the evolutionary dissipation of confrontational politics, as well as its sensitivity to cultural difference, can be confirmed.

One of the themes of this book has been the participation of queer film and video, either directly or indirectly, in the political struggles both around sexuality in the political arena and, somewhat contradictorily, around the access of Canadian filmmakers to the audiences of the cultural marketplace. The toilet sex trajectory, in conclusion, seems like a microcosmic index of the shifting terrains of these two struggles. If the uncompromising political construction of toilet sex in *In Black and White* and *Ten Cents a Dance (Parallax)* coincides with the bleak Capital Cost Allowance period, these two films' entrenchment in avant-garde aesthetics and distribution echoed in many ways the lingering marginality of queer politics in the Canadian landscape (Quebec remained, for example, the only province with Charter protection until the long, bitter Ontario struggle finally triumphed in 1986, the year after *Ten Cents*). Onodera's breakthrough into the international queer-festival circuit, still in its early stages in the mid-eighties, did, however, herald a promising upsurge of queer cinema in Canada and elsewhere, with the end of the famine of the seventies finally in sight (and the regular programming thereafter of Canadian queer cinema in community festivals abroad, first in San Francisco and soon everywhere else). The instransigeant *Urinal* offered contradictory signals, summing up the era of the avant-garde at the same time as it signalled a shift to feature-film theatrical accessibility by winning the prize at Berlin. Yet distribution problems remained critical, as discovered by Greyson's Canadian distributor, Full Frame, which had been experimenting with the coalition of queer politics within its labour, international solidarity, and feminist catalogue but soon went belly up, a devastating closure to alternative film distribution in Canada and to *Urinal*'s access to the big screens that do it justice. The film's currently restricted availability in Canada from its U.S. distributor is of course symptomatic, and it is no accident that even Bruce LaBruce's work is extremely difficult to come by in his own backyard, for commercial, rather than legal, reasons.

Later political dynamics have been ultimately dictated or shaped by Supreme Court interpretations of the 1982 Charter of Rights and Freedoms, with the governmentality in the politics of rights that we gained from the Charter matching the governmentality in national cultural funding. As discussed in chapter 6 and elsewhere, the impact on queer political culture has been fundamental, and it is impossible not to connect, at least symbolically, Wheeler's enshrinement of the couple and LaBruce's love-hate critique of the couple in their respective toilet sex scenes as a response to this dynamic. If our minimal progress in capturing theatrical screens, at least in English Canada, remains precarious, there has clearly been a breakthrough of queer visibility accompanying this progress since the midnineties, as the prizewinning visibility of *Le Confessionnal*, *Better than Chocolate*, *The Hanging Garden*, *Forbidden Love*, and *Lilies* testifies (see portrait gallery, CANADIAN FILM AWARDS). Some would argue that this presence has had its cost in terms of a depoliticization of sexuality in the cultural landscape, since a normalization is clearly built into the romantic comic toilet sex episode of *Chocolate* that even Katherine Monk approved of as "positive" – however refreshingly subversive the film is in its discourses about postmenopausal female sexual pleasure, sex toys, transgender rights, state censorship, and its advocacy of butt plug initiations for teenage male heterosexuals. Feature film visibility does not necessarily evacuate the politics of sexuality – as we saw with *Bubbles Galore* and *Urinal* – rather, it mixes it into a contradictory discursive ferment that may be the best one can hope for from a feature film sector itself sentenced to remain in its present marginal context. If toilet sex has disappeared from the queer political radar in the face of same-sex marriage as I write this in 2003 (temporarily one fears), the next step in the trajectory, perhaps reflecting Gonick's intraqueer dynamics, is no doubt waiting in the wings.

OF CUTS AND CONCLUSIONS

We have toured several different zones of queer sexual representation on film and video in English Canada and Quebec. We have explored out-and-out commercial hard-core porno and non- or quasi-commercial community-focused variants of the same formula. We have explored also the gamut of art film and video, from features to shorts, most of which have their cake and eat it too, brazenly showing more or less explicit representation but at the same keeping a distance, not so much *inhabiting* the hard-core of hard-core as *scrutinizing* or *dissecting* it from the side or from above or from within editorial parentheses. Together we have discovered that this eclectic corpus is united by its common preoccupation with money, as well as with images of fucking across a whole spectrum of intensities. The works share the compulsion to transmit a strong sense of the materiality of sex, both the economics of sexual exchange and relationships and the economics of sexual representation, from the commodification of fantasy to the marketing of sexual identities and practices. This preoccupation with the materiality of sex is in turn inflected by a cluster of shared cultural characteristics, whether on the anglophone or francophone side of the Canadian cinematic watershed: all more or less involve the cross-fertilisation of the impulse to show and give erotic pleasure with the aims to instruct, transform, provoke, document, and mobilize.

If these aims sound like those of the National Film Board, it's no accident, for these discourses of sobriety, I have repeatedly claimed, intersect obliquely but distinctively, much like the board's output itself, with a Canadian context overwhelmed by our documentary cultural heritage. Could Canada really be one of the places that bring together Foucault's famous polarities of sexual knowledge, his "two great procedures for producing the truth of sex": on the one hand, *ars erotica*, erotic art, which the philosopher (somewhat simplistically) situated willy-nilly within almost all non-Euro-American, non-Judaeo-Christian traditions, and on the other hand, *scientia sexualis*, the science of sexuality? The latter is descended in so-called Western societies from the Christian ritual of the confession and deploys "the transformation of sex into discourse" through the disciplines of modern science, psychiatry, and law, etc. (Foucault [1976] 1990, 6). Can it be that the generations of Canadian artists we have seen struggling to produce the truth about pleasure at the same time with the discourses of science and sobriety have finally brought *ars* and *scientia* together above the forty-ninth parallel?

I'm being facetious as well as wistful, for the fairy tale of *ars* and *scientia* living happily together ever after is considerably dampened by our overwhelming context of cultural and economic dependency, impacting across the board on factors from the impoverishment of artists, to the denial of audience access, to the dumping of foreign sexual commodities (from commercial porn, including the progressive queer variety, to the avant-garde) on home turf. We have seen how this latter context of dependency has itself been illuminated repeatedly by various strategies of the artists that I have spotlighted, from the casting of hyperbolically American performers and the appropriation of patently American pop culture (including pornography) to the conspicuous foregrounding of the indigenous spaces, bodies, languages, and iconographies that have arisen over thirty years from the marketplaces, movements, and cultures that constitute the queer Canadian here and now.

When we talk about dependency, we are talking about a kind of economic censorship, and to conclude, I would like to highlight one more time this further important environmental element shared by all the works in this chapter, the rocky terrain of censorship. This terrain comprises, on the one hand, the economic censorship of the marketplace and the legal censorship of our colonized state apparatuses and, on the other hand, the social, cultural, institutional – and psychic – constraints that amount to a perhaps more insidious form of censorship. There is no space to treat this issue exhaustively, and fortunately, an excellent subliterature and filmography on the history of the censorship of the arts in Canada has emerged – a history that, incidentally, overlaps irretrievably with the history of queer sexual representation (Gilbert 1999; Cossman et al. 1997; Fuller and Blackley 1996).

Suffice it to offer a few centrifugal arrows, by way of tying together some of the threads that are still loose. Within a culture in which sexuality is at the centre of both personal identity and the regulation of citizenship, censorship is drawn like a magnet to sexual representation, whether *ars* or *scientia*, and the works in this chapter that hover near or within the dread zone of the explicit are particularly scarred by its effects. As just one example, look at the two versions of Bruce LaBruce's 1999 film, *Skin Flick* and *Skin Gang*. Though neither version responds to specifically Canadian constraints, the two versions fulfil the conventional requirements of the soft-core U.S./British market and the hard-core German/U.S. market respectively. They thus offer a concise object lesson in how both censorship and self-censorship can radically transform a work, with regard not only to the nitty gritty of penetration and money shots but also to the vaguer cultural dynamics that render the former truncated work the sharper and even hotter work of erotic art and social critique. (Aside from this comparison, what does it mean that a Toronto boy wonder couldn't – or couldn't be bothered to – distribute these fantasies in Canada?) Within the present corpus, censorship and self-censorship have taken on many other forms as well. John Greyson, whose videos and films *Jungle Boy, Moscow Doesn't Believe in Queers,* and *Urinal* have been examined here, later produced the full-length film *Un©ut* (1997), on the subject of censorship itself (leaving aside for now the apt but complex metaphorical connection to circumcision he drew out in the film), licking the wounds left by the outright suppression of one of his breakthrough works, *The Making of Monsters* (1991). This suppression had as its pretext copyright enforcement, rather than sexual censorship. But same difference: obviously the American rights holders might have been more tolerant of Greyson's parodic appropriation of their intellectual property were it not within a work on queer public sex!

Looking at our corpus, it is clear that this issue of copyright censorship, while not at first glance necessarily or directly related to sexuality, is responsible for the ghettoization of whole swatches of artistic work based on the "scratch" aesthetics of intertextual appropriation (which, ironically, appropriates pictures from the south-of-the-border Babylon 90 percent of the time, like naughty but not very dangerous colonial bandits); "scratch" video artists are therefore relegated as a result to the alternative gallery circuits and educational margins where copyright is often not policed, rather than to the broadcast, cable, and video-rental audiences they clearly have the moral right to access.

At the other end of the spectrum, on a more conventional level we have also seen the more direct effect of legal harassment, actual and potential, of distributors, producers and consumers by the state and its organisms – vice squads, courts, lawyers, licensers, enforcers of zoning, fire, and liquor regulations, customs agents, and film surveillance boards (the latter two apparatuses, ironically, impeding our right to import mostly U.S.-originating sexual imagery). Beginning as far back as the 1950s but reaching its full rhythm in the 1970s, this state-ordained harassment has continued sporadically ever since. Its legacy is the wholesale stunting of the development of an indigenous erotic art and science, industry and infrastructure.

One of the lessons to be learned is clearly the arbitrariness of censorship in all its guises. The attack on the Banff Centre for the Arts by the Alberta government and the Alberta right-wing media in 1992, provoked by Sylvie Gilbert's brilliant exhibition of mostly feminist sexual film, video, art, and performances, ("Much Sense: Erotics and Life"), demonstrates this lesson well, along with its inseparability in our social-democratic heritage from the crucial stake of public arts funding (Gilbert 1999). The vulnerability of one of the most prestigious arts cultural centres in the country to this demagog attack is symptomatic. Equally significant is the fact that none of the bountiful lineup of American works in the show or any of the film and video works programd were the butt of the hatchetmen, only the most vulnerable of live indigenous bodies in performance, the "radical lesbian" Vancouver collective Kiss and Tell. A major moral is that the powers of silencing, hatred, and fear include the power to set the agenda, the stakes, the victims, the criteria, and the battleground at whim and to keep artists, consumers, and sexual marginals constantly on the defensive on shifting terrain, creating the conditions for a culture of shame, vulnerability, paranoia, self-doubt and self-censorship. The parliamentary attack on *Bubbles Galore,* with which I introduced this chapter, is another illustration of the same principle of the arbitrariness and unaccountability of censorial power over a work chosen accidentally and after the fact from among literally thousands of potential sexual works funded by our network of public arts councils, broadcast and film investment schemes, museum infrastructures, etc. Set up as the centrepiece of a demagogical ideological campaign, inflamed by words like "radical," "lesbian," and "pornography," *Bubbles* provided a pretext to close down public debate about, and support of, culture, diversity, and minority empowerment.

Still, it is misleading to overstate the dynamic of suppression, too tempting to develop a repressive hypothesis, to borrow another Foucauldian concept, to describe the overwhelming weight under which the exciting, rich, and energized twenty-five-year sexual corpus has struggled to assert itself. One needs, rather, to use the conceptual tool that Foucault used to counter the repressive hypothesis, a dynamic through which the naming of "radical lesbian pornographers" by hate mongers, for example, is part of the prototypical interaction of control and resistance he described as the "spiral of power and pleasure." The pleasure and sobriety we have found *chez* Roberts, LaBruce, Greyson, Fung, Reinke, Dirty Pillows, and the toilet artists are distinctly analogous to the pleasure that the French philosopher summed up in the context of the nineteenth century: "pleasure that kindles at having to evade this power, flee from it, fool it, or travesty it ... power asserting itself in the pleasure of showing off, scandalizing, or resisting." Concretely, Foucault's model of science's interactive role in the spiral seems felicitously parallel – *too* felicitously? – to the operative relationship between censorship in Canada and the sexual artists caught up in its web:

There is no question that the appearance in nineteenth century psychiatry, jurisprudence and literature of a whole series of discourses on the species and subspecies of homosexuality, inversion, pederasty, and "psychic hermaphrodism" made possible a strong advance of social controls into this area of "perversity"; but it also made possible the formation of a "reverse" discourse: homosexuality began to speak in its own behalf, to demand that its legitimacy or "naturality" be acknowledged, often in the same vocabulary, using the same categories by which it was medically disqualified. ([1976] 1990, 45, 101)

The literal applications, at once hypothetical and concrete, of the "'reverse' discourse" model to the corpus at hand are rich and bountiful. The unprecedented cablecast of *Bubbles Galore*, subsequent to the parliamentary brouhaha, reaching an audience unimagined at the time of its production several years earlier and reviewed in every major daily, is just one example of the pleasure of "scandalizing" power.

On the level of textual rather than contextual meaning, the protocols of confidentiality, protecting the identity of the guilty, are most interesting and constitute another kind of complex censorial effect: would Greyson's proud and forthright testimony from the Oakville toilet arrest survivor in *Urinal* have had the same impact without the diabolical delirium of the absurd mask on the other witness, the hyperbolic double-edged satire on the anonymity that a patronizing and complicit media culture and social-sciences establishment imposed on those who revolt and dissent on the pretext of protecting them? Surely Greyson has punctured better than anyone else a whole cultural infrastructure of shame, embodied elsewhere throughout our corpus by the mise-en-scène of bodies without identifiable heads, of credits peopled only by pseudonyms. And across town a few years later, did the absurd Alice-in-Wonderland conviction of *Bad Attitude* in Toronto (Cossman et al. 1997) not lead directly to even badder attitude in *Pornograflix*, a work that can be seen as an absolute celebration of the "degradation" around which the Butler decision revolved, not to mention as a serious boost for an entire indigenous network of dildo-and-harness lesbian image production? Finally, the interwoven pressures of economic censorship and dependency may be the toughest dynamic to understand as part of a Foucauldian spiral: Bubbles's entrepreneurial revolt against the patriarchal porno industry is a fictional echo of the real-world self-reliance espoused by Priape and Bruce LaBruce with their foreign markets and revenue-driven ethos, which the free-enterprise bigots would surely approve of, but their relationship to our imperilled heritage of public arts funding is inextricable all the same. Neither can exist without the other.

If Katharine Monk is right that Canadian cinema is full of "kinky, dark, quirky and obsessive sex," her explanations of bonding mechanisms in a frigid climate or absurdly monolithic national personality constructions such as a "national insecurity complex" need to be qualified. She is closer to the truth when she declares that "all straight sex in Canadian film is downright bent," for the intense queer sexual energy that we have been exploring in this chapter infuses the whole landscape. And the spiral is an appropriate figure for it. These films and videos embody this irreversible choreography, which sets up artists and spectators – desiring, fantasizing, discoursing, learning, engaging, mobilizing – in a whirling concatenation of feints, clashes and dashes, and pas de deux with the governmentalities of exclusion, violence, and constraint, as well as those of rights, beneficience, and legitimation; with the marketplace as a stage where alienation, fetishization, and satiation square off with impulses of diversity, choice, and fulfilment, as well as the co-opted and orgiastic pleasure of consumption; where censorial mechanisms have not smothered but, rather, fanned the politicization of desire and the violence of legality and interdiction engages in a hesitation waltz with the sobrieties and affirmations of community and collective self-knowledge, revolt, and ecstasy.

9

Anti-Retroviral: "A Test of Who We Are"

Many well-meaning souls ... have claimed that the AIDS crisis is resulting in a cultural renaissance – that old "great art is born of suffering" line. Well, thanks but no thanks. Concepts of "great art" ultimately benefit only those collectors who want hefty returns on their investments, rarely the communities that originate such production. Renaissances are usually identified after the fact, claimed by bystanders who have achieved a safe, contemplative distance. The romance of suffering is affordable only to the bourgeoisie, who vicariously consume it, but by definition never do it.

For us artists in the midst of the maelstrom, it's a matter of supreme indifference to us to learn, as another critic has suggested, that our collective body of work from this last decade will one day be studied with the same reverence and fascination currently reserved for the literature of the Second World War.
~ John Greyson, "Parma Violets for Wayland Flowers," 1992

INTRODUCTION: THE MAELSTROM

As I started to write an early version of this chapter in October 2000, Canadians had been plunged into an election, but I was more interested in the minister of immigration's preelection announcement of a new policy of compulsory HIV testing for all immigration candidates. I was reflecting on the history of our settler territory, which was driven, we must not forget, by overcrowded, unsanitary boatloads and planeloads of immigrants and refugees and contoured by the propagation – both infectious and environmental and even military – of the scurvy, smallpox, cholera, typhus, typhoid, syphilis, tuberculosis, influenza, polio, cancer, AIDS, and SARS that lay in wait for those immigrants and for the land's unimmunised original inhabitants. It is as if *Plague Years*, the title of Mike Hoolboom's collection of film writings (1998), could serve equally as the title for a history of Canada. Yet the government was responding to the urgent warnings of planetary crisis coming out of that year's Durban International AIDS Conference by ineffectually trying to block it at the border and winning an election with the same stroke. It was as if, after two decades of the longest and most costly and fractious – and perhaps most unnecessary – epidemic in modern Canadian history, we had learned nothing. As I undertook the final version of this chapter in the winter of 2003–04, more than three years later, Montreal Catholic seminarians become the new demographic target for HIV testing, in a far more duplicitous policy manoeuvre than even that of their friends in Ottawa. And the administration of our local children's hospital blundered its way into a public scandal around the practice of a recently deceased PWA surgeon and the infinitesimal theoretical risk to which she might have exposed her hundreds of patients. Yet instead of public outrage, we go on with our lives with resigned indifference to these flagrant acts of bureaucratic scapegoating and brutality.

At such moments I always think of moving images, in particular the images of those film and video artists who have acted as a kind of conscience within Canadian culture and society. I think not of a cultural renaissance but of a cultural reckoning, these artists' unforgettable images of social otherness, corporeal abjection, psychic intensity, and political provocation that summed up the challenge of the Pandemic. Their images have synthesized for me the experiences of people living with AIDS, whenever teaching, fundraising, buddying, activism, volunteering, and funerals left me enervated, as our society moved through the more than two decades of the retrovirus. This chapter is devoted to some of those images that inspire, that summon us not only to action against state cynicism but also to morality, lucidity, and affect vis-à-vis the medico-social crisis that we allowed to happen and to a visual and narrative identification with the corporeal and existential meltdown – and illuminations – it has entailed.

I would like to consider one by one in this chapter three Toronto men whose films and videos have stood out among the strong generational current of artistic responses to the Pandemic – John Greyson, Richard Fung, and Mike Hoolboom – basing my reflection on three works by each. All three artists I know personally and with great affection, and I am in awe of their extraordinary commitment and magnetism as public intellectuals/artists – personae all too lacking in the public sphere of an English Canada seemingly mobilised around Ralph Klein, Don Cherry, and Paul Martin. For some reason the AIDS-myopia of the Liberals' immigration policy made me think immediately of Hoolboom rather than the others, not only because he is a child of immigrants (like Fung) and an artist who (like Greyson) has done his share of raging along the way against stupidity, power lust, and greed in Ottawa (*Kanada*, 1993; *Valentine's Day*, 1994). I thought of him mostly because, of my three selected artists, he alone is infected like thousands of other Canadians with the retrovirus that is besieging bodies and continents. (Both Greyson and Fung have PWA life partners: Greyson's partner since 1997 has been the prominent visual artist Stephen Andrews, whose work has often appeared in AIDS- and queer-themed shows; and Fung's since 1977 has been activist educator Tim McCaskell, who in addition to being a subject of *Sea in the Blood*, has been a key collaborator for many of his lover's works, as well as for several of Greyson's works.) Hoolboom's serostatus no doubt factors into the unusual power of his films, his voice, and his person to engage a nonspecialist, interdisciplinary audience with no interest in experimental cinema, something that in fact all three of these artists have a knack for doing. But their charisma, prolificacy, and profile notwithstanding, their work makes sense only, they would all agree, as part of that larger cultural community and trajectory focused on and by the retrovirus over the last two decades. Accordingly, I would like to begin by charting the first generation of Canadian AIDS audiovisual activism, the turbulent groundwater of oeuvres and artists that surged up in the 1980s and continued into the 1990s.

GROUNDWATER

> It's not happening to us in Canada, it's happening to them.
> ~ *Letters from Home*, Hoolboom

After its "discovery" in 1981, what is now called the human immunodeficiency virus and the devastation it caused were commonly perceived here in Canada as an "American" phenomenon, and a strictly "gay" one at that, but one mercifully lagging, epidemiologically speaking, several years behind the skyrocketing crisis in the States. Despite the futile alarms raised by *The Body Politic* and others, the virus soon infiltrated the bloodstreams of Canadians – but all too slowly their cultural consciousness. In the United States by middecade, a major counteroffensive of long and short films and video documentaries and even porno films about AIDS was in place, most from within the lesbian and gay "community"; the most visible mainstream cultural texts were the sanctimonious TV movie of the week, *An Early Frost*, and its spitting sister, Larry Kramer's pioneering Broadway play *The Normal Heart* (both 1985). Around 1984 Canadian media artists, initially in Toronto, then elsewhere, inaugurated an at first tentative trickle of cultural work about

AIDS. The first Canadian documentary prophetically appeared in Toronto in 1985 (*No Sad Songs* [NIK SHEEHAN, co-produced by the AIDS Committee of Toronto, 26]), a survey of gay community mobilisations intercut with dramatised fantasy vignettes and sewn together around a mournful portrait of a gay man with AIDS preparing for the end with campy humour and courage. AIDS media work picked up momentum immediately after Sheehan's bold venture forth; it was most commonly community-based but with arts networks also well represented, reaching its peak at the end of the decade. For example, GLENN WALTON's Halifax-based documentary *Life after Diagnosis* (1990, 30), funded by federal ministries, was a heartfelt and accomplished example with stirring coast-to-coast encounters with more than a dozen eloquent voices and faces.

Almost two decades of fevers and lulls in AIDS-related cultural production since *No Sad Songs* can, alas, be divided into periods and genres. As I myself have recounted (1992), the popular melodrama genre, the "tearjerker" – and I do not use the term in any pejorative sense – was the first, most lasting, and popularly most effective of the cultural formats deployed in the international arena, unashamed in its aestheticisation of suffering, its narrativisation of loss, and its elegiac solicitation of mourning. The first cycle (*An Early Frost*; *Buddies* [Arthur Bressan, United States, 1985]; *Parting Glances* [Bill Sherwood, United States, 1986]; and somewhat later, *Longtime Companion* [Norman René, United States, 1990] and *Together Alone* [P.J. Castellaneta, USA, 1991]) bounced off its brilliantly cranky German mirror opposite *A Virus Knows No Morals* (Rosa von Praunheim, 1986). The cycle moved to the mainstream, culminating in the international critical and box office hits of the early nineties: *Les Nuits fauves* (*Savage Nights*, Cyril Collard, France, 1992) and *Philadelphia* (Jonathan Demme, United States, 1993), followed by a sputtering of indie latecomers, notably *Jeffrey* (Christopher Ashley, United States, 1995) and *It's My Party* (Randal Kleiser, United States, 1996).

Canada's two distinctive entries into the melodrama current, both musicals, came late: LAURIE LYND's miniature narrative elegy, the crystalline *RSVP* (1991), and John Greyson's rambunctiously hybrid agitprop feature, the comedy-romance *Zero Patience* (1993). Like many of the above works, *Zero* was eloquent in its elegiac portrait of PWAS' courage and rage, but it was also close to von Praunheim in its spunky irreverence and beyond even him in its deployment of spectacle, eroticism, humour, and experimental effects adapted from art video – and puppet animation! *Zero* was also both an essay on the epistemology and politics of the epidemic and a cathartic melo engagement with two pairs of lovers challenged and ennobled by crisis and finally parted by death. But it is as a musical that I shall come back to this great work in the next section. A follow-up Toronto feature by

PWA Jim Black stares at the camera with serenity in this production still from Nik Sheehan's bold and prophetic documentary *No Sad Songs* (1985), the Canadian cinema's first major confrontation with AIDS. Production still, the Canadian Filmmakers Distribution Centre

CYNTHIA ROBERTS, *The Last Supper* (1994), an impressively controlled adaptation of a PWA theatre piece by Hillar Liijot about the dancer protagonist Chris's ritualised assisted suicide, featured a real-life actor, Ken McDougall, performing his own final struggle, as it turned out. Shot in real time at Casey House, the Toronto hospice, *The Last Supper* garnered positive notices and the Teddy Award at Berlin yet immediately disappeared off the radar screen of Canadian canon formation – it is unfortunately not even available on video. The Vancouver video feature *The Time Being*, by KENNETH SHERMAN (1997), was also noteworthy for its achievement and innovative in its narrativisation of a gay couple's encounter with sickness, death, and mourning. Neither Roberts's nor Sherman's films succeeded in having

The Last Supper (1994): Chris (PWA actor Ken McDougall) performs the last choreography of both actor and character in Cynthia Roberts's AIDS melodrama, two years before the treatment breakthroughs transformed Canadian AIDS image making. Production still, Greg Klymkiw and Cynthia Roberts, Horsy Productions 1996

an impact beyond their festival launches, and the tearjerker momentum might have seemed spent. Yet somehow it carried on, and led to two major English Canadian feature films at the start of the new decade, *The Perfect Son* (LEONARD FARLINGER, 2000) and *The Event* (THOM FITZGERALD, 2003), both assisted-suicide narratives (why do they appear in three-year intervals?). Both of these latter two films were greeted with critical respect and box office indifference, alongside cautious rumblings from within the queer press and elsewhere: was there perhaps just a smidgen of anachronism about fully wrought AIDS suicide melodramas set within privileged North American white gay male milieus in the rapidly evolving global context, which was shaped by new treatment realities and the geopolitical land-scape of pharmaceutical blackmail? As we shall see with the work of Greyson, Fung, and Hoolboom, melodramatic desire settled much more fruitfully somehow and intervened more concretely in the "marginal" works of the avant-garde indie scene than with Telefilm Canada (with one "movie musi-cal" exception).

Melodrama was only one of the genres favoured in the wave of artistic productivity around AIDS in the late eighties and early nineties, and *Zero* was not Greyson's first contribution to it. "AIDS is a war," this indefatiga-ble anticensorship activist and wunderkind of the Toronto video and film scene had announced in 1990, summarising the political urgency of so much AIDS media activism, "there's no time for artsy debates about formal issues." He then went on to paraphrase the contrary view that "AIDS is a war, not just of medicine and politics but of representations – we must reject dominant media discourses and forms in favour of a radical new vocabu-lary that deconstructs their agendas and reconstructs ours" (1990).[1] In fact, his own prolific video work was an energetic embrace and negotiation of both positions simultaneously. Greyson must also be seen as a facilitator, critic, and impresario, working infectiously behind the scenes of the first wave of Canadian film and video work. In the article just quoted, he also listed the genres of AIDS media activism and contributed to virtually all of them, either through directing or off-screen support: cable access, documents of performances, memorial documentary portraits, experimental decon-structions of mass media, educational tapes on prevention and other urgent topics for specific audience targets, documentaries about AIDS service organizations, safer sex tapes; activist documents of demonstrations and so forth, and PWA-directed tapes on such issues as alternative treatments. The Toronto video cable project that Greyson organized with PWA video artist MICHAEL BALSER encompassed most of these genres and enfranchised a whole diverse lineup of young artists and community voices before being shut down by Rogers Cable's kneejerk censorship in early 1991.

It could be argued that a no less palpable contribution by Greyson around the time of Montreal's V International AIDS Conference in 1989 was strictly curatorial. Affirming that the wave of in-the-streets, in-your-face community-activist video originating mostly in New York was on a par artis-tically with the more culturally prestigious and visible utterances – and in fact he didn't care whether it was or not, as we saw in the epigraph to this chapter – he compiled and circulated a cornucopia of tapes for cultural, educational, and community work. His package *Video against AIDS*, co-curated with American Bill Horrigan in 1990, contained seventeen Ameri-can, two British, and three Canadian videotapes (Greyson's own *The ADS Epidemic*, to which I shall return; Michael Balser and Andy Fabo's allegorical

Survival of the Delirious [1988]; and *Another Man*, by "Youth against Monsterz" [1988, 3], a Toronto collective effort aimed at high school students that is part media rebuttal and part safe sex-clip). The overall package ran the gamut from obscure art video to encyclopaedic grass roots assemblages of raw documentation and dramatised community agitprop, enshrining alternative media as the place where the action was. VAA literally changed the face of AIDS in North American arts landscapes.[2]

In 1992, *Les nuits fauves* impacted on the cultural environment of the Pandemic not because it was a melodrama but because of its status as posthumous autobiography. Collard's film was unique for a feature-length work of cinematic fiction, but it echoed a crucial genre in both PWA literature (Hervé Guibert, Paul Monette, Michael Lynch, Ian Stephens) and fine art (David Wojnarowicz, Robert Mapplethorpe, GENERAL IDEA). Yet Collard's stupendous and indulgent film had been surpassed in its epochal raw intensity by another posthumous first-person work that appeared the same year, the small-format video documentary *Silverlake Life: The View from Here* (Tom Joslin with Peter Friedman, United States, 1992). The following year saw both Derek Jarman's *Blue* (United Kingdom) and Gregg Bordowitz's *Fast Trip, Long Drop* (United States), two very different self-referential works, film and video, ascetic and carnivalesque, testamentary and "the-world's-my-oyster," respectively, works that cemented the emerging autobiographical cycle of independent nonnarrative film and video as the most significant of the 1990s. (Certainly the activist wave of the late eighties had had autobiographical tendencies, but this wave submerged in its collectivist ethic most individualist discourses of makers' lives as creative raw material.)

Canada's distinctive representation within this international convergence of autobiographical work around the beginning of the nineties had in fact preceded the above autobiographies and was manifold. In addition to short experimental video pieces by Balser and Fabo in Toronto and ZACHERY LONGBOY in Vancouver,[3] there were two principal longer works. The tender and lyrical video essay *Récit d'A* by ESTHER VALIQUETTE (1990), an apparently conventional PWA portrait discreetly layered over the artist's own "coming out" as infected and over her reflections on the body, mortality, and landscape, announced a new voice and a new departure beyond the demographics of Canadian AIDS artwork in the 1980s (male, gay, and anglophone).[4] According to CHANTAL NADEAU (1997, 32–6), Valiquette's work was "an intense, powerful voice telling of the difficulty of seeing oneself as a 'positive' body ... making a representation of the virus merge with a representation of her body, appropriating the aesthetic of science as a code of self-representation."

Esther Valiquette leaving her footprints in the symbolic desert landscape of
Récit d'A (1990), an apparently conventional PWA portrait discreetly layered
over the artist's own "coming out" as HIV+. VHS frame grab, *Récit d'A*, by
Esther Valiquette, 1990 Distribution Vidéographe

Another Canadian contribution to the genre was from the West Coast:
Dr PETER JEPSON-YOUNG, a gay doctor with one of the pioneering Vancouver AIDS practices, who was himself diagnosed in 1986, began producing weekly broadcasts for the Vancouver CBC station in 1990, and a lively
and inspiring series of 111 short vignettes appeared before his death in
1992. Repackaged that same year for the CBC by David Paperny as *The
Broadcast Tapes of Dr. Peter*, this cumulative work preserved the broadcasts' diary format and showed, among other things, the undaunted hero,
literally blinded, like Jarman, by an opportunistic cytomegalovirus infection, veering cheerfully down a British Columbia ski slope. *Tapes* was less
about the then cutting-edge video activism and analysis than about giving
the "general public" a brave and dignified face for the syndrome. Its Academy Award nomination and U.S. broadcast on HBO reflected this mainstream viability. Otherwise, neither *Récit* nor *Tapes* registered within the
international AIDS cultural vanguard, and not only for the usual factor of
their "Canadianness." Valiquette's beautiful work had the disadvantage of
being in French and English at once and almost inaccessible in either language versions, as well as feeling a bit literary for anglo tastes and both

dated in its political innocence and ahead of its time in its confrontation with the metaphysics and iconographies of corporeal mutability. Jepson-Young's work, which went on to a book version by Daniel Gawthrop (1994), went by virtually unnoticed by the movement's New York and London–centred gatekeepers, Douglas Crimp, Paula Treichler, Cindy Patton, and Simon Watney,[5] perhaps because of its mainstream marketing or else because the image of a privileged gay white man dying of AIDS, an Anglican to boot, seemed no longer "front line." We shall see how Hoolboom's and, later, Fung's entry into the autobiographical modality pushes this energy towards its most productive level.

Meanwhile down the St Lawrence, the NFB was stirring, belatedly and half-heartedly, as we saw in chapter 6, but their first product devoted to the Pandemic left more than a little to be desired. *The Karate Kids* (Derek Lamb, 1990) is a narrative cartoon produced for an NGO called Street Kids International, which aimed to tell urban street kids of the third world about AIDS risks and safer sex. The cartoon shows resilient boys named Pedro and Mario and their heroic older buddy named Karate, who all hang out in the market and watch for rich tourists and other ways to survive. Karate warns them about HIV transmission and especially about the dangers of a fat, rich older pedophile in sunglasses named The Smiling Man, who is seen haunting the market for sex for hire with the street kids and who may be an AIDS transmitter. He is first seen pushing a girl out of his fancy car and taking off but then coming back to lure Mario and Pedro with expensive gifts. "That man wanted to fuck you. And maybe you would get sick with AIDS … He looks okay," Karate says, "but some people carry AIDS inside them for many years before they start to look sick" (Connolly 1990). Mario finally succumbs to the lure of the Smiling Man's money and goes off with him in his car. Karate and the others follow in hot pursuit on his red scooter: "We'll go and get that bastard." Mario is saved, but the Smiling Man's car crashes in the frantic chase and "explodes in a ball of fire. And that is the end of the Smiling Man." Nothing could have been more important at the end of the 1980s than campaigns of information, demystification, and empowerment among impoverished risk groups in the developing world. But this triumph of mystification and scapegoating, in its reductive vilification of queer predators like the incinerated Smiling Man and its murderous fantasy of populist lynching for those suspected to be infected, did not fit the bill. Now that gays and lesbians were making demands of the studio, pedophiles were still legitimate scapegoats – and what could be a better target than a pedophile john?

Partial amends were made in 1993 with TAHANI RACHED's French-language consciousness-raising epic *Médecins de coeur*, but it was perhaps too little, too late for the government studio (see chapter 6), now that the initial energy and urgency of the AIDS audiovisual wave had wound down. Nevertheless, this portrait of a clinic of burnt-out (mostly gay) Montreal doctors at ground zero of the national AIDS crisis opting for a therapeutic palaver is a masterpiece of its kind. Rached, the veteran social issue documentarist of the French program, is at the listening post as the doctors with heart hash out professional ethics and personal values and responsibility. So are we, for this film offers as much, if not more, talk than perhaps any other NFB film. Though the *Globe and Mail* found the film "pretty dull viewing," the magic of the doctors with heart works for spectators with heart: the subjects visibly achieve individual grace and catharsis, as well as collective strength, and so do we. One of the gay doctors himself dies of AIDS during the shoot, and the film unexpectedly switches gears, with Tahani's poetic refrain of Montreal's AIDS memorial park throughout the seasons suddenly heightening its concrete elegiac force and the doctor's funeral service closing a reflective, analytic film with a gush of emotion.

Drs Réjean Thomas (right) and Michel Marchand (who died during production) in the NFB French studio's 1993 consciousness-raising epic *Médecins de coeur*: exquisite but too little, too late for the government studio. Production still, used with permission of the National Film Board of Canada

Outside of the NFB in the early 1990s, production was stabilizing at the same time as it was domesticated and diversified, ranging from the perennial elegiac genre (of which JUSTINE PIMLOTT's prize-winning, heart-wrenching tribute to gay PWA men's revitalization of a hinterland resort community, *Laugh in the Dark* [1999], is the most striking example) to the portrait to the melodrama and before too long to a renewed, reshaped geopolitical agitprop vocation, maintained well into the 2000s and epitomized by Greyson's South Africa–themed video opera *Fig Trees* (2003). But before that was to happen, the introduction of the new multiple therapies around the time of a later Canadian conference, the Vancouver International AIDS Conference of 1996, had spelled a paradigm shift of AIDS discourse, as well as a turning point in the work of all three of the artists I am considering. The shift entailed, among other things, what Paula Treichler (1999, 325) has called a "transition from a concept of AIDS as a classic epidemic of acute infectious disease to that of AIDS as a chronic, potentially manageable disease" (at least in the privileged and medicared pockets of the so-called developed world).

This miraculous return – at least for now – of many of the sick to the ranks of the working populace – including Hoolboom, Andrews, and McCaskell – and of the arts critic from the job of necrologising dead artists to the luxury of monitoring continuing oeuvres and maturing artists, occasioned a parallel shift in the symbolics and genres of AIDS texts. *Destroying Angel* (1998, 32), a short film by Hoolboom's old Sheridan College colleague Philip Hoffman, co-directing with American PWA Wayne Salazar, would in some ways epitomise this shift. Pursuing familiar diaristic and autobiographical conventions by expanding the frame into both co-authors' "families," the film's narrative and real-world dénouements confound the AIDS mortality cliché and viewers' expectations: the PWA turns out to be a survivor mourning Hoffman's partner, Marion MacMahon, the third artist in the diaristic triangle, who has fallen to cancer. By 2000, the AIDS melodrama was for all intents and purposes obsolete, such that one critic, José Arroyo, could welcome the pill-popping French feature film *Drôle de Félix*, which he calls an "AIDS romance," in the following terms (2001): "to my knowledge at least, [it is] one of the first films with an HIV+ protagonist who is offered the expectation of a future, however delimited. In this charming romantic tale … the final clinch between the lovers isn't a death-bed scene but the beginning of an idyllic holiday."

Indeed the "expectation of a future" precisely described a presumption in the post-1996 AIDS-related work of Greyson, Fung, and Hoolboom alike, but in very distinct ways, as we shall see. Space does not permit me to treat all three AIDS-themed oeuvres in any comprehensive way. Accordingly, since all three film/video makers use music, document, and autobiography in their works, I shall selectively, and perhaps arbitrarily, focus on the use of music by Greyson, documentary by Fung, and autobiography by Hoolboom, as a means of organizing the next three sections devoted respectively to these three artists. I will line up these three corpuses to delineate their subject of the HIV-infected body in a symmetrically complementary manner as agent/object, respectively, of utopian pleasure (music), of sobriety, knowledge, and power (documentary), and of identity (autobiography).

GREYSON AND "MUSICALS ABOUT AIDS"

> Taking difficult subjects – like two assholes talking to each other about assholes and ass-fucking – how do you make that something an audience, straight and gay, can listen to and get engaged by? My solution is that you make it a duet and the two assholes sing to each other.
> ~ John Greyson

When *Zero Patience* came out in 1992, it was commonly assumed or implied in the promotion and critical response that there was something paradoxical or even iconoclastic about "A Musical about AIDS" (as the tagline for the feature put it). In fact, nothing could be further from the truth. Not only do most cultures marshal some kind of music to deal with mortality, but filmic and videographic representations about AIDS since the very early days of the Pandemic had almost all integrated music into their aesthetic structure and discursive address. Three principal genres that I have elaborated in part I all had made concrete use of music, both instrumental and vocal – agitprop, elegy, and melodrama (as its name implies). And two sublime Toronto melodramas from that dark period of proliferation and despair between the Montreal and Vancouver conferences, *RSVP* and *The Last Supper*, both made concrete use of a prerecorded classical female aria for their essential affect: the CBC radio broadcast of Jesse Norman's recording of Berlioz's "Spectre of the Rose" unites Lynd's community of mourners in *RSVP* and the playing of Purcell's "Remember Me (Dido's Lament)" for Chris's deathbed dance, which celebrates love and art in *The Last Supper*. This is not to forget the no less sublime British counterexample, the music video package *Red Hot and Blue* (1990), which lined up international pop singers and groups performing video covers of Cole Porter songs for the benefit of AIDS organizations: here rock met Broadway in an uneasy alliance but the classic torchy contributions by k.d. lang and Annie Lennox virtually stole the whole show, rock video commandeered by Tin Pan Alley. What is surprising is that there are not even more AIDS musicals.

Perhaps I am being disingenuous in eliding the difference between music films and "musicals," between the structural use of music in film and the

"Our mourning together, this must be the thing we call country." Hoolboom's dictum demonstrated by a bereaved woman tuning into the CBC's cross-country radiophonic wake in Laurie Lynd's miniature AIDS musical elegy *RSVP* (1991). Production still, Film Reference Library

specific historical genre "the musical." The latter implies considerable formal, cultural, and contextual baggage, from its utopian energy as defined by Dyer ([1977] 1992) and its serial structure of discrete "numbers" to its roots in popular entertainment. Discussion of the genre also assumes the context of its historical decline since the 1960s, both in Hollywood and in the art cinemas of the world (a decline so decisive that *Zero Patience*'s tagline might have been no less emphatic as simply "A musical" or, even more, "A *Canadian* musical," a species so rare that I could count its members on one hand). But I insist that in the Canadian contexts of thwarted access for both audiences and artists to the continuous cultural dialogue intrinsic in the notion of "genre" and of unevenly developed popular cultural energies of any sort (here I am speaking principally of English-language culture), the elision between the standard musical genre and the one-off analogue that takes a futile stab at building an indigenous musical tradition is appropriate.

Furthermore, in case it might also be a concern that the topic of AIDS disqualifies a film from belonging to the musical genre, *au contraire:* when we call a genre "utopian," this does not of course mean "upbeat." Indeed, many of the great works of the movie musical's ancestor, the opera (the form at which Greyson ends up, more or less, with *Fig Trees*, in 2003, but I'm getting ahead of myself), were tragic, not the least of which were operas about the AIDS of the nineteenth century (tuberculosis), *La Bohème* and *La Traviata* (it is no accident that composer David Wall [2003] compared Zackie Achmat, the PWA nonfiction hero of *Fig Trees*, to *La Traviata*'s consumptive diva Violetta). And even the movie musical heritage of the twentieth-century cinema has been much more tragic in its orientation than is commonly acknowledged, from *A Star is Born* (1954) to *Carousel* (1956), *West Side Story* (1961), *Les Parapluies de Cherbourg* (1964), *Cabaret* (1972), *Nashville* (1975), *New York, New York* (1977), *Yentl* (1983), *Velvet Goldmine* (1998), *Dancer in the Dark* (2000), and *Hedwig and the Angry Inch* (2001), and … that other major Canadian musical, *The Saddest Music in the World* (GUY MADDIN, 2003).

So *Zero Patience* is a musical about AIDS, no big deal, and in fact I would argue that it was one of several that Greyson made. In this section I would like to focus on these musical AIDS utterances by this director, instances of his development of a sui generis subgenre, the AIDS musical – loosely Canadian, generic and queer, it goes without saying. I am doing so for several reasons other than the works' obvious interest as an underexamined seldom-assembled corpus. First, this provides a way of considering Greyson's unique and specific intervention in Canadian culture, queer and nonqueer, without engaging with the comprehensive book-length treatment of this major artist that would otherwise be required, a book too big and too close for me at this time. Second, Greyson's AIDS filmography in general is large, arguably the expansive nucleus of his oeuvre (his first video dates from 1979, the eve of the outbreak, and his entire career moved forward in its shadow (can one think of even *Law of Enclosures* [2000], a late feature ostensibly about heterosexual marriage, aging, cancer, and the Gulf War, as *not* being also, subtextually, about AIDS?). For these reasons, it is convenient to zoom in on his musical works about AIDS.

Further triage subdivides Greyson's musicals into two further categories. First, the "appropriation" musicals, which recycle appropriated numbers within a postmodern intertextual framework, an omnipresent practice within 1980s art video and art cinema, as we have seen, but one for which he was an important innovator. These numbers were either commandeered "as is" through lip sync (*The Kipling Trilogy*, 1984–85) or extradiegetically. An ideal example of extradiegetic appropriation is *Andy Warhol's Blow Job (New York and Toronto)* (1989, 2), part of Greyson's series of safe-sex shorts doubling as homages to the queer film canon (from *Un chant d'amour* to *Querelle*), which were distributed autonomously, as well as integrated into his *Pink Pimpernel* (1989). In this delectable miniature, two tandem vignettes of the titular activity, first latex-protected and then not, offer both an allusive, open-ended debate on risk practices and a clear, graphic demonstration and domestication of condom use; all is laid under high-tenor Michael Callen's cover of Connie Francis's 1961 wailer "Where the Boys Are." The PWA superhero's recording is itself an appropriation that already "queers" the Hollywood teen mash song but is further transformed by Greyson into a campy, pleasurable, sex-positive core to his debate-cum-cautionary demonstration.

The appropriation musical can also *reconstitute* its source as parody and/or pastiche, and Greyson's most striking experiment in this category was *The Making of Monsters* (1990, not an AIDS musical in the strict sense, but alongside *Zero*, Greyson's most classical movie musical). *Monster's* refashioning of Brecht and Weill songs within a bite-size *Lehrstück* led, notwithstanding, to a catastrophic legal crisis and the withdrawal of the film from circulation (due to copyright issues around the Weill tunes). A work intended to be about homophobic violence and the crisis in masculinity became also an object lesson in intellectual property (as *Un©ut*, 1997, did not fail to analyze in depth).

The second category consists of those AIDS films for which nonappropriated, *original* music was composed and positioned as the structural core of the film. I will devote the rest of this section to this manageable subgroup of basically three masterful works, staggered across Greyson's career, *The ADS Epidemic* (1987, 5), *Zero Patience* (1993, 100), and *Fig Trees* (2003, a seven-number, seven-room video opera installation, 37). In terms of generic form, the works progress from rock video to the classical Broadway/Hollywood "integrated musical" idiom, to avant-garde opera, and in some sense they thus represent a search for a musical form resonant with indigenous realities and the international AIDS crisis. The first two works were collaborations with composer Glenn Schellenberg, and the third with composer David Wall. (I am not including in this roster two others of Greyson's collaborations with Schellenberg, his score for Greyson's first feature *Urinal* [1988], a thin, nonvocal synthesizer concoction that is by no means either a structural component of the film or an enduring contribution to film scoring, and the rap anthem "What We Want Is [AIDS Action Now!]," which is used as extradiegetic lead-in/wrap-up theme for both of the 1989 AIDS conference tapes, *The World is Sick [Sic]* and *The Pink Pimpernel*. This latter number has a rousing, raucous energy perfectly matched with the incantatory rhythms of the demonstrators' chants within the documentary world of the tapes, but on the whole it also does not operate as either work's structural core.)

The ADS *Epidemic* (1987) was one of the earliest works in the safe-sex surge of the late eighties and early nineties (preceded only by the New York Gay Men's Health Crisis package *Chance of a Lifetime* from the previous year and the dubious example of the 1985 porno film *Inevitable Love,* which promotes condom use but mentions AIDS only once). The five-minute single-song format of Greyson's tape points to another contextual factor, as I've suggested, the overwhelming influence the new pop genre and the technology of music video, then in its first decade of existence, was having on both art video and queer political media practices (the influence arguably went in the opposite direction also). But Greyson's cinephile reference could not be more esoteric: another great music film, if not musical, Luchino Visconti's ravishing 1971 literary adaptation and "dead queer movie" *Death in Venice,* which is based on Thomas Mann and Gustav Mahler. Greyson does not exactly stick to the original parable of Aschenbach, the great artist who succumbs to Apollonian ideals and ephebophile passions for young Tadzio and dies of cholera. Rather, following Greyson's hallmark practice of bringing queer historical or fictional figures back to life in the present, Aschenbach is reconstituted as an elderly, repressed puritan haunting Toronto's Harbourfront and being shocked into a fatal attack of Acquired Dread of Sex by the sight of ephebes playing with condoms. Greyson retains from Visconti the harbour steamer that took Aschenbach to his fateful tryst with Tadzio (reincarnated as the Toronto Island ferry), and the strong visual tropes of iconic Edwardian costumes (including the boys' bulging maillot-style bathing suits), the beachfront setting where Aschenbach ruins his makeup and expires in the deck chair from an exploding heart, and Tadzio's silhouetted final transcendent gesture on the beach, pointing to the Resurrection for Visconti (but Greyson's ephebe holds up a condom, symbol of more earthly pleasures).

Greyson's clarion warning about the erotophobic backlash threatened by the Pandemic, doubling as a safe-sex promotion, is channelled through his and Schellenberg's titular song, "The ADS Epidemic." This agitprop ballad with a catchy pop melody and rhythm is complete with a narrative stanza ("Aschenbach a liberal fellow ... ") and alternating didactic stanza ("You can get ADS from doctors and cops / You can get ADS from high school jocks"). The song, the first of Schellenberg's many collaborations with Greyson, plays out over the full length of the tape, its sprightly cadences edited perfectly to match the parodic narrative and the agitprop inserts. The latter are enacted bouncily by Leena Raudvee in dance-like vignettes, decked out with the usual Greyson array of toys and masks (the "high school jock" doing lumberingly macho aerobic-like movements, gesturing in time with the music with beer bottles, wearing shades and a headband).

Conceived of as a work of public art by the Public Access "Lunatic of One Idea" project, which brought fifteen downtown artists to a sixteen-monitor video wall in suburban Mississauga's Square One Mall, Greyson's tape used a format carefully aimed at infiltrating public space with queer music video and AIDS-prevention messages. In particular, an adapted karaoke (or "singalong") device adding key words and phrases (such as "using condoms") as subtitles,was apparently intended to heighten the pedagogical role of the lyrics for an audience that at best would consist of strolling shoppers attracted by the novelty of the video wall. Greyson intended the tape to seduce an undifferentiated public with jokily benign homoeroticism and condom iconography of the kind still very rare in public arena at the time (Calvin Klein offered male bulges aplenty throughout the 1980s of course, but no kisses and certainly no condoms).

The ADS Epidemic could thus not benefit from the target-audience principle that was essential to the growing momentum of prevention messages, nor could it fully avail itself of the graphic literalness about using condoms and affirming eroticism that characterize the Gay Men's Health Crisis series of 1986 and 1989, and even of Greyson's own safe-sex miniatures of the same year (with their literally in-your-face roll-on demonstrations). Mississauga had to do without the matter-of-fact frankness that the activist consensus of the late eighties considered to be indispensable for gay vernacular effectiveness. Even worse, the "Public Access" project design was weak in both groundwork liaison and follow-through in terms of positioning (no pilot projects or test studies?), and Greyson hardly felt that his effort had been validated:

It was a video wall suspended above the main entrance, in other words framed by glass, with tons of daylight competing with our salacious images – long before we arrived, sound was always kept to a minimum by the mall, following complaints from various store owners who didn´t want any competition for their tasteful muzak – so when I did my first scout of the place, it took me 3 cycles of the advertising loop (McDonald's, Levis, KFC) to realize that the furniture store ad featuring a young yuppie couple was actually a public service announcement for safe sex (in the vague terms of "get the facts" but of course offering no facts) – so my Mann-ian intervention was perhaps "muted" by such limitations – no headsets, maybe an hour-long loop – ADS was 5 min – I seem to remember being sandwiched between an ad for American Express and an ad for Toyota (which of course was the reason for the title – ADS – in the first place). (email 12 January 2004).

Accordingly, the most significant distribution for the tape no doubt took place after Mississauga had come and gone, as a cassette within the queer/arts network of the willing and predisposed. Competing with Levis ads was clearly not a way to go.

Although Greyson continued to collaborate with Schellenberg on ensuing projects (*Urinal* [1988], the AIDS conference diptych [1989], and *The Making of Monsters* [1991]), their next AIDS "musical" in the sense that I have determined is *Zero Patience* (1993), a film that has gradually come into its due as a canonical paving stone of Canadian cinema of the 1990s. The tale of the Québécois flight attendant Gaétan Dugas, vilified by early tabloid science and by Randy Shilts as the person who introduced HIV into North America,[6] is rendered into a fruitful and contradictory narrative essay-mosaic by Greyson's traditional tools, now honed for the first time on a "decent" feature budget:

- dizzying formal play and techno-wizardry,
- densely self-reflexive and allusive intertextuality, including media deconstruction,
- camp anachronism that problematizes the historiography and historicity of culture, science, and sexuality,
- unabashed didacticism born out of the artist's personal activist trajectory (a typical hostile review begins, "I don't like being preached to"),
- a related realist frame of urban landscape and diaristic observation that ensured the situatedness of political discourse (including the *human* landscape registered in Greyson's typical aggressively p.c. diversity casting),
- melodramatic narrative that reveals the queer romantic deep down and enables and affirms affect, pleasure, and desire,
- and of course the equally related, unabashedly heady eroticism that was also one of Greyson's many trademarks.

Greyson renamed Dugas Zero and took up where Shilts had left off, parachuting him from his afterlife as a ghost into the Toronto gay ghetto of the nineties to "Tell my story, clear my name." Opposite, he constructed as co-star the figure of Sir Richard Burton, the Victorian orientalist explorer, who is converted in the course of the film from the epitome of bad sensationalist scientist to an AIDS activist and Zero's love interest. Finally, Greyson assembled around the pair the members of an ACT UP–like activist cell that includes an HIV+ ex-junkie called Typhoid Mary and an elementary school teacher, George, Zero's former fuck buddy, who is going blind from opportunistic cytomegalovirus. My summary is only a linear skeleton for a typically centrifugal narrative/expository structure that dashes off self-reflexively in all directions.

Studded throughout are the film's set pieces, Greyson's and Schellen-berg's nine glittering musical numbers. Along with the conjugal dynamic enabled by the strong lead casting, chemistry, and performances by Normand Fauteux and John Robinson, this structure allows an essential coherence to the film – playing somewhat the same anchoring role that Greyson's six documentary minifilms played within the film in *Urinal* (which was even more centrifugal than *Zero* – see chapter 8). On one level the orderly unfolding of nine numbers, plus three reprises, of diverse genres and styles makes *Zero*, despite its many "meta-" levels, into a loose but relatively conventional integrated musical – in the sense that it comprises a balanced spectrum of numbers all more or less advancing the "plot," including a "character development" solo self-portrait, a love duet, a full-company "Act One curtain" showstopper, a comic or novelty number, an inspirational or motivational number, etc. – so much so that many critics identified the film as an homage to the classical musical, and they were not wrong.

Though hitherto Greyson's taste had been far more pop-eclectic (witness "To Sir With Love," the appropriated core of the first of the Kipling Trilogy, *Perils of Pedagogy*), here he clearly shows his openness towards slightly earlier gay generations' fixation on MGM show tunes. But the two collaborators also reinvented the form to meet their discursive agenda, cross-fertilizing Gershwin/Porter/Rodgers with Brecht and Weill, and of the nine songs, four are baldly programmatic Brechtian discourses on Greyson's two topics *du jour*:

1   The ideology of science and epidemiological scapegoating
    "Culture of Certainty," Burton's solo apologia for empirical science as the solution to the Pandemic;
    "Control," a novelty group number by the five PWA members of the ACT UP group, elaborating their one-word strategic platform, both for survival and activism;
    "Contagious," another group number, a song/ballet riposte by the rain-forest creatures scapegoated by science for the spread of the virus, come back to life in the Natural History Museum displays.
2   Sexuality/anality/patriarchy
    "The Butthole Duet," a duet between Zero's and Burton's nether orifices, incarnated as puppets, serving triply as an affirmation of gay sex, a parody of the love duet, and a programmatic rebuttal (as it were) to Leo Bersani's famous article "Is the Rectum a Grave?" (1987) – arguably also a novelty showstopper, given its shock value and video male aero-

bics chorus number that it is liberally larded with the only frontal nudity in the film.

The other songs fit more easily into conventional, less discursive, musical dramaturgy: the bawdy comic number "Pop-a-Boner"; the torchy romantic duet of love, separation, and loss, "Six or Seven Things" (not surprisingly, the song that received outside recognition, a nomination from an online awards organization called Fennec);[7] and the introductory and wrap-up thematic numbers "Just like Scheherezade (Tell the Story)" and "Zero Patience," respectively. But for all their traditional lyrical and narrative priority, these other songs are bustling with ideas and comment beneath the layers of intense lyrical or narrative animus.

For the purposes of this brief section, however, I would like to discuss one song that is my personal favourite: "Positive," a thematic number that doubles as a portrait and performance setpiece for the George character (played by Grenadian Canadian Richardo Keens-Douglas, who had also starred in The Pink Pimpernel but who is best known as a prizewinning dramatic author). This song for George's solo voice, supported by a chorus of his pupils, expresses the anxiety, confusion, and intense fluctuation of feelings from doubt to courage of prototypical PWAs of the late 1980s, feelings that had surfaced repeatedly in documentary portraits of PWAs in both Greyson's own work and those he curated in his VAA package. "Positive" is not a showstopper (like the reprise of "Scheherazade" that features garishly costumed blood cells floating about in a pool set, only to be scattered by Miss HIV, Michael Callen again, in drag and singing his heart out on a Streisandian high note held forever). Rather, George's solo, counterpointed by the children's refrain, is a relatively intimate number, formally rigorous and almost ascetic, set in both the classroom workplace and the most private recess of the home, the shower. It is the kind that classically transforms everyday objects like school desks and shower curtains into magical accoutrements of spectacle and affect. George's direct one-on-one performance of his feelings, first to his pupils and then from his shower to us his privileged spectators, bears the qualities of both intensity ("experiencing of emotion directly, fully, unambiguously, 'authentically,' without holding back") and transparency ("A quality of relationships – between represented characters [e.g., true love], between performer and audience ['sincerity']") that Dyer identifies as among those intrinsic to the traditional film musical's formulaic construction of utopian feeling ([1977] 1992, 20-1). In contrast to others of the songs, which are often energized by Greyson's compressed archness, self-reflexive wit, and allusion, this dialogue between a man, a lineup of children, and a virtual audience – between two spaces, private and public – is simple in its theme and direct in its appeal to pathos, desire, and solidarity

("I want to plan ... I want to know ... I want to live"). This directness is mediated only by quasiBrechtian captions, which Greyson could not resist, in the form of the contradictory media headlines about AIDS that are plastered across George's shower curtain (which I don't recall even noticing until about the third viewing of the film).

Formally, the mise-en-scène elegantly builds on a tension between the gliding high-angle frontal tracking shots of the row of children doing abstract desktop choreography with pencils, rulers, and apples and the also high-angle but very diagonal views of George at the blackboard transmitting knowledge and then in his shower wracked with agnosticism – all playing with the contradictory valence of "positive" as "certain" (of knowledge) and "positive" as HIV+, hence "uncertain":

> They're positive that I'm positive,
> They're sure that these doubts are a curse,
> I'm supposed to be certainly certain,
> Well, I'm sure I'm getting worse.

Meanwhile, the children's chorus "I know I know that I don't know ... Je sais ... " – conjugating the French verb *savoir* for bilingual Canadian content no doubt, but perhaps also to evoke the Cartesian ancestry of the enigma around knowing, existing, not knowing, and dying.

Why the shower? On one level this is beefcake, undeniably present as the water streams down on George's face and strong chest. On another level the imagery constructs an up-front affirmation of the body beautiful in a discursive context of bodily degradation. Indeed, one can look at all the choreography of the film in this light, from the dreamily exquisite synchronized water ballet at the start to the famous "pop-a-boner" bathhouse trio in a communal shower room – so coy it's male burlesque – to the film's standard publicity shot showing head-on the shirtless Zero/Fauteux in another shower scene (under the deluge of the sprinklers, in the final "Ascension" moment of the film), singing intensely, arms above his head, armpits flaming. But in addition there is something pleasurable and sensuous, even sacramental, about the naked man singing so intensely of the contradictions of his life as the water cascades over his body.

As a song also about teaching, about the contradiction of a human subject wracked with uncertainty yet hired to transmit certainty and knowledge to young minds, "Positive" falls into line with the theme of intergenerational education and socialization that appealed to Greyson, the erstwhile artworld twinkie, almost from the start, surfacing in *Perils of Pedagogy, The Making of Monsters, After the Bath,* and *Lilies,* among others (and of course it grips me on this same personal level as a teacher, as well). Thus, when the

PWA George's shower song in *Zero Patience* (1992) appeals directly to pathos, desire and solidarity. VHS frame grab

most mischievous of the schoolboys comes later to visit George in his hospital room, the wordless moment of caring and reconciliation and further knowledge transmission becomes one of the narrative's several climaxes of melodramatic resolution.

"Positive," then, this beautiful number performed by a supporting character, encapsulates many of the dynamics of the film and of Greyson's oeuvre, a utopian fusion of corporeal pleasure and desire within the infected body, of feeling, knowledge, and empowerment both within the world of the film and the world of its audience. "Immediate" and "transparent," it builds on a musical and filmic vernacular that Bongani Ndodana may well dismiss as "populist" (2003). But this label would be one that Greyson would affirm in its positive, politically progressive sense as a handle for his artistic and political deployment-cum-dissection of a hoary but magically accessible filmic genre, the musical.

The decade-long passage from Broadway/Hollywood to "serious" or avant-garde contemporary music did not take place overnight, and if we are looking for a stepping stone between *Zero* and the 2003 video opera *Fig Trees*, perhaps we can point to the medieval-style polyphonic motet by Mychael Danna that scores *Lilies* in 1996 (see chapter 5), buoying up that film's intertexts of saintly martyrdom and homosocial community. In fact, the continuity is striking, a reminder that Greyson's celebration of vocal harmony in the euphonious *Trees* goes back very far indeed – beyond the "populist" three-voice harmony of "Pop-a-boner" in *Zero*, beyond the melancholy cruising park chorus of wandering men-in-heat in *Making of Monsters*, beyond the modified group rap idiom of *The World is Sick (Sic)*, as far back as the lip sync cowboy quartet of *Kipling Meets the Cowboys* (1985, 22) ... and even further? Greyson's composer-collaborator for *Trees*, David Wall, proposes the notion of vocal harmony as a political analogy (2003, 18–19): "the tradition of operatic ensemble ... incorporates one of our central theoretical motifs: that real social change, such as the gaining of readily accessible anti-retroviral drugs for people with AIDS in South Africa, is achieved by a vast multitude, not by singular, indeed 'operatic' heroes. Musical polyphony in our context represents the ultimate democratization of history's rich and layered narrative." *Trees* pushes Greyson's avant-garde interests and roots in new directions with a mosaic complexity that is even more allusive, dense, and formally playful than two decades of allusions, densities, and play. Nevertheless, its continuity with Greyson's preceding work lies not only in this vocal "democratization" but also in the structuring through music of utopian feelings of revolt and liberation, community and desire, elements that invested his earlier works, above all *Zero*.

What is more, *Fig Trees* applies this political and aesthetic vision once again to AIDS. While Greyson had been taking a decade-long sabbatical from the theme – at least as an explicit motif, rather than as a nagging undercurrent – the sad descending spiral of the Pandemic had not been on pause. It even seemed that the hiatus of hope around the 1996 Vancouver conference and its aftermath, though responsible for the plummeting of mortality within populations with access to health care in the West, had been but a blip on the planetary screen. The already catastrophic picture in sub-Saharan Africa had been qualitatively exacerbated, and new epicentres had emerged around the globe, from China to southern Asia to the former Soviet bloc. In the cultural arena, although a stream of productions was maintained, as we have seen and shall continue to see in this chapter, Western artists by and large retreated into a denial of the geopolitical disaster that evoked the dark days of silence in the mid-1980s, preferring at best, like Farlinger and Fitzgerald, to develop domestic imagery that seemed to retread familiar territory.

Greyson had been to South Africa several times throughout the nineties, first on his trips to queer festivals. There he had encountered not only queer arts impresario Jack Lewis, his eventual collaborator on the 2003 co-production feature *Proteus*, but also Lewis's partner Zackie Achmat, a PWA who was assuming a leadership role in the Treatment Access Campaign, which had been set up to bring the expensive new drugs to the country's infected millions. Was Greyson really a solitary voice crying out in the Western wilderness about the continent's struggles for all the things sung about in 1993: control, a science of conscience, access to health, zero patience, and the will to live? No, of course, but within the trickle of development documentary films that gradually became available, especially after the Durban conference of 2000 (including some even from the Johnny-come-lately NFB), Greyson's voice was unique in channelling the fierce energy of the queer/AIDS cultural movement of the late eighties and early nineties into the exacerbating geopolitical crisis.

Not easily reduced to a plot synopsis, *Trees* is based on a narrative around Achmat, a founder of the Treatment Access Campaign who is carrying on his personal medication strike to force the African National Congress government and the pharmaceutical cartel to provide the new antiretrovirals to his compatriots. Buoyed by Nelson Mandela's support of his cause and by a symbolic concession by President Mbeki's embarrassed government, Achmat's resumption of his treatment serves as a kind of denouement for the narrative. (Mbeki finally yielded fully to the campaign on 12 August 2003, three and a half months before the premiere of the opera at the suburban Oakville [Ontario] Galleries.) Interwoven with this documentary thread is another self-reflexive narrative line: Gertrude Stein and Virgil Thomson, pioneers of twentieth-century modernist literature and music, respectively, and co-creators of the 1928 avant-garde opera *Four Saints in Three Acts*, come back to life in contemporary Oakville alongside St Teresa and several martyrs of the South African AIDS cause. In this more blatantly Greysonian fantasy, the two queer ancestors deliberate on material for a remake of *Four Saints*, the tie-ins being the question of martyrdom in both operas – spiritual and political, respectively – and of racial politics as well.

Each of the seven unique numbers in *Trees* is installed in its own room, to be "consumed" in random sequence, each incorporating its own specific musical-dramatic strategy, or "game" (as Wall puts it). Though all seven offer music and lyrics rigorously inspired by Stein's modernist principles of formalist composition, all fall musically within Wall's "wholly conservative, indeed counter-revolutionary perspective" that occupied the "necessary middle ground between maudlin Broadwayism and barely listenable post-Schoenbergian chromaticism" (2003, 18). The cumulative musical fabric is richly playful and accessible (once pop- or showtune-shaped ears acclimatize to the trained voices of the classical vocal idiom), as well as dramatically gripping and, politically speaking, charged with both effect and affect. The gallery tour of seven different variations of operatic format echoes in its way the classical movie musical (and *Zero*), which also offers after all a gamut of musical styles, genres, and pretexts.

In terms of affect, two numbers from *Trees* surmount most dramatically the arcane and rigorously intellectual conceptualism of the premise – in other words, "immediacy" and "transparency" again – as well as confronting most explicitly and directly the politics and thematics of the Pandemic.

"The Queen's Throat," Achmat's "operatic" sickbed solo with chorus, is a rendition of a video-conferenced speech he sent to the Barcelona AIDS Conference of 2002, when he was too sick from his strike to travel. "T-Shirts," no doubt the work's most conventionally agitprop piece, showcases a quartet of the work's characters performing a vocal transcription of Greyson's short documentary on the TAC struggle. The quartet and the documentary unfold simultaneously by means of parallel screens with overlapping soundtracks.

"The Queen's Throat" might be thought to most resemble "Positive" in its melodramatic solo performance of PWA emotion and defiance, and the chorus this time is comprised not of schoolchildren reinforcing the theme but of translators creating comic interference with their various language versions of the speech, transformed by Google's translation software into ever more nonsensical versions. Greyson formulates his theme as "the lures and limits of martyrdom" (2003, 12), and it is as if he is using the Steinian games to modulate, mediate, or blatantly back off from its "lures" – or what Wall calls "the operatic tradition as a means of grand heroification"[8] – while playing up its "limits" (2003, 21). Another way of looking at this is to see it as an artist deploying the self-reflexive formal procedures of modernism to create what Dyer has called (in relation to Judy Garland, evoking a tradition of precursor gay cultural critics as well) an important aspect of the so-called "gay sensibility":

What both Jack Babuscio and Vito Russo bring out is the way that the gay sensibility holds together qualities that are elsewhere felt as antithetical: theatricality and authenticity. Equally I'd want to suggest that the sensbility holds together intensity and irony, a fierce assertion of extreme feeling with a deprecating sense of its absurdity ... This passion-with-irony is another inflection of the gay sensibility, a doubleness which informs equally Russo's living-on-the-edge, Babuscio's theatricalisation-of-experience and indeed the whole suffering-and-strength motif. (1987, 154–5)

"T-Shirts," the most programmatic AIDS number, follows in this same model, using a kind of contrapuntal musical structure, as well as Greyson's ever self-reflexive schema, to again capture this paradoxical double-edged sensibility. The room for this "number" is set up as a drive-in theatre in which spectators sit in a van that evokes the Treatment Access Campaign vehicle and through the windshield watch the documentary element projected onto a large suspended composite T-shirt, the eponymous agitprop garment used by the treatment activists in their street theatre demonstrations. Projected onto this "screen" is first the large purple logo HIV Positive, which as a T-shirt inscription operated in the campaign as slogan and performative declaration of personal, corporeal implication or of solidarity through the symbolic assumption of the label of infection. As a political tactic the T-shirt incorporated the strong confessional element of early ACT UP activism and of artists from Valiquette to Hoolboom, but it was rooted in a brutal political context in which PWA Gugu Dlamini, reincarnated as a character in *Fig Trees*, was beaten to death after "coming out" as PWA in 1998.

Then the documentary unfolds, offering several sit-in and demonstration scenes and two charismatic solidarity *darshans* by Mandela: his visit to the Achmat residence, followed by a press conference out front and in another setting his silent but symbolically articulate donning of the T-shirt. Captured in black and white small-format video (filmed mostly by Lewis but with a contribution by Greyson), the work is framed by an activist rock group, "The Generics," whose indigenous pop idiom tribute to Achmat clashes pleasantly with the quartet. Through freeze frames and stutter editing, Greyson accentuates Achmat's momentous frontline declarations and Mandela's T-shirt demonstration. The raucous noise of the documentary overlays the musical performance, seen on a dashboard monitor for the "drive-in" spectators seated in the van, and its voice elements are transcribed into choral motifs for the four singers, either in duets or quartet formation (shot frontally in colour, their lineup keyed in against Toronto's Gardiner Expressway, as if to underscore the cultural and geographical gap between Toronto and Capetown). The banal cadences of both ultimatums and everyday speech are transformed into musical lyrics, effecting, as Wall puts it, "a kind of elevation of the everyday into the mythic realm." For example, Mandela's press conference appeal to the reporters, "I don't hear typical questions," becomes not so much an elderly hard-of-hearing statesman working on the acoustics but as reprised by Gugu Dlamini's voice, a self-reflexive pointer about the whole process of hearing, typicality, and questioning.

In short, both numbers extend the discursive complexity and experimentation of the other two AIDS songs of Greyson that I have discussed ("The ADS Epidemic" and "Positive") as dynamic counterpoints of narrative and agitprop, private and public, individual solo and "democratic" chorus, the queerly heroic and the queerly ironic, comic, contradictory, or camp. At the same time all have a strong element of immediacy and affect, mediated but not diluted by the familiar layering of metapolitical analysis. With *Trees*, Greyson was intent on avoiding what he saw as the way *Zero*'s audiences and critics had responded only to the musical elements rather than to the self-reflexive aesthetic and political discourse (email, 10 May 2004). With *Zero*, his mistakes had been "all interrelated, which have to do with trying to occupy a popular genre wholesale – though it's meant to be a meta-musical, in fact it became merely a musical, and therefore could be judged on

Fig Trees (2003), the "т-Shirts" number: South African treatment activist Zackie Achmat, Nelson Mandela, and chorus perform counterpoints of narrative and agitprop, private and public, heroic and camp, Capetown and Toronto. CD frame grab.

those terms (quality of music/dance/production value, but most of all, narrative simplification …)." In his view, the fully achieved quality of the *Fig Trees* package more rigorously implements his artistic intent without the compromises built into the feature film industry: "[it is] the project that I'm most proud of, in my entire life … Truly the best thing I've ever done, I do believe" (email 12 January 2004).

It is hard to disagree with Greyson's pride in the video opera, whether or not we can agree that *Zero* fell so completely on stony ground (and I for one do not). Whether the compromises of the avant-garde gallery scene and the perils of suburban exhibition (Oakville, granted, was not Mississauga, on the other side of the Gardiner Expressway/Queen Elizabeth Way) also entered into the artist's considered comparison of his two major works on AIDS, not to mention their different contexts more than a decade apart, is another question. Needless to say, the package included a palpable documentary dimension that has been maintained throughout all the meanderings of Greyson's twenty-five-year career, but the issues of documentary must now be considered in relation to the work of the actor who plays Achmat's filmmaker lover Lewis in *Trees*, Greyson's frequent collaborator Richard Fung.

FUNG: THE DOCUMENTARY IMPULSE

> One of the most important things in doing prevention education is to empower people with knowledge, skills and choices.
> ~ Alan Li, Toronto AIDS activist, in *Fighting Chance*

A subjective hand-held camera set to an upbeat disco-ish soundtrack moves attentively through a gay-male sauna, past towel-wrapped clients in the corridor and the cubicles. The subject, soon revealed as a slim, young Chinese man in a jaunty baseball cap, considers several potential sexual partners and is declined by others before finally coming to an unspoken agreement with a South Asian man of the same age. In the latter's mirrored cubicle, the two begin kissing and caressing and then engage in anal intercourse, the seated Chinese man penetrating his partner, who is astride his lap. The men's bodies, as well as their condom and lubricant, are all carefully and graphically shown in close-up operation. Safe-sex slogans scroll by first in English, and then in French, as well as in several Asian languages and then the final credits.

The 1990 safe-sex videotape thus described, *Steam Clean*, has a symptomatic place in the videography of Richard Fung, positioned halfway through the eleven-work career spanning from 1984 to 2003. But it has sometimes been absent from Fung's own personal c.v., perhaps because it was a commission produced jointly by the Gay Men's Health Crisis (GMHC) of New York and the AIDS Committee of Toronto, perhaps because it is so bluntly didactic in its public service announcement (PSA) appeal. Another community-commissioned tape, Fung's documentary on AIDS within Asian North American communities, *Fighting Chance* (1990, 31), which was released the same year, and *Sea in the Blood* (2000, 26), his synthesis of his own biography in relation to illness, are both more substantive and more personal confrontations with the retrovirus, a full-fledged enlistment of the documentary impulse. But out of what might seem to be my intellectual perversity, *Steam Clean*, the steamiest, slenderest, least personal, and least documentary of Fung's three AIDS documentaries opens this section on his oeuvre as a discourse of "sobriety ... instrumental power ... domination and conscience, power and knowledge, desire and will," to deploy once again Nichols' handy formulation (1991, 3–4). Neither my auteurist training nor my affinity towards social-activist documentary allows me to discount commissions, especially those undertaken with community organizations. Furthermore, I enjoy going against the grain of the growing literature on Fung that prefers to canonize the postcolonial queer hybridity of his more complex autobiographical and historical essays like *The Way to My Father's Village* (1988, 38), *My Mother's Place* (1990, 49), and *Dirty Laundry* (1996, 31), rather than something as straightforwardly instrumentalist as *Steam* or as expository as *Chance*. This literature also downplays the sexual discourse and performance – queer at that – that I think are at the centre of Fung's production, as well as his strong sense of rootedness in place, both of which are part of his essential documentary vocation, thus downplaying the full constellation of intersecting artistic, identity and political practices.

To repair this oversight, I would first like to reclaim *Steam Clean* as the key to Fung's oeuvre and then approach his two other AIDS-themed works, viewing all three in terms of both sexual imagery and discourses of place and thereby affirming the documentary sensibility and instrumentalist sobriety that they embody. Let me make several initial points about *Steam Clean*, first by quoting SARA DIAMOND's Foucauldian reading of the tape: "In *Steam Clean*, a safe sex tape addressed to Asian men by Richard Fung, a surveillance camera happens to discover two men having sex in a steam bath" (1996, 203). An obvious error (mistaking the large mirrored perspective that concludes the tape for a one-way mirror?) arising not only because the author presumably prefers French theory to Greek active but also because like most of us academics and theorists, Diamond writes about the works *she* would like to see and make rather than what is on the screen – as if a self-reflexive overlay about Foucault's panopticon could possibly help Fung in achieving his activist goals of encouraging safer sex, of saving lives among the gay Asian community in North America.[9]

Here is a typical example, I am afraid, of the demotion of the sexual in academic discourse around queer culture. Sexual representation, in fact queer sexual performance, is an important but unacknowledged commonality that Fung shares with a disparate body of contemporary work in hybrid documentary and that Nichols has lumped together as performative (1994), from Pratibha Parmar's *Khush* to Marlon Riggs' *Tongues Untied*, and one can certainly add queer Canadian artists from STEVE REINKE to CLINT ALBERTA and LORNA BOSCHMAN to his grouping. Laura Marks has called

Richard Fung's *Steam Clean* (1990): a tender couple demonstrating condom use, as well as "constructing an alternative erotics ... articulating counterhegemonic views of sexuality," a utopian pan-Asian sexual subject. VHS frame grab, VTape

the sexual element in so many of these works the "engaging [of] desire," the "reclaiming [of] sexual pleasure on their own terms (1993, 23)." But the critical reception of all of such artists often reveals a symptomatic soft pedalling of the hanky-panky: typically, one reviewer of Fung's *Dirty Laundry* of 1996 repeatedly intones the trimmed mantra "race and gender," when he clearly should be saying, at the very least, "race, gender, and sexuality" and no doubt even "nationality" – but we'll come back to that elision of location in a moment (Steven 1996).

Thanks to narrative conventions and expectations aroused by the charming chemistry of the two actors, *Steam*'s smiling, tender, and safe coitus reproduces the distinctively romantic narrative of couple formation epitomized by all Fung's queer Asian tapes. They may be so shaped obliquely, as in *Orientations* (1985, Fung's first tape, a queer pan-Asian CR documentary in which AIDS has not yet been broached), or explicitly, as in *Chance*, in the sense that individualized talking heads of PWA activists from around the continent are gradually transformed in the editing into situated talking couples who had once thought their diagnosis meant they'd never get another shot at love. With both the anonymous and dramatized libertines in *Steam* and the committed real-life couples in *Chance*, Fung literally accomplishes his goal, announced repeatedly in his writings, of moving beyond "pulling apart" sexual discourses to "constructing an alternative erotics ... articulating counterhegemonic views of sexuality," constructing a utopian pan-Asian sexual subject (1991, 165).

Diamond played a formative role, of course, as an executive producer of artists' work about safe sex in this country, namely the two series of PSAs about AIDS that she enabled from her throne at the Banff Centre (including its pioneering segments on lesbian sexual practice). Her comparatively trivial mistake about *Steam* no doubt slipped into print because few people look seriously at sexual imagery, and this whole network of so-called performative work in which Fung is usually situated is a slippery commodity, susceptible not so much to state censorship as to discursive manipulation in the academic marketplace, partly because of its cultivated open-endedness and obliqueness. Fung's own articles amusingly recount his own personal appropriability as artist persona, not only by GMHC and the Canadian cultural hierarchy (more of that later) but also by those dreaded institutions of the opportunist liberal academy, the "bomber crew" panel and the multicultural anthology. In these settings, he is drafted to wear the Asian hat today, and tomorrow the queer hat, the video hat, the leftist hat, occasionally the Canadian hat, and sometimes, within our pathological Canadian confederation, the Anglo hat. Fung is the ideal postcolonial panelist – so what if the specifics of his practice and his identity are sacrificed?

Coming back to what is on the *Steam* screen, first of all the camera's point of view wanders down the bathhouse corridor, and who should pass with a characteristic cruise of the lens but that hairy-chested WASP hunk McCaskell, Fung's real-life partner. Then who should be busy reading in cubicle number two but pioneering Toronto video artist COLIN CAMPBELL, and who should be seen in cubicle number four by what is now revealed as the embodied look of our fetching protagonist but Fung himself, together with a certain aspiring filmmaker named Greyson, and McCaskell again, no doubt too busy plotting their next collaboration to engage in a hot foursome with the camera. No, we do not meet any other Toronto video art stalwarts in the next cubicle. But as the protagonist passes an unwilling white (presumed) racist and a willing black leather man in their respective cubicles, to end up in the arms and anus of the well-prepared stubble-chested South Asian man, it is clear that we are not only having real sex but we are also doing so in a real place. We are in the middle not only of the incestuous universe of the Toronto art video community, not only of a community education network staffed by activists from Toronto's queer Asian and antiracist education organizations, but also of a real Toronto sauna, the Spa on Maitland. The sense of networking and location for this fully dramatized and useful piece of instructional porn is thus as strong as in any of Fung's more conventional realist documentaries, all set at least in part in Toronto and dealing with political refugees, police racism, and conscious-ness-raising by Asian gays and lesbians. So strong that the Asian sector of the intended audience in the United States must have felt a sense of bewilder-ing dislocation, not only from the admonition in formal French to "enculer en sécurité" seemingly towering over the messages in Tagalog, Hindi, Chinese, and Vietnamese but also from the documentary specificity of this space, all the more since American viewers caught up in the panic mentality of the debate around bathhouse closures in the major centres (San Francisco closed, New York mostly did) must have found this Toronto location very matter-of-fact. Indeed, this is not a virtual panopticon or a porno set but an earnest, brightly lit space that feels less like a sauna than a seminar conduct-ed by sober young community educators – which it is, along with every-thing else!

We can also think of the Spa on Maitland as the setting for what we might call the "homoscape" or, more generally, the "eros-scape." In doing so, we would be borrowing Arjun Appadurai's figure of the "scape" – as in ethnoscape, mediascape, financescape, technoscape, and ideoscape. From the Indo-American anthropologist's viewpoint, "scapes" are "different streams or flows along which cultural material may be seen to be moving across national boundaries," which resonate through the perceived stabili-ties and localities of our everyday lives (1996). Shifting the notion's applica-tion from the ethnic diasporas to that of the differently constituted queer diasporas, the "Homintern" (Waugh 1993), the queer global village, the eros-scape, is the transnational scene of sexual spaces, commodities, com-munications, and identity performance. The eros-scape is shaped, as in Fung's tape, by flimsy partitions, corridors, half-opened doors, and mirrors and textured by easily inflected (and disguised) accoutrements of – in this case – baseball cap and towel, stubbled chest and leather harness, condom and lubricant. It is inhabited by the coded rituals of looking and cruising, the negotiations of consent, and ultimately of course the protocols of sexual exchange. In the space of the sauna, the scape is stable because it is so her-metic, scarcely disrupted by the performance of rejection, racist or other-wise, channelled down the corridor through the serial process of selection and culminating in the mirrored space where sex is enacted, the conjugal drive is resolved, and community is consolidated.

With its relatively conventional narrative construction, the unitary eros-scape of the Spa on Maitland is a far cry from the hybrid scapes of Fung's other, more complex works. In those videos, in the spatial complexity of trans-bordered community networks, present space and historical space, documentary space of interview and dramatized space of reenactment, as well as the various mediatic spaces employed (from email to Super 8 home movies), there is what Appadurai calls the "fundamental disjuncture" of scapes. The clash of eros-scape with ethnoscape articulates more vividly than ever the identity disjuncture of queer and Asian that Fung has been so expressive in documenting since 1984. Such a disjuncture had been epitomized in the moments in *Chinese Characters* where Asian gay men, anchored in the foreground ethnoscape, are video-keyed against the imaginary background of a white porno eros-scape commodity (see chapter 8). In fact, we can see all Fung's works as documentary apprehensions of Chinese diasporas repeatedly coming together with the queer nation.

But I would like to approach the question of scapes and place/space in Fung's work from a slightly different angle. Critical attention to postcolonial narrative and performative video alike has frequently underlined the uprootedness, the dislocatedness of space. For José Muñoz, an Hispanic American publishing in the British journal *Screen*, Fung's *Mother* and other tapes are situated in "contact zones," "locations of hybridity" such as the Asian community in Toronto and are "uniquely concentrated on issues of place and displacement." That is, "Fung's place, in both Canada, Trinidad, gay-male culture, documentary practice, ethnography, pornography, the Caribbean and Asian diasporas, is not quite fixed." (1999). In a similar vein, Appadurai can generalize on behalf of a whole body of postcolonial theory about "deterritorialization," "human motion," and the ethnoscape as the "landscape of persons who constitute the shifting world in which we live: tourists, immigrants, refugees, exiles, guest workers, and other moving groups and individuals." He argues in general that cultures are no longer nationally and spatially centred but that locality is felt globally rather than spatially (1996, 33, 183–99).

These descriptions are certainly apt if we think of Fung's cast of migrants, both fictive and real, whose spatial coordinates are indeed "not quite fixed." *Chance*, for example, includes within its "talking heads" tour of the pentagram formed by Toronto, Vancouver, San Francisco, Los Angeles, and Boston two poetic interludes whose spatial coordinates are decidedly nonspecific. The space of these interludes, shot also in the ever helpful Spa on Maitland and accompanied by a poetic voice-over, is largely symbolic: the mise-en-scène of Buddhist ritual folding and burning of gilded funeral papers, suggestive imagery of a group shower scene, and a nude man's gestural play stripping a flower of its petals, which then scatter around his comely feet. These "not quite fixed" interludes all together invoke the subjective tropes of memory, mourning, and lingering desire. In *Sea in the Blood* also, underwater swimming footage taken in Lake Simcoe functions as the rosy, sensuous symbolic space of memory and conjugal comfort, as well as a sensual evocation of blood. Even in the nitty-gritty of *Steam* there is a return to a symbolic voyage or quest narrative structure already used in *Chinese Characters* and Fung's two autobiographical tapes, where he literally travels to the homelands, both mythical and material, of his parents. Equally connoting a sense of "not quite fixed" is his deft use of the video key for confronting two disparate spaces, as we have seen in *Chinese Characters*.

But these readings of Fung's spatial imagery as "deterritorialized" cannot explain his work fully. We must also think of the specifically North American mandate and referent of both *Steam Clean* and *Fighting Chance*, the concrete community space of the sauna in the former and the specific urban geographies of the latter. For if we look at his oeuvre as a whole, and even within the works that we might call most deterritorialized, the hybrid shifting space of the migrant is always anchored in a strong sense of locality and rootedness. *Chance*, for example, may well move erratically among the five different North American metropoles, but it encounters faces, bodies, and voices in each that are all vividly situated within the recognizable space, both private and public, of these settings. For example, in the Vancouver sequences centred on "Lim," the dignified Malaysian immigrant delivers his measured and clear testimony about his personal struggles with the virus and with his family as he is seated on a bench by the sea wall in the West End, with first the bay and then the skyline as backdrop. Initially, certain well-worn documentary clichés might be anticipated – the interlocutor framed by generic urban landscape, etc. – but we soon learn that it is the bench, rather than the picturesque setting, that is the key spatial referent. The bench is a memorial to Lim's departed lover, set up in the spot he frequented while dealing with his diagnosis, and it is soon metamorphised into a row of similar benches along the wall testifying to other lives lost. Diasporic and unfixed perhaps, this image of the hard and bolted wooden object of solace for the bereaved migrant is *also* an indicator of a specific urban site of personal and collective history, the documentary apprehension of place. The Vancouver sequence reveals, here as elsewhere, the situatedness of the social activist whose documentary aesthetic integrates the postmodern and the nonreferential performative within a strong realist, instrumentalist framework of localized agendas of city and nation. Fung once casually mentioned to me the "pedagogical strategy" that had dictated the relatively conventional interview-based format for the tapes on refugee rights and police racism, respectively *Safe Place* (1989, 32) and *Out of the Blue* (1991, 28). This clearly applies as well to the two 1990 AIDS tapes, which are among his two most pragmatic works in terms of connecting specific localized audiences and short-term community goals with the North American urban environment within which Fung has worked since the 1970s. Subtending the autobiographical searches for "my father's village" and "my mother's place" in his hybrid canonized work, then, is the inscription of "*my* village" and "*my* place."

Unfortunately, the *Screen* article on Fung's queer hybridity introduces the question of the national as an afterthought, mistakenly identifying the artist as Chinese American and pointing the reader in footnotes to a couple of hookups between postcolonial theory and the Canadian entity. My intention is not to reclaim another internationally recognized artist for the Canadian pantheon à la William Shatner but rather to point out that it is as limiting to disregard crucial settings of Fung's documentary practice – the urban locality and the national arena – as it is to soft-pedal his sexual imaginary. These Toronto and Canadian settings have seen Fung's canonization and co-optation in the name of multiculturalism, to be sure, but they have also felt the benefits of his strong and influential interventions on cultural and social debates and policies. In short, Fung's brilliant marshalling of the ethnoscape and the eros-scape, their overlaps and convergences, cannot properly be understood without reference to their rootedness in the metropolitan and the national, dynamic places not only of hybridity and dislocatedness but also of community rootedness, coalition, and intervention.

A decade after these two 1990 AIDS videos, after traversing a prolific and creative period strengthening his command of scripting and narrative with his railway video *Dirty Laundry* (1996), Fung departed in bold new directions with *Sea in the Blood* (2000). A personal epic that brought metaphysics to my soul and tears to my eyes, *Sea* highlighted the continuity and the growth in Fung's documentary trajectory, extending his experimentation with representing both sexuality/conjugality and place. A work that has met universal acclaim, *Sea* also completes the arc of the elegant triptych of autobiographical/familial works, adding his late sister Nan to the portrait gallery that already includes his mother and his father.

Sea is structured on the artist's voice – both audio and typographic – as it narrates his lifelong voyage through the life-threatening illnesses first of Nan, a victim of the rare hereditary blood disorder thalassemia, and then of resilient PWA lover McCaskell. Larded with the standard materials of postmodern autobiography, home movies and slides, the tape follows five members of the Fung family over five decades and four continents, perhaps the classic canvas of postmodern, diasporic narrative. Its primary agenda is to set up illness both as a metaphysical and physical element and as a political issue – a familiar preoccupation in AIDS arts, as we have seen. But here I want to emphasize the work's documentary confrontation with sexuality and place.

The erotic discourses of the tape are based on the parallel between Nan and Richard as desiring subjects: Fung remembers the teenaged Nan's despair that a chronically sick girl could never have a boyfriend and contrasts it with his whispered confession – now, not then – that he also wanted a boyfriend. Later one of Nan's dying wishes is to meet her brother's lover, as if in surrogate fulfilment of her childhood fantasy. The beach imagery, both vintage and reconstructed, seems to connote this shared desire, but only in Richard's case does it come to fruition as a discourse of adult conjugality in the sensuous and celebratory underwater imagery of Tim and Richard swimming together. The lush iconography of air bubbles, slowly waving limbs, graceful gymnastics, and glowing naked skin echoes in a diffuse and ambiguous way the intense and playfully complicit relationship of brother and sister. As in Fung's other AIDS tapes, this conjugal imagery takes the politics of sexual identity for granted, rather than constructing it as a contestatory or affirmative claim. Instead the tape uses it to subtly undermine ideological assumptions around the heterosexual family that are constructed through the vintage home movies and then destabilized through the melodramatic unfolding of the narrative, with its elements of maternal castration and blackmail, filial revolt and exile, the manipulation and exorcism of guilt and confession, tenacious silence, and retroactive revelations. This narrative must be read in the larger context of the Asian extended family, which Fung locates elsewhere as the crux of difference:

In the context of North American racism, families and communities can have particular significance for Asians in affirming identity. So while white gays and lesbians can avoid personalized homophobia by separating from their families or formative communities and still see themselves reflected in the society around them, their Asian counterparts do not always share this mobility and often find their sexual/emotional and racial/cultural identities in conflict. (1991, 64)

Fung has had to face just that conflict in all his work, but he does so most vividly here, as he gradually discloses his narrative with all the measured calmness of the master storyteller and deceptively unfrenzied adult he has become.

Recalling his skulk back too late to Toronto in 1977, the evening after Nan had died, Fung establishes Toronto as the end of the narrative, after its peregrinations through Trinidad, Turkey, India, Nepal, Ireland, and London. The Queen City is the most concrete of all, the site where the core conjugality of the film is initiated and lived and the site of Nan's brief adulthood and her final encounter with mortality. One of the most resonant images in the film is the sunny colour snapshot of the smiling adult Nan after she has visited the queer communal house on Seaton Street where her rebel brother has put down roots, a vivid capsule of both melodramatic narrative and documentary discernment of place.

Obviously *Sea* is less literally activist and instrumentalist in its orientation than the other two AIDS tapes. In fact it is an AIDS tape that almost takes AIDS for granted. *Sea* nevertheless maintains a strong documentary articulation of politics, not only in the confrontation of queer conjugality with heterofamiliality but also in its critique of the epidemiology of thalassemia. Paradoxically, it is also political in the matter-of-factness of its glimpses of McCaskell as he transforms his HIV infection into AIDS activism and a political constituency of the infected. The video thus extends the balance that I have argued is intrinsic to Fung's work – the balance between aestheticism and activism, between Fung the diasporic's elusive postcolonial, postmodern canonicity and Fung the Torontonian's pragmatic social realist roots, between the eros- and ethnoscapes and the sense of rootedness in place.

This section on Fung was first started as part of a festschrift in honour of the late Erik Barnouw, my old teacher at Columbia University (Waugh 1998). Erik had first presided over my awakening interest in documentary in the early seventies, and I was thrilled to be able to pay homage to him through deciphering Fung's works about AIDS and queer sexuality in the shadow of a towering heritage of documentary imagery of lives and places. Homo-age as well as homage, for there was also a perverse thrill in discussing the vivid nonfiction anal penetration amid the sober academic encomia for my heterosexual mentor who'd introduced me to the documentary pioneers Flaherty and Vertov back in the seventies. But I knew he would understand, a twinkle in his eye, how a 1990 three-minute safer-sex video was a direct descendent of Vertov's revolutionary Soviet newsreel *Kino Pravda* (Cinema Truth, 1922–25), which was not without its own kind of role-model dramatizations and didacticism.

What brings sexuality and place together in Fung's documentary oeuvre is not only politics but also Fung himself, his personal voice and autobiographical impulse. I can't help noticing in *Sea*, alongside the gorgeous effects and strong affect, the simple unaestheticized presence of the shamed queer school kid that was Fung himself, the home-movie figuring of a slight and hyperactive son returned to repeatedly by the editor. From this frenzy performed by the original "school fag" (to borrow the title of another of his tapes, 1998) for his parents' camera, we can trace the performative trajectory of his learning to be "close to illness." Fung's voice-over says he was "painfully shy" away from the family (and its home-movie camera evidently), but we are only left to imagine the extent of that pain. Amid the guilt-ridden elegiac strain for his sister the medical exhibit, the nostalgic love poem to infected commie backpacker Tim, and the dignified laconic encore of Mother Fung snipping castratingly away at her plants (in her third tape?), *Sea* ends up being the most autobiographical of Fung's works. He certainly appears on-screen more than he has since his uncredited faux interview way back in *Chinese Characters* (1986, see chapter 8), and he is now literally in the eponymous sea throughout (at the beach with Nan, capturing 1970s skinny-dipper Tim on camera, embodied by a boy actor in 2000, cavorting underwater with Tim in the haunting metaphoric title footage). I learned a lot I didn't know about my friend Richard in this auto-biographical tape, but it is the issue of autobiography that I would like to address in the next section and in reference to another Torontonian.

HOOLBOOM: THE AUTOBIOGRAPHICAL IMPULSE

because you don't belong to yourself any longer ...
~ Mike Hoolboom, *Positiv*, 1997

Having scanned the groundwater of AIDS cultural activism in Canada in the 1980s and 1990s and then zoomed in on Greyson the musicalist and Fung the documentarist, in this section I would like to focus on Mike Hool-boom the autobiographer. I will examine his three principal short works about AIDS from the 1990s and to do so, must move back from the 2000s of *Fig Trees* and *Sea in the Blood* to consider the earlier decade's triptych as an epitome of the autobiographical thrust in Canadian queer AIDS work. I included my take on Hoolboom's AIDS triptych in this volume with some trepidation, for I knew that AIDS certainly does not comprise the entirety of Hoolboom's contribution as an artist (any more than it does for Greyson and Fung), nor does it define him as a human being – far from it. This ver-satile artist, no less prolific than the other monumental presences in this chapter, is the focus of a large critical literature that has enlisted many of Canada's finest (and worst) film critics, curators, and fellow artists.[10] Hool-boom is also a productive film writer and curator in his own right, so a nar-row focus and selection is both necessary and appropriate. Furthermore, as he himself put it after his 1988 diagnosis, HIV provided "a kind of unifying locus for my identity" (Bailey 2000, 277), and without a doubt his postdi-agnosis work transformed his mission and vision as an artist. It also found him a new and expanded audience, shifting his position within national and international cinemas. At the centre of this transformation is Hoolboom's AIDS triptych of the 1990s: *Frank's Cock* (1993), *Letters from Home* (1996), and *Positiv* (1997), which falls in the middle of the chronological span that I have already constructed in following Greyson and Fung from the 1980s right through to the 2000s.

Hoolboom's 1988 diagnosis took place in St Paul's, the same Vancouver hospital where Dr Peter's practice and final years were lived out. Known then as a twenty-something Toronto experimental filmmaker with a reputation for formal rigour, celluloid purism in the age of video, and film community activism, Hoolboom fluctuated in his work between structural minimalism and excess. Having discovered the writer within, he was increasingly pushing the "new talkie" tendency of eighties avant-gardism to its limit, developing clear talents as raconteur, diarist, and aphorist. An ardent collaborator, then as now, Hoolboom moved to Vancouver at the end of the decade to nurture his working and personal relationship with Ann Marie Fleming, an emerging figure in that city's experimental scene. Hoolboom's seroconversion, that critical moment of truth later rehearsed repeatedly in his 1990s films, not only altered his life but also resituated him as an artist in the international and Canadian context I have been sketching:

So one Saturday afternoon we trooped off together to have our juice drained [at a Red Cross blood drive] and that was that. Until a letter came for me in the mail. Saying there was a problem with my donation. My blood. That I should go see my doctor. That's when he told me I was HIV positive. He was a young guy who worked in the clinic and he handed me a bunch of pamphlets and said, "I don't really know anything about this disease, I've never talked to anyone who's had it before but read this." I didn't handle the news all that well. I kept it to myself and waited to die. Drank a lot. Phoned up a bunch of people I'd slept with and passed the word along. And began a frantic tear of short films that's lasted till now. Never wanting to make anything bigger than my head because I didn't figure I'd be around to finish it. I just didn't know. (de Bruhn 1993, 5)

The first generation of AIDS artists, from Bressan and Valiquette to Vito Russo, as well as the writers and visual artists I have mentioned above, had passed or were passing the torch, almost all dead by the time of this interview, given just after the shooting of *Frank's Cock*. With this film, Hoolboom found himself, for better or worse, among a second generation of figureheads of the AIDS arts movement, one of its first male artists *not* to have emerged from gay cultures and communities. Though the era of in-the-streets activism seemed to be passing – at least in North America – many of the other artistic concerns I have inventoried would be taken up and reinvented in Hoolboom's AIDS triptych: the melodramatic impulse, the recycling and reconstruction of received media images, the metaphysical thrust, the negotiation between agitprop urgency and formal innovation; and the exploration, transgression, and affirmation of sexuality.

Vancouver was also where Hoolboom encountered Joey, a fellow member of a PWA group, whose story would become dramatised as *Frank's Cock*, the first panel in Hoolboom's AIDS triptych. Despite its risqué title, its marketing as experimental, and its consumer warning of "extremely explicit," *Frank's Cock* is basically a populist melodrama, a narration of a gay romance and its impending end in Frank's imminent death, notable for its power of affect and identification. The narrator, played by then unknown Western Canadian actor Callum Keith Renney, tells of his first encounter with his lover Frank and their mentor-novitiate relationship of ten years, a love story embellished by feats of raconteur braggadocio. The eponymous appendage – described but unfortunately not seen – signals Hoolboom's appropriation and celebration of same-sex desire, which had been at the core of the queer arts counteroffensive for almost a decade but was relatively new within Hoolboom's hitherto flamingly heterosexual sensibility.[11] Hoolboom's visually and narratively intricate format, which was based on a direct-address on-screen narrator and a four-way split-screen mosaic structure, struck an immediate chord. The unnamed Renney character occupies the upper-right quadrant, frontally addressing the camera in informal, voluble, confidential close-up. After the upper-left awakens with a montage of physiological microphotography (no doubt connoting the invading micro-organisms or all the swimming cells that Hoolboom repeatedly tells us in film after film die every day in the body), the lower-left quadrant recycles Madonna's banned *Erotica* video, and eventually the lower-right chimes in with close-up excerpts of anal and oral coupling from commercial gay pornography. All three peripheral quadrants are more or less synchronised with the ebb and flow of Renney's tale and are visualised complementarily with Hoolboom's characteristic tinted black and white. The soundtrack includes his unabashed appropriation of romantic, if not outright sentimental, music, including that of another Frank, Mr Sinatra. Conciseness is perhaps the key to the film's impact: one hardly believes that such layered narrative complexity, visual virtuosity, and emotional wallop have all been demonstrated in only eight minutes. Hoolboom would basically return to variations of this tight polyphonic formula for his subsequent two films, but his authorial discretion, channelled through, or perhaps hovering behind, *Frank*'s dramatized premise, would soon dissipate.

If Hoolboom's breakthrough, rewarded with festival prizes and wide circulation, had come out of an interpersonal encounter and a discovery of other sexualities, the next film was more about a retroactive Mike-come-lately discovery of the political movement that had grown up within the epidemic in the 1980s. A visit to an ACT UP rally in New York[12] had occasioned yet another transformation in Hoolboom, by his account, from a living-room observer of the AIDS crisis to a participant in a collective belonging:

we realized that most of us – and there were thousands – were positive ... a congregation of those who had laid their beloveds into the ground, and come here still daring to hope ...

Vito Russo was the last to speak, and I'd never heard 20,000 people cry at the same time – leather giants and drag queens holding each other in the flood. Something that day changed for me. (1998, 112)

Hoolboom subsequently discovered a speech that Russo had made in Albany in the summer of 1988, the text of which became the core of *Letters from Home* (1996). The elements of direct address, narrative excess, and melodramatic affect have been extended from *Frank*, but this time the multilayered polyvocality is sequential rather than simultaneous, and the unitary dramatized narrative premise is lifted. The narrative now migrates from voice to voice in a multiracial, multiaccented, multigenerational procession of protagonists and narrators, on-screen and off (mostly figures from the Toronto arts scene, where Hoolboom had by this time reestablished himself). *Frank*'s individual-focused simplicity was set aside, and the film now aspires in its allegorical casting beyond gay community to the collective universality Hoolboom experienced that day with ACT UP. Russo's text is a narrative of his and his friends' experiences as PWAs, and an accusatory indictment of the avoidance, indifference, and stigmatization of state (ACT UP's usual target) and society. Hoolboom fleshes out the speech with his own characteristic dream narratives of a diagnosis (borrowed from Herman Hesse) plus a bodily revelation, a personal anecdote, some Canadian content, and even more high-contrast visual flair than before.

Most importantly, for the first time in this series the rotating first-person voice includes Hoolboom himself, briefly superimposed over water images and sounds, appropriating Russo's words "As a person with AIDS" for himself. The procession finally culminates with Renney, this time recounting first-person a sickbed encounter between the PWA character he plays and a friend, incorporating the melodramatic tropes of flowers, embrace, and epiphany sealed in a mutual looking-into-eyes. All this unfolds beneath the most manipulative rendition of "Amazing Grace" imaginable, frail piano transposing into organ swelling polyphonically under a glorious sunrise that blazes out Renney's face. The effect of this anthem is as devastating as it is absolutely true, having migrated from the nineteenth-century abolitionist movement to the twentieth-century antiaddiction movement and most recently to both AIDS culture and Oprah-land. But that's not all: the final shot catches Hoolboom, in extreme close-up, looking into the lens – a shot that retroactively takes over the film qualitatively.

Rather than making a transformative appearance as a voice or a coda, Hoolboom is the absolute *centre* of the next work the following year. Furthermore, his third AIDS panel, *Positiv,* was for the first time to offer the expectation of a future, to use Arroyo's phrase, going into circulation both separately and as part of the six-film package *Panic Bodies* in 1998. With its

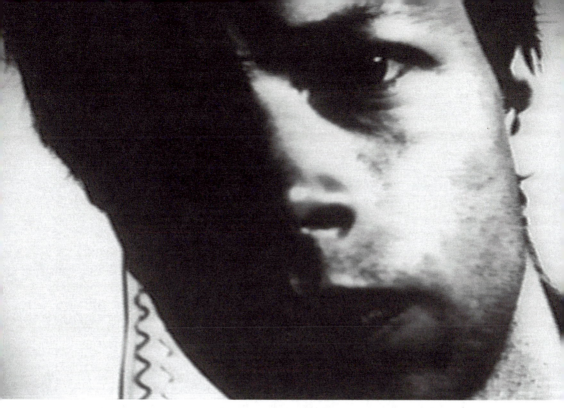

Mike Hoolboom checking the lens in the final frame of *Letters from Home* (1996): the work's melodramatic affect and multilayered polyvocality include the artist's first person voice as PWA for the first time. VHS frame grab, still production provided by the Canadian Filmmakers Distribution Centre

serene image of acceptance, bliss (both carnal and spiritual), and eternity and its presiding collaborator, the serene PWA Tom Chomont, *Bodies* was to seem to provide a symmetrical counter-answer to Hoolboom's previous long work, the scandalous *House of Pain* (1995, whose resident collaborator had been the raging artist of extreme sensation, Paul Couillard). This latter film, a nightmare inferno of visual intensity, erotic extremes, and corporeal abjection, part Dantesque, part Rabelaisian, had been put together for release after *Frank's Cock* in 1994–95, partly out of earlier shorts. It was as if *Panic Bodies*' riposte to *House of Pain* symbolically articulated the 1996 shift, itself symbolically associated with the Vancouver Conference. Appearing as it did in 1997, *Positiv* would of course not have had the full retroactive distance to assess in explicit terms this paradigm shift brought about by the new treatments, yet the film still articulates an important evolution in Hoolboom's AIDS conception all the same, as if demonstrating and updating Russo's original ultimatum that AIDS is about living: "Because we already know how we're going to die. What we don't know, what we're asking you now, is how we're going to live ... AIDS is a test of who we are as a people."

Hoolboom's self-reflexive insertion into the text is now fully realised, no longer vicariously embodying "Joey" (Frank's real-life lover), Callum Renney, or Vito Russo but maintaining a continuous presence on the screen, his own face, his own body, his own biographical trajectory, his own personal circle of family and friends. *Positiv* returns to *Frank*'s four-panel split-screen structure, and not only does he fully take over Renney's place as the frontal on-screen narrator in the upper right but he "performs" in the other quadrants as well. He recycles self-reflexive narrative fragments from earlier, apparently uncompleted projects that evoke his memories of growing up and moving away (one fragment where he is decked out in angel wings on a lonely highway), as well as his more recent experience of medical tests and treatment (Hoolboom engaged in the prophylactic inhalation of aerosol pentamidine to ward off pneumocystis pneumonia; shots of this treatment curiously extend the orality of the earlier panels). Of this experience of medicalisation, the narrator pronounces that

There's not much the doctors can do for you, except draw (your) blood out for tests. In fact the more your condition worsens the more tests (they seem to need.) are demanded, as they seek ever finer ways to monitor your decline. Your identity is clinging to these numbers, your viral loads, the ratios of enzymes and tissues that continue to betray you. [The passage scored out appears in the *Plague Years* version of the script only, while the parenthetical clause is in the final film version.]

At the same time the "found footage" strands veer in their relation to the voice from exact synchrony (shots of detached hands matching the narrator's memories of his childhood piano efforts and conceptions of his unintegrated body parts) to delirious arbitrariness. The consistent thread through all the found footage, from sci fi and pedagogical films alike, is corporeality, gleanings from pop culture's neurotic obsession with bodily transformations, from Ken Russell's *Altered States* to Fred Astaire and Ginger Rogers's *Shall We Dance*.

The least successful of the three works in terms of mainstream festival audience impact and prizes (at least as an autonomous short film), *Positiv* is in many ways the most challenging and original of the three, departing from the land of melodrama and finality into its own distinctive personal territorial flux, where "I guess I'm gonna have to wait it out" – part holding pattern, part stock taking, part manifesto: "just all of a sudden it comes to you – a new word has taken the place of your body … the little sticker on your chest doesn't say, 'Hi I'm Mike,' it only says 'AIDS' because you don't belong to yourself any longer, and as you get older it's not you they're talking to anymore it's the sickness."[13]

It remains for me to revisit Hoolboom's AIDS triptych as a whole, and focus on his performative autobiographical articulations of the sexualised, infected, abject body, in short, the *queered* body as locus of identity. In the 1980s I had associated Hoolboom with a masculinist wing of Toronto experimental cinema, a certain Sheridan College–Bruce Elder cohort, approximating the network that Hoolboom himself had once termed the "escarpment" school (1991, 43). Within the discipline of film studies, a tempest in a teapot called "The Cinema We Need" had gripped the mid-eighties and summed up for me many of the aspirations of this cohort.[14] The polemics had endowed a particular cultural aesthetic with imperial cultural and political pretensions on a national scale, without any serious ramifications for the rest of the cultural struggles going on elsewhere within these national borders. It was a *dialogue des sourds* by straight white anglo male intellectuals living in Toronto (and Ottawa) and pushing a kind of intellectualized modernist experimentalism as the solution to the [English] Canadian cinematic impasse. Of course the cohort's unquestioned masculinism was only part of the problem, but for me it was the start and end of the debate. However, Hoolboom later affectionately credited the cinematography of *Letters from Home* to his longtime collaborator Steve Sanguedolce, the "cream of the eyejocks" (with whom he had also made the prediagnosis road movie *Mexico*, in many ways Hoolboom's most masculinist movie).[15] In so doing he accidentally touched my queer Montrealer's nerve, which had blocked me out of the Toronto jock avant-gardism of the previous decade. The Hoolboom of *Letters* had long since moved beyond this jockdom, despite the vestigial traces of athletic metaphors in the AIDS films, for example, "Joey" wanting to be "Wayne Gretzky with a hardon" in *Frank*, his fascination with the size of the titular cock, and Hoolboom's receptivity to ACT UP militarist and fire fighting rhetoric in *Letters from Home*. Even at the time of his diagnosis in the late eighties, Hoolboom had already been moving beyond the eyejock visual primacy and intellectualism of his earliest work. He was entering the territory of sexual iconoclasm with his heterosexual diary and performance films, where his female partners of the day, from KIKA THORNE to Svetlana Lilova to Anne Marie Fleming, were offering the camera their bodies, sexual engagements, or relationships with the filmmaker – as well as artistic input.[16] In this territory of the body, the cracks in the machismo, its vulnerability, volatility, and relativity, seemed to be spreading.

I do not mean to overwhelm Hoolboom's frenzied productivity of the first postdiagnosis years with a teleological trajectory, all the more so since many of the short films that came out one after another had been based, like *Mexico*, on material shot earlier. Still, what is clear is that the 1993 Hoolboom of *Frank's*

Cock was a vastly different species. The transformative effect of his diagnosis was repeatedly being confirmed in interviews: "Our identity hinges on our body. Now what happens to that image once you become HIV positive? ... I worked harder. Finished more films. And quite unconsciously began a series of films that take the body as its subject." (de Bruyn 1993, 6).

It does not require a simplistic biographical reading to recognise throughout the triptych the obsessive repetition of this diagnosis moment. I think of the charged use of Billy Holliday's "You've Changed" on the soundtrack of *Letters* or of the opening dream narrative of *Letters from Home*, punctuated by ominous flash close-up shots of a man in a surgical mask:

as I get closer I can see a man stooped over a small set of crystals gathered on a table. He doesn't look up as I get close and I understand each of these crystals represent a part of myself ... He looks up then and for the first time I can see he's wearing a doctor's surgical mask. He says, "I'm sorry. I'm afraid you're HIV positive," pointing down at the pile, and sure enough, right in the middle of the glow, there's an off-colour stone slowly wearing down everything around it. I guess the future's not what it used to be.

This whole sequence is topped off by found footage of conflagration and catastrophe. The spectator also repeatedly experiences variations of this trans-/per-formative pronouncement that are more social than medical, the enactment of stigma through speech or, even more profoundly, through the look. Reflected in the haunting look back at the lens of the speakers in *Letters* and of Hoolboom himself in *Positiv* and in the proliferating eyes in all four quadrants as *Positiv* moves towards its end, this stigma is repeatedly recapitulated by the voice: "If I'm dying from anything, it's from the way you look when I see you with that funny kind of half smile on your face" (*Letters*). "[Y]ou read the whole cruel truth on their faces. You watch yourself dying there" (*Positiv*).

At the same time, indissociably, there are the moments of knowing constituted by "coming out" tropes, those Foucauldian exercises in reversing and reclaiming stigmatising discourses, once the sacrament of gay liberation, now the political ritual of the constituency of the infected. As in Bordowitz's *Fast Trip* four years earlier, Hoolboom repeatedly performs his identity on-screen through the continuous confession, or rather affirmation, of seropositivity and illness. Taken together the three narrations of his triptych include about a dozen such affirmations, either enacted or narrated. Hoolboom's performance of identity through transgressive sexuality is even more obsessive, not only spoken but also visual. This is the zone where even Cronenberg fears to tread, the zone beyond Greyson's flopping penises and anal puppets of *Zero*, the "extremely explicit" zone of throbbing indexical flesh, from the porno display and the romantic anecdote that creates worship of rimming in *Frank* to the intensely ecstatic sequence of kissing and lovemaking by nude male couples under the shower in *Letters* to the variously farcical and transcendent masturbatory frenzy of *A Boy's Life* and *Moucle's Island*, the two lusty chapters that seemingly counterbalanced the comparatively chaste serenity of *Positiv* in the composite feature *Panic Bodies*. In *Bodies*, Hoolboom, the narrative and autobiographical subject with intense eyes, earnest voice, and blistered flank, joins a processional fresco of a dozen of so other panic bodies through its six episodes.

The erotic performances in *Panic Bodies* panicked more than one lazy film critic. Commenting on *Bodies*'s receiving the best Canadian feature award at Montreal's 1999 Festival du nouveau cinéma et des nouveaux médias, *Le devoir*'s Odile Tremblay did not hesitate to collapse sexual gesture into literal embodiments of authorial identity and personality, *showing* into *being*:

How the devil could this confused film have seduced a jury, endlessly pushing its experimental side towards the land of the marginal? Excessively ambitious, this narcissistic documentary woven out of homosexual obsessions (we are forced to watch countless masturbation scenes) seems to want to demonstrate for the sake of demonstrating, upset for the sake of upsetting, provoke for the sake of provoking, without delivering any coherent message at the end of the road. (9 February 2000, BIO)

Paradoxically, out of the mouths of homophobic incompetents comes something approaching an understanding of the artistic effect of Hoolboom's performative, autobiographical marshalling of sexual imagery. The performances of two discrete identities, sexual and sero-, whether verbal or gestural, are relayed separately or in tandem. Hoolboom produces or archives, looks at, shoots, shows, and speaks both the gestural repertory of sexual marginality *and* the bodily performance of immuno-marginality. But the two identities tend to merge in their instability, all the more so within the formats of split-screen, sound-image counterpoint and narrative identification, as if together they constitute an expanded and fluid identity configuration. Beyond the post-Stonewall notion of fixed sexual essence, this is a sphere of abject stigma and otherness, in short, of queerness. Each of the three films is structured by these performative moments, where voice confronts body and sexual act, image confronts image, speech and sound confront images, and all together enact identity. *Positiv*, the final panel of the AIDS triptych, the most fully realised consummation of Hoolboom's autobiographical discourse, is the ultimate stage in his confrontation with both his body and his identities. It seems the perfect demonstration of what Annamarie Jagose has called "the multi-directional pressures which the

AIDS epidemic places on categories of identification, power and knowledge ... a radical revision of contemporary lesbian and gay politics ... a radical rethinking of the cultural psychic constitution of subjectivity itself" (1996, 94–5). The social subject known as Mike Hoolboom may or may not be bisexual, but Mike Hoolboom the filmmaker is here and queer.[17]

In the postmodern 1990s and 2000s of multiple and crossover audiences, identities and practices, hybrid forms and influences, and queerly volatile political and cultural configurations of mainstreams and margins, Hoolboom joined Greyson and Fung in affirming narrative as part of a new aesthetic hybridity. His embrace of autobiography and documentary, performance and eroticism, melodrama and activism – in short, his growing detachment from the hyper-intellectualized avant-garde – enabled the discovery of new audiences and constituencies for whom Greyson and Fung were already household words. The darling of both experimental and mainstream festival audiences, as well as AIDS community and educational organisations, Hoolboom was embraced, even appropriated, perhaps most enthusiastically by queer audiences anchored in the worldwide queer festival networks. For the copywriters at Montreal's *Image + Nation*, who offered Hoolboom a retrospective in 1998 and an updated tribute program in 2000, the Toronto filmmaker had "a unique vision of living as a gay man with AIDS ... a revolutionary subject ... Described by some as the most important Canadian filmmaker of his generation, this adventurous and challenging experience will change the way you look at film forever."[18]

As I put finishing touches on this chapter during the spring of 2004, the election of four years ago that had maintained the regime of shame is ancient history, the policy of scapegoating silently continues its course, and Canada has increasingly become a pale copy of Hoolboom's 1993 *Kanada* (with "There's No Business like Show Business" now enthroned as the national anthem). The South African and Barcelona AIDS conferences of 2000 and 2002 made the Vancouver Conference's momentary space for paradigm shifts and hope seem a distant memory, as the dimensions of the global castastrophe – and the soaring infection rates in Canadian backyards – become increasingly clear. Yet the new election on the horizon has suddenly ushered in get-those-drugs-to-Africa legislation and brought new money for the global AIDS fight out of rejuggled budget hats, complete with appearances by U2 singer Bono: the appearance of the Pandemic as a positive election issue in 2004, in contrast to rather than the backlash ploy of 2000, has struck some as cynical and others as a sign of hope. We shall see. Meanwhile, showing *Positiv* in recent years to various groups, I found that audiences and I don't cry as we did for *Frank's Cock* and *Letters from Home*. Instead, dry-eyed but no less profoundly moved on other levels, we engage with Hoolboom's serene acceptance of the organic otherness of his body, his movement beyond the concrete particularity of seropositivity, sickness, and sexual identities towards a generalised queerness that he performs together with his perplexed sickbed visitors and film spectators alike. After *Panic Bodies* (1998), Hoolboom's prolific creative energy showed no signs of abating, bringing forth various writing projects and a diversified film and video output. This included the major docu-biopic on his old gay comrade-in-arms from New York, PWA filmmaker Tom Chomont (*Tom*, 2002, 75, TIFF), a film that encompassed both the AIDS thematic and an autobiographical hook, as well as shorter work, seemingly unrelated, about the childhood of the human organism (*Jack*, 2002, 15) and of the cinema (*In the Dark*, 2003, 8). The queer identity performed through the AIDS triptych is clearly in no danger of calcifying.

Having looked in this chapter at the AIDS work of three major Toronto artists – Greyson, Fung, and Hoolboom – we have seen outgrowths of the surge of cultural activism sparked by the Pandemic in the 1980s, the momentum maintained until the present day of this writing. Greyson's and Fung's extended series spanning the 1980s and the 2000s, and Hoolboom's more concentrated triptych of 1993–97, can be seen, not as dated texts sealed off hermetically from history (as I've repeatedly emphasised), but rather as artistic encounters with the rapidly evolving context of the Pandemic. In 1993 Mike Hoolboom said, "It used to be that we thought meaning was contained in the work but now we understand that the work is part of a social relation that is always changing. Always alive" (de Bruyn 1993, 4). Of course with Greyson's and Fung's formation within on-the-streets queer and anticensorship activism of the early eighties, they never had any doubts about their work being part of a social relation. But it's interesting how Hoolboom's personal and artistic crisis, as inscribed in his films, awakened him to this intrinsic dynamic.

All three artists at the ground zero of the Pandemic, marshalling different resources – music, documentary, and autobiography – intervened on an immediate level in the relations of individual social conscience within cultural currents and institutions. If for Greyson *Fig Trees* "both questions and demonstrates the troubled relationship between an elite art form and a kind of grubby street activism" (2003, 13), it can be said that all three men energized their work to trouble relationships between cultural ghettos/audiences and broader social dynamics. Who could have predicted during the heyday of the New Queer Cinema that Greyson would soon be immersed in Durban sit-ins and Oakville Galleries openings or that Fung, the talking-heads chronicler of Asian diasporic coalitions, would end up in the National Gallery and the Bell Video Award pantheon or that during the doldrums of the avant-garde in the mid-eighties, the fringe eyejock Hoolboom would end up as the bad boy vilified by *Le devoir* for jerkoff shots and at the same time the darling of Image + Nation? No, these three artists and their nine works responding to crises of bodies and continents have neither constituted a cultural renaissance nor dislodged *Return of the King* from its throne, but they *have* maintained the edge of transgression, marginality, and struggle so palpable in the angry, desperate, and committed low-budget tapes assembled by Greyson light years away, in 1990. Don't forget that *Positiv*, Hoolboom's title, is still a marker of stigma and shame, both in Red Deer and in Soweto. We shall explore further this transgressive tradition of titles and words that wound, defy, and construct community in the next, concluding chapter of part 1.

10

Conclusion: Of Bodies, Shame, and Desire

Oh my God, I'm a body!
~ Mike Hoolboom, *Positiv*

Hoolboom's *Positiv* and Fung's *Sea in the Blood* have brought us back to the microscopic constituents of the organism and have thus brought us back to the body. Despite the overarching theories, spectrums, historical dynamics, and national imaginaries that have tempted us throughout this book, bodies (and bottoms) are the bottom line. The artist's cry that I have used as an epigraph for this chapter could have been echoed by all the artists assembled in this book in their fashion as his voice-over continued:

Which is funny because ever since becoming HIV positive, I've felt like a virus that's come to rest in this body for a while. That it really doesn't belong to me anymore. Like I'm trying on a new suit that won't fit ...
I realized that despite all the chaos and upsets and frustrations, my life possessed a shape after all, a unity of design, and that shape was my body ...
You imagine your body like those maps of the second world war, with arrows marking movements of troops and tanks, with trenches dug and landmines buried ...
When I come to, they have this terrible expression on their face like, "Are you all right? And of course I am. I'm fine. I've always been fine, only they can't see that. My body keeps getting in the way.

As a conclusion to this section of *The Romance of Transgression*, this roughly chronological sequence of essay chapters, I would like to focus, as Hoolboom does in *Positiv*, on the body at its most palpable and visible level. But I can't do that with any presumption of the neutrality or benignity of the body, for as the reader of this book and the spectator of *Positiv* and these hundreds of films and videos know all too well, the body is a particularly charged site of contradictory and ambivalent meanings and identity discourses in our culture – and no doubt any culture – and not only for the seropositive.

Within Judeo-Christian Euroamerican cultures, specifically within the queer or counternormative traditions that this book attempts to elaborate, Hoolboom's sense of misfit between body and self (or identity or soul), or to perhaps put it another way, his corporeal feeling of shame, traditionally abounds and prevails. And for all the last decades' breakthroughs in the social and constitutional realm by which we have made such progress in legitimizing our queer identities, relationships, and communities – and indeed our bodies – that shame is still a fundamental dynamic of our romances, our transgressions, our comings of age and comings out, our daily lives and cultural engagements and constructions of community and space, as the hundreds of artists encountered in this volume continuously remind us, consciously or unconsciously.

As I pointed out in tying up chapter 9, *Positiv* is a work that evokes immediately in its title, even before it plays, the encounter with the body and the workings of shame, in this case the stigma of infection, and as such it is one of the whole processional constellation of works that deploy a similar strategy, knowingly or unawares. The exercise might seem frivolous or indulgent, but I have discovered almost by accident that it is extremely fruitful simply to look at large swaths of the titles produced by artists discussed in this book. Together these titles take on an overwhelming and concrete cumulative meaning, which I display unedited in all their astonishingly literal poetry of excess (I have organized them in loose category clusters, made up of sequences of titles organized more associatively than chronologically or alphabetically):

1   Of general corporality, bodily attributes, and abjection: *Bodies in Trouble, Corps et âme* (Body and soul), *Corps souviens toi* (Remember, my body!), *À Corps perdu* (Headlong), *Corpusculaire, Panic Bodies, In the Flesh, Tremblement de chair* (a pun: approximately, Fleshquake), *Meat Market, Mother's Meat Freud's Flesh, Prime Cuts, I Know What It's Like to Be Dead, Love among Corpses, House of Pain, Flesh of My Flesh; Big Fat Slenderella, Fat World, Fat Chance, Hard Fat, Big Girl Town; Confused: Sexual Views, Survival of the Delirious, Spent, Panic,*

Panic, In Tens Sity; Quiver, Aberrant Motion, Oral, Dish, Crush, Touch, Don't Touch Me; Choose Your Plague, The World Is Sick (Sic), Sick World, Sick & Nasty: Too Much Ginger Spice Will Make You Sick, Frostbite, A Cancer Video, Cancer, HIV Rollercoaster, Récit D'A (pun: AIDS story), *Deaf, Dizzy, Fever, Anhedonia, Hamartia, Itchy Ya-Ya, 60 Unit Bruise, Tattoo, Needle, Pricks, An Adventure in Tucking with Jeanne B.; Body Fluid, Turbulence of Fluids, Canada Sperm Bank of Satan, Wads and Wads, Cream Soda, Smudge, Dirty Laundry, Underwear, Love and Human Remains, Shiteater, Salvation Army, Pus Girl, My Personal Virus;*

2   Of body parts: *Blood River, Fresh Blood: A Consideration of Belonging; Straight in the Face, Red in the Face, Danny Kaye's Eyes, Thick Lips Thin Lips; Skin, Skin, Laws and Skin, Skin Deep, Skin Gang/Skin Flick, Scars, Shirley Pimple, Cold Sore, Gerçure* (Chapped [lips]); *Frank's Cock, French Canadian Horse-Cocked Pornstar, Rubber Gun, This Is an Erect Penis, Surfer Dick, Hose, Peckers, 2000 Bites* (2000 cocks), *Super 8½, Un©ut, Canada Uncut; We're Talking Vulva, Pussy Galore, Pussy Goes to Party, C.L.I.T., Cherries, Cherries in the Snow, Below the Belt; My Left Breast, Boots, Boobs and Bitches: the Art of G.B. Jones, Boobyz, Baby Boobs; No Skin off My Ass, The Asshole Is a Very Tense Hole, Jane Gets Her Butt Done; The Hand, Handy Man; The Heart Exposed, Highway of Heartache; Black Heart; Belly, Femur, Femur, Belly; Deep inside Clint Star; Men on Fur on Men, More than Hair Care Products, Shave Your Legs, Audrey's Beard, Keltie's Beard, Five O'Clock Shadow;*

3   Of erogenous or other bodily functions: *That Thing We Do; Desire, Cruising, Larking, Only Enough to Ignite (Some Unpreventable Adventures in Lesbian Flirtation), An Objective Measure of Arousal; Candy Kisses, Alien Kisses; Wake Up, Jerk Off, Etc., Master Libation, Hand Job, Rub, Suck, The Daisy Chain Project, Penetration, Assplay, Fuckfest, Peter Fucking Wayne Fucking Peter, Emission, A Nation Is Coming, Coming to Terms, How to Fake an Orgasm; Transmission, Scratch, Seuls les éternuements sont éternels* (Only sneezing is forever), *Smash, Slam, Fall, You Can't Beat It Out of Us, My Addiction, Crever à vingt ans* (Croaking at twenty), *This Narrative Is Killing Me;*

4   Of places: *Toilet, Urinal; Hanging Garden; Sous-sol* (Basement), *Basement Girl; Laugh in the Dark, Bed Space; Track Two, Il était une fois dans l'Est* (Once upon a time in the East [End]), *Montreal Main* (red light district);

5   Of labels connoting sexual difference and stigma (by far the longest and most overwhelming list): *Being Different, Les Autres* (The others), *We're Funny That Way, Sticks and Stones, One of Them, Or d'ur* (pun:

"hard gold" and "garbage"), *Tainted, Infidel, Outrageous; Dangerous Offender, Illegal Acts, Violent, Untouchable, Dysfunctional, Queen St West: The Rebel Zone, The Troublemakers, Boy Crazy, God's Fool, Le dément du Lac Jean-jeunes* (The madman of Jean-jeunes Lake), *The Devil's Toy; Where Lies the Homo, True Inversions, The Fruit Machine, Class Queers; Queer across Canada, Queercore, Moscow Does Not Believe in Queers, Queer Things I Hate About You; Wild Woman in the Woods, La demoiselle sauvage* (The wild maiden), *Bad Girl, Bad Girls; Pink in Public, Touch of Pink, The Pink Pimpernel, The Pinco Triangle, Pink-eyed Pet; Forbidden Love, Stolen Moments, Secrets, Open Secrets, How to Be a Recluse, Quiet Man, Solo, Alone, Seuls, Ensembles (Alone, Together), Lonely Boy, Closet Case, Behind the Veil: Nuns; Little Faggot, School Fag, Faggot, Drag on a Fag, Gay Boy ... We Do Not Go Extinct, Michael a Gay Son; Female Sex Perversions, The Lonely Lesbian, Disposable Lez, Amazones d'hier, lesbiennes d'aujourd'hui* (Amazons yesterday, lesbians today), *Dike; Gendertroublemakers, Can You Say Androgynous? Les Feluettes* (Lilies, i.e., sissies), *Boy Girl, Nancy Boy vs Manly Woman, Femme, Butch, Butch/femme in Paradise, Old Butch, Butch Magnet, Baking with Butch, Not like That: Diary of a Butch-a-phobe, Kings, Girl King, Day in the Life of a Bull Dyke, Your Mother Wears Combat Boots, The Bisexual Kingdom, Switch; Barely Human, Voyage de l'ogre* (Voyage of the ogre), *The Making of Monsters, Adventures of Ponygirl, Pussyboy Trilogy, The Misadventures of Pussy Boy, Porcaria, I Was a Rat, Wild Dogs, Alice Is a Bitch, Beastboy, Jungle Boy; Erotic Exotic, Miss Chinatown, Banana Boy, Refugee Class of 2000, Queen's Cantonese Conversational Course, Soulsucka, Rude, Save My Lost Nigga Soul, Media Blackmale, Sackhead, French Canadian Horse-Cocked Pornstar, Hayseed, Fresh off the Boat, Straight from the Suburbs; Hookers on Davie, Go-go Boy (Prelude), Night Shift, L'escorte, Hustler White, Mirha-Soleil Ross's Gut-Busting, Ass-Erupting & Immoderately Whorish Compilation Tape! Yapping Out Loud: Contagious Thoughts from an Unrepentant Whore, Beefcake, Christian Porn, Watching Lesbian Porn; Positiv, Positive Men, Symptomatic, Zero Patience; Shiteater, I'm a Voyeur, Bondage Television, Motherfuckers.*

This queer epic of titles is not so much Whitmanesque as veering rather between Burroughs and Ginsberg, and it has Cronenberg beat hands down and also echoes the wonderfully inventive and colourful titles in porno, that tradition on the lowest rung of the cultural hierarchy (for example, to mention titles cited in this volume alone, *Classy Cunts, French Erection*, and *Sure Shot*). In the present queer Canadian corpus, for every title of affirmation like *Proud Lives* and *Fighting Chance* or of melodramatic promise like

I've Heard the Mermaids Singing, there are twenty of these blunt, irreverent, and smutty manifestos, often one-word, about lust and the dust. One might be prompted to ask at the end of this exhausting litany what on earth is going on here, if it were not more than abundantly clear. Focused much more on transgression than romance, much more on abjection than idealization or liberation, artists are clearly using film and video, among other things, as a means of confronting the body, of managing stigma, of working through shame.[1] They are doing so either on an individual, almost therapeutic level or on a collective cultural level, either on the level of small-scale autobiographical enunciation or on the level of six- or seven-digit-budget Telefilm Canada feature projects (*Hanging Garden*) and prestigious Genie-winning nonfiction (*Hookers on Davie*).

There is much glib and vacuous talk by designer pundits (mostly Toronto journalists) of the "end of gay" (Archer 1999). Same-sex marriage or not, the bill to include sexual orientation in antihate legislation is being held up in Parliament as I write,[2] Focus on the Family Canada are flooding national newspapers with full-page ads ("We Believe in Mom and Dad"), HIV and other STD transmission among young gay men is rising because of still not fully understood dynamics of self-esteem (not to mention bug-chasing and gift-giving subcultures), male nude dancers and bathhouse managers and patrons are under trial in Montreal and Calgary, respectively, thanks to Victorian bawdy-house laws, queer teenagers are still committing suicide, and the remains of dozens of sexworkers are still being sifted in Coquitlam. Did a single mainstream editorialist trying to comprehend the 2004 Baghdad prison torture scandal acknowledge that it was homo sex being used to "shame" Iraqi POWs?[3] Not surprisingly then, shame does not seem to have abated on the artistic agenda, and in fact it spreads: according to legend, Hoolboom's title *Frank's Cock* caused more embarrassment than mirth at the Toronto Film Festival when the Government Film Commissioner announcing its award, had to enunciate the four-letter word. As Sedgwick declares: "at least for certain queer people, shame is simply the first, and remains a permanent, structuring fact of identity: one that has its own, powerfully productive and powerfully social metamorphic possibilities" (1993a). Artists are demonstrating that her statement has lost little of its applicability.

Hoolboom's *Positiv* in many ways exemplifies my selection of short works for discussion in this closing chapter on shame, in the performative operation of a title that enacts not only diagnosis, stigma, and identity but also (at least until the last half of the 1990s) the death sentence ("you watch yourself die"). Despite the displaced "you" of Hoolboom's commentary, the author's body is vividly present on the screen, notably in his passive reception of the medical apparatus or in the almost sacramental unveiling of the authorial skin like miraculous stigmata, in the explicitness of the authorial voice narrating this identity process ("you read the cruel truth on their face"). Sedgwick's understanding of the operation of shame is basic and persuasive: "shame and identity remain in very dynamic relation to one another ... The forms taken by shame are ... integral to and residual in the processes by which identity itself is formed."

To conclude this section of the book, I would like to further explore this basic connection between identity and shame through profiling a half dozen works similar to Hoolboom's, all autobiographical, and I will do so in chronological order. They are autobiographical in the same very specific sense as Hoolboom's work: the author's first-person voice is accompanied by the author's body on the screen. It is a truism that autobiographical work has had heightened importance within cultures of sexual minorities, in film and theatre especially since World War II, in literature much earlier. In the indexical forms of more recent independent film and art video, this role is heightened all the more. The self is performed without the usual mediations of discretion or self-censorship, the obliqueness of fiction or the impersonal third person of expository documentary. Thereby, the management of corporeal shame is visible as a most accessible and palpable process. In these works, the author's body, and inevitably voice, serve as text, as medium for the inscription of identity, as crucible for the processing of shame. But in each work they do so in a unique and specific way. For, as Sedgwick adds, "the shame-delineated place of identity doesn't determine the consistency or meaning of that identity, and race, gender, class, sexuality, appearance and abledness are only a few of the defining social constructions that will crystallize there, developing from this originary affect their particular structures of expression, creativity, pleasure and struggle" (1993a, 13–14).

The eight artists discussed here come to their art form and institutional and geographical context each from a specific combination of personal-identity determinations. They thus enact shame in a unique creative manner, bringing forth works that vary widely in their discursive means (from performance to compilation) and generic/aesthetic affect (from high-camp comedy to intense melodramatic assault). This vivid range of authorial voices and bodies has obvious implications for the concept of the author and the role of authorship in our moving-image cultures. I and many others have considered how fashionable poststructuralist ideas of the death of the author are most resisted or adapted most radically within various subaltern nodes and cultures, whether women's, postcolonial, queer, or other minority, marginal, and diasporic cultures. It suffices here to stress the importance of autobiographical works, with their performance and processing of shame and identity, in both the vibrancy of resistant and minority cultures and in queer moving-image cultures in Canada and elsewhere. However much

Colin Campbell's *I'm a Voyeur* (1974), a precursor to the body/shame current of the 1990s: through his neighbour's window frame, the artist plays both voyeur and "voyee," nude and clothed. VHS frame grab, VTape

first-person voices continually reinvent traditional romantic notions of authorship, they are indispensable wherever erasure and silence are hovering at the edge of globalized cultural marketplaces.

The seven Canadian works I shall briefly describe here (in addition to *Positiv*) are all from the 1990s and 2000s, but they have important precursors, especially from the first art video wave of the 1970s: I am thinking of such tapes as COLIN CAMPBELL's *I'm a Voyeur* (1974, 15), in which the artist plays both voyeur and "voyee," nude and clothed, or PAUL WONG's 1976 *60 Unit Bruise*, a minimalist video "body art" performance with a title connoting both bodily injury and blood technology, either medical or illicit, showing an injection of "white blood" spreading its colour across Wong's "yellow" back. Such precursors reflect a time and context when conceptual games in the new medium of art video were becoming increasingly infused with the tensions of sexual marginality and which seem like light years away from the raw populist nineties – beyond-conceptual, beyond-art-world-ghetto.

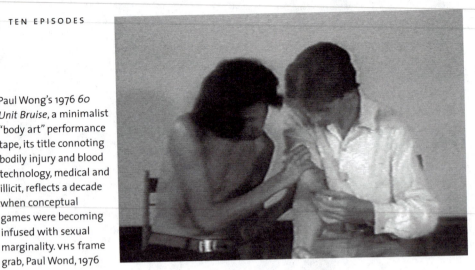

Paul Wong's 1976 *60 Unit Bruise*, a minimalist "body art" performance tape, its title connoting bodily injury and blood technology, medical and illicit, reflects a decade when conceptual games were becoming infused with sexual marginality. VHS frame grab, Paul Wond, 1976

We're Talking Vulva (Shawna Dempsey with Tracy Traeger, 1990, 5) is one of the films that brought to an end Studio D's chronic anxiety about sexual identity in one fell swoop. The package in which it appeared, *Five Feminist Minutes* (see chapter 6), featured sex workers and lesbians of colour, rappers, and all the excluded and dispossessed of the 1970s middle-class white-feminist agenda. A work that cross-pollinates street-theatre performance, rock video, and rap music, *Vulva* might be thought to mask its sexual provocation through the very traditional NFB vocation of addressing youth about sexual hygiene in their own vernacular. Indeed, fifteen years later it still looks slightly chary as it feels the water of the lesbian continuum, with its lesbian content reduced to a matter-of-fact line or two and no explicit image: "Some of us gals like other women, Touch and suck and do tribadism, That's lesbianism!" This language play is as strategic as it is self-reflective, and the film is noticeable now for the absence among all the words for vulva of the essential Anglo-Saxonism "cunt":

When I first wrote the piece, as a live performance in 1986, it was at the very beginning of the sex radical movement, when things like S&M, and lesbian sex practices in general were first being talked about. I don't think we had yet reclaimed the word "cunt." I don't remember using it before 1987 (when I came out and was sleeping with a dominatrix Wiccan). By then the piece was written and rhyming couplets are hard to change ... I don't know what Studio D would have thought of "cunt" in 1990. Certainly the local film funding agency, Manitoba Film and Sound, wouldn't let us put the word "vulva" in the title. So we said that the film would be called "The Rap," got the money ($15,000 which we are still paying back) and then titled it exactly as we wanted (same title as the performance). (Email 25 May 2004)

Dempsey's latinate names for genitals and sexual acts have been standard camouflage since the rise of vernacular languages post-Gutenberg in the early-modern period. Although the word "cunt" would have more aptly anticipated Hoolboom (seventy years after D.H. Lawrence introduced it into "serious" English literature), Dempsey does resort to "fuck" once or twice, and the Studio at least went one better than Manitoba Film in allowing the word "vulva," rather than pudenda, "things to be ashamed of." One of the only things I've retained from my undergraduate course in Anglo-Saxon in 1968 was that our linguistic ancestors did indeed use a word for genitals, "scamu," or shame, of which pudenda was a literal translation. At the time, among the straight men in my dorm "You're a cunt" was one of the worst taunts imaginable, an accusatory though jocular assignment not only of gender transgression to a male hallmate but of the very fleshly and performative embodiment of that anatomical "lack" that according to Dempsey "remind[s] them of Mother – we all come from here, this hole and none other. Vagina!" ("Cunt-eye" was another favourite slur among my dormmates, but we won't venture into reflections on the no doubt fruitful association of organs of sight and sexual pleasure/procreation.)

In any case, the lingering power of "cunt" by other names, the aggressive flaunting of this shame, is deployed by Dempsey in the name of sex education and feminist community, joyously, visually, and theatrically, not only in the studio but also in the street, the marketplace, and the workplace where she had originally performed the piece – even on the steps of the Manitoba legislature. In fact, we are not only *talking* vulva, as the blunt title trumpets, we are *looking at* vulva, and Dempsey's large pink rubber genitalia suit is at the centre of the screen the entire time. Since the cunt is an external masquerade, not surprisingly it is clitoral, not vaginal, pleasure that is literally foregrounded – all the more so since Dempsey's face seems to operate as the getup's clitoris – and penile penetration takes a decidedly secondary role in long lists of vulvar things and activities. The accelerated, zoom-happy, wildly mobile camera accentuates her orgasmic twirling, hopping, and gesturing, and even the nonsexual operations of urination and pubic shampoos take on a queer aura. Dempsey wears sunglasses, and her body is covered from head to foot with this genital mask, and the film is not autobiographical in the sense of individual identity. Rather, a sense of collective identity is transmitted, the agile, voguing clown standing in for the gendered queer body. Her public corporeal transformation into the "scary" "hole," from the shameful lack into a convex and proud presence, shatters the ideological divide between public and private, performatively transforms the artist as well as the space in which she flaunts it, queering both – as well as the spectators on screen and in the audience. However, the still-cautious mid-eighties period and place in which the work was conceived

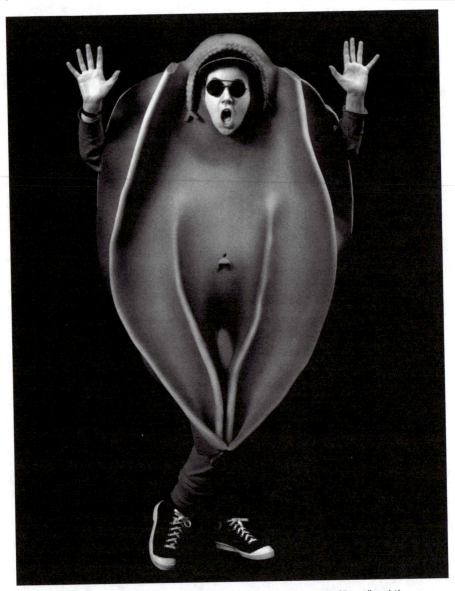

Latin notwithstanding, *We're Talking Vulva* (1990) deploys the power of "cunt" and the aggressive flaunting of this shame, in the name of sex education and feminist community – joyously, visually, and theatrically. Production still

("very beginning of the sex radical movement") and its ultimate institutional context may have dictated that Dempsey's work (she was still in her early twenties at the time) seems to navigate shame the most cautiously of all the works I have selected for this chapter.

Fat Chance (Anne Golden, 1994, 6) is another matter. Here the title announces a shame that is less sexual in the literal sense than broadly corporeal, but also gendered in its social implications of waste and excess in our gynephobic and anorexia-genic culture. Here also Sedgwick must be brought in, namely her investigation with Michael Moon of associations of queerness and obesity through the filmic persona of Divine (1993b, 215–51). Exploring the contradictory stigma of fatness in an evolving historical context, they argue that "the modern fat female body represents both the efflorescence and the damaging incoherence of a social order," as well as "a certain interface between abjection and defiance ... interlocking histories of stigma, self-constitution, and epistemological complication proper to fat women and gay men in this century." They refer finally to identity processes related to fatness and queerness that are both distinct (in terms of visibility) and analogous:

there *is* such a process as *coming out as a fat woman*. Like the other, more materially dangerous kind of coming out, it involves the risk – here, a certainty – of uttering bathetically as a brave declaration that truth which can scarcely in this instance ever have been less than self evident. Also like the other kind of coming out, however, denomination of oneself as a fat woman is a way in the first place of making clear to the people around one that their cultural meanings will be, and will be heard as, assaultive and diminishing to the degree that they are not fat-affirmative. In the second place and far more importantly, it is a way of staking one's claim to insist on, and participate actively in, a renegotiation of *the representational contract* between one's body and one's world. (230)

Curiously, Moon and Sedgwick don't touch on associations of fatness and lesbianism, whether as an erotic preference or as an aesthetico-ideological style, whether butch or femme (cf., k.d. lang's "big-boned gal," chapter 5), in defiance of the hegemonic feminine regime. In this tape and later works, Golden proudly performs and incarnates both desire and style as a handsome woman of proportions that are both square and Rubenesque, rather than gargantuan à la Divine. At the same time, Golden literally embraces the abjection of fatness in her title – especially with the sarcastic innuendo of the declaration "fat chance!" that she appropriates and inverts. The tape is autobiographical in the sense that the author performs on-screen for its entire duration, in costumes of both nudity and pendulous urban butch that are in striking contrast to Dempsey's rubber armour. Moreover, Golden also effects both instances of the "coming out" that Sedgwick and Moon point to, coming out as queer and as fat, renegotiating the "representational contract" of each. These two instances are constructed through the work's interpolated threads, first a vigorous stand-up erotic performance between the author and her slightly slimmer butch partner, in a black and white rendition of an industrial warehouse set, and second, a colour kitchen scene where Golden interacts solo with both a refrigerator and its bountiful stock and the camera. In the latter, languid and at times supine, she looks intently into the lens – the eye contact that absolves shame in its most fully confessional coming-out mode – and repeatedly and intimately intones, "I love my body." In short, the stigma of fat is transformed into a celebration of pleasure, both sexual and gastronomical. The two registers merge, as Golden spreads out victuals among her breasts and as her lover amorously gobbles up her generous belly, almost swallowed up in its amplitude.

A film made in Montreal later in the decade, JEAN-FRANÇOIS MON-ETTE's *Where Lies the Homo?* (1998, 34) enacts a different conception of coming out and of autobiography as well. Never so shamelessly exposed or vulnerable as Golden, Monette embraces for his title an abbreviated and outdated medical-moniker-turned-insult, "homo," and a pseudo-poetic question that perhaps carries the punning connotation of falsehood. If Golden

"I love my body!": Anne Golden coming out as "Rubenesque" in *Fat Chance* (1994), transforming the stigma of fat into a celebration of pleasure, both sexual and gastronomical. VHS frame grab, G.I.V.

Jean-François Monette's *Where Lies the Homo?* (1998): a boy actor performs the artist's pre-pubescent self in acts of flight, confrontation, and flaming gender dissidence. DVD frame grab, camera Michael Wees, Bare Bone Films Inc. 2000

performed the self as gourmand, lover, and narcissistic poser, through food and on-screen bodily configurations, it is Monette the *editor* who performs the self here, mostly off-screen, brilliantly assembling a kaleidoscope of filmic extracts from both inside and outside the queer canon, from Cocteau's *Sang d'un poète* (1930) to Friedkin's *Cruising* (1980). These clips register Monette's coming of age and growth of identity consciousness through his identificatory attachment to and consumption of them. Amid the shots, both luminous and camp, of an entire galaxy of role models from Snow White to Audrey Hepburn and Sal Mineo, the author's own body appears in two guises: first by means of the home movie repertory that is the standard raw material of the glut of autobiographical work of the last generation (taken almost always, as with Monette, by the absent father) but that somehow never loses its power to fascinate; second through a boy actor that Monette had impersonate his prepubescent self in black and white acts of flight, confrontation, and flaming gender dissidence. Both guises are retroactive in that they fit into the chronology of his life lived that Monette narrates in the classic chronological thrust of literary autobiography, and both perform the shame of gender transgression. First there is the unconsolably weeping toddler of the home movies in his gender-ambiguous red shorts, devastated, we are told (no doubt with a certain amount of licence), because his uncle disapproves of his choice of Barbie over GI Joe and brands him a "sissy." These shots fully connote what Sedgwick calls "the terrifying powerlessness of gender dissonant or otherwise stigmatized childhood" (1993a, 4), made all the more resonant because he is first seen sheltered on the lap of the mother, who will herself go through a coming-out process, also thanks to the home movies reedited by her shamed baby who grew up to be a filmmaker. Second, through the mediation of dramatization the eleven or twelve-year-old actor embodies a preteen Jean-François peering through a metaphorical chainlink fence or, most flamingly, marching up the steps to a church entranceway in his mother's wedding gown, compounding the transgression of Gender Identity Disorder with the shame of public sacrilege.

Meanwhile the first-person narration impels a tale of self-realization over these Hollywood and art film narratives of entrapment, violence, and awakening. Through these mediating images, the author persona comes out, not once, but three times, a waltz of hesitation brought on by the AIDS trauma that ineradically complicated gay-male identity-formation in the 1980s. The insistent repetition of the coming out tropes, in combination with the visual tropes of flowering and self-realization (everyone looks up when once-mousy Audrey, as *Sabrina*, arrives at the high-society party, transformed into a butterfly in her strapless New Look gown), constructs a kind of excess and insistence. The film's hyperbolic identity fixity is expressed in a language of rebirth that jars slightly with the fluidly queer nineties: the author joins "my kind," learning "everything I needed to know as a gay man," a teleological thrust and essentialist certitude of adult identity that no doubt compensates for the terror of the boyhood narratives.

School Fag (RICHARD FUNG and Tim McCaskell, 1998, 17) is not literally autobiographical except in the sense that the eponymous motormouth performer who completely dominates the work, nineteen-year-old Shawn Fowler, is clearly an uncredited co-author. *School Fag* was at the same time a highly personal work for Fung in that it was his first (credited) co-directing project with his life partner of twenty-five years, and it comes out of McCaskell's long-standing work around homophobia and racism within the belly of the Toronto public-school system. Fowler, veteran of the Triangle Project and LGBT Youth Toronto, is clearly one of Tim's wards. His run-on monologue/oral history, intercalated with in-drag performance moments as Wonder Woman and a Ru-Paul-inspired prom queen, plus soundtrack whooshes and fast-forward vogues, is a brave, insightful, and inspirational reclamation of the humiliation inflicted on him within the school system (lockers blazoned with graffiti'd abuse, etc.). *School Fag* may be the only one of Fung's works entirely about a white protagonist, but it fits all the same into his postcolonial framework, for few "ethnicities" are as visible and problematized as that class-determined ethnicity of Shawn, who grew up "white trash" in a "white-bread neighbourhood" in Toronto with "no car" (the *shame*!). But the melodrama of this "white trash" sissy fixated on heroines both white and black is somehow all the richer in its tension between race/class stigma and gender/sex ostracism, and in his performative transcendence through shame-managing struggle, glamour, community, and art.

Shawn says "fag" is one of the five big bad words, but it is a label he relishes. (He also is fond of the *real* meaning of the initials for his affinity group Lesbian and Gay Bisexual Transgender Youth of Toronto, namely, Lying, Gossiping, and BacksTabbing Youth of Toronto.) His delight in the ugly syllables of his vehicle's title, like the eponymous embrace of "spoiled identities" in the other films I've mentioned, whether linked to body type, age, race, gender, identity, legality, sexual practice, sero status, sociopsychiatric brand, etc., is not only about an ideological appropriation of a formerly nasty epithet that is now second nature to social movements from fats to whores to cripples but also about the political force of shame.

Richard Dyer noticed Fung's tendency with his earliest works to move beyond gay-lib-style essentialist "affirmation" towards a postmodern "awareness of surface, construction and play [combined] with a sense of urgency and edge" ([1990] 2003, 284, 295). Paradoxically, the sudden flood of NFB-produced documentaries that emerged at the beginning of the nineties by and large resuscitated the 1970s political aesthetic (see chapter 6), from *Out: Stories of Lesbian and Gay Youth* (David Adkin, 1990) to the groundbreaking (for the board) transgender documentary *In the Flesh* (Gordon McLennan, 2000). It is significant that the mega-hit *Forbidden Love: The Unashamed Stories of Lesbian Lives* had a subtitle that literally disavowed the *shame* of the *forbidden*, for this skirting around the transformative political energy of shame through affirmative images may point to the only liability of this otherwise wonderfully fresh and paradigm-shifting film. The NFB's "unashamed-ness" reflects, among other things, both the state studio's appropriation and de-fanging of 1970s/1980s identity politics/aesthetics and the state's agenda of deploying rights jurisprudence in the mainstreaming of sexual marginality. Unsurprisingly, some of the recent NFB documentaries – unlike *School Fag* no doubt – seem to be getting into the schools these days, where Shawn and the other fags can finally see them.

Sadomasochism (DEANNA BOWEN, 1998, 14) was discussed in chapter 5 as part of a cluster of Caribbean-diasporic films and videos imaging memories of island girlhood, but it must also resurface here with its "scary" title and with an authorial performance that incorporates Bowen's firm, unshod legs as they slowly stride along the moist sand of a beachfront. Though in colour, this performance of the authorial body is visually the most ascetic in this chapter, especially in comparison to the in-your-face Dempsey and Fowler. Her most fluid, oblique, and volatile – in short, *queerest* – conception of identity is constructed by the four other discursive threads in Bowen's uneasy weave:

1 her first-person voice-over, like the others in this selection, dense and overwhelming in its intensity and weight, searching her body and her ancestry for her identity and her "path";

2 the other colour visual refrain of a match being lit in close-up and slowly burning out;

3 black and white still news photos of racist political violence from the historical context of the U.S. civil rights movement, found images that create a strong affect, like those of Monette, but revulsion, empathy, and anger on an obviously different register from his intimate fantasy projection of identification upon Hepburn and the other queer stars;

4 a dialogue script of graphic sexual violence between a male dominator and a female submissive, delivered typographically on black and white screens, at the top and the bottom of the screen respectively, one all the more disturbing in that it is unclear whether this brutality constitutes abuse or consensual role play and furthermore whether the sexual/gender violence metaphorizes, symptomatizes, or simply parallels the racist social violence we are seeing alongside.

I'm sorry Daddy, really I am.

I'll make it up to you.

Let me show you that I'm good

Deanna Bowen's *Sadomasochism* (1998) offers typographically delivered dialogue of graphic sexual violence between a male and a female, disturbingly unclear in its reference: role-playing or violence, metaphor or symptom or fantasy script? Frame grab strip

In fact, this is not the only extreme ambiguity of the work: is the title an identity label or a political figure or a moral judgment (a reading that I have encountered from a student or two, however unlikely it is, based on textual evidence)? Whatever the case, the title *Sadomasochism* simply names one of the most stigmatized sexual-identity practices, and the repetitive structure of the tape emphasizes the performative, reiterative nature of identity. Although we can know of Bowen's lesbian identity from the context of production and distribution (in queer community festivals), the title extends "queer" beyond the stable identities of post-Stonewall sex-object-choice political essentialism towards the gamut of what Sedgwick calls "performative identity vernaculars, flushed with shame-consciousness and shame creativity ... butch abjection, femmitude, leather, pride, sm, drag, musicality, fisting, attitude, zines, histrionicism, asceticism, Snap! culture, diva worship, florid religiosity, in a word, *flaming* ... And activism" (1993a, 13–14). (Had Bowen read this before imaging the flaring match refrain?) And we would add to the list (in addition to "fat defiance," which Sedgwick curiously seems inadvertently to have left off) *combinations* of her terms, as well as the different "shameful" identities of diasporic, refugee, immigrant, and exile, which racialize sexual identity and sexualize racial identities through a mix that is all the more potent for its instability.

The colour shot of Bowen's feet is repeated several times as a visual refrain in an otherwise stark, mostly black and white video and thus acquires a nonspecific metaphoric tenor to match the ambiguity of the author's voice-over declaration of the openness of her destination, as well as her identity: "Awestruck and fearsome, my feet carry me to places I have not seen on the maps that my ancestors had made ... I now walk in my own, knowing that I want to go to places that I know nothing of."

MIRHA-SOLEIL ROSS, Toronto's prolific transgender/sexwork queen bee, performance/video artist, and author of *Yapping Out Loud: Contagious Thoughts from an Unrepentant Whore* (2002, 74), has always had the record for stigma-drenched titles, held until recently by her compilation tape *Mirha-Soleil Ross's Gut-Busting, Ass-Erupting & Immoderately Whorish Compilation Tape* (2001, 30). However, *Yapping*, the video adaptation of her 2002 Toronto performance contains in its title fully six self-stigmatizing epithets of social opprobrium, with zoological, acoustical, epidemiological, moral, and sexual connotations respectively, and her script throws in dozens more, from "prostitute" and "pariah" to "freak."

There is also, interestingly, "coyote," not only the acronym of the first prostitute rights organization in the 1970s, Call Off Your Old Tired Ethics, but also the yapping predator of the agricultural hinterlands, the scapegoat of agribusiness and the martyr symbol of the animal rights movement (one of Ross's many activisms). The coyote's iconic image in borrowed footage of both sacrificial slaughter and wilderness sociality (including communal yapping and solo dancing!) was both the projected backdrop of the theatrical performance and the woof of the video work, projecting eloquent associations that are both metaphoric and political. The stand-up performance encompassed several of Ross's personae, most importantly her garter-belt-bedecked, long-haired self, the trannie prostitute who offers many moving anecdotes of her childhood and her adult professional activities, as well as machine-gun political tirades rich in the discourses of class resentment (as with *School Fag* but often with a Québécois inflection), as well as of professional pride. She even throws in discourses of shamed heteromasculinity on behalf of her clients:

I don't know if it is because they stand in such extreme contrast to the way they are portrayed by feminists but there is something in my clients, in their tenderness and gestures towards me that I find deeply moving ...

For the most part it is in their courage to see me, a transsexual woman, again and again, 'cause yes in this culture it takes courage for a man to get so close, so intimate with an individual whom a large percentage of the population considers a freak ...

Whether I am working with a 600 pound disabled man who can't reach his penis to masturbate or an intersex guy whose genitals are nothing like the ones you're used to dealing with or simply the average Joe Blow who wants to start under the blankets cause he's too shy, the men I meet force me to be sensitive to a certain reality: That I am not dealing with objects here but with complex and vulnerable individuals who can be stricken by as many body image problems, self-concept issues and fears of sexual inadequacy as anyone else.[4]

In between, Ross also incarnates and demolishes several of her personae, including Bridge It Taylor, a "radical feminist anti-porn activist" in tasteful pant suit and short blond wig, expert in disenfranchising real working women:

Poverty and lack of access to education has, of course, been a tremendously significant factor in terms of the reasons why these women have turned to prostitution ... Unfortunately lack of education means lack of agency, which regrettably means lack of wisdom, which roughly means inability to articulate one's experiences in a politically viable way. So I, Bridge It Taylor, have no other option tonight than to completely put myself at the service of these women and speak on their behalf.

She also incarnates and demolishes a phobic male hunter figure whose psychopathic anti-whore virulence is matched only by the disturbing unfolding slaughter of a coyote hunt in the rear projection. Ross's work is a vivid

Mirha-Soleil Ross's *Yapping Out Loud: Contagious Thoughts from an Unrepentant Whore* (2002), record-holder for stigma-drenched titles, features the artist's proud garter-belted trannie hooker persona. VHS frame grab

example of the incursion by queer artists into new territorializations of shame in the 2000s.

With *Solo* (2003, 54), ATIF SIDDIQI transitioned from the world of transgressively gender-bending, performance-based personal video to the sedate world of NFB documentary for his thematic search for conjugality (aka Mr Right), thanks to the state studio's diversity competition scheme. The euphemism of the title *Solo* is thus not surprising: one shade more benign than "single" and more neutral than the like-sounding "lonely" (see chapter 2 for a spotlight on a not dissimilar earlier NFB film that *does* use this terrifying word, *None But the Lonely* [1957]) and certainly more benign than "desperate" (a word Siddiqi uses in the film). "Solo" still connotes the horror of nonconsensual unmarried status in a relationship-commodifying culture (and with just a nuance of the additional transgressiveness of the masturbation porno genre that "solo" has come to signify as well).

Like Dempsey, Fowler, and Ross, Siddiqi dominates every shot, but his slight, fey but dignified presence is more restrained than that of his gut-busting fellows, or as his therapist says in reference to his relationship impasse and blockage of childhood trauma, shy and reserved, if not "numb and tight," "not present," even "half-dead." Many of the setups depict him immobile in an unpopulated landscape, pensively surveying a lake or the

Vieux-Port or even his clothes spinning dry in his cruisy local laundromat. The docu-narrative follows Siddiqi in improvised courtship dinners with a camera crew on hand; consultative outings and conversations with friends and a role-model couple; heavy-duty sessions with the therapist, where the element of personal authorial confessionality has a breath-catching aura of shame; and perhaps most painfully, encounters with his Pakistani but diaspora-bound parents, seated confrontationally in front of the camera. The couple's dismissal of their son not only as homosexual but as adult human being, buoyed purportedly by religious and cultural codes ("Allah produced you as a normal human being"), returns the artist to the place of childhood abjection and disempowerment that is glimpsed repeatedly in the snapshots of the shy and pretty boy.

Alongside the observational scenes, the NFB budget allowed Siddiqi to shuffle in dramatized fantasy interludes that evoke his earlier over-the-top artistic indulgences in such tapes as *Erotic Exotic* (1998). However, moments where a winged angel hunk conducts Siddiqi to the ideal Mr Right seem anticlimactic in comparison to an earlier scene that parodies makeup commercials: framed by generic "third world" black and white found footage of donkeys, desert, and turbans, a stentorian ayatollah-ish voice intones "120 lashes to the sinner for sodomy." The star is tied to the stake amid all the sand, where, dolled up in lavish glitter makeup, boas and a feather Mohawk on his shaven skull, he transforms the lashes of the whip into his own luxuriantly encrusted eyelashes and proclaims to the lens in what Divine would have called a glamour fit, "If I must have lashes, make them For Real. For Real Mascara helps you to look good even in the worst situations." This moment of delectable performance based on a simple pun, of the transformation of shame into the affirmations of shared aesthetics and politics, sums up in many ways the achievement of all eight of these artists who invest their bodies and their shame in their art.

The above eight works by Hoolboom, Dempsey, Golden, Monette, Fowler/Fung/McCaskell, Bowen, Ross, and Siddiqi have all in distinct ways dramatized the possibilities of shame and bodily performance as an artistic and political resource, and I would add several final observations to their eloquent individual testimonies. Most importantly, their works are obviously not the final word on transgression or its romance and signal neither the "end of gay" nor the dissipation of the force of shame in the queer imaginary in Canadian cinemas and videos or anywhere else. Far from it, the expanded territorializations of shame into the "outer limits," to come back to Rubin's phrase, staked out especially by Bowen, Ross, and Siddiqi, remind us dramatically of its continued force.

In formal terms, we can also say that these and similar artists suggest caution with respect to the proliferation of new media and any tempting

Solo (2003): NFB cameras capture a winged-angel hunk conducting the artist-performer Atif Siddiqi to Mr Right. The fantasy resolution is anticlimactic after Siddiqi's lashings by childhood trauma and present-day parents and ayatollahs. Production still, used with permission of the National Film Board of Canada

utopian reading of the helter skelter evolution of digital and cyber media in terms of their potential for enfranchising queer cultural energy. Yes, cruising, dating, courtship, and sexual exchange, as and well as community and affinity construction have all gone cyber, in both commodified and noncommidified forms, and yes, Golden and Bowen have worked, like Greyson and Onodera and many others, in every medium from installation to web art and every other imaginable new constellation of representation and audience along the way. But Dempsey, Fowler, Ross, and Siddiqi also belong to a tradition of theatre and stand-up vocal performance that long predates photography (and even literature!). Moreover, the phenomenon of queer community festivals that have stabilized as thriving institutions in a dozen localities across Canada and hundreds elsewhere are essentially old-fashioned hybrids of town halls, carnivals, (meat-) marketplaces, and hoedowns (see CALGARY, KINGSTON, LONDON, MONTREAL, etc.). They provide a classical communal audience experience whose mandate all the downloading and video streaming in the world do not seem to be jeopardizing. For all their various degrees of formal innovation, these eight artists retain important elements of layperson accessibility, classicism, and continuity in their works, which I would reductively summarize under three headings:

The indexical. Digital, iconic, and virtual-image construction are Big Things and here to stay. But the vibrancy of these works and their figuring of the body, authorial or otherwise, in all its fleshly impertinence, suggest that indexical representation, that is, the construction of "images both moving and still, that mechanically record through photochemical, electronic, and digital processes, the 'real' bodies and 'real' spaces of the 'real' world" (as I attempted to define this concept recently [2002, 12]) is also here to stay – for reasons we might never fully understand. Once again, "O My God I'm a body" was Hoolboom's cry in *Positiv*, and it deserves much repetition. For the essential dynamic of indexicality, of corporeal referentiality, of the insistence on real bodies as the raw material of the moving image, of the fleshly body, of the sexual body, of the shamed body, must remain with us.

The verbal/oral. In many ways, the eight works operate as oral histories, some obviously more linear and chronological than others, some more explicitly self-referential than others. They are all characterized by an excess of speech, of vocal performance that celebrates the power of words and language (to which Bowen adds the power of the written text, as if in competition with her voice). This vocal excess was anticipated by certain artists of earlier generations, for example by COLIN CAMPBELL, MICHEL TREMBLAY, and CRAIG RUSSELL in the 1970s (see chapter 4), whose measured scripts and stand-up numbers, respectively, through brilliant in their riffs on queer and Québécois oral idiom, now appear absolutely laconic in comparison to the dense verbalizations of Monette, Bowen, and Ross.

The narrative. Where there are words, there is often story, and all of these eight autobiographers are strong storytellers – even the most abstruse of the group, Bowen, and the most didactic, Dempsey. Interestingly, Hoolboom has connected the general shift towards narrativity in his own works and elsewhere to articulations of identity, both as sexual outsider and, in his case, as infected:

many of those traditionally excluded from even marginal modes of expression – women, people of colour, gays – have an abiding interest in a narrative practice because their experience must be accounted for in their stories so long ignored given shape [*sic*] by communities of interest … I guess I've rediscovered stories over the last few years as I've had to come to grips with my HIV status, my own imminent decline … The time I've got. I have to make resolutions quicker, to go back and try to make explicit the patterns of dissent that have narrated my own confusions. This looking back is undertaken with the hot breath of The End on my back, and occasions my own need to tell stories again. To recount what happened and why. (de Bruyn 1993, 2, 9)

Whether these stories are told vocally or visually, through fictional or non-fictional modes, through relatively conventional format as in a feature film like *Better Than Chocolate* or through Hoolboom's experimentalism, as in *Positiv*, the narrative impulse at its most fundamental – here is my life – is clearly an ongoing core of queer imaginaries here and abroad.

I have been using the word "political" advisedly. Despite the consumerist cooptation of Siddiqi's fastidious and subversive eyebrow care by *Queer Eye for the Straight Guy* and despite the lonely and frantic individualism of self-fulfilment discourses, pop therapeutic cultures, and the current tidal wave of commodified confessionalism, I hope to have demonstrated the political import of this corpus, despite all its contradictions, complacencies, and rough edges. The raw self-renewing group of eight texts in this chapter foreground eight bodies and voices that are on the line, their shames and abjections tempered into gestures of knowledge and vision, questioning and indictment, mobilization and community, coalition and outreach. These texts are at the core of *Romance of Transgression*'s broad, unmanageable corpus of several thousand films and videos, demonstrating many technologies, provenances, and audiences.

Despite this brash and rebellious political energy that Canadian queer work shares with much that comes from below the border and across the planet, a certain troubling but ineffectual backlash against political art and queer cinema/video in particular has raised its head within academia, buoyed by some of the more abstruse corner dynamics of queer theory. For example, although Ellis Hanson, in his *Out Takes: Essays on Queer Theory and Film* (1999), is oblivious to the flood of Canadian image making taking place a three hour's drive from his Ivy League shelter at Cornell University in upstate New York, there is no doubt that he would apply much of his blanket condemnation of queer indie political cinema, especially of the 1980s, to these eight voices and most of the present corpus – in fact he does so by his very obliviousness. Ellis's first target is the "prescriptive," "moralistic," and "edifying" "seventies tone" and (horrors!) "multi-cultural complaint" of much "gay and lesbian" film studies, starting with founders Vito Russo and Richard Dyer themselves (1999, 1–19). (If this reductive caricature of an entire intellectual heritage smacks a little too much of the neocon attacks on diversity education in the United States since the Reagan years, it is ironic, for Hanson's own teaching on youth sexuality at Cornell has been vilified by the neocons on the Internet.) Next, our cinematic heritage of the affirmation and postaffirmation periods comes in for no less totalizing a dismissal: "preachy radical politics, cheap irony, and low production values," as well as "films that are politically impeccable, but visually and sexually illiterate," not to mention "amateurish." One question emerging out of Hanson's spew of vilification for cultural workers who are identity allies, as one of my readers has commented, pertains to the question of shame itself and to the impulse to elucidate and self-represent through shaming others.

One butt of Hanson's diatribe is *She Must Be Seeing Things* (Sheila McLaughlin, 1988), the American feminist feature about power and perversity within an interracial relationship, to which Hanson prefers *Basic Instinct* (1992) and *Bound* (1996). Hanson's habit of hierarchising lavish Hollywood features over low-budget indies is entrenched when the groundbreaking AIDS melodrama *Longtime Companion* (1990) becomes his next straw text, lumped in with *Philadelphia* (1993), the movie that this milestone film made possible, and with Hollywood's post-*Cruising* penitential *Making Love* (1982). All are then tossed out with the entire bathwater of indie realist fiction and experimental and documentary shorts. No matter that it was the pre-queer indie cinema, painfully financed and distributed during the Reagan-Thatcher-Mulroney years and the first ravages of the Pandemic, that enabled the growth of 1990s New Queer wunderkinder like Americans Tom Kalin and Todd Haynes, whom Hanson approves of (though not enough to search out essays on them for inclusion).

Hanson is right in wanting to reclaim pleasure and is certainly entitled to prefer big budgets, fantasy, style, and erotics over sermons, of course, but these last three qualities were not in as short a supply as he claims in the 1980s, as Canadian works such as *The Wars* (FINDLEY, 1982), *Or d'ur* (SHBIB, 1983), *La Cage* (PARADIS, 1983), *Jungle Boy* (GREYSON, 1985), *Pouvoir Intime* (SIMONEAU, 1986), *I've Heard the Mermaids Singing* (ROZEMA, 1987), *Sortie 234* (LANGLOIS, 1988), *The Width of a Room* (TUFF, 1989), and *No Skin off My Ass* (LABRUCE, 1990) would have tipped him off. And no one I know finds these qualities missing in *Chinese Characters* (1985) and *Ten Cents a Dance (Parallax)* (1986), to mention only two prescriptive and moralistic pamphlets by uppity young Canadian multiculturals first heard from in the 1980s.

Ultimately, I can't explain Hanson's revisionist forebear-baiting other than by hypothesizing his personal distaste for nonfeature, non-mass-market narrative formats and for melodrama (to each his own, though the importance of melo genres within queer cultures in the first decade of the Pandemic cannot be understated – see chapter 9) and by wondering again about generational biases (born in 1965) and that particular ideological/cultural dynamic of provincialism (has anything other than *Basic Instinct* ever played amid the Taco Bells of Ithaca, NY?). But it is less productive to complain about American and ideological tariffs in these cultural- and sexual-trade imbalances than to resist them by exploring and cultivating the home-grown crop over the five or more decades of the present history, which I hope I have managed to do in this book.

When I wrote the introduction to this volume in Chennai, I wondered whether I would end up coming back to that city in my thoughts at the moment of writing its conclusion. Then I went that very evening to see, with my companion Nagarajan, a new Tamil feature that he was very proud and excited about and wanted me to see. *Autograph* (2003, 154) is a very long autobiographical feature about serial heterosexual crushes and passions, as well as unusual heterosocial friendships, on the part of the male hero, played by director/scriptwriter Cheran, all of which culminates in an arranged marriage with a beautiful, shy bride whom we, like Cheran, have hardly met. Of course, Cheran's performance of his body and dramatized humiliations at the hand of his various girlfriends give *Autograph* a certain common ground with this chapter's eight works, but I will not pronounce on whether Cheran's multitasking was a brilliant tour de force à la Charlie Chaplin, Orson Welles, and Atif Siddiqi or a display of rampant egotism, bombastic pectorals, and mediocre talent à la Sylvester Stallone and Mel Gibson. Regardless, this innovative sleeper hit was a forceful reminder of the cultural relativity of the autobiographical impulse in the arts, a tradition spinning out of Western romantic individualism and virtually unknown in Indian documentary or cinema history as a whole, as I commented in my 1989 stock-taking of the field (1990, 28–39).

It is curious to reflect that the raw subversion of those eight Canadian bodies performing before the camera was, after all, a perfectly logical outgrowth of Western culture, rather than some kind of rupture. Be that as it may, it is no longer true that the autobiographical form is absent within Indian independent documentary, for in the fifteen years since my original observation, small-format video technology and seismic but (strictly metropolitan) cultural shifts have produced a whole crop of first-person work. This has inevitably included "queer" work, of which the best-known in North America is *Summer in My Veins* (1999, 41), by the Harvard-trained, Chantal Akerman–mentored Delhiite, Nishit Saran (1976–2002). This first-person coming-out saga cum diasporic road movie fits perfectly into my "performing shame/performing the body" subgenre: its first scene shows the author undergoing an HIV test after a risky encounter and then taking the subsequent half hour to come out on camera painfully to mother and a carful of aunts, before learning the (negative) results. Not exactly Richard Fung but in the same cricket park, this work evidences the uneven emergences of romantic individualism in pockets of South Asian cultural elites, along with the liberalization of the economy, as well as the globalization of Western-style queer shame and bodies throughout what I called in chapter 9 the homoscape or the eros-scape (Delhi and Mumbai have both joined the network of cities boasting sporadic queer film festivals). The transcultural traffic in queer image making is both locally rooted and culturally inflected, which the current Western taste for decontextualized diversity has not unproblematically encouraged, and I had also participated therein by showing *Sea in the Blood* this trip and *Lilies* on an earlier one. This traffic is energized by geopolitical strains and the marketplace, no doubt, but also by desire, and I would like to segue into desire in order to sew up these final pages of this increasingly personal and tender chapter.

Having excitedly shown me *Autograph*, Nagarajan departed and left me in Chennai in that liminal stage of waiting a few days for my plane, winding down my film research and tourist activities, as well as the intense flurry of desire – both erotic (homo-) and social (homo- and hetero-), intellectual and political, that sustains the queer traveller, or at least me, outside Plateau Mont-Royal. Writing the introduction to this book in the moment of that winding down was different from writing this conclusion a few months later in the rainy Canadian election spring. But desire is still colouring this process of synthesis and reflection on bodies and shames, authors and their works, although now differently configured, together with the deepening realization of its determining impact upon this entire project. In *Hard to Imagine* (1996) I also reflected on desire in my conclusion to that history of pre-Stonewall homoerotic photography and film, polemically declaring that "as a scholar who shares my generation's skepticism about the possibility of objectivity in the social and biological sciences, I would go even further than snorting at the positivist, empiricist principle of sexual research swallowed so innocently by 1950s jurisprudence. Instead I propose outright that the stance of prurience is one of the fundamental principles of gay cultural and sexual research, then as now, a science legitimized, energized and prioritized by desire." (1996, 398).

It would be easy to apply this principle to a reading of *The Romance of Transgression*, for the reader has no doubt already deduced how an erotic response has shaped and deepened my takes on many works in this survey, colouring responses as diverse as my rage at CRONENBERG, my troubled identification with *Cornet at Night* and *Dreamspeaker*, my guilty complicity with *Hi I'm Steve* (KENNEDY) and *Lonely Boy* (REINKE), and my uncritical rapture with *In Black and White*, *Sortie 234*, and *Steam Clean*. Yet this book is not about that desire in the way my book about erotic image making was. I realize now, thinking about sharing a Tamil movie excursion with Nagarajan and in showing my friend Richard's queer Canadian autobiography in Jaipur, that my 1996 declaration of the intrinsic prurient desire behind gay scholarship inadvertently downplayed other kinds of desire, intellectual desire for knowledge and understanding ("desire" was after all one of the terms of Nichols's definition of the documentary discourses of sobriety [1991, 3–4]), political desire for empowerment and utopia, and perhaps especially the social desire for community and friendship.

Another person now familiar to the reader, John Greyson, has also linked Richard in print to the concept of friendship: "The ongoing autobio of Richard B. Fungus is all about everybody else. This is his artistic intervention and political triumph. His friends are his politics, his politics are his friends, and his tapes the proof that such an ecology is possible, and necessary" (2002, 11). Both Richard and John have indulged in film criticism and theory and would be the first to admit that looking at and writing about, collecting, and showing films and videos is also part of the inseparable ecology of art, politics, and friendship.

While conjugal couples are in the headlines and nuclear families are in the hate-mongering focus ads of the current electoral campaign, this other, more amorphous and fluid ecology is often overlooked, and it is this realization of the inextricability of the desire of friendship from the intellectual work of this book that I would like to emphasize as a parting shot. By coincidence or not, I count Mike, Shawna, Anne, Jean-François, Deanna, Richard and Tim and Shawn, Mirha, Atif, and the sorely missed Nishit among my friends (though I met Shawn only virtually, met Deanna only when she presented in my classroom, and know Mirha only through a few rather hyper email exchanges). They are all my bosom friends indeed, to quote another queer Canadian, Anne, the slim one, red-haired, from Prince Edward Island. I've learned a lot I didn't know about my friends through their autobiographical and other works, made hundreds of new friends whom I will likely never meet, thanks to the identificatory seduction of film and video (and research communications) and in forcing myself to perform and fulfil the desire of friendship through writing about them, my own form of autobiographical processing of thought and affect. The dynamic of pedagogical desire must also be acknowledged, though that is a matter for further reflection; suffice it to acknowledge the thrill to see surfacing throughout this volume those like Anne, Jean-François, and Atif (and Colleen and Denis and Joe and Maureen and Manon and Wendell and ...) whose faces I have seen in slightly younger and less world-troubled incarnations staring back at me in the classroom.

It is a shameful secret I suppose that friendship and its discovery is inextricable from the process of arts funding, criticism, scholarship, curating, and history. This is all the more the case within the small independent arts/queer/academic circuits of this country, especially in the age of email, where personal acquaintanceship goes hand in hand with professional cultural networking and growth, all the more so when the processes of criticism and historiography are enacted, as in this case, within now conjoined networks of old friends, virtual and real. In one of the nastier and philistine debates within the *Bubbles Galore* kefuffle, *Toronto Sun* columnist Michael Coren flailed out at the conspiracy of friends that has pornographized Canadian culture: "I have been around long enough to know how these things work. Look, these [public agency funding] juries are made up of a very small number of people. The movie industry is very small. They know one another. Movie makers sit on the jury. Other people they know come in to get a grant. Of course you get a grant. And then you'll be sitting on a jury in a few months' time and then I'll get a grant from you. They give money to people they know. It doesn't work."[5]

While this image of the cultural industries infrastructure as a combination of a masonic underground and the Liberal sponsorship trough is ludricous, how did this bigoted demagogue know about the fundamental mortar function played within the arts scene by "knowing" and friendship and tissues of collaboration, affinity, neighbourliness, and conjugality (and ex-conjugality) – and in particular within the queer arts scene? It is all the more so when, as in this final chapter, artists' lives are the subject matter as well as the psychic shell of the work and its networks of support, response, and dissemination. All the more so when autobiography triggers the broadening and deepening of significations and affects of home and diaspora, sexuality and shame, illness and mortality, the nuclear family and, indeed, the desire for friendship itself. And this book also is caught up in this community of desire, erotic, intellectual, and political, and, my final realization in this process, the desire for friendship – all of which, as John says, are ultimately the same thing.

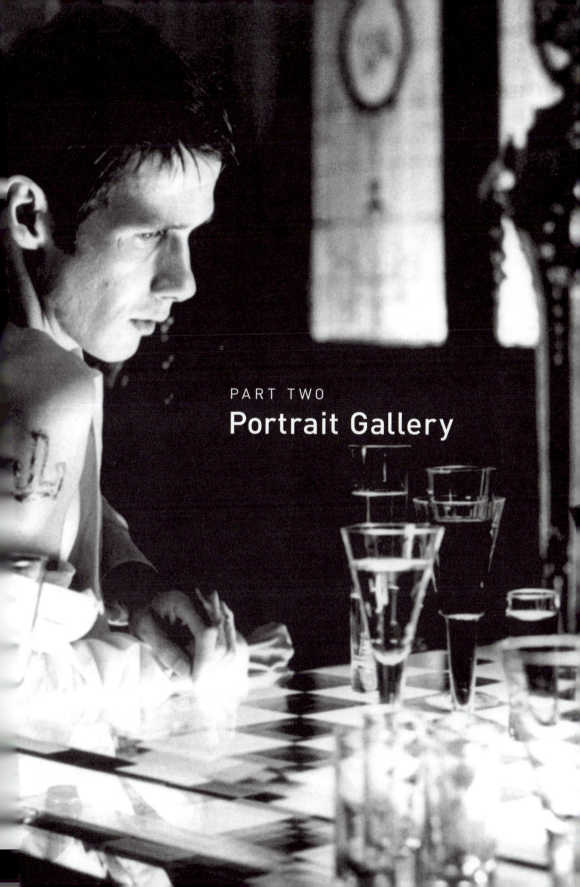

PART TWO
Portrait Gallery

ABBOTT, SARAH, b. 1969. Film- and videomaker, installation artist. Trained at Queen's and Syracuse University, NY, Toronto-based Abbott started with conceptually rigorous celluloid shorts in the 1990s before moving into art video. Her most narrative-based works were popular at queer festivals, especially the prizewinning film *Why I Hate Bees* (1997, 4), a comic reminiscence of girlhood. The videos *Knee Level* (2002, 7) and *Rug* (2001, 19) are about space and point of view: in the latter, a floor-level camera accidentally captures out-of-focus fucking during a thunderstorm, and gender and duration are forgotten in a kind of sensuous queer Warholian minimalism.

ABDUL, HANA, b. 1979. Toronto-based, York-trained Abdul is known for several short videos on the community festival circuit in the 2000s. Personal in tone and experimental in design, *Written on the Body* (2001, 12) and *Middle of East ... and North of the Continent* (2002, 9) both reflect articulately on women of colour struggling to reconcile queer identity with a heritage of political violence and cultural difference. *Written on the Body*, a colourfully stylized narrative about a thirteen-year-old discovering menstruation, smarmy sex educators, and other unhelpful female mentors – and finally a glimpse of lesbian possibilities – was honoured at Inside Out 2003.

ACHBAR, MARK, b. 1955. Documentarist. Queer-friendly codirector of the prizewinning dissident epic *Manufacturing Consent: Noam Chomsky and the Media* (1992), U.S.-trained Achbar is familiar to the queer audience for his 2 *Brides and a Scalpel* (Vancouver, 1999, 55). This video diary recounts the Nanaimo-based loves and lives of MTF Georgina Scott and "lesbian bio-girl" Linda Fraser, who by the sequence of marriage first and surgery later became the first married lesbian couple in Canada. A hit of the 2000 international queer festival season, this work vindicates small-format digital video as a sensitive and astute chronicler of our lives, apt for both melodrama and comedy. Editor-facilitator Achbar skilfully integrated Scott's and Fraser's quotidian perspectives to offset his own outsider liabilities and ensure *Brides*'s place among transgender representations in Canada.

ACHTMAN, MICHAEL (b. 1961, actor, playwright, videomaker), and R.M. Vaughan, (b. 1965, writer). Harvard- and Ryerson-trained Achtman and Saint John–bred, UNB–trained Vaughan, both Toronto-based, have collab- orated on almost ten short videos since 1998, mostly experimental narra- tives with a hard queer-political thrust. Their powerful *MASH Notes for Private Kyle Brown* (1997, 11), directed by Achtman and based on Vaugh- an's poem, takes off from the 1993 Somalia affair in which a civilian pris- oner was tortured by Canadian soldiers. An interracial lineup of angry voices and faces piece together a culture of homophobia and racism. The duo's more subdued *Shinto* (2000, 11) focuses on a gay relationship, and a soundtrack lovers' quarrel belies deeper dynamics of aggression. Working solo, Achtmans queerly updates the Cain and Abel story in *Flesh of my Flesh* (2001, 11). Achtman also starred in John Greyson's *Un©ut* (1997).

ADAMS, EVAN TLESLA, b. 1966–67. Actor, playwright, activist, documen- tarist, dancer, doctor. Calgary-based Adams is of Coast Salish heritage from near Powell River, Vancouver Island, and was educated in Victoria, Vancouver, and Calgary. A teenaged poster boy and community health facilitator for the 1986 National Native Alcohol and Drug Abuse Pro- gramme, the role model came out only to see the poster withdrawn. As a playwright, Adams achieved early international success shortly thereafter and the AIDS-themed play *Snapshots* (1989; Adams 1992) became the flagship piece for Adams's ongoing AIDS-education campaign within native communities. In the 1990s, his writing activities took him onto native drama slots on the CBC. As an actor, Adams won attention as the hero of the TV movies *Lost in the Barrens* (1990) and *Curse of the Viking Grave* (1993), followed by his role as Thomas-Builds-the-Fire in the U.S. indie feature *Smoke Signals* (1998). Although this trickster sidekick role had a queer aura in this prizewinning Native American film, it was the followup feature by the *Signals* scriptwriter Sherman Alexie, *The Business of Fancy*

Dancing (2002), that brought Adams his first starring explicit queer role. His award-winning performance as a successful writer who makes a conflicted return visit to his reservation roots brings out Adams's versatility in scenes ranging from tender relationship-work with his white lover to brittle confrontations with ghosts from his past. As a documentarist, Adams collaborated with white Powell River lesbian filmmaker JAN PADGETT on *Kla Ah Men* (2003, 88), focusing on the treaty process engaging his birthplace community, the Sliammon First Nation.

ADAMS, KATHLEEN PIRRIE. Critic, curator, videomaker. Trained at the University of Toronto, York and Ryerson, Adams is an influential voice on the Toronto queer/arts scene. Her intelligent analyses and assessments of lesbian culture have appeared in print venues ranging from *Take One* to *Fuse*. During the 1990s, Adams was also involved in queer video production and often curated thematic programs at Inside Out and local galleries. One production venture was *Excess Is What I Came For* (with Paula Gignac, 1994, 5), a deliriously *noir* dream of Toronto dyke nightlife.

ADKIN, DAVID, b. 1968. Documentarist. Saskatchewan-bred, York-trained Adkin established himself at the NFB's Toronto office with a series on media before pitching his groundbreaking 1993 documentary feature, *Out: Stories of Lesbian and Gay Youth*. Together with *Forbidden Love*, *Out* consolidated the inertial institution's historic turnaround and was the only gay-male-authored entry in the 1994 and 2003 Lesbian and Gay Video packages (see chapter 7). Adkin's subsequent major films include the much-praised documentary *Jim Loves Jack: The James Egan Story* (1995), about the Canadian gay-liberation pioneer, his long-term relationship, and his historic Supreme Court spousal-benefits lawsuit. Adkins then made a concerted foray into the U.S. market with *We're Funny That Way* (1998), on standup comics, and worked for the Toronto leather circuit. Adkin's committed relationship with his subjects and uncompromising development of full-length formats is palpable in the historical and emotional impact of his work.

AGUILA, MELANYA LIWANAG, b. 1971. Cultural activist, videomaker. OCAD-trained and Toronto-based Aguila has made half a dozen short videos and one hour-long work since 1993, all exploring the political realities of the Pinay (Filipino/a) diaspora and homeland struggles, often intersecting with feminist and lesbian-identity points of view, ranging in formats from documentary to didactic narrative. *Kislap ng Pera (The Glitter of Money)* (2003, 7) features a late-night couple in conflict in their conjugal bed. Issues of colonization, assimilation, and acceptance of difference problematize the romanticism of the scene, but clasped hands give clues to positive resolutions. Aguila produced, directed, edited and wrote her work, and collaborated as camera with other community activist projects in both the United States and Canada.

AITKEN, WILL, b. 1949. Critic, writer, teacher. One of Canada's longest-standing openly gay film critics, Indiana-bred, McGill-trained Aitken cofounded Montreal's L'Androgyne bookstore in 1973. An incisive, uncompromising commentator on movies on the CBC, as well as in mainstream and queer print media such as *TBP*, Aitken's purview is international cinema, queer and otherwise. As a scriptwriter Aitken's contribution to Canadian queer cinema was a futile St Sebastian subtext in the 1996 Japanese rowing coproduction *Rowing Through* (Masato Harada), an endless and repressed *Chariots of Fire* imitation. His novels, such as the erotic, memoiresque *Terre Haute* (1989), have fared much better.

ALBERTA, CLINT, 1970–2002. Documentarist. A dazzling young shooting star of personal queer/Native cinema, the Alberta-bred director uncovered pain and beauty within himself and his generation of young aboriginals before his 2002 suicide. Also known by his birth name, Clint Morrill, and several other *noms de caméra*, the most recent being Jules Karatechamp, Alberta will be remembered mostly for his NFB feature, *Deep Inside Clint Star* (1999, 89). In this unclassifiable documentary he interviewed six of his male and female friends, gay and straight, as well his mother, most casually posing for the camera on Day's Inn beds or standing or driving amid the city- or rez-scapes they inhabit. The questions about sexuality, identity, and personal history are frivolous and indiscreet, and sometimes the gorgeously androgynous and charismatic director seems more intent on primping directly into the lens in his satin cowboy shirts or aestheticizing his mundane wanderings with his hyperkinetic camera. Yet the depth of revelation and intimacy reached wowed audiences at Sundance and at queer, documentary, and aboriginal festivals around the world, as well as receiving a Gemini. Alberta's first film, *Lost Songs* (1999, 25), was a somewhat more routine documentary short about tuberculosis among prairie First Nations people. This was followed by a short indie autobiographical fiction, *My Cousin Albert: Portrait in Shades of Black,* about a gay and a straight teenage-boy duo (Alberta's character gets pounded out when he develops more than a feeling of friendship for his pal). His last film, *Miss 501 (A Portrait of Luck)* (2001, 82), is a portrait of an ageing Toronto drag performer named Burger in the queer underground bar scene.

ANDERLINI, KEN, b. 1962. Director, videomaker, curator, teacher. SFU– and UBC–trained Anderlini has been a presence in the Vancouver queer film/video scene since the early 1990s, committed to the aesthetics and politics of sex and to the themes of homophobic violence and the Pandemic. Essentially a collagist of images and voices, Anderlini launched his experimental triptych *Tangled Garden* (1992–94) from a lavish chiaroscuro assemblage of contemporary gay-male bodies posing against a backdrop of Western homoerotic painting, from Michelangelo to Demuth, under voices dissecting masculinity and desire. *Threnody, a Wailing Song for Carl* (1991, 20) is a densely textured elegy for Vancouver artist Carl Watson (d. 1991). *Hose* (1998, 9) plays with the semantics, erotics, and politics of piss, deliriously dousing the commoditization of queer sexuality.

ANDERSON, BARBARA K, b. 1952. Producer, writer, documentarist. UBC– and University of Toronto–trained Anderson has been a prolific maker of broadcast documentaries with Vancouver's Amazon Communications since 1992. Some of her projects reflect her background in Africa and in feminist and church-based organizations, including the prizewinning AIDS documentary *No Regrets: King Thobani's Journey towards Healing* (1996) and *Gay Spirit* (1996, 52), an encounter with queers emerging from traditional faiths. *Fighting for the Family* (1997, 47) is a journalistic essay on political struggles over family definitions, pitting blond she-wolves from Real Women–type groups and suburban school boards against a friendly assortment of queers and experts. In a lighter vein is *Casablanket* (2000, 44), an inspired butch-femme parody of the 1944 Hollywood classic. Refugees from Surrey hang out in Chick's Café on Commercial Drive, dodging Fraser Valley vigilantes, while waiting for refugee airlifts to San Francisco.

ARCAND, DENYS, b. 1941. Director, scriptwriter. Université de Montréal– trained, Oscar-winning heterosexual Arcand is Quebec's most famous director. As a critic and documentarist early in the 1960s, he displayed the phobias (xeno-, eroto-, homo-) of his educational cohort, among other things queerbaiting his fellow filmmaker CLAUDE JUTRA, ten years his senior. Two decades later, *Le Déclin de l'empire américain (Decline of the American Empire*, 1986) finally put Arcand on the international map. Although most gays found the gay character Claude (YVES JACQUES) fairly laughable in the main (an art historian who prowls the Mountain, pisses blood, comforts women, likes rough trade, and is a superb cook), few denied certain redeeming characteristics, especially retroactively when the same character turned up defanged in Arcand's *Invasions barbares* (2003; see chapter 9). In 1989 Arcand's *Jésus de Montréal* queered Jacques again in the supporting role of the (literally) devilish media lawyer. In 1993, Arcand directed his queerest film, *Love and Human Remains* (100), an adaptation of BRAD FRASER's 1989 play. In this first English-language film, Arcand underwhelmed with his apprehension of Fraser's angst-ridden urban landscape haunted by serial killers and AIDS. Arcand was apparently oblivious to those "other countries" of English Canada and homosexuality: the yuppie specificity of Fraser's unnamed prairie city and his insider tenderness for his queer characters were lost in translation.

ARCHAMBAULT, LOUISE, b. 1970. Director, scriptwriter. Concordia-trained, Montreal-based, queer-friendly Archambault is known to queer audiences around the world for her prize-winning short fiction film *Atomic Saké* (1999, 35mm, 33). In this felicitous convergence of insightful scriptwriting, *mise-en-scène*, and cinematography, three hip young women friends around a saké-lubricated dinner stumble upon the homoerotic underpinnings of homosocial friendship.

ARMATAGE, KAY, b. 1943. Documentarist, programmer, critic/historian. University of Toronto–trained, queer-friendly Armatage has taught women's and film studies at her alma mater since the early 1970s and was a principal programmer at TIFF, beginning in 1983. Her two fine short films from the late 1970s were among the first Canadian independent films to recognize the political centrality of lesbian history and culture: *Jill Johnston: October 1975* (codirector Lydia Wazana, 1977, 30), a cinéma-vérité account of the University of Toronto visit by the New York lesbian star writer, and *Gertrude and Alice in Passing* (1978, 8), an experimental narrative about the historical lesbian icons Stein and Toklas. The career of the former film fizzled when Johnston, author of *Lesbianation*, later showed up in Toronto, refused Armatage the distribution rights outside of Canada, and according to TBP (October 1977, 16), generally offered "the most patently reactionary anti-woman statements ever heard in that setting." Both films deserve more frequent revivals.

ARROYO, JOSÉ, b. 1962. Critic, teacher. McGill- and SFU–trained José Arroyo was an influential interpreter and champion of Canadian queer cinema in the 1980s while a reviewer for the *Montreal Mirror* and later as associate editor of *Cinema Canada* from 1986 to 1988. He has taught in England since 1992, publishing and media-guesting frequently on Canadian and international queer cinema.

AUDY, MICHEL, b. 1947. Director, scriptwriter. One of the pioneers of Quebec queer cinema, this Trois-Rivières native started developing ambitious feature projects in 8mm while still a teenaged film-club fanatic. With the support of Radio-Canada and the NFB, he went on to his first 16mm feature, *Jean-François-Xavier de ...* (1969), a free-form meditation depicting male and female adolescence in confrontation with the constrictions of family, religion, and, of course, death. The film was notable for its lyrical views of young men in sylvan settings, usually nude – and its struggles with taboo sexual desires through ambivalent symbolism and inarticulate challenges to family and church. Trounced by critics, Audy persisted in 1972, this time in 35mm: *Corps et âmes* (1971) fared even worse than the previous film, despite Audy's movement towards a more conventional narrative world of male adolescents ambiguously connected to a single young woman. The film broods about loss, guilt, trauma, and death again, but the painful, unreciprocated longing is recognizable to any queer spectator. Undaunted, Audy went on to court personal bankruptcy with yet another feature, *La Maison qui empêche de voir la ville* (1974), yet another variation on the male-male-female triangle and a downbeat narrative of trauma and memory. Offering a gorgeous hitchhiker and long scenes of unconsummated male intimacy (the guys have to get drunk to put their arms around each other, but their eyes have no such inhibitions), the film scarcely survived its preview screenings.

Audy bounced back to feature filmmaking in the early 1980s, usually in educationally oriented and financed projects. Best known is *Luc ou la part des choses* (Luc or His Share of Things, 1982, 90), a coming-out drama set in a Trois-Rivières working-class milieu, an engaging low-budget feature about a 20-year-old mechanic's crisis of self-discovery notable for its intensity and resourcefulness. Who knows what is more surprising: that the stubborn director was able to wrest funding for this film from the Quebec Ministry of Education budget or that he actually pulled it off as a nonprofessionally acted, tender, and positive melodrama? Audy deftly observes the steamy and conformist small-town setting, teenage male friendship, familial bonds and pressures, the trauma of sexual awakening, and ultimately personal growth, stigma management and identity reconstruction. *Luc* also has its sexy moments, not only in an encounter with the blue-eyed, dark-bearded stranger post-skinny-dipping on the banks of a river but also in the bonding among shirtless buddies on those long, hot summer evenings. Yet another tragedy of the queer exodus from the stifling heartland, the film's sentimentality is offset by its working-class hard-headedness, a unique and lovely work unavailable in any form in English or French (see chapter 5).

The second work of the decade, *Crêver à vingt ans* (Croaking at Twenty, 1984), is a hustler melodrama of overwhelming pathos, also undistributed and un-subtitled. After a few more educational commissions Audy apparently withdrew from filmmaking.

AYANOGLU, BYRON, b. 1946. Playwright, chef, video maker. Istanbul-bred, McGill-trained, Toronto-based Ayanoglu is the prolific writer of plays, cookbooks, and restaurant guides. He circulated several videos on the queer circuit in the 1980s, including *Chichenitz Ah* (1987, 16), an idio-syncratic allegory about evil spells and gay-lesbian rivalry, and two collab-orative works about the doomed queens *Marie Antoinette* (1985, 10) and *Imelda* (1987, 9). Ayanoglu's performance in NIK SHEEHAN's *Symposium* (1996) is well-seasoned and well-sauced.

AYOUP, COLLEEN, b. 1968. Filmmaker, video maker. A promising young luminary of Montreal dykedom. Concordia-trained Ayoup is best known for her documentary *Kings* (2001, 20), a spirited docu-encounter with a local drag-king troupe. Her other experimental narrative miniatures in film and video reflect the same irreverent take on gender illusion and perform-ance, with sex added and stirred: *Oral* (1998), a hot silent strap-on tryst contextualized by gabby maternal interference and some lesbian/Lebanese wordplay that may not be as trivial as it sounds; *Me Myself Bound & Jackie* (2002), variations on a sexy and self-reflexively layered "Honey, I'm home!" involving a stunning drag king.

BAILLARGEON, PAULE, b. 1945. Director, actor. Trained in the theatre, queer-friendly Baillargeon's *La Cuisine rouge* (codirector, Frédérique Collin, 1979, 82) was an experimental feature and the furthest incursion of the feminist avant-garde into the Quebec feature in the utopian 1970s. An East End wedding party goes awry when the women desert the kitchen and opt out, conducting a lazy counter-party on the balcony, half dream and half nightmare, and indulging in a slow-motion orgy of bathing, danc-ing, [un]dressing up and down, storytelling and good old sisterhood. Meanwhile, all the guys can do is complain, talk about Guy Lafleur and nationalist politics, and eventually pull off one of their own halfhearted stripteases. My queer postmillennium students found the film a little too trapped in seventies New Age macramé and declared the homoeroticism intrinsic in the rites of homosociality to be as skittish as it was abundant. But the improv troupe of emerging Quebec stage and film actors, headed by actresses Baillargeon and Collin, deftly posed questions of sexuality within the cultural feminism of the day and built a challenging and origi-nal movie around them.

Baillargeon next attracted the queer audience with *Le Sexe des étoiles* [*Sex of the Stars*] (Montreal, 1993, 100), one of the first Canadian dramatic features with a transgendered protagonist. But in some ways it's less the story of Marie-Pierre than the coming-of-age story for her adolescent daughter Camille, who is discovering not only her transformed father but also the wide world of astronomy, diverse sexuality, family conflict, and urban subcultures. Based on Monique Proulx's 1987 novel, *Sexe* met with acclaim, including a best-actor prize for Denis Mercier as Marie-Pierre. The "art film" aura of *Le Sexe des étoiles* is seductive, and its forthright view of the urban sexual underworld (including a movie-stealing teenage male hustler Lucky in a supporting role) rings true. But something jars in Marie-Pierre's submission to bullying by her ex-wife and by her obsessive but well-intentioned daughter, and when, at the latter's insistence, the transsexual awkwardly resumes male attire for some obscure reasons, the film seems to pause in midair and lose its engines. Scholar Viviane Namaste critiqued what she saw as the film's mangled nationalist metaphors (2000, 93–131). Olivia Jensen, another MTF academic, was more focused on the film's betrayal of the original novel's "incredibly positive and sympathetic understanding" and critiqued the "Y-chromosome-hating violence" underlying the assumption, emerging in the scene where Camille discovers her first period, that "one can only become a woman by female birth." The too-masculine casting of Marie-Pierre didn't go over very well with the transgendered audience either (email, 4 September 2003). The Quebec acting community has often been caught up in the Tom Hanks syndrome, relishing plum roles based on outsiders' "invisible lives" (to cite the title of Namaste's book on transgendered people) and deliver-

In one of the first trans-themed Canadian dramatic features, Paule Baillargeon's *Le Sexe des étoiles* (1993), Marie-Pierre submits to her daughter's bullying, resumes male attire, gets an acting award, and leaves trans audiences cold. Production still, Cinémathèque québécoise

ing dignity (if we're lucky) and angst, while leaving the invisible constituency caught up in conflicted feelings of elation, vulnerability, and continued hunger. Bruce LaBruce prefers kickass spunk to dignity, and sad, tony Marie-Pierre makes me want to agree.

Baillargeon's feature bio-doc on her film industry colleague and neighbour, *Claude Jutra: Portrait sur film* (*Claude Jutra: An Unfinished Story*, 2002, 82), was tender, respectful and resourceful in its incorporation of unfamiliar images of the great queer director but took too few risks in apprehending the role of sexual identity in the creative process.

BALASS, JOE, b.1966. Documentarist. Concordia-trained Montrealer Balass has made two films since leaving film school in the early nineties, but these two unique video documentaries earned him a respectful following within two religions, three languages, and many sexualities. The first, *Nana, George and Me* (1997, 48), was autobiography disguised as separate but intertwined interview encounters with an elderly woman and man belonging, like Balass, to the Iraqi Jewish diaspora. The two couldn't be more apparently different, the filmmaker's ninety-year-old traditional grandmother and a maso bon vivant who likes being playfully trampled by his "trade" retinue. But Balass's subversive probing of their respective sexualities as fully as their Bagdadi ancestry is what brings them together as foils for the filmmaker's own faux-naif off-screen self-exploration. Subversive of inherited documentary ethics and visual styles (who says you can't ask your grandmother about her bridal deflowering over extreme close-ups of the skin folds of her neck that may mimic what you saw as an infant in her arms?), *Nana, George and Me* is one of the boldest entrants in the queer autobiographical wave of the 1990s.

The Devil in the Holy Water (2002, 94), made in collaboration with Balass's partner Giampaolo Marzi, has a playfully superficial, journalistic edge that seems to cloud its intensely personal stake and style. The quirky, insightful investigation of Catholic institutional homophobia and a definitively Italian street theater of everyday life all crystallize in the clash of the 2000 Vatican Jubilee with the Word Pride counter-demonstration taking place in the Holy City at the same time.

BALSER, MICHAEL, 1952–2002. Video maker, curator, producer, AIDS activist. New Brunswick–bred Michael Balser was part of the experimental video and Super 8 scene in Fredericton and Ottawa before finally putting down roots in Toronto in 1985. His early video *Jerungdu* (1986, 13) was already autobiographical, an expressionistic collage, but his diagnosis with HIV that same year suddenly provided him with a life crisis and a personal/political theme that would shape the rest of his prolific, restless, and

In *Survival of the Delirious* (1988), Michael Balser and Andy Fabo use the aboriginal personae of the Windigo and the warrior huntsman to narrativize the AIDS crisis, as well as come out as HIV+. VHS frame grab

committed artistic career. Continuing in the postmodern collage vein with his two-channel piece *Fear of Everything in the Universe* (1987, 25), Balser met his life partner, Alberta-bred visual artist Andy Fabo (b. 1953), during production. Their fruitful artistic collaboration led to several of Balser's best-known works, including *Pogo Stick Porno Romp* (1987, 9, see chapter 8), a playful essay on culture and nature laid over with Fabo graphics and, among many other things, a sexually explicit celebration of the couple's young relationship. Their *Survival of the Delirious* (1988, 14), while an equally inventive collage, had a more sombre register, using the personae of the native warrior huntsman and Windigo to narrativize the personal and community crisis around AIDS, as well as to come out as HIV+: Fabo is seen in dramatized conversation with his doctor discussing the new and controversial AZT therapy options, one element in the poetic mosaic about danger, fear, and resolution.

Balser's later works continue to reflect his AIDS activism (see chapter 9), works that include *Toronto Living with AIDS*, the cable series he coordinated for cable starting in 1992, whose impact was thwarted by censorship; two compilations of AIDS Public Service Announcements (1993), for which Balser, in collaboration with the Banff Centre, enlisted the contributions of queer video artists from coast to coast; *Positive Men* (1995, 50), a mosaic of dramatic scenes about a gay-male community affected and responding, together with documentary portraits of PWAs; and the autobiographical "cybertour" *Treatments–Adventures in AIDS and Media* (1996, 43). Late work sometimes returned to the absurdist vein of earlier years, as in two busy, wacky riffs on space travel, acting auditions, and the infiltration of Canadian TV by robots, *Rocket Science* (2001, 11) and *Popular Science* (2002, 23). Otherwise, two DVD collaborations with Fabo veered towards an almost zen apprehension of the male body, mortality, aesthetics, and desire (*Motion of Light on Water*, 2001, 12; *Imperfect Proportions*, posthumous, 2002, 5). Balser continued his prolific output, combining activist documentary with experimental narrative and collage, until his death in 2002. Dialogue said by an "AIDS Activist Action Figure" in *Treatments* might be thought of as his parting words: "if I'm going to go, at least I'm going to go out fighting."

BARRY, MICHAEL EDWARD (a.k.a. Mike EB), b. 1980. Filmmaker, performer, critic, Toronto-based Barry's three experimental shorts made since 2001, including *Late Night Visitor* (2001, 3), have been popular in international queer festivals. *Visitor*'s boisterous satire of "Heritage Moments" remade a tale of secret homosocial "training partners" busted by paternal repression, acted out by Barry and his codirector EVGENY ZBOROVSKY in their underwear – all amid artefacts of the pre-Stonewall homoerotic physique movement that are "Part of Our Heritage"! Barry codirected the rambunctious *Wads and Wads* (2003, 5) with JOHN CAFFERY and has also collaborated with PETER KINGSTONE.

BARTH, ANNE, b. 1951. Video maker, teacher. Trained at UQAM (where she now teaches), prizewinning Montreal artist Barth produced several works during the 1990s committed to exploring and finding video art equivalents for French-language feminist and lesbian-feminist literature. Best-known was her adapation of NICOLE BROSSARD's poetic essay-novel *La nuit verte du parc labyrinthe* (*The Green Night of Labyrinth Park*, 1993, 24). The writer is seen and heard performing and writing her dense, personal words amid resourceful visual and auditory strategies for communicating their evocative multilingual complexity.

BARTLETT, RENNY, b. 1955. Director, scriptwriter. A queer-friendly Ottawa native, Bartlett was trained in London and is known chiefly for his accomplished debut feature *Eisenstein* (2002, 96), a German-Canadian coproduction biopic of the queer Soviet film pioneer. Shot with bright and Brechtian epochal flair on location in Russia, Ukraine, and Mexico, *Eisenstein* is irreverently camp and deadly serious about the historical betrayal of Bolshevik ideals, aesthetics, and revolutionary desire. It may be the second Canadian feature to depict the queer Soviet director (after GREYSON's *Urinal*, 1998) but the first to show him astride a phallic Mexican cactus, ripping the clothes off his beefy blond collaborator Alexandrov and fending off DANIEL MACIVOR as a Hollywood homophobe named Stalker.

BEARCHELL, CHRIS, b. 1953. Journalist, critic, activist. As one of the minority lesbian element on the collective of Toronto's influential gay-liberation monthly, *The Body Politic* (1971–87), Bearchell was one of the most listened-to voices in the magazine, the most pro-sex, anticensorship feminist in Toronto. Her in-depth analysis of the 1981 CBC documentary debacle *Sharing the Secret* is typical of the insight and expressiveness she consistently offered (see CANADIAN BROADCASTING CORPORATION/ RADIO CANADA): "The Kastners' camera does not just passively record and reflect; it selects, frames and shapes. They are formula filmmakers specializing in 'sensitive' issues, complete with closeup invasions of private pain. When they don't find exactly what they want or expect they're not above using a little creativity to achieve the desired effect." Other than her articulate testimonies in such documentaries as *Track Two* (SUTHERLAND, 1982) and *Stand Together* (NICOL, 2002), Bearchell performed a flirtatious cameo in *Another Man* (Youth against Monsterz, 1988, 3), an early safe sex video for high schools.

BEAUCAGE, MARJORIE, b. 1947. Documentarist, teacher, activist. A Manitoba-bred Métis, Ryerson-trained Beaucage is one of Canada's most distinguished First Nations media artists. Beaucage worked from 1992 to 2000 in Saskatoon and is known for her prolific body of collaborative and personal work documenting and inspiring First Nations experience, voices, and struggles. Her *Bingo* (1991, 18), a "heavily coded incest film" about the victim mind, was programmed at Image & Nation 1995 as part of a group of women's documentary and experimental videos, "History from the Inside Out." Beaucage's *China ... through One Woman's Eyes* (1996, 28) includes an evocative look at lesbians claiming representation at the 1995 Beijing NGO Forum, and her *Proz Anthology* (with Susan Risk, 2000) included strong lesbian voices within its streetworkers' diary notebook format. Otherwise, references to queer issues are usually subsumed under her visionary spectrum of feminist and aboriginal voices.

BEAUDRY, LISE, b. 1972. Director, photographer, community arts animator. Concordia-trained, Toronto-based Beaudry won queer festival awards at both Toronto and Dublin for her personal, humorous but intense mash note to Jeanne Moreau, *Le Tourbillon* (2002, 6). Not just a fan montage of the French star's legendary moments, this bilingual cinematic whirlpool is also an appropriation of Moreau magic into the artist's queer fantasy life as she accompanies her on her guitar and joins the race across the bridge from *Jules et Jim.*

BÉLANGER, FERNAND, b. 1943. Documentarist. Long known as the NFB French studio's rebellious in-house anarchist and specialist in the alienations and passions of youth, Bélanger's first works like *Ti-coeur* (1969) and *Ty-peupe* (1971) were pulsating with homoerotic subtexts. But he is best known for his boldly innovative and risk-taking *Passiflora* (codirector, Dagmar Teufel, 1985, 85; see chapter 6). On the eve of the great NFB turnaround, this daring graffiti essay on the Pope, Michael Jackson, the Olympic Stadium, and the manipulation of the masses gave a spunky glimmer of hope in a decade of institutional complacency. Named after the anesthetic tropical passion flower, *Passiflora* deploys animation, "new music," street theatre, and dramatization laid over its observation of the two media stars' simultaneous visit to their Montreal faithful. It celebrates resistance by a coalition of the disobedient: gays, transpeople, the young, battered women, the "psychiatrized," and abortion activists and clients. In the face of such irreverence, the studio brass moved quickly into damage control mode, nixing an English version, discouraging festival exposure, quietly dumping the film into short-lived release, and effectively banishing the two directors to Canadian film Siberia. Today the film is not even available for purchase – *quelle coincidence*!

BELL, RICHARD, b. 1975. Director, scriptwriter. Born in Port Coquitlam and trained at Vancouver's Langara College theatre program, Studio 58, Bell surprised with his first feature *Two Brothers* (2000, 60), an unusual DVD marketing success story that used the $545 budget as a publicity ploy. Shown internationally in queer community festivals, the intense melodrama about sibling conflict – gay vs. straight, country vs. city mouse – feels soapish, with every issue lined up, from AIDS to alcoholism. But Bell pulled it off through sincerity, fine performances, and black-and-white urban realism. Bell has served with Out on Screen.

BENNER, RICHARD, 1946–1990. Director. An American expatriate who made it in Toronto, Richard Benner is remembered chiefly for his brilliant low-budget hit *Outrageous!* (1977, 96), about a Toronto drag queen who makes it in New York.

Based on Margaret Gibson's story "Making It," the feel-good story of the friendship of a female impersonator/hairdresser and a "real" female schizophrenic on the lam from psychiatry featured real-life drag performer Craig Russell, who became a star as a result. This *Casablanca* of English Canadian cinema reflects an almost perfect synchrony of talents brought together almost by accident at just the right moment, auguring so much for Canadian feature production then mired in the "tax shelter" void. Gibson had based her sharp original story on her friend Russell, and Benner transformed it into a witty script and *mise en scène* that more than deserved its Berlin Silver Bear and its sleeper success in New York. The climactic numbers featuring Russell reincarnated as Davis, Bankhead, and even Ella Fitzgerald ("It's not tacky drag. I do real impressions. No records. My own voice") are so wonderful that they make you forget what a fine little, very Canadian movie about the redemption of outsiders and the emergence of community has proceeded them. Championed more by mainstream critics and audiences than by queer communities, *Outrageous!* is still a positive and moving narrative of emerging queer identities. No longer available on video, this classic is a prime candidate for DVD release, in fact for a 35mm sing-along version, so that the youngsters can bellow along with Robin such immortal lines as "Mad as a Hatter Darling" (see chapter 4).

Benner went on to another Toronto-centred adaptation, *Happy Birthday, Gemini* (1980), which managed to maintain a modicum of gay sensibility despite its U.S.-studio financing. The sequel *Too Outrageous!* (1987) also failed to impress, despite Russell in comeback mode, but was not as bad as all the critics said. AIDS robbed us of both Benner and Russell shortly thereafter.

BEVERIDGE, SCOTT, b. 1964. Film- and video maker, scriptwriter, AIDS activist. CFC-trained Beveridge, an award-winning veteran of the Toronto indie queer media scene, made the defiant claim that his half dozen short films and videos since 1992, often starting out as Super 8, were all self-funded. His uncompromising experimental narratives, such as *Quiver* (1999, originally Super 8, 5, TIFF) and *Odessa* (2000, 5), were encounters of first-person voice with allegorized performance, provocative politicizations of AIDS, violence, homophobia, and queer normalization. The former constructed an analogy between a masochist prisoner's eroticized brutalization by his master and an HIV patient's submission to corporal invasion, while the latter was a ceremonial polemic against sexual science and sexual identities/bodies – from "third sex" to hypothalmus.

BEZALEL, RONIT, b.1969 Documentarist. Based in Montreal in the early 1990s, McGill-trained social activist Bezalel is best known for *When Shirley Met Florence* (1994, 27), her affecting, deceptively simple film about friendship between two elderly Jewish Montrealers, a married heterosexual woman Shirley and her pal Florence. "Music was one of the glues," they say, and it's clear from this documentary how singing and playing together sustained their friendship for twenty-five years, throughout each's attachment to life partners and conformist pressures. Originally an independent project, *Shirley* was taken under the NFB's wing and made part of its lesbian/gay package, and it became a favourite of both the queer and the Jewish festival circuits. Bezalel's earlier work had included a reflection on lesbian stereotyping (*Tearing the Veil*, 1990), as well as the raw

372 | PORTRAIT GALLERY

You Can't Beat It Out of Us (codirector, Chris Martin, 1991), about the Montreal police's brutal crackdown on queers during the Sex Garage affair. Bezalel relocated to Chicago where her housing activism led *Newsweek* to name her one of the top fifteen women of the twenty-first century!

BLACKBRIDGE, PERSIMMON, b. 1951. Interdisciplinary artist, performer, actor, video maker. Blackbridge's pioneering contribution to queer video in Canada began with *Still Sane* (directors Brenda Ingratta and Lidia Patriasz, Vancouver, 1984, 60), a video version of Blackbridge's 1984 Vancouver sculpture show together with Sheila Gilhooly, inspired by the latter's three-year psychiatric incarceration in the seventies. Blackbridge's ceramic sculptures of Gilhooly's tortured and ultimately triumphant body are inscribed with diary entries. The video adaptation of these three-dimensional forms and words created a new work, a stunning survival narrative that reached an international crossover audience, in conjunction with the book version (1985). This important early tape confirmed the essential role that both the genre of autobiography and format of video would play within lesbian culture and queer communities. Gilhooly and the sculptures would reappear in MARGARET WESCOTT's NFB epic *Stolen Moments* (1997). In the 1990s, Blackbridge was most visible as a leading member of the Lesbian sex/art collective Kiss and Tell (others were Lizard Jones, b. 1961, and Susan Stewart, b. 1952). Their touring erotic arts exhibition "Drawing the Line" helped turn the tide in the feminist sex wars – pro artistic sexual expression, anti-censorship (the video version of *Drawing the Line* was by LORNA BOSCHMAN, 1992). In the same vein, Kiss and Tell's groundbreaking exhibition "True Inversions," presented at the Banff Centre in 1992 sparked a confrontation in the Alberta political environment around arts funding and freedom of expression (Gilbert 1999). In the video version, also by Boschman (1992), crammed with the event's carnivalesque swings, costumes, and makeup, as well as delirious couplings, vocal performances, and political analysis, Blackbridge preserved her legendary "in-your-crotch" performance for posterity. Blackbridge also acted in Boschman's child abuse narrative *Family Secrets* (*Five Feminist Minutes*, 1990), and codirected her *Sunnybrook* (1995). Kiss and Tell published a book-format elaboration of the issues raised in their work: *Her Tongue on My Theory: Images, Essays and Fantasies* (1994).

BLUTEAU, LOTHAIRE, b. 1957. Actor. New York–exiled, Québécois Bluteau was a distinctive star presence in the international queer cinema beginning in the late 1980s, most memorably in the gay Holocaust love story *Bent* (Sean Mathias, United Kingdom, 1997). His best-known Cana-

International queer star Lothaire Bluteau as tortured photographer Pierre seeks his
hustler brother and his family's secrets in *Le Confessionnal* (1995). His lean body and
weary face usually connote asexuality, rather than awakened gay desire. Production still,
Film Reference Library

dian queer role is Pierre Lamontagne, the tortured photographer searching
for his hustler brother and his family's secret history in ROBERT LEPAGE's
Le Confessionnal (1995, Genie nomination). Sometimes tending to be
typecast along the same angsty lines, Bluteau's Giacometti-lean body and
his lucidly weary face usually connote a repressed asexuality rather than
an awakened gay desire. In lighter cameo roles he has graced international
queer movies from *Orlando* (Sally Potter, United Kingdom, 1992) to *I Shot
Andy Warhol* (Mary Harron, 1996). Although Bluteau has never publicly
indicated his sexual identity, even his "non-gay" lead roles, such as the
enigmatic mystic *Jesus of Montreal* (1989, Genie) and the repressed Father
Laforgue in *Black Robe* (1991), tend to be ... well, not exactly *straight*.
Montreal and London (England) theatre-goers will never forget his excori-
ating performance as Yves, the hustler who has killed his lover in *Being at
Home with Claude*, but queer movie-lovers have etched indelibly on their
hearts the set-piece in *Confessionnal* where Pierre dawdles through a
labyrinthine gay sauna in pursuit of his brother, who finally tells him in the

steam room that this is not his place (rather implausibly), or the transcendent scene of hands-off orgasm in *Bent*.

BOCIURKIW, MARUSYA, b. 1958. Video maker, writer, teacher/lecturer. NSCAD-trained Bociurkiw has worked for over two decades in all three Canadian metropoles and has been based in Vancouver since the mid-1990s. Early works addressed the interface of gender, class, and geopolitics, while sexual identity emerged as a theme of an essayistic and narrative hybrid practice with *Playing with Fire* (1986, 75). *Bodies in Trouble* (1990, 15), an attempt to situate lesbian eroticism in the context of right-wing backlash, was full of the positive imagery of an ideal couple, equal parts sensual bed-play and defiant demonstrations, equal parts Toronto, Montreal, and the no-dyke's-land in between, full of images of borderlines, passengers in transit, and very Canadian transportation images, full also of a sensibility of exile, liminality, and melancholy. In the long-gestated *Nancy Drew and the Mystery of the Haunted Body* (1999, 45), Bociurkiw developed the playful format of the ideological essay narrative, setting the girl detective up for an investigation of the politics of sexual abuse and the "false memory syndrome." Since 1990, Bociurkiw has concentrated increasingly on her writing, often accenting her Ukrainian heritage. She has also given illustrated lectures on lesbian resonances on television and in music video, which have been popular on the queer community festival circuit, and has taught at Concordia, York, SFU, and UBC.

BOSCHMAN, LORNA, b. 1955. Video maker, editor, camera operator, curator. Since 1986, prizewinning video artist Boschman, trained at Video In and ECIAD, has been one of the most visible, influential, and prolific presences on the West Coast lesbian-feminist arts scene. Her work showed the primary influence of feminist documentary, as in her searing investigation of women who "slash" in *Scars* (1987, 12). At the same time, she developed her skills in fantasy (the five-minute *Butch/Femme in Paradise*, 1988, follows a sullen butch chasing an elusive femme sprite along the scenic British Columbia coast, one of the most popular shorts on the international queer community circuit of the 1990s) and in wacky comedy (*Dr Lorna's Seven Day Poodle Diet*, 1998). Boschman's work on lesbian eroticism in collaboration with the collective Kiss and Tell (*True Inversions* and *Drawing the Line*, both 1992) impacted favourably on the continent-wide debates in the early nineties about sexual representation and censorship, both in the feminist community and the mainstream. Not shy of probing the traumas of the body alongside its pleasures, Boschman artistically investigated a wide range of body issues beyond sexual identity in the narrow sense, from cancer and abuse to disability and fat. The personal docu-

Lorna Boschman's work on lesbian eroticism in collaboration with "Kiss and Tell" (*Drawing the Line*, 1992) intervened in the 1990s debates about sexual representation and censorship, both in the feminist community and the mainstream. VHS frame grab, Drawing the Line, Lorna Boschman, 1992

mentaries on the politics of fat (*Big Fat Slenderella*, 1993, and *Fat World*, 1994, in addition to *Poodle Diet*) demonstrated Boschman's excellence as editor as well as camerawoman with their interludes and backdrops of graceful choreography by round marine mammals. A community activist, Boschman has collaborated with many artists on the Vancouver queer scene, from SHANI MOOTOO to PAUL LANG.

BOUCHARD, MICHEL MARC, b. 1958. Playwright, scriptwriter. Among the best-known of post-Tremblay Quebec playwrights, the prolific Bouchard became one of our most visible queer theatrical presences in the 1980s. Adaptations of his work have become mainstays of Canadian queer cinemas, namely, the prize-winning *Lilies*, the turn-of-the-century tragic teenage love story set in Bouchard's native Lac-St-Jean region and reenacted by an all-male jailhouse ensemble fifty years later, which Bouchard adapted from his 1987 stage hit *Les Feluettes* (JOHN GREYSON, 1996; see chapter 5), and *Les Muses orphelines* (*The Orphan Muses*, Robert Favreau, 2000, 107), adapted by the playwright from his 1989 play, a contemporary rural dysfunctional family melodrama, this time with a strong lesbian theme. Bouchard also adapted his 1991 children's play, *L'Histoire de l'oie*, as a TV movie (*The Tale of Teeka*, Tim Southam, 1998).

BOWEN, DEANNA, b. 1969. Video and installation artist, arts administrator, curator. Caribbean-born, SFU- and ECIAD-trained, Toronto-based Deanna Bowen has shown her complex works, often Old Testament–inspired narratives of intrafamilial sexual/power dynamics, in both queer community festivals and independent film and arts settings. Queer audiences have been most struck by the uncompromising video *Sado-masochism* (1998, 14; also an installation, 2000, see chapters 5 and 10), a montage of ritual words and images that confront sexual role-playing with violent familial abuse dynamics, corporal performance, and personal and racial political histories. Even *The Toronto Star*'s Peter Goddard spoke of "frightful irony" and of the "spare imagery and the narrator's richly evocative text bound tightly together by a fiercely focused intelligence" (31 March 2000). Bowen has collaborated with many other Toronto queer artists, such as DEBORAH KIRKLAND, and served with Inside Out.

BRADLEY, MARK, b. 1976. Director. Trained and based in Regina, Bradley circulated one of the more interesting entries in the experimental home-movie recycling genre in queer and experimental festivals worldwide in 2001, the prizewinning *Family Outing* (5), an autobiographical reflection on portents of future queer identity in scenes of fishing with Dad, piano lessons, and weddings – optically printed to bring out both ominousness and banality.

BRADLEY, MAUREEN, b. 1967. Video maker, teacher. Trained at Concordia and UBC and recently teaching at the Universities of Regina and Victoria, Bradley is a talented and prolific satirist who has specialized in the vagaries of identity labels, eroticism, memory, and coupledom. Bradley loves voice-over narration, and this, whether confessional, political, poetic, or erotic, always amplifies or counterbalances her visual flair, which has oscillated between experimental virtuosity and documentary directness. Often an onscreen performer in her own work, Bradley is the star of *Defiance* (1993, 6), possibly her most explicitly political work: here she is seen engaged in intensifying slow-motion liplock with another woman, all overlaid with a chorus of homophobic voices to the tune of "I'm not homophobic but ... " and then wrapped up by a scrolling Foucault quote about the spiral of power and pleasure. *The Chosen Family* (2001, 13), a hilarious tale of queer siblings, a wedding, and a coming out, and *You Fake* (2003, 7), a miniature about simulated lesbian orgasms, both indicate a promising new direction in narrative.

BRAND, DIONNE, b. 1953. Poet, documentarist. Official profiles of prizewinning Trinidad-born poet Brand are coy about her lesbianism and its relevance to her writing, although she and her work itself are not. Toronto-based Brand has had a significant involvement with film, both as writer and director, especially with works about African Canadian women's history and culture made in collaboration with the NFB's Studio D. As director, Brand is best known for *Long Time Comin'* (1993, 52), a warm and vivid portrait of two black lesbian artists, Grace Channer and Faith Nolan. But her more personal and perhaps more profound work as director is *Listening for Something ... Adrienne Rich and Dionne Brand in Conversation* (1996), a filmic reading and discussion between herself and the American elder lesbian writer that brings out rich synchronies. Most recently Brand wrote the script and text for *Under One Sky ... Arab Women in North America Talk about the Hijab* (Jennifer Kawaja, NFB, 1999, 44).

BRIAND, MANON, b. 1964. Director, scriptwriter, art designer. One of the rising stars of Quebec features, Concordia-trained Briand has her finger on the pulse of her generation of hip urban gays, lesbians, bisexuals – and even heteros – for whom sexual identity is an affair of the heart and as a political issue ranks up there with hairstyles. Her talent for sprightly narratives of sexual ambiguity and torch-carrying among the Plateau intello-bohemia came to critical attention with the prizewinning short narrative *Les Saufs-conduits* (1991, 56), about an unreciprocated male-male-female triangle. Her contribution to the stylish black and white episode film *Cosmos* (1997), by six upcoming Quebec directors, is one of the most memorable: "Boost" recounts a surreal urban journey in which a woman drives a gay buddy to the clinic in her broken-down convertible to get the results of his HIV test – never revealed, but everyone has a feeling ... With Briand's first feature, *2 Secondes* (1998), more prizes came her way and the queer community festival circuit as well, as she moved into the big-budget arena with this skilfully wrought melodrama about a dykey, washed-up bike racer who finds fulfilment as a courier in Montreal's mean streets. She also finds solace in an unusual friendship with an older (male) Italian bike repair specialist and eventually in the arms of an unidentified (female) heartthrob. *La Turbulence des fluides* (2002) was less queer and more star-driven (Pascale Bussières and Geneviève Bujold!), and its reception reflected the "second feature" syndrome, with some critics lying in wait with sharpened knives. All the same, the film is an imaginative melodrama about an international seismologist who finds tidal and human mysteries and (hetero-) romance in her home town of Baie Comeau (as well as her lesbian old friend still carrying a torch for her). Meanwhile, an English-language TV biopic about the Toronto marathon swimmer, *Heart – The Marilyn Bell Story* (2000) allowed Briand to refine her directing skills,

An unreciprocated male-male-female triangle in Manon Briand's prizewinning short
Les Saufs-conduits (1991), one of her smart narratives of ambiguity and torch-carrying among
her hip urban omnisexual generation. Production still, Cinémathèque québécoise

as well as her interest in female bodies, athletic challenges, and sexual ambiguity.

BRITTON, ANDREW, 1952–94. Critic, writer. British-born film writer Andrew Britton was an influential queer-film scholar who contributed to Canadian and international queer-film culture from his Toronto base during the last fifteen years of his life. Occasional reviewer for *TBP* between 1979 and 1983 and a frequent contributor to *Cineaction!*, Britton was known for his fiercely intellectual confrontation with the entire spectrum of the cinema. Author of books on Cary Grant (1983) and Katharine Hepburn (1984), of influential articles spanning horror cinema and queer Eisenstein, his widely cited 1978 denunciation of "camp" exemplifies a political moralism that was out of fashion a quarter century later but is worthy of revival: "'Subversiveness' needs to be assessed … as a relationship between a phenomenon and its context – that is, dynamically … In a contemporary context, gay camp seems little more than a kind of anaesthetic, allowing one to remain inside oppressive relations while enjoying the illusory confidence that one is flouting them" (1978–97).

BROSSARD, NICOLE, b. 1943. Writer, documentarist. A prizewinning Montreal poet, essayist, and novelist, Brossard has had several connections to lesbian film and video. The codirector of MARGARET WESCOTT's pioneering "lesbian continuum" documentary *Some American Feminists* (1977), Brossard appeared twenty years later as a witness in Wescott's sapphic epic *Stolen Moments* (1997). Brossard was also one of three subjects in Dorothy Todd Hénaut's marathon portrait of three Quebec lesbian writers, *Les terribles vivantes – Louky Bersianik, Jovette Marchessault, Nicole Brossard (Firewords*, 1986). Finally, Brossard collaborated with and appeared in ANNE BARTH's respectful and imaginative video adaptation of her multilingual, multilandscape poetic text *La Nuit vert du Parc labyrinthe (The Green Night of Laybrinth Park*, 1993). In all, Brossard performs her allusive poetic writing and champions lesbian-feminist literature.

BROWN, DANNY. Porn star. Franco-Ontarian Brown, a.k.a. Daniel LeBrun, Danny Gibson, and Robert French, made it big in California gay porn videos, beginning at the end of the 1980s (Bradley 2004). The five-foot-seven-inch curly-haired brunette was notable for his Québécois accents in dialogue scenes, but dialogue was not his principal attraction. Directed by Chi Chi La Rue and Jean Daniel Cadinot, among many others, Brown graced almost fifty films between 1988 and 1995, including WILLIAM DUFFAULT's *Les hommes au naturel* (1995), produced on Montreal turf, where he has remained active.

BRUNO, WENDELL, b. 1967. Film- and video maker. Born in Trinidad and Tobago, Ottawa-bred, Concordia-trained Bruno's short experimental works of the 1990s explored the interface of black and queer experience, desire, and representation. *Media Blackmale* (1994, 5), a frequent queer festival programmer, responds to Mapplethorpe in its confrontation with images of black masculinity and bodies. *I and I Outlook* (1994, 8) pursued these themes on a more personal tack in a poetic coming-of-age narrative about a boy's relationship with his father.

BRYAN, T.J, b. 1968. Writer/poet, activist, film- and videomaker. Born in Barbados, University of Ottawa–trained, Toronto-based Bryant, "a.k.a. Tenacious," is a self-taught, self-styled immigrant, working-class, black, queer, femme "militant mama from hell on a mission of radical societal transformation," who was published in many anthologies. Her two films of the early 2000s challenged festival audiences, including *No You Cyan't Touch It* (2001, 3), on one level a close-up documentary about the artist's locks set in an ice-stormed Toronto, but on another level it's an in-your-face manifesto about hair as "revolution," overlaid by strong spoken lyrics written and performed by Bryan: "this hair marks me as a nomad, not just black, queer or female ... eternal, twisting, undulating, dread, dark, dangerous and true."

BULMER, ALEX, b. 1966. Theatre artist, videomaker, teacher. Bishops- and Ryerson-trained, Toronto-based Bulmer's identity as a vision-impaired lesbian informs her artistic work on stage, on radio, and on the small screen, all of which excels in rich auditory artistic compensations for images that come and go. Her first video *Beauty* (1998, 12), plays with voice recognition devices and striking visual fluctuations to line up sensory memories – and assessments – of her lovers over the years, from the frivolous me-person to the deep, silent, beer-drinking butch who likes *The Sound of Music*.

BURGESS, MARILYN, b. 1960. Interdisciplinary artist, arts administrator. Concordia-trained, Montreal-based Marilyn Burgess is remembered most by queer audiences for her early experimental videotape *A Woman in My Platoon* (1989, 20). This minimalist manifesto reflected Burgess's background in parallel art spaces but was a resonant capsule of late eighties queer political art. Appropriating and eroticizing NFB women's recruitment images from World War II, Burgess added a first-person audio account of a woman's expulsion from the Canadian forces oceanography unit for her sexual orientation plus official House of Commons video shots of parliamentarians spewing homophobic hatred, all cemented together by zen-like waves on the shore. In fact, Canadian women soldiers in World War II were not the American WAVES but the Canadian Women's Army Corps; nevertheless, Burgess made her point. In the 1990s and 2000s, Burgess worked at the Canada Council before shifting to Telefilm Canada.

BURT, AMY, 1952–2003. Director, writer, art designer. Ohio-born, Halifax-based Burt moved from industry set decorating to personal filmmaking late in her life and left one narrative short honoured at Inside Out in 2003. Based on a 1964 autobiographical incident, *This Boy* (2002, 22) shows an eleven-year-old tomboy and John-Lennon-wannabe named Kit, who gets into deep trouble, all because of her crush on her rosy-cheeked girl friend, but the cops and the collateral damage are all worth it when the crush turns out to be reciprocal!

BUTLER, ALEC, b. 1959. Playwright, video maker, performer, curator. Brought up on Cape Breton as Audrey, Toronto-based Butler is best known for critically acclaimed plays such as *Black Friday* (1990). His video work includes the *Pussyboy* trilogy (with Terri Robertson, 2000, 4), which is comprised of short animated works that depict the trauma and isolation of growing up trans in the 1970s. *Audrey's Beard* (2002, 3) is a time-lapse record of the growth of exactly that, a reflection on a former life as butch dyke. In collaboration with activist Vlad Wolanyk and others, Butler curated Inside Out's groundbreaking trans series "Gender Euphoria" in 2003.

CAFFERY, JOHN, b. 1978. Filmmaker, rock performer. Self-taught, Hamilton-born, Toronto-based Caffery presented three low-format experimental shorts in the 2002 and 2003 queer festival seasons, including a sexy performance-piece, Super 8 work entitled *Wads and Wads* (codirector MICHAEL BARRY, 2003, 5), in which the Freudian equivalence of money and come is amusingly imagined. *All the Right Moves* (2003, 5, Inside Out Digital Video Project), an edgy first-person ethnography, features a nonplussed cat that doesn't care whether gay men or straight men dance better. *Doppelganger* (5) was programmed as part of the Best of 2002 works at Toronto's experimental venue Pleasure Dome.

CAINES, MICHAEL, b. 1964. Video- and filmmaker, expressive arts psychotherapist, painter. Toronto-based Caines, trained at Dalhousie and York, contributed several late 1990s experimental shorts that echoed his day job. *Fever* (1998, 7) is about dreaming and paranoia, with the camera caressing the body of a tormented naked sleeper with an ambiguous relationship to his dreams. *Symptomatic* (1998, 5) hypnotically explores the interface between desire for the hunky urban loiterer gazed at and addressed and a mysteriously remembered childhood in a desert landscape.

CALGARY INTERNATIONAL LESBIAN AND GAY FILM FESTIVAL, Fairy Tales, founded in 1998 and held over a weekend in early summer, was a late, sporadic entry to the string of metropolitan queer festivals with impressive staying power. Brenda Lieberman is the most recent director. The festival's predecessor was the shortlived, "The Fire I've Become" organized by KEVIN D*SOUZA at the Glenblow Museum in 1995.

CAMPBELL, COLIN, 1942–2001. Video artist, filmmaker, writer, professor. The influential pioneer of English Canadian video art, Campbell was bred and educated in Manitoba and first taught at Mount Allison University before settling in Toronto, where he was a pillar of the art video community, teaching at OCAD and later University of Toronto. Over thirty years, the prolific Campbell produced more than fifty works, often incorporating his own brilliantly restrained transgender performance in such pieces as the wry *Woman from Malibu* (1976), and pushed the possibilities of video narrative towards unprecedented ambiguity and complexity without ever allowing it to lose its immediacy and direct impact.

Video pioneer Colin Campbell acting in the coming out melodrama thread of John Greyson's
naughty video *Jungle Boy* (1985), competing with the artist's pioneering hardcore inserts.
Video frame grab, VTape

One of the artist's earliest and queerest tapes, *I'm a Voyeur* (1974, 15),
came at a time when conceptual games with the new medium of art video
were becoming increasingly infused with the sexual tensions of voyeurism,
performance, and identity mutability. A minimalist long-take stare at the
narrator's neighbour's window yields minimal return at first as the lithe,
long-haired intellectual restricts himself to typing. But the prurient narrator's incantatory voice-over whispers to his target – "Do you know I've
been watching you? … do you see me? … I'm a voyeur." – seem to yield
fruit as the mysterious neighbour's banal everyday activities segue more
and more towards bathing and undressing, until he finally stares right back
at the voyeur-narrator. The mindfuck punchline for insiders or those
who've read the description is that the voyeur is really the exhibitionist –
both are performed by the artist – and that the two activities are inextricably caught up with each other. But even for non-insiders, the tape is an
intriguing and artful tease.

Fascinated by soap opera and voyeurism and always gently satirizing
the arch antics of art world denizens and the queer rebels alike – the bad,

the beautiful and the superficial – Campbell contributed perhaps more and earlier than anyone to the consolidation of video as a queer stronghold within the not always hip art scene in Canada in the seventies (see chapter 8). Honoured here and abroad, his collaboration with many other artists, including his former partners LISA STEELE and JOHN GREYSON, resulted in many vivid roles in others' works, such as the latter's *Jungle Boy* (1985) and *The ADS Epidemic* (1987). Campbell's anomalous 1991 film *Skin* (18) dramatized testimonies by women with AIDS, and he was awarded the prestigious Bell Canada Award in Video Art in 1996.

At Campbell's death, Greyson summed up the last two of ten basic lessons from "The Woman from Malibu's Video Art Academy and Finishing School" thus: "[number] 9, bad drag. Bad drag is better than good drag. Bad wigs are better than good wigs. Bad drag skips the surface and slams you right into the hunger of gender, the ten-year-old boy with the towel over his tits in the bathroom mirror pretending to be Elizabeth Taylor, terrified of being caught. Which brings us to [number] 10, narcissism, video as mirror, camera as confessional, the screen a pool of mercury: darkly beautiful, tremulous, on the verge of wonder, on the brink of tears. Only a narcissist as unflinching as Colin could stare into the lens with such honesty, and see himself so clearly. And know that through such a mirror he could see us" (2002b).

CANADA COUNCIL FOR THE ARTS. Among our slew of centralizing heritage and cultural institutions, scorecards for representing sexual diversity diverge greatly: National Gallery of Canada, B+; Canadian Broadcasting Corporation, C+; the Canadian Museum of Civilization, F; the National Film Board of Canada (see chapter 6), B. The Canada Council for the Arts gets A as the only agency with a steady and positive record of living up to its mandate of reflecting the sexual diversity of Canadian history, culture, and populations. Inaugurated in 1957, the council acknowledged cinema as a distinct discipline only in 1969, and video shortly thereafter. The council's grant-awarding protocol of peer juries composed of artists and its commitment to "parallel" institutions ensured that its largesse was always one step ahead of the so-called "taxpayers" in its support of artists belonging to sexual and gender minorities. The majority of the individuals and institutions in this portrait gallery have benefited at some point from council largesse, from TIMOTHY FINDLEY to DEANNA BOWEN, and although the community festivals were sometimes slow in figuring out a funding angle, they too all eventually lined up at one council spout or another. Though its sexual-diversity mandate has never been explicit, unlike its affirmative action programs around gender and around racial and aboriginal minorities, the council has been a principal funder of queer moving-image culture from coast to coast to coast for the last quarter century. Over the years, the council's defense of its arm's-length relationship to the powers that be has been steady, through vilification by the *Alberta Report* for its support of Kiss and Tell (see PERSIMMON BLACKBRIDGE), through Reform Party MPs' attacks on CYNTHIA ROBERTS's *Bubbles Galore*, through hell and high water.

CANADIAN BROADCASTING CORPORATION/RADIO CANADA. The public broadcaster founded in 1936 has an uneven record in addressing and reflecting its queer constituency. It's simplistic of course to generalize across current affairs and arts and dramac programming in a bicultural institution that is far from monolithic in the first place, with many central-izing and decentralizing pulls and voices. Nevertheless, the scorecard of the French side is somewhat better than the uptight anglo side, with its chronology of queer visibility in sitcoms, soap operas, and TV movies stretching back to the seventies (see MONTMORENCY and TREMBLAY). But does the unrestricted forum provided to arch-homophobe Denise Bombardier in the Radio-Canada current affairs division since the 1980s take away what the left hand hath given? If on the English side we should be thankful for Anne Murray and K.D. LANG specials, Kids in the Hall (see THOMPSON), CODCO, and Svend's coming out on *The Journal*, was it all cancelled out by the genocidal erasure of *Canada: A [Straight] People's History* (2000–01)? No, but ...

As an example of the public broadcaster's schizophrenic relationship with queer Canadians, take the network's offerings during that epochal winter of 1981, in which the attack on gay men by the Toronto police (see SUTHERLAND) shifted the paradigms of Canadian queer history. In Janu-ary, twenty-five days before the bathhouse raids, the network proudly broadcast John Kastner and Rose Kastner's "documentary," *Sharing the Secret*. This was its first-ever serious focus on sexual-identity politics, twelve years after Stonewall and following hard on the heels of the notori-ous CBS reportage *Gay Power, Gay Politics* (which had inaugurated the Reagan era by trial-ballooning the devastating backlash "special-rights" line on gay-lib politics). The Emmy-award-winning mother and son team's production up here was a "softer," "liberal" version of the U.S. backlash. But their ninety-minute portrait of a half dozen male Toronto subjects was carefully planned to weed out "activists" and to enable a sensationaliza-tion of maladjustment and melodrama, not to mention the usual media obsessions: promiscuity and tormented parents. Subsequent reporting in *TBP* uncovered instance after instance of manipulation and ethical viola-tion and unanimous feelings of violation among the subjects of the film, several of whom had been ludicrously disguised by the documentary duo. What is more, in a symbolically potent coincidence, the Kastners' camera had voyeuristically traced the exact route down the sauna corridors that the police were to follow with their bludgeons (Waugh and Rock 1981)!

Seventeen days after the raids, the network followed up with the broadcast of a second effort, this time in its prestigious "For the Record" docudrama slot, a prizewinning one-hour coming-out fiction, *Running Man,* directed by hetero-macho veteran documentarist Donald Brittain. The CBC's first queer-themed dramatic film depicted a married high-school track coach whose closet walls start crumbling when his star athlete comes out to him and then commits suicide. Guilt pushes the protagonist to confront his own identity. Brittain's hard-edged style did credit to a well-researched script, filmed on location in Toronto. Dialogue like the pickup line "Are you a pitcher or a catcher?" or the whispered confession "How many Hail Mary's for going down on a guy at the bus station?" were the talk of the pre-AIDS gay cocktail circuit from coast to coast. Anticipating the following year's Hollywood breakthrough *Making Love* in its focus on the breakup of a heterosexual marriage, *Running Man* faced criticism from *TBP* for its oblique angle on homosexuality and its all-straight collective authorship (December-January 1980–1, 28–9). But *Le Berdache*'s Bernard Courte praised the work for being "intensely realist," "non-exploitive," and salutary in its probing of the anguish of the closet (April 1981, 59). Courte would have probably been more in synch with the general response of gay audiences had it not been for the recent pogrom. As if in penance, Radio-Canada offered its own first lesbian-themed TV movie the following year (see MAHEUX-FORCIER). In short, three baby steps forward and one giant step back sums up the history of the *televisual* romance of transgression in Canada, a comprehensive book that remains to be written.

CANADIAN FILM AWARDS. A more or less continuous tradition since 1949 has honoured Canadian films in yearly awards and ceremonies, surviving almost six decades of the perennial industry doldrums and intranational flareups. The CFAs became the Etrogs in 1968 (after the trophy sculptor), and in 1980, with the founding of the industry-run Academy of Canadian Cinema and Television, they became the more bilingual-sounding Genies.

Not surprisingly, a considerable sampling of the more virulently homophobic output of our so-called national cinemas received major honours over the years, thanks to the forever erratic nomination and selection process, especially after the silence on sexual diversity lifted in the 1970s: *The Ernie Game* (Don Owen, NFB, 1968), *The Silent Partner* (Daryl Duke, 1978), *L'homme à tout faire* (Micheline Lanctôt, 1981), *The Bay Boy*

(Daniel Petrie, 1985), *Un zoo la nuit* (Jean-Claude Lauzon, 1988, a thirteen-award sweep including best film; see chapter 8.). And then there's the Academy's love affair with DAVID CRONENBERG, who received accolades for three of his more phobic outbursts, oozing anal typewriters and all: *Dead Ringers* (1989, best film, directing, screenplay), *Naked Lunch* (1992, best film, directing, screenplay), and *Crash* (1996, directing, screenplay).

What may be surprising is that, alongside this hall of infamy, so much of the queer canon has also received major nods: *Mouvement perpétuel* (CLAUDE JUTRA, 1950), *À tout prendre* (CLAUDE JUTRA, 1963), *Walking* (RYAN LARKIN, 1969, animation), *Fortune and Men's Eyes* (JOHN HERBERT, scenario 1971); *La vie rêvée* (MIREILLE DANSEREAU, 1972); *Dreamspeaker* (CLAUDE JUTRA, 1977, four awards), *Running Man* (DONALD BRITTAIN, CBC, 1981), *P4W: Prison for Women* (JANIS COLE and Holly Dale, 1982), *The Wars* (scenario TIMOTHY FINDLEY, 1984), DON HAIG (1985, outstanding contribution), *Perfectly Normal* (YVES SIMONEAU, 1991), *Le singe bleu* (ESTHER VALIQUETTE, 1993), *The Fairy Who Didn't Want to be a Fairy Anymore* (LAURIE LYND, 1993), *Exotica* (ATOM EGOYAN, 1994, including best supporting actor for the gay character), *Love and Human Remains* (BRAD FRASER, 1994, screenplay), *Le Confessionnal* (ROBERT LEPAGE, 1995), *Fiction and Other Truths: A Film about Jane Rule* (LYNNE FERNIE and AERLYN WEISSMAN, 1995), *Lilies* (John Greyson, 1996), *Maman et Ève* (Paul Carrière, 1996), *Sous-sol* (PIERRE GANG, 1996), *The Hanging Garden* (THOM FITZGERALD, 1997), *The Five Senses* (JEREMY PODESWA, 1999), *La Face cachée de la lune* (ROBERT LEPAGE, 2003), *Ryan* (Chris Landreth, 2004).

Ultimately, no doubt, the awards measure most the box office–driven whims of industry insiders from year to year, skewed as ever by Toronto-Montreal rivalries and by the collective low self-esteem that ensures knee-jerk valorization to those who make it abroad. But the awards also reflect – somehow ... inevitably – the centrality of the queer imaginary to the Canadian cinematic traditions.

CARDONA, DOMINIQUE, b. 1955, and Colbert, Laurie, b. 1958. Directors, scriptwriters. This Toronto-based, internationally recognized team contributed three films to the queer festival and feminist film circuits in the 1990s. Their documentaries *Thank God I'm a Lesbian* (1992, 55) and *My Feminism* (1997, 55) both received critical approval internationally for their lively and fresh spectrums of voices and issues (the former is more Canadian in focus, the latter international). The prizewinning *Below the Belt* (1999, 13 , TIFF) moved into new territory: it was a superbly crafted teenage-relationship drama showing lovers acting out their ups and downs in the boxing ring before the unexpected discovery that heterosexual mothers too are caught up in similar passions.

CARVER, BRENT, b. 1951. Actor. British Columbia–bred Carver is known best for his three-decades-long career as a leading man at Stratford and on Broadway (Tony Award, *Kiss of the Spider Woman*, 1993). In addition to *Kiss*, his contributions to queer theatre have been many, from FRASER to *Bent* to FINDLEY. However, Carver's major contribution to queer Canadian cinema rests on three strong lead performances alone, each indelibly marking a different decade and showcasing a different aspect of his prodigious talent: in Robin Phillips's star-crossed adaptation of Findley's World War I narrative *The Wars* (1982) as Robert, a tortured young officer whose angst about his masculinity and the world goes much deeper than shell shock; in JOHN GREYSON's *Lilies* (1996) as the cross-gender Comtesse, a deluded mother overwhelmed with love for her gay son; and in THOM FITZGERALD's *The Event* (2003) as Brian, the unflappable and committed director of a Manhattan AIDS community organization implicated in the assisted-suicide deaths of his terminally ill charges. A fey, trim blond whose intensity never leaves his sharp-featured face, however

Brent Carver in the first of three performances that have marked queer Canadian cinema: as Robert in Timothy Findley's *The Wars* (1982), a young officer whose angst about masculinity and violence goes deeper than shell shock. Production still, Cinémathèque québécoise

restrained his histrionics, on-screen Carver expresses a distinctly queer mix of melancholy, strength, risk, and obsession.

CHAPMAN, ALEXANDER, b. 1964. Actor. Quebec-bred, Dawson College-trained, Toronto-based Chapman is best known for his Genie-nominated role in JOHN GREYSON's *Lilies* (1996). As the lustful and lucid French aristocrat Lydie-Anne, the African Canadian Chapman was cast against type but burned up the screen in his liaison with St-Sebastian wannabe Simon. DANA INKSTER cast him next in a more subdued role as her community-building gay bartender in her short *Welcome to Africville* (1999). Also known by his nom de drag, Titty Galore, Chapman was brought back by Greyson for a supporting role as South African activist Simon Nkoli in his *Fig Trees* (2003). On stage, Chapman also played in Can-Stage's *Angels in America* and on TV on "Kids in the Hall" (as a drag queen who takes over the world).

CHONG, CHRISTOPHER, b. 1972. Animator. Toronto-based DIY film-maker Chong plied the queer festivals at home and abroad with quirky and experimental shorts in the late 1990s, often based on a deft and witty use of claymation. The most narrative, personal, and popular was *Crash Skid Love* (1998, 4), about a crush on a punk boy that ends up in a Christian Science Reading Room and in a dream about a dick that swings like a pendulum.

CHOW, SAMUEL, b. 1980. Video maker, visual artist. Hong Kong-bred, University of Toronto–trained Chow was an *Xtra!* prodigy coverboy in 2003, the year he produced three intimate queer video shorts on themes of cultural- and sexual-identity adjustments. The most ambitious, *Banana Boy* (2003, 7), successfully integrated English with Cantonese and personal family melodrama with Tienanmen Square massacre footage, all culminating in a coming out that is like bursting out of a bathtub full of water where you can't breathe.

CICCORITTI, JERRY (GERARD), b. 1956. The co-founder of Toronto's Buddies in Bad Times Theatre way back in the early 1980s (with SKY GILBERT), queer-friendly Ciccoritti went on to become a dependable commercial genre director, moving more or less effortlessly back and both between TV movies and the big screen and between Canada and the United States. Ciccoritti is an interesting example of a director who makes discreet and not-so-discreet queer films about nonqueer subjects, for example, that allusive campfest of a political biopic *Trudeau* (2002). Or his prizewinning *The Life before This* (1999), an observant Toronto comedy-drama about

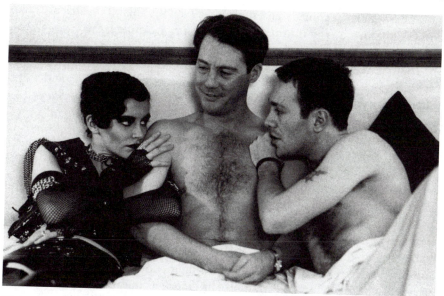

Triangular ambiguity in the queerest feature ever made by a queer-friendly maker, *Paris France* (Jerry Ciccoritti, 1993). The bisexual boxer-poet (right) fucks the whole cast and can't keep his clothes on or his pubic hairdo consistent. Production still, Film Reference Library

the randomness of everyday life and relationships, which surprises halfway through when a romantic hetero-flirtation scene suddenly shifts into a bold but nuanced coming-out scene. My all-time guilty pleasure is the queerest feature ever made in Canada, if not the world, *Paris France* (1993), an inspired, literate and expertly performed melodrama about horny, needy writers. Peter Outerbridge plays a hot, bisexual boxer-poet who can't keep his clothes on and has wild sex with everyone else in the movie. Understandably, this scary, arty, sexy potboiler divided the critics like nothing else, appearing on both ten-best lists and ten-worst lists – an important accomplishment in itself.

COBURN, WENDY, b. 1963. Sculptor, teacher, videomaker. Trained at Concordia and OCAD (where she went on to teach), Toronto-based Coburn is best known for such unsettling public art objects as her cunnilingus allegory *The Spirit of Canada Eating Beaver*, cast in bronze for Pride 2000. Her two videos circulated within artists' spaces and queer community festivals in the early 2000s. *My Heart Divine* (2001, 4) was both part of NIKKI FORREST and NELSON HENRICKS's enigmatic conceptual "heart" series and a fleshed-out, autonomous gloss on the ancient art of water dowsing, where the analogy between the divining rod and the strap-on seems highly metaphysical.

CODCO. Television comedy ensemble. The Newfoundland theatrical troupe, founded in 1973, initially included, among others, the Jones siblings, Cathy and Andy, as well as the gay sometimes couple Greg Malone (b. 1948) and Tommy Sexton (1955–94). Their outrageous satire was first recorded on celluloid through the St John's film co-op Nifco and was remarkable for its distinctly queer edge, whether in *Sisters of the Silver Scalpel* (1981, 13), which inaugurated a distinctively Newfoundland version of queer-nun drag, or in *Outport Lesbians* (1985, 4). After intermittent appearances on the small screen, Codco finally got a regular full-season slot on the CBC in 1989 and lasted seven seasons, despite frequent censorship, until Sexton's death from AIDS in 1994. As a troupe, their caricatures often depended on gender masquerade (Malone's Barbara Frum and Queen Elizabeth were the highlights). The gay partners' queer-themed sketches were much more politically topical than the equivalent material being presented during the same period by Kids in the Hall (Andy Jones quit in 1991 after the network squelched their Mount Cashel pedophile priest sketches). Sexton and Malone's brilliance as queer satirists is memorialized in *Tommy: A Family Portrait* (Mary Sexton and Nigel Markham, NFB, 2001, 71; see chapter 6.). After his partner's death, Malone maintained his career as an actor, director, and political activist. In Mary Walsh's CBC extension of the Codco legacy, *This Hour Has 22 Minutes* (1993+), Rick Mercer (b. 1969) continued the troupe's tradition of openly gay performers, but his repertory lacked the explicit queer sensibility of his mentors.

COHENE, ALEESA, b. 1976. Videomaker, visual artist. Inspired by the political import of found footage, Toronto-based Cohene was trained at York, OCAD, and the International Academy of Design. Her three videos of the early 2000s challenged the received configuration of both the planet and the body. Programmed at Inside Out, *Absolutely* (2003, 8) took on globalization in its intermingled iconography of protestors dragged away by police, clips from *Soldier Girls* (1981) showing young female black and Latina recruits at a U.S. boot camp chanting their fanatical desire to kill "an Iranian," and strange expert interviews that fade in and out of their critical edge. Cohene has often collaborated as photographer and otherwise on the Toronto queer radical circuit.

COLE, JANIS, b. 1954; HOLLY DALE, b. 1953. Documentarists. This pioneering feminist documentary team has produced a rich and diverse oeuvre, together and apart. Largely steering clear of explicitly lesbian projects, their films, almost always independently financed, have consistently shown a deep, impassioned, and unconditional identification with women who

Brilliant queer satirists Tommy Sexton (left) and Greg Malone in Codco clip excerpted in *Tommy: A Family Portrait* (2001). Video frame grab, used with permission of the National Film Board of Canada

are on the edge, whether sexually or socially. Cole and Dale started their collaboration at Sheridan College in the 1970s and already expressed an interest in sexual and social marginality in their early shorts: *Cream Soda* (1976), about sex trade workers; *Minimum Charge No Cover* (1976), about Yonge Street sexual outlaws; and *The Thin Blue Line* (1977), about detainees in an institution for the criminally insane.

Cole and Dale's important first feature breakthrough may also be their most explicit lesbian work, but it followed the day's fashion for treading ambiguously along the line of homosociality: *P4W: Prison for Women* (1981, 58 , Genie). This documentary version of *Caged* and its dozens of B movie "women behind bars" genre successors is more gripping than the lot of them combined. It wasn't easy for Dale and Cole to get permission to film within Kingston's notorious Prison for Women, but they were finally allowed in. Basically a portrait of five of the women, the film never uses the L or D words, perhaps out of a sense of ethical commitment to the subjects, perhaps because the early-1980s context still favoured discretion. But things are very clear, and long before butch-femme became fashionable again, the subcultural universe is full of codes of sexual identities, tonsorial and other. Most compelling is the portrait of the devoted couple Janise and Debby, lipstick lesbians before their time, who will be separated for twenty years as soon as the latter's imminent discharge comes up. They perform croquet and makeup for the camera, but the intensity of their relationship cannot be so easily avoided. Unlike similar institutional documentaries, such as those of the American Frederick Wiseman, *P4W* was not interested in the banal and benign prison officials, concentrating on the prisoners, their stories, their experiences, and their relationships between each other. When this low-budget independent work bowed at the 1981 Toronto Festival, its groundbreaking importance was immediately recognized by more than one lesbian critic:

It is the first time in Canada, to my knowledge, that the love of two women for each other is presented as entirely positive, a needed support, growthful, with no compulsion to discover why this came about or whether they couldn't find greater satisfaction with men or any of the qualifiers normally attached to a lesbian relationship if it ever manages to find its way onscreen. It is undoubtedly not coincidental that this "first" is in the context of a women's prison, so that in fact there is an implicit qualifier – there are no men available to these women. If this makes it easier for the audience to accept the relationship as valid, well, it's a first foot in the door. (Martineau 1981)

One particularly heart-wrenching portrait in the film, of Marlene Moore, a self-abusing "slasher," led to Cole's prizewinning, more experimental follow-up profile *Shaggie: Letters from Prison* (*Five Feminist Minutes*, NFB, 1990), an elegy for a victim not only of society but also of her own hand (the basis also for the duo's prizewinning later TV movie *Dangerous Offender*, CBC 1996).

After *P4W* came *Hookers on Davie* (1984, 86), an ahead-of-its-time exploration of the Vancouver world of street prostitution (female, male, and transgendered). Winning the pair their second Genie, this "direct cinema" epic on the world of street prostitution in Vancouver maintained Dale and Cole's exemplary solidarity with marginal and disenfranchised – and resistant – subjects. Confronting taboos of moralism and invisibility at the height of the sex wars, the filmmakers' ethnography/manifesto coincided with the Trudeau government's investigation into prostitution and pornography through the Fraser Commission. After two months in Vancouver's famous tenderloin area, Dale and Cole convinced their half dozen lively subjects to work while hooked up with radio microphones, and the result is both tender and in your face, even coming perilously close, were it not for their customary intense complicity, to the risks of voyeurism. *TBP* gave the film its fervent thumbs up – "the chance to compare our own sexual-minority-turned-subculture with another" – but had reservations about its ambiguity around "contradictions that could have been enlightening if they'd been explored." CHRIS BEARCHELL also suggested an interesting remedy in her *TBP* review: "political analysis can best be done from the inside, looking out. Next time, the prostitutes should step out of the roles

Inmate couple Janise and Debbie, lipstick lesbians before their time, soon to be separated, perform makeup for the camera in the Kingston toilet, in Janis Cole and Holly Dale's carefully ambiguous but compellingly clear *P4W: Prison for Women* (1981), VHS frame grab

of characters, subjects, victims, get their hands on the cameras and aim them not simply at each other, but at the world that shapes the lives of hookers on Davie Street" (no. 103 [May 1984], 31). Two decades later, prostitution has still not been decriminalized, and bawdy house laws are still used against both their subculture and ours.

The duo's next major project, *Calling the Shots* (1988), treated women directors in the film industry but lacked the edge of their earlier work, perhaps because women filmmakers have their guard up in front of the camera, perhaps because the intensity of marginality was missing. The two women's working and personal partnership dissolved in the late 1980s, and Dale attended the CFC, eventually trying her hand at a less-than-successful vampire film, *Blood and Donuts* (1995). Although both artists worked in individual directions throughout the 1990s, occasional collaborations were possible. In her definitive article on the duo, Kay Armatage found that despite its generic disparity, *Dangerous Offender* was typical of the two women's oeuvre as a whole in its confrontation with class and its "commitment to realism coupled with empathy and an exacting refusal of liberal mythologizing" (2002). Armatage, however, perhaps because of the filmmakers' discretion, did not consider sexual orientation a relevant category for Canadian cinema's most sustained and resilient oeuvre about lipstick lesbians, bulldykes, transpeople, and hustlers. Over the last decade,

Dale worked largely on commercials and television series, while Cole taught writing at OCAD.

COLE, KEITH, b. 1965. Performer, director, producer, public relations person. Thunder Bay–bred, York-trained, LIFT p.r.-person Keith Cole is sometimes referred to as *the* "tap-dancing drag queen" and came into film and video through theatre and performance. His first video was *Toilet* (1996), based on a performance about surveillance and pornography. He then moved into celluloid, producing and starring in *Nancy Boy versus Manly Woman* (director Erwin Abesamis, 1997, 27), a maniacal narrative about a fey superhero and comic strip artist who likes popsicles, psychotherapy, and pounding schnitzel. Subsequent works such as *I Think I'm Coming Down with Something* (about crabs, 2003, 4) continue in a similar performance-based vein. A cameo cast performer from the first *Queer as Folk* season, Cole has collaborated with local queer experimentalists from MICHAEL CAINES to SKY GILBERT, who called him "just about the gayest man on earth besides moi."

COLLINS, DAVID (b. 1961, videomaker, writer, theatre director, activist), and Ian Jarvis, (b. 1969, videomaker, drag performer, curator, activist). University of Toronto–trained Collins and OCAD-trained Jarvis have made many short videos, both separately and as a prolific team, since the beginning of the nineties. Among their recurrent themes are memory and loss, desire, aging, and the vulnerability and innocence of youth (*Something Died with Johnny*, 1998, 4; *My Springtime Days*, 1999, 2; *Honey Bunny*, 1999, 2 , starring gay Toronto's elder statesman George Hislop). Among their best works is the moody, nocturnal *Love Sex Poetry* (1996, 5), about romance and jazz. Collins and Jarvis are also astute documentarists, whether with the tongue-in-prepuce *Peckers – Patrick and Paul Get Pierced* (1997, 7) or the respectful essay on haircutting as a queer profession, *Vain but Cheap* (1998, 7). A frequent collaborator with the duo is ED SINCLAIR.

COMEAU, RICHARD, b. 1960. Editor. A talented stalwart of the hip young queer mafia of Quebec cinema, Concordia-trained Comeau was a part of MANON BRIAND's creative team on all her films, edited JEANNE CRÉPEAU'S innovative *Le Film de Justine* (1989), and more recently edited such big-gun queer-flavoured commercial fare as *C't'à ton tour Laura Cadieux* (original novel by MICHEL TREMBLAY, director Denise Filiatrault, 1998) and ÉMILE GAUDREAULT's *Mambo Italiano* (2003).

COUNTING PAST TWO. Toronto's Transsexual, Intersex and Transgender Film/Video/Arts Festival was founded in 1998 by activist/artist MIRHA-

SOLEIL ROSS, in recognition of the distinctive cultural and economic situation of trans communities. Taken over in 2002 by multimedia artists Boyd Kodak and Cat Grant for its most recent rendition, at the University of Toronto, the event billed itself as the largest trans festival in the world and offered a rich multiformat lineup. Kodak and Grant's own lively media work includes *The Misadventures of Pussy Boy* (2001, 4), as well as the well-known activist video broadside *Shadsmith Manzo Performance* (1998, 6), about the eponymous Mexican Canadian trans community activist deported that year into a Mexican context marked by murdered transgendered women and the campaign to bring her back.

COWELL, LAURA, b. 1968. Video- and filmmaker, playwright, performer. OCAD-trained, Toronto-based Cowell may be Canada's Sadie Benning, a prolific producer since 1990 of handmade personal miniatures, often based on her own performances. *Can You Say Androgynous?* (1991, 1) is a static one-shot manifesto showing the topless artist flipping placards to offset the hasslers who question her public butch persona ("Why is it so important to know if I have a penis or not?"), with a final teaser glimpse of authorial breasts before it's all over. Cowell founded the Splice This Super 8 festival in 1998 with KELLY O'BRIEN and has also collaborated with MICHAEL ACHTMAN, ROBERT KENNEDY, R.M. Vaughan, and CHRISTINA ZEIDLER.

COYOTE, IVAN E, b. 1969. Writer, musician, video maker. Whitehorse-bred, Vancouver-based, gender-indifferent Coyote is a distinguished fiction writer who won the Gerry Brunet Award at Inside Out for her video *Transmission* (1998, 7), a snapshot of a fantasy transgendered family: "Sometimes I want to be just like my Dad when I grow up – but without the scars." His tape "crosses gender boundaries with a Western feel," said the catalogue for the eastern TranSpective: The New England International Transgender Film and Video Festival.

CRANSTON, TOLLER, b. 1949. Figure skater, painter. This book is not about figure skaters, but when Ontario-born, Quebec-trained Cranston innovated, transformed, and outed male figure skating in the 1970s, he did so as a queer international television star. His defiant insistence on "being myself" allowed future generations of boys and men to transcend the uptight skating world and express androgynous styles, bodies, and feelings. Cranston was the subject of the biodoc *InTollerance* (Sylvia Sweeney, CBC, 2001, 42), which despite a wooden narration and denial discourse from both filmmaker and the recycled painter in his Mexican refuge ("[figure skating] has nothing to do with sexual orientation ... movement, feeling, emotion doesn't have a gender"), includes awesome period performance footage and tributes from Cranston's successor, outed champion Brian Orser.

CRAWFORD, JEFFREY, b. 1965. Arts administrator, curator. UNB-trained Crawford has been the indefatigable distribution coordinator at Toronto's CFMDC since 1995. Curating programs of Canadian queer film at community festivals at home (from Vancouver to Toronto) and abroad (London, Toykyo, Miami, South Africa, Melbourne, etc.), Crawford is responsible more than anyone else for Canadian short filmmakers finding an audience, usually funded by federal agencies that Crawford has diligently wooed and won. In 2001 Crawford offered San Francisco's Frameline, on the quarter-century anniversary of this mother of all queer community fests, an assortment of Canadian queer kitchen films called "Cooking with Canucks," which may take the cake.

CRÉPEAU, JEANNE, b. 1961. Director, video maker, scriptwriter, producer. Trained at the NFB and the CFC, Jeanne Crépeau was the first openly lesbian filmmaker from Quebec to make the rounds of international queer community festivals with her prizewinning short films and videos. In them, urban gals are caught up in romantic relationships and *peine d'amour*: *L'usure* (By Attrition, 1986, 8), *Gerçure* (The Flu, video, 1988, 18), and *Le film de Justine* (Justine's Film, 1989, 45).

Reflected in these short works, Crépeau's interest in lesbian romance, her skill at directing actors in both dialogue and gestural comedy, and her aesthetic taste for hybrid forms all resurface in her first feature *Revoir Julie* (*Julie and Me*, 1998, 92; see chapter 5). A whimsical and tender postmodern romance shot in the tranquil Cantons de l'Est, the bilingual, bi-zonal *Revoir Julie* is much more of the quintessential Montreal lesbian feature than Léa Pool's entries into the stakes. Blonde Anglo twenty-something Juliet is recovering from a bad breakup and goes to find her old school friend, brunette Julie, esconced in the *pure laine* heartland where birds sing and hammocks swing gently. Instead of sympathy Juliet discovers love and brings Julie back to her funky Plateau apartment for a happy ending. A perennial presenter of her short films about stressed relationships since the 1980s, Crépeau was not able to cobble together a bare-bones budget for shooting this first feature until the end of the 1990s and then had to cut scenes and characters that might have sketched in a little more texture and context. But Crépeau made up for modest means with sparkling dialogue, resourceful intertextuality, and spirited performances (especially by the Chaplinesque STEPHANIE MORGENSTERN). Crépeau is also a strong activist in the Montreal milieu for artisanal and independent cinema.

CRONENBERG, DAVID, b. 1943. Director. English Canada's most famous and prolific heterosexual feature filmmaker is poet of the flesh in mutant revolt, nightmare imaginer of interfaces of body and machine. Far from including Cronenberg as an honorary queer, this listing simply can't exclude the obsessive homophobe who can't stay away, the publicly funded Canadian exporter of images of corporeal and sexual perversity around the world, whether as strip miner and sanitizer of queer canons (e.g., *Naked Lunch*, 1991; *M. Butterfly*, 1993) or as mythologizer of queer revulsion (*Dead Ringers*, 1988) and existential despair. Traumatized by fantasies of penetration of the male body from the start, whether via phallic parasite (*Shivers*, 1975), pulsating mutant video cassette (*Videodrome*, 1982), or errant tongue/plug (*ExistenZ*, 1999), Cronenberg resolves the stress by littering the landscape with dead queers (to name only a few of the most recent and prominent, the brothers Mantle in *Dead Ringers*, 1988; Song Liling in *M. Butterfly*, 1993; Vaughan in *Crash*, 1995), as Christine Ramsay has shown [1999]).

CUTHAND, THIRZA, b. 1978. Videomaker. Cuthand is one of the most inventive and prolific of young video artists of the baby dyke generation. Born in Saskatchewan of Cree and Scots descent, she broke into the international queer festival circuit with the wry, self-reflexive three-minute *Lessons in Baby Dyke Theory* (1995) even before completing her fine arts degree at Vancouver's ECIAD. Recipient of many distinctions, her work is raw, intimate, ironic, sexy, and taboo-shattering, as in the SM-charged *Helpless Maiden Makes an "I" Statement* (1999) or *Untouchable* (1998), an autobiographical reflection on intergenerational eroticism. Her tapes were featured in First Nations contexts such as the exhibition Exposed: Aesthetics of Aboriginal Erotic Art (Regina, 1999). That same year's *Through the Looking Glass*, an allegorical video pageant, is her most explicit confrontation with her native heritage and the identity and cultural conflicts entailed. With *Anhedonia* (2001 – the title is a technical term for a symptom of depression, the inability to experience pleasure), she branched out into new territory, dealing with characteristic frankness with her own bipolar condition, assembling a tough visual and verbal iconography of corporal abjection and psychic despair. In the 2000s, Cuthand relocated to Montreal, the site of her 2000 solo retrospective, curated by GIV and La Centrale Galerie Powerhouse.

CZACH, LIZ, b. 1965. Curator, critic. Toronto-based, University of Toronto– and Concordia-trained Czach was an important force in the early years of Inside Out and led a successful lobby to maintain Toronto Metro Council funding for the beleaguered festival. From 1990 to 1995 Czach also programmed at the Pleasure Dome, Toronto's edgy indie venue, the home of innovative year-round queer lineups. Starting in 1995 Czach was programmer for Perspective Canada at TIFF, collaborating with DAVID MCINTOSH

Thirza Cuthand broke into the international queer-festival circuit with her student video, the self-reflexive and self-presenting *Lessons in Baby Dyke Theory* (1995). Video frame grab, Working Baby Dyke Theory: The Diasporic Impact of Cross Generational Barriers, Thirza Cuthand, 1997

in support of up-and-coming queer auteurs from GREYSON to LEPAGE (though lesbian features emerged more slowly) and thus reinforcing a local queer film culture that resonated from the metropolis to the hinterland and abroad.

DANSEREAU, MIREILLE, b. 1943. Director, scriptwriter, editor, producer. Educated at Université de Montréal and London's Royal College of Art and mentored at the NFB, prolific feminist filmmaker Dansereau is best known to queer audiences for the first independent feature made in Quebec by a woman, *La vie rêvée* (Dream Life, 1972, 85). This modernist, feminist narrative of two young women's friendship soon became appropriated by lesbian audiences, especially in English Canada, for the sensual ambiguity of the characters' friendship and personal/political awakening. The reading of the film's lesbian subtext by such critics as Jean Bruce (1999) was all the more compelling since 1970s lesbian feminism itself had built on the political continuum between homosociality and homo-eroticism and Canadian lesbians had to wait until well into the 1980s for their first explicitly insider lesbian feature film, whether in English or in French. Upon reviving the film thirty years later, Dansereau emphatically declared her heterosexuality, but retroactive authorial intention or identity

The homosocial heroines of Mireille Dansereau's oft-subtexted 1972 narrative feature *La vie rêvée* (Dream Life, 1972). This bedtime consciousness-raising scene suggests why this friendship film became appropriated by lesbian audiences. Production still, Cinémathèque québécoise

do not always determine a work's meaning for a generation crossing the cinematic desert.

DAVIES, NICHOLAS, b. 1970. Critic, programmer, actor. McGill-trained, Toronto-based Davies has been an influential programmer for both TIFF and Inside Out, as well as a juror for queer film festivals both at home and abroad. As a frequent film critic for *Xtra!* since the late 1990s, he is known for his broad cinematic culture, reliable taste, and unflinching hype avoidance. In a former life, Davies was known for key roles (pseudonym Klaus von Brucker) in Bruce LaBruce's *No Skin off My Ass* (1991) and *Super 8½* (1994). The "These Boots Are Made for Walking" dance and bathtub sex scenes in the former film alone guarantee a place in this book, if not immortality.

DAY, DENNIS, b. 1960. Videomaker, editor. Newfoundland-bred, Toronto-trained, Montreal-transplanted Dennis Day is one of the leading lights of the OCAD pomo homo video movement. His sensibility is distinct, and it's as an editor and collagist that he shines, enamoured of bright primary colours, pink pastiche and 'ppropriation, sexy allegory, frontal perform-ance, and the precise, technically flawless but nongimmicky deployment of all those 1980s art video gimmicks. My favourite is *Auto Biography* (1994), a witty reconstruction of a Newfoundland queer coming-of-age, complete with swishy fashion struts chroma-keyed onto the runway of the local wharf (see chapter 5). For all his playfulness Day has also been capa-ble of profound emotion, as in his AIDS cycle, coproduced with Montreal dancer Ian Middleton and culminating in the elegiac, prizewinning *Heaven or Montreal* (1997). Finished four years after Middleton's death from HIV, this tape features an austere and intense Middleton performance editorially paired with another, older woman dancer and many conditional state-ments of intent ("If he had not died, we would have ...). After a pause, Day returned in 2001 with the prizewinning *This Narrative is Killing Me,* a self-reflexive story of a gay vampire wandering and channel-surfing through history and mythologies. Day's virtuoso editing was also behind the haute couture of JOHN GREYSON's *Un©ut,* and contributed to the work of numerous other artists, including BALASS, BOCIURKIW, FERNIE, FUNG, and HOOLBOOM.

DEACON, CHRIS, b.1965. Director. Montreal-bred, Ryerson-trained Deacon presented several short comic fiction films within the queer festival circuit in the 1990s, including *Twisted Sheets* (1996, 14), a well-crafted comedy about a scriptwriter exacting lesbian revenge on her unfaithful boyfriend by stealing his new girlfriend, and the Genie-winning *Moving Day* (1998, 23; TIFF), about a heterosexual couple in crisis. Queer-friendly Deacon's earlier drama *Between Friends* (1991, 13) treated the subject of women and AIDS, and she also established television credits in the United States and Canada, including *Degrassi: The Next Generation* (see SCHUYLER).

DEMAS, PETER, b. 1963. Director, scriptwriter, actor. Trained at the University of Western Ontario, Ryerson, and the CFC, Toronto-based, award-winning Peter Demas contributed several short comedies to the fes-tival circuit beginning in 1993. *The Soldier Boy* (1995, 27, TIFF) anticipat-ed the Australian *Head On* in its anguished melodrama of sexual diversity and errant offspring within a Greek immigrant family (including the son's black boyfriend, who eventually turns up in Greek national costume). *Straight in the Face* (2002, 12, TIFF) overturns family melo conventions in depicting two gay dads' worries that their daughter's chosen boyfriend might not be straight enough.

Pomo homo video artist Dennis Day's *Auto Biography* (1994) is a witty reconstruction of a Newfoundland queer coming-of-age, complete with swishy fashion struts chroma-keyed onto the runway of the local wharf. VHS frame grab

DEMERS, GLORIA, 1941–89. Scriptwriter, editor. Originally trained as an editor at the NFB, Montreal-bred Gloria Demers was one of the pillars of, and unobtrusive lesbian creative forces within, the flourishing women's Studio D throughout the 1980s (see chapter 6). She first made her mark as the writer for the epic feminist documentaries *Behind the Veil: Nuns* (MARGARET WESCOTT, 1984), *Speaking Our Peace* (1985), and *Goddess Remembered* (1989), all discreet explorations of the homosocial/homoerotic continuum.

Demers may be remembered chiefly as the scriptwriter for the hit homosocial docudrama *The Company of Strangers* (1990, director Cynthia Scott, Studio D/NFB, 101). One of the most critically acclaimed, canonized, and popular Canadian features of the 1990s, this work follows eight elderly women marooned in the splendidly pastoral countryside of the Laurentians – *Survivor* before its time. Director Scott is a queer-friendly heterosexual, and only one of the characters is openly lesbian (MARY MEIGS), but another, Catherine, is openly butch, talented at motor mechanics, and, er, married to God. Nevertheless, *Company* was successfully marketed as part of the NFB lesbian and gay package of the nineties, perhaps because Meigs and, above all, Demers had vital input. Otherwise the film is less about explicit sexual identity than about the blurred boundaries within a diverse Studio D "bomber crew" community of women. Meigs's coming out scene to her pal Cissy while bird-watching in the marsh is one of the most understated and sweet-tempered in queer film history ("That's nice, dear!"). But otherwise Meigs is mysteriously absent when the others talk about such things as falling in love.

Demers's recruitment of Meigs as the ensemble cast's not-so-token "out" lesbian was affectionately recounted in the latter's memoirs of the production after Demers's premature death from lung cancer at the peak of her creative career. *Company* and both of the other explicit NFB dyke epics of the 1990s, *Forbidden Love* and *Stolen Moments* are all dedicated to her, and that speaks.

DEMPSEY, SHAWNA (b. 1963), and MILLAN, LORRI (b. 1965). Videomakers, performance artists. The zany Winnipeg performance art duo caught everyone's attention in 1990 with *We're Talking Vulva*, their rap music film about female genitalia (codirector Tracy Treager), which as part of Studio D's anthology *Five Feminist Minutes*, brought the clitoris into a lot of unexpected places and is estimated to have reached more than a million viewers worldwide. The most rambunctious of the series's "implicit" shorts, *Vulva* came from the spunky Winnipeg arts scene but tied in well with the NFB's historical educational mandate as a vernacular work instructing its audience about female genitalia. The throwaway lesbian references in the performance come within the traditional inclusive feminist spectrum, even though such bold and naughty cunt-in-your-face subversiveness left no one guessing (see chapters 6 and 10).

Fleeing the NFB nest, Dempsey was to follow up, in collaboration with Millan, with a series of irreverent videos that moved rather quickly from the feminist implicit to the dyke explicit. Dempsey and Millan, erstwhile life partners, went on a prizewinning roll of ten video productions, most featuring their own inimitable performances. Each tape is unique, but all deployed the women's famous deadpan wit, their pop postmodern flair for sculptural costume and décor, their genius for pastiching trash narrative forms such as nature documentary, and their delight in sending up the foibles – as well as the pleasures – of identity conformism, community, and essentialism. Hyperactive, pixie-like Dempsey was equally evocative in a day-glo Medusa fright wig (*Medusa Raw*, 1992, 9) and a 1950s cutout housedress (*Good Citizen Betty Baker*, 1996, 27). Millan's distinctively solid and earthly body is up front in tattoo and undershirt in *Day in the Life of a Bull Dyke* (1995, 10) and has also moved through videos by Montreal's ANNE GOLDEN, such as *Brothers* (1998). Among the most popular and perennial Canadian lesbian voices at queer community festivals around the world, Dempsey and Millan also have had a symbiotic relationship with artist-run spaces from coast to coast, especially their motherhouse, Winnipeg's Video Pool.

D'ENTREMONT, PAUL ÉMILE, b. 1966. Documentarist. Moncton- and Dalhousie-trained Acadian d'Entremont, a Halifax-based Radio-Canada director, is familiar to queer audiences primarily for his tender and lyrical film on identity and difference, *Seuls, ensemble* (*Alone, Together*, NFB,

2000, 25). D'Entremont's portraits of a gay man's and an adopted woman's search for roots and belonging are parallelled with each other in the context of questions of Acadian community and heritage. The result is one of the more quietly seductive queer documentaries from the Atlantic region.

DIAMOND, SARA, b. 1954. Video maker, producer, arts administrator, curator, teacher, critic. An SFU graduate and teacher at ECIAD (1985–91), the New York–born "red diaper baby" was brought up in Toronto and settled in 1978 in Vancouver, where she became a key figure and pioneer in Vancouver video art and activism. As one of the five-member feminist collective Amelia Productions, Diamond contributed to what is probably the earliest dyke-activist videotape in Canada, the rough-hewn but passionate conference document *Lesbians against the Right* (1981, 45). Although the main thrust of Diamond's own video art within such frameworks as the Women's Labour History Project is less interested specifically in queer identities, its exploration of the artist's personal genealogy, as well as gendered and class history in British Columbia, situates both in relation to the lesbian/homosocial continuum. She assumed the influential post of artistic director, media and visual arts, at the Banff Centre in 1992, where her legendary support of queer video and interdisciplinary media art made Banff a queer cultural garrison in Alberta. There Diamond stamped a whole generation of Canadian and international queer video work, from the AIDS-activist safe-sex series of the early nineties to residency-produced tapes such as RICHARD FUNG's *Dirty Laundry* (1996) and the American Gregg Bordowitz's *Fast Trip Long Drop* (1993). Diamond received the Bell Canada Award in Video Art, 1995, and became president of OCAD in 2005.

DICKIE, BONNIE, b. 1947. Documentarist. A veteran of CBC radio and TV in the Northwest Territories and then feminist director/producer at Winnipeg's Prairie Centre of the NFB, Bonnie Dickie is best known for *Sandra's Garden* (1990), part of the government studio's original Gay & Lesbian Video Collection (1994; see chapter 6). A lyrical and emotional portrait of women gathered around abuse survivor Sandra (who has cowriter and codirector credit), the eponymous garden is a healing space full of music, flowers, water, courageous first-person voice-over, and lesbian alternative families. A perennial social-issue activist and collaborative filmmaker, Dickie pursued her interest in abuse recovery in her award-winning, aboriginal-themed documentary *Hollow Water* (2000).

DIONNE, LOUIS, b. 1964. Video maker, AIDS activist. Montreal-based, self-trained Dionne converged his two vocations and in the 1990s made a distinctive contribution to queer cultural politics in that city. *Le Bain de M. Soleil* (The Bath of Mr Sun, 1994, 35) is a participatory excursion to a parkland cruising area that becomes a sex-radical investigation of queer sex – part porno, part ethnography, part lyrical landscape art, part political analysis of safe sex, video voyeurism, and risk. In the next year's *Comment vous dirais-je?* (How Would I Tell You?, 32), a bold and unsettling documentary, the artist comes out to his parents as HIV+ on-camera. Active in Montreal's Image + Nation festival, Dionne facilitated short videos by five HIV+ authors that were presented at the 1995 festival as *Le Sida n'est pas une maladie honteuse ... N'est-ce pas?* Since then Dionne's camera has been active in both the Montreal HIV/AIDS community and the porno network, shooting and editing *2000 bites* (2000 Cocks, Paul Finaki, 2001).

DIRTY PILLOWS. The Toronto-based trio composed of York-trained Mishann Lau, Concordia-trained Angela Phong, and "Miss Bea" caught attention in 2003 with the first Toronto lesbian porno production *Pornograflics* (see chapter 8). This slick collection of raunchy episodes set in shops, kitchens and bedrooms, and garages of the queer city maintained the impulse of erotic pedagogy and community responsibility alongside the horny fun and became a hit at the major Canadian queer video festivals. Earlier, Lau was known for *Come and Go* (1998, 13), an erotic dyke-bar fantasy, and Phong for *Far Away* (1992), a one-minute nuclear family encounter around a very large zucchini.

DI STEFANO, JOHN, b. 1963. Video and interdisciplinary maker, curator, teacher. Montreal-bred, Concordia-trained, New Zealand–based di Stefano is best known on the queer circuit for *Tell Me Why: The Epistemology of Disco* (1991, 24), a funny and celebratory but political analysis of the role of disco culture in queer identity. His 2000 video HUB (2000, 22) was about airport space, not surprisingly a personal issue for the artist, and his 2002 exhibition "Je me souviens" treated his hero, Pier Paolo Pasolini, the Italian queer communist filmmaker/poet.

DONOVAN, PAUL, b. 1954. Producer, director. Dalhousie- and London Film School–trained Donovan is best known as the Halifax mogul who since the 1980s has run, with his brother Michael, the private-sector regional success story Salter Street Films, responsible in recent years for *This Hour has 22 Minutes* (see CODCO). The presumed heterosexual Donovan merits a footnote in Canadian queer film history for *Siege* (a.k.a. *Self-Defense*, 1982), one of the early, rare queer-positive features during the capital-cost-allowance period. Programmed at one of the first Toronto queer festivals (Harbourfront, 1985), *Siege* is a prizewinning, self-financed low-budget actioner, inspired by the recent Halifax police strike, pitting vigilante thugs against gay and lesbian characters, who (uncharacteristically, for the time) fight back.

DOUGLAS, DEBBIE, b. 1961, and GABRIELLE MICALLEF, b. 1960. Video makers, AIDS activists. These Caribbean-Canadian, Toronto-based arts activists are known to queer audiences chiefly for their impressive debut video *AnOther Love Story: Women and AIDS* (1990, 30). This strongly scripted and acted didactic narrative about a Caribbean-descended lesbian community and an interracial couple coming to grips with fear, denial, and prejudice about HIV was produced within the cable access project spearheaded by BALSER and GREYSON at the end of the 1980s. After being blocked from the airwaves, the tape circulated nonstop within educational and community organizations and its happy ending, dental dams and all, stayed relevant as the years exacerbated the gendered epidemiology of HIV.

DOUGLAS, WILLIAM, 1953–96. Choreographer, dancer. Nova Scotia–bred, Toronto- and New York–trained Douglas led dance companies in New York and Toronto and before his AIDS-related death lived a final five years in Montreal with his life partner, dancer José Navas (b. 1963, star of his own queer dance film, *Lodela* [Philippe Baylaucq, NFB, 1997, 27]). Douglas's prizewinning career is amply documented on video, but the most enduring record is the video *Emotional Logic: William Douglas Transformed* (Lisa Cochrane, 1994, 24). The couple talk frankly and eloquently of art, life, love, and death, and three dance numbers are generously excerpted. The most effective moments are solos by Douglas, improvised dance-wading on the Cape Breton shore, and a final unveiling of his agile body as he moves allegorically towards the camera, into the darkness.

D*SOUZA, KEVIN, b. 1968. Video maker, activist, writer. Pakistan-born, Calgary-trained D*Souza was a mainstay of Prairie queer arts/culture and antiracism political scenes in the 1990s before moving to Australia. His video work showed in queer venues from New Delhi to CALGARY, where he was instrumental in setting up the first queer video and film festival in 1995. He specialized in compilations of diverse vignettes of, or by, South Asian gay men, each bringing different sensibility and styles to issues of identity and sexuality. Key examples were *his distance between us* (1999), an enigmatic series of emotions and portraits. His best-known work, *Puri* (made with his frequent collaborator, Toronto writer/activist/broadcaster Arif Noorani, 1998, 6), sensuously strings together experimental and narrative glimpses of subjective, erotic experiences, ranging from a fantasy of a stern math teacher being ploughed on his own desk by a precocious student to a memory of furtive teenage Hindi-movie-sharing between best buddies, all under a Bollywood male-male song-and-dance duet.

DUBOIS, RENÉ-DANIEL, b. 1955. Playwright. One of Quebec's conspicuous pantheon of openly gay playwrights, the NTS graduate Dubois's language-drunk universe has been translated to the screen much less than that of Tremblay, Bouchard, or Lepage. To film audiences, Dubois is known chiefly as author of the play *Being at Home with Claude* (1985), brought to life with respect and flair (1992, 84) by the mainstream heterosexual director Jean Beaudin (b. 1939). The character of Claude, the hustler who murders his lover at the peak of ecstasy, fearing that they will not be able to live with less, is incarnated viscerally on-screen by queer-friendly matinee idol ROY DUPUIS (b. 1963). The role had been played on stage by the even more intense (and also more ascetic and queerer) persona of Lothaire Bluteau, but it was Dupuis's box office clout and calfcake glamour that financed the film. Fortunately for the star, MARC PARADIS volunteered to show him real hustler bars to get him in the right mood, and Dupuis rose to the occasion. Beaudin opened up Dubois's claustrophobic chamber drama by showing the fatal sex in graphic detail, as well as its frenzied summer-in-Montreal setting, as if Dubois's dynamic crescendo of cross-examination and confession could not sustain a film. *Claude* was a modest success at home. Foreigners had trouble keeping up with the subtitles during the screaming matches between the interrogating detective and the hustler, but queer audiences approved of this interesting entry in the New Queer Cinema stakes of the early 1990s.

DUCHARME, CAROLE, b. 1963. Director, scriptwriter, lawyer, producer. Trained at the Université de Montréal and a Québécois refugee in the Vancouver film industry, Ducharme is best known to queer audiences for her prizewinning one-of-a-kind *Straight from the Suburbs* (1998, 25). The only work on the international queer circuit to have been shot in the north-shore Montreal suburbia/siberia of Laval, this cartoonish satire of social-guidance films and homophobia turns the tables in a primary-coloured place where the women wear terrible wigs and where, worst of all, it's an embarrassing shame for the Barbie-doll heroine to start having erotic feelings for the opposite sex. Brimming with political darts (a sharp one at Customs Canada, who ended up buying her film for their employees' resource centre), one scene was put in clearly to explain why Ducharme's amateur cast are all speaking their cheery satirical English with a Québécois accent: this is Quebec and everyone here once spoke

French, but that disappeared and only the accent remained. Ducharme has also made documentaries, including a probably less campy work for TV Ontario (French) on Vancouver's Downtown Eastside, *Les enfants du quartier* (1999).

DUFFAULT, WILLIAM [Jacques Millet, 1961–95]. Porn video maker. Laurentians-bred hardcore wunderkind of the early 1990s, Duffault made four or more porn videos, popular both at home and with American consumers, most produced or distributed fully or in part by Montreal outfits such as Wega and Priape. Involved romantically with a U.S. porn star, Duffault had a short but intense career, demonstrating a good feel for the passionate superficiality of the genre. He gave his work a unique Quebec stamp, whether with the bilingualism run amuck of the early *Au Maximum/French Erection* (1992) or the hockey theme of *Sure Shot* (1994): "Do you wanna puck?" The promotional description for his *Northern Exposures* (1993) assured customers that the actors' "sensuous accents will get you worked up" and that *Les Hommes au Naturel* (1995) went in "the far reaches of North America [where] there are wild men just dying to get action." Duffault died of AIDS shortly after his final shoot.

DUPUIS, ROY, b. 1963. Actor. Trained at the NTS, Quebec leading man Dupuis is a queer-friendly heterothrob of the large and small screen who got his start playing intense stage and screen roles that never flinched from intense physicality, erotic performance, and queer identities. Dupuis is known by queer film audiences, in particular, for two explicit roles of lumpen obsession in MICHEL LANGLOIS's *Sortie 234* (1988) and RENÉ-DANIEL DUBOIS's *Being at Home with Claude* (1992). A completely different matter is the homophobic *J'en suis* (Claude Fournier, 1997), in which Dupuis plays a yuppie who dangles his wrist in order to access the job market that fags have all sewn up. Can the star who read his scripts too lazily be forgiven when the hate movie of the decade includes his to-die-for wrestling scene followed by a long and lingering bare-all shower scene?

EGOYAN, ATOM, b. 1960. Director, writer. Victoria-raised Atom Egoyan is the most queer-friendly of the Toronto canon cabal of straight-male feature auteurs, the one that understands most the volatility of desire and the ambiguities of obsession and voyeurism. *Exotica* (1994, 102) was both his queerest movie and, not surprisingly for a film about a jailbait [female] stripper, his big international box-office breakthrough. The queer plot in this multilayered narrative about trauma, parent-child bonds and the sex industry (centred in the eponymous elaborate sex club), features Don McKellar playing Tomas, a hairy and handsome but shy pet store owner

Queer-friendly Quebec star Roy Dupuis, an obsessed country boy in love with his buddy in Michel Langlois's *Sortie 234* (1988), has never flinched from intense physicality, erotic performance, and queer identities. Production still, ACPAV, photographer Céline Marchand

specializing in exotic contraband and in the scam of using extra ballet tickets to pick up tricks who all just happen to be men of colour. Tony Rayns found the gay twist "credible and charming" and was encouraged by Egoyan's "progress" in dealing with queerness, with which "more than an aspiration to political correctness has been driving him to come to terms" (1994). *Exotica* was multiprized at Cannes and at the Genies, and McKellar got the Genie for his supporting role.

ELLIS, ANDREW (a.k.a. Dreux). NSCAD-trained, Halifax-based Ellis got his start codirecting with fellow student and erstwhile boyfriend THOM FITZGERALD on their first feature, *Movie of the Week* (1990, 71), an ambitious intertextual effort, which the *Globe and Mail* described as a flamboyant mess ... "a strong idea about television versus reality in the life of a young gay man ... smothered under a mix of ideas alternately sophomoric and pretentious, and a fascination with film and video techniques which outlasts that of the audience ... [but in which] the dialogue shows flair and the would-be TV commercials are very funny ... (29 September 1990). Ellis went on to the world of shorts with *Dance of a Totally Unified Person* (1991, 10) and *Video Boyfriend* (1992, 13), a prophetic comic fantasy about the possibility of mail-order video sex partners replacing relationships in the nineties. Ellis had a cameo role in his old friend's *Hanging Garden* (1997) and was associate producer of his next film, *Beefcake* (1999), relocating to San Francisco.

ERBACH, JEFF, b. 1973. Director, scriptwriter, music video maker, programmer, arts administrator. Winnipeg Film Group stalwart Erbach is best known to queer audiences for his first feature *The Nature of Nicholas* (2002, 100). The film burst into the film festivals unannounced in 2002, was greeted by unanimous raves, and confirmed that there is definitely something in the waters of the Red that attacks the Canadian realism gene. A queer, Gothic coming-of-age narrative about the eponymous twelve-year-old-hero, *Nature* marshals an unsettling mix of spin-the-bottle games with girls, a dead father, a passive mother, a creaky farmhouse, insects, and zombies – all presumably set off by a kiss between Nicholas and his best friend Bobby. Puberty was never meant to be easy, and Erbach, self-styled "straight-ish" in orientation, masterfully commanded child performances, interior and exterior landscapes, surreal fantasy effects, and a sense of pace that belies his music video sideline. All add to the film's seismic terror of the body and its changes.

ESTDELACROPOLIS, DEMETRI, b. 1962. Director, scriptwriter. Concordia-trained Montrealer Estdelacropolis (pseudonym Demetrios Estathopoulos) was the toast and scandal of the Berlin festival in 1985 with his queerish *Pink Flamingos* redux, *Mother's Meat Freud's Flesh* (97), which was in fact the *only* Canadian feature there that year. In a fit of "positive image" outrage at TBP (108, November 1984), I was not amused by the hetero-sexual filmmaker's coming-of-age tale of a mostly nude heterosexual film-maker/gay porn star: "Assimilated partly from old-fashioned camp à la Warhol, and absorbing much of its violence and stridency from punk, the sensibility is more often than not characterized by both gay elements and virulent misogyny – so often in fact that the two seem to go hand in hand. They do not." But the *Globe*'s JAY SCOTT praised the film's "hilarious vignettes" and "quirkily laconic dialogue" (20 August 1984). Estdelacrop-olis's substance troubles, widely broadcast in the media, delayed for fourteen years the completion of his second feature *Shirley Pimple* (1999), which sank like a lead balloon. Thereafter Estdelacropolis put down roots and project development feelers in Rotterdam.

FARLINGER, LEONARD, b. 1962. Director, scriptwriter, producer. CFC-trained Torontonian Farlinger made a strong impact with his first feature, *The Perfect Son* (2000, 93), an AIDS melodrama built around the conflict-ual relationship of two brothers, a respectable older brother who is gay and dying of AIDS and a younger black sheep brother who is neither. Queer-friendly Farlinger based the script in part on the story of his own late brother and received respectful notices at both mainstream and queer festivals around the world, above all for the effective chemistry between heavyweight Canadian actor Colm Feore as the PWA and TV hunk Sean Cubitt as his brother. The film handles sexuality and the pandemic with humour and sensitivity, but *Xtra!* critic DAVID COLLINS commented on Farlinger's timing: "People die of AIDS, even today in the world of invasive drug treatments. People die and it is horrible. But do we really need another film at this point in the history of AIDS that maps the death of a person with AIDS as inevitable? ... *The Perfect Son* is unmistakably a well-crafted, passionately told film – unfortunately, a decade late" (25 January 2001).

FARROW, JANE, b. 1961. Video-, film- and radio maker, producer, writer, teacher. Toronto-based Farrow started in the queer punk underground, and showed several irreverent, low-budget short films in the late nineties on the queer festival circuit, before settling increasingly at CBC radio. She collaborated with many others in the Toronto queer media milieu, including ALLYSON MITCHELL and KELLY O'BRIEN, with whom she made *Nice* (1995, 9), a fierce anti-lifestyle comedy in which Farrow stars as the lesbian geek who, after making the rounds of the gym, Mazda showrooms, Wal Marts, and other dyke consumerist hot spots, discovers she "never knew it costs so much to be a lesbian." Farrow also produced ROY MITCHELL's *I Know a Place*.

FAVREAU, ROBERT, b. 1948. Director, documentarist. Originating in union activism and social work before making a mark in Quebec political documentary in the 1970s, queer-friendly Favreau was responsible for two important and accomplished queer-ish features of the 1990s, the heritage biopic *Nelligan* (1991, 104) and an adaptation of BOUCHARD's *Les muses orphelines* (*The Orphan Muses*, 2000, 107; see chapter 5). Émile Nelligan (1879–1941) is often considered Quebec's national poet and just as often claimed as a queer ancestor. Favreau's interpretation of Nelligan's tragic life, most of it spent in a psychiatric hospital, buoys up both claims, and the elaboration of his driven young hero's friendship with gay poet Arthur de Bussières and their interaction with turn-of-the-century Montreal's queer scene (rapacious, drunk sailors and lamp-lit bathing scenes) is inspired.

FERGUSON, MATTHEW, b. 1973. Actor. Toronto-bred and -trained Ferguson started on the stage but was the revelation of the film *Love and Human Remains* (DENYS ARCAND, 1993) as Kane, the crush-stricken gay busboy. Building on the same type, Ferguson was next the earnest and passionate long-haired teenager in *Eclipse* (JEREMY PODESWA, 1995) who feels hurt when his lovers treat him like a twink. John Greyson further developed his petulant queer side in *Lilies* (1996), where as the young

Bilodeau, his envy and repression lead to destruction, and in Un©ut
(1997), where as one of the circumcision-obsessed Peters, his queer persona becomes updated – urban and political but still passionate. The
queer-friendly Ferguson got Genie nods for most of the above queer roles,
but this potential was to be largely wasted in commercial television and
cameo film roles.

FERNIE, LYNNE, b. 1946. Documentarist, artist, programmer/curator.
Fernie was an active and versatile member of the Toronto interdisciplinary
arts scene when Studio D boss Rina Fraticelli recruited her to direct
what would become the NFB's most important queer film and one of their
biggest hits of the 1990s, *Forbidden Love: The Unashamed Stories of Lesbian Lives* (1992, Montreal, 85). Together with codirector AERLYN WEISS-
MAN, she injected a fresh postmodern aesthetic and politics – and erotics!
– into the feminist studio in its final years, leading to standing ovations
wherever the film was shown. There had been raves at queer community
film festivals before, but never had a new Canadian film been so well-
timed nor the rush of response so unanimous, charged, and deserved. Perhaps the Pandemic and the Tory regime had worn queer audiences down,
or perhaps it was the element of surprise that the homophobic government
studio had finally put out. What was the common ground shared by the
two topics brought together by the filmmakers – imported American lesbian-themed pulp novels in the postwar era and the emerging network of
lesbian or lesbian-friendly bars in the three Canadian metropoles in the
1950s and 1960s? The dominant tone of nostalgia for the abject aura of
the "underground," present in both the seedy watering holes and the sensationalist pulp. This past was reclaimed both by the film's slew of aging
dyke witnesses and by the linking fictional narrative of the country girl
who discovers the urban subculture and ends up as her own pulp cover
illustration in the arms of a butch brunette. No doubt the discovery of forbidden history was felt as an antidote to the growing normalization of a
love that was not quite as forbidden in 1992 as it once was – and this at a
time when same-sex marriage was scarcely a gleam in the collective eye!
(See chapters 5 and 6.)

After 1992, Fernie went on to make two independent documentaries
on the elderly lesbian writer Jane Rule (*Fiction and Other Truths*, 1995
[Genie]; *Jane Rule … Writing*, 1997, director credit once more shared with
Weissman), again marshalling a creative hybrid approach to a topic now
somewhat less risky. Fernie came back to the board for two spirited shorts
aimed at antihomophobia work in schools, the documentary *School's
Out* (1996) and *Apples and Oranges* (2003), a fresh, innovative mix of
animation and classroom listening/observation.

FINDLAY, DAVID, b. 1967. Video maker, curator, performer. First introduced to queer audiences as a voluptuous African Canadian actor in JOHN GREYSON's videotapes, such as *Kipling Meets the Cowboys* (1985) and *Andy Warhol's Blow Job (New York and Toronto)* (1989), as well as in his antiapartheid film *A Moffie Called Simon* (1986), the queer-friendly Findlay is responsible for the oft-programmed *Gender Lace and Glass* (1992, 3), a poetic meditation on race, masks, and gender-ambiguous desire. A busy participant in the Toronto artists' video network, in 2000 Findlay curated a sound-oriented program on "language, the body, performance and freedom of personal choice," titled "Queerly on the Ears."

FINDLEY, TIMOTHY, 1930–2002. Novelist, playwright, scriptwriter. Ontario's great gay writer will obviously not be remembered most for his cinema connections, though they were far from negligible. His first appearance was as a handsome young actor in a very suggestive moment with Alec Guinness in the NFB's *Stratford Adventure* (1954, 39). Among several later ventures into writing for film/TV was the forceful script for *Don't Let the Angels Fall*, a pre-CFDC feature (1968) about the implosion of a Westmount nuclear family (see chapter 3). Among Findley adaptations is the dutiful 1985 NFB fiction about boyhood initiation into adult geopolitical violence, *Going to War* (Carol Moore-Ede, 24).

Not unrelated in theme is Findley's greatest contribution to film, his 1982 script of his own 1977 prizewinning novel *The Wars* (1983, 123), Robin Phillips' expensive and Stratfordish "heritage film." Phillips (once and future Stratford Festival honcho) assembled a mass of high-powered talent, including leads Martha Henry, William Hutt, and BRENT CARVER as the Toronto aristocratic couple and their tormented "sensitive" son Robert, caught up in the Great War. The film flopped castastrophically, and its gorgeous period art design and performances seemed overwhelmed by acrimonious production squabbles. But it was more likely also scuttled by discomfort on the part of the distribution/public relations nexus with Phillips' forthright exploration of Findley's themes of masculinity in crisis, including bountiful beefcake – though the crucial scene of Robert's rape by Canadian soldiers was a little too tactfully elided. All the same, Carver is excellent as the young officer who can't face up to human mortality or his own desires and who, transported to the trenches of Flanders, rescues his squadron from poison gas and a troop of cavalry horses in a fiery spectacle of martyrdom. This underrated Canadian queer film from a period when they didn't grow on trees, unavailable in any format, is an essential link in our queer heritage – cinematic as well as literary.

Findley and his partner Bill Whitehead, their life together as well as their collaborative relationship, are astutely and unabashedly portrayed in the NFB biodoc *Timothy Findley: Anatomy of a Writer* (Terence Macartney-Filgate, 1992, 58).

FITZGERALD, THOM, b. 1968. Director, scriptwriter, producer, actor. Atlantic Canada's great gay hope, New York-bred, NSCAD-trained Fitzgerald is one of the most prolific, distinctive, and unpredictable filmmakers of his generation.

Fitzgerald was catapulted to international attention with the multi-prizewinning *The Hanging Garden* (Halifax, 1997, 91, see chapter 5), the prodigy masterpiece of a scarred and fat queer boy coming-of-age in a dysfunctional family. The diverse narrative elements – coming of age, return of the native, law of the father, compulsory heterosexuality, sibling complicity, homosocial triangle, the bush garden (seashore mode), the wedding explosion, and even the reconstitution of the (queer) family – all come together in a richly symbolic web that moves as much as it challenges. A superb script, *mise-en-scène*, cast, and performances, plus a walk-on fiddle performance by ASHLEY MACISAAC and a tender, daring teenage sex scene shattered by a shrieking grandmother in the attic: what more could anyone want? This postmodern collage of flowers, bodies, families, and regional place is one of the great features of the nineties.

Fitzgerald never looked back or repeated himself thereafter. Trapped in the "second-film syndrome," Fitzgerald's underrated second feature *Beefcake* (1999), a hybrid recreation of the pre-Stonewall golden era of physique eroticism, met with bewildered and lukewarm critical response despite its lurid canvas of jiving musclestuds and DANIEL MACIVOR's sterling performance as the conflicted beefcake impresario. Next came a bread-and-butter U.S. TV genre assignment *Blood Moon* (2001) about a freakshow teen wolfgirl whose Rumanian location inspired the next, more personal feature *Wild Dogs* (2002). This strange melodrama of not-so-innocent Canadians abroad in Bucharest, fucking – and fucking up – each other and the locals, is notable for a vivid sense of space and charismatic nonprofessional performances by Roma beggars Fitzgerald had "discovered." Self-professedly "fucked up" on the Kinsey identity scale (Hays 1998), Fitzgerald's own nuanced performance as a chubby pansexual blackmailer recalls a similar scene of bad sex in *Garden*, seemingly light years earlier. But this one doesn't lead to an exhilarating reconstitution of the family – unless the Fitzgerald character's final reunion with his Rumanian orphan puppy counts.

Fitzgerald's 2003 feature, *The Event* (2003), a meandering AIDS "assisted suicide" drama set in post-9/11 Manhattan, maintains the melo mode. The film was greeted by the now predictable critical dismay, despite some kickass drag queen moments and moving performances by Canadian perennials BRENT CARVER, Sarah Polley, and Don McKellar that stand apart from the U.S. leads.

Fitzgerald's whole trajectory can no doubt be traced back to his training at NSCAD. In fact his first feature, now quietly dropped from the filmographies, was his 1990 student production *Movie of the Week* (codirector ANDREW/DREUX ELLIS), a zero-budget tale of a young gay man's coming-of-age, self-reflexively straddling the line between performance art, video forms, and narrative cinema.

FLANDERS, ELLEN, b. 1966. Film- and videomaker, photographer, curator, arts administrator, activist. Brought up in Toronto and Jerusalem and trained in the studio program at New York's Whitney Museum, Flanders was well known to TORONTO queer audiences as executive director of Inside Out from 1996 to1999, a period when the festival grew up and out. As an artist, Flanders has explored the intersections of lesbian and Jewish identities, as well as the photographic image, in two enigmatic autobiographical essays in black and white and colour: *Surviving Memory* (1996, 9), a political and erotic confrontation with the weight of the Holocaust, the couple, and sexual transgression, and *Once* (2001, 12), about Yiddish language, identity, and heritage, from a queer granddaughter's point of view. Her 2003 work-in-progress, *Zero Degrees of Separation*, encounters Israeli and Palestinian lesbian and gay couples in the overall context of peace initiatives.

FORREST, NIKKI, b. 1964. Video maker. Born in Scotland, trained at the University of Saskatchewan and Concordia, Forrest has been active in the Montreal experimental-video scene since 1989. A staple of queer community festival "local heroes" programs, her eight or so tapes are mostly ascetic but luminous and personal. *Static* (1995, 7) was more explicit and narrative than most in its citation of queer-baiting media discourse over oblique everyday images of a dyke couple. Seen first sleeping, then getting dressed, they make their way around grey subdued Montreal in the artist's characteristic slow motion, and then a quietly poetic but defiant female voice takes over from the hatred, spoken over the scarcely perceptible gesture of two hands grazing each other as the women walk, part of a process the voice calls "reconfiguring."

FRASER, BRAD, b. 1959. Playwright, director, broadcaster. English Canada's leading playwright of his generation, the Alberta-born, Toronto-based Fraser got his first taste of directing only in 2002, adapting his own *Poor Superman* (1995) as *Leaving Metropolis*. Savaged by critics, this creditable directorial debut is a fiercely unapologetic urban tale of desire, relationships, and mortality that struck a chord with festival audiences despite some greenhorn stiffness behind the camera.

Before that, in 1993, Fraser's script of his own *Unidentified Human Remains and the True Nature of Love* (1989) was brought to the screen with somewhat more finesse by DENYS ARCAND as *Love and Human Remains* (100). Arcand produced a respectable though underwhelming transmission of Fraser's universe of cynical young gay and straight singles in an urban universe threatened by violence and the virus. Arcand's research on English Canada and homosexuality left something to be desired, and Fraser's uncanny knack for capturing the yuppie inner core of an unnamed prairie city was completely lost on the Montrealer. The film's vaguely abstract Toronto setting, peopled by imported minor stars, had American critics talking of "interstates." Others, however, recognized a very un-American quality in Fraser and Arcand's "depiction of mature relationships between various genders and sexual identities, while still examining the undercurrents of a damaged generation."[1]

Fraser's name was also attached to several short videos, including *Parade* (codirector DANIEL MACIVOR, 1996), an Ecstasy-laced Pride Day love story. Meanwhile, Fraser has been a charismatic talk show host on PRIDEVISION cable and in NIK SHEEHAN's 1996 "postmodern" documentary *Symposium: Ladder of Love,* where he discusses his views on love – in bed. Fraser supplied the voice and narration for the NFB's queer sexual-history essay *Anatomy of Desire* (JEAN-FRANÇOIS MONETTE, 1995).

FUNG, RICHARD, b. 1954. Video maker, teacher, curator, activist. For almost two decades, Trinidad-born, OCAD-trained Torontonian Richard Fung has been a leading light of Canadian video art (Bell Canada Award in Video Art, 2000). His work oscillates between a spectrum of modes: auto-biographical (*The Way to My Father's Village*, 1988), narrative (*Dirty Laundry*, 1996), activist documentary (*Orientations*, 1984), and erotic (*Steam Clean*, 1990). No other artist has probed the intersections of sexual and ethnic/racial identities as honestly, as fruitfully – as undogmatically – as this community-based, activist artist visionary. Fung's *Chinese Characters* (1986), a pioneering essay on sexual representation and queer Asian identities, was acquired by the National Gallery of Canada and greeted by a racist and homophobic outcry during its 1988 exhibition, a brouhaha that demeaned the media and Parliament and had the contrary effect of vindicating Fung's centrality to the arts in Canada.

The best was arguably yet to come: Fung's *Sea in the Blood* (2000, 26), twelve years later, was in many ways his most self-revelatory work in an oeuvre of autobiographical tapes, as well as his most aesthetically accomplished. Most of the intertextual ingredients tested elsewhere are present, from home movies to textual titles to interviews and appropriated "found" materials, but there's also a heightened visual lyricism rising to the tape's surface like its rosy underwater bubbles, embroidering the artist's voyage through the life-threatening illnesses, first of his late sister Nan and then of his resilient PWA lover Tim. Sexual identity weighs in, of course, but in a way utterly inconsequential to the web of familial and conjugal love in this exquisitely mature and profoundly affecting work.

Fung has taught at the California Institute for the Arts, the State University of New York at Buffalo, OISE, and, most recently, OCAD (see chapters 8 and 9).

GABORI, SUSAN, b. 1947, and Janet Walchewski (Dawigowiecz), b. 1949. Documentarists. Queer-friendly Gabori and Walchewski were behind an anomalous and quirky documentary, *New Romance (Aspects of Sexuality and Sexual Roles)* (1975, 34), which has the distinction of being the first NFB film to use the L and G words and present up-front, real live self-affirming lesbians and gays on the screen. The two women made the film on the sly using "short ends" (waste film stock), presenting the producers with a fait accompli, a finished film, which the brass then took on and distributed (it *was* the seventies!). The documentary offers, in sequence, a consciousness-raising session of young straight women talking about emerging sexual mores and losing their virginity, followed by a portrait of a rather inarticulate plaid-shirted pipe-smoking lesbian couple, then interviews with straight Italian-Canadian wrestlers talking about masculinity and enforced sports socialization for boys, then a couple of proudly swishy Montreal hairdressers, then an interview with a straight-looking man who talks about kissing other men, and finally a glitzy glamour party with lots of dressing up, acting out, and genderfuck, climaxing in a lingering same-sex kiss. Intercut, a young woman has her head shaved so that people will not base their impressions on her looks. The film's improvised and subjective origins and outsider perspective are evident in its lack of thematic or cinematic structure and in the way it substitutes impressions for research. In the late seventies, I was furious that this flaky "first" was a bungling assortment of what were then considered negative stereotypes, not to mention its total obliviousness to the then consolidating queer political movements. Almost three decades later, the film has improved with age, providing invaluable imagery of people and lives from an undocumented period and place.

GAGLIARDI, LAURENT, b. 1948. Filmmaker, scriptwriter, arts administrator. Montreal cinephile Gagliardi is best known to queer audiences for *Quand l'amour est gai* (*When Love is Gay*, NFB, 1994, 49), a resourceful documentary that finally brought the French studios of the NFB up to date on the wide world of male homosexuality. A survey of current issues in the gay community, Gagliardi's film offers a lively urban cardiogram that is distinctive for its respectful attention to older men and its frank depiction of sexuality, both dramatized and documentary (including a performance by a legendarily well-hung danseur from Club Taboo). The NFB nervously added the warning "This film contains scenes which could shock certain people" to its description. The film was broadcast in both Quebec and France, and indeed certain people could be shocked, and they did make official complaints to the Canadian Broadcast Standards Council when the film aired (the complaints were thrown out by the council after careful consideration). This politicization of sexual imagery was part of Gagliardi's conscious intent, but Éric Fourlanty, the gay reviewer for Montreal's weekly *Voir*, found the film weakened by its mandate as the first film to do everything all at once and by a related vagueness about its intended audience (15 September 1994). YVES LAFONTAINE, of *Fugues*, defended the film's simplicity and its manner of showing "Montreal gays, ordinary, intelligent and articulate, never ridiculous, most of the time right on, sometimes disconcerting in their frankness, but always interesting" (July 1995).

Gagliardi worked for the NFB in the late 1980s, collaborated with JEAN-FRANÇOIS MONETTE and MICHEL LANGLOIS, as well as with LÉA POOL on two of her less queer projects along the way, served with the *Archives gaies du Québec*, and is most recently project head at Quebec's film-funding agency SODEC.

GANG, PIERRE, b. 1957. Director, scriptwriter, producer. Shaped by the Montreal theatre world that initiated him in the 1980s, Pierre Gang first attracted attention with his finely crafted, semiautobiographical feature *Sous-sol* (1996). René, a prepubescent, working-class Montreal boy, is caught in a conflicted and voyeuristic relationship with the sexuality of his mother, a blowsy widow and waitress who finds a hot boyfriend with a fascinating dick, but René eventually manages to grow up all the same. With one of the best Quebec queer coming-of-age movies as a calling card and a Genie for best screenplay under his arm, Gang was hired as an eligible Quebec resident to direct the U.S. gay cable sequels, *More Tales of the City* (1998) and *Further Tales of the City* (2001). His Canadian backers rescued this project from a U.S. funding chill around the explicit queer stuff in the queer-bashed part 1, parachuting Montreal locations and Canadian actors like Jackie Burroughs delightfully but somewhat improbably into the mythic San Francisco of Armistead Maupin's original epic. Along the way Gang directed BRENT CARVER in another English-language, U.S.-focused film, *The Legend of Sleepy Hollow* (1999). Gang is a talented scriptwriter and director of actors, as well as another example of the prophet-in-his-own-country syndrome.

GAUDREAULT, ÉMILE, b. 1964. Director, scriptwriter. Montreal-based Gaudreault's *Mambo Italiano* (2003), the queer Canadian box office sensation of 2003, was the most successful popular gay comedy since *Outrageous!* Coscripted by Gaudreault and Steve Galluccio, the author of the 2002 hit play in both English and French, *Mambo*'s commercial success was due in part to the flashes of authenticity and over-the-top humour tapped from Galluccio's own experiences growing up and coming out in Montreal's Little Italy, and in part to timing. The film was sold around the world to distributors eager for a repeat of the humungous 2002 G-rated ethnic sleeper *My Big Fat Greek Wedding*. So eager was the all-powerful American distributor to recap the earlier success that it forced the removal of the two on-screen kisses between the protagonist Angelo and his closety cop lover Nino, interfering considerably with the coherence of the film. Like *La Cage aux folles* in the seventies, *Mambo* divided its audience between the outsiders who found the caricatural humour the most hilarious thing they'd ever seen and queers who recognized the moments of truth but found much of the gaps and excesses troubling, not the least of which was the downbeat ending, which had been much more satisfyingly ambiguous in the play. In the play, the hunky but traitorous Nino ends up, not as Gaudreault's unrepentent and unproblematical hetero paterfamilias but as the troubled and still-closeted man haunting a gay sauna when his new wife is not looking. Gaudreault attempted to alter the tone by adding a romantic ending for Angelo with a gay helpline activist, based on the director's own experiences as a volunteer years earlier, but with mixed success, and the scenes making fun of the helpline's distressed young clients is less uproarious than tasteless.

Gaudreault is a commercially proven scriptwriter and director, whose notable earlier hit, *Nuits de noce* (2001), had already established his knack for directing ensemble comedy and familial farce. It had also incidentally proven more current than he had probably expected: sending a boisterous Québécois extended family to Niagara Falls for a hetero wedding, Gaudreault wove in as supporting characters a gay male couple who decide to tie the knot as well and seem to be surprised when they're refused a licence by the Ontario civil service. Two years later, the script would have needed some updating.

GELLMAN, DARA, b. 1975, and LESLIE PETERS, b. 1974. Videomakers, curators, arts administrators. Australia-bred Gellman and OCAD-trained Peters, both Toronto-based, have initiated curatorial projects and new-media exhibition venues in Toronto since 1997. Gellman has presented ten or more video and video installations in international film festivals, as well queer community sites. Her *Alien Kisses* (1998, 3) processes a girl-girl kiss stolen from mainstream sci fi TV and rarefies it into the realm of abstraction. Gellman and Peters's many collaborations theorize their joint contention that "We are all voyeurs in our daily lives. Video is an extension of the desire to watch and be watched ... Video is addictive" (1999). *Interference* (2003, 17), an abstraction of crime-solving reality TV locations – mysterious bungalows and spooky shrubbery – pushes compulsive voyeurism to its limits and can also be read as outsiders' queering of a depopulated suburbia. Peters's *surge-o-matic* (with Lisa Foad, 2002, 10), a colour-saturated, juicy close-up symphony of 1950s style cooking, cleaning, and grooming (pale blue cupcake icing!) perpetrated by two contemporary gals unspooled at Image + Nation as a prototype of lesbian high-and-dry camp.

GENERAL IDEA. Interdisciplinary arts collective, video makers, Toronto. AA Bronson (Michael Tims, b. 1946), Felix Partz (Ronald Gabe, 1945–94), Jorge Zontal (Slobodan Saia-Levy, 1944–94). The homo pomo team's best-known video was *Shut the Fuck Up* (1985, 14), an analysis of the relationship of artists and the mass media the collective had been coyly flirting with since their inception. Incorporating imagery from *Mondo Cane* to *Batman*, the tape climaxed in a ringing challenge: "The pieces of the puzzle don't add up, they just don't add up. Are you listening? Are YOU listening? Do you get the picture, do YOU get the picture? Do you know what to say? Do you know what to say when there's nothing to say? When there's nothing to say, shut the fuck up. Shut the fuck up." Thereafter, this new activist orientation became increasingly visible in their work, especially around AIDS, as Partz and Zontal became sick. Underexposed in queer film and video festivals, perhaps because their work's arch high conceptualism often lacked "capital-G" gay content or feel-good crowd-pleasing immediacy or, as Bronson charged, because they were suspected of being politically incorrect with their much-flaunted icon of a poodle (Carr 2003), General Idea were among the Canadian artists best known on the international contemporary arts scene and received the Bell Canada Award in Video Art, 2001. After his partners' death, Bronson constructed a prizewinning solo career.

GILBERT, SKY, b. 1952. Playwright, actor, film- and video maker. Once called by the *Toronto Sun* "a 6-foot, hairy-chested 220-pound drag queen," in 1979 Gilbert founded Toronto's indispensable institution of queer culture, Buddies in Bad Time Theatre. In 1994 the organization moved into its spiffy Alexander St space, and in 1997 Gilbert passed on the reins as artistic director. Gilbert occasionally brought his universe of histrionic excess, social marginality, and explosive sex/gender subversion to the large and small screen: his best-known work as filmmaker is his 1992 adaptation of *My Addiction* (1994), a zany *ronde* of scenes by an assortment of "addicted" characters, from a hustler complaining about his fucked-up johns, to his obsessed and closeted john (played by long-standing collaborator DANIEL MACIVOR), to the latter's neurotically codependent wife. *I Am the Camera Dying* (1998, 30) offered a gender-warped tale of Marvette, a recently deceased heroin addict, who returns to this world as a gorgeous gay sailor who just wants to cruise boys but keeps encountering weird Toronto heterosexuals. Gilbert also lent his legendary performance talent to other queer film and video projects, from MIKE HOOLBOOM's *Kanada* (1993) to CYNTHIA ROBERTS's *Bubbles Galore* (1996).

GIRARD, SUZANNE, b. 1949. Photographer, activist, filmmaker. Known chiefly as a photographer before becoming the long-standing coordinator of Montreal's Divers/cité (Pride) celebrations in the 1990s, Girard's one film appeared in several retrospectives. *Rest-O-Rant* (1987, 10) is a stylish portrait of what seems like an ordinary neighbourhood greasy spoon, animated by astutely kinetic still photographs, oscillating between saturated and washed-out as the staff washes up. But look at that staff! This is a dyke work space, and Girard's film is in fact a pulsating document of the legendary La Paryse snack bar in Montreal's Quartier latin, a celebration of butch energy and community among the deep fryers.

GLAWSON, BRUCE, b. 1954. Documentarist, television producer. York-trained Torontonian Glawson is best known for the pioneering *Michael, A Gay Son* (1980, 27). An activist hybrid documentary about coming out, the prizewinning *Michael* was the first major independent queer work of an educational orientation in Canada, and as the first to get TVO broadcast and NFB distribution, had an important impact throughout the 1980s. Expanding on the feminist documentary formula, the earnest eponymous hero does c.r. with his peer group and then another peer group role-plays his family members in crisis, an effective trompe-l'oeil strategy that usually had first-time audiences thinking they were watching Michael's real father freaking out and real mother conciliating. TBP critiqued the film's excessive "typicality" and "talking heads" fixation (February 1981), but this nit-picking underscored the fact that *Michael* was almost all we had in 1980. In the 1990s Glawson put his name as producer on much queer pro-gramming, such as the queer stand-up documentary *We're Funny That Way* (DAVID ADKIN, 1998), and starting in 2001 was briefly a pillar of pre-cutback PRIDEVISION.

GLOVER, GUY, 1908–88. Producer of approximately 290 NFB films over almost thirty-five years beginning in 1941. A bilingual Alberta-raised poet and critic, Glover is remembered as a witty party-thrower, NORMAN MCLAREN's open but discreet lover for all of that time and his survivor by only two years when he died in 1988, and above all as a producer passionately engaged with the ideas and images of his films. One of the most influential figures in Canadian film history, he has no entry in the standard English-language reference books. Among many roles, he was a long-standing collaborator with the board's pre-Studio D women filmmakers, including GUDRUN PARKER, scriptwriter for subtextually suggestive films like *The Stratford Adventure* and *Being Different*. Many of his other titles also suggest discreet subterfuge, wordplay, and open secrets, the search for alternative masculinity, and even the possibility of sexual transgression, from *The Inner Man* to *Opera School*. My weird delectation of such titles aside, a thematic analysis of the films also reveals Glover's commitment to intercultural exchange, nonconformity, progressive causes, and especially the performing arts. Glover, a ballet and theatre lover, had been hired by Grierson possibly because he wanted his boyfriend and he thought hiring a Canadian wouldn't hurt; though by the end of the war Glover had already made his mark as a producer, he had also been typecast by the boss as a performing-arts specialist. The performing arts had always provided a safe space for the expression of subterranean homoerotic affiliation and desire both in themselves and through cinematic and photographic adaptations, and looking at Canada film history from this point of view opens up a whole new field of enquiry. Look at the punctilious tenors and willowy young men in wire-rim glasses and suits who wander through Glover's arts films as accompanists and you will know about nonmacho models of masculinity before their time. Meanwhile, Glover's narration and voice-over for the irreverent Oscar-nominated cartoon *Romance of Transportation in Canada* (Colin Low, 1952, see chapters 1 and 2) bared his queenly wit and inflections for all to hear.

McLaren would later claim that his closetry was in deference to Glover, and one of Glover's rare public utterances implicitly corroborates this. Glover's 1967 article "How to Make a Canadian Film" was an ironic scolding of the new waves of the late sixties as uttered by an old-guard producer of the tradition of quality. Among his Swiftian barbs at the indiscipline, modernist editing structures,and narcissism of the baby-boomer Fellinis around him was a note about themes: "Youth in revolt is a perfect subject-area. Post-teens in revolt is perfect for a post-teens director. Departures from mental and sexual norms (so-called) are especially desirable" (1967). In that parenthetical "so-called," by which Glover qualified "sexual norms," there nevertheless seems to be a hint, two years before the decriminalization of sodomy, of the relativity of those norms, one of the few cracks in this public armour of mentorial disdain where the private queer elder glints indulgently through.

GOLDEN, ANNE, b. 1961. Video maker, documentarist, curator, arts administrator. High priestess of the coven of lesbian and feminist video activists at Montreal's GIV since 1989, Anne Golden was a pillar of Montreal's women's film festivals of the 1980s and one of the founding programmers of that city's Image + Nation festival for much of the 1990s. Golden is also an accomplished electronic conjuror of wry lesbian camp, astute sexual politics, and versatile video aesthetics. She began her video production career as an AIDS activist, producing *Les Autres/Women and AIDS/HIV* in 1991 (31), an early dual-language encounter with women commenting on the media and research silence around women and AIDS and on safe sex, a topic tackled again the following year with the spoofy thirty-second mock commercial *Safe Soap (PSA)*. *Fat Chance* (1994, see chapter 10) followed, both an installation and an autonomous tape, which inaugurated Golden's characteristic use of self-reflexive bodily performance in her work, this time exploring fat, shame, and lesbian identity. A later series, including *Brothers* (1998, 6), played with gender masquerade and ambiguity, again featuring Golden herself as deadpan androgyne performer, and the same year's spaghetti Western send-up *Big Girl Town* (25) offers a related riff on drag and "size." Golden has most recently tackled "lesbian insomnia" in *Somme* (2003, 12), a disorienting and poetic fantasy of the artist as sleep clinic addict, plus somnambulent zombie queers, pastoral dreams, and … cheesies.

GONICK, NOAM, b. 1971. Director, scriptwriter. The most prominent of the younger generation of ultra-realist cinephile campers from Winnipeg, Gonick eschewed his elders' prairie-fed sexual ambiguity for pure queer pride. The scion of leftist activist intellectuals, Gonick's first short *1919* (1996, 8) queerly repositioned the saga of the 1919 Winnipeg General Strike in a homosocial immigrant steambath (Gonick himself plays a rather cute wire-rimmed Jewish Bolshevik). Gonick's Winnipeg mentor was the subject of his next film, *Guy Maddin: Waiting for Twilight* (1998), a spoofy one-hour homage shot among the ostriches on the set of *Twilight of the Ice Nymphs,* completely reinventing the "making of" genre.

In 2000 Gonick changed the landscape of Canadian queer cinema, literally, with his long-awaited Cinemascope rave epic *Hey Happy!* (2000, 75) Ten years in development, Gonick had been forced by funders to change the title from *Fuckfest 2000,* but the spirit of his Super 8 epic about a guy sleeping with 2000 other guys before the millennium remained intact despite the 35mm. *Happy* is a homage to Pasolini's carnivalesque medieval frescos, as well as to his mentors Maddin, LABRUCE, and Waters' gospels of provocateur histrionics, hallucinogenic narrative, and trash aesthetics. The narrative offers an apocalyptic Rabelaisian container for what is really a very simple triangular love story: two battle-scarred boys named Sabu and Happy fall in love and want to fuck, but a jealous vixen named Spanky delays the gratification. Come to think of it, it's the same story as in a not too dissimilar film by another of Gonick's mentors, JOHN GREYSON's *Lilies*, but this one substitutes upbeat prairie rave euphoria for Quebec martyr melodrama. But *Hey Happy!* was far from the typical gay romantic comedy of the nineties. Gonick's vision of the flood-threatened postindustrial outskirts of his hometown, the CPR continuously rumbling past, led to some of the most innovative landscape work in recent Canadian film. Its flora and fauna were also an essential part of the dream, including a statuesque trannie sexworker who turns out to be an intergalactic space goddess presiding over Sabu's climactic pregnancy (sic). The set pieces alone guaranteed *Hey Happy!*'s place in the pantheon, from Sabu's interlude in a dream pool swimming among a dozen naked hotties, the most exciting underwater erotics since *The Blue Lagoon* (via *Zero Patience*), to the uninterruptedly teeming, swarming rave scenes (does any other Canadian feature credit fourteen "audio artists"?).

GRÉGOIRE, PIERRE, b. 1954. Director, production officer. Concordia-trained Grégoire contributed the feature narrative *Adramélech* to Quebec theatrical distribution in 1986, but its lacklustre reception seems to have blocked further directorial ventures. The eponymous hero is wardrobe designer to Satan, and the film's hellish universe is aestheticized and post-modern, with a queer aura that clearly disturbed the *Le devoir* reviewer for its undercurrents of morbid aestheticism and evil-laced fetishism (1 February 1986). Time to revive a neglected treasure?

GREYSON, JOHN, b. 1960. Director, videomaker, curator, writer, performance artist, teacher, activist. The London, Ontario–bred, art school dropout burst onto the Toronto art scene with his sexy and politically enflamed performances and videos in the early eighties and never looked back. One of the first to bring together traditional left solidarity activism (unions, Central America) with queer politics in an energized art form that was pulsating with formal invention, ideas, and fun, Greyson's political causes ranged from censorship, apartheid, and AIDS to the more specifically queer issues of public sex and ghetto culture. Everyone has their favourites from this period, but mine has to be *Jungle Boy* (1985, 15), which manages to intersect Kipling-derived Orientalist jungle and wolf-

In Noam Gonick's *Hey Happy!* (2000), Spanky, the baddest homo of them all, self-styled "biggest bitch in the world" and demonic opposite of tragicomic 1970s hairdressers, is the composite of all evil movie fags and hates relationships. Production still, Clayton Godson as Spanky O'Neil in *Hey Happy!* (Noam Gonick, 2001) Big Daddy Beer Guts, Inc.

boy metaphors, a Mexican pop song, and a taut coming-out narrative miniature, starring Greyson's soon-to-be partner, video artist COLIN CAMPBELL. Greyson's six-hour curated package of twenty-two international AIDS videos (*Video against AIDS*, 1989, with Bill Horrigan), jumpstarted the North American arts community's implication in the health crisis. Meanwhile the anthology *Queer Looks: Perspectives on Lesbian and Gay Film and Video* (coedited with Martha Gever and Pratibha Parmar, 1993) revved up international film culture at the heyday of the New Queer Cinema. Greyson's video style, a convergence of techno-wizardry, dense allusiveness, camp anachronism, unabashed didacticism, melo narrative, urban diaristic observation, heady eroticism, and media collage, stuck with him as he moved into film in the late 1980s, his first feature being the prizewinning *Urinal* (1988) (see chapter 8). Greyson's distinctive style and vision endured but became more polished and accessible as he emerged from a residency at the CFC, where he produced the dazzling Brechtian musical about queerbashing and masculinity, *The Making of Monsters* (1990), only to see it suppressed by mean American lawyers.

Greyson's next feature, the AIDS musical masterpiece *Zero Patience*

(1993), has gradually come into its due as a canonical paving stone of Canadian cinema of the 1990s (see chapter 9). Thereafter, Greyson moved into less personal projects like the Telefilm Canada adaptations *Lilies* (Genie for best Canadian film, 1996; see chapter 5) and *Law of Enclosures* (2000), devastatingly underrated and touted by the media as his first straight film, despite its queer probing of heterosexual marriage and the first Gulf War. But the 1980s Greyson was most palpable in the more personal Canada Council projects that he developed in the intervals between the big bucks, such as the brilliant docu-narrative essay on censorship and circumcision, *Un©ut* (1997), and even in the iconoclastic CBC docu-drama *After the Bath* (1995). The 2003 South Africa coproduction *Proteus*, another underfunded, more personal work (coproduced and written with Jack Lewis), offered old and a new Greyson at the same time in a profound update on queer heritage cinema. Not Merchant-and-Ivory but based on a historical eighteenth-century interracial sodomy trial that the filmmakers had found in the archives, *Proteus* reversed Greyson's usual anachronism, problematizing the story's inherent queer martyrology with postcolonial lust and Foucauldian angst. South Africa remained the setting for Greyson's next major work, a video opera installation based on the Treatment Access Campaign, a complex and ambitious return to the AIDS theme that Greyson rightly considers one of his best works (see chapter 9). Greyson joined the film production faculty at York in 2004.

GUILBERT, CHARLES (b. 1964, video maker, musician, writer, critic), and SERGE MURPHY (b. 1953, video maker, interdisciplinary artist). The prizewinning Montreal video art team Guilbert and Murphy are well known on both the Quebec art scene and the international queer festival circuit as reinventors of everyday storytelling and song. Their minimalist frescos detail the lonely and restless lives of the young intellectual fauna and flora of the Plateau-Mont-Royal. The bittersweet *Homme aux trésors* (Man of treasures, 1988) may be their best known and their queerest video, and when I discovered it in 1989 for my "Images '89" programming, I waxed rhapsodic: "New narrative and new social/sexual identities, but the old old patterns persist: triangles and (vicious) circles, romance and betrayal, naked breakfasts and men who have hammers instead of penises. Murphy and Guilbert expertly modulate both the delirous rush of language and the excruciating plenitude of silence." Pushing the same direction even further, their *Sois sage ô ma douleur* (1990) was honoured at the 1991 *Rendez-vous du cinéma québécois*. Known in international venues, the local heroes were accorded retrospectives at both Image + Nation (1995) and the *Rendez-vous* (1998). Queerness was always matter-of-fact in their work, but by the time of the existential bitch session between a straight young woman and her gay male friend in *Au verso du monde* (*Outside looking in*, 1994), it's so cool that it's almost invisible. Always at the core of their work, music became increasingly important and *Rien ne t'aura mon coeur* (1997) has been described as a "kaleidoscopic musical comedy." Michel Grou (b. 1964) was the technical director/editor of the first four of the duo's videos and codirected *Rien*.

GUPTA, NILA, b. 1961. Filmmaker, writer, community activist. India-born, Ryerson-trained, Toronto-based Gupta has provided four shorts to the queer and diaspora festival circuits since 1998, documentary and experimental negotiations of diasporic and lesbian-feminist identities in the context of globalization. The prizewinning *A Phone Comes to Jammu* (1998, 7) is a handsome autobiographical black-and-white essay on the author's link – by telephone and gender, as well as by kinship – with a female contemporary in northern India, destined for an arranged marriage. Personal questions of cultural relativism and responsibility are interwoven with mysterious narrative fragments, while the artist's present Toronto positioning, lover and all, is laid out in the here and now.

HAIG, DON, 1933–2002. Producer, editor. Eulogized upon his death as one of the most influential presences within Canadian cinema, Don Haig was remembered as a key editor during the formative sixties at the CBC, as an independent Toronto-based producer during the seventies and eighties, and as English studio kingpin at the NFB in the nineties. The eulogizers did not mention that this handsome, openly but quietly gay Winnipegger, happily partnered with Bill Schultz for 47 years, who started his career distributing and *loving* MGM musicals, also produced one of the momentous but sadly unreleased English Canadian queer features of the seventies, *125 Rooms of Comfort* (1974).

One of the lost children of Canadian cinema, queer or straight, this low-budget but ambitious feature film showed apparently only once or twice and then met undeserved oblivion. *125 Rooms* was directed by Patrick Loubert (b. 1947), a York-trained, queer-friendly pioneer of Canadian animation and cofounder in 1971 of the legendary Ottawa studio Nelvana. The film is about a dilapidated hotel in St Thomas, Ontario, the site for both a stand-up comedy gig at a stag party (by a has-been named "Johnny Canuck," based on Loubert's vintage Canadian comic strip hero), and various wheeler-dealings around the sale of the place to rapacious U.S. buyers. One co-owner, Billie, on leave from a mental hospital and scandalously queer, won't go along with the sale and becomes a rather distinctive martyr for Canadian economic autonomy (metaphors of American imperialism were not unheard of in Canadian films of the 1970s). The rather heavy climax intercuts two scenes: the hotel MC introduces the "beautiful vivacious" new stripper to her rowdy and appreciative male audience; meanwhile, outside the hotel other drunken patrons discover Billie in drag and prevent him from getting away, shouting "faggot!" They beat him up, rip off his wig, kick him when he is down in the grungy alleyway, douse him with beer, and leave him for dead – which suits the other co-owner and the buyers just fine. According to Loubert, Billie was basically Haig's contribution to the film, a character based on a brilliantly outrageous queen character the filmmakers knew on Toronto Island, who had provided screen tests but seemed too unstable to count on for the project (telephone interview, 10 December 2003).

The film's failure was attributed partly to CFDC interference (the funders kept removing the sex and violence scenes from the script, and Loubert and Haig basically restored them, including the queerbashing scene, on the set). But the interwoven plot lines are also somewhat murky, even in the context of 1970s art film narrative structure. One critic homophobically equated Canada's colonized national identity with what he calls Billie's "goofy sexual incompetence," responding to the climactic fatal queerbashing with the question, "is Billy's transvestism an image of the total `feminisation' of the son and heir of the Canadian mansion, an expression of an unconscious desire to be raped?" (Fothergill 1975, 58). Rather than transposing a little too deftly the sexist myth of the woman who wants to be raped to the queer who wants to be bashed and in the same breath to the Canadian who wants to be colonized, he might have reflected on the silencing of embryonic queer cinemas, however conflicted, just as they were beginning to stir.

In his next career as Toronto producer, Haig was also behind the great queer hit of the eighties, *I've Heard the Mermaids Singing* (1987), and, during the final productive and influential civil servant phase of his career, supported emerging queer filmmakers and projects such as *Anatomy of Desire* (JEAN-FRANÇOIS MONETTE, 1995) and *When Shirley Met Florence* (RONIT BEZALEL, 1994).

HALIFAX. The Halifax Lesbian, Gay & Bisexual Video & Film Festival, organized by filmmaker MICHAEL WEIR, in collaboration with the Centre for Art Tapes, offered a bold week-long program in June 1992. Rich in local fare such as THOM FITZGERALD's early work, the 1992 festival led to the follow up Peggy's Film Festival in 1993, affiliated with Pride activities. But the Nova Scotia capital was thereafter able to sustain only localized and one-off manifestations of queer film and video, based in artist-run centres or local universities.

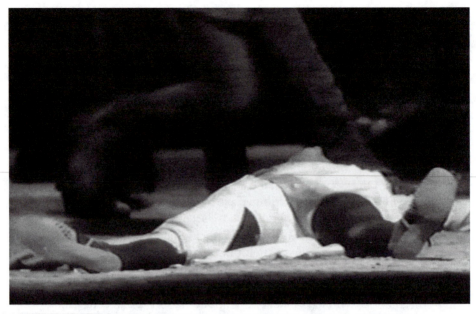

One of Canadian queer cinema's lost children, Don Haig's and Patrick Loubert's *125 Rooms of Comfort* (1974): Billie the gender-dissident hero is fatally queer-bashed outside the family hotel that is being eyed for takeover by American predators. VHS frame grab, special permission of the estate of Don Haig (Film Arts) – W.W. Schultz

HALL, STEV'NN, b. 1966. Videomaker, editor. A Concordia-trained Maritimer, Hall is based in Toronto but also worked in Vancouver, contributing to both arts festivals and mainstream TV production, as well as an irreverent and reflective indie sideline in SM fantasy. *Bondage Television* (1999, 10) pushed the TV trailer format to its fiendishly self-parodic extreme, including everything from 1950s physique spanking to Mel Gibson emoting from his armpits, strung up in a Hollywood dungeon. *Red in the Face* (2000, 6) is also about extremes, but in a different mode: a disturbingly subjective and matter-of-fact narrative of sequestration and murder, all blamed on the psychopath narrator's excess of TV socialization (*Bionic Woman!*) within his 1970s nuclear family.

HALLIS, RON, b. 1945. Documentarist, teacher. McGill-trained, Montreal-based, queer-friendly Hallis, a pioneer of independent social-issue and "third world" documentary in English Quebec, broke ground in 1970 with his early work on sexual marginality. *Toni, Randi and Marie* (1971, 48) was a cinéma-vérité trilogy about the everyday lives of the eponymous female impersonator, transvestite hustler, and female prostitute. The section on Randi also circulated separately as *Night Shift* (1970, 20). Risks of voyeurism aside, the work stands up as a respectful and unique encounter with its proud but stigmatized subjects.

HALPRIN, SARA, b. 1943. Critic, documentarist. As Barbara Halpern Martineau, American-bred Halprin was a key political and intellectual voice in lesbian feminist criticism on the Toronto scene in the late 1970s and early 1980s, writing a regular column in the Toronto women's magazine *Broadside* and contributing reviews and articles to Canadian film magazines such as *Cinema Canada* and *Take One*, as well as several in the United States. As a filmmaker, Halprin was responsible for several of the early queer documentary chestnuts, including the still-circulating prototransgender manifesto *Keltie's Beard* (1983, 9) and *Heroes: A Transformation Film* (1983, 23). Halprin later married and settled with her husband in Oregon.

HANNON, GERALD, b. 1944. Journalist, activist, film critic, video maker, actor, teacher, sexworker. New Brunswick–born, Ontario-bred Hannon is one of Canada's most notorious queers of the post-Stonewall generations. A member of Toronto's original TBP collective, Hannon twice set off moral panics that effectively put national media, gatekeepers of sexual and cultural politics, and queer community leaders to a test that many failed: as the author of the 1977 TBP article "Men Loving Boys Loving Men" (1977–78), which led to the gay lib paper being dragged before the courts in a three-year ordeal, and as the central figure in the 1995 "Ryerson Prof: I'm a Hooker" scandal, which led to his being fired from teaching journalism.

Hannon was also a player in the three-decade drama of Toronto queer cinemas. As standby film and culture critic at TBP during the 1970s, his forceful writing injected sexual politics into the cultural debates that were shaping queer communities. His 1975 review of the pioneering U.S. gay lib feature *A Very Natural Thing* at the time of its Toronto run, saw it as a patriarchal plot: "We have been had. *A Very Natural Thing* is a heterosexual movie – only the sex of one of the protagonists has been changed. This time, to corrupt the innocent." (October 1975, 21). Hannon developed a relationship with Toronto's indie queer film scene, appearing in NIK SHEEHAN's *Symposium* (1996), in which his episode from his life as a mature hustler contributed much shit to the fan. His acting skills were also confirmed as the brutal master in SCOTT BEVERIDGE's *Quiver* (1999). Finally, Hannon tried his hand at directing, and his 1999 video short *Cousin Mike* (1999, 10), starring the author and Beveridge, an explicit tale of sort-of-intergenerational sort-of-incest, moved into my top-ten list of queer Canadian short fiction.

HARMSEN, LEIF, b. 1967. Interdisciplinary/web artist, filmmaker, writer, anticensorship activist. Trained at Concordia and the University of London, Leif Harmsen has been a hyperactive stalwart of the downtown Toronto Super 8/arts/sex radical scene since the late nineties. His quirky personal/experimental miniatures circulated in many arts/queer film spaces. Among them, *Electrical Discharge* (1999, 1, with Greg Woodbury) is a miniature riff on two guys with electrical jitters leading to a climactic kiss; *Cruising* (1999, 7) is a frenetic six-frame-per-second appropriation of Toronto downtown and island urban space for the titular activity; *Penetration* (2001, 10) is jubilant and inspired meta porn where queer and non-queer come together.

HAYES, LISA, b. 1967. Director, arts administrator, producer. Trained in Michigan, as well as at Ryerson, and active in Toronto's LIFT, queer-friendly Hayes has been a prolific director of personal short films in various modes and sensibilities – comic, experimental documentary, political, and narrative – since the mid-nineties. *Lez Be Friends* (2000, 13) narrates confusions and ironies around sexual labels and perceptions, while the prizewinning *Dike* (1996, 9) tackles compulsory heterosexuality and excessive perspiration.

HAYS, MATTHEW, b. 1965. Film critic, journalist. Edmonton-bred, Concordia-trained journalist Hays has had an important impact on the emergence of queer cinemas and cultures in Canada. Regular film critic at the *Montreal Mirror* beginning in 1993, Hays was also known for his in-depth interviews with filmmakers in Canadian film magazines like *Take One* and *Cinemascope* (not to mention *Xtra!*, the *Globe and Mail*, and other Toronto media). In the L.A.-based *Advocate,* Hays also successfully pushed profiles of FITZGERALD, ROZEMA, FRASER, and LEPAGE upon American readers whose international culture sometimes gets stuck with Chastity Bono. Hays always confronts issues of sexual identity with his subjects and is known for finally having got Rozema to come out.

HENRICKS, NELSON, b. 1963. Video and filmmaker, writer, teacher. Alberta-bred and trained at the Alberta College of Art and Design, as well as Concordia, Montreal-based Nelson Henricks received the Bell Canada Award in 2002 for his wry and rigorous, long-standing and prolific contribution to video art in Canada, queer and otherwise. Author of almost twenty-five short films and videos since 1985, Henricks has a wide range: from the ascetic (*Window*, 1997) to the luxuriantly erotic (*Handy Man*, 1999), from documentary (*Murderer's Song*, 1991) to narrative (*Crush*, 1997, SODEC prize), from the abstract to the autobiographical (*Shimmer*,

1995), from rigorously intellectual (*Legend*, 1988) to high camp (*Planétar-ium*, 2001) – appealing both to community festival audiences and to high-Derridean theorists. Does *Comédie* (1994) remain my favourite simply because that's the one I programmed in my queer-Canada retrospective at Cinémathèque Ontario in 1994, because its obsessive and deluded attachment to Métro station walls and Hydro-Québec meters echoed my own integration into Montreal years earlier, because it's queer without being gay, or because I have an enduring soft spot for Petula Clark? Working in English and French, Henricks often collaborates with his partner, interdisciplinary artist Pierre Beaudoin.

HENRIQUEZ, PATRICIO, b. 1948. Documentarist. Henriquez, bred in Chile and imprisoned by Pinochet, is a Québécois queer-friendly filmmaker who is known chiefly to queer audiences for his *Juchitan Queer Paradise* (2002, 65). This bold, subjectively ethnographic encounter with a queer-embracing Zapotec culture in southern Mexico also appealed to Latino audiences and human rights constituencies in North America. Henriquez, a prizewinning political chronicler of Latin American struggles, affirmed the politics of sexual identity with verve, though he understandably faltered in translating the vocabulary of sexual identity among four languages. He also left one question unanswered: where are all the "straight" men that must be having sex with the film's flaming, charming stars?

HERBERT, JOHN, (1926–2001). Playwright, scriptwriter. The English Canadian theatre's great gay pioneer Herbert is known most for his international stage hit *Fortune and Men's Eyes* (1965), which is based on his experiences in the Guelph Reformatory on "gross indecency" charges. Herbert participated in the adaptation of his play to the screen under the same title during the first surge of publicly financed Canadian feature film production (director Harvey Hart, Montreal, 1971). This Hollywood-financed, CFDC-backed project feature had its hopes pinned to the momentum of the commercial gay cycle of 1969–70 (*Midnight Cowboy, Women in Love*) but it ran into production squabbles and mixed reviews and failed to live up to the success of the play. Trained in CBC drama, director Hart (1928–89) was parachuted into the production but managed to deliver a creditable narrative. Despite a few rough patches (due in part to the imported American leads and to changes in the original play, such as the suicide by the gay rapist bad guy Rocky), *Fortune* was carried by the intense conviction of the original property (*The New York Times* grudgingly conceded the film's "depressing authenticity" [17 June 1971]). The innocent, "straight" hero Smitty, imprisoned for pot rather than Herbert's original charge, discovers a prison world of gang rape, sexual blackmail, and corruption, which is portrayed with brutal honesty, but he also discovers bonds of tenderness and loyalty. Smitty ends up corrupted, but along the way he also discovers the possibilities of resistance incarnated in the ebullient character of Queenie. This bottle-blonde is usually thought more than Smitty to represent Herbert's own persona and is played by swishy American actor Michael Greer, who had starred in the New York theatrical productions of the play and effectively steals the movie. Filmed in the same decommissioned Quebec City prison as that other canonical film *Lilies* a quarter century later, *Fortune and Men's Eyes* was removed from its Canadian context and severely and undeservedly chastised in Vito Russo's *Celluloid Closet* (1981). The film remains an underrated milestone in the trajectory of Canadian queer narrative cinema.

HILL, BILLY, 1928–79. Canada's first international queer beefcake star, Hill was Mr Montreal and Mr Canada (1954) and a favourite model of Montreal physique photographer ALAN B. STONE throughout the 1960s. Hill's international appeal to pre-Stonewall gay men was based mostly on magazine spreads and black-and-white glossies, but he also delivered several immortal pump and pose performances on the St Lawrence riverfront for Stone's Super 8 softcore shorts, unfortunately never well distributed. Ironically his motion picture charisma lingers most accessibly in a scene from our homophobic state studio's snarky fitness documentary, *I Was a Ninety-Pound Weakling* (Georges Dufaux, Wolf Koenig, NFB, 1960, 24). The bodybuilder takes the oblivious filmmakers on a rather static tour of the Billy Hill Gym, in what is now the heart of Montreal's *Village gai* and stiffly twitches his magnificent muscles for himself in the mirror and for the camera. If you look hard, the location's function as a covert nexus of gay community networks is evident on the screen, an all-male landscape of bared skin and bulging torsos, proud display and covert looks, and especially the long and charismatic shot of magnificent Billy himself, who, despite his forced smile and slight cross-eye, clearly loves being worshipped. (See chapter 7).

HOE, HUNT, b. 1961. Malaysian-born, Concordia-trained Hoe is a Montreal-based, queer-friendly filmmaker interested in the fluidities within masculinity and diasporic cultural identities. The two areas came together in his two best-known works: the NFB documentary about Asian masculinity, *Who is Albert Woo?* (2000, 52),which is a lively collage of excerpts from Jackie Chan movies and interviews, including a "brown queer activist," and the controversial feature film and queer festival perennial, *Seducing Maarya* (1999), a masala stew set in Montreal's Indian-restaurant underground, with a main course of familial stress, incest, rape and other potboiler spices. An interracial gay male couple is dessert, the most authentic of the various dishes.

HOLLINGS, GRAHAM, b. 1962. Filmmaker, musician. Self-taught, University of Toronto–trained, Toronto-based Hollings is a prolific short filmmaker and Pleasure Dome activist who has made six naughty shorts for the queer and the Super 8 circuits in the 2000s, both here and abroad. *Canada Sperm Bank of Satan* (2002, 12) is a rollicking political allegory made on the Niagara Peninsula about a Georgia prowler deflowering Canadian boy hitchhikers after pouring maple syrup over their buttocks – all transpiring under Jimi Hendrix subverting "The Star-spangled Banner" and Celine Dion defiling "God Bless America."

HOOLBOOM, MIKE, b. 1959. Director, writer, curator, cinematographer, AIDS activist. Sheridan College–trained, Toronto-based fringe filmmaker Hoolboom has been described as "major," "protean," "prolific," and "disturbing," and he is all of those things, plus queer-friendly and PWA and much more. Conspicuous on the Toronto independent scene since 1980, whether at the Funnel or the CFMDC or TIFF (two prizes), Hoolboom was the author of the indispensable interviews in *Fringe Film in Canada* (1997, 2001). He has also been accorded retrospectives at queer community festivals in recognition of an oeuvre that excoriates the desires and stigmas of the queer body (see chapter 9).

HULL, ANDREW, b. 1963. Director, scriptwriter, interdisciplinary video artist. Carleton-trained architect-turned-filmmaker Hull works in both Germany and Toronto and has provided several accomplished short narratives to queer and other showcases since the late nineties. *Dizzy* (1999, 19) reflects the author's cosmopolitan base in its parable of a dizziness brought on by airports, lost luggage, barf bags, and the childhood memories they evoke, and above all German boyfriends; *That Thing We Do* (2002, 16) is more about queer identity in middle-class Toronto, coming out at the cottage, and finding a support network in childhood, this time real rather than remembered.

INKSTER, DANA, b. 1972. Filmmaker, interdisciplinary artist. Ottawa-bred, Queen's- and Concordia-trained Dana Inkster is best known for *Welcome to Africville* (1999, 15). Africville was the African-Canadian community in Halifax that was razed for "urban renewal" in the late sixties. Against a backdrop of black and white archival footage of this neighbourhood under demolition unfolds a slice-in-time narrative set on the eve of destruction. Highlighted are three generations of women in an Africville family, including a proud and lustful, thirty-something dyke, plus the friendly and queer local bartender (ALEXANDER CHAPMAN). Lushly photographed against brightly coloured settings, the film raises the question not only of a lost community history but also of lost sexual histories and identities. Well known on both the queer international and the African diaspora circuits, Inkster's 2003 documentary is *The Art of Autobiography*.

JACQUES, YVES, b. 1956. Actor. Known chiefly outside Quebec as the sensitive, gay art historian who shares with his straight colleagues his erotic experiences of Mont-Royal cruising and of boy's buttocks and then pisses blood in DENYS ARCAND's *Le Déclin de l'empire américain* (1986), Jacques has in fact had a sustained career on stage and screen in Quebec and France. Often identified with queer roles, most notably the drag role of Lydie-Anne in BOUCHARD's *Les Feluettes* on stage, Jacques came out publicly after years of quiet solidarity on screen, going against the grain of Quebec's queer but often apolitical arts scene.

JAMES, SHEILA, b. 1962. Theatre artist, video maker, writer, musician. UBC-trained James is a multitalented, multidisciplinary, multicultural fixture of the Toronto queer/diasporic arts scene. Since 1998, four of her videos have made the rounds of the community festivals from Montreal to Berlin to Delhi, all exploring queer desire and cultural hybridity through experimental and fantasy narrative. *Lakme Takes Flight* (with Melina Young, 2000, 12) is an over-the-top appropriation of the operatic flower duet from the eponymous French orientalist opera (trademark of other lesbian fantasies such as *I've Heard the Mermaids Singing*, as well), adding airborne coupling in a rickety turboprop, a postcolonial political edge, and Bollywood delirium. The prizewinning video poem *Unmapping Desire* (1999, 7), about social and geographical impediments to women loving women, was broadcast in Germany.

JEAN, RODRIGUE, b. 1957. Director, scriptwriter, video maker. Trained in biology, sociology, and literature but with a professional background in dance and choreography, Acadian Rodrigue Jean was the revelation of French-language queer feature film in the late nineties. Founding member of the dance troupe Les Productions de l'Os, Jean lived in London for ten years, and his first video, *La dèroute* (1990), was based on his choreography. Subsequent tapes include the prizewinning *La mémoire de l'eau* (1996, 11), a disturbing narrative of a man who drowns his dying lover and is haunted by his memory, and *L'appel/Call Waiting* (1998, 16), a gay telephone breakup melodrama inspired by Cocteau.

Jean's feature film debut was *Full Blast* (1999, 92), based on the prizewinning Acadian novel *L'Ennemi que je connaîs*, by Martin Pître. A blast of fresh sea air when it hit mainstream theatres and queer festivals in 1999, *Full Blast* is a downbeat art film with a pop feel about five hinterland characters whose lives are going nowhere. *Blast* was shot in Bathurst New Brunswick's beautiful setting on Chaleur Bay, where the pulp and paper mill is closed and everyone smokes way too much (tobacco and pot). Three down and out buddies, Piston, Charles, and Steph, reunite and dream of starting up their old band again. Piston's ex Marie-Lou is a superb singer, the only thing the band has going for it, but she's resisting because Piston is a dealer, a pothead, and a loser who won't accept responsibility for their daughter. All is presided over by the bar owner, Rose, a wise and tough lady who can't say no any better than anyone else in this town: she's played by Louise Portal, whose involvement ensured Jean a generous budget and big names for this first feature (not that the producers didn't end up balking when they finally saw Jean's superbly directed, contemplative, and sexually transgressive film – until audiences actually liked it!). It turns out that the film revolves less around Charles the gay man returning to the setting from which he once escaped than around Steph, the beautiful bisexual who seems to have just a little more resilience and integrity than his pals and who fucks – and is fucked by – almost everyone else in the circle but can't find what he's looking for. Charles escapes again, but Steph and everyone else is stuck (see chapter 5).

Jean continued in the same skilfully drawn melodrama of regional sexual, existential, and social marginality with his next feature, *Yellowknife* (2002, 117). This time it's a road movie and Jean's frustrated and lonely characters are anything but stuck in a backwater, miraculously driving from Moncton to Yellowknife with scarcely more than the usual roadkill, robberies, brawls, and orgies. A broodingly handsome young man, Max, rescues his sister Linda from a psychiatric hospital, and they set out in their pickup truck, picking up anglophone twin-brother hitchhiker-strippers as well as a blowsy lounge singer (Patsy Gallant, the Quebec disco star in a much-praised comeback) and her driven omni-sexual manager, as well as, eventually, somewhere along the way, a straight and narrow aboriginal cop who bonds with Linda. They make it to Yellowknife, but as the genre requires, encounter much more than expected along the way. *Yellowknife* is even more of an encyclopedia of sexual marginalities than *Full Blast*, complete with incest, sexwork, sexual assault, a compulsive masturbation-exhibitionism-voyeurism symbiosis, and even a scary kind of conventional heterosexuality with the cop, as well as implied homoerotic self-discoveries by both brother and sister. This seeming lapse into art film pansexual perversity drove a few critics off the deep end, but by and large *Yellowknife*'s critical reception as a confirmation of Jean's impressive originality was better than its disappointing boxoffice results.

JEPSON-YOUNG, DR PETER, 1957–92. Trained at UBC and Ottawa General Hospital, Jepson-Young was a gay doctor with and for AIDS affiliated with Vancouver's St. Paul's Hospital, the only local institution caring for AIDS patients in the early 1980s. Diagnosed with Kaposi's Sarcoma in 1989, Jepson-Young began producing weekly video diaries on his daily struggles for local CBC broadcast, and 111 short vignettes appeared before his death in 1992. Eventually repackaged for the CBC by David Paperny as *The Broadcast Tapes of Dr Peter* (1992), the broadcasts' diary format was preserved. Its Oscar nomination and U.S. broadcast on HBO reflected the brave and amiable diarist's mainstream viability. After his death a Vancouver AIDS foundation took his name, opening the Dr Peter Centre Day Health Program at St Paul's in 1997 (see chapter 9).

JIVAN, KASPAR, b. 1965. OCAD-trained, Toronto-based Jivan, a.k.a. Kaspar Jivan Saxena, began working in the late 1980s in wry animated shorts, which were shown at international queer and diasporic festivals, signed Gita Saxena. The artist moved into personal video, concerned with diasporic heritage and identity, and was especially noticed for *Second Generation Once Removed* (1990, 19) and *Bolo! Bolo!* (1991, 31, with IAN IQBAL RASHID), an imaginative cable documentary on AIDS in the context of the South Asian community that led to Rogers Cable censoring the *Toronto Living with AIDS* series, of which it was a part. Among later works, the work-in-progress *Only Enough to Ignite (some unpreventable adventures in lesbian flirtation)* (signed Gitanjali, 1996-98, 13) was a rich and playful, multilingual assemblage of interviews and performances by women of colour. Starting in 1998, Jivan's work was programmed in transgender festivals in Toronto and abroad, and his current new-media museum documentary in progress, *Creatures of Terra Incognita,* spotlights the "natural history of monsters."

JONES, ADAM GARNET, b. 1982. Video maker. British Columbia–bred, Toronto-based Jones, one of Inside Out's initiates, has received training from the Gulf Islands Film and Television School, as well as Ryerson. Jones made three accomplished dramatic tapes in 2003 about relationships and rupture. *Erin & Eva* (10) is a discursive standoff between two cousins that reflects the artist's First Nations origins, while *13 Minutes* is a four-minute gem with very sharp edges about a brittle young man who has a lot to learn and uses video and ultimatums to dump his boyfriend: "You can do whatever you want to do. I just gotta do my hair … I'm standing strong, you're gone."

JONES, G.B., b. 1965. Video maker, performer, interdisciplinary artist, musician. Emerging out of Toronto's queer core underground in the 1980s, Jones founded the influential zine *J.D.'s* with BRUCE LABRUCE and collaborated with him in his iconoclastic small-format queer punk filmmaking of the late 1980s. Jones went on to deliver memorable Warholian performances as driven and exploitative up-and-coming lesbian filmmakers in both of LaBruce's first features, *No Skin off My Ass* (1991) and *Super 8½* (1994). These filmmaker roles paralleled her own practice as maker, and her rough-hewn punk narratives like *The Yo-Yo Gang* (1991), *The Lilipop Generation* (1993, 2), and *The Troublemakers* (1992/1997, 20) were popular programmers in queer, alternative, DIY, and women's festivals. For her visual works, launched as zine illustrations of baby-butch bikers, Jones was called the female Tom of Finland, and her stride as an artist exhibited throughout North America and Europe soon overtook her filmmaking career.

JUTRA, CLAUDE, 1930–86. Director, scriptwriter, actor. Ancestor, enigma, and martyr of queer cinema in Canada, Jutra's prodigious oeuvre contained only one explicit queer moment. But that moment, in *À tout prendre* (1963), was accompanied by gongs and zooms (see chapters 3–5). Well, there was also that lesbian parenting comedy with Patty Duke (*By Design*, 1981), quite explicit enough, which TBP called "Laverne and Shirley have a baby" (January/February 1983).

I have written many times about Jutra and still can't get him out of my system. The first time (1981), Jutra was still alive and a mutual friend told me he liked being called the E.M. Forster of Quebec cinema (which I did because of his problematical silence following *À tout prendre*). I next wrote about Jutra just after his 1986 Alzheimer's-clouded suicide, a two-in-one eulogy for both Jutra and his mentor NORMAN MCLAREN, who had died the same winter, a celebration of the two founding queens of our national cinemas ([1988a] 2000). I came back to the pair in 1994 when I programmed the legendary Jutra-McLaren collaboration, *A Chairy Tale* (1957), as the inaugural text of Canadian lesbian and gay cinemas in my retrospective "The Fruit Machine" at the Cinematheque Ontario; playfully, I encouraged the audience to read the playful pixillation as an allegory of relationships (the chair, skittish about being bottom, is non-gender-specific). That queer film subcultures have not beatified Jutra can be ascribed not only to his belonging to a minor national cinema and speaking the wrong language. The obliqueness of his representations of sexual identity also consign him to the canon's antechambers already crowded by

Arzner, Murnau, Whale, Cukor, Eisenstein, Carné, Minnelli, and other discreet members of an earlier generation.

Otherwise, thirty-five years of tidal undercurrents began when the teenager Claude went out with his birthday-present camera and made two "amateur" films, *Le dément du lac jean jeunes* (The madman of Jean-Jeunes Lake, 1948, 40) and *Mouvement perpétuel* (1949, 15). The two films vibrate not only with precocious cinephile aestheticism but also with intense and conflicted undercurrents of homoerotic desire – whether conscious or unconscious, we may never know. They demand an exploration of such undertheorized concepts as clandestinity, stigma, and transnationality as both authorial and spectatorial positions.

They also force us to confront the issue of intergenerational eroticism as a historical social construction and artistic energy. In fact, this issue and the taboos it generates within our culture are no doubt responsible for the anomalous and contradictory position that this most-canonized artist holds within the Canadian/Quebec film heritage. Consider the following: Jutra film stills grace the covers of no less than four major textbooks on Canadian film, and *Mon Oncle Antoine* remains firmly entrenched as number one on the all-time Canadian ten-best list; in Quebec a memorial cult set off by his tragic premature death left us an auditorium, two national film prizes, and an urban park in his name. Since his death a monograph on his work has appeared in English, as well as a full-length documentary on his life and work, yet neither Leach (1999) nor PAULE BAILLARGEON's *Claude Jutra, portrait sur film (Claude Jutra, an Unfinished Story*, NFB, 2002, 82) treat seriously the issue of sexual identity in his artistic biography.

For years the textbooks have repeated Jutra's centrality in the historical trajectory and generic makeup of Quebec and Canadian cinemas, in particular his theme of youth and the passage from innocence to knowledge. Yet this centrality has been constructed by the literature through codewords and stereotypes that range from the veiled judgements of "self-indulgence," the "Quebec Cocteau," and "masochism" to "mental, moral and romantic confusion that we were all going through at the time ... what is the secret, what is the key to the vault?"[2] And then there are the subjournalistic idiocies that have more in common with *Toronto Sun* profiles of child molesters. Savour this 1970s excerpt from Martin Knelman, launched by an acknowledgement of Jutra's sovereigntist sympathies:

When you think of a shy, plump, forty-six year old film director with granny glasses dancing in the street [after the 1976 PQ victory], it's impossible not to think of it as a delicately humorous scene from a Claude Jutra movie ... the personality of the man is more openly, more fully expressed in his movies than in his behaviour in what used to be called real life. As a human being, Claude Jutra is rather shy and understated. His smiles suggest that he has marvellous little secrets, and perhaps that's why he appears to communicate more readily with kids ... his mild little smile and his subtle, cheerfully ironic remarks hint that there are things going on in his head that he's not quite ready to tell you. (1977, 56)

Knelman's jokey affection also resulted elsewhere in a panic reaction to Jutra's late English-language masterpiece *Dreamspeaker* (see chapter 5), whose climax happens to be an ecstatic skinny-dipping scene between the blonde pubescent hero and his adult mentor, a mute native giant.

The posthumous memorial cult was equally symptomatic: journalists who wanted to discuss Jutra's homosexuality were threatened with lawsuits, and a telefilm bio-project that included scenes of adolescent peer-group sexuality was vetoed. The Cinémathèque québécoise's memorial booklet, a series of eulogies by heterosexual co-workers and friends, is crammed with odd embroiderings of their confusing discovery that they hadn't really known him after all:

WERNER NOLD (Jutra's frequent editor): Today after he has gone, I realize that despite the fact that we worked together, having been what one can call without contradiction true friends, I don't know him very much. Can one have a secret nature to the degree of leaving his friends outside of a decision such as his? His last one. A decision that I admire. I wasn't aware of this courage of his ...

Claude was always interested in children; he established with them very privileged relationships. He had succeeded in creating an absolutely special communication with my own children, a relation that I otherwise felt envious of...

Claude was always on a diet; he ate Metrecal cookies. One day he arrived with a tube of Swiss sweetened condensed milk: "Well Werner, I've found the sperm of the Alps." We put it in coffee, he even had some from the tube to wash down his cookies, *a funny diet* ...

CLAIRE BOYER: Claude adored children. When he came to my place, he would roll on the floor with my children and their dog Lupin. Screams and laughter would fill the house where he would suddenly become the youngest. It was one of the sadnesses of his life not to have any children.

CLÉMENT PERRON (scen. for *Antoine*): We had known each other already for several years but I was not close to him. I would say even that quite a few things, naturally, separated us ...

LORRAINE DU HAMEL: He died as he lived, alone and discreet.[3]

Was this tone of surprise and patronization based on a misapprehension o f Jutra's artistic self-revelation as the real thing? Take his persona as an actor, for example, in his own films and those of others, in which he had

Peter (Ian Tracey), an orphan whose burst at freedom is doomed in Claude Jutra's *Dreamspeaker* (1976), a role that epitomizes the centrality of intergenerational eros and mentorship in the author's oeuvre. Production still, CBC

no qualms about performing wrenching vulnerability and self exposure, even in the literal sense of the frontal nudity that happened to go along with several of his performances. Did his colleagues think because they had seen his *zizi* that they had seen the man? That this childlike auntie's entire life was on the screen and behind the camera?

Looking more closely at Jutra's first two films can help. *Le dément,* amateur cinema in the etymological sense of the word, declares itself a campfire melodrama for boy scouts, and it certainly is that, a *child abuse* melodrama. The film's first-person narrator, a twelve- or thirteen-year-old scout recounts the troop's rescue of an abused boy from his drunken hermit father, who eventually falls to his death from a cliff, pursued by the troop, who become a vigilante mob of astonishing violence. The film is also, thanks to Jutra's and his lifelong collaborator Michel Brault's precocious handling of Claude's Bolex, a lyrical essay on the summer forest and on teenage male bonding and socialization, punctuated by not one but three bathing sequences, deliriously long and sensual, the *Lord of the Flies* gone *Boys in the Sand.* The abusive family is a demonic opposite of the idealized scout troop, that same-sex parental substitute and institution of male socialization, but the narrator's reference to the passive son-victim muddies the neatness of the opposition: "He must be his son, he seemed to love him even if he was brutal." At the end, their mission of normalization completed, the scouts abandon their now-domesticated orphan at a foster home of stultifying tranquility.

Mouvement, Jutra's second film, is a dream narrative of a triangular romance that resolves itself in a violence that once again surprises. A hetero couple are menaced by a charismatic male, bare-chested and oiled to kill, felicitously labelled "the other," who pursues the hero through the woods, across bridges, and along roads and waterfronts, killing him four times. The heroine is ineffectual and basically figures as currency in the real narrative exchange of the film, the intense attraction/repulsion between the two men. *Mouvement* is influenced by, among others, Maya Deren, Eisenstein, and Cocteau but most surprisingly by Kenneth Anger's *Fireworks,* still wet from the lab in 1949. It is not surprising that Maurice Huot from *La Patrie* found *Mouvement* morbid, bizarre, obscure, surreal, and "sensation for the sake of sensation" (December 1949). The jury at the first Canadian Film Awards disagreed and gave the teenager his first prize.

Much more is going on in these two films than fun with Claude's birthday Bolex. It doesn't take a psychoanalytic PhD to wonder what the young artist is working out in the obsessive repetitiveness of the narrative and the dramatic excess of the violence by which the figures of heterosexual romance and the nuclear family are dispatched in the two films. And there is the blatant beefcake of both films, or should I say calfcake, with the hunky bad guy coming back as obsessively as Nosferatu, and the scouts rushing into the water for ritual communion at the blow of a whistle, even in the midst of orphan rescue (the narrator performs his own striptease for the camera early on, throwing each garment in turn from off-camera into the frame). Clearly the scophophilic fantasies of bathing, of same-sex combat and pursuit, of male mortality, represent tentative and contradictory confessions and disavowals, steps back and forth on the cultural continuums that span from homosocial male bonding to same-sex genital exchange, from parental love through same-sex mentorship to intergenerational eros.

Skipping back and forth across his filmography, I am drawn to the critical and commercial failure of Jutra's two ambitious features about doomed heterosexual passion, *Kamouraska* (1973) and *Pour le meilleur et pour le pire* (1975). These films more or less reconstitute *Mouvement*'s boy-boy-girl triangle, and in their failure led to Jutra's final period of exile and disarray and films like *By Design* in English Canada. I prefer to see these works in the larger context of Jutra's Forsterian silence following *À tout prendre.* Certainly, the instability of the last fifteen years of his oeuvre was inextricable from the obliqueness with which he felt obliged to approach his homoerotic sensibilities and preoccupations. This may have been due in large part to the hurt he felt after the public queerbaiting he faced, not only from critics but from collaborators and peers DENYS ARCAND, Jean-Claude Labrecque and even Michel Brault in the decade after coming out in *À tout prendre*, his only venture in explicit autobiography, a hurt compounded by the censorship later imposed on the film's gay voice for its CBC broadcast. How *not* to make a Canadian film? he asked in 1968. "Choose a non commercial subject, so personal it is indecent, banal, futile, immoral, sordid." was the first prescription. We can never know to what extent this bitterness was coloured by his awareness of the monstrosity with which society would brand the erotic sensibility he expressed on celluloid, a closet within a closet, a closet that was *not* to be decriminalized the following year, 1969.

Silence is relative, and it is essential to move back to the documentaries of the fifties and sixties, counterposing them to his late feature films, in which adult mentorship would be increasingly problematized – remember *Mon oncle Antoine*'s drunken Antoine and frivolous Fernand (played interestingly by Jutra) – or futile, as in *Dreamspeaker* (see chapter 5), *Pour le meilleur ou le pire* (1975), or *La Dame en couleurs* (1984). The earlier nonfiction inevitably aligns the idealist openness of children and teenagers with the beneficent nurturing of adults. The Age of Aquarius increasingly ushered in the blind destructiveness of adult authority, for example the cops who clamp down on the humpy Westmount skateboarders in *Rouli-roulant (The Devil's Toy*, 1966, 15), a film dedicated, appropriately for those who read such things between the lines, "to all those who are victims of intolerance," or the range of authority figures excoriated in *Wow!* (see chapter 3). In this broader view of the documentaries and features as complementary visions of these same processes of growth, education, and socialization, one thing is incontrovertible: Jutra's sense of these processes, the most profound within our two national cinemas in which youth films have long been a privileged genre, is channelled and deepened through the physicality of his pubescent heroes and through his eroticization of their pedagogic interactivity. Jutra the poet of youthful learning cannot be separated from the Jutra whose erotic fulfilment derives from engagement in that process. This is the essence of Jutra's work. Here is the terror it has held for critics and film historians, here are the secret and the courage that his closest collaborators couldn't face.

The final word I give to Jutra himself, a testamentary line from the commentary of Jutra's finest documentary *Comment savoir* (1966, 71), a film purportedly about new technologies of learning but one really about the persistence of the intergenerational human dimension within the encroaching techno-cybernetic order. The line was written and read by the director over a magistral scene in which a boy is taking a lab dish to a sunny classroom windowsill in order to watch crystal formation: "What I will have learned, what I will have understood, are, along with love, my most precious possessions, and like love are the best things to receive and to give. It is with these religious precautions that this afternoon I have just placed this in a ray of sunlight."

KEARNS, PATRICIA, b. 1957. Documentarist, programmer. One of Montreal's distinct independent Anglo lesbian voices, Concordia-trained Kearns is known chiefly within the queer circuit for two films, *If the Family Fits* (1994, 51) and *Choir Girls* (1998, 52). The latter was a loving, sprightly communal portrait of a Montreal women's choir, whereas the former was a measured, aesthetically resourceful essay on alternative families, including cutaways to Real Women spokesdemogogues, who hang themselves with their own microphone cords. Kearns's interest in the "lesbian continuum" and left/feminist politics surfaced in her NFB production *Democracy à la Maude* (1998), a portrait of antiglobalization activist Maude Barlow, which had the distinction of being baited for its state-funded "partiality" by the parliamentary right. Kearns more recently has been an activist within women's new media arts organizations. In 1988 Kearns helped found Image + Nation and continued her involvement into the 1990s.

KELLY, KEVIN, b. 1958. Interdisciplinary artist, video maker. Trained at Lethbridge, Victoria, and Rutgers, Montrealer Kelly contributed two videotapes to the queer festival circuit, *A Super Natural Premiere* (1997, 6) and *Autobiology 15* (2002, 2), in addition to a wealth of video installation work on the international art scene. Kelly's first tape is an autobiographical narration of sexual initiation by his thirteen-year-old elder brother, laid over the otherworldly backdrop of the 1960s television images that provided the imaginary context for a small boy's coming-of-age, from *Bewitched* to *Lost in Space*.

KENNEDY, ROBERT, b. 1962. Director, video maker, actor, and editor. This prizewinning and prolific artist has produced almost thirty short experimental and documentary works in 16mm, 8mm, and video within the Toronto queer and activist communities since 1986. A contributor to the work of filmmakers from BRUCE LABRUCE to Ron Mann, he has been popular on the international festival circuit from New Zealand to Barcelona, as well as TIFF. His films range from activist documentary to self-reflexive media analysis and queer comic experimentalism. In the last category, my favourite is *Hi I'm Steve* (1999, 7), a comic gem about a baldish, skinny thirty-something everyman who gives up on the telephone dating services and finds love and happiness as a dolphin. Shot on crystalline black and white Super 8, *Hi I'm Steve* features the artist's own speedy run-on voice-over, and his edgy performance sums up perfectly a whole universe of neurotic relationship insecurity and ever-hopeful fantasy-reality management. "Hi I'm Steve. I confuse intimacy and sex but is that really so terrible?"

KINGSTON, ONTARIO. reelout queer film + video festival. Queer-film exhibition activity in the heartland of Tory Ontario, the hub of prisons, military bases, and crusty Upper Canada academia, began around 1980 with a focused program at the National Film Theatre entitled "Images of Social Reality: Gay Issues and Film" and featuring mostly male-oriented films such as *Montreal Main*. After two decades of intermittent stirrings, "reelout" was launched in the rented backroom of the region's only gay bar in 1999, followed by a strong weekend of mostly alternative fare the next spring. Since then, strong student organizing energy, supported on campus by the Ontario Public Interest Research Group and the Film Studies Department, has ensured steady audience development based on intense annual one-weekend packages of indie features, visiting Canadian presenters, local-talent panel discussions, and imaginatively programmed shorts.

KINGSTONE, PETER, b. 1974. Video maker, writer, curator. Trent- and York-educated, Toronto-based Kingstone was the prolific producer of more than a dozen video shorts and installations in the early 2000s – about growing up/out queer, family, art, the media, relationships, and of course sex. My favourite, *Driving* (2003, 14), is about all of those things: fragments of the artist filming his (fictional?) boyfriend breaking up with him as he's driving aimlessly through and around Toronto on the sixteen-lane 401, captured on a traffic surveillance camera loop that seems as circular as the relationship process itself.

KIRKLAND, DEBORAH, b. 1950. Filmmaker, cultural administrator. Toronto-based Kirkland, one of the LIFT queer circle, made two shorts that innovate narrative structure for the exploration of relationships and desire. *Slip* (1999, 7) humorously recounts erotic dreams that a woman and her therapist just happen to be having about each other at exactly the same time. *Letter to Margot* (2001, 8) deals more with memory and loss; it's an exquisitely minimalist cinematic letter to an "ex" from a despairing but slowly healing narrator: "I do not know how to let go of you."

KLASSEN, KATHRYN, b. 1954. Documentarist, film development officer. Saskatchewan-bred, Concordia-trained Klassen, often a collaborator of JOSÉ TORREALBA, provided the queer community festival circuit with *Out of the Shadow Into the Sun* (2001, 78) after several years of preliminary versions. In this elegant documentary history, Klassen celebrates women within the macho ranks of Spanish bullfighting. Her eroticization of her bold heroines is implicit (L-words avoided), whether in her sustained analogy to a statuesque flamenco dancer or in her awestruck gaze, often slow motion, at the *toreras'* grace and daring.

KNEEBONE, TOM, 1932–2003. Actor. New Zealand–born, Toronto-based Kneebone was one of English Canada's best-known comic performers in cabaret and in theatre, where his queerish roles included Noel Coward, Peter Pan, Hans Christian Anderson, and Puck. In addition to many guest performances on the CBC over three decades, Kneebone (Order of Canada) stood out on film for a cameo as Robert Shaw's agile and sympathetic co-worker in the pioneering Montreal feature *The Luck of Ginger Coffey* (1964), characterized mincingly in a tavern scene as a momma's boy. But the actor got far fewer film roles than he deserved.

KOKKER, STEVE, b. 1965. Video maker, critic, writer. Montreal-bred, Estonia-based Steve Kokker is the ardent chronicler of the erotic undercurrents of homosociality, fandom, and voyeurism – in both word and image. Popular on the queer community festival circuit and occasionally within mainstream festivals, his personal video documentaries *Komrades* (2003) and *Birch* (1995) reflect his troubled encounters with Russian military subcultures and masculinity in general. *Happiness Is Just a Thing Called Joe* (1998) is the ultimate found-footage fan homage to Joe Dallesandro by way of Judy Garland. His decade of film reviewing beginning in 1987 in Montreal weeklies, as well as other publications, championed emerging queer cinema by such directors as Gus Van Sant, as well as quirky eruptions of homoerotic desire in unexpected corners of the media.

LABERGE, YVES, b. 1961. Director. Reports from Cannes in May 1981 by both dailies and the gay press were thunderstruck that Canada was represented at the world's most prestigious film festival not only by Gilles Carles's multimillion-dollar superproduction *Les Plouffe* but also by a five-hundred-dollar twenty-minute Super 8 film by the unknown Trois-Rivières Cégep student Laberge. A coming-out narrative of a young man, *Tous les garçons* showed, according to my report in *Le Berdache* (October 1984, 34), its hero struggling with memories of earlier rejected overtures and experiments with drag, and finally his decision to be himself. A precocious blip in Canadian queer film history, Laberge seems to have disappeared from the radar screen thereafter, despite announced plans for a second feature.

LABRUCE, BRUCE, b.1964. Director, scriptwriter, ziner, columnist, critic. Toronto's most in-your-face queer filmmaker, Bruce LaBruce holds many records: one of our best-known auteurs internationally, his four feature films are the most difficult to access nationally; the only Perspectives Canada perennial honoree to have been omitted from Rist (2001) and Wise (2001) (which includes Neve Campbell!); the only auteur to have sucked and been fucked in close-up on-screen *and* to have included Bergman on his all-time "top ten" list for *Sight and Sound* and published academic film criticism on Peewee Herman and HIV/AIDS (under the name of Bryan Bruce for Toronto's *Cineaction!* in the 1980s); the only major Canadian filmmaker never to have received any government arts grants.

A small town Ontario boy made good in Toronto, LaBruce started his filmmaking career with underground Super 8 sex films such as *I Know What It's Like to Be Dead* (1987) and scored his first feature hit with the no-budget Warhol-esque romance *No Skin Off My Ass* (1991), featuring LaBruce in love with a skinhead street boy and his far-out sister making a movie about it. *Super 8½* (1994) was a kind of remake of elements of that film, more ambitious and complex with its interwoven narratives of Bruce the down-and-out porn star being exploited by up-and-coming lesbian filmmaker Googie for her new film and including a fine repeat perform-ance by his skinhead consort. *Hustler White* (1996) followed, with LaBruce's obsession with sexwork crystallizing in a pseudo-quasi documentary shot on Santa Monica Boulevard. For his next feature, LaBruce's perennial German producer Jorge Brüning took him across the Atlantic, and their skinhead potboiler entitled *Skin Flick* (1999), with a hard-core version called *Skin Gang*, was shot in London and Berlin. Assaulting audiences with its deliberately provocative transmission of skinhead violence and racism and implicating them in its eroticization, *Skin Flick/Gang* demonstrated an edge that few artists would risk. Mean-while, with scarcely any pauses in his fierce, astute and witty journalistic output (from the underground zine *J.D.s* of the 1980s to the biweekly columns/critiques for Toronto's *Eye Weekly* since 1997), LaBruce's unremitting artistic growth has been as priapic as it has been profound (see chapter 8).

LAFONTAINE, YVES, b. 1965. Critic, programmer, filmmaker. As editor and film writer for Montreal's *Fugues* monthly since 1994, Université de Montréal–trained Lafontaine is Quebec's most influential gay film critic and advocate. Valued for his reliable *tours d'horizon* and encyclopedic knowledge of international queer cinema, Lafontaine offers impeccable judgment and catholic taste. As a programmer, Lafontaine was at the centre of the Image + Nation programming team and leadership during its growth period from 1993 to 2000 and codirected (with René Lavoie) the important AIDS-solidarity Festival international du film VIH et Sida in 1995. Wearing his filmmaker's hat, Lafontaine was responsible for four prizewinning experimental shorts, including the meta-porn *Corpusculaire* (1990, 11) and *Homme hippocampe* (1992,18), a hypnotic construction of dreamlike pools, sleeping and swimming bodies, and pulsating abstract collages, with a whispered voice declaiming the fantasy mystery of the eponymous seahorse man. Filmmaking's loss was film culture's gain.

LAMBERT, ALAN (pseudonym Alain Lebeau), 1967–92. Porn star, sex-worker. A suburban boy from Montreal's South Shore who went to Los Angeles around 1988, Alan Lambert – 5′8″, brown hair, uncut – made about two dozen porno films for such studios as Falcon, including *Beach Dreamer*, *Hard to Be Good*, *Bound for Lust*, and *Wolfboy*. As his career took off, his roles increasingly played up his specialty as a bottom and the scripts never tried to explain his noticeable Québécois accent, other than casting him as a New Zealander or a Frenchman. Around 1990, Lambert studied public administration at UQAM but did not persist. As he developed plans to kill himself at the peak of his physical perfection, his small network of friends tried to talk him out of it, but to no avail. He shot himself publicly in Square St-Louis just before Christmas at the age of twenty-five – less than a year after he'd posed as coverboy for the Valentine's Day issue of *Fugues*. Long suicide communications in French and English focused on incoherent radical, apocalyptic beliefs, insisting that AIDS was not a factor and that his spirit was still alive. After Lambert's death, Los Angeles experimental filmmaker William E. Jones made *Finished* (1997), a beautiful experimental reflection on the performances, friendships, idiosyncratic beliefs, and premature death of the charismatic man he never knew – eighty-five elegiac minutes that never show the cock and the ass that ensured his livelihood and immortality.

LANG, K.D., b. 1961. Singer, actor. The Grammy-winning "torch and twang" vegetarian cowgirl from Consort, Alberta is the biggest international Canadian lesbian star of the last two decades. This book is not about singers, but lang's visibility as a performer and icon in the visual media is such a part of her impact that her inclusion is incontrovertible. Lang is officially considered to have finally "come out" shortly after the release of her 1992 album *Ingenue*, when the thirty-year-old superstar did

a generic interview and cover for *The Advocate* (16 June 1992) and soon
after posed for a shave by supermodel Cindy Crawford on the cover of
Vanity Fair (August 1993). However, anyone who remembers her queer-
flirtatious work and gender-transgressive image years before that wonders
what the fuss was all about. Her major film role was in Percy Adlon's
prizewinning *Salmonberries* (Germany, 1991) as an alienated part-Inuit
foundling androgyne named Kotzebue who develops a crush on and eventually wins over the German librarian Roswitha in remote Alaska (throwing her books around, bringing her a big fresh fish, and giving her and us
her own frontal nude scene). (She also appeared in 2000 in Stephan
("Priscilla") Elliott's UK-Canada coproduction flop *Eye of the Beholder*,
and reportedly the less said about her performance the better.) No doubt
more prized on the lesbian circuit is her legendary but rare CBC duet
of "I Want To Sing You a Love Song" (1991) with our other country
singer/lesbian icon Anne Murray (heavy eye contact and explosive subtext), which MARUSYA BOCIURKIW kept alive with her touring lecture
"Cross-Sexing the Narrative: Lesbian Subtext in Music Videos." Lang's
music video performances contributed to her charisma, alongside that
phenomenal voice. Her cover of Cole Porter's "So in Love" in the AIDS-
fundraiser *Red Hot and Blue* compilation (1990), with its explicit same-
sex elegy narrative and its heart-wrenching vocal interpretation, is my
favourite version of my favourite song from my favourite musical. The
let-it-all-hang-out, Gemini-winning CBC special "k.d. lang's Buffalo
Café," (writer as well as star, 1989) is a must for Canadian content aficionados (a duet of "CA-NA-DA" with Stompin' Tom Connors himself).
(See chapter 5.)

LANG, PAUL, Videomaker. Ontario-bred, Vancouver-based Lang is one of
the most articulate voices on Vancouver's AIDS-activist artistic front. In
1993 an early collaboration with ZACHERY LONGBOY led to *Choose Your
Plague* (6), an often-programmed poetic tape in which the two artists literally eat (and spit out) the words that determine their existence as HIV+ gay
men, from "fear" to "racism." In 2001 Lang solo'd HIV *Rollercoaster*
(27), a disturbing, open-ended essay on the culture of barebacking, in
which testimonies and performances by a range of "stake-holders" (one
enthusiastic participant brags that he measures the unprotected loads he
receives in litres), interpolated with porno clips. Two visual metaphors pre-
dominate, the famous rollercoaster in the Pacific National Exhibition site
and a less familiar one: the rosy, anal *Fantastic Voyage/Innerspace* landscape of colonoscopy images. Lang has collaborated as camera with most
of the Video In queer artists.

LANGLOIS, DENIS, b. 1960. Director, scriptwriter. The most ambitious and persistent of Montreal's feature film interpreters of young urban gay identity of the AIDS generation, Concordia-trained Langlois was a stalwart of Main Film co-op before breaking through with his twenty-one-minute *Ma Vie* (My Life, 1992). Programmed by TIFF and queer festivals around the world, this dramatized, semiautobiographical life of Jeannot (played by Langlois) stretches from the hippie sixties through the disco years to the AIDS-panicked start of the nineties. *Ma vie* allegorizes post-Stonewall gay history, as well as laying out the themes of Langlois's subsequent two features, both cowritten with his life partner Bertrand Lachance (b. 1948).

L'Escorte (1996, 91), Langlois's first full-length feature, expands the scrutiny of loves, relationships, art, loss, and mortality among the coke-sniffing young urban queers of the filmmaker's generation. The twenty-something gay men who are the focus of the film inhabit the Plateau and live lives that have been irremediably affected by AIDS. The gay male friendship circle comedy-melodrama, often set in West Hollywood, has been a staple of the festival circuit, but this tale of a callboy's destabilization of an interlocked network of a couple and their artsy exes and friends is one of the few Canadian prototypes. Paradoxically, for all Langlois's strong sense of urban place, *Escorte* made more of a splash in festivals and theatres abroad, from Winnipeg to Paris, than at home, where some critics baulked at the plot contrivances and other low-budget first-feature symptoms. But audiences appreciated Langlois's persistent, sincere, and observant canvas of everyday life and love in the gay nineties.

Funded with great difficulty, *Danny in the Sky* (2001) portrays a confused, straight male stripper with a gay father and prods the ambiguities within sexual identities and the industries of desire. True to form, despite *Danny*'s glittery showstoppers and resonant landscape of the Village gai, this film did less well in Quebec than abroad, dive-bombing undeservedly at the box office in the prophet's own country. In 2003 Langlois determined to change all that as he doggedly moved into production with the queer amnesia melodrama *Amnésie: L'Énigme James Brighton*, with financing finally in his pocket after a decade of struggle.

LANGLOIS, MICHEL, b. 1945. Director, scriptwriter, professor. Neither the most prolific nor the most explicit presence in the Quebec queer film scene, Langlois's films will be among its enduring legacies. First making his mark as co-scriptwriter with such auteurs as Jacques Leduc and LÉA POOL, his scripts sometimes registered queer nuances and characters, as in Pool's homosocial dream *La femme de l'hôtel* (1984, 89), but more often not, exploring instead general themes of aging, mortality, relationships, and

A callboy destabilizing an urban gay couple in *L'Escorte* (1996), the first feature by Denis Langlois, the most ambitious and persistent of Montreal's feature film interpreters of young gay male identity in the AIDS generation. Production still from film stock shot on Super 16 by D.O.P. Stefan Ivano with actors Robin Aubert and Paul-Antoine Taillefer, Cinémathèque québécoise

psychological torment. Such was the case with his first feature, *Cap Tourmente* (1993, 115), a melodrama about a rural family agonizing over its secrets in which a mysterious stranger played by heartthrob ROY DUPUIS fucks [with] everyone in the family, including the son, and delivers the obligatory nude scenes.

However, Langlois's most unforgettable queer contributions are three exquisitely rendered nonfeature films. The prizewinning *Sortie 234* (Exit 234, 1988, 25) was a rural bisexual triangle narrative. When I programmed in Toronto in 1989 this short first film showcasing a scriptwriter and a young actor unknown outside Quebec, I showed no restraint: "Full-blown archetypal narrative at its most dreamily gorgeous. James Dean finally tells Robert Mitchum he's in love with him and Dorothy Malone lights another cigarette … Langlois … is a filmmaker to watch out for if not to die for." *Sortie 234* remains as ravishing as it was in 1988 and not only because it featured Dupuis in his first screen role (and best gay role) as the conflicted country boy in love with his best friend who ultimately has to take Exit 234 for the big city. Langlois wove flickers of Jean Genet's *Chant d'amour* into his fierce love story, as well as dialogue worthy of *Casablanca*.

Lettre à mon père (1992) was a poetic autobiographical coming-out essay, addressed to the filmmaker's dead father. *Le fil cassé* (*The Broken Thread*, NFB, 2002, see chapter 6) continued in this vein with its moving reflection on genealogy and the continuity the author has interrupted as a childless gay man. Langlois has taught at Montreal's Institut de l'image et du son since 1996.

LANTEIGNE, KAT, b. 1975. Director, actor, screenwriter, playwright. Vancouver Film School–trained Lanteigne started in the nineties as a playwright produced in Vancouver before making two skilled narratives of female coming out/of age, both showcasing her own effectively nuanced lead performances. *Wilma's Sacrifice* (1998, 15) is a gothic rural period piece about the fanatical familial and religious repression of lesbo teen romance caught red-handed in the barn, which fortunately leads to escape and a happy ending. *Maids* (2001, 17) is a hilarious comedy about compulsory hetero-socialization unfolding within a wedding from hell.

LARKIN, RYAN, b. 1953. Animator. Bred in Dorval and trained at the Montreal School of Fine Arts, the precocious Larkin was taken under the wing of the NORMAN MCLAREN circle at the NFB at nineteen. He is known chiefly for his inspired study of human motion, *Walking* (1968, Oscar nomination, 5), which, among other things, domesticated the male nude for the still-skittish animation studio. After four films, Larkin dropped out in the 1970s and has since lived on the Montreal streets, as recounted in Chris Landreth's Oscar-winning animated portrait *Ryan* (2004, 14). Larkin was famous again, and his ex-girlfriend wondered on-screen about the links of his homosexuality to his extraordinary life and art.

LAVOIE, ANDRÉ, b. 1966. Critic. Université de Montréal–trained Lavoie wrote a thesis on queer representation in 1980s Quebec cinema and has been a contributor to the film magazine *Ciné-bulles* since 1990 (editor 1995–99), as well as stringer for *Le devoir*. A public lecturer and panelist on queer cinema, including queer Quebec soaps, Lavoie is a connoisseur of international auteur cinema, but never a proselytizer for its queer element at the cost of quality and vision. Covering Image + Nation 1992, Lavoie lambasted Studio D for TV-style visuals in its documentary about disabled women's sexuality, *Toward Intimacy*, and summed up the new era of queer film abundance: "Trying out all genres and formats, gay and lesbian filmmakers, despite a sure marginalization of their works in official distribution circuits, prove that, just as with their straight colleagues, they are capable of the best and the worst, of the most surprising boldness as well as of the most sterile conformity" (1993).

LAWSON, STEPHEN (b. 1969), and AARON POLLARD (b. 1967). Trained at NTS and at ECIAD and Concordia, respectively, Winnipeg-bred Lawson and Montrealer Pollard are also known both as Gigi L'Amour and Pipi Douleur and as 2boys. This creative team and real-life couple work in video-supplemented performance and in video itself, based in Montreal, and have presented in arts and queer spaces in North America and Europe. The tandem are known above all for extravagant and intense stage spectacles such as *Battle Hymn* (2002), where Gigi incarnates Judy Garland singing her traditional patriotic showstopper before Pollard's video backdrop of showering lollipops as symbols of infantile regression and the capitalist work ethic. Translated to strictly electronic format, the duo made *Teddy Bears' Picnic* (2001, 6), capturing a perverse Goldilocks flirting with drag king bears, and ventured into new territory with *15 Questions (Something Blue)* (2002, 3), a raunchy collage assault on same-sex marriage.

L'ÉCUYER, GERALD, b. 1962. Director, scriptwriter, interviewer. Trained at Concordia and the CFC, L'Écuyer is known chiefly for his experimental autobiographical feature *The Grace of God* (Toronto, 1997, 75). Wildly uneven like the hypnotically beautiful kaleidoscope that is its principal visual refrain, *Grace* was hemmed together over a decade, thanks to its initial production push at the CFC in the late eighties and, as its voice-over narration claims, to the intervention of four psychiatrists. Prequels or earlier versions included prizewinning student films from the 1980s. Popular on the queer circuit and in specialized settings like Toronto's Rendezvous with Madness festival, *Grace* is a haunting quilt of confessions, fragments, and stories, many about a boy's discovery of parental power and beneficence, of erotic obsession, of the institutions of psychiatry and filmmaking, and of the therapeutic power of storytelling itself. David Cronenberg's star turn as an evil psychiatrist in *Grace* and L'Ecuyer's cameo appearance in an episode of David Lynch's *Twin Peaks* were by-products of an earlier career as a starfuck interviewer for glossy celeb magazines such as *Interview*. L'Écuyer has more recently worked for TVO.

LEE, PAUL, b. 1963. Director, producer, curator. Hong Kong–born, raised in Toronto after 1976 and trained at University of Toronto and New York University, Lee made three short films in the 1990s that were staples of mainstream, queer, and diasporic festivals. The prizewinning *Thick Lips Thin Lips* (1994, 6) is an experimental close-up study of an embrace between two men of Asian and African descent respectively, in the context of racist and homophobic violence and communicated through music rather than language. *The Offering* (1999, 10, 35mm) is narrative, both ascetic and lush, set in traditional Japan, about a relationship between a monk and a novice that is mirrored by the transition of the seasons (inspired by the Jean Cocteau ballet *The Young Man and His Death*). Lee's films are characterized by their sensuality combined with tight formal precision. Lee was the coordinator of the first edition of Inside Out in 1991 and thereafter also committed himself to producing first films by other directors, as well as curating thematic series.

LEFAVE, LAURA JEANNE, b. 1963. Videomaker, installation artist. University of Ottawa–trained lefave has been part of the Montreal experimental interdisciplinary arts scene since the early nineties. Known for her delicately orchestrated feminist/formalist minimalism, lefave's most explicitly queer work may be *Seuls les éternuements sont éternels* (Only sneezing is forever, 1998, 9). This reflection on the optics of watching an eclipse as a blinding vertical stripe through a camera obscura on a beach also reflects the artist's own identity and perception plus the silhouette of a strolling dyke couple enjoying the beach in a less theoretical way.

LEPAGE, ROBERT, b. 1957. Of all Quebec's major gay artists, theatrical wunderkind Robert Lepage is perhaps the least *politically* gay. His first three adaptations of his marathon theatrical productions, as Peter Dickinson has argued (2005), involved considerable straightening out of characters and situations: *Le Confessionnal* (1995, Genie best picture and director), *Le Polygraphe* (1996), and *Nô* (1998). Whether or not the straightening process involved simply compression or also sanitization, the first two, furthermore, tackled the ideologically tricky theme of queer suicide. Nevertheless, Lepage's universes of shifting historical times and transcultural spaces seemed very queer in many ways: *Le Confessionnal* has become one of the more enigmatic, meaty works of the international queer canon.

After *Polygraphe,* the frothy *Nô* was high camp from beginning to end, with its requisite queer joke scene leaving no more bitter an aftertaste than all the péquiste, fédéraliste, and FLQ jokes. Lepage's fourth feature *Possible Worlds* (2000), a British coproduction based on another author's play for the first time, was his coldest, straightest work, though beefcake detectors go off intermittently. *La face cachée de la lune* (*The Far Side of the Moon,* 2003), another Lepage theatrical adaptation, continued the director's habit of matter-of-factly incorporating queer references and characters with little interest in sexuality as a theme in its own right, but this time there are additional resonances: *Face* is the most autobiographical of his films and the queerest one since *Confessionnal*. Lepage himself plays both of two brother protagonists, one a space-theory geek who has a female "ex" but is apparently asexual, despite strange behaviour with his brother's lover in a sauna he is "trying out." The other brother is a pompously unsympathetic guppy weather man "who happens to be gay but no big deal." The lover Carl is more interesting, a bodybuilder covered below the shoulders in piercings and tattoos, but above the shoulders he is a Quebec City civil-servant bureaucrat. Perhaps it's political after all.

LEVIN, MELISSA, b. 1958. Film- and videomaker, documentarist, teacher. Bred on the U.S. East Coast and living in Chicago and San Francisco before migrating to Toronto, Levin has been a prolific and prizewinning chronicler and satirist of urban lesbian lifestyles since 1997. Often featuring Levin's partner, visual artist Nina Levitt, her works are popular in queer festivals, including the *Baking with Butch* series (2000–01, episode 1, 5; episode 2, 10), a comic clash of cooking show inanity with subcultural stand-up. *Cherries in the Snow (An Ode to Joan Nestle)* (2002, 4) is an artier initiative, a symbolic celebration of lesbian herstory through the transformation of a traditional housewife activity into a public cruising ritual: hanging out the undies to dry. Levin taught video at Toronto's Triangle queer high-school program before making *Class Queers* (codirector and writer Roxane Spicer, 2003, 53) a one-hour documentary on three of the program's brave students, an intimate and risk-taking vérité account that was broadcast on CBC *Newsworld* and other cable venues, marred unfortunately by the curse of the CBC voice-over. Levin has also been active in Inside Out.

LEVY, JOSHUA, b. 1974, director, writer. The Ontario-bred, York-trained filmmaker is known for his auspicious feature debut *Hayseed* (1997, 90; codirected with queer-friendly Andrew Hayes, b. 1971), which played TIFF and Sundance as well as the international rack of queer community festivals. In this *Candide*-style parable, Gordie, a diminutive blond cutie from a matriarchal rural farmstead, follows his lost beagle to big-city Toronto and never stops smiling despite all the gay white-slave traders and other corrupt, exploitative, and lustful wackos encountered there (cameos by the Toronto queer cabal THOMPSON, MACIVOR, and LABRUCE), as well as the requisite whore with a heart of gold whose profession oblivious Gordie narrowly escapes joining. Levy had worked on "Kids in the Hall," and other than Thompson, secured "Kids" backing in the form of a cowriter credit for Paul Bellini and a cameo by Mark McKinney. *Hayseed* somehow missed entering the Canadian canon, perhaps because the fresh, folksy but sex-savvy satire of innocence adrift was hard to pigeonhole as either queer or otherwise or because the Egoyan-Cronenberg tastemakers prefer to keep our frothy comic sensibilities on television and reserve the Art Cinema for world-heavy themes.

LILIEFELDT, LOUISE, b. 1968. Performance artist, teacher, video maker. South Africa–born, OCAD-trained Liliefeldt has been active in Toronto queer-artists networks since the early 1990s, collaborating as performer and otherwise with many video artists, including CHRISTINA ZEIDLER, MOORES and TRAVASSOS, and a group called Machine Sex Action Group. Her 2001 video collaboration with Michael Caines, *Hamartia* (11), programmed at Inside Out, is a minimalist confrontation with trauma, blood, spectatorship, and a woman's face staring back at the camera, with "a scrap of cloud" visible behind the eyes.

LIM, DESIREE, b. 1971. Videomaker, writer. Malaysia-bred, Tokyo-trained Lim worked for a decade within the Japanese lesbian movement, making several videos (such as *Disposable Lez*, 2000, 7) and a feature film, all notable for their lighthearted satirical humour and busy, colourful sense of the frame. Having settled in Vancouver in 2002, she is involved in TV development projects and codirected with WINSTON XIN the resourcefully comic documentary *Salty Wet* (2002, 9), in which local Chinese-Canadians debate adaptations of queer language in Cantonese, including the strange phrases "eating the carpet" and "hitting the airplane!"

LIVE PEACH PRODUCTIONS, a.k.a. Poison Ivy and Eden, a.k.a. Jane M. [Jane Meikle, b. 1976] and Emily M. [Emily West Cummins, b. 1977]). Porneastes. Cummins and Meikle, then enterprising McGill/Concordia students, are known for *Classy Cunts* (1999, 45), a DIY porn anthology of three flavourful episodes. Shot in a fetish club in the Village gai and shuddering with an aura of community initiative and zero-budget creative excitement, *Classy* inaugurated a new phase in Canadian lesbian eroticism (see chapter 8).

LOGUE, DEIRDRE, b. 1964. Filmmaker, curator, arts administrator, performer. Trained at NSCAD, Banff, and Kent State (Ohio), Toronto-based experimentalist Logue is best known to queer film audiences for a series of nineteen DIY primal monodramas she performed and directed under the title *Enlightened Nonsense* (1997–2000, 22). The series explores gender ambiguity, as well as the maso physicality of assailing one's own body with basketballs, whipped cream, gaffer tape, and gravity. Logue ran Toronto's indie Images festival (1995–99) and moved on to head CFMDC, both essential enablers of queer cinema/video. Logue played the butch metalworker in Moores and Travassos's *Dog Days* (1999).

LONDON LESBIAN FILM FESTIVAL. The annual two-to-four-day spring event in the conservative Southwestern Ontario university city, continuous since 1992, is unique in Canada for both its longevity, its specific focus, and its hinterland bravado. The most recent coordinator was Kerry Kearns.

LONGBOY, ZACHERY CAMERON, b. 1963. Videomaker, performance/installation artist. Born in Churchill, Manitoba, of Sayisi Dene lineage, ECIAD-trained artist Zachery Longboy places his multiple identities as a white-adopted/native gay HIV+ Vancouverite at the centre of his multidisciplinary practice. His intensely felt, hybridly layered videos often use his complex performance-installations as a departure point. Among his best known is *Water into Fire* (1994, 10), based on a Banff Centre performance of the previous year: amid a candle-lit, native-iconed space littered with AZT bottles and echoing with traditional drumming and vocals, Longboy himself performs a nude choreography as a giant, shrieking bird, and one unforgettable shot features his whole body perched on one leg, his eagle eye staring right into the lens. The image-track is varied with Longboy's signature recourse to natural image of flowing water, woods, and meadows, and PWA voices intrude on the soundtrack, meditating on a mortality that is like "climbing a ladder." Longboy coordinated the First Nations Video Access Programme in Vancouver. His other AIDS-themed works included *Choose Your Plague* (with PAUL LANG, 1993, 6), and the PSA *Living Tree* (1993, 30 seconds). Those works concentrating most on the clash of his native heritage with his white urban cultural environment include *Eating Lunch* (1992, 12), *Confirmation of My Sins* (1995, 12), and *The Stone Show* (1999, 9). Longboy is nationally honoured and widely shown in queer and First Nations venues, as well as in public collections.

LOZANO, JORGE, b. 1950. Documentarist, videomaker, activist, curator. Colombia-bred, self-taught Lozano has been a prolific producer and organizer within the Toronto video and Latino communities since 1980, offering works with a strong political and personal sense of the hemispheric context. Especially well known within queer festival audiences for his documentation of the Latino female-impersonation subculture, the bisexual-identifying Lozano's *Samuel and Samantha* (1993, 21), a warm and profound portrait of his articulate codirector, Salvadoran-Canadian Samuel Lopes, as he dons his other persona, was an early celebration of diversity within Toronto's queer communities. Lozano's *Latinos en Tacones "The Pink Triangle"* (1999, 19) provided vivid documentation of the College St Latino club scene of the early 1990s. Lozano collaborated with other members in the queer video art community, such as ANDREW JAMES PATERSON.

LUBRIK, STANLÉ (pseudonym Jean-Denis Lapointe), b. 1955. Director, scriptwriter, impresario, magazine editor, cartoonist. Renaissance man

Zachery Longboy's choreography as a giant, shrieking bird in his native-iconed AIDS performance tape *Water into Fire* (1994, 10). VHS frame grab, film still compliments of Videopool

Lapointe is best known as a prolific energizing force within Montreal's commercial erotic culture; he's director of the Festival des arts du Village and has been principal collaborator at the skin magazine *Zipper/Zip* since 1994. As Lubrik (his connection to *2001: A Space Odyssey* is unknown), Lapointe was a chief artistic contributor to Quebec's two most successful porno features, *Alex et Bruno* (1999) and *Fuck Friends* (2000, director). The former, a narrative of an urban peeping tom finding farm work, love, and orgies in the country, was a hit on both sides of the Atlantic. The latter, a populist fresco of gay-next-door roommates topping each other's erotic escapades, was less meteoric commercially but more artful, with its low-key improvised performances, down-home snowscapes, long johns, and horny firemen.

LYND, LAURIE, b. 1959. Director. Toronto-based Lynd is best known for his prizewinning trilogy of gay-male narrative miniatures, the breakup musical *Together and Apart* (1985), *R.S.V.P.* (1991, 23), and *The Fairy Who Didn't Want to Be a Fairy Anymore* (1992, Genie, Best Short Fiction). Their masterful orchestration of music and affect is not surprising, given Lynd's acknowledged inspiration in Virginia Woolf, Barbra Streisand, and Julie Andrews, and *R.S.V.P.* is arguably the masterpiece. Thanks to the Pandemic, the 1980s and 1990s were drowning in elegies, an ancient art form that that lost generation had to reinvent. But this short fiction about the lover, friends, and family of a Toronto man who has died of AIDS is perhaps the simplest and the most beautiful and heartfelt of all. Thanks to CBC Radio, the deceased man's musical request becomes a posthumous reminder not only of his personal taste but also of music's power to heal, and, thanks to the broadcaster's national constituency across the time-zone grid, the song is a repeated ritual as new listeners are added each hour to the community of the grieving. R.S.V.P. reached an international audience as part of the 1993 package *Boys' Shorts: The New Queer Cinema* (see chapter 9).

DANIEL MACIVOR's performances are foundations for both R.S.V.P. and the whimsical allegory of self-hatred and affirmation *Fairy*. The collaboration of director and actor continued with Lynd's adaptation of MacIvor's one-person play *House* in 1995, which was funded, like *Fairy*, through the CFC. Built on the actor's provocative sensibility and stage charisma, *House* received mixed reviews, and Lynd moved on to directing mostly TV episodes (*Queer as Folk*, *Degrassi: The Next Generation*) and TV films (the children's fantasy *I Was a Rat*, BBC/CBC, 2002; and the New Brunswick health-care social melodrama *Open Heart*, 2004).

MACDONALD, ANN-MARIE, b. 1958. Playwright, novelist, actor. Prizewinning author MacDonald, bred in Cape Breton but Ontario-based, has been sparing in her involvement in film as a writer. As an actor, she won a Gemini for her lead performance as the sympathetic straight teacher in the CBC's lesbophobic native residential-school melodrama *Where the Spirit Lives* (1989). But MacDonald is remembered best by queer audiences for three strong supporting roles in feature films: as Brent Carver's ill-fated paraplegic little sister in *The Wars* (1983), as the sulky artist girl friend of Polly's boss in *I've Heard the Mermaids Singing* (1987), and as Frances, the repressed bookstore employee who finds a cause in the anticensorship struggle and true love in the arms of transsexual Judy, in *Better Than Chocolate* (1999). She narrated the Studio D hit *Forbidden Love* (1992), and also wryly embodied the closety power dyke from Bay Street in CASSANDRA NICOLAOU's *Interviews with My Next Girlfriend* (2001).

MACISAAC, ASHLEY, b. 1974. Musician, actor. This is not a book about brilliant but naughty Cape Breton Celtic fiddle players. But MacIsaac's cameo performances in two feature films from the queer canon, THOM FITZGERALD's *The Hanging Garden* (1997; MacIsaac also contributed much of the film's music) and the DANIEL MACIVOR-scripted *Marion Bridge* (2003) – not to mention a somewhat dazed appearance as himself in an episode of the CTV hockey miniseries *Powerplay* (1999) – more than qualify the deft-fingered queer rebel for these pages.

MACIVOR, DANIEL, b. 1962. Actor, playwright, scriptwriter, director. Cape Breton–bred MacIvor, the prolific wunderkind of the Toronto-based English Canadian theatre scene since the 1980s, has been an indispensable presence in queer cinema and video in English since his stunning performances as the AIDS-bereaved CBC listener in *R.S.V.P.* (1991) and the allegorical title character in *The Fairy Who Didn't Want to Be a Fairy Anymore* (1992), both by LAURIE LYND. As an actor, MacIvor's range is broad indeed, from the grand guignol pornocrat whose penis just can't stay in his pants in *Bubbles Galore* (1996) to the textured pathos of his role as Bob Mizer in THOM FITZGERALD's underrated *Beefcake* (1999). MacIvor acted for most of the other luminaries of the Toronto queer film scene, including GILBERT, PODESWA, and GREYSON. Far from a ghettoized artist looking inward only on the queer community, MacIvor's work as scriptwriter and, ultimately, director (*Past Perfect*, 2002) delivered complex insights into heterosexual family and relationships, as in the 2002 Cape Breton sisters melodrama *Marion Bridge* (which also included a finely drawn dyke character; director Wiebke von Carolsfeld). MacIvor has also supported emerging queer filmmakers, playing the ambiguous customer in JEAN-FRANÇOIS MONETTE's *Take-Out* (2000).

MACSWAIN, JAMES, b. 1945. Director, video maker, interdisciplinary visual artist, teacher, arts administrator. A distinctive queer voice within the Halifax independent film and arts network for more than two decades, as well as a pillar of the Atlantic Filmmakers Co-operative, MacSwain was trained at Mount Allison and teaches at NSCAD. His uneven and eclectic output includes *The Executor* (1996), a short narrative video touching on AIDS, triangles, and transgender; *Mother Marilyn* (1997), a whimsical cut-out animation about astronomy and Marilyn Monroe's secret son; and most powerfully, the raw first-person documentary *Amherst* (video, originally Super 8, 1984), a jeremiad about his hometown, where the artist awakened in the 1950s and early 1960s to sexuality and self-knowledge, as well as to capitalism, ostracism, and exile (see chapter 5).

MADDIN, GUY, b. 1956. Director. The unique Winnipeg conjuror of faux vintage melodramas from our collective cultural unconscious, Maddin is not gay, but his titles sure are mighty queer, *Twilight of the Ice Nymphs* (1997) being the one that raises the most plucked eyebrows. Maddin's arch re-creation of primitive imaginary worlds populated by llamas, Shelley Duvall, legless matriarchs, and virginal heroes gives the camp aesthetic a reinvented and perversely self-conscious charge and at the same time projects an intense sincerity that other camp followers don't get. Camp has long since ceased to be an exclusive queer game preserve, of course, but

Daniel MacIvor, clutching the lover whose AIDS death he would mourn in the Laurie Lynd's *R.S.V.P.* (1991). Wunderkind of Toronto theatre since the 1980s, MacIvor has established a commanding presence as a queer film actor and director. Production still provided by the Canaidian Filmmakers Distribution Centre

what about those explicitly homoerotic moments like the intergenerational pedagogical eros in *Archangel* (1990) (that even the *Guide to the Cinema(s) of Canada* noticed [Rist 2001, 134–5]) or all that full-frontal shower action in *Coward Bend the Knee* (2004)? And then there are those luridly apochryphal towel-boy anecdotes of kneeling locker room encounters with Soviet hockey players recounted to his gayboy acolyte NOAM GONICK in his ultra-fan movie *Guy Maddin: Waiting for Twilight* (1997). Few other nonqueer auteurs have gone beyond "trafficking in queer chic" (to use John Greyson's phrase [email 27 October 2003]) to include so generously and unself-consciously a queer constituency in their world. Scopophilia, paraphilia, pedophilia, cinephilia: there are enough philias pulsating through the Maddin mindscreen to make him honorary lifetime resident of *The Romance of Transgression*.

MAHEUX-FORCIER, LOUISE, b. 1929. The award-winning Montreal-based novelist created a stir in 1982 when her television drama *Arioso* played on Radio-Canada one cold winter primetime, reportedly the first French-

language lesbian-themed program to air on the state network. Writing for
TBP (no. 87, April 1982), I found fault with the slick flashback tale of a
paralyzed writer remembering her lover killed in a car crash caused by a
rejected male suitor, full of outsider ideological messiness and even reminiscent of *Emanuelle* in its exotic "misty pastel ambience." But I defended
its frankness, reminding readers that the author had been writing positively
about lesbian themes since the sixties (though she had declined to disclose
her sexual identity to me when asked). Pioneering dyke activist Jeanne-
d'Arc Jutras wrote a furious open letter to the writer in *Le devoir*, calling
the car crash "a negation of our right to exist and to love" (6 February
1982)," but in the same pages two other queer writers Jean Basile (2 February) and Gloria Escomel (13 February), defended Maheux-Forcier's
"nuanced" tragic theme.

MARKOWITZ, MURRAY, b. 1945. Director. Heterosexual Markowitz's
claim to fame in this volume is as director of *August and July* (1973, 92).
A commercial feature film coming out of the late sixties cinéma vérité aesthetic, this documentary narrative of a month in a country farmhouse with
two women in love raised a lot of expectations and then dashed them.
TBP's Linda K. Koch was typical: "I went to see *August and July* genuinely
wanting to be shown something by this film – I left, having been shown
how *not* to make a movie and *still* waiting for the first Canadian lesbian
movie" (no. 8, Spring 1973). The film's sensationalist publicity blitz belied
the "serious" nature of this attempt to probe a relationship through observation and improvisation, which meant that in order to get to the skinny-
dipping and sex scenes, you had to listen to hours of relationship
wrangling. Markowitz, who made four other features in the 1970s before
disappearing from view, candidly admitted to the energy of jealousy in
interviews. *Cinema Canada*'s presumably straight reviewer hit the nail on
the head: "*August and July* has a slight perversion to it ... that of allowing
men who are totally bewildered by lesbianism to thrust aggressive-yet-
frightened cameras into the lives of two women – whose reality they could
not and would not accept" (Ibranyi-Kiss 1973).
   Still, it's an important document of a lifestyle lesbianism of the immediate post-Stonewall period, a time when people actually said things to each
other like "Making love to a woman isn't having a fuck you know. It has
to be a very powerful force that attracts two women together." Thirty
years later, the film feels as interminable and annoying as it felt in 1973,
with the now-distant 1973 post-"flower child" narcissistic sensibility making it seem like a diabolical parody. Those waiting for "the first Canadian
Lesbian movie" would have to wait at least another decade.

MARTIN, CHRISTINE. Videomaker, actor. Concordia-trained Chris Martin made a splash on the Toronto and Montreal queer/art/politics scenes before moving to New York in the 1990s. Her *Laws and Skin* (Montreal, 1990, 6) explores sexual identities constructed through public body performance. With the tape *Pleasure Police* she participated the same year in artists' responses to the Montreal Sex Garage confrontation between cops and queers. Martin is perhaps best known by her actor alias, Chris Teen, the radical hooker dyke Wednesday Friday in LABRUCE's *8½* (1994) who has her penetrative way with innocent disabled male hitchhikers.

MAURICE, GAIL. Actor, scriptwriter, director. A northern Saskatchewan Métis, the statuesque, gleaming-haired Maurice is best known to queer audiences as the charismatic protagonist in the prizewinning prison drama *Johnny Greyeyes* (2000, 76) directed by Chilean-born, queer-friendly Torontonian Jorge Manzano (b. 1968). Maurice was a contributor to the script, with its central element of the tragic behind-the-bars love story between Johnny and Lana, a native "lifer." Her strong performance was matched by the intense conviction of the violence-wracked narrative material and the effectiveness of the location shooting, especially on Northern Ontario reserves. Audiences forgave the rawness of the mise-en-scène and script, as well as inevitable continuity problems incurred by extensions of the cinematography over five years as the funding from various public sources dribbled in. Festival showings at Sundance and Berlin culminated in awards at Inside Out and American queer festivals, as well as distinctions at the American Indian Motion Picture Awards, followed by a modest commercial release and DVD distribution. Maurice went on to roles and script development in native-themed projects with both Canadian public and international producers.

MCBRIDE, JASON, b. 1968. Filmmaker, film critic and journalist. University of Toronto– and Vancouver Film School-trained, Toronto-based McBride won a prize at the 1999 Inside Out festival for *Stargaze* (1998, 12), a well-wrought fiction about a Peterborough youth, Derek, undergoing shock aversion therapy in Toronto at the start of the 1960s to cure his homosexuality. Based on a story by Ontario writer Derek McCormack, this melancholy black and white narrative constructs an effective period context and a sympathetic, resilient character in the boy. McBride's *Alter* (2001) is another short, this time with a female protagonist and a transgender, multiple-personality hook.

MCGARRY, MICHAEL, 1954–89. Director. SFU-trained filmmaker McGarry is important chiefly for one all-but-forgotten film. *In Black and White*

(Vancouver, 1979, 10), one of the handful of Canadian queer film master-pieces of the 1970s, is an experimental short from the SFU film program, a manifesto of liberation politics, postmodern aesthetics, and defiant erotics. Narratively speaking, two young men, one married and the other an "out" seventies clone, meet in a public toilet and have hot sex, but they're caught through video surveillance. McGarry stepped into the clone role when his actor for this student production didn't show, and his straight cameraman played the married hottie with real conviction (see chapter 8). McGarry was to move to Toronto and die of AIDS, with only one apparent follow-up to his masterpiece: the poetic film *The Front Lawn*, also ten minutes long, was inspired by queer anarchist Spanish playwright Arrabal and completed posthumously in 1990 by McGarry's SFU classmates for Van-couver's *Moving Images Distribution*. *The Front Lawn* featured Pietà-like choreography by a female-male couple against a variety of urban and natural cliff-like backdrops: the male dancer was McGarry's life partner, Jorge Hoguin, who also died of AIDS.

MCINTOSH, DAVID, b. 1952. Programmer, critic, teacher, scriptwriter, edi-tor. Carleton- and York-trained, Toronto-based McIntosh was one of the more influential behind-the-scenes presences in Canadian film, queer and otherwise, as curator for the prestigious Perspective Canada series at TIFF 1992–97, showcasing works ranging from BRUCE LABRUCE's *Super 8½* to Tahani Rached's *Médecins de coeur*, and thereafter for the Hot Docs documentary festival. A champion of Latin American solidarity, McIntosh curated Toronto retrospectives for queer Mexican filmmakers Jaime Hum-berto Hermosillo and Arturo Ripstein in 1991. He has also published definitive criticism on such canonical queer filmmakers as LaBruce and MICHAEL BALSER, as well as collaborating with JOHN GREYSON as editor on *Urinal* (1989) and with NOAM GONICK as story editor on *Hey Happy!* (2001) and scriptwriter on the follow-up feature *Stryker* (2004). McIntosh has taught at OCAD since 1994.

MCLAREN, NORMAN, 1914–87. Animator. All of us have flickering grade-school memories of the work of McLaren, the National Film Board's great animator (see chapter 2). When the world-famous artist died at the age of seventy-three after a forty-three-year career and sixty films, his career had been crowned with distinctions (including the Order of Canada, the Oscar, and the Palme d'or). In many ways Norman McLaren fit one stereotype of the gay artist perfectly – not the tormented self destroyer but the sensitive, fastidious, and solitary craftsman and visionary. One colleague commented on his "soft, sad, watching eyes, that sometimes searched me furtively and then left me for his heart of hearts." Others found a similar sense of mystery and unstated sexual tension in both his work and his personality (Cutler 1983):

So complex is McLaren that people who have worked with him for decades say frankly they don't understand him. The symbolism of his movies offers a fertile field for psychoanalytic interpretations. His humanitarianism, which led one writer to call him "a saint," has a touching childlike quality to it, of one reaching out to be loved as well as to love. He dresses like a college boy, looks twenty years younger than his age, and has kept the youthful innocence and enthusiasm common to great artists. Far from taking seriously any thought he might express about giving up filmmaking, one shudders to think of what life would be for him without it; the necessity brings him in to work sometimes when he is so mentally depressed and physically ill that he frightens those around him.

McLaren and his longtime partner, NFB producer GUY GLOVER, became a respected fixture within the NFB's otherwise homophobic social world. Their fresco-covered apartment became a legend, and one story of the early fifties told of the Hallowe'en party when the two men both showed up in full Spanish senorita drag, complete with white lace mantillas. Otherwise their careers pursued separate trajectories at the government studio, almost never overlapping. Among McLaren's many disciples were filmmakers CLAUDE JUTRA and RYAN LARKIN.

McLaren had been at the NFB since almost the very beginning, recruited by his fellow Scotsman John Grierson in 1941. He very quickly established a worldwide following for his lively un-Disney abstract choreographies and radically innovative techniques of scratching and painting right on celluloid, equally at home interpreting wartime propaganda commissions, Quebec folklore, the risky cause of peace during the Cold War, and the latest in contemporary minimalism. In the midsixties, McLaren turned to a new series with a processed photographic style that would celebrate the human body with an unprecedented sensuality. The three films in the series, *Pas de Deux* (1967), *Ballet Adagio* (1971), and *Narcissus* (1984), all used ballet as the basis for haunting evocations of movement and gesture, and, through the use of various technical procedures, magnified the ballet's inherent eroticism (all the more so since the skimpy male costumes revealed the sexualized male bodies more than the comparatively chaste female getups). Ultimately though, *Pas de deux* and *Ballet Adagio* dissect and celebrate a ritualized convention of heterosexual mating.

With *Narcissus* (1983, 22), McLaren was less cautious: this sensuous retelling of the classical myth of the self-absorbed dreamer is McLaren's only explicitly queer film. A sensuous retelling of the classical myth of the

McLaren and Jutra, mentor and acolyte: two of the NFB's discreet homosexual artists at the animation stand c. 1955. Sandals are not visible, but is that a fishnet T-shirt on twenty-something Claude? Production still, used with permission of the National Film Board of Canada

self-absorbed dreamer youth, *Narcissus*, completed two years before his death, is considered McLaren's most autobiographical work and his testament. Some version of the Narcissus myth had been on McLaren's drawing board for over thirty years, and he was not the first artist to use it as a cover for male eroticism. But it was perhaps a good thing that it took so long to come to fruition, until the social climate and McLaren's unassailable status would permit a relatively explicit exploration of the sexual signification of the story. To an inquisitive gay journalist, the late Robin Hardy, McLaren indicated a long genesis for the film:

I think I can say with certainty that twenty years ago I would have regretfully dropped [the "homo-eroticism"] as not being "acceptable" in an NFB film for general public distribution ... Around 1970, when I was making a 35mm b & w rough sketch of the film with Vincent Warren ... I came across a version of the [Narcissus] legend that contained the homo episode (in fact it recounted that Narcissus was besieged by hosts of girls and young boys). The three or four other versions I had read up til then had mentioned only Echo ... When I discovered the encounter with Ameneius, I got very excited and dead set on including both the girl and youth encounters, as they would not only throw Narcissus' auto-philia into even greater relief but would give me a very justifiable opportunity to portray a homosexual relationship on the screen. A thing I had often wished to do. I am not sure if at that time (1971) stirrings of gay lib had filtered into the backwoods of my secluded life!

An intervening didactic project put *Narcissus* on the back burner, all the more since McLaren was feeling "schizophrenic & neurotic" about both content and narrative cohesion in the project. He returned to the project in 1979 but assured Hardy that the 1972 film would have included the queer content despite pressure from Glover's presence to put the brake on earlier impulses toward such delicate themes: "I myself would gladly come out (& officially), but I wish to respect the feelings of my partner – someone whom I have lived with for the last forty-five years!" McLaren also claimed that the final *Narcissus* would have been even gayer than it turned out had it not been for factors beyond his control:

In 1979 on returning to work on "Narcissus," what with the prominence of the Gay Lib Movement in the meantime, felt I would surely be a traitor, if I were to have left Ameneius [sic] out. The choreographer, Fernand Nault [b. 1921] who is one of us, handled that sequence of the film very gently. I would have wished for him to have done it a bit more boldly, but I didn't see his choreography until the first days of rehearsal and it was impossible to ask for any radical changes, since we were so pressed for time. (1982)

The final 1983 version offered a simple three-part narrative structure in which a dreamy and exquisite youth engages in two romantic pas de deux, first with a female partner, a "nymph," and then with a male partner, "a hunting companion" (according to the ludicrous official summary). The two pas de deux may be equally luscious, but the male duet has a stunning effect as an unprecedented representation of gay male sexuality. Of course McLaren covers himself by equating the two gender options for the tragic hero, and both options are equally rejected, but there is no doubt what side the weight of centuries of wish-fulfilment is leaning towards. In keeping with the story, the ending is tragic: the hero rejects his two lovers, dances with himself (in another breathtaking homoerotic pas de deux!), and is finally revealed to be imprisoned by iron bars and a brick wall.

It would be too easy to dismiss this film as yet another arty piece of closet beefcake and to see McLaren's lavish stylization as yet another mechanism of avoidance. Still, the prison-bar ending comes across as an image not so much of the tragedy of self-absorption but of sexual repression, even of the thwarted self-realization of the closet. As tragic as it is beautiful, *Narcissus* stands up well as the testament and the yearning of the shy Scottish-Canadian civil servant who was one of the more isolated queer contemporaries of Visconti, Cadmus, and Burroughs.

MCLEOD, DAYNA, b. 1972. Videomaker, performance artist. Alberta-bred, Concordia-trained McLeod is well known in the Montreal queer performance milieu as the pruriently costumed "beaver girl." Her five comic short videos since 1998, often built around McLeod's on-screen monologues, have brought the house down at queer festivals around the world. The prizewinning *How to Fake an Orgasm (whether you need to or not)* (1999, 9) is the ultimate how-to video, delivering McLeod's carefully systematic instructions and glib asides through a particularly, in-your-face, kinetic relationship with the lens. *Watching Lesbian Porn* (2001, 11) throws in satirical asides about the "issues" raised by women's studies, as well as lurid but coy background shenanigans, including much shrieking, thwacking, and assorted accessories.

MEAD, WRIK, b. 1962. Toronto's prolific poet of pervert pixillation, Sheridan College–trained Mead has since 1987 made a unique body of more than twenty miniatures of manic queer narrative fantasies, parables, and dreams. Some are frothy fun, such as *Cupid* (1998), the fable of the adult cupid lurking at a party scene who shoots his arrow at a hunk who throws it back on-target, whereupon the cupid is enveloped in his own snake-like cock and dragged off-screen. Some betray the erotic intensity of the closet romantic, such as *Frostbite* (1996), in which a lighthouse keeper rescues a frozen dreamboat sailor, bathes him, and cares for him and lives happily ever after – not without a gorey moment along the way. Other works are fraught with more painful material, such as two later, ambitious works combining more conventional narrative and documentary discourses, reflecting on the heaviness of queer history: *The Fruit Machine* (1998), about the postwar RCMP antigay purge, and *camp* (2000), about the queer Holocaust. Often based on single-frame images in Super 8 and other formats, Mead's work offers a distinctive vision of the gay body: jerky, acrobatic, impulsive, passionate. Mead has combined his production with teaching at OCAD.

MEHTA, DEEPA, b. 1949. Director. Toronto Indo-Canadian Mehta would have a place of pride as honorary queer in this listing on the sole basis of her ground-breaking lesbian feature *Fire* (1996, Toronto, 104). This lavish but astute melodrama of sisters-in-law in love was shot entirely in Delhi with Indian leads and a Canadian supporting cast but without any Canadian public investment. One of the most talked-about films in Indian history, *Fire* led to theatres being stormed and boosted the local queer movement to new levels of visibility. But it is actually a rather modest love story set within a labyrinthine extended family, elevated by star power (actresses Shabana Azmi and Nandita Das) and the rich visual symbolism of sensuous fabrics and purifying flames. Furthermore, as *Xtra!*'s headline put it, "*Fire* is hot!" (11 September 1997). The heterosexual director Mehta's third feature received standing ovations at North American festivals, despite carping by straight white male critics and some lesbians, in both North America and India, who challenged what they saw as a contextual theory of lesbianism, women driven into each others' beds only by husbandly neglect. But a larger context of a transnational artistic milieu where courage is rare and a turbulent planetary traffic in sexual identities increasingly calls into question cultural and national borders confirms *Fire*'s status as a historic moment in Canadian – and *Indian* – queer film history.

In fact, *Fire* is not unrepresentative of Mehta's oeuvre as a whole: her half dozen features show a consistent commitment to probing the delicate borders between homosociality and homoeroticism, male (*Sam and Me*, 1991; *Earth*, 1999) as well as female. Mehta is especially astute at dissecting the volatile construction of diasporic masculinity, and the explorations of drag and transgressive gender performance in *Sam and Me* and *Bollywood Hollywood* (2002) are vivid and unsettling spectacle.

MEIGS, MARY, 1917–02. Writer, painter, performer. The distinguished U.S.-born Montreal writer, for many years companion of prizewinning writer Marie-Claire Blais (b. 1939), was recruited by writer GLORIA DEMERS to join the bomber crew cast of the hit feminist docudrama *Company of Strangers* (1990, NFB, 101; see chapter 6). For queer audiences Meigs stole the movie right out from under heterosexual director Cynthia Scott's nose, despite just a soupçon of Studio D tokenism in that country air. Her coming-out scene, using ye olde birdwatching excursion as a pretext, was an understated feel-good masterpiece of comic improvisation,

Toronto Indo-Canadian Mehta broke ground with her 1996 feature *Fire*, an astute melodrama of sisters-in-law in love set within a Delhi extended family, igniting debates in both Canada and India about cultural specificity and contextual lesbianism. Production still, Seville Pictures

but all was not easy on the set. Never let a writer act in your movie – she'll outlive you and write a book about it (1991):

The day I became the magnet for Gloria's attention, she saw me as the lesbian she had dreamed of for the film. She believed that wishes have magic power ... I felt the pressure of her wish ... I didn't like the ambiguity of my role. Would I be in the film because I was a lesbian? Would I have to act the part of a lesbian? I could only be myself, I said. My letter, which seemed so reasonable to me, reduced Gloria to tears. "I was happy to have a lesbian," she said, "Your not being in *The Bus* [the working title then] is like trying to paint a picture without red paint." As it turned out, I was happy to be some brushstrokes of lavender paint, part of the whole composition, and not the swatch of red that Gloria had wished for. But Gloria's first wish came true; I became a piece of the structure of the film. (98)

Later on the set, "Gloria was there, hoping I'd proclaim lesbian rights and disappointed by my silence, which she blamed on everybody except me. They hadn't drawn me out, she complained; they had treated me as though I was invisible. I felt her hopeful eyes on me, quavered out that I wasn't interested in sex any more and looked fixedly at the floor" (124). The rest is queer Canadian film history.

MELNYK, DOUG, b. 1952. Video maker, interdisciplinary visual and sound artist, critic, arts administrator. University of Manitoba–trained Melnyk, a pillar of the Winnipeg queer arts community, made five videotapes in the late 1980s and early 1990s, which, like *Auld Lang Syne* (1988, 9), present intercalated talking heads whose deadpan narratives are fraught with oblique queer sexual undercurrents. The "queerest" is *Danny Kaye's Eyes* (1994, 7 and 14), in which a scene from a movie featuring the closeted star is reconstructed as a looped and multiframed wet dream of cowboy action and sexy nude nighttime visitors.

MENTLIK, GAIL, b. 1960. Film- and videomaker. Trained at the State University of New York (Buffalo) and based in Toronto, but maintaining roots in Buffalo, Mentlik has worked in experimental and personal documentary forms since 1990, producing ten short works, some broadcast on the Women's Television Network, as well as showing at experimental, Super-8, Jewish, and queer venues. Alongside her colourful and affectionate portraits of her mother, an elderly Holocaust survivor, her frequent collaborations with Anne Borden have more explicit connections to the queer constituency. For example, *Rub* (2002, 2), a bouncing black and white, positive and negative, close-up paean to masturbation, set under Dusty Springfield's "Just a Little Lovin'," was a queer festival favourite.

MILLS, PAT, b. 1976. Director. Ryerson-trained, Toronto-based Pat Mills came out of nowhere with her first feature *Secondary High* (codirectors Emily Halfon, b. 1979, and Hazel Bell-Koski, b. 1977; 2003, 90). A rough-edged graduation film from Ryerson students, *Secondary High* is the demented triptych of pubescent revolt, trauma, and desire that *Degrassi High* and the NFB antihomophobia films should have been. Among countless high moments is Sally the Vampire's rejection of a blond jock from her lineup of straight football victims because she recognizes a kindred closet case. He then immediately falls into passionate liplock with the annoyingly cheerful "Gay Straight Alliance" proselytizer guy under the rainbow flag as the lesbo punk band "Six Healthy Fists" escalate their cacaphony to new levels of decibel defiance. The filmmaking team's manifesto reads, "Continuity is for pussies," which explains the snow on the street all year round. This ebullient queer Canadian update on *Blackboard Jungle* was a sleeper hit of the 2003 queer festivals. Mills's earlier fiction short was *The Affected Turtleneck Trio* (2002, 18), whose jist is resisting the artistic establishment!

MITCHELL, ALLYSON, b. 1967. An animator with a sweet tooth committed to hands-on frame-by-frame filmmaking, Mitchell's dozen or so shorts since 1996 have been bittersweet miniatures that specialized in the world of relationships, girlfriends, and other torments of everyday life, often imagined as metaphors of treats ("MONO GAMY SUX" spelled out in gumdrops and jellybeans in *Candy Kisses*, codirector Jane Farrow, 1999). TV *Did This to Me* (1999) substitutes media addiction for sugar highs. Mitchell has collaborated with LIFT and many others, including her unrelated namesake Roy, on the Toronto queer DIY scene.

MITCHELL, ROY, b. 1959. Film- and video maker, arts administrator. Maker of a dozen short videos and Super 8 films, University of Toronto–trained Mitchell is the epitome of the low-tech personal artist whose work is about his life and his community. Mitchell is best known for the prizewinning *I Know a Place* (1998), a personal documentary about his hometown, Sault Ste Marie, and the history of its queer social networks in the person of a voluble steelworker/queen bee (see chapter 5). Mitchell's rough-hewn videos often incorporate his indulgent and perceptive Super 8 footage of the world around him and range from the sentimental (*Friend*, 2002, a reflection on an evolving friendship with a dog and a guy) to the wry and the quirky (*Christian Porn*, 2000, amiable performances for the camera alongside a fundamentalist nuclear family lined up to protest the Regina queer film festival). Mitchell has also run Toronto's Trinity Square Video since 2001.

MOFFET, FRÉDÉRIC, b. 1971. Film- and video maker, documentarist, teacher. Trained at Concordia and the Art Institute of Chicago, prizewinning artist Moffet is known for risky probings of queer subcultures and sexual performance on screen. I discovered this with *Alice Is a Bitch* (1993), in which the artist transgressed several borders at once, entering a video screen and fellating a masturbating man therein – not a typical undergraduate film. Experimental, personal confrontations with desire and transgression continued in the multiscreen *Three Page Letter to an Ex-Lover* (1995, 4) and in the prizewinning documentary on sexual offenders, *An Objective Measure of Arousal* (2001, 6). Always interested in corporal and erotic performance, Moffet has focused in the 2000s even more on extremes, collaborating in several videos with Montreal choreographer of physical intimacy Manon Oligny and making a provocative documentary on the gay male "feeder" and "gainer" subculture, *Hard Fat* (2002, 23). Moffet settled in Chicago in 1998, where he teaches at his alma mater and addresses an international queer constituency in both languages.

MOHABEER, MICHELLE, b. 1961. Video- and filmmaker, teacher. Guyana-born, Carleton- and York-trained Michelle Mohabeer was a stalwart of the Toronto indie film scene after bursting into view with *Exposure*, her entry in Studio D's *Five Feminist Minutes* (1990). The first up-front lesbian film from the NFB was also the first Canadian work by a lesbian artist of colour (see chapter 5). Mohabeer's prizewinning next work, *Coconut, Cane and Cutlass* (1994, 30) explores her Indo-Guyanese cultural and political heritage with its layered and poetic use of landscape, voice, dramatization, and movement to evoke displacement and diaspora. These themes and this sensual hybridity of documentary, autobiographical, narrative, and experimental modes continued to dominate Mohabeer's approach in her imaginative subsequent works such as *Two/Doh* (1996, 5), an erotic connection between two women of different cultural origins, and *Child-Play* (1997, 14), the dream-state of an elder woman remembering childhood abuse.

MONETTE, JEAN-FRANÇOIS, b. 1967. Documentarist, director, editor, producer. Versatile Concordia-trained Monette is a rare combination: a favourite of the queer community festival short-film circuit who actually earns a living making bread-and-butter queer documentary programming for cable. His prizewinning shorts *Where Lies the Homo?* (1998, see chapter 10) and *Take-Out* (2000,) are both about the pain and excitement of coming out, respectively an autobiographical documentary and a moody urban fiction about a teenager whose meeting with a mysterious adult male sparks self-discovery. *Where Lies the Homo?* offers an innovative use of movie clips, home movies, and dramatization to articulate troubled memories of self-affirmation: *Snow White* will never look the same again! The same talent as a compilation editor had already surfaced in the NFB documentary *Anatomy of Desire* (1995, sharing the directing credit with then partner Peter Tyler Boullata), about the evolving modern science of sexual identity – undervalued despite its festival prizes. Equally at home working in English and French, Monette has also been responsible for several "reality" documentaries, including the feature *Coming Out* (2000–01) and the series *Out in the City/Out à Montréal* (2000–02), all for cable-cast but popular at the queer festivals. One highlight of the latter diverse panoply of urban queers transpires when the straight dancer son of the gay cop whose coming out we've been following finally reveals that he's not so straight after all – not that sharp-eyed spectators ever doubted.

MONK, KATHARINE, b. 1965. Critic. Montreal-born, UBC-trained Monk was movie reviewer at the *Vancouver Sun* from 1990 to 2003 and thereafter nationally with CanWest. Her book *Weird Sex & Snowshoes and Other Canadian Film Phenomena* (2001) brought the discussion of sexuality in Canadian film into the mainstream and even ended up on screen itself (2004). Valiantly grasping the hypothetical "national" sexual psyche by the horns, Monk proposes that "kinky, dark, quirky and obsessive sex in Canadian film" (120) is one of "our" bonding mechanisms in our frigid environment and, moreover, that as a "dysfunctional national family" our "propensity for complete sexual denial could be reflecting our continuing national insecurity complex" (124). Writing from an implied but never explicit queer point of view, Monk acknowledges the positive energy and diversity in queer sexualities on Canadian screens – at least in comparison to the "downright bent" heterosex (144). Her explanation for this falls short of linking up the political movements, cultural activism, and community construction that have enfranchised queer artists and audiences, but is a suggestive starting point: "Why gay sex gets a better shake than straight sex should be easy to explain at this point because it reaffirms, symbolically, what we've already come to understand about the larger systems at work in Canadian cinema – particularly our attempts to reconcile all the varying manifestations of "other" that occur in Canadian society at large" (148).

MONKMAN, KENT, b. 1965. Filmmaker, visual artist, theatre designer. Of part Cree ancestry from northern Manitoba, Toronto-based, Banff- and Sundance-trained Monkman first attracted attention from queer audiences with the prizewinning experimental dance video *A Nation Is Coming* (codirector Michael Greyeyes, 1996, 24). This sensuous imagining of a ghost dancer's clash with contemporary society is homoerotic without being explicitly queer. His next video *Blood River* (2000, 23) was more conventionally narrative, but still strikingly visual, in its portrait of an adopted young native woman reaching out from her suburban shelter for her roots and discovering the troubled, bloodied hustler who is her blood brother.

MONTMORENCY, ANDRÉ, b. 1939. Actor, television host. One of Quebec's most beloved television personalities and most visible queer cultural icons, Montmorency appeared already as a teenager on the CBC's long-running series *Le Survenant* in the 1950s, becoming a small-screen regular for four decades thereafter. On stage he appeared in most Montreal theatres, eventually taking up directing, and played MICHEL TREMBLAY's most famous queen in a 1996 revival of *La Duchesse de Langeais*. On the big screen, Montmorency played Sandra, the bitchy club hostess in the epochal *Il y était une fois dans l'Est* (1973, see chapter 4), almost stealing the film. Later that decade, Montmorency finally became enthroned as Quebec's most famous homo in his TV soap role as swishy hairdresser Christian Lalancette in Denise Filiatrault's hit series *Chez Denise* (1979–82). In his 1992 autobiography *De la Ruelle au Boulevard*, Montmorency made his coming out official, as if there was any need, and shortly after became celebrity host on Quebec's queer public affairs show *Sortie gaie*, on cable.

MONTREAL. Image + Nation: Festival international de cinéma gai et lesbien de Montréal. Efforts to organize a regular outlet for queer cinema in Montreal go back to the 1970s, with Concordia's *Conservatoire de l'art cinématographique* offering in 1977 Images of Homosexuality on the Screen, a month-long series of twenty-five films with an enterprising but mostly male mix of European art cinema (Fassbinder, Visconti, and Fellini), dead queer bashers (*The Sergeant*, 1968), and recent breakthroughs such as Frank Vitale's *Montreal Main* (1974). The first initiative to come out of the queer community itself, coinciding with Fierté gaie and the Fête nationale in June 1980, La Semaine du cinéma gai, was organized by Le groupe sortir, BERNARD ROUSSEAU, and others, a for-profit initiative connected to the commercial interests growing around the sex shop Priape in the then embryonic Village gai. The Semaine ran into the issue of bicultural representation that would underly all future Montreal initiatives (namely, the inaccessibility of French-language product). But to their credit the organizers recruited several filmmakers from France and put together a diverse program of 1970s features and shorts, mostly male in orientation. The event took a dive commercially, and the organizers would not return to exhibition until later in the 1980s when they took over a theatre in the Village.

Two years later, in June 1982, the Association pour les droits de la communauté gaie repeated the initiative, this time on a noncommercial basis, with films showing at the Cinémathèque québécoise and the new medium of video showcased at the association's own space. I curated the program together with a network of collaborators, attempting a more comprehensive program and a fifty-fifty gender balance (including screen-

André Montmorency, one
of Quebec's most beloved
queer cultural icons, as Michel
Tremblay's Sandra, almost
stealing the whole movie, *Il
était une fois dans l'Est* (1973;
see chapter 4). Production still,
photo by Attila Day from the
Cinémathèque Québécoise
Collection, COPYRIGHT Les
Productions Pierre Lamy

ings by *Réseau vidé-elle* for lesbians only!), plus a special Super 8 sidebar
and many of the up-and-coming international directors showing their
early works, from Terence Davies to Su Friedrich. Canadians represented
included MARC PARADIS, COLIN CAMPBELL, and the duo of JANIS COLE
and Holly Dale. Sporadic smaller ventures continued, often on university
campuses (Concordia and Université de Montréal) or within the local
film festivals, especially the Festival du nouveau cinéma. The next major
autonomous event took place in 1986, organized by René Lavoie (b.
1955), again at the Cinémathèque, but this time adding the NFB venue.
This latter festival was notable for its conspicuous AIDS-related program,
sponsored by the local AIDS committee CSAM, and for the now usual
element of a strong French and Québécois representation (MICHEL AUDY,
BASHAR SHBIB).

Lavoie, a Concordia-trained activist, provided the continuity between
these precursor initiatives and the establishment of Diffusions lesbiennes et
gaies du Québec, the organization that launched Image + Nation in 1988.

MONTREAL 1980
26 juin – 2 juillet

PROGRAMME
GRATUIT

SEMAINE DU CINEMA GAI

Program cover for Montreal's 1980 Semaine du cinéma gai: a commercial dive that tested the water for Image + Nation eight years later

That year, in collaboration with Pierre Chackal and programmer PATRICIA KEARNS, a new era in community audience development got underway, riding the tremendous boom of the New Queer Cinema and the grass-roots proliferation of makers born after Stonewall. For the first years the fall festival was dependent on the Cinémathèque, the Goethe Institut, and the NFB and in the midnineties relied increasingly on universities, before finally putting down roots at the heritage multiplex Le Parisien in 1997. Lavoie had remained at the helm until 1991 but continued to contribute to the programming until 1995, when he produced the admirable AIDS-related sidebar event, Festival international du film VIH et sida, in partnership with a French organization, one of the most significant and varied AIDS cultural events ever held in this country. Thereafter he moved on to direct the prevention organization Séro-zéro. Lavoie's chief collaborator at DLGQ in this middle period had been video artist and impresario ANNE GOLDEN, and other programmers in the early years included seasoned AIDS arts programmer Allen Klusacek and bad girl CHRISTINE MARTIN, as well as Kearns. YVES LAFONTAINE and SUZANNE GIRARD joined the enterprise in 1993 (with Lafontaine remaining in the leadership cluster until 1999), bringing cinephile catholicity and business acumen, respectively, before returning to focus on the magazine *Fugues* and on Divers/cité.

UQAM-trained video artist and activist Charlie Boudreau (b. 1961) first contributed to the programming in 1995 and the next year moved into the overall coordination of the festival, at Lafontaine's side and with the assistance of her then girlfriend Katherine Setzer (b. 1969). Like most of their predecessors Boudreau and then Concordia communications student Setzer had tried their hand at production (respectively, Boudreau's *Stepping Out Smartly*, a snazzy 1993 contribution to the Banff-commissioned safe-sex PSA series [see chapter 9], and Setzer's SM-flavoured *Trust You*, 1992, 2). They worked in collaboration with Lafontaine until 1999, and thereafter became the executive duo in charge of both administration and programming. As the institution professionalized and corporate sponsorships became increasingly important, DLGQ as a collective entity with a community board receded from view, and Image + Nation assumed the personality-driven pyramid structure of other mainstream Montreal festivals.

Throughout its history, Image + Nation maintained its distinctive plug-in to European francophone cinema, reflected the strong populist but cinephile taste of its audience (for example the frequent revival of European classics or the 2002 Fassbinder retrospective), maintained the legacy of Lavoie's commitment to AIDS-related programming, and, since 1999, developed a youth-oriented lineup and matinee schedule. By and large missing the strong auteur-based orientation of other festivals, as well as Toronto's and Vancouver's success with free-lance curating, youth mentorship, Q & A's, panels, and interview-type programming, Image + Nation nevertheless became noted for its strong festive atmosphere and large, loyal following, instituting a juried competition for features in 2002.

MOORES, MARGARET (b. 1955, director, writer, curator), and ALMERINDA TRAVASSOS (b. 1957, director, cinematographer, teacher). OCAD-trained Moores and York-trained Travassos, erstwhile life partners and artistic collaborators, have been internationally acclaimed pioneers of the independent women's/queer film scene in Toronto for over two decades. Involved in New Left and lesbian activism during the seventies, the pair segued into lesbian film and video production through curating the 1980 Feminist Film Festival at the Funnel. They first created a strong impact with *Labyris Rising* (1980, 14), a gentle satire of Kenneth Anger's *Scorpio Rising* displaying a lesbian ten-speed instead of the Harley, the Michigan Women's Festival instead of a Hells Angels rally, and a lesbian cat instead of … well, you know. Over the years the film has acquired historical value as a document of the late-seventies Toronto lesbian scene, including pool-playing and the infamous Fly By Night Lounge (see chapter 5). Usually the labour was divided up between Moores, the writer-director, and Travassos, the cinematographer-director, and included documentary and more experimental fare, as well as comic narrative. My personal favourite among their works of the 1980s is another classic, *Frankly, Shirley* (1987), about a one-night stand that turns to romance in the strangely empty public spaces of wintry Toronto and ends when Jane and Wendy actually start to talk. The film shocked some because it was one of the early works to envisage public sex as a dyke fantasy and reality. Their more ambitious, campy, and very queer *Dog Days* (1999, 40) revisited the utopian Michigan pastoral fantasy with a narrative about big-city dykes (played by a who's who of Canadian lesbian video, from SHAWNA DEMPSEY to DEIRDRE LOGUE) discovering their relationship to the land and the invisible queer past. The two artists increasingly worked separately, as in Travassos's collaborations with CAMPBELL and GREYSON and Travassos's *Bianca Comes Out* (2002, 9), a personal confession about predilection for soap operas, subtitled in Portuguese in homage to the artist's grandmother. Travassos has taught media at OCAD since 1999.

MOOTOO, SHANI, b. 1958. Videomaker, writer, visual artist. Trinidad-bred, Vancouver-based Shani Mootoo is best known as a Booker-nominated novelist (*Cereus Blooms at Night*, 1998). But she is familiar to queer community festival audiences thanks to a handful of experimental short videotapes that interrogate cultural and gender hybridity, diaspora, and Canadian identities and landscapes, both urban and rural. Of these tapes, most produced in Vancouver artist-run spaces and in collaboration with LORNA BOSCHMAN, the work most shown is the rollicking *Wild Woman in the Woods* (1993, 14). *Woman* is a postcolonial parable set in the snowy woodland mountainsides around Banff: a butch South Asian in bowler hat, played by Mootoo, pursues a flirtatious South Asian forest sprite, decked out in henna, saffron sari, glitzy jewellery, and come-hither choreography. What ensues are a cross-country ski chase in saris and all and a bacchanalian dance among nautch girl muses in a clearing high up on the slopes, through which the heroine finds her true femme Indian self.

MORGADO ESCANILLA, CLAUDIA, b. 1962. Director, writer, producer, curator. Born in Chile and trained at Concordia, SFU, and the CFC, Vancouver-based Morgado made a dozen short films since coming to Canada in 1986, all but one on celluloid, which, according to Elena Feder, "evince a quest for a language with which to manifest multiple marginalized desires." Morgado's prizewinning films established her as "a *transfrontera* (border crossing) subject with an unabashedly sexually polymorphous Latinø persona" whose use of the typically torchy Spanish love-song forma of the *bolero* "enables her to displace to a lesbian register forms of masochistic desire that were originally articulated for a heterosexual audience" (2003). A case in point was one of her more ambitious and queer-explicit works, the 1997 *Sabor a mí (Savour me)* (35mm, 22), a sensuous narrative of voyeurism, flirtation, role playing, and lust between a married woman and her butch neighbour, full of painterly tableaus of bodies and furnishings and showered, literally, with petals. Winner of five festival awards, the experimental docudrama *Unbound* (1994, 19) also evoked painting and presented women of different cultures, races, and ideologies – including Morgado – offering their breasts and their cultural meanings of breasts to the camera. *Martirio (Sufferance* 2000, 19, coscripted by Aaron Martin [see SCHUYLER]), is perhaps Morgado's kinkiest work, a hothouse melodrama of lesbo twin trapezists and paraplegia masquerade.

MORGENSTERN, STEPHANIE, b. 1965. Actor, filmmaker. Swiss-born, Montreal-bred, McGill- and Banff-trained, Morgenstern is known for strong performances in several iconic lesbian films, notably the landmark features *Forbidden Love: The Unashamed Stories of Lesbian Lives* (1992, 85) and *Revoir Julie* (JEANNE CRÉPEAU, 1998, 92), plus several shorts, such as *Why I'll Never Trust You (In 200 Words or Less)* (CASSANDRA NICOLAOU, 1995, 11). The diminutive, bilingual, queer-friendly blonde is best known as the naive but fast-learning country girl in *Forbidden Love*, but she also demonstrated a flair for repartee in *Revoir*. In all her roles Morgenstern merges transparency and playfulness, and in some of the hottest sex scenes in the Canadian lesbian canon, vulnerability and fire.

MORIN, ROBERT (b. 1949, videomaker, filmmaker, cinematographer), and LORRAINE DUFOUR (b. 1950, videomaker, producer, editor). Queer-friendly pioneer-founders of Montreal's Coop Vidéo in 1977, Morin and Dufour, recipients of the first Bell Canada Award in Video Art in 1991, are known to queer audiences chiefly for an early work, the beautiful and complex point-of-view queer narrative *Gus est encore dans l'armée* (Gus Is Still in the Army, 1980, 21). An unnamed narrator, a teenaged working class guy, tells about joining the Canadian Forces, simply because their commercials are so good, and discovering unexpected attractions to another ordinary soldier named Gus while filming their training camp at Petawawa in Super 8. In 1980, the consequences are inevitable, especially after the army psychiatrist looks at his footage. Morin became a prize-winning feature film director, where his personal stamp of left-wing machismo includes an exploration of masculinity in fluidity and crisis.

MOSSANEN, MOZE, b. 1958. Television director, scriptwriter (Toronto). Trained as an actor in the United States, Toronto-based Mossanen first caught the attention of the queer audience with the drama *Illegal Acts* (1982, 21), an unsettling allegory of the gay community by way of a chicken-processing plant. He also caught the attention of the CBC, where he eased into arts programming focused on dance, the field where he has fortified his reputation ever since. The CBC did not like his 1992 departure outside the tony realm of ballet however: his 1992 collaboration with SKY GILBERT, *The Jane Show*, in which Gilbert interviews his rather over-the-top drag alter ego was rejected for a prime-time slot, and then a "sanitized, toothless version" was eventually broadcast. "The artistic resonance of the original [was] brutally excised," according to *Xtra!*, though there was some redeeming value "in seeing an openly queer artist discussing his work and the responsibilities of the gay artist on national television" (27 November 1992). Mossanen's scrapes with censorship and artistic interference got roasted in his Gemini-nominated *My Gentlemen Friends* (1999, 68), an unprecedented and insightful drama about three elderly gay-male ex-dancers who reminisce about their golden years as queer pioneers, both onstage and off. All is framed by the story of a TV program production around them being sabotaged by a nasty and gutless, closeted television executive. Hmmm. Next came another CBC-supported program, *The Rings of Saturn* (2002), a "contemporary dance drama" about love and romance, including a homo-romantic tour de force: a repressed and lonely male doctor has trouble hearing the heart of a hunky patient (chest hair evidently interferes with stethoscopes), and a to-die-for pas de deux ensues. Inspired by *Les Liaisons dangereuses*, the follow-up, *Year of the Lion* (2003), was judged by *Xtra!*'s NICHOLAS DAVIES to be a "hugely successful" improvement on *Rings* (9 January 2003), despite inequitable gender dynamics in the roles: there are some lesbo flirtations around a pool table, but it's the wonderful male-male pas de deux interpretation of cruising and game-playing (literally – it's a frisbee!), as well as romance, that steals the show.

MOSSOP, ROWLEY, b. 1959. Video maker. Mexico-born, OCAD-trained Mossop was well known on the Toronto queer video scene in the late 1980s, showing works on sexual identity and on AIDS, before ending up as a producer on the CBC's *The National*. His popular *Pleasure* (1987, 11) was about a passive young man being swallowed up in the "perfect world" of TV spectatorship, scarcely interrupted by his homoerotic fantasies.

MYERS, BO, b. 1967. Filmmaker, scriptwriter, cinematographer, editor, teacher, curator. McGill- and ECIAD-trained, Vancouver-based Myers, an Out on Screen board member, is best known for the multiple prizewinning *Tiny Bubbles* (1997, 5), a tender and whimsical, hand-crafted 16 mm homage to the women in the artist's life, from mother to "ex," well received in Jewish and experimental venues, as well as queer.

NADEAU, CHANTAL, b. 1963. Teacher, critic, author. Leading arbiter of Quebec queer and feminist film culture, Université de Montréal-trained Concordia communications professor Nadeau wrote astutely in the 1990s in both French and English on LÉA POOL, JEANNE CRÉPEAU, and ESTHER VALIQUETTE in relation to the patriarchal nationalist thrust of Quebec cinema, as well as on international lesbian cinemas and the queer film festival phenomenon. Her book *Fur Nation: From the Beaver to Brigitte Bardot* (2001) was a witty analysis of our founding resource-based industry, fur, and its gendered sexualization within postcolonial Canadian cultural history.

NEWBIGGING, MARTHA, b. 1966. Animator, curator, children's illustrator, activist. OCAD-trained, rural Ontario-based Newbigging was well known in the 1990s for her spots on gender and environmental politics, often made in collaboration with Almerinda Travassos. Beginning with *Dress-code* (2003, 3), a funny riff on the pissed-off ideograph on the ladies's room door, Newbigging also plugged into the international queer community circuit, for which she co-curated, with Travassos, a hit program of animated shorts by artists the next year.

NICOL, NANCY, b. 1951. Video documentarist, teacher. A prolific pioneer of feminist video documentary in Canada, Toronto-based Nicol began her career in the late seventies but first impressed with her momentous 163-minute, five-part marathon on the history of the reproductive rights struggle in Canada, *Struggle for Choice* (1986). Excelling at documenting grass-roots organizing and resistance, Nicol assembles her materials into epic vistas of historical processes, interpreting struggles over gender and sexuality through the lens of materialist class politics.

Her first major queer-themed work, *Gay Pride and Prejudice* (1994), situated the 1994 Ontario battle for same-sex benefits and equal families in the shadow of nineteenth-century "queer" historical figures Austen and Wilde. Gary Kinsman, reviewing the one-hour two-channel tape in *Fuse* (1995), concluded

I was not in Toronto during the final debates over the defeat of Bill 167, so I was delighted that this video allowed me to "live" some of this through the TV screen. *Gay Pride and Prejudice* ends with the vote result and the resulting protest in the House. Security guards wearing latex gloves are shown throwing lesbians and gay men and supporters out of the Queen's Park gallery with chants of "Shame, shame!" in the lobby as Queer activists regroup. I at first could not believe that large numbers of people chanted 'Burn down the house!' at the angry assembly at Queen's Park that night, but here it is recorded as part of our Queer histories. The video closes with Talking Heads' "Burning Down the House." The spirit of Stonewall lives!

Nicol's *Stand Together* (2002) is an even more ambitious historical overview of the struggle for queer equality in Ontario from the 1960s to 1987, the aftermath of Ontario's acceptance of sexual orientation in its Human Rights Code. More than thirty-seven hours of oral histories went into the completed two-hour video, alongside historical archival material. Nancy Irwin described the tape as "an inspiring tale of the struggles and victories of the Ontario gay and lesbian movement. Nicol has been able to capture the urgency and drama of key events by integrating the stories of individual artists with captivating re-enactments and archival media" (2002).

Trained at Concordia and York, Nicol teaches new media at York.

NICOLAOU, CASSANDRA, b. 1968. Director, scriptwriter, production coordinator. Toronto-based, CFC-trained Nicolaou is known on the queer community and mainstream festival circuits for her witty narrative shorts about lesbian coupledom, all luxuriously shot by queer-friendly cinematographer Kim Derko. Nicolaou's films were based on strong performances, and their titles speak volumes: *Why I'll Never Trust You (In 200 Words or Less)* (1995, 11) and the award-winning *Interviews with My Next Girlfriend* (2001, 13) are, respectively, uneasily romantic and broadly comic takes on relationships and community. *Dance with Me* (1997, 9) is more lyrical and personal about generational relationships, ethnicity, and pleasure among women within the family.

NIKOLAI, CLARK, b. 1961. Video maker, curator. Vancouver-based Nikolai is a veteran independent video artist who got his start on the Saskatoon artist-run scene. His miniature videos offered a comic take on talk and a rough-hewn flair for colour, dance, and trash culture. Most recently he explored bear culture with a 2002 Pacific Cinematheque program and offered his own virtuoso, microcloseup celebration of body hair erotics and identity, *Men on Fur on Men* (codirector Martin Borden, 2003, 8).

OBERLANDER, WENDY, b. 1960. Video and installation artist, teacher. Prizewinning California-trained, Vancouver-based Oberlander was a regular at Jewish and queer festivals worldwide in the late 1990s and 2000s. The daughter of Holocaust refugees, her best-known works incorporate elements of family history and autobiography, namely, *Nothing to Be Written Here* (1996, 47) and *Still (Stille)* (2001, 25). A member of the Out on Screen board, Oberlander has taught at ECIAD and SFU.

O'BRIEN, KELLY, b. 1966. Director, teacher. OISE-trained Kelly O'Brien is a Toronto Super 8 advocate whose politically savvy experimental shorts have been a staple of queer film festivals since 1995. Perhaps most successful was the droll diaristic narrative *After Morning* (1999, 5), in which the filmmaker discovers she's forgotten the stress around pregnancy risk when she's stranded in a New York City weekend on a futile and expensive hunt for "morning-after" contraception after a certain slip with a guy and a broken condom.

ONODERA, MIDI, b. 1961. Director, scriptwriter. For two decades one of Canada's most internationally recognized, prolific, and versatile lesbian film- and video makers, Onodera was trained at OCAD, where she established her roots in the Toronto arts community.

Onodera's first major film, *Ten Cents a Dance (Parallax)* (1985, 30) immediately established her international reputation. This experimental narrative triptych about sex, games, and money was also one of the most controversial works of the decade, eliciting strong reactions wherever it was shown. Three semisatiric vignettes glimpse lesbian, gay male, and hetero sexual exchange, from cool to hot. Twenty years later we're still debating what it's all about and what Onodera's two distinctive overlapping frames might have to do with that, and that's a sure sign of a masterpiece (see chapter 8).

The next major film was entirely different, *The Displaced View* (1988, 52), a chaste but innovative documentary essay on Onodera's Japanese-Canadian heritage, on her grandmother and the other women in successive generations of her family, and on the interface of history, memory, race, gender, and sexual identity. These themes recur in the subsequent series of short films and videos, along with her commitment to renewing experimental, autobiographical, and narrative forms. *Basement Girl* (2001, 12), for example, is a multiple-formated, multiple-languaged narrative about a jilted young woman who holes up in her basement apartment with TV and junk food and who eventually emerges to "make it on her own," thanks to the inspiration of the Bionic Woman.

Onodera's one initiative in the feature film sector led to the enigmatic *Skin Deep* (1995, 85), which had a mixed critical and commercial response. *Skin Deep* intrigued audiences with its narrative of an Asian-Canadian filmmaker trying to balance her art with her rocky personal life and its themes of gender identity and transgression, tattooing, pain, and desire.

Most recently, Onodera experimented with digital, interactive, and performance-based media, continuing to confound audiences and critics who want sexual and racial identity in neat, lucid, and affirmative representational packages and to delight those who want to be challenged.

OTTAWA. Making Scenes. The capital's Queer Film and Video Festival was founded in 1992, and rivalled the big three metropolitan festivals in its innovative programming and hinterland community energy, evolving into a two-weekend event by 1998 and developing a year-long parallel screening profile. The original programming team was headed by the indefatigable Donna Quince and in the 2000s by Carleton-trained Dan Grummisch and José Sanchez. The capital region's queer festival included the National Library as its venue and its important Canadian vocation was reflected in an ambitious Canadian retrospective in 1999. In 2003, after its twelfth season, Making Scenes ceased operations, victim of burnout and deficits, and is sorely missed.

PADGETT, JAN, b. 1946. Documentarist, animator, writer. Activist in the rural Vancouver Island film community and queer support network, children's literature/film specialist Padgett was responsible for two of the imaginative antihomophobia trigger films in the NFB "Celebrating Diversity" package of 2002: *Sticks and Stones* (2001, 17) and *In Other Words* (2001, 25), for elementary and high-school students respectively. She also collaborated with queer native actor EVAN ADAMS in directing *Kla Ah Men* (2003, 88), a documentary shot around her Powell River base about the latter's Sliammon First Nation community, intended as an intervention in the British Columbia treaty crisis of the 2000s.

PARADIS, MARC, b. 1955. Videomaker. The most important Québécois gay male voice in video in the 1980s, the pioneering and prolific Paradis is known for his moody, obsessed, and poetic reflections on the male body, passion, taboos and limits, relationships, and loss (see chapter 8). Internationally known and respected on the international art video circuit, Paradis is less well known in English Canadian queer networks, perhaps because of the sometimes specialized standards and miniature formats of art video, because of the unfamiliar combination of hard-core imagery and subtly layered aestheticism (including his studied music tracks, combining original compositions with his indulgence of liturgical vocals), or because his morose, philosophical voice-overs seem excessive in translation. Paradis's first work, *Voyage de l'ogre* (1981), an essay that connects the horror of Chicago serial killer John Gacy to testimonies of nubile young Montrealers on their experiences and fantasies of hustling, is his most socially conscious work. Most others unfold in the intensely personal and hermetic universes of individual desire, such as Paradis's triptych on lost love, *L'incident Jones* (1986), *Délivre-nous du mal* (Deliver Us From Evil, 1987), and *Lettre à un amant* (*Letter to a Lover*, 1988), the latter with its masturbatory lyricism being one of his finest works. Paradis was also an influential curator and active member of the video network during the 1980s. His narrative *Harems* (1991), a delirious dreamlike love story between a screenwriter and a go-go boy, was his longest work, almost an hour, as well as, apparently, his last.

PARKER, GUDRUN, b. 1920. Director, documentarist, producer, teacher. One of the earliest women directors at the National Film Board during World War II, queer-friendly Parker was in the MCLAREN and GLOVER circle, and her gentle, practical feminism was a force behind several of the more subtextable NFB chestnuts of the 1950s. Her astute interrogations of masculinity in the age of enforced gender obedience (see chapter 5) included, above all, *The Stratford Adventure* (1954), memorable for a dramatized cruising scene over coaching and cigarettes between bisexual stage star Alec Guinness and gorgeously queer novitiate actor Timothy Findley. But *Being Different* (director Julia Murphy, script Parker, 1957, 10) is one of the queerest Canadian films of the 1950s famine, an NFB remake of *Tea and Sympathy* and protofeminist challenge to monolithic machismo and gender conformity. An elementary teacher trying to encourage nonconventional gender performativity reads aloud twelve-year-old George's essay on the pleasures of butterfly catching, and his hockey-loving buddies on the paper route are merciless in their harassment of the transgressor. According to the convention of the "trigger film," we don't see George making up his mind, but he knows he has to choose, and no film before or after has ever so compassionately captured the cruelty – and the potential freedom – entailed in that choice. Towards the end of her career, Parker produced in the Montreal independent sector and taught film at Vanier College.

PATERSON, ANDREW JAMES, b. 1952. Videomaker, interdisciplinary artist, critic, performer. University of Toronto–trained Paterson has been an omnipresent and prolific fixture of the Toronto queer/art video scene for more than two decades, on-screen and off. His tapes are complex experimental essays, often with self-reflexive narrative elements, formulating political issues from inside the arts and queer communities. *Pink in Public* (1993, 20) was a witty and colourful intervention in the "outing" controversy of the early nineties, in which an entertainment journalist, played by Paterson, must choose between playing along with institutionalized closetry or taking a stand, while focus groups on the club floors of the nation argue the political ins and outs. *Cash and Carry* (1999, 6) offered a debate on capitalism, globalization, and the new barter economy, illustrated by a toilet blow job between a waiter and his customer/john.

PELOSO, LARRY, b. 1956. Documentarist. Trent-trained, Toronto-based Peloso is known chiefly for the broad international success of *Prom Fight: The Marc Hall Story* (Toronto, 2002, 58, TIFF), a feel-good but engaging documentary on the Oshawa teenager's victorious battle in the media and the courts to force his Catholic school board to let him take his boyfriend to his prom. Structured around a day-by-day account of the struggle, *Prom Fight* was buoyed by the exceptional charisma of dewy-eyed, blue-haired angel Marc and his family, not to mention its prophetic input into the same-sex marriage swell of the following year. Supportive family aside, there's an odd reverse-oedipal dynamic to Marc's seduction of the avuncular United Auto Worker elders while the bigot stepmother/school board chair sheds alligator tears as she sharpens the castration gavel with her blood-red nails. Still, there are lots of nice mothers around, including a rouge-cheeked PFLAG organizer who seems to have stepped right out of *Queer as Folk* (which also makes a guest appearance ...).

Meanwhile, the titular hero's growing vulnerability to the seductions of the vividly portrayed media frenzy creates a sinking unease in the film, and the concluding update on the romantic couple's postprom breakup adds just the right modulation for triumphalist readings. Nevertheless, when one of the gang opines at the moment of victory (in Ontario valleyspeak), "This is, like, history, guys," only the hardest-hearted queer cynic can resist a tear or two. The film was, not surprisingly, a big hit on the community festival circuit around the world and on specialty cable broadcasts in Canada and the United States. Peloso preceded his breakthrough with his prizewinning *Coming Out of the Iron Closet* (1995, 40), about queer life in former Soviet bloc societies.

PIETROBRUNO, ILEANA, b. 1965. Director, scriptwriter, producer, editor. After several prizewinning experimental shorts, Montreal-bred, McGill- and SFU-trained, Vancouverite Pietrobruno made two deliriously stylized short features that were standards on the queer festival circuit and broke into the mainstream international festivals but failed to follow through into broader distribution. Her first feature, *Cat Swallows Parakeet and Speaks!* (1996, 75), is a feminist gothic narrative, eerily subjective and lusciously stylized in both black and white and colour, about a paranoid model and an anorexic ballerina bonding within a creepy hospital (shot on location in an abandoned asylum). Along the way the film probes tabloid narrative and women's body issues from eating disorders to menstruation. LIZ CZACH, programmer for TIFF 1996, was effusive: "Part feminist fable, part surreal dream and part horror flick, this hallucinatory first feature shows Pietrobruno is a director full of promise." Pietrobruno's next feature was seven years in the waiting: *Girl King* (2003, 80), a gender-bending buccaneer flick that charmed queer festival audiences with its swashbuckling butch-femme comic strip sensibility plus multiracial casting. *Xtra!*'s Rachel Giese opined, "Post-queer and post-feminist (and post just about everything else), it manages to tackle the complicated terrain of gender with insight and humour" (15 May 2003). Meanwhile, Pietrobruno edited five West Coast NFB documentaries, including PADGETT's two 2001 queer works for youth *In Other Words* and *Sticks and Stones*.

PIKE, PAM, b. 1962. Videomaker, interdisciplinary artist, curator, designer. NSCAD-trained, Halifax-based Pike is known for *The Absence of Us* (1986, 19), an essayistic, diary-based video manifesto that circulated among festivals in the late 1980s and early 1990s. Textured by words, names, and writing, *Absence* also constructs in its claustrophobic studio set a minimalist narrative around an on-again off-again couple and a search for community. Its climax is a bold graffiti action, on-location in night-time Halifax: "Women Loving Women."

PIKE, PHILLIP, b. 1962. Documentarist. Lawyer-turned-filmmaker Pike struck a strong chord with his first work *Songs of Freedom* (Toronto, 2002, 75). This gripping, low-budget video is the first documentary about queer life in Jamaica. Structured around "talking head" interviews with a network of brave men and women active in gay social and political life in Kingston, *Songs of Freedom* ranges from a historical overview to detailed and moving personal experiences. The video is notable for resorting regularly to the digitalization of all but two of its subjects' faces to protect their anonymity, testimony to the menacing climate, as well as an unsettling aesthetic device. Pike showed his groundbreaking work in festivals about "same-gender loving people of African descent" he organized in Toronto, Montreal, and U.S. cities, as well as, discreetly, in Kingston.

PIMLOTT, JUSTINE, b. 1962. Documentarist, soundperson. Technical support on many feminist and lesbian documentaries since the mid-1980s and a frequent collaborator of such directors as FERNIE and WEISSMAN, Toronto-based Pimlott brought out her first documentary as director in 1999. *Laugh in the Dark* (47; see chapter 9) is a prizewinning low-budget documentary about community – and its loss – in the hinterland of Southern Ontario. Crystal Beach, not far from the Fort Erie border crossing on Lake Erie, used to have claim to being our Coney Island, and under vintage images of its rollercoaster glory days, Pimlott narrates a small group of gay men arriving from Toronto in Crystal Beach's days of decline in the early 1980s. They undertake the resort town's rejuvenation, overcoming local prejudice through their charm and sincerity, and gradually build up a kind of community consisting of "four fags, two dykes and a seventy-eight-year-old 'former practicing heterosexual' woman." The image conveyed of this unusual friendship circle, whose energy is devoted largely to sprucing up their digs and putting on AIDS fundraiser cabaret benefits, is both sentimental and wry: "your friends are God's apology for your family," says the elderly fag hag Doris. But, as AIDS rears its head, feelings of sunlit nostalgia are soon replaced by tearful expressions of loss, for three of the four men eventually die, and the alternative family must pack up and leave. The documentary about the transplantation of queer community into the boondocks has shifted gears and has become one of the most unpretentious, effective, and affecting elegies in Canadian queer cinema. In 2003 Pimlott went on to make *Punch like a Girl*, a well-received TV documentary series on women boxers, coproduced and codirected with her partner Maya Gallus.

PODESWA, JEREMY, b. 1962. Director. An essential figure in the New Queer Toronto Wave of the 1990s, Ryerson- and American Film Institute-trained Podeswa first attracted attention way back in 1983 with *DAVID ROCHE Talks to You about Love*, an engaging monologue and sketch performance by the eponymous actor about love, same-sex, and otherwise. Podeswa's first feature, *Eclipse* (1994), a trilingual carousel of horny but alienated Torontonians fucking their way through a solar eclipse, was very queer in its omni-sexuality, as well as a masterful exercise in mise-en-scène, directing, acting, and gazing in rapture at long-haired newcomer Matthew

Ferguson. The second feature, *The Five Senses* (1999, Genie Best Director), followed in a similar vein with interwoven narratives, multisexual labyrinths (and beefcake), high-powered acting, and evocative urban symbolism. Both films literally embody Podeswa's resistance to the pigeonhole of "gay filmmaking" in the narrow sense:

> my sexual orientation is one element among others. I believe that the experience of belonging to a minority, whether tied to sexual orientation, religion or race, changes your perspective you can have on our environment and things in life. My orientation is only one part of me: I am Jewish, my parents are immigrants, I am North American. All these things and many others make what I am. It would be very restrictive, even a mistake, to say that my work or any other filmmaker's can be reduced to the dimension of sexual orientation. (*Fugues*, 16–9 [December 1999], 88)

Podeswa followed up with bread-and-butter exercises in TV movies (the period prairie melodrama of heterofamilial dysfunctionality *After the Harvest*, 2000) and directing queer cable episodes (*Six Feet Under*).

Podeswa then stunned everyone with a brilliant short fiction about the masochistic eroticism of an abused and sequestered teenager, *Touch* (2001, 29), by far the new decade's best queer short fiction in English. This half-hour narrative follows the first-person narration of Richard, who emerges from his trauma to crave the eroticism of pain. Richard turns away from his restored family and the flirtatious high-school boy at the next locker towards the nighttime world of street-corner hustling for johns who will hit him. Based on the story "My Lover's Touch," by Vancouver writer and ex-sexworker Patrick Roscoe and starring Brendan Fletcher, the intense sandy-haired revelation of *rollercoaster*, *The Law of Enclosure*, and *The Five Senses*, *Touch* was compared to Genet by an online commentator when it bowed at TIFF in 2001: "Raw, beautiful and haunting, it may be Podeswa's best work."[4] No one who saw the film disagreed.

POIRIER, ANNE CLAIRE, b. 1932. Director, documentarist, editor, producer, scriptwriter. The long career of the grande dame of Quebec (hetero-) feminist cinema was not exactly queer-positive – surprisingly, nary a dyke over thirty-five years of production – and coughed up only one gay male character, a strained and melancholy portrait of a middle-aged man in *La quarantaine* (1982). Accordingly, her 1988 redemption in the low-budget and unsentimental feature film about the gay male elderly, *Salut Victor!* (NFB, 84) was all the more refreshing. The warm-hearted feature love story between two elderly inmates of a "home" was based on *Matthew and*

Chauncey, by the Montreal gay anglophone novelist Edward O. Phillips. With its high-powered cast (the crotchety, closety Philippe is played by Jean-Louis Roux, one of the pioneers of classical theatre in Quebec), *Salut Victor!* was popular at foreign queer festivals and on domestic TV.

POOL, LÉA, b. 1950. Director, scriptwriter. Swiss-bred, UQAM-trained Pool is Quebec's most prolific and visible queer woman feature filmmaker. Her official public identity, oscillating between gay and bisexual, was reflected in her continuous fascination with border zones between homoerotic and homosocial friendships among women (as in her prizewinning first major success, the poetic *La femme de l'hotel*, 1984) and with amorous triangles, usually set off against the interfaces between desire and outsiderness – a subject of considerable personal authority for a director who knows what it is to be Jewish, an immigrant, and a single mother in the land of *pure laine*. Pool has suffered the instabilities of the marketplace as much as any art cinema auteur but with a lion's share of state funding over the years, has brought forth a sustained and original series of nine feature films, assorted documentaries and TV films and plus one short fiction, *Risponde-temi*. The latter, a sensuous and flawless narrative of a woman accident victim being transported to hospital in the arms of her lover on an oddly circuitous and scenic route through Montreal, is considered by some her best work, and it's certainly her most unambiguously lesbian one (part of the anniversary anthology film *Montréal vu par ...*, 1991). Otherwise, her weakest films are those most caught up in the lethargies of international coproduction and heterosexual romance (*La demoiselle sauvage*, 1991, *Mouvements du désir*, 1994), and most recently in the English language (*Lost and Delirious*, 2001).

Few would dispute that Pool's strongest features are those closest to her own personal experience (*Anne Trister*, 1986, a cultural feminist tale of a bisexual immigrant artist with parent issues that was a mainstay of the first crop of international queer community festivals in the mideighties; and *Emporte-moi*, 1998, 95). Her rare treatment of gay male experience, *À corps perdu* (1988), is a resourceful and controlled adaptation of French gay novelist Yves Navarre's *Kurwenal* and has aged well. Pool was not the easiest filmmaker for everyone to admire: promised breakthroughs into the American market never materialized, and lesbian film scholar Chantal Nadeau chided her for depoliticizing gender and sexuality, for "oscillating between the desire for sexual difference and the representation of (lesbian) sexuality as socially indifferent" (1999, 206). However, *Xtra!*'s Shane Smith considered the autobiographical *Emporte-moi* "a sublime coming-of-age-drama and a tribute to the transformative power of cinema" (7 October 1999). (see chapter 5.)

Salut Victor! (1988) is a warm-hearted feature love story between two elderly inmates coming out in a "home." Popular at home and abroad, the film redeemed for queer audiences feminist director Anne Claire Poirier's dyke-oblivious career. Production still, used with permission of the National Film Board of Canada

POSTOFF, SHAWN, b. 1974. Director, scriptwriter. University of Toronto–trained Postoff is a scriptwriter who directed three well-crafted narrative shorts circulating through the festivals in the early 2000s. *Coming to Terms* (2000, 16) is a classic coming-out tale, well-acted and well-written, within the white middle-class cottage-owning Ontario world, all unfolding within telephone conversations between an undergraduate and his uptight parents. *Talk Salo* (2002, 10) is more complex and original, a shaking up of a boy-boy friendship, again within the Toronto college set, through the sharing of Pasolini's disturbing Sadean masterpiece *Salo: 120 Days of Sodom* (1975). Postoff has a scriptwriting credit on *Queer as Folk* and instructed screenwriting workshops at the University of Toronto.

PRIDEVISION TV. Toronto's specialty "all-GLBT" cable channel was approved by the Canadian Radio Television and Telecommunications Commission in 2000 to much fanfare and launched on 7 September 2001.

The doomed lovers in *Rispondetemi*, Léa Pool's sensuous short about a woman accident victim being transported to hospital in the arms of her lover. Pool's best work, or only her most unambiguously lesbian one (part of *Montréal vu par ...*, 1991)? Production still, Cinémathèque québécoise

Its parent company, Headline Media Group Inc., owned by straight businessman John Levy, promised twenty-four-hour queer-focused digital entertainment and public affairs broadcasting but got off to a bad start when cable companies immediately began gouging customers. An encouraging lineup of charming queer media stars-in-development included book show host Mathieu Chantelois, call-in health show host Dr Keith, public affairs journalists Rachel Giese and Michael Serapio, and sports queen Paul DeBoy ("Locker Room"), alongside glamorous trans host Nina Arsenault, and even BRAD FRASER as a talk show host – plus the inevitable weird and ever increasing selection of cheap late-night imported porno (without the fast forward feature, of course). But the company never came anywhere close to its year one target of sixty thousand subscribers and hemorrhaged huge losses from the very beginning. Stripping itself bare of most innovative and all expensive programming (the talented and smart Giese and Serapio were among the first to go), as well as community-based producers such as BRUCE GLAWSON, and keeping only the most essential staff members, Pridevision struggled valiantly to hold its own despite widespread predictions of catastrophe, relying on increasingly grating filler programming. Syndicated gay columnist Richard "Three Dollar Bill" Burnett had long since cancelled his subscription and pulled no punches in his explanation for *Hour* readers: "I was spending eight hard-earned bucks a month for a bunch of lousy reruns and midnight porn interrupted by commercial breaks at the most inopportune moments. You could hear the groans in living rooms right across the Great White North and, honey, they weren't groans of pleasure" (15 April 2004). Repeatedly announcing plans to move into the U.S. market, Headline's real agenda was to sell, and it finally did so at the end of 2003. New owner Bill Craig is gay as well as a bi-national (Canada and the United States) TV veteran, and he promised to tackle the channel's weak link, distribution.

QUANDT, JAMES, b. 1956. Programmer, critic. University of Saskatchewan–trained Quandt, one of Toronto's most influential and award-winning cinematic arbiters, first caught attention as an occasional *TBP* critic in the late 1970s, chastising French director François Truffaut, a "smug, self-congratulatory egoist," for having "vindicated" the "superiority" of heterosexuals in his most recent "fluff" movie (March 1980). Quandt went on in 1985 to curate film at Harbourfront, where he launched Toronto's second major queer festival the following year. It included the first Rosa von Praunheim retrospective and stirred up the momentum that would culminate five years later in Inside Out, where Quandt was also part of the initial team. At the helm of Cinematheque Ontario beginning in 1990, Quandt commissioned me in 1994 to curate the first ever retrospective of Canadian queer film and video, the fourteen-program "Fruit Machine." Quandt otherwise has presided over an elegant international crossroads of art cinema and auteur revivals, preparing retrospectives and/or monographs on major queer filmmakers from silent-era closet cases Murnau and Stiller to modernist icons Fassbinder, Schroeter, and Bresson. His work was notable for an impeccable cinephile rigour and comprehensiveness often livened, as in the case of the Russian Sukorov, with a queer eye for the subtext.

RAFFÉ, ALEXANDRA, b. 1955. Producer. Singapore-bred Raffé migrated from the United Kingdom in 1978 and was soon collaborating with PATRICIA ROZEMA on the production of *Passion: A Letter in 16mm* (1985). Their relationship as lovers lasted only a year, but Raffé had discovered a knack for producing and went on to produce Rozema's first big hit, *I've Heard the Mermaids Singing* (1987), as well as her less successful next feature, *The White Room* (1990), a symbolic heteromelodrama. Raffé is known also for executive producing the queer masterpiece of the 1990s, *Zero Patience* (John Greyson, 1994), as well as other prominent Canadian features of the decade, such as David Wellington's tortured reflection on masculinity, *I Love a Man in Uniform* (1993). Appointed director of the Ontario Film Development Corporation at the peak of its glory in 1995, Raffé then had to preside over the savaging of the important organization by Mike Harris's Tories, serving until 1998. In 1995, multiple-Genied Raffé was honoured for her extraordinary contribution by Toronto Women in Film, and she then returned to producing features about dysfunctional masculinity *(Flower and Garnet,* 2002).

RAMSAY, BENNY NEMEROFSKY, b. 1973. Videomaker, visual artist. Montreal-born, York-trained, Berlin- and Toronto-based Ramsay was named Toronto ArtFag in 2000, and his prolific output of short videos showcasing his performance as singer and groover validated the title. A rare combination of perennial festival favourite and rigorous high-concept experimentalist, Ramsay's work built on a fascination with pop music and the singing voice, as well as the mediation of musical emotion through linguistic translation and media technology, not to mention a queer indulgence in postmodern camp and transgendered voice. My favourite is *Je Changerais D'Avis* (2000), a cover of Françoise Hardy's 1966 yé-yé standard, with multiple frames à la CNN, multiple language subtitles, and the surprisingly effective pathos, through all those layers of cable clutter, of the odd tear wiped away by a singer who really feels it.

RANCOURT, ÉRIC, b. 1968. Videomaker. Québécois Rancourt confirmed himself as a strong, original presence on the Montreal and international queer video scene with *L'Homme gruau/Oatmale* (2001, 50), a devastatingly deadpan, semiautobiographical narrative about a depressed, jilted, and horny guy on the dole (unabashedly performed by Rancourt himself). Trained at Vancouver's ECIAD, Rancourt produced his first two tapes in Lotusland and, not surprisingly, they probed a precariously transplanted identity within the sexual networks of the West End ghetto: *Bed Space* (1995) figured a cramped relationship as a too-narrow apartment bed, and *French Canadian Horse-Cocked Pornstar* (1996) initiated the pattern of Rancourt literally embodying his own narratives of sexual alienation.

RANDERA, SAFIYA, b. 1973. Filmmaker, multidisciplinary artist. OCAD-trained, Toronto-based Randera had two complex, personal films circulating on the queer festival circuit at the turn of the 2000s. *Jangri* (1998, 7) was a personal essay confronting the uneasy mediation of lesbian identity through the heritage of South Asian culture. Erotic interludes tangle with layers of received imagery and on-the-street interviews with women in Toronto's Little India who say it's "unnatural" and "everybody hates."

A more autobiographical mosaic is *Health Status Survey* (2000, 12), which uses a questionnaire to tenderly but frankly narrate the shifts in power within a lesbian relationship when a disabling injury turns one partner into caregiver and the other into reluctant "patient."

RASHID, IAN IQBAL, b. 1964. Director, scriptwriter, poet, activist. Of South Asian Ismaili descent via Tanzania, Toronto-bred Rashid was active on the local queer activist/arts scene in the late eighties. His first poetry collection, *Black Markets, White Boyfriends and Other Acts of Elision* (1991) was well received, and queer audiences remember him for *Bolo Bolo!* (codirector Gita Saxena, 1991, 30), the irreverent but deep-probing queer South Asian entry into the Toronto AIDS cable series project. In 1991, Rashid moved to Bristol, England, to pursue his writing and film-making career and distinguished himself with several fiction film shorts that were popular on the queer community network as well as on U.K. public broadcast. *Surviving Sabu* (1998, 16) is a much-praised intersection of coming out/of-age narrative with cinephilia, diasporic cultural clash, and queer sexual affirmation. In 2003 Rashid came back to Toronto to develop these themes in feature-length format in his Canada-U.K. co-production *Touch of Pink* (2004, 91) – finally an excellent queer subversion of the oppressively heterocentric diasporic wedding cycle of the 1990s and 2000s. *Pink* is an intercontinental, intercultural couple comedy-romance and family melodrama in which the hero's queeny and closety Cary Grant guardian angel wonders what people actually do in this Toronto that wasn't exactly his first choice for a vacation destination.

REGAN, FRANCIS, b. 1964. Director. An Edmonton-bred, Vancouver-based dentist trained at ECIAD and UBC, as well as the New York Film Academy, Regan has contributed well-received celluloid shorts to international queer and mainstream festivals since the late nineties: *Still Life* (1997, 4), a narrative about a birthday football, and *Back at the Bar* (2002, 4), an experimental focus on the alienations and desires of queer youth.

REGINA. Queer City Cinema. Founded in 1996 by Gary Varro, Saskatchewan's principal lesbian and gay film and video festival has been held biannually in the late spring since then, with Banff-trained Varro (b. 1961) at the helm. QCC makes up in innovative programming for the relative dispersal of its demographic base. A legendary political brouhaha was sparked in 2000 by its "taxpayer funded" "Community and Pornography" sidebar, which saw pan-national panel participants posing with evangelical protesters in front of the Public Library Film Theatre. Programs have toured also to Saskatoon, Winnipeg, and Edmonton.

REINKE, STEVE, b. 1963. Videomaker. Trained at the NSCAD, Reinke has been a major queer presence in Canadian video art since 1990. His legendary *One Hundred Videos* (1989–96), an ambitious, epic project whereby he committed to producing one hundred short videos before the millennium (he beat the deadline by almost four years!), is his demented serial masterpiece (see chapter 8). The appropriation of fragments from the archival dumpster is one of the principal strategies in this massive agglomeration of miniature works, but there are also many dexterous examples of interactive or observational personal camera work, as in *Request* (1993), where he knocks on the door of a half dozen ostensible strangers, who all happen to be male hunk co-conspirators, and asks them to disrobe for his video, which they all do without hesitation. Reinke's recurrent voice-over is not autobiographical in the literal sense, but his personal sensibility shines through this miraculous and self-reflexive encyclopedia. Among Reinke's preoccupations are the artistic process and the image-bank unconscious of civilization; the body, the self, and identity; childhood and regression; narrative and humour; and same-sex desire, obsession, transgression, fetishism, and above all, voyeurism. Sometimes the titles alone tell all, and my favourite is *Eighty Prominent Dermatologists* (1992). Since the completion of the hundred videos, Reinke has continued his prolific output, despite occasional bluffs about ceasing production, in general offering longer, more complex works that often extend his traditional themes. For example, *The Chocolate Factory* (2002) develops his 1995 fascination for gay serial-killer Jeffrey Dahmer. Originally Toronto-based, Reinke teaches at the University of Illinois at Chicago.

RÉSEAU VIDÉ-ELLE. This radical lesbian video production collective, undoubtedly the longest still-active queer arts activist group anywhere, with more than fifty tapes under their belts, was launched in 1975 by Diane Heffernan (b. 1942) and Suzanne Vertue (b. 1947). Both had been NFB-trained community activists involved in Vidéographe, the state studio's pioneering community video program, and had been active since 1972 with documentaries of women's voices, lives, and causes, from feminist theatre to nude dancers' political mobilizations. Perhaps their best-known title is *Amazones d'hier/ Lesbiennes d'aujourd'hui* [Amazons yesterday, lesbians today], the name for a documentary tape (1981, 105, French and English versions), the production group formed to make it, and the group's magazine of "political reflection," undertaken in 1982. Among the names associated with these activities over the years, many coming out of another earlier, 1970s collective Coop-Femmes, were Ariane Brunet, Ginette Bergeron, Danielle Charest, and Louise Turcotte. AHLA was about politics and everyday life within Montreal's "radical lesbian" networks, shot often in diaristic fashion between 1979 and 1981 by the group, sometimes also called the Collectif Vidéo-Amazones. According to Turcotte, the videotape "invited about ten Montreal lesbians to express themselves in front of the camera about their personal life, their conception of lesbianism and of feminism, and on themes such as work, relationships and sexuality" (Demczuk and Remiggi 1998, 363–98).

Oriented towards French, as well as North American, directions in theory and activism, the group at first restricted its video work to lesbian-only audiences but loosened the conditions later in the 1990s. Other representative titles were *Tout qui sort de l'ordinaire* (Everything that's out of the ordinary, 1979, 60) and *Espaces lesbiennes. Vivre dans un espace* (Lesbian spaces; living in a space, 1982, 40). An intense but irregular series of video productions followed over the next decades, some maintaining the rigorous radical stance of the group's original inspiration, others branching out into emerging concerns like eroticism. In 1990 Heffernan risked controversy with Montreal's first lesbian erotic video, *Orgasmes à la crème fouetté* (Whipped Cream Orgasms, codirector Patrizia Tavormina, 28; see chapter 8). The group continued to be active, but maintaining its ability to address younger generations of lesbians interested in such things as diversity and AIDS activism was increasingly a challenge.

RICHTER, SUZY, b. 1963. Filmmaker, singer. A graduate of the Universities of Toronto and Berlin, self-taught, Toronto-based Richter is a veteran of the underground/Super 8/DIY film scene, and a perennial of queer community festivals since the early 1990s. The camp aesthetics of abjection are her forte, whether the stench of bars (*Infidel*, 1999, 13) or cleaning out the tub (*Old Butch*, 1995, 2). Richter, a sometime drag king performer, celebrated uniform drag in *Dressed to Drill* (2002, 4).

ROBERTS, CYNTHIA, b. 1965. Director. Montreal-bred, Carleton- and Ryerson-trained, Toronto-based, queer-friendly Roberts has contributed two major but underrated and underdistributed features to the queering of Canadian cinemas. *The Last Supper* (1994, 96) was a compelling adaptation of an AIDS assisted-suicide stage melodrama about a dancer who choreographs from his bed his last performance for his lover and his doctor. *Bubbles Galore* (1996, 86) brought porn queens Annie Sprinkle and Nina Hartley together at last with the Canada Council for the Arts and sent jitters through the very foundations of public arts funding in Canada, distracting from its own considerable virtues as a pink-filtered erotic feminist-lesbian hooker trash melodrama. (see chapters 8 and 9.)

ROCHE, DAVID, b. 1951. Actor, writer. Concordia-trained Roche has been a fixture of the Toronto queer theatre scene since the late 1970s. An early film appearance was in the pioneering *David Roche Talks to You about Love* (JEREMY PODESWA, 1983, 22), a version of Roche's quirky and flamboyant stage act. The actor followed up as the hyperkinetic fireman who pontificates on death and dying in another pioneering film, Nik Sheehan's AIDS documentary essay *No Sad Songs* (1985). Roche later starred in John Greyson's two 1989 AIDS tapes, *The World Is Sick (Sic)* and *The Pink Pimpernel*, in the former in drag as a ditzy and reactionary CBC reporter who is kidnapped by AIDS activists at the Montreal AIDS Conference and joins her kidnappers à la Patty Hearst. More recently, Roche has been a frequent collaborator of Michael Achtman, performing in his tapes *MASH Notes for Private Kyle Brown* (1997) and *Shinto* (2000).

ROGERS, GERRY, b. 1956. Documentarist, producer. A veteran producer and director of feminist documentary for the NFB, especially for Studio D, in the 1980s and 1990s, Rogers moved from the invisible lesbian end of the feminist spectrum to the matter-of-fact up-front variety with *My Left Breast* (2000, St John's, 57). The first Canadian documentary breakthrough and bestseller of the new century, *My Left Breast* is Gerry Rogers's account of her struggle against breast cancer. Based on over seventy hours of diaristic, low-format video material shot by Rogers and her life partner Peggy Norman, this ebullient but challenging independent film (financed by CBC Newsworld) is a brilliant demonstration of the potential of low-format video for exploring the personal politics of intimacy, desire, and self-representation. The L word is taken for granted as Rogers and Norman follow the community empowerment and the late night tears of their everyday lives; the camera and microphone validate sexual identity as intrinsically inseparable from other social issues, such as women's health. Rogers, a roundish ex-nun and veteran producer of some of Studio D's more harrowing essays on such subjects as sexual abuse (*To a Safer Place*, 1987), reveals her wackier Newfoundland side, rolling around and clapping flippers on a dramatic oceanfront precipice a with other hairless survivors, seals. Showered with Genies and Geminis, along with dozens of other prizes, *Breast* was the toast of U.S. talk-show-dom and one of the most successful queer Canadian videos ever.

ROMILLY, JASON, b. 1970. Director, writer, producer, editor. Toronto-based Romilly was part of the LIFT network of queer young indies in the 1990s, contributing two stylized fiction shorts to the queer festival circuit before moving into music video: *Alone* (1996, 20), "an amazing ambitious video piece about violence, sexuality and shortness of vision," according to

Eye (10 July 1997), when the tape was programmed as part of a 1997 African Canadian series; and *Spent* (1998, 27 , 16mm), a noirish descent narrative, well-crafted and stylish, about a delusional bisexual young hunk who thinks he can manipulate and betray his tricks and his mother because he's a secret agent.

ROSS, MIRHA-SOLEIL, b. 1969. Performance artist, videomaker, transsexual activist, curator, sexworker. Transplanted Québécois Ross is Toronto's most visible and prolific transgender cultural voice. The star of the National-al Film Board's well-intentioned documentary *In the Flesh* (Gordon McLennan, 2000, 47), Ross's own sixteen or so video productions have much more raw artistic energy and political bite – "gut-busting, ass-erupting and immoderately whorish," as she says in the compilation of video excerpts. The tapes, often made in collaboration with Xanthra MacKay and Mark Karbusicky, blur boundaries between document, demonstration, performance, narrative, autobiography, representation ... and provocation. From her own personal body, history, and experience to the political fields of reproductive technology and animal rights, Ross's restless art covers a broad landscape of politics and desire. Ross founded Toronto's COUNTING PAST TWO trans-arts festival in 1998. (see chapter 10.)

ROSS, SINCLAIR, 1908–96. Our canonical literary ancestor, known for his fiction of coming-of-age, repression, and masculinity on the Depression-era prairies, came out as an elder queer lion in the years before his death and helpfully suggested rereadings of his writings from decades earlier. Subtextual readings of film versions of his short stories thus became all the more legitimate, especially Stanley Jackson's *Cornet at Night* (NFB, 1963, 15) and Anne Wheeler's adaptation for Atlantis of his famous story *One's a Heifer* (1984, 24). (See chapter 5.) His crypto-queer novel *As For Me and My House* (1941) has rich potential and remains lamentably untackled by cinematic recyclers.

ROUSSEAU, BERNARD, b. 1950. Entrepreneur, exhibitor, programmer, producer. Partner in Montreal's legendary gay sex-shop Priape (est. 1974), Rousseau has been a leading Canadian purveyor of gay porn, first on Super 8, later on Beta and VHS, and eventually on DVD (as well as in magazines, of course) for almost thirty years. A film buff, Rousseau was part of the team who in 1980 in East-End Montreal put together the Semaine du cinéma gai, a financial disaster for the inexperienced programmers but a pioneering event as the first major queer film festival in Canada. When a Chinese community cinema closed soon after, the undaunted Rousseau persuaded his associates to open the first (and only?) gay cinema in Canada,

Le Cinéma du Village, in the then burgeoning Village gai. Wanting to show "non-stereotyped" gay cinema, the theatre opened in 1984 with Arthur Bressan's harrowing *Abuse* (1983), a serious downer for the new audience, but a run of the more upbeat and sexier *Ernesto* (1979) was more successful. Still, the theatre was a financial sieve and after six months converted to porno, where such hits as Matt Sterling's *The Bigger, the Better* (1984) packed them in – benevolently approved by the Régie du cinéma du Québec at a time when gay hardcore was available licitly nowhere else in Canada. The Cinéma du Village finally closed in 1993, as home video clinched its domination of the market (Priape and its new rival Wega were the largest Canadian rights holders), and porn *production* was beginning to emerge as a possibility. Priape financed and distributed several of the half dozen *pure laine* Québécois porn videos that appeared as the nineties wore on – a strange universe in which bilingual porn stars wore hockey pads during their fuck scenes. Priape was one hundred percent investor in the last and best of the lot, *Fuck Friends* (2000), which dropped the bilingualism (contrary to the implication of the English title) and kept the skates but flunked at the cash register (see chapter 8). A lifelong opponent of censorship, Rousseau is a committed stakeholder in the commercial viability of queer culture.

ROY, ANDRÉ, b. 1944. Poet, film critic, teacher. One of Quebec's most famous living poets (Governor General's Prize), whose multiply translated works express unabashedly his gay male subjectivity, Roy has also been an award-winning film critic since the 1970s. An art film traditionalist, Roy is author of several books on film and a pillar of Quebec film culture, writing for *Le Berdache* and *Fugues*, as well as mainstream publications. Seldom if ever focused on queer cinema in itself, Roy was unrivalled in the depth of his understanding of queer filmmakers, from those abroad like Fassbinder and Almodovar to those at home like Rodrigue Jean: "[The latter's] characters are neither conventional nor folkloric; he doesn't normalize them any more than he naturalizes them. However they are very present, bodily present. This filmmaker knows how to film bodies, not only through their purely fleshly sensuality ... but also their faces and their looks that bespeak spleen and tenderness as much as savagery and triviality ... It's a cinema where beings are overwhelmed, disconnected from the world, where despair is near, a cinema between affliction and affection" (2001).

ROZEMA, PATRICIA, b. 1958. Director. The most prominent of English Canadian lesbian feature filmmakers, Rozema has Southwestern Ontario Dutch Calvinist roots, which surfaced in the repressive settings in which the engaged heroine of *When Night is Falling* (1995) discovers the lesbian within. Trained in college theatre and on American TV/film sets, Rozema's first short, *Passion: A Letter in 16mm* (1985, 28), a first-person breakup drama, was notoriously cagey about gendered pronouns, and in fact Rozema would come out publicly only in 1999.

Rozema's ambiguity dissipated only a little with her first feature, *I've Heard the Mermaids Singing* (1987, 81), the international box office hit that catapulted her into the Canadian canon, a whimsical postmodern fable of a Toronto office gal who fantasizes about art, romance, identity, and flying. This low-budget first feature by an unknown director was the Canadian sleeper success story of the 1980s, as much in the reviews as at the box office, all the more so since it was the most forthright and successful lesbian film on the national scene in English to date. The heroine Polly, played by a pert and charismatic comic genius, the queer-friendly Sheila McCarthy, develops a crush on her lesbian boss and expresses herself both through her dreams of Victorian ladies' picnics and through her camera lens. Queer media welcomed the film eagerly, but its ambiguities created controversy at the same time: *The Advocate* welcomed *Mermaids*' "laissez-faire lesbianian" with its "just happens to be … not a problem … casual, offhand" treatment (7 September 1987), while the more political *Gay Community News* "cringed" at the director's insistence that the film was "not about" lesbianism or dykes (September 1987). *Mermaids* holds up well two decades later despite some 1980s video diary mannerisms and maintains its place as a milestone in Canadian queer cinemas. Coproducer was Alex Raffé, with whom a fertile artistic relationship would continue.

When Night is Falling (Toronto, 1995, 93) was another major landmark, a coming-out melodrama that is an international queer festival favourite. Applauded by mainstream critics and queer audiences, as well as boffo at the art cinema box office, Rozema's torrid romance between a theology professor and a circus performer has everything you could want: stars (Pascale Bussières, Rachael Crawford, and Henry Czerny, all delivering superbly), a coming-out narrative, an (underplayed) racial theme, even heteroeroticism between Bussières and her soon-to-be-abandoned fiancé that is almost as hot as the now legendary same-sex steamorama. *Xtra!* opined that Rozema's "refusal to vilify the straight white men, will annoy those who prefer a simpler, less messy political spectrum" (28 April 1995). Not everyone's cup of tea is Rozema's tortured Calvinist triangle or her magic realism (from the laundromat to the big top and a frozen puppy that comes to life when love is reborn!), but all the elements come together so well that the seduction was almost universal. *The Lesbian Film Guide* effused, "Superb, captivating, tender, often funny and frequently beautiful … like a lyrical poem, deeply felt and perfectly formed. Rich, vibrant colours, romantic images – naked women swimming in clear blue water –

Voyeur Polly's view of her boss (Paule Baillargeon, right) and girlfriend (Ann-Marie MacDonald, left) in Patricia Rozema's *I've Heard the Mermaids Singing* (1987), the most successful lesbian film not about lesbianism ever. Production still, *I've Heard the Mermaids Singing*, Cylla Von Tuedeman, 1987, VOS Productions, Ltd.

a dusting of snow, a half-moon and always the night just a moment away ... Unmissable" (Darren 2000, 219). Did anyone ever say all of that about *Desert Hearts*? After *Night*, Rozema moved back and forth between a successful major studio Jane Austen adaptation (*Mansfield Park*, 1999) and an assortment of Toronto shorts, including an artful first-person segment in NIK SHEEHAN's *Symposium: Ladder of Love* (1996).

RUSSELL, CRAIG, 1948–90. Gender impressionist, star. Female impersonator/performer Russell had once been part of Mae West's household in Hollywood, and his best friend back home, Margaret Gibson, wrote a story called "Making It" based on her friendship with the Toronto boy who wanted to make it as a star like Mae. The story somehow turned into a movie script in the midseventies and was brought to the screen with Russell in the starring role as Robin. The rest is history, and Richard Benner's delirious and sentimental *Outrageous!* became a sleeper smash and a cinematic platform for Russell's stupendous real-voice incarnations of everyone from West to Ella Fitzgerald (see chapter 4).

La Russell, the hot new star with a Berlin Best Actor trophy tucked into his bra, soon ran into hard times, personally and professionally, even got married (to a woman) in pumps and tights in front of TV news cameras, and Benner didn't do much better. It was only ten years later that the two careers converged again and were given their ill-fated second chance, a sequel called *Too Outrageous!* (1987). Sequels apparently just don't seem to come naturally to a national cinema whose hard-won success stories, in the States or elsewhere, are so few and far between. Benner lacked practice, Russell lacked discipline on set, and ambiguities about intended audience and miscalculations about how to set up interactive cabaret-type performances on the big screen all contributed to the commercial and critical failure of the film, despite the gala premiere at TIFF 1987. References to AIDS, of course, had had to be worked into the script, but the notes were false, and the retrovirus got even by robbing us of both Benner and Russell in 1990.

SANDLOS, KARYN, b. 1968. Filmmaker, curator, educator. York and OISE-educated, Sandlos is active in Toronto experimental film. Two of her films have played in queer and experimental festivals at home and broad: *Passing Through* (1998, 12) is an experimental first-person film about memory and an evocative dialectic of butch boots and wedding dresses, girlhood remembered and caburetors exploding, rural values and urban lifestyles, while sloshing through a beautifully hand-tinted meadow of pink flowers in Mount Forest, Ontario; *Still Here* (2001, 7), mediated through hand-processing and single-take performances, eulogizes the artist's uncle, a gay painter who was murdered.

SARAHAN, JOE, b. 1962. Video maker, installation artist, arts administrator, curator. Winnipeg-born, ECIAD-trained but self-taught Sarahan has been a pillar of Vancouver's Video In and queer video circle since 1983, a frequent collaborator of PAUL WONG, PAUL LANG, LORNA BOSCHMAN and, most recently, painter Attila Richard Lukacs (2002). Celebrated for his confrontational aesthetics of sexual and social outsiderdom, Sarahan's best-known work was his urban dirge *Holy Joe* (1987, 11), whose acquisition and presentation by the National Gallery in its inaugural video show in 1988 (also showcasing FUNG and PARADIS, curated by queer-friendly Su "Mother Courage" Ditta) led to a major censorship kefuffle involving yellow media and the Ontario Censor Board, partly in response to Sarahan's fleeting glimpses of an SM dungeon (Ditta 1999). Sarahan's most ambitious project, *West Coast Sailor Love Story* (1997, 45), is a loose and spicy narrative about a blond American sailor (played by the prolific artist himself) on shore leave and fulfilling his queer fantasies in a Vancouver underworld of glory holes and homophobic bikers. The political discourses about everything from safe sex to hegemonic white masculinity keep bubbling to the surface.

SARRA, SAMANTHA, b. 1980. Videomaker, critic, curator, activist. Toronto-based Sarra, an initiate in the Inside Out Queer Youth scheme in 1999, has provided the community festivals with several video shorts about identity, relationships, and the body, including *What She Is* (1998, 5), about homophobia; *C.L.I.T., Certified Lesbians in Training* (writer/producer, 2000, 8), a mocu-mentary; and *Baby Boobs*, 2001, 10), a PSA for lesbians about breast cancer. A veteran of Pridevision, Sarra's voice as a journalist and arts critic is heard frequently in *Xtra!*, and she has curated for Inside Out.

SAUNDERS, JOYAN, b. 1954. NSCAD- and San Diego-trained Newfoundlander Saunders was a distinctive and rare presence within the lesbian video scene in the early eighties before relocating to the University of Arizona. Her enigmatic and wry narrative or conceptual pieces epitomized dyke camp ahead of their time. In its sunbaked desert iconography, *Here in the Southwest* (1984, 23) showed that you can take a girl out of the Rock but you can't take the Rock out of the girl.

SCHRODER, ELIZABETH. Videomaker, scriptwriter. Torontonian Schroder made half a dozen feminist experimental videos over a decade beginning in the mideighties, interrogating gender and cultural difference in the media and the art world. Among them was one of the few Canadian works to have articulated an explicit bisexual identity, *The Bisexual Kingdom* (1987, 22), a comic coming-out fantasy based on the TV show *The Animal Kingdom*. Schroder later relocated to the United States.

SCHUYLER, LINDA, b. 1949. Television producer. The queer-friendly, Toronto-based creator of *The Kids of Degrassi Street* (1982–86), *Degrassi*

Junior High/Degrassi High (1986–92), and *Degrassi: The Next Generation* (2001+) has been a legend of Canadian television and a major cultural export industry for almost a quarter of a century. Honoured by the Order of Canada and Emmies and Geminis galore, Schuyler got it right from the very beginning, capturing kids' points of views in her chronicle of Toronto East End kids growing up. At the same time she developed occasional queer story lines in memory of a fellow teacher's gay son's suicide. With *The Next Generation*, 1980s caution was thrown to the wind and queerness was handled with all of the up-front matter-of-factness that half-hour episode lengths and interwoven leukemia subplots allowed. Executive story editor and script contributor to *Next Generation* was Aaron Martin (b. 1972), Brantford-bred, trained at Queen's and the CFC, and co-scriptwriter of a queer festival favourite, *Martirio* (*Sufferance*, CLAUDIA MORGADO ESCANILLA, 2000, 19). In the interests of realism Martin defended his gay tenth-grader Marco's stereotypical artsiness and the bloody Church Street queerbashing he gets in the episode where he comes out. But all was forgiven when Martin soon provided an out and proud hockey-player boyfriend, and added a kiss! Serial coming-of-age melodrama for teens makes different structural demands from those made by either documentary (*Prom Fight*, 2002; *Class Queers*, 2003) or dystopian punk/cult films (*Secondary High*, 2003). Toronto in the 2000s has nurtured a symbiotic stew of all three, giving Canadian queers the luxury of choice. The L.A. entertainment queer-media watchdog group GLAAD honoured *The Next Generation*, and *The Advocate* called it another reason to love Canada (20 January 2004).

SCOTT, JAY (pseudonym Jeffrey Scott Beaven), 1949–93. Film critic. Nebraska-born draft dodger Scott joined the *Globe and Mail* in 1977 and presided as Canada's most influential English-language film critic until his death in 1993 from AIDS. Scott took his role and the objectivity it entailed seriously. Though he was not especially committed to either queer or Canadian cinema (in his two published collections of approximately two hundred film reviews [1985, 1994], there are only a handful of each), he did them justice and was part of that energized moment when both the Canadian New Wave and the New Queer Cinema came into their own.

Scott's early review of an early film that was both Canadian and queer, *Track Two* (SUTHERLAND, 1982), started out with the *Globe*'s then compulsory "homosexual" but switched to "gay" in the fourth paragraph and never turned back, an understated boost for this documentary denunciation of police terrorism: "In the interests of thoroughness, Sutherland's decision not to interview the police is regrettable, but the director may have felt – and the position is defensible – that in conducting raids on six bathhouses and in arresting 304 men, the police had already released a statement. *Track Two* is in the nature of a reasonable and unexpectedly low-key response" (1 July 1982). The same year, Scott was virtually the only major critic to come to the defense of *The Wars* (TIMOTHY FINDLEY, scenarist, 1983) as "a historically important event and, like so many important historic events of late, it bruises the heart." Even before he gradually came out as a gay public persona, the occasional campy nuance and ironic insight gave him away. Only the most flaming could end their review of *Mommie Dearest* (1981) thus: "This is theoretically a modern horror movie about mother love, but it is actually one of the funniest movies about how *not* to make a movie ever made. The moral? CRAIG RUSSELL reports Joan Crawford sent a message to all movie stars from beyond the grave: 'Don't die: people'll dish ya.'"

SECTER, DAVID, b. 1943. Winnipeg-bred Secter was a University of Toronto theatre major when he made the breakthrough feature for which he is most known, *Winter Kept Us Warm* (1965, 81). The first queer Canadian feature film in English is a tale of triangles on campus whose audacious perspicuity and discreet eroticism still make you hold your breath four decades later (see chapter 4). Big Man on Campus Doug meets frosh Peter in September, Doug realizes something and plays guitar love songs to Peter in his dorm room, Peter meets Sandra, Doug loses Peter, April is the cruelest month. Secter took *Winter* to Cannes, and for once a few contemporary international critics got it right both on the queer and the Canadian angle.

Secter went on to make another Toronto feature, *The Offering* (1966, 80), an interesting interracial romance that expresses his sensibility but lacks the previous film's punch, before relocating first to New York and then to California, where his media career was been intermittent. Joel Secter's affectionate feature documentary biopic about his uncle (*The Best of Secter and the Rest of Secter*, 2005, 58) fills in the gaps in the subsequent career of a cinematic and sexual rebel whose artistic promise was not to be fully realized.

SEGATO, LORRAINE, b. 1956. Musician, documentarist. Sudbury-bred, Toronto-based, socially conscious rock star of the 1980s (Parachute Club), Segato's 1983 hit "Rise Up" was appropriated as an anthem by the Toronto queer community, McCain's french fries, and the NDP. Her feisty documentary about her old Toronto stomping ground, *Queen St. West: The Rebel Zone* (2002, 51), starring GREYSON, FERNIE, et al., was honoured at Inside Out. Segato's other contributions to queer film in Canada included an early "daring" film venture into lesbian sexuality entitled *Larking*

(1980), as well as her role in the Sudbury documentary *The Pinco Triangle* as a repressed housewife who metamorphoses into a dykey rocker belting out "Out from the Underground" in front of the Big Nickel. Segato's catchy theme song for Fernie's anti-name-calling cartoon *Apples and Oranges* (2003) is "It's Not Cool to Be Cruel."

SELWAY, SHAWN, b. 1948. Director. Hamilton-based Selway was the queer-friendly McMaster student who produced *A Son of the Family* (1977, 29), a pioneering short fiction, unique for its time, that was distributed by the CFMDC within the gay-liberation movement circuit in the late seventies but that has now vanished. Based on the true coming-out story of Selway's high-school best friend and developed in consultation with another gay friend who had fled to Montreal, the film's official catalogue description read: "A dramatic account of several crucial months in the life of Mike Norris, a young homosexual. Mike's 'coming out' and departure from family and girl friend are his first steps in asserting his right to be gay outside the gay milieu. The drama unfolds as he faces new social and employment trials." Seeing the film for the first time in 2003–04, I am impressed with how well *Son of the Family* holds up, perceptively shot in 16mm black and white by queer-friendly producer-cameraman James Aquila with a strong sense of place (winter in Hamilton!). Mike's relationships with his male and female support networks around him, and even with the blasé Torontonian who provides him with his first amour and then dumps him, are subtly delineated. The film ends with an unexpected counterstereotype twist plus a witty ideological parting shot: a window display of mannequins mechanically enacting the heteropatriarchal institution of marriage.

SHBIB, BASHAR, b. 1959. Director, screenwriter, producer. Syria-born, Concordia-bred Shbib (a.k.a. Chbib) has been an obsessive and prolific filmmaker since the early 1980s, dividing his activities between Montreal and Los Angeles, a conjuror of Warholian universes of sexual fluidity and marginality. The most impressive of his early Montreal shorts, *Or d'ur* (1983, 44) is a delirious faux-vérité narrative of the world of male hustlers, complete with an over-the-top madame and bordello. Next came the transgender-themed *Betsy* (1983) and *Amour impossible* (starring Montreal transpersona Michelle DeVille, 1984). The subsequent stream of anarchic low-budget features such as *Memoirs* (a lesbian love story, 1985) and *Evixion* (denizens of a large apartment building caught up in voyeurism and AIDS panic, 1986) usually included a canvas of sexual dissidence and social diversity – not to mention hot men. In the stream of features produced through the nineties in the United States, Shbib's world became somewhat more mainstream, but occasionally recalls the provocations of his youth, as with the trans-themed *Panic* (1996). More recently, Shbib has returned to academia, but at the time of writing is in postproduction on *Wedding Murders* (2004), about a gay serial killer in love with the police officer on his trail. Repudiating definitional labels, the "operationally bisexual" Shbib straddles borders, whether cinematic, national, or sexual.

SHEEHAN, NIK, b. 1960. Documentarist, journalist. One of Toronto's distinctive queer documentary voices, Algonquin College–trained Sheehan made a big first splash as the director of Canada's – and possibly the world's – first major documentary about community response to AIDS, *No Sad Songs* (1985), an impassioned, eclectic essay centred around a profile of PWA Jim Black (see chapter 9). This work's AIDS theme and its formula of mixing vérité documentary with dramatization was developed further in 1996 in Sheehan's next major work, the unusual, feature-length *Symposium: The Ladder of Love*. Here a sprinkling of Toronto's queer glitterati, from BRAD FRASER to PATRICIA ROZEMA, imitate Plato and talk about love, showing films-within-the-film, all directed by Sheehan, to explore their ideas. When *Symposium* was broadcast, the *Globe and Mail* called it "imaginative and candid" and a vindication of the role of CBC in "this country's broadcast landscape and essential to the intellectual health of [TV]" (21 October 1996). Sheehan's 1997 *God's Fool* (98) was a biopic of Canadian queer iconoclast and globe-trotting novelist Scott Symons, which *Xtra!* called "Sheehan's best work to date" (8 October 1998) and which also got broadcast.

SHERMAN, KENNETH, b. 1966. Director, writer, editor, multimedia artist, teacher. ECIAD-trained Sherman teaches at Vancouver Film School and is best known in the queer festival circuit for his meticulously crafted AIDS melodrama *The Time Being* (1997, 52). Within the small subgenre of the assisted-suicide narrative, *Time Being* is much more about the bereavement and lingering desire of Sebastian, the partner left behind, than about the choices of his late lover Michael. Their relationship and their support network are also vividly captured in simulated home video, and the affect is strong and honest. More recently, Sherman made the prizewinning *Go-Go Boy (Prelude)* (2002, 13).

SIDDIQI, ATIF, b. 1970. Video artist, documentarist, performance artist. Karachi-bred, Los Angeles-inflected, Concordia-trained Siddiqi is an artist whose film, videos, and performances could not easily be separated from his public/private transdisciplinary, transcultural, trans(ultra-?)gendered persona. His first major video, based on early performance work, *Erotic*

Exotic (1998), used poetry, song, dance, and costume to develop a personal outsider erotics within both South Asian and Montreal urban contexts. *M! Mom, Madonna and Me* (2001) offered to worldwide festival audiences a loose narrative line based on Siddiqi's semi-autobiographical performance as a transglobal artist in search of love (from both Mother and several on-the-road hunks), artistic fulfilment, and stardom. For *Solo* (2003), Siddiqi had his first chance at a "professional" budget and resources, thanks to the National Film Board's Reel Diversity competition, and produced once more an autobiographical narrative (see chapters 5 and 10). Here he wove together memories of childhood trauma brought out in on-screen therapy sessions, familial encounters and confrontations, fantasy interludes from underwater ballet to eyelash extravaganzas, and even improvised efforts at on-camera dating. Canadian queer cinemas have sheltered many artists for whom life itself is a work of art, but Siddiqi may well be one of the most risk-taking, focused, and unique.

SIEGEL, LOIS, b. 1946. Filmmaker, teacher. U.S.-bred Siegel has taught filmmaking and made personal independent films, sometimes more documentary than experimental and sometimes vice versa, since the seventies in Montreal and most recently in Ottawa. Known for her zany humour and taste for the exceptional as a social observer, queer-friendly Siegel was familiar to queer communities, especially for her *Lip Gloss* (1993, 75), a full-length cinéma vérité exploration and oral history of Montreal's legendary world of drag club performance and trans identities, taxed by some with voyeurism but valued by historians as a document of a disappearing world.

SIMARD, KIM, b. 1980. Director, scriptwriter. Concordia-trained, Montreal-based Simard presented in queer festivals her prizewinning *Shave Your Legs* (2001, 10), a well-crafted and evocative coming-of-age narrative about a young girl who encounters mortality in the shape of a dying grandmother, unwelcome gender socialization in the character of a stepsister who spends hours in the bathroom razor in hand, and, worst of all, betrayal in her best friend who discovers boys' kisses – all one snowy winter.

SIMONEAU, YVES, b. 1956. Director, scriptwriter. Trained at Laval and within Radio-Canada, queer-friendly Simoneau directed two exceptional queerish features, shot in Montreal and Toronto respectively, before he relocated to Hollywood in the 1990s. *Pouvoir Intime* surprised audiences in the boom year of 1986 with its freshness as a noir heist film with a theme of gender-bending and sexual marginality. Christian Rasselet may have found the film, with its deliriously satisfying post-bloodbath happy ending, to be "too perfect to be convincing" (*Sortie*, May 1986), but almost everyone else was impressed (see chapter 8).

Perfectly Normal (1990, 104) was a warmhearted Toronto fable of hockey, assembly-line alienation, male bonding, real estate, ethnicity, and ambiguous masculinity. But to this typical English Canadian recipe add the unsettling ingredient of opera, and you have the stylish queer-straight sleeper hit. The perfunctory heteroconjugal resolution for the shy hero Renzo, who ends up in operatic drag as Bellini's Norma, hardly dilutes the film's predominant homosocial energy. It's really an off-balance love story between Renzo and his larger-than-life uninvited roommate (played by larger-than-life British comic star Robbie Coltrane), a shyster who bursts in on him in the shower, transforms his life, and moves on – just as Simoneau did.

SIMPSON, MOIRA, b. 1947. Documentarist, cinematographer. Prolific pillar of West Coast feminist documentary for almost a quarter century, Simpson is known chiefly for her large output for the NFB, documentaries about everything from growing up and adolescence to geopolitical peace and justice. She directed the mid-eighties series on addiction that was the context for one of the first NFB portraits of a woman "who happened to be" a lesbian, *Lorri: The Recovery Series* (1985, 14), made at a time when Simpson was a "queer-friendly heterosexual." Meanwhile, she also specialized in films for and about gender socialization and sexual education for children and youth, such as *The Growing Up Family Video* (1989, 75). As a cinematographer she shot such films as Peg Campbell's ground-breaking docudrama on young sexworkers, both male and female, *Street Kids* (1985, 22), and, with her evolved lesbian identity long since on her sleeve, JAN PADGETT's effective antihomophobia work *Sticks and Stones* (2001, 17).

SINCLAIR, ED, b. 1968. Videomaker, producer, editor. York-trained, Toronto-based Sinclair has been a frequent collaborator with the Ian Jarvis–David Collins duo and also with queer-friendly fellow York graduate Karen Kew, with whom he has frequently explored issues of Asian identity and sexuality. Their *Chasing the Dragon* (1993, 22) is a provocative experimental narrative about phone sex between a white man and a fantasy Asian transwoman, Cherry, that symbolically merges exotic food discourse with sex fantasy; it's followed by a talking heads forum by young Asian Canadians, gay and straight, men and women, on orientalism and desire. Sinclair also edited NANCY NICOL's epic *Stand Together* (2002) and has made several bread-and-butter music videos.

SINGER, LIZ, b. 1962. Montreal-bred, Chicago-trained Singer is a prolific Toronto-based artist who has made over a dozen short films and videos since 1998, in formats from Super 8 to video. A perennial of Inside Out and other festivals, she pursues a whimsical view of childhood, culture, memory, and consumer environments. One of her most popular works is an unusual three-minute Super 8 miniature, *Snap* (1998), in which vintage snapshots and laid-back shots of elderly, smiling Nova Scotia women (no doubt with secrets) are piled up under rhyming valentines, all received from different women by a mysterious Dorothy in the 1930s and 1940s, while Anne Murray booms out "I Wanna Sing You a Love Song." The film is dedicated to Murray's classmate and fan, the artist's mother. *Malled* (2003, 9) is a more straightforward and affectionate portrait of Tyler, a multiply-pierced, blue-haired teenage butch who works (and flirts) in a mall clothing store and wants to be a blacksmith.

SISLER, CATHY, b. 1957. Video maker, performance artist, musician. U.S.-bred, OCAD- and Concordia-trained Sisler was a prolific, prizewinning video artist working in Montreal throughout the 1990s. Her most recognizable trope was the "spinning woman," an over-the-top (literally) conceptual role that she herself performed on street corners and in other public spaces, as recorded in many of her tapes, such as the four-part *Aberrant Motion* series (1993–94). In these works, in Julianne Pidduck's words (2004, 93), "she uses her (lesbian) body as an intervention in the everyday flow of 'normal' traffic, pedestrians, thought … imprint[ing] her aberrant body and ideas in the 'normal movement' of urban public space … [and] present[ing] *unfashionable* modes of deviation and risk," in contrast to the hip "outsider-ness" of so much so-called New Queer Cinema of the early 1990s. *Twala* (1996, 17) moved on to assail the comforts of happiness and coupledom – the only Canadian queer work to append a helpful bibliography?

SMITH, SCOTT, b. 1969. Director. Trained at SFU (both Fine Arts and Marketing), as well as the CFC, Vancouverite Smith's *rollercoaster* (1999, 90) was another in the staggering roll of breakthrough queer first features on the Canadian landscape of the 1990s. The feature is also an update to the fifty-year Canadian tradition of sensitive and earnest films about the alienations of youth. Handling with authority a set of unknown young actors, Smith follows five young rebels on the lam from a group home who spend a day in an off-season midway (a set piece filmed over twenty-seven days at Vancouver's Pacific National exhibition site), acting out the tension around the drives of sex and death. Brendan Fletcher's trajectory as the awakening teenage pervert is especially heart wrenching. However implausible its compression into the cinematic logic of the One Day Crisis Resolution and its triggering through the pedophile-ex-machina, the film's trajectory is majestic and true – all the more so since queerness is set up as one of a range of teenage agonies and ecstasies, rather than as the usual isolated volcano. Smith broke through with *rollercoaster* at festivals internationally, both mainstream and queer, and where it really counted, in modest independent theatrical deals.

Coming after bread-and-butter assignments on U.S. TV (*The Chris Isak Show*), Smith's follow-up feature, *Falling Angels* (2003), is based on a novel by Barbara Gowdy. Here he returned to his theme of coming-of-age (girls this time) against a backdrop of social tension, nuclear paranoia, and sexual confusion, and again explored a complex queer character within a strong ensemble cast.

STAGIAS, NICKOLAOS, b. 1971. Film- and videomaker. Trained at Concordia, San Francisco State, and UBC, versatile and prolific Montreal native Stagias is among the few of the Canadian queer cohort (along with BOCIURKIW, SUTHERLAND, and WEISSMAN) to have worked in all three Canadian metropoles, most recently in Toronto. Beginning with his experimental student essay on queer slang, *Drag on a Fag* (1992), transgender performance and disguise were perennial themes, whether in the short semidocumentary *Femme* (2001), in which a trannie hooker is filmed on Vancouver's real mean streets and blows a john in his car, or in the ultrasitcom episodes *The Dress* (2002) and *The Elevator* (2003), both starring Toronto's irrepressible Lucy Ricardo–inspired drag queen stars The B-Girlz. A popular queer festival programmer was the ambitious narrative *Out and About* (1999), an absurdist road movie about four fey Vancouverites trying futilely to butch it up to cross the U.S. border and running into SM fantasy interference. Stagias's frequent collaborator is Vancouver poet, playwright, performer, and eroticist Michael V. Smith, whose enigmatic narration accompanies the recent *Butch* (2003), an experiment with "male drag," multiframed screens and the cyclical choreography of park cruising.

STEELE, LISA, b. 1947, and KIM TOMCZAK, b. 1952). Artists, activists, curators, arts administrators, teachers. Honorary queer couple Steele and Tomczak were founders of the Toronto media arts centre VTape, one of Canada's primary disseminators of queer video, and together constituted thereafter one of the forces of Canadian video art as well as unflinching champions of queer culture and the fight against censorship. Their own queerest video is undoubtedly *Legal Memory* (1992, 80), an underappreci-

rollercoaster (Scott Smith, 1999): teenagers on a lark at an off-season midway are unprepared for the moment of both trauma and self-truth that awaits the macho Stick (Brendan Fletcher, right) in the toilets. Production still, Film Reference Library

ated feature-length docufiction about an unremembered incident in Canadian history that is at the intersection of queer desire and community, the law, and social control. Leo Mantha was one of the last people to have been executed in Canada, in 1959 for the murder of his boyfriend on a naval base near Victoria. Steele and Tomczak tell Mantha's history through a riveting present-day investigative narrative probing legal culture, collective memory, and gay community. Tomczak plays Mantha as a hottie in a white T-shirt, and Steele plays a contemporary journalist. She has also performed in queer videotapes by such artists as COLIN CAMPBELL and JOHN GREYSON.

STIKEMAN, GINNY, b. 1941. Producer, administrator, editor. Ottawa-bred Stikeman trained in editing, research, and directing at the NFB beginning in 1968 and cut her teeth in the social-action Challenge for Change program before entering Studio D as director and editor in 1975. She left her mark on many internationalist feminist projects and is best known for having led the studio in its swan song years from 1990 until its 1996 shutdown, a period when it took huge strides toward cultural and sexual diversity (see chapter 6). Stikeman has producer credit on many films in the lesbian canon, including *Forbidden Love* (1992) and *Listening for Something* (1996).

STONE, ALAN B., 1928–92. Photographer. Montreal beefcake genius Stone was principally an artisan of still images that recorded the soft-core erotic fantasy of the pre-Stonewall gay male generation. Technically, he belongs in this book only by virtue of a couple of drawerfuls of Super 8 posing films made in the 1960s, films never fully marketed or distributed. Stone's Mark One Studio, ensconced in his suburban Pointe Claire basement, was the most successful Canadian purveyor of that censored era's glossy mail order photos of smiling, oiled-up, and coyly bulging male beauties. His films, such as *On the Rocks*, starring his diminutive studio heartthrob Mike Mangione, or several presenting the international star and former Mr Canada, BILLY HILL, are more amateurish but at the same time more playful than the photographs. Super 8 allowed Stone's stable of studs to improvise little strut-and-flex choreographies on the shore of the St Lawrence, leap in and out of those Laurentian forests and streams, deftly change tacky swimsuits between shots, and in general turn on that flirtatious charm that became the epitome of Canadian maleness for Stone's thousands of international customers.

SUTHERLAND, HARRY, b. 1948. Documentarist, producer. A rare example of a truly pan-Canadian documentary film- and videomaker, Sutherland worked in social-action documentary in Halifax, Montreal, Nunavut, Toronto and Vancouver. His queer activist work began in the midseventies in Montreal under the indirect rubric of the NFB's community activist program Challenge for Change, and the passion for community interaction has remained.

This passion led to the first gay-liberation activist documentary in Canada, *Truxx* (1978), a short manifesto of collective resistance to police oppression in the wake of the historic 1977 raid on the Montreal gay bar Truxx. In 1976 the City of Montreal launched a pre-Olympic cleanup of gays and prostitutes, a new wave of persecution that shocked the gay community, both francophone and anglophone, out of its complacency, and whole-scale organizing started up again, energized by the simple exigency of self-defense. The police responded in October 1977 by swooping with machine-guns into the Stanley Street bar and made the largest mass arrest since the October Crisis. One hundred and forty-six men were forcibly given VD tests (a Q-tip punitively inserted into the urethra), crammed incommunicado all night into tiny cells with standing room only, and charged the next day under the familiar vague and discriminatory bawdy-house and gross indecency laws. That night, three thousand protesters blocked the streets of what was then the West End Peel-Stanley gay ghetto for several hours, and as the *Journal de Montréal* headline screamed, "Les Homos et la police: c'est la guerre!" No more than three hundred demonstrators had ever shown up for a gay lib demo before, and two months later an embarrassed and still-idealistic PQ government (only one year in office) passed Loi 88, the first human rights legislation protecting lesbians and gays anywhere in the world (Norway joined Quebec in 1981). The charges hung over the heads of the accused for several years thereafter, before finally being dropped.

Truxx appeared the year following the events and narrated them simply and directly. Made on a shoestring and transferred from then rare video to 16mm, the film aimed at bolstering organizing in the gay community around the issue. Sutherland used still photos, a voice-over, and interviews with two victims and two activists and concluded with footage of subsequent demonstrations. The editing and pace are rough, and the dubbing is cheap – two interviews are in English and two in French, but only the English version was ever released, because of lack of funds. The effect of the two interviews with victims, one an anglophone musician and the other a francophone bicycle repairer (a division of labour that did not always appeal to francophone spectators), was stunning for tearful audiences who saw their communal experience and anger on the screen for the first time. The film holds up well a quarter century later – a reminder for many that little has changed in police-community relations in Montreal, as elsewhere – but has not been available for many years. A spinoff of *Truxx*, aimed at the high-school market, was the directors' documentary short *Paul/David*, which caused the nineteen-year-old TBP film critic JOHN GREYSON some consternation for falling short of that tough audience's high standards (no. 58, November 1979).

Relocated to Toronto, Sutherland and his collaborators Gordon Keith and Jack Lemmon continued in the same vein, producing the pioneering epic *Track Two* (1982), about community defiance of the police in reaction to the 1981 bathhouse raids. The documentary recounts queer Toronto's coming-of-age in that cold winter after the historic 5 February swoop by Toronto police on four local bathhouses and their violation of 286 gay bodies and the rights of an entire community. The film was inaugurated as a document about George Hislop's doomed 1980 aldermanic campaign, but the team suddenly found themselves with a much larger project on their hands. Trained in fast response, they caught everything on film: the quiet testimony of one victim who says, credibly, that he now understands how his parents felt at Auschwitz; the huge and defiant rallies and nighttime street demonstrations; the plainclothes agents provocateurs who actually held the banner out in front! (The raid itself was reenacted on location in the Richmond Street Spa.) While a few mainstream media homophobes saw nothing but a "boring documentary that's little more than a series of talking heads" (*Montreal Gazette*, 30 October 1982), most other viewers were caught up in the electricity of history in the making. JAY SCOTT, the *Globe and Mail*'s not-yet-out reviewer, called it an "admirable comprehensive consideration of the late seventies and early eighties, years during which Toronto's homosexual community evidently underwent unprecedented radicalization" (1 July 1982). But Michael Lynch, in TBP, best captured the hushed but euphoric impact of the film on Canadian and, especially, Toronto queer audiences: "As a historical document, it confirms who we are and what we've been through. I heard a cry from deep within myself: yes, this is and was my life, our lives. I felt gratitude to the film for returning what time takes away; our history our heart ... the most intelligent gay thesis film I know ... An instrument which not only documents a community creating itself but, itself, further creates that community ... it creates a fresh universe by adding nothing but itself" (1982). Two decades later the film holds up fairly well as a vivid period piece, still capable of fomenting strong responses, although some spectators born around the time of the raids themselves find the low-budget celluloid vérité style somewhat rough-hewn and the fervent plaid-shirted talking-head activists creatures from another planet – as indeed they are.

A decade after this historic work, *Memo from Church Street* (1993) covered similar territory, taking stock of the evolved and more confident community, but met with lukewarm response in the era of burgeoning queer media and film festivals. In more recent years, based in Vancouver, Sutherland concentrated on producing rather than directing, contributing to key documentaries, from DAVID ADKIN's *We're Funny That Way* (1998) to Aerlyn Weissman's *Little Sister's vs Big Brother* (2002).

SWENSON, LAUREL, b. 1967. Video maker, graphic designer, curator. One of the Vancouver school of bad-girl video artists, the SFU-dropout Swenson is known for the in-your-face defiance of her sensibility and her hard-talking dyke subjects, and at the same time for the poetic delicacy of the way she brings words and images together. The prizewinning Swenson's identity as a mother comes out in such works as *MotherFuckers* (1995, 4) and, most ambitiously, *Marking the Mother: Mothers, Tattoos & How We Break All the Rules of Motherhood* (2000, 25). This latter documentary essay on the stigma of marginality within the social networks around mothering is animated by six voices and well-decorated bodies. *How to be a Recluse (7 easy steps)* (1998, 5) is a wry and ironic, as well as sensual, rumination on the assets and liabilities of social isolation.

TAM HO, b. 1962. Video maker, interdisciplinary artist. Hong Kong-born, McMaster- and U.S.-trained Tam was a prolific producer on the Toronto queer/art video scene before relocating to New York in the late 1990s (continuing to exhibit in Canada). His works usually merge Asian queer identity issues with high-art conceptualism, often with a compelling personal overlay. *Season of the Boys* (1997, 4), a slow-motion gaze at a Chinatown basketball match, infuses the mix with eroticism. The nostalgic documentary *La Salle Primary* (1998, 5) visits the artist's old Catholic boys' school in Hong Kong, from the empty shower rooms to the corridors bustling with uniformed little boys caught up in intimate private talk.

THOMPSON, HOPE, b. 1963. Director. Trained at Mount Allison, as well as Ryerson and OCAD, Thompson was part of Toronto's LIFT queer film network in the late 1990s, when her four well-crafted narratives made an impact on queer festivals. Her most accomplished work, *Switch* (1999, 22, TIFF), was a skilfully periodized lesbian film noir set in 1949 in Toronto's underworld of telephone exchanges, race tracks, ambiguous cabarets, and sudden escapes to Niagara Falls. In 2000 Thompson moved to Pittsburgh with her artistic and life partner, visual artist Simone Jones, where the two continued their creative collaboration.

THOMPSON, SCOTT, b. 1959. Brampton-born, York-educated and -expelled, the self-styled "fag comedian" was the biggest international Canadian gay male star of the nineties. Starting in 1984, Thompson joined up with four straight improv stand-ups from Toronto, the Kids in the Hall were born, and the rest is television history. First in Canada and then beginning in 1989 on U.S. cable and eventually broadcast, the group revolutionized TV comedy with their manic, beyond-satiric gender-bending sketchwork, finally bowing out in 1995. Thompson's most regular persona among a whole menagerie of characters both in and out of drag was the immortal Buddy Cole, as GERALD HANNON described him in Thompson's 1989 outing in the *Advocate*: "an acerbic, effeminate gay man with a cigarette and martini, holding forth from a stool in any gay bar anywhere." "Me and my friends had always prided ourselves on being *special* fags," Thompson told Hannon, "We never 'femmed out'; we never called each other 'sister' or used girls' names. But I started developing Buddy, and I was terrified: I was afraid that once I started femming out, I wouldn't be able to stop ... I had to let the queen in me out ... Buddy's my conscience. He tells me that effeminacy is not bad ... You don't laugh at Buddy because he's stupid. You laugh because he's wise and smart and always wins. Buddy's the one who ridicules – make fun of *him*, and he'll rip your face off" (1989). Thomas Haig went even further, aligning Buddy's queerness with national identity: "Through the figure of Buddy Cole, then, I can imagine the particular 'queerness' of Canada as a place in which we thoroughly enjoy and craftily deploy our fabulous ambiguous and excessive identities" (1994).

Hollywood feature film exposure for the troupe followed in the less-than-mega-hit *Kids in the Hall: Brain Candy* (1996), which the *Advocate* described as "bogged down in its darkness and its determination to be clever, wacky and pithy" (30 April 1996). Thereafter, Thompson went solo on U.S. cable and the Internet, but never abandoned Hoserland, gutsily lending celebrity support and irreverent energy to local queer political causes and appearing in cameos in films ranging from his old high-school buddy BRUCE LABRUCE's *Super 8½* (1994) to the NFB's *Out: Stories of Lesbian and Gay Youth* (1993).

THORNE, KIKA. Film- and videomaker, curator, activist. Toronto-based, OCAD- and ECIAD-trained, bi-/queer-identified Thorne is a prolific maker of unclassifiable, sex-radical shorts that have made her a pillar of the Toronto indie film/video world, as well as what KATHLEEN PIRRIE ADAMS termed "coy mistress of the local queer arts community." One of Thorne's early collaborators was Mike Hoolboom, who described her work as "[following] a trajectory from the private to the public. Each of her films carries a diary address and arises from personal encounters, or as Kika describes it – just hanging out. These casual, low-tech documents of the underclass come armed with a barbed politic, whether in the sexy feminism of her early work or the address to urban homelessness in her more recent efforts" (2001, 265). In her prolific output of almost twenty works since 1991, Thorne offered "magical condensations that come from rushing headlong at the controversies surrounding sexual identity and sexual freedom. She veers off into personal reflections, then back out onto skid-marked vistas paved with collective memory and mass desires" (Adams 1997).

Sister (1995, 11) is an aggressive and enigmatic utterance of mourning for a sister who killed herself, bursting with the images and speech of queer eroticism and corporal satiation, while *Year Book* (1997, 3) is more fun, an abrasive fantasy of four Catholic schoolgirls who play patty cake and much more. Other collaborators have included KELLY O'BRIEN, with whom Thorne made *Suspicious* (1996, 5), an irreverent "talking heads" riff on the traps of identity politics.

TIERNEY, JACOB, b. 1979. Director, scriptwriter, actor. Montreal-bred, Toronto-based Tierney is a queer-friendly former child actor (best known for the lead in queer British director Terence Davies's *The Neon Bible*, 1996). Tierney burst onto the feature film circuit at TIFF and Venice with *Twist* (2003, 97), an adaptation of *Oliver Twist* set in the gritty Toronto world of junkie hustlers. A promising debut, especially in the acting and urban-location departments, *Twist* did not fully work out how to update Fagin and his gang of kiddie thieves into contemporary rentboys and their pimp, whether in terms of scripting, social realism, or sexual politics. All the same, this tragic queer love story is a worthy addition to the robust Canadian film/video gallery of hustlers and johns and the first dramatic feature entry since the more resonant *Hustler White* (BRUCE LABRUCE, 1995) – set, after all, in sunny L.A., not the filthy, freezing streets of the Queen City.

TORONTO LESBIAN AND GAY FILM AND VIDEO FESTIVAL, INSIDE OUT. Efforts to create a regular venue for queer film and video programming in Toronto were anticipated as early as the late seventies with efforts by MAR-GARET MOORES, Elan Rosenquist, and ROBIN WOOD and more concretely in the 1980s by such events as the film and video program at the Sex and State Conference held alongside the International Gay Association Conference in the summer of 1985. At this major event, seven programs, mostly shorts and organized by the usual suspects, including CAMPBELL, FUNG, GREYSON, and Moores, ranged from Barbara Hammer to Pasolini and included an AIDS program by UK activist-artist Stuart Marshall. The following year JAMES QUANDT organized the "first international festival of gay cinema" at Harbourfront, which was short on women's cinema but surrounded by the respectability that the previous hot summer had lacked. Quandt's celluloid-centric selection of more than thirty items managed to include only one Canadian feature and four shorts but introduced Torontonians to the emerging international canon, not yet called the New Queer Cinema, including then little-known Gus van Sant and Derek Jarman. Thereafter, the Images Festivals took up the slack with strong queer programmes starting in 1988 (works by BOSCHMAN, Greyson, PAUL WONG, etc.). TIFF also offered an increasingly important queer presence, thanks to such dedicated queer programmers as David Overbey and DAVID MCINTOSH.

It was not until 1991 that, following in the footsteps of Montreal, Ottawa, and Vancouver, Inside Out was finally born, with a ten-day blow-out at the Euclid Theatre, coordinated by PAUL LEE, and with JEREMY PODESWA on both the steering and programming committees. A strong diversity agenda, AIDS activist focus, and commitment to Canadian works, especially shorts, were all reflected in the programming. Joanne Cormack minded the store between 1992 and 1996, aided by Francisco Alvarez, LIZ CZACH, Chris Eamon, and others. Professional organization, effective collective decisionmaking, and accountable community liaison ensured quantum growth throughout the nineties. The move to a "real theatre" (the Cumberland, in Yorkville) happened in 1997, in the first of ELLEN FLAN-DERS' three influential years as uber-boss. Along the way influential programming coordinators were Fung (1997), JANE FARROW (1998), and

Shane Smith (1999–2000; Smith was later reincarnated as regular and reliable film critic for *Xtra!*). Kathleen Mullen, formerly of the Vancouver festival, came on board in charge of programming in 2001, with Scott Ferguson at the executive director job. (Mullen's imaginative curating of Canadian queer media benefited other festivals around the world at the same time.) Allen Braude, transplanted from Vancouver in 2000, and Howard Fraiberg also provided valuable administrative leadership (1997 to 2001) before moving into producing (*Class Queers*, 2003).

Innovative scholarships and subsidy schemes for young media artists, youth and trans outreach, symbiotic liaison with local artists, and inspired roles for local curators, as well as awards that reflect the diversity of programming formats, were all part of the success story. In 2002, sixty-five works over fifty minutes (cf. seventeen in 1991) were shown, together with two hundred shorts (sixty-six in 1991), not to mention lecture and "interview with artists" presentations. Billing itself as the largest queer festival in Canada (hotly contested by Montreal), the festival's financial success (the galas moved to the glitzy Paramount in the Queen West district in 1999), with corporate sponsorships galore, led to some carping about selling out. But on the whole the festival has stayed faithful to its community roots and political commitment.

TORRANCE, JENNIFER, b. 1949. Producer. Queer-friendly, British-bred Torrance joined the Vancouver regional office of the NFB in 1972, engaged in that office's women's production, and by 1980 began to produce films about youth and education, developing a particular interest in sexual abuse. Working with such West Coast filmmakers as MOIRA SIMPSON and Colin Browne, Torrance added her credit as producer to several films in the first NFB lesbian and gay video collection, including *Lorri: The Recovery Series* (1985, 14) and *Father and Son* (1992, 88) (see chapter 6). For her the discourse of sexual identity was a natural extension of youth filmmaking, and one of her films in *The Growing Up Series* (1989) was banned from many schools because an elementary pupil asks on camera what happens when a man loves another man. Eventually relocating to the NFB Prairies office, first in Winnipeg and then in Edmonton, Torrance produced the antihomophobia high-school drama *One of Them* (Elise Swerhone, 2000, 25), the coming-out story that became part of the curriculum in British Columbia and elsewhere.

TORREALBA, JOSÉ, b. 1961. Documentarist. A presence on the Montreal documentary scene in both languages, Concordia-trained Torrealba made his mark with two video documentaries on gay male culture. *Limites* (1995) imaginatively documented the homoerotic photography of fellow

XTRA! PRESENTS
INVERTED
IMAGE
TORONTO'S FIRST INTERNATIONAL FESTIVAL OF GAY CINEMA
NOVEMBER 7 THROUGH 15, 1986
STUDIO THEATRE, YORK QUAY CENTRE
235 QUEENS QUAY WEST, HARBOURFRONT
INFORMATION: 364-5665
HarbourFront

Toronto's second major queer film manifestation (1986) at Harbourfront was curated by James Quandt and featured Derek Jarman's *Angelic Conversation*, stirring up the momentum that would culminate five years later in Inside Out.

Latino-Québécois Carlos Quiroz, while *Got 2B There* (1999), a stylish feature, journalistic but personal, surfed the international AIDS benefit "circuit party" phenomenon and was shown in queer festivals everywhere. In 2003, Torrealba brought out his most ambitious documentary thus far: *Open Secrets*, a fifty-five-minute NFB essay on gay men who found community and persecution in the Canadian military during World War II, a riveting assemblage of interviews, archival footage, and suggestive vintage paintings, all inspired by the research of historian Paul Jackson. Torrealba was born in Venezuela, where he has also worked on feature films.

TOUMA, ZIAD, b. 1974. Director, producer, writer, music videomaker. Concordia-trained La Pasionaria of Montreal nightlife, Touma is best known for his feature *Saved by the Belles* (2003, 90). A boisterous paean to Montreal's club scene, *Saved* is an urban epic whose glitter belies its warm heart and has in fact a strong documentary orientation – not the least because it's based on a 1998 incident when an amnesiac young man showed up in the Montreal after-hours landscape and the queer community took him to its heart. Touma shapes over-the-top nonprofessional performances by gender illusionists, "cyberpunk fag hags," wide-eyed boy nymphets, hookers, and cynical bisexual impresarios into a rather classical tale of coming out/coming-of-age: a young everyman named Chris/Sean finds community, his repentant homophobe father, and himself. Star Sheena/Brian Warren (who also cowrote) does a creditable run as a black Divine with feelings and vulnerability, and the rest of the gang are also inspired. Touma's *dernier cri* music-video background, evident in the never dull visual and audio flair and stunning design, doesn't hide the film's place in the Waters/Warhol/Morrissey genealogy of marginality, and there are lots of queer Montreal ancestors as well, from *Il était une fois dans l'Est* to *Montreal Main*. But in contrast to those glum ancestors, this generation's update set within the 2002 Divers/cité parade is very upbeat. Some of the individual sequences stand on their own as truly inspired, such as an interlude set in an all-night veterinary clinic for clubbers. The concluding ice-blue dreamlude, in which the two halves of Chris/Sean are married, is a fine wedding set piece that uncannily ended up with its finger on the pulse of the nation when the film premiered in 2003. Earlier, Touma's *Dinner at Bubby's* (1994, 11) had given queer festival audiences a preview of the director's interest in the tense interface of conjugality and familiality

TRELEAVEN, SCOTT, b. 1972. Videomaker, writer, zine producer, performer. OCAD-trained Treleaven was a prolific and omnipresent pillar of the Toronto sex radical/handmade media underground starting in the midnineties. An early work is the cheap but aggressively illuminating documentary on queer dynamics within the punk music and zine subcultures, QUEERCORE *(a punk-u-mentary)* (1996, 21). About *Salivation Army* (2001, 21), the *Village Voice* waxed rapturous: "a rantumentary about his wannabe-revolutionary homocore faux-gang. DIY grungy and surprisingly subtle, *Salivation* smartly links world-changing ambitions to perverse desires for purity and innocence. 'I have seen the new face of radicalism,' Treleaven narrates, 'and it is cute.' Like Dennis Cooper with a heart, he keeps outside fires burning. In your face *Will and Grace*" (20 November 2002).

TREMBLAY, MICHEL, b. 1942. Playwright, novelist, scriptwriter. Inveterate cinephile, Quebec's most famous living writer and arguably its most famous queer was always in love with the movies and included a scene at his habitual hangout, the Festival des films du monde de Montréal, in his TV-movie gay romance, *Le coeur découvert* (1986).

The record of Tremblay's involvement in filmmaking, most often in collaboration with his habitual theatrical director, André Brassard (b. 1946), is lamentably sporadic. Their collaboration led to one dazzling and raucous masterpiece, a pioneering manifesto of queer desire based on several of the author's theatrical works, *Il était une fois dans l'Est* (Once upon a Time in the East, 1973, director Brassard, scenarist Tremblay, 100; see chapter 4). This pioneering feature of life on the Main is still as cruel and exhilarating, loud and tender, as when it was released thirty years ago. *Il était* brings together narratives from several classic plays, including *Hosanna* and *Les Belles-soeurs,* and assembles the brilliant Tremblay stage ensemble, a who's who of Quebec theatre, as well as a host of local drag queens. TBP found the film cold, irritating, clichéd, and irresponsible – "just one more film showing gay people sinking under the burden of being alive; and as such has little justification for having been produced at all" (July/August 1975) – but the national gay newspaper couldn't be right all the time. Pre-queer – even pre-gay – in its sexual politics, *Il était* may suddenly be back in fashion. Number one on the crying-out-for-DVD-release list.

The 1980s saw *Le Coeur découvert* (The Heart Exposed, director Jean-Yves Laforce [Radio-Canada], Montreal, 1986, 107). I found this TV-movie melodrama, based on Tremblay's script of a gay neo-family, "a delightful tour de force" when it first came out. It now even seems ahead of its time in its probing of queer parenting (not one risk-taking adult-child bathtub scene, but two!). Scintillating dialogue, strong per-formances, and an alert sense of urban space – all combine to make this film, winner of the audience prize at the San Francisco queer festival, one of the treasures of the eighties.

Tremblay also participated in a few other joint film projects that were more interested in gender melodrama than queer politics in the literal sense. Others of his scripts have been directed by other queer-friendly filmmak-ers, where interesting supporting gay characters have usually been at hand, for example, in *C't'à ton tour Laura Cadieux* (It's Your Turn, Laura Cadieux, 1998), directed by Denise Filiatrault (who played the unforget-tably spunky lesbian waitress in *Il était*). Michel Moreau's TV film *Les trois Montréal de Michel Tremblay* (The Three Montreals of Michel Tremblay, 1989) was a reverential but spirited exploration of the artist's attachment to his three neighbourhoods – the working class Plateau, the queer tender-loin of the Main, and tree-lined Outremont – and offered an effective cinematic portrait of one of Tremblay's most memorable characters (also featured in *Il était*), the great tragic Duchesse de Langeais.

TRÉPANIER, TANYA, 1971–2003. Filmmaker, interdisciplinary artist. Bred in the Comoro Islands, Malawi, and Trinidad, Halifax-based Trépanier produced nine short videos in the last seven years of her life. Her work often pondered the tension between her South Asian cultural heritage and bisexual identity, as in the colourfully effective comic narrative *Sugar and Spice* (1997, 10), in which lovers Radha and Anna futilely try to hide their dyke posters and dildo before the former's aunt comes for lunch, only to discover that Durga Aunty may be much hipper than they thought (at least according to one of the alternative endings!). Trépanier received retrospective tributes in 2003 from both Image + Nation and Halifax's Ladyfest feminist arts event; her other works included experimental documentaries and narratives about relationships and desire.

TRIPTYCH MEDIA. Production company. Robin Cass, Louise Garfield, and Anna Stratton first came together to produce JOHN GREYSON's first "real" feature, *Zero Patience* (1993), beginning in 1991. Queer-friendly Garfield and Stratton had been in the producing program at the CFC, where the former had associate-produced Greyson's *The Making of Monsters* (1990). Encouraged by the artistic success of the *Zero* venture, the three Torontonians (Cass came from the television production milieu) incorporated Triptych Media in 1994, with the goal of producing quality films and television in the Canadian context, and became a mainstay of queer Canadian feature filmmaking. Their next big success was Greyson's *Lilies* (1996), from MICHEL MARC BOUCHARD's prizewinning play *Les Feluettes*, and the costume drama of teenagers in love won the Best Picture Genie award. Triptych was also behind THOM FITZGERALD's breakthrough feature *The Hanging Garden* the following year, continued with another Bouchard adaptation *Tale of Teeka* (1998), and also produced films by SCOTT SMITH and DEEPA MEHTA.

TUFF, DAVID, 1959–92. Film- videomaker. Calgary native Tuff studied film and video at ECIAD and in his short career before being struck down by AIDS, showed exceptional verve and promise. Among other works, his video installation *Are We Going Backward?* (1987–88) is an activist documentary collage of plague imagery and voices, together with angry street theatre denouncing the then Social Credit BC government's proposed legislation setting up an AIDS quarantine. In a diametrically opposite tone, Tuff's nine-minute graduation film, *The Width of a Room* (1989), is a dreamlike narrative of a man alone in a hotel room, exalted by a fantasy (or memory?) of an erotic encounter.

VALIQUETTE, ESTHER, 1962–94. Videomaker, director. The first major Quebec visual artist to testify to her personal struggle with HIV and AIDS, honorary queer Valiquette's oeuvre is among the most-treasured artist statements on AIDS to have been produced in this country. After a start as camera assistant and lighting technician, Valiquette brought out her first videotape, *Récit d'A* (1990, 19). This remarkable hybrid documentary builds on an audio interview with a gay American PWA, Andrew Small, and by the time it's over you have participated in a rich philosophical reflection on mortality and coming out as PWA. Valiquette incorporated autobiographical elements, such as the artist's travel diary through a California desert, as well as graphic traces of MRI's as a visual motif and theoretical musings by Susan Sontag and Edmond Jabès, together with the Small interview. Incorporating both English and French, *Récit* is perhaps the quintessential Montreal work (its title is a pun, translating as "Story of A" but sounding like "sida," the French word for AIDS). *Récit d'A* had the impact of a thunderbolt in 1990, catching up for almost a decade of Quebec artistic hibernation on HIV.

Valiquette's next work, *Le singe bleu* (*The Measure of Your Passage*, 16mm, 1992), is an award-winning poetic essay on mortality and impermanence disguised as an NFB programmer on Cretan archeology. Valiquette's final work was the evocative experimental short video *Extenderis*, released the year before her death. In 2003 Valiquette was honoured posthumously as Hero by the Fondation Farha, the first artist to have received this distinction.

VANCOUVER. Out on Screen, Vancouver Queer Film and Video Festival. Canada's third-largest queer film festival may actually be our earliest. At least an embryonic gleam-in-the-eye version took place at the Pacific Cinematheque in the fall of 1976, an all-imported, almost all-male, five-program series emphasizing queer independent authorship, curated by Cinematheque programmer and experimental film aficionado Tony Reif (b. 1944). Reif daringly incorporated three hard-core American porno features by Arthur Bressan, Fred Halsted, and Wakefield Poole, respectively. Bressan and Halsted came in person, the latter with boyfriend/porno star in tow, and made unprecedented waves. The experiment was repeated the following year, but then a dozen years of relative famine followed (interrupted by such one-off events as a 1988 lesbian film festival) until the founding programme of Out on Screen took place in 1989, then called Vancouver's Gay and Lesbian Film Festival and still based at the Cinematheque.

Initiated by community activists such as Daniel Collins, along with Chris Adkins, Keith Clarkson, Mary Ann McEwan, Robert Rothon, and others, the four-day August 1989 event, originally conceived as a lead-up to the cultural celebration that was to accompany the 1990 Gay Games, was an unexpected hit, despite a projector breakdown the first night. Of twenty-six films, the favourite was ANNE CLAIRE POIRIER's senior-citizen romance *Salut Victor!*, while JOHN GREYSON's "controversial" *Urinal* ran at midnight.

The 1990 blowout matched the games in its ambitions, expanding to two venues and, buoyed by Worst Movie Marathon fundraisers, actually finished in the black (as had the initial series). But the organization scaled back to a five-day run, before going for broke with ten days again in 1995, and then continued at this level (the event was to oscillate between late spring and late summer before finally settling into its August slot in 1996). Among the most visible early leaders for the organization were Louise Pohl (taking over from Collins as president, she held the helm for five years and is remembered for getting community businesses on board), James Roberts, Rothon, and filmmaker Katherine Sharp.

As the enterprise began to grow, a network of community-based artists and curators began to provide essential energy, a network including KEN ANDERLINI, MAUREEN BRADLEY, PAUL LANG, ZACHERY LONGBOY, Seanna MacPherson, CLAUDIA MORGADO ESCANILLA, Kathleen Mullen (see TORONTO), ERIC RANCOURT, LAUREL SWENSON, GORDON WONG, WINSTON XIN, and WAYNE YUNG. No doubt the broad community involvement and the diversity imperative led the festival to be among the first to change its name officially to Queer in 1996. In the years of consolidation in the late nineties, especially with the tenth anniversary celebrations in 1998, various individuals came forward into coordinating positions, including Allen Braude, Jennifer Fisher, E. Centine Zeleke, Michael Barrett (who has been programming coordinator since 2000), and Drew Dennis (who first joined in 1996 and has been festival director since 2000).

Throughout, the principle of programs personally curated by local makers has been maintained, plus a strong commitment to cultural diversity and to BC and Canadian product. The most momentous event of the 2000s occurred around the 2002 opening gala presentation of AERLYN WEISSMAN's historic feature *Little Sister's vs Big Brother*, about the notorious state effort to squelch the local bookstore. The BC censor tried at the last minute to close down the gala, for want of a permit that had never been required in the history of that festival or any other. As the BC Civil Liberties Association joined the fray, tension mounted over the intervening twenty-four-hour period, and crowds assembled for the showdown at the Granville Street Theatre. In the face of public outcry, the government backed down at the last minute and the opening proceeded on the basis of this important precedent. We won, and the country's third-largest queer festival got a lot of international headlines, as well as a vindication for their strong commitment to anticensorship policy and cutting-edge sexual programming.

INCITEMENTS
DELIGHTMENTS
ENLIGHTENMENTS

"...I HAVE ALWAYS HOPED THAT CINEMA COULD BE A GREAT LIBERATION MACHINE..." JAMES BROUGHTON

VANCOUVER'S SECOND ANNUAL
GAY AND LESBIAN
FILM FESTIVAL
AUGUST 2 TO 12, 1990

out on
screen

GALA EVENING AT THE RIDGE THEATRE ● 3131 ARBUTUS STREET, VANCOUVER ● AUGUST 2, 1990
ALL REGULAR SCREENINGS AT THE PACIFIC CINEMATHEQUE ● 1131 HOWE STREET, VANCOUVER

SHOWTIMES 7:00PM AND 9:30PM PLUS SPECIAL FRIDAY MIDNIGHT SCREENINGS

● FOR MORE INFORMATION CALL 684-ARTS ●

An early incarnation of Vancouver's Out on Screen, the year the Gay Games came to town.

VANSLET, DEBORAH, b. 1961. Video maker, performer, technician. Concordia-trained, Montreal-based VanSlet has inflected most of her tapes since 1991 with her charming on-screen or on-soundtrack personality as a voluble and whimsical storyteller. Perhaps best known for her *Sick World* cycle (1991–94), VanSlet got personal with the third instalment *Sick World III: The Baby* (1994, 20), where she recounts on-screen her then partner Erica Courvoisier's giving birth to their daughter Auguste, and the world of sperm donations, epidurals, and breast feeding seems less sick than warm, physical, and infused with queer tenderness, for all the raconteur jokiness. VanSlet stayed behind the camera for collaborations with choreographer/dancer Sarah Williams in two lesbian pas de deux dance tapes, *Link* (1996, codirector Lisa Graves, 6) and *Twitch* (1999, 5), both smart, kinetic riffs on Montreal urban space. In the 2000s, VanSlet's interest in the weather found a characteristic approach, as in the quirky and poetic *Weather Permitting* (2001, codirector PATRICIA KEARNS, 27). She has also performed in others' tapes, most notably as the "Clint Eastwood" character in ANNE GOLDEN's *Big Girl Town* (1998).

VAUGHN, LEX, b. 1972. Filmmaker, comic performer, visual artist, rock musician. U.S.-bred and -educated Vaughn, Toronto-based since 1999, has performed live comedy in many Canadian venues, appeared as a heterosexual in *Queer as Folk*, and is part of the Toronto handmade film/badgirl circle. An inspired collaborator, Vaughn cosigned and coperformed with John Caffery the perky techno dance/body manifesto *Doppelganger* (2002, 5); with Megan Stanton, the pixillated Super 8 action film *Slickster Fixter* (2001, 4), in which hyperactive Vaughn herself rescued maidens in distress in the Westside Y locker room; and with her girlfriend ALLYSON MITCHELL, a host of handmade confections, including *Pink Eyed Pet* (2002, 3), more slapstick fare about a woman and her "pet." Vaughn was crowned Toronto's Art Dyke of 2001.

VERABIOFF, MARK, b. 1963. Videomaker. The work of Halifax-bred, NSCAD-trained Verabioff was visible as part of the Toronto and Halifax queer video scenes in the 1980s, before he abjured further art production in 1991 (tongue in cheek?) and relocated to Northern California. Influenced by music video and frankly erotic in his sensibility, Verabioff's most popular of a half dozen tapes was *Crossing the 49th* (1985, 10), a whimsical and colourful play on the iconography of sexual patriotism and the conceit of "queer nation" before its time.

VERRALL, ANN, b. 1959. Video maker. NSCAD-trained, Halifax-based Verrall was coordinator of the Centre for Art Tapes in 1992 when it hosted the first Halifax queer film festival. Her own contribution to the festival consisted of two evocative exercises in feminist experimentalism, *Remembering Anna* (1988, 10) and *Natural Birth* (1991, 10). In *Anna*, a reflection on history, memory, and desire, an unidentified vintage photo portrait of an old woman sparks a time-travel encounter between the jeans-clad narrator and an unknowable ancestor in her lonely frame house and Edwardian skirt ... and a fleeting touch that might be a fantasy flirtation.

VIRGO, CLEMENT, b. 1966. Director, scriptwriter. Jamaican-born, CFC-trained Virgo is one of the most distinctive voices within his generation of thirty-something Toronto auteurs. Queer-friendly Clement's early shorts, such as *Save My Lost Nigga' Soul* (1993, 24), made clear his deftness at intermingling African diasporic thematics with narratives reflecting issues of masculinity and both erotic and consanguineous relations. *Rude* (1995, 89), the first African Canadian–directed feature film, was a critical triumph but ran into the usual Canadian "first-feature" box office sluggishness. Its four interwoven narratives present inner city characters struggling to prevail against social, economic, and cultural constrictions, including Jordan, a gay boxer enacting a stunning coming-out process, which infallibly made every audience "lose it," according to the director. Rinaldo Walcott has argued that Virgo's effort "to bring a critical discussion of sexuality to black Canadian cinematic representations is mangled" by his inability to be "pedagogical about the ethical relations of race, sexuality and community in a way that does not necessarily produce a victim" (2003, 96). But guts is guts, and the decidedly nonvictim bashee's defiance of his "muscle-bound steroid-taking pussy-eating freak" assailants, based on a real-life character recollected from Clement's adolescence, has already ensured the story's status as one of the most resilient queer film fictions of the decade: "You know what you niggers' problem is? – no one's ever come in your mouth." Virgo's prizewinning subsequent features, the TV children's film *The Planet of Junior Brown* (1999, 91) and *Love Come Down* (2000, 99), a remake of *Saved*, continued Virgo's probing of the faults within masculinity and homosociality in the context of urban black culture.

VITALE, FRANK (b. 1945, director, cinematographer), and ALLAN MOYLE, (b. 1947, director, scriptwriter). American-bred Vitale and Moyle, both McGill-trained, were the sexually ambiguous *enfants terribles* of anglophone Montreal indie feature filmmaking of the 1970s and together were responsible for two of the anomalous milestones in English-language queer narrative film.

Montreal Main (director Vitale, scenarist Moyle, 1974, 88) was an unexpected breath of fresh air in the early seventies and stands up well thirty years later as a brave and original tale of intergenerational love and betrayal. Vitale had already been noticed within the video community for his original and sexually ambiguous episodic narrative *Hitchhiking* (1972). In *Main,* Vitale cowrote, directed, and starred as the intense bearded photographer who falls for twelve-year-old, long-haired Johnny from the suburbs, whom he meets hanging out on The Main with his hip artist and counterculture friends, and it's mutual (though apparently never consummated). Amazingly well received both here and in the United States (the knee-jerk hysteria over intergenerational relations apparently hadn't yet taken over), *Montreal Main* met an ambivalent response in the embryonic gay media of the day: TBP's Ron Dayman (November/December 1974) called the film a "real cocktease" in its "repressed" sense of homosexuality, leaving its audience hoping the characters "would finally come out," but he praised the way the "sensual though latent character of [the couple's] relationship comes across beautifully" and the film's recognition of their entrapment "in an ageist, homophobic world where freedom is impossible."

Rubber Gun (director Moyle, cinematography Vitale, 1977), a low-budget heist film set within a queerish countercultural setting, follows in the same vein. My analysis in 1980 was appreciative: "Because homosexuality is peripheral to the quasi-thriller narrative of *Rubber Gun*, this film's acceptance of gayness is much less problematical [than in *Main*]. A fascinating image emerges of a micro-milieu where sexual marginality is taken for granted. Gayness is not a privileged or challenged or suppressed terrain, it is just there. The plot is a pretext for a collage of warm, breathing portraits of characters, most of whom happen to be gay, but are usually too tired or too familiar or too drugged out to fuck each other." I valued *Montreal Main* and *Gun* as "vivid documents of that world, seen from the inside, and of its inhabitants, each one incarnated in the improvised autobiographical mode," but I had reservations about their politics of taken-for-granted apolitical ambiguity, oblivious to the heightened political tension of the "Olympics cleanup" period in local history (1981 27). My students in 2002 had other political reservations, surprised by the misogyny of the Vitale-Moyle universe.

Both features presented in a supporting role fast-talking flamboyant local queer fixture Stephen Lack, who would later go on to a sporadic 1980s career acting in U.S. feature films, as well as in Cronenberg's *Scanners* (1981). Vitale soon returned to his American roots and disappeared from view. His Canadian collaborator Moyle, who plays his awkward, "straight" jerk-off buddy in *Main* and who was involved in what I called "a wonderful comic seduction scene" with Lack in *Gun*, continued acting in supporting roles in other Canadian films, including *Outrageous!* (1977), before also relocating in the States. There, Moyle has been sporadically active as director ever since, and his *Times Square* (1980), a teenaged-girl homosocial love story, was to show up in queer community festivals. All his subsequent films, including the Canadian *New Waterford Girl* (2000), excelled in depicting the confusion and passions of (basically straight) young people.

WAGNER, ANTON, b. 1960. Documentarist, producer. Indefatigable ethnographer of Toronto queer scenes and other dissident subcultures since the 1970s, York- and University of Toronto–trained Wagner may be best known for his biodoc on Jamaican-Canadian queer photographer Michael Chambers, *The Photographer: An Artist's Journey* (1997, 45), an in-depth journalistic exploration, broadcast on the CBC, of the artist and the controversies around his Afro-centric, often homoerotic, nudes. Queer and black festival audiences also appreciated Wagner's lavish and loving documentaries on "diva" worlds of drag performers: *Forbidden Fruit Unfinished Stories of Our Lives* (1999, 27), whose oral histories of white

Twelve-year-old suburban Johnny, whom Frank Vitale, an intense photographer, falls in love with in his own *Montreal Main* (1974). The film was amazingly well received before the intergenerational taboo became a panic later in the 1970s. Production still, photo of Johnny Sutherland by Frank Vitale, Cinémathèque québécoise

Ontario stage stars uncovers a forgotten narrative going back to the post-war period; *Latin Queens: Unfinished Stories of Our Lives* (1999, 55), which injects inextricable refugee politics into the formula; and *Divas: Love Me Forever* (2002, 48 and 81), a worshipful encounter – on stage and off – with six Toronto black performers, most of whom trace their roots back to Caribbean childhoods. The latter was produced by Wagner and directed by the Cuban-bred former dancer Edimburgo Cabrera (b. 1960), Wagner's frequent, talented videographer on earlier works.

WALTON, GLENN, b. 1952. Documentarist, director. NSCAD-trained, Halifax-based Walton is known principally for his moving 1990 documentary *Life after Diagnosis* (30), an encounter with a rainbow spectrum of fourteen proud and out men and women with HIV or AIDS from coast to coast. Aimed principally at boosting the morale and survival skills of the recently diagnosed, and funded by Ottawa with Nova Scotia Persons with AIDS Coalition sponsorship, *Life* soft-pedals queer identity (in words, but not in the personal sensibilities of most of its witnesses, nor in a sentimental scene where a PWA male couple sing love songs together at the piano). The film is otherwise notable for accomplished in-studio dramatized interludes in which an allegorical everyman wrestles with dark hooded figures before discovering the cheery community of your local support group. In the 2000s, Walton branched into drama with *Chamberpiece* (2004, 30), a tale of gay-straight urban voyeurism.

WATT, JOHN. Videomaker. Little is known about Mount Allison–trained Watt, a student of COLIN CAMPBELL and a prolific video artist on the Toronto scene between 1972 and the mideighties, focusing primarily on experimental conceptual work. His early *White on Black, Black on White* (1972, 35) is catalogued evasively at Vtape as using "the body as a painting tool for sculptural body forms." But RICHARD FUNG found it "homoerotic and sensual," showing black and white men's nude bodies lying on top of each other until, thanks to their hands smearing paint over each others' skin and crevices, "everyone's switched colour" (email, 26 October 2004). A 1974 work features the artist's girlfriend.

WEIR, MICHAEL, b. 1965. Filmmaker, editor, curator. Halifax-based Weir, trained at NSCAD and the Rhode Island School of Design, was known for several short videos of the late 1980s and early 1990s. *The Quiet Man* (1989, 5) sets off John Wayne's heterosexual coupling from the eponymous 1952 John Ford movie against similar swoonings by a contemporary male-male couple, to eloquently absurd effect. Weir also headed efforts to launch a Halifax queer film and video festival, which got off to a bang in 1992 but soon petered out. Weir ultimately collaborated as editor on THOM FITZGERALD's *Beefcake* (1999; Genie nomination) and *Wild Dogs* (2002), having relocated to the United States.

WEISSMAN, AERLYN, b. 1947. Documentarist, soundperson, teacher. Best known as the codirector with LYNNE FERNIE of the breakthrough NFB hit of the early nineties *Forbidden Love: The Unashamed Stories of Lesbian Lives* (see chapter 6), Weissman was bred in Chicago and trained in sound recording in the U.S. documentary milieu before coming to Canada in 1970. One of her earlier experiences was recording sound for JANIS COLE and Holly Dale's *P4W: Prison for Women* (1981), an activity repeated for the team's next film, *Hookers on Davie* (1984). After the success of *Forbidden Love*, Weissman went on to further collaboration with Fernie, namely, documentary work on lesbian writer Jane Rule, including the Genie-winning *Fiction and Other Truths: A Film About Jane Rule* (1995), and her own project on women surviving violence, *Without Fear* (1993). With almost thirty sound credits at the NFB over two decades starting in

1975, Weissman was also one of the filmmakers' collective who signed the pioneering feminist feature *A Winter Tan* in 1989, the controversial semi-fictional account of a washed-up (shamelessly heterosexual) writer's sex odyssey to Mexico. Weissman's indie documentary *Little Sister's vs Big Brother* (47), a stirring and comprehensive epic of the bookstore's struggles against state censorship, premiered in 2002. Included in the NFB's 2003 queer pedagogical package, this film's heroic portraits of the bookstore's activist triumvirate Janine Fuller, Jim Deva, and Bruce Smyth (and writer/employee Mark Macdonald) are already enshrined in the Canadian queer pantheon. Since 2001 Weissman has also directed for the TV documentary series *Kink*, as well as making *WebCam Girls* (2004, 52).

WERDEN, RODNEY, b. 1946. Videomaker. Self-taught, queer-friendly Werden was a prolific pioneer on the Toronto video art scene for two decades beginning in 1973, specializing in documentary portraits of sexual and gender marginality and notable for his "scrutinizing camera gaze of a Diane Arbus, mostly fascinated, occasionally identified" (Diamond 1996, 191). Several tapes encounter male or female prostitutes, but *"I'll Bet You Ain't Never Seen Noth'n Like This Before ... "* (1980, 36) remains one of his more startling works, living up to its title in its encounter with solitary heterosexual male anality.

WESCOTT, MARGARET, b. 1941. Documentarist, editor, producer (NFB). The discreet but brave lesbian voice within the NFB for almost three decades, Wescott made up the lonely queer fifth column, along with writer GLORIA DEMERS, at the feminist Studio D before the skittish government studio's great belated awakening around 1990. Trained as an editor at the beginning of the seventies, Wescott became a staff director with the new women's studio around 1975, delivering an undercover lesbian punch with *Some American Feminists* (codirector NICOLE BROSSARD and Luce Guilbeault [1935–91], 1977, 16 mm, 56).

A pioneering feminist documentary produced by an almost all-lesbian team (except for the queer-friendly actor Guilbeault), *Feminists* was in many ways typical of the studio's ostrich-like queer politics of the period, subsuming sexuality within gender politics in the general sense. But anyone who saw the filmmakers' in-your-face encounters with American lesbian feminist stars Rita Mae Brown, Kate Millett, Ti-Grace Atkinson, and, above all, defiant political prisoner Susan Saxe could hear – to paraphrase Brown's immortal words – the testicles rolling all around the floor of the government film commissioner's office. The film's lone voice cried out within the lingering wilderness of lesbian and gay silencing, not only in Canada but everywhere as the late-seventies backlash picked up steam.

(Well, not quite *alone*, since it came out in the same year as *Outrageous!* and *Word is Out* and the year before *La Cage aux folles*.)

Wescott's next major film, the epic *Behind the Veils: Nuns* (1984), retreated somewhat in the naming department, but this intense exploration of female homosociality and spirituality featured some very dykey sisters in T-shirts and butch haircuts. After the Studio D shake-up at the end of the decade, Wescott and the other staff directors were pushed out into the patriarchal cold, and she was slow in finishing, elsewhere at the NFB, her final film, *Stolen Moments* (Montreal, 1997, 92), a cross-cultural and transhistorical tour of lesbian feminist communities, cultures, and sexualities in the cities of Europe and North America. When it finally appeared, this monumental essay, shot in lush, classical NFB style, may have seemed dated and idiosyncratic in its politics and aesthetics, all the more since it had been upstaged by the hip megahit *Forbidden Love* five years earlier. But the glimpses of lesbian cultural and political mobilizations, both current and reconstructed from the distant past, from Paris to San Francisco (Vancouver and Montreal provide the Can Con), are evocative. And any hesitation about the wooden narration that refers to lesbians in the third person, if any remains after the boldest on-screen cunnilingus scene ever financed by Canadian taxpayers, dissolves when the boys' anthem "Somewhere over the Rainbow" is appropriated at the end, swelling up over this summation of a utopian dream and lived history, the preretirement legacy of a pioneer.

WHEELER, ANNE, b. 1946. Director, producer. English Canada's most prominent woman feature filmmaker, the Albertan director was trained in feminist prairie documentary. Most accomplished in the portrayal of women's friendship, unforgettably in *Loyalties* (1986), Wheeler is also skilled in developing narratives of male homosociality, as in the underrated teenage rodeo melodrama *Cowboys Don't Cry* (1988). Along the way she also excelled at short fiction, often queer-auraed, if not explicitly queer-themed, like her SINCLAIR ROSS adaptation *One's a Heifer* (1984, see chapter 5). But this long-married heterosexual mother belongs most in this list as honorary lesbian for *Better than Chocolate* (Vancouver, 1998, 98), the celebrated baby dyke comedy romance. *Chocolate* is in some ways a contender for the title of the Canadian *Desert Hearts*, a breakthrough romantic comedy that filled the void in mainstream lesbian representation and became an instant classic. Perhaps it's a measure as much of the director's track record in sketching women's social worlds as of her sexual orientation that she's able to fill in so deftly all the sexually diverse narrative borders around her core relationship story, from the heterosexual middle-aged mother's discovery of pleasure to the bookstore subplot inspired by the Little Sister's bookstore's never-ending battle to the teenage hetero brother who discovers butt plugs. Supported by an accomplished cast, including Peter Outerbridge's fine torchy performance as transsexual, *Chocolate* simply all comes together as a politically correct feel-good love story with a strong sense of time and place – ours!

WILD, GREGORY. Director, art designer. Calgary- and UBC-educated, Vancouver-based filmmaker Gregory Wild was hailed at the time of the 1994 release of his feature *Highway of Heartache* (86) as part of the new West Coast Wave of Canadian cinema. But this brilliant *Female Trouble* meets *Coal Miner's Daughter* meets *Peewee's Big Adventure* camp/country musical was a one-off effort. Wild, apparently bogged down in the project he announced back then as "Jane Blond Glamour Spies" in vintage technicolor, thereafter disappeared from view. The movie's big draw for the 1994 Toronto International Festival and many queer community fests was not only the high-energy visual artifice but also the straight and strong songs composed and performed by Seattle-bred singer/star Barbara Chamberlin, later based in Whitehorse. They may have titles like "I Got the Burning Beaver Blues," (about the heroine Wynona Sue Turnpike's green and viscous STD attack), but the voice and the emotion are true. Funders were less than enthused, however, about Wild's eagerness to court offense through anti-p.c. discourses around race and gender. The *Village Voice* opined that camp had died in the 1980s and that "this turkey-fisted satire grinds its gears down a highway to headache (10 September 1996)," but the *Montreal Mirror*'s STEVE KOKKER recognized "a satiric take on the Christian right, sexism in the workplace, the male sex role, oppression and tabloid TV" and an overdue desecration of the "sanctity of Canadian cinema" to boot (n.d., 1996). Wild's earlier shorts entitled *Cry ... Baby Boom* [1990] and *Meat Market* [1991] already attracted the attention of queer festival programmers to his high camp sensibility, as well as high production values and frissons of John Waters.

WILSON, PENDRA, b. 1964, Toronto. Video maker, porn maker, radio psychic. Toronto-born, Vancouver-based Wilson, sometimes credited simply as Pendra, self-defines as a pro-sex feminist, transgender female, a pro-democracy activist, and a porn director. Shaped by the Toronto queer punk zine scene, as well as Freud, Marx, and San Francisco, her half-dozen iconoclastic video shorts explore sexual marginalities within queer cultures from SM to bears to porn (often with a good dose of theory mixed in, whether psychoanalytic or Jungian) and have circulated in queer and lesbian festivals internationally since the early nineties. *Kore Cara Mia* (1999, 18) is an erotic narrative about SM and safe-sex practices between a woman and her HIV-positive lover. An earlier work, *Granny's Bedtime Story* (1992, 19), subverts SM lesbian hardcore through a narration "like Mr. Roger's Neighbourhood but gone bad, bad, bad and pornographic."

WINNIPEG GAY AND LESBIAN FILM SOCIETY. This persistent film activist hub in Winnipeg dates back to 1985, when the group incorporated and pioneered periodic screenings for such fare as Fassbinder and *The Times of Harvey Milk*. But a presentation later that year of the 1955 Liberace clunker *Sincerely Yours*, then being recycled as high camp, brought out only twenty spectators, and the organizers all had their coats stolen. But commitment is commitment, and a benefit showing of the first Canadian AIDS film, Nik Sheehan's *No Sad Songs*, followed in 1986. Starting in the spring of 1987 regular annual festivals were held, called Counterparts, including ambitious programs and visiting filmmakers and even a lecture by me on erotic cinema (my strongest memory remains having to classify my porno clips with the provincial film board). From there a dedicated core of organizers maintained the event through funding and mission crises, switches back and forth from spring to fall, and the intermittent growth of audience, holding festivals in 1988, 1989, 1991, 1992, and 1994. After a hiatus of six years, the society got a new lease on life with emerging president David Wyatt, bridging over the years when the lights were out. They rechristened their henceforth annual events Reel Pride, hooking up with the local Pride activities, but still being indecisive about spring or fall. In October 2003 the program of Reel Pride x billed itself the Tenth Winnipeg Gay/Lesbian/ Queer Film & Video Festival, offering a six-show weekend of international features scaled down in ambition and scope from "last year." After sixteen years, the films were still rated and the local board deemed TOUMA's *Saved by the Belles* to contain "coarse language."

WONG, GORDON, b. 1976. Video maker, interdisciplinary artist. ECIAD-trained, Toronto-based Wong has worked with personal documentary, dramatic narrative, and found-footage stop-motion animation since 1997. His prizewinning *Beyond These Walls* (1999, 7) is a lusciously crafted personal narrative about a male survivor of sexual assault reflecting on the physical and psychological aftermath in which the innocent details of everyday living, like a drop of soup on a table cloth, bring back the fear. When living in Vancouver, Wong was active with the Video In/Out on Screen mentoring program.

WONG, PAUL, b. 1955. Video maker, interdisciplinary media and performance artist, curator, anticensorship advocate. Once known as the "Chinese Canadian Warhol," Vancouver's prolific video pioneer, a founding member of Video In, has played off queer and Asian identities against both West Coast cultural politics and the international high art conceptual scene like no other for almost three decades. Wong's 1976 *60 Unit Bruise* was made in collaboration with artistic partner and erstwhile "boyfriend" Ken Fletcher (1954–78), a minimalist video performance showing an injection of the white, blond Fletcher's blood spreading its colour across Wong's back. When Fletcher committed suicide, Wong continued his engagement with body art and performance: *In tens sity* (1979) is a twenty-three-minute video distillation of a five-hour document of Wong's Vancouver Art Gallery performance in a padded cell "trying to get inside [Fletcher's] head space" (Milroy 2002), a shocking elegiac work of improvised corporal flailing.

Then identifying as bisexual, Wong became increasingly interested in sexual identities and lifestyles and his video installation work *Confused: Sexual Views* (1984), nine hours of twenty-seven people "yakking" about sexuality, was meant to inaugurate the VAG's new video space but instead became the decade's most celebrated censorship scandal when the gallery pulled the plug at the last minute, claiming the work was not art. The incident galvanized the arts community across the country, where other censorship battles were also waging in the context of an overall right-wing drift. The courageous and persistent artist sued, then lost the courtroom battle, but ultimately won the war, receiving the Bell Canada Award inVideo Art in 1992, a retrospective at the National Gallery in 1995 ("On Becoming a Man"), and a vindication exhibition at the VAG in 2002.

Scarred by the *Confused* ordeal, Wong maintained his interest in sexual identity but at the same time intensified his interest in Asian Canadian arts and politics, curating the ground-breaking "Yellow Peril" touring exhibition of Asian Canadian film, video and photography in 1990–91. Racial and sexual issues come together in *So Are You* (1995, 28), which at the same time revives *Confused*'s fascination with talk and storytelling, and in *Refugee Class of 2000* (2000), a series of antiracism television ads, which also bring out the comingled presence of sexism and homophobia in the discursive British Columbia atmosphere around immigration. The 1990s also saw Wong intervene as an AIDS activist in *Blending Milk & Water – Sex in the New World* (1996, 28), a documentary compilation of views of sexually diverse Chinese Canadians on AIDS and sexuality.

Wong's description of Yellow Peril contributors can be applied to its author: "In retrospect they are the brave survivors of a generation that had to kick ass. Perhaps it is that drive that is at the very foundation of making art that attracts the so-called misfits and disenfranchised. It is those souls adrift and in search that often make the most worthy and brilliant statements of our time" (1990, 12).

WOOD, NATALIE, b. 1965. Videomaker, visual artist. Trinidad-born, OCAD-trained, Toronto-based Wood has made two nonfiction tapes that reflect her African Canadian identity. *Enter Hailey* (2002, 8) explores queer-positive possibilities for the extended nuclear family through the presence of an ebullient niece, while *The Dozens* (2004, 7) uses "blaxploitation" iconography to reflect on black masculinity.

WOOD, ROBIN, b. 1931. Critic, scholar, teacher. A founder of academic film studies in Canada, British-educated Wood was one of the first major voices in film studies to come out and to publicly reflect on the implications of a queer perspective for understanding film (1978). His headquarters was first Queen's University and in recent decades York. There he founded the Toronto journal *Cineaction!*, a locus for much debate about queer cinema in Canada, as well as a vehicle for Wood's unique version of a "radical" film theory that includes Vincente Minnelli. Wood also frequently contributed to *TBP*, cowriting with his long-standing domestic partner Richard Lippe (b. 1941), often bringing out the contradictions between humanist artistic judgments and political agendas. In the case of Michael Cimino's controversial Vietnam movie *The Deer Hunter*, they declared that "It seems to us ... to be a great movie, and like other great reactionary movies it can be *used* progressively, as a means of understanding and clarifying the changes society is undergoing ... One must always be able to say, 'I'm strongly opposed to it ideologically, but I love this film'" (1979).

Curiously, Wood and Lippe, an expert on classical Hollywood queer director George Cukor and *Cineaction!* coeditor, have a blind spot for most queer Canadian cinema (e.g., GREYSON). But Wood was one of the first to lambaste CRONENBERG's sexual phobias, and his influence on how we look at Hollywood and European art cinema, from Hitchcock to homosociality, has been immense.

XIN, WINSTON, b. 1965. Video maker, curator, writer, arts administrator. Malaysia-born, Toronto-bred, Vancouver-based Xin has been a stalwart of both Out on Screen and Vancouver's video cooperative Video In, as well as a collaborator with local queer makers such as DESIREE LIM and KEN ANDERLINI. His short contribution to the broken-heart autobiographical video genre *Boulevard of Broken Sync* (1996, 3) offers inventively processed and animated imagery, as well as witty retribution upon a certain ex who thought they could still be friends.

YAEL, B.H., b. 1957. Video maker, teacher, curator, peace activist. Israel-born, Toronto-bred Yael has been active on the Toronto video art scene for two decades starting in 1985 and teaches at OCAD. Her tapes, hybrids of experimental narrative and documentary elements, were preoccupied with gender and sexuality from the start, and issues of lesbian identity gradually surfaced. While *The Lonely Lesbian* (2002, 5) is a whimsical allegorical piece about a middle-aged accordion player wandering through the streets of New York towards the beach, *Fresh Blood: A Consideration of Belonging* (1995, 55) is a autobiographical essay. Here Yael explores Iraqi-Jewish heritage and queer identities, rooted in landscapes of Israeli deserts and her own face, and encounters three generations of women in her family, as well as the voluptuous iconography of belly dancing.

YUNG, WAYNE, b. 1971 Videomaker, writer, curator. Edmonton-born but transplanted to Vancouver in 1994 and most recently based in Germany, the prolific Yung was the most compelling queer video voice of his generation on the West Coast. Yung's dozen or so intense short works produced since 1994 have tended to dissect intersections of queer and Asian identity, cramming the screen with layers, captions, visual embroidery, and intertextuality gone berserk. In 1998 he produced three lessons in an over-the-top *Queen's Cantonese Conversational Course* in which smarmy hostesses present basic points about Chinese grammar, culture, and vocabulary, all illustrated through witty scenes of Vancouver gay life: ways of saying "good-bye" are illustrated through a hysterical bathhouse melodrama in which a jilted character shrieks "Get out, you slut!," all dutifully transcribed by subtitle. That these language games are available in both English and French versions is itself fitting comment on the politics of bilingualism in a multicultural, postcolonial society. In many others of his tapes, Yung puts himself on the line as performer, for example, as the lucky protagonist in *Field Guide to Western Wildflowers* (2000, 6) who kisses over sixty guys in a series of busy vignette variations, each illustrating a keyed-in wildflower backdrop with an attribute, while documentary voice-over interviews each recount their "first Asian kiss." In other works, like *Peter Fucking Wayne Fucking Peter* (1994) and *Davie Street Blues* (1999), this self-reflexive froth yields to a less-camouflaged expression of vulnerability, passion, and desire. Yung is one of the most-encountered queer Canadians at international queer and diasporic festivals.

ZBOROVSKY, EVGENY, b. 1981. Filmmaker. USSR-born, Toronto-bred, Concordia-trained Zborovsky, a sometime collaborator of Mike E.B. [BARRY], showed *Christopher* (5), a narrative of fantasy prevailing over isolation, at Inside Out in 1999, before moving into 16mm with several further works about fantasy, including *The Paper Dress* (2002, 6), a well-crafted tale of a boy's dreamworld that fuses *Pink Narcissus* and *Swan Lake*.

ZEIDLER, CHRISTINA, b. 1968. McGill- and OCAD-trained, Toronto-based Zeidler's short comic videos and Super 8 films have been popular at queer and handmade festivals since 1994. Her talent for parody has prevailed over such macho genres as blaxploitation (*Soulsucka*, 1995, 3), Xtreme sports cablecasting (*Dogboganning*, 1998, 3) and porno (*Desire*, 1994, 5), where the reflecting object of lust is a sensuous chrome teakettle. Zeidler collaborated with other stalwarts of the DIY community, including ALLYSON MITCHELL, with whom Zeidler formed the Freeshow Seymour collective in 2003 to indulge each other's obsessions with sweets and pets respectively.

ZUCKERMAN, FRANCINE, b. 1958. Documentarist, director, scriptwriter, producer. McGill- and Columbia-trained, Toronto-based Zuckerman is best known for her prizewinning documentary on women and Judaism, *Half the Kingdom* (NFB, 1989, 59), as well as for other broadcast documentaries on feminist and Jewish themes. A new departure was *Passengers* (producer Paula Fleck, 2000, 15, TIFF), a lyrical and well-crafted narrative about a woman driving with her lover to her father's funeral, full of memories of their special relationship and of regrets for never having come out to him. Zuckerman continued thereafter to work in cable broadcast drama and documentary.

Notes

CHAPTER ONE

1 Renamed for political reasons Regina, Kitchener, and Boulevard René-Lévesque, respectively.
2 For an analysis of such patterns in the neighbouring Malayalam-speaking state of Kerala, see Osella and Osella (2004).
3 For names of artists and institutions printed in small caps throughout the text, the reader is referred to the corresponding entry in the portrait gallery in part 2.
4 Passed by Parliament on 14 May 1969, the Omnibus Bill reformed the sexual offenses portions of the Criminal Code, including the removal of clauses dealing with "buggery" and "gross indecency" (but not the full removal of the state from the bedrooms of the nation, since group sex, intergenerational sexualities, and other "perversions" remain criminalized to this day). The modern period of Canadian queer/sexual politics was thus given its symbolic start. Six weeks later, Greenwich Village drag queens and other queers rose up against police harassment at the Stonewall Tavern, giving the symbolic start of modern American queer politics a more dramatic and revolutionary flavour – at least in comparison with a partial reform handed down by paternalistic, homophobic politicians in colonial imitation of a British reform law from two years earlier (Kinsman, 1996). Hereafter in this book, "Omnibus/Stonewall" will be the shorthand to denote this watershed year of 1969 in North American queer history.

CHAPTER TWO

1 I am grateful for a few of the research leads in relation to some of this chapter's sources to my research assistant Jon Davies and the students in my 2000 MA seminar in English Canadian Cinema, in particular André Caron, Éric Bourassa, and Brian Crane.

2 This is not to say, of course, that later on in the sixties and seventies Canadians would not develop robust and distinctive modes of resistance to the prevailing regime of gender, cultural, and political conformity, especially in metropolitan and campus areas.

3 "Cornet at Night " was later adapted for the board under its original title, somewhat less successfully, by Stanley Jackson in 1963.

4 *Being Different* made the rounds of the queer community festivals in 2002–04 as part of a compilation program curated by Vancouverite Bill Taylor entitled "Lock Up Your Sons and Daughters! Anti-Queer Films from 1950–90." It was misidentified as an anonymous American antiqueer propaganda film. This misreading of a sensitive, protofeminist work from 1957 by a living artist is an object lesson for all of us in the importance of conscientious historical research.

5 The only explicit *Playboy* consumer I've spotted in the 1950s corpus is the furtive raincoater who patronizes the drugstore where the *Howard* protagonist has an after-school job: "Mustn't interrupt him until he's ready. He's going to rifle through the picture and photography magazines. Have a good look at the nudes and cheesecake. On the sly. Then when he's seen all there is to see, he'll finally find the magazine he was really looking for. A *Saturday Post*." In fact he loyally opts for Canadian content instead: *Macleans*.

6 Official catalogue description for the recycled film, *How They Saw Us: Is It a Woman's World?*, series director Ann Pearson, National Film Board of Canada, 1977.

7 These two unusual films are fascinating beyond their prophetic elaboration of the issue of substance abuse: their image of Toronto and Montreal urban undergrounds is a unique audiovisual boon for historians of social marginality in Canada.

8 Citation from a review of *Feeling of Rejection* in the *Journal of the American Medical Association*, 22 May [1948], excerpted in response analysis document, typescript. Archives of the National Film Board of Canada, Montreal.

9 "Kindly woman professor" is the descriptor of hostile Clare's "faculty editorial representative" provided by a unmarried professional female spectator in the expert feedback compiled by the board in response to an early version of the film, "Criticisms of Script on 'Hostility,'" 2; Archives of National Film Board of Canada, Montreal. The final commentary for the film describes this character, a portly white-haired woman, thus: "She has been fortunate in finding someone who understands her, a wise teacher who recognizes her limitations, as well as her endowments, who helps her and is happy over her successes without in turn using her or making the demands her mother made. Through her Clare gains some understanding."

10 *Drug Addict* was refused import to the United States because of its lenient views of addiction as deserving of treatment rather than criminalization. *The Street* was withdrawn at the last minute by CBC brass from its Sunday 5:30 P.M. broadcast slot, 27 January 1957. Their pretext was that the work was "not suitable for family viewing," in an atmosphere exacerbated by the recent screening of the "Perspective" film on interracial marriage, *Crossroads*, and a panel discussion about the suitability of Elia Kazan's *Baby Doll* for Canadian theatres. McLaren's version of the bowdlerization of *Neighbours* by educational film distributors in the fifties and its restoration during the Vietnam war is illuminating: "they thought this short scene at the climax of the film robbed the film of a lot of its guts and message, and that it should be put back. It was a very vapid film without that … though another reason for having cut it out originally was that I believed in the formal structure of

the film, because I'm a stickler on a strict form, that *the film dealt with two men and a flower.*" (McLaren, 1978, my emphasis). All three cases are documented in primary documents in the respective title files in the National Film Board of Canada Archives, Montreal.

11 Adolfas Mekas, "Excerpt from *Hallelujah the Hills!*" in Gretchen Weinberg, "MC et Moi (A Spiritual Portrait of Norman McLaren)," *Film Culture* 25 (summer 1962): 46. Rounding out Mekas's profile of the animator on this page are other suspect descriptors: "Bashful, slim, full-eyed ... a lonely artist ... presenting us with a world bizarre, gay, merry and charming." Thanks to André Caron for bringing this to my attention. Mekas wasn't born yesterday; he was a filmmaker/intellectual from New York where they knew about such things. His brother Jonas, the high priest of the New York experimental film scene, went quickly from denouncing in 1955 the fifth column homos within the scene to respectfully acknowledging their contribution eight years later (Dyer [1990] 2003, 134).

12 Cf. The interviews cited in Maurice Leznoff, *The Homosexual in Urban Society*, MA thesis, McGill University, 1954 (cited Kinsman 1996, 118).

13 Charles E. Israel (1920–99) was scriptwriter for *The Street, Crossroads* (interracial marriage, 1957), *None but the Lonely* (urban bachelor, 1957), and *Borderline* (teen issues, 1956). In Lucie Hall, "An Interview with Charles E. Israel," *Cinema Canada* 108 (June 1984): 14–18, Israel is evasive about possible political motivations for his migration.

CHAPTER THREE

1 "Sex in the U.S.: Mores & Morality. The Second Sexual Revolution." *Time*, January 24 1964, 54–9. The first sexual revolution had followed World War I. The article is most striking forty years later for its reliance on clerical commentary and its total silencing of/silence on homosexuality.

2 I use Ballantyne and Tree together as the director's surname throughout, combining her maiden and married names respectively, to avoid the confusion that followed her midcareer name change and the inability of sources (including the NFB itself) to follow a consistent or logical pattern ever since.

3 The phrase is of course taken from Ehrenreich (1983), which presciently and definitively established the terms of the cultural study of the recent history of sexuality.

4 Produced in the spring of 1968, Lefebvre's shot of the racially motivated rifle shooting is clearly an explicit echo of the Martin Luther King Jr assassination. If I am right that Canadian culture in the sixties had the reflex of assigning minority perturbations to "elsewhere," it was of course deluded, for Canadian media were increasingly searching out their own domestic examples of sexual marginality; cf. "Canada's Leading Homosexual Speaks Out," *Weekend Magazine*, 13 September 1969, 6–8. Nineteen sixty-eight was also the year of what was essentially a black uprising in Montreal itself, at my own Concordia University, as it turns out. Caribbean students accused a biology professor of racism, the situation was botched, it deteriorated, and the computer department was trashed, leading to enormous damage, jail terms, and deportations.

5 The *Toronto Star*'s critic refers to the passage of "homosexuals embracing," in the context of his virulent denunciation of the film: "insufferably boring, self-indulgent montage of disconnected shots and sequences," "utter chaos," "limp satirical arrows," "arbitrary and sophomoric montage," "painfully embarrassing ...

amateur home movie," "an insult to the Toronto public." Clyde Gilmour, "*Jusqu'au coeur:* Chaos from Quebec Never Goes Right to the Heart," 5 July 1972, unpaged clipping, Cinémathèque québécoise.

6 The Front de libération du Québec was the ultranationalist organization that had set off several bombs in the wealthy anglo enclave of Westmount and elsewhere during the sixties and that would be responsible for the kidnapping and political assassination that sparked the October Crisis of 1970, nearly toppling the federal state.

7 The use of U.S. iconography by these films had been was a consistent pattern at the NFB since its origins and is evident in the U.S.-centric address of well-known films from later periods, such as *Not A Love Story: A Film about Pornography* (1981). This pattern arguably belies the board's mandate and no doubt reflects export marketing considerations as well as Canadian cultural dynamics.

CHAPTER FOUR

1 Cited dialogue excerpts from VHS versions of *À tout prendre*, *Winter Kept Us Warm*, and *Outrageous!* and from published scenario *Il était une fois dans l'Est: Un film de André Brassard* (Montreal: L'Aurore 1974), my translation.

2 The two "system" formulations belong respectively to Eve Kosofsky Sedgwick (1992) and Gayle Rubin ([1982] 1993).

3 The single public-sector film from this period that approaches any degree of explicitness towards a queer – in this case lesbian – thematic, is *Some American Feminists* (1977; see chapter 6 and WESCOTT). If that is an urban fairy tale, it is one of New York, and it is of course no accident that the first queer-authored queer film to see the light in the NFB desert should be one of exile. See also Waugh 1981. See also the outsider-voiced *New Romance* (GABOR and Walchewski, 1975).

4 Much (but not all) Canadian film studies in English and in French assumes the discrete autonomy of the cinemas in the two official languages. There is a respectable subliterature on Canadian "regional" cinemas (e.g., in Véronneau, 1991), but very little research has been done identifying the urban contexts of Canadian regional or national cinemas as the determining cultural variables.

5 The exceptions come from Quebec, of course, and consist of a couple of Anglo-Montreal ambiguities (*Montreal Main* [FRANK VITALE, 1974] and *The Rubber Gun* [Allan Moyle, 1977]) and a couple of Trois-Rivières obscurities by MICHEL AUDY (for example, *La maison que empêche de voir la ville*, 1975).

6 For a history of "the Mountain," see the late Luther A. Allen's "L'aventure sexuelle clandestine: le cas du mont Royal," in Demczuk and Remiggi (1998, 81–102); for an outsider's cinematic mythology of "the Mountain" see ARCAND's *Déclin de l'empire américain* (1986).

7 The Tremblay plays providing characters and situations for the film are *Les Belles-soeurs* (1968), *En pièces détachées* (1970), *À toi pour toujours, ta Marie-Lou* (1971), *Demain matin, Montréal m'attend* (1972), *Hosanna* (1973), and *La Duchesse de Langeais* (1973).

8 Alfred Hitchcock's *Strangers on a Train* (1951) and Kenneth Anger's *Scorpio Rising* (1963) are cited explicitly by Jutra, his fellow *Nouvelle vaguiste* François Truffaut makes a guest appearance, and Jutra's sometime mentor Jean Cocteau is an easily identifiable ancestor of this parabolic tale of a tormented artist. *Winter*'s intertextual relationship with T.S. Eliot's *The Wasteland* (1922) and Henrik Ibsen's

Ghosts (1881) is made explicit in the narrative, and a Harry Belafonte concert at O'Keefe Centre gives Doug the pretext for his first date with Peter, as well as for a telling impulse to stroke the handsome and exotic singer's face on the concert poster, as Peter looks on. Brassard has cited Ingmar Bergman's *Cries and Whispers* (1972) as an inspiration, but a more significant Genet lineage is apparent in his transgressive characters' frontal theatricality in both his film and stage work. Benner's precise cinematic culture and references beyond the gay lore of *All About Eve* (1950), etc., obviously shared with star CRAIG RUSSELL, are unknown.

9 The geometry of both Jutra's and Secter's girlfriend/boyfriend setups are variations of Sedgwick's Girardian triangulation model of male homosociality: "a calculus of power that was structured by the relation of rivalry between the two active members of an erotic triangle" (1985, 21). Interestingly, a man rather than a woman is the object of rivalry in the case of Secter's two overlapping triangles.

10 Two familiar sources on gay politics of the sixties and seventies are, respectively, D'Emilio (1983) and Altman (1981).

11 For a history of a homosocial athletic facility as queer space see Gustav-Wrathall (1998). For a cultural studies–inflected, rather than historical, account of related phenomena closer to the University of Toronto's Hart House gym itself, by a professor of physical education at that very institution, see Pronger (1990).

12 Such insider/outsider communication is a familiar dynamic in pre-Stonewall film history, which has a continuous record of closeted or not-so-closeted directors and writers offering two-tiered works simultaneously to the initiated and the uninitiated, from *Mädchen in Uniform* (Leontine Sagan, 1931) to *Rope* (scen. Arthur Laurents, 1948), from *Ossessione* (Luchino Visconti, 1942) to *The Left-Handed Gun* (scen. Gore Vidal, 1958).

13 For a skeletal history of the development of the Toronto gay community see McLeod (1996); for a cinematic view of the Toronto gay community and ghetto c. 1980 see the feature-length documentary *Track Two* (HARRY SUTHERLAND et al., 1983); for scholarly accounts of Toronto queer history and geography see Grube (1997), Maynard (1994), and Ross (1995). The websites established by Rich Bébout through the Canadian Lesbian and Gay Archives are also exceptionally helpful: http://www.clga.ca/archives/what/papers/docs/toronto/tor1971.htm and http://www.clga.ca/archives/what/papers/docs/toronto/morecw.htm.

14 In fact, Brassard shot *Il était une fois dans l'est* in the *West*, in the then empty Hawaiian Lounge on Stanley Street, which ended its twenty-five-year intermittent vocation as a gay-welcoming space in the 1980s when it became a hetero strip club catering to NHL hockey players. For more of the evolution of Montreal queer geography, see Demczuk and Remiggi (1998); see also Higgins (1995, 1997, 1999a, 1999b).

15 Leap (especially Higgins, 1999) and Ingram (especially Grube, 1997) are useful introductions to theories, histories, and ethnographies of queer urban space.

16 Peter Morris (1993) has commented on the odd resistance of *À tout prendre* to canonization, but he does not attribute this to Jutra's discourses of sexual marginality. The film made it onto a "best" list recently for the first time (Wise 1998). The film also receives extended treatment in Leach (1999) and Marshall (2000), though only the latter adequately problematizes Jutra's queer sensibility. It is not clear whether this listing and these books can effectively re-canonize a work not available on video with English subtitles. *Il était une fois dans l'Est* is not available on video at all.

17 For analysis of the papering over of class and cultural difference in the "national" Quebec cinema of the 1960s, see Houle (1980). See also legal theorist Carl Stychin's analysis of Quebec since the 1970s (1998, 89–114).

18 For the role of the anticensorship battle in the Quiet Revolution see Hébert 1970.

19 *Outrageous!* even goes to bat for biculturalism, incorporating in its pan-national allegorical frieze a nasty and hyperfeminist Québécois dyke-in-exile – a full decade before a more elaborated version of the same character in *I've Heard the Mermaids Singing* (a film that shared Secter's taste for T.S. Eliot–inspired titles). *Mermaids* is similar to *Winter* in other ways as well, with its post-Stonewall exploration of ambiguous borders between homosociality and homosexuality. *Outrageous!*'s nasty dyke is a far cry from the brave, strong, and sexy lesbian couple in *Il était*.

20 In fact, to this day the most comprehensive history of the Toronto "lesbian and gay community" of the 1970s and early 1980s is a compendium of *The Body Politic* journalism: Jackson and Persky (1983). For a documentary source see also Bébout's site http://www.clga.ca/archives/what/papers/inven/tbp/tbpint.htm.

21 Discreet gay critic Basile does not mention Jutra's queer confessional, but certain suggestive keywords and phrases appear: "Narcissus," "adolescent," "too personal" … "even exposes himself bravely – here is everything! – in all his complexity."

22 One of the most detailed and measured "positive image" critiques of *Outrageous!* also came from abroad, from Richard Dyer (1979), British pioneer of gay film studies, whose groundbreaking *Gays and Film* (BFI) came out in 1977, the same year as the film. Dyer mentioned the Toronto locale only in passing and focused instead on comparing *Outrageous!* with the American *Word is Out – Stories from Some of Our Lives* (Mariposa Film Group, 1978) in terms of discourses of realism, utopia, and gender categories.

23 Jutra probably saw *Scorpio Rising* (1963) in a preliminary version, since he had clearly been following Anger's career since its beginning, having echoed Anger's *Fireworks* (1947) in his own *Mouvement perpétuel* (1949).

24 For a contemporary gay lib perspective on these two films see my own "Films by Gays for Gays: *A Very Natural Thing*, Word is Out, *and* The Naked Civil Servant" [1977], in Waugh (2000, 14–33); see also Dyer ([1990] 2003) for a discussion of "affirmation" gay cinema of the 1970s.

CHAPTER FIVE

1 My student Scott Preston read *Cornet* in terms of the Diefenbaker government's "save rural Canada" platform (Film Studies 605, 1999).

2 Critic Jim Leach (1999) and filmmaker PAULE BAILLARGEON in *Claude Jutra, portrait sur film* (NFB, 2002, 82) both fail to fully acknowledge Jutra's sexuality as an indispensable filter for looking at his life and his work.

3 The boyfriend, by coincidence, was played by the same Luke Kirby who two years later would play Angelo in *Mambo Italiano* (GAUDREAULT, 2003) and would finally learn what it's like to have one's beloved stolen by an opposite-sex rival.

4 So named because Hollywood war films during the 1940s and thereafter would often set up a homosocial collective protagonist in its bomber mission or infantry outpost or wherever, scrupulously composed to offer a demographic and regional spectrum of [usually white] American society and opposing the Jewish boy from Brooklyn and the Irish boy from Boston to the midwestern Wasp farm boy, etc.

CHAPTER SIX

1 A French pun that combines the word for pope "pape" with the word for faggot "tapette."

2 Cited correspondence and documents related to the *Passiflora* affair are from the author's personal archive.

3 I am obviously borrowing the title of the late Toronto activist and professor Michael Lynch's poetry collection *These Waves of Dying Friends: Poems* (Bowling Green, NY, 1989).

4 "Open Letter to Mr. François Macerola," *Cinema Canada* 141 (May 1987): 4. This was the issue that presented on its cover then closeted Patricia Rozema and arch-homophobe Jean-Claude Lauzon gloating over their forthcoming trip to Cannes, with the first lesbian feature *I've Heard the Mermaids Singing,* and the most antigay film yet made, *Un zoo la nuit,* under their arms, respectively.

5 Somerville showed her true colours on sexual-minority politics in the late 1990s, campaigning against adoption and reproduction rights for queer parents and against same-sex marriage. See her *The Ethical Canary: Science, Society and the Human Spirit* (Toronto: Viking 2000).

6 John Greyson, "Flaunting It!" unpublished documentary film proposal, 10 August 1987.

7 Harry Sutherland, "Our Body Politic: An Outline for a Feature-Length Documentary," unpublished documentary film proposal, 3 August 1987.

8 Untitled document for "investigate" re "Flaunting It," (September 1987). The anonymous consultant is referring to Gerald Hannon's notorious article about men-boy relations (1977–87), which had sparked *The Body Politic*'s three-year ordeal in criminal court in the late 1970s.

9 Canadian Broadcast Standards Council, Quebec Regional Council, "CFJP-TV (TQS) re 'Quand l'amour est gai'" (CBCS Decision 94/94-0204), 6 December 1995. http://www.cbsc.ca/english/decisions/decisions/1995/951206c.htm.

10 The eight films and tapes I futilely recommended for NFB pickup (alongside the already handled *Michael a Gay Son* [BRUCE GLAWSON, 1980]) were 1 *Still Sane* (PERSIMMON BLACKBRIDGE, Brenda Ingratta, and Lidia Patriasz, 1985); 2 *Orientations* (RICHARD FUNG 1985); 3 *Heroes* (SARA HALPRIN, 1983); 4 *No Sad Songs* (NIK SHEEHAN, 1985); 5 *Luc ou la part les choses* (MICHEL AUDY, 1982); 6 *Track Two* (HARRY SUTHERLAND, 1982); 7 *Ten Cents a Dance* (MIDI ONODERA, 1985); 8 *David Roche Talks to You about Love* (JEREMY PODESWA, 1985). Lest the unwary reader conclude that the first half of the 1980s were a fertile era for Canadian queer film and video production, it should be known that these six shorts and two features were virtually the *only* queer productions here in those years.

CHAPTER SEVEN

1 See Waugh (1996, 92, 258–69) for an analysis of the pre-Stonewall crypto-wrestling beefcake genre.

2 Literally, "undrinkable." This typical response was from Caroline Barrière, "La virilité sur patins," *Le Droit,* 13 December 1997, A4.

3 Other than Barrière, the two most influential of the female dissenters from the *Les Boys* phenomenon were from Montreal dailies: Odile Tremblay (*Les Boys* et moi,

Le devoir, 23 December 1998, B15) and Nathalie Petrowski ("La broue des *Boys*," *La Presse*, 15 December 1998, C13). The latter tempered her disdain by admitting that the film reflected reality in Quebec, where "beer and hockey are the two founding teats of our imaginary ... the Quebec collective unconscious has never passed the oral stage of beer consumed in a tavern or fermented in a lockerroom ... [The film] projects onto these bankrupt temples, through these loser characters who skate on their boots ... this collective powerlessness to rise up above our pathetic misery ... Once again, this powerlessness is what defines our society, and it always will. That's why one can hardly denounce a film that reflects us so well."

CHAPTER EIGHT

1 This exceptionally literate insight came from John Griffin, *The Gazette*, undated review of *Bubbles Galore*, c. 1999, cited in press kit provided to the author by producer Greg Klymkiw, 20 August 2003.

2 Cited by Glen McGregor, "Bubbles Galore Speaks," *Ottawa Citizen*, 29 May 1999 (final edition) B1.

3 Comment by typical online critic regarding *No Skin off My Ass* (1991), filethirteen.com (http://www.filethirteen.com/reviews/noskin/noskin.htm), accessed 5 May 2004.

4 John Allemang, "*Bubbles Galore*'s Satire Is Only Skin Deep," the *Globe and Mail*, 10 June 1999, D2; Claire Bickley, "The Trouble with *Bubbles*," *Toronto Sun*, 17 June 1999.

5 David MacDonald, *The Z Review* (http://www.angelfire.com/movies/davidsmovies/, 23 June 1999). MacDonald is apparently a UK-based Canadian.

6 Cynthia Roberts, cited in Katherine Monk, "Sex and Women – They're Finally Getting Together on Screen," *Vancouver Sun*, 6 October 1996, C1.

7 Chris Cobb, "Reformers Just Enjoy 'Sex Talk': Filmmaker Cynthia Roberts Responds to Criticism of Her Film *Bubbles Galore*," *Ottawa Citizen*, 28 January 2000, A3.

8 Among several excellent volumes analysing the Canadian history of obscenity law and censorship in the arts is Johnson 1997: note particularly an especially valuable focus on the Butler Decision and its context in Brenda Cossman, "Community Standards, Artistic Merit and the Censorship of the Arts," 85–98.

9 Two standard reference works on Canadian cinema are Rist (2001) and Wise (2001). Astonishingly, both lack entries on LaBruce and a glance at a half dozen recent monographs and anthologies comes up almost completely short on any extended treatment beyond a passing list reference or two. *Cineaction!*, LaBruce's old magazine, featured *Super 8½* on its cover (no. 36, 1995) and reviewed three feature films of the 1990s but has run no major articles.

10 David McIntosh's most thorough treatment is his (1997); LaBruce features have all received serious critical attention in *The Village Voice* (New York) and *Sight and Sound* (London); an example of a pro-Bruce critical voice in Paris is Bourcier (2001).

11 "Lodger," anonymous online film review site, U.S. accessed 28 June 2004. http://www.filethirteen.com/reviews/noskin/noskin.htm.

12 Interview with supplier by the author, 2004, source confidential.

13 I have been unable to identify this footage, but Fung and I agree that the likely culprit is 1970s porn auteur William Higgins. Email communication, September 2003.

14 Matthew Hays, 1999, "Lesbo Lust: Local Dykes Launch their Porno Short *Classy Cunts*," *Montreal Mirror*, 10 June.

15 Greyson likely had in mind the fake eyelasses in *Sharing the Secret*, the CBC's scurrilous 1981 documentary on the gay community by John Kastner and Rose Kastner, which among its many political, aesthetic, and ethical lapses disguised several of its subjects with fake names, fake whiskers, and eyewear (see CBC). The potted palms first appeared as camouflaging in 1960s American television reporting on "Homosexuality."

16 For a more detailed analysis of this scene in terms of abjection, masculinity, and nationalism, see Parpart (1997, chapter 1), Reading the Permeable Male Body in Jean-Claude Lauzon's *Un zoo la nuit*, 24–77. While her reading is insightful and authoritative, she omits some details and does not take the gut-wrenching homophobia of the scene far enough.

17 Compare Schwartzwald's analysis of nationalist tropes of homophobia in literature (1991, 175–95) and in sociocultural theory (1993, 264–99). Parpart has also suggested the parallel offered by *Un zoo* to Frantz Fanon's androcentric and homophobically displaced anticolonialist discourses (1997, 7–8, 26, 46).

18 This interesting and pioneering assemblage of short narrative vignettes is based on "Underground," the source of my epigraph above and other poems, including "BomGay," in R. Raj Rao, *BomGay* (London, New Delhi, Toronto: Aark Arts 2005), 16.

19 Elizabeth Pincus, "Crime and Melancholy," *Gay Community News*, undated clipping, 1987.

20 The reference, of course, is to the notorious nabbing of British gay pop star George Michael with his pants down in a Beverly Hills public toilet in 1998.

CHAPTER NINE

1 AIDS-related video works directed by Greyson in those prolific years of the late eighties include *Moscow Doesn't Believe in Queers* (1986), *The Ads Epidemic* (1987), *Four Safer Sex Shorts* (1987), *Angry Initiatives, Defiant* Strategies (1988), *The Pink Pimpernel* (1989), and *The World is Sick (Sic)* (1989). See Folland (1995) for a useful contextualisation of this early Toronto AIDS video activity within international theory and practice.

2 Chicago's Video Data Bank and Toronto's VTape sold up to two hundred copies of the three-cassette package to arts and educational institutions, but its impact was even wider than the sales suggest, since it was often handed over free to community organisations. Data kindly provided by the two organisations, December 2000.

3 Respectively, *Survival of the Delirious* (1988) and *Choose Your Plague* (1993).

4 The lag in Quebec artistic responses to the Epidemic is curious. In 1985 Denys Arcand and his cast put together the first mainstream Quebec cinematic portrait of a PWA in *Déclin de l'empire américain* (released in 1986): the portrait of the "tragically" gay sex-addict art historian who pisses blood and thereby absolves/exculpates the promiscuity of his heterosexual friends. This erroneous and pernicious image figment would later be justified by the actor YVES JACQUES after his own coming out a decade later by claiming that little had been known at that time of AIDS – the same year that universal HIV screening was introduced into the blood donation system in the "industrialised" worlds, Montreal AIDS community

Yves Jacques as Denys Arcand's implied PWA in *Déclin de l'empire américain* (1986), the "tragically" gay sex-addict art historian who cruises the Mountain (above, right), pisses blood, and exculpates the promiscuity of his heterosexual friends. Production still

organisations were already under way, and Rock Hudson's diagnosis and death became the number one media story! My hypothesis is that the resignation of the postreferendum arts scene, articulated in an apolitical formalism, did not spare *Déclin* and, coupled with cultural insulation from the North American media's AIDS crisis of conscience, allowed Quebec artists and writers to slumber on in the city with the highest infection rate in Canada until the V International Conference on HIV/AIDS in Montreal in 1989. The first Quebec French-language audiovisual work of any substance, *Récit d'A* appeared the following year: a personal masterpiece by a seropositive heterosexual woman making her first tape, a woman who nonetheless somehow felt compelled to journey to San Francisco to interview a person with AIDS ... When in 2003 Montreal gay journalist MATTHEW HAYS developed a piece for the *Toronto Star* on the Jacques PWA character's amazing resilience in Arcand's sequel to *Déclin* seventeen years later, *Les invasions barbares*, Arcand hotly denied that the original character had anything to do with AIDS, contradicting an interview he'd done with the same critic a decade earlier. The article was effectively killed but salvaged by *Take One* (Hays 2004).

5 *Tapes* is also ignored by Catherine Saalfield, the compiler of the videography in Juhasz (1995), as well as by Juhasz herself, a surprising omission in the light of the book's aspirations to definitive historiography. However, a paragraph's attention was accorded in Baker (1994, 84–5).

6 The most influential critique of Shilts (1987) is Crimp (1987).

7 http://awards.fennec.org/

8 Wall (2003), 21.

9 In fact, Diamond *has* made this tape, or rather film, or rather she *participated* in this film. *In Black and White* (MICHAEL MCGARRY, 1979) is an undeservedly neglected short from the seventies about gay toilet sex, captured by surveillance

cameras, and offers Diamond's uncredited voice on the soundtrack (see chapter 7).

10 Among the contributors to the superb critical material on Hoolboom are Cameron Bailey, Michael Dorland, Peggy Gale, Marc Glassman, Noreen Golfman, Robert Everett Green, Janine Marchessault, Laura Marks, Tom McSorley, Geoff Pevere, Steve Reinke, Catherine Russell, Barbara Sternberg, William Wees, and Mike Zryd.

11 Exceptionally, Hoolboom plays with drag in *Man* (1991) and *The New Man* (1992), codirected with the feminist Fleming.

12 In the company of Tom Chomont, the gay PWA experimental filmmaker from New York, a key collaborator of the 1990s, whose letter about a near-death experience would become the basis of *Eternity*, part of Hoolboom's *Panic Bodies* in 1998, and who would be the subject of Hoolboom's portrait *Tom* (2000).

13 This excerpt appears in the *Plague Years* (1998) version of the script (159) but not in the final film.

14 The principal texts in the "The Cinema We Need" debate (authored by Bruce Elder, Bart Testa, Piers Handling, Peter Harcourt, Michael Dorland, and Geoff Pevere and published in the *Canadian Forum* and *Cinema Canada* in 1985) are collected in Fetherling (1986, 260–336). Hoolboom also made a less-known contribution to the debate: "The Cinema We Have: Rumblings from Canada's Other Cinema," *Innis Herald* (November 1986) and *Splice* (newsletter of Saskatchewan Filmpool, spring 1987).

15 *Mexico*, released in 1992 out of material shot around the time of Hoolboom's pre-Vancouver, pre-diagnosis days, was an ambitious and disturbing exploration of continental politics just as the Tories were pushing through NAFTA, but also an ambivalent immersion in the culture of the bullring and industrial landscapes.

16 The availability of the Hoolboom filmography sometimes seems to be in constant flux: most of the sex-diary films, including *From Home* (1988), *Was* (1989), *Eat* (1989), and *The New Man* (1992, with Anne Marie Fleming), have apparently – symptomatically? – been withdrawn from circulation. Still in distribution are *Two* (1990, with Kika Thorne) as well as *Man* (1991, with Fleming).

17 Hoolboom currently does not publicly acknowledge a fixed sexual identity, but this feels as much like queer fluidity as coy evasiveness. At Concordia University, 25 November 1999, a journalist asked him publicly whether it is true that he is straight, and he deflected the question with a big grin, hip motion, and "I wouldn't say *straight*," drawing out the final word in a three-syllable phonetic performance of butch camp.

18 *Image + Nation: Festival international de cinéma gai & lesbien de Montréal*, catalogues 1998 and 2000, 49 and 25, respectively.

CHAPTER TEN

1 I am indebted to Eve Kosofsky Sedgwick's recirculation and repoliticization of the notion of shame and of 1950s sociologist Erving Goffman's related concept of the "management of spoiled identity" in (1993a, 1–16; 1993b, 177–214, 215–51).

2 Svend Robinson's private member's Bill C-250, adding gays and lesbians to a list of groups legally protected from incitement of hatred and genocide under the Criminal Code, was finally passed by the Senate on 28 April 2004 and given royal assent the next day, despite massive lobbying by the evangelical right. Not a single media report of the firebombing of a Montreal Jewish school mentioned the filibuster of the anti-hate bill going on at exactly the same time.

3 Cf. Brenda Cossman, "Iraqi Prisoner Abuse a Queer Concern," *Xtra!*, 15 May 2004, 20.
4 This and subsequent excerpts from "Yapping Out Loud," unpublished performance text, 2002, were kindly provided by Mirha-Soleil Ross, email communication, 23 May 2004.
5 Michael Coren, "Public Funds Used to Create Alleged Porn Debate," television forum, *Canada AM,CTV*, 12 May 1999. Record 16 of 22, Cdn NewsDisc 1999, Disc 3.

PORTRAIT GALLERY

1 Unsigned capsule review on queer website Planet Out (U.S.), accessed 28 June 2004. http://www.planetout.com/popcornq/db/getfilm.html.
2 Excerpts, respectively, from David Clandfield, *Canadian Film* (Toronto: Oxford, 1987), 63; Pierre Patry, in *Claude Jutra* (1987, 22); Jutra, citing responses to *À tout prendre* in Pâquet (1967, 13); Jean Chabot, in Conseil québécois pour la diffusion du cinéma, *Cinéastes du Québec 4: Claude Jutra* (1971, 3).
3 Testimonies by Nold, Boyer, Perron, and du Hamel, in *Claude Jutra: filmographie et témoignages* (1987, 24, 26, 27, 30).
4 http://eyetap.org/cyberman/cyberman_eye_tiff_movie_rating_printer.htm. Accessed 27 November 2003.

Bibliography

This bibliography is restricted to monographs and major scholarly articles consulted in my research for and writing of this book. Short reviews, interviews, web materials, and other similar sources are cited within the text. Otherwise, the principal primary sources for this book are of course the almost fifteen hundred Canadian films and videos studied in its preparation. It is not possible to provide a detailed database for these works, including titles, authors, dates, format, and distribution information, but all are referenced in the text upon first appearance, and most authors are profiled in the portrait gallery. Also cited in the text or endnotes if appropriate, but not in this bibliography, is the extensive correspondence (email, telephone, in person, and regular mail) carried out with individuals and groups. Citations of French-language texts are my translation unless otherwise indicated.

Adams, Evan. 1992. "Theatre and AIDS Education in a North American Native Community." In Ken Morrison and Allan Klusacek, eds., *Leap in the Dark: AIDS, Art and Contemporary Cultures*, 247–63. Montreal: Véhicule.

Adams, Kathleen Pirrie. 1997. "Sex is Inevitable." *Xtra!* Unpaged, undated clipping, c. July.

– 1998. *"Stolen Moments" Take One* 6, no. 18 (winter): 17.

Adams, Michael. 1998. *Sex in the Snow: Canadian Social Values at the End of the Millennium*. Toronto: Penguin.

Alioff, Maurie. 1997. "Sexual Utopia: Cynthia Roberts's *Bubbles Galore* [interview]." *Take One* 5, no. 14 (winter): 36–8.

Allen, Beverly, ed. 1982. *Pier Paolo Pasolini: The Poetics of Heresy*. Saratoga, CA: Anma Libri.

Allyn, David Smith. 2001. *Make Love, Not War: The Sexual Revolution in America, 1957–1977*. New York: Routledge.

Altman, Dennis. 1981. *Coming Out in the Seventies*. Boston: Alyson.

Anderson, Elizabeth Susan. 1996. "Pirating Feminisms: Film and the Production of Post-War Canadian National Identity." PHD diss., University of Minnesota.

Appadurai, Arjun. 1996. *Modernity at Large: Cultural Dimensions of Globalization.* Minneapolis, MN: University Of Minnesota Press.

Arcand, Denys. "Cinéma et sexualité." *Presqu'Amérique* 1, no. 3 (1964).

Archer, Bert. 1999. *The End of Gay (And the Death of Heterosexuality).* Toronto: Doubleday Canada.

Armatage, Kay. 2002. "Janis Cole and Holly Dale's Cinema of Marginality." In Jerry White and Bill Beard, ed., *North of Everything: English Canadian Cinema since 1980,* 122–44. Edmonton: University of Alberta Press.

Armatage, Kay, Kass Banning, Brenda Longfellow, and Janine Marchessault, eds. 1999. *Gendering the Nation: Canadian Women's Cinema.* Toronto: University of Toronto Press.

Arroyo, José. 1986. Review of *Passiflora. Cinema Canada* 128 (March), 28.

– 1992. "Bordwell Considered: Cognitivism, Colonialism and Canadian Cinematic Culture." *Cineaction!* 28: 74–88.

– 2001. Review of *Drôle de Félix. Sight and Sound* 2, no. 1 (January): 47.

Bailey, Cameron. 2000. Interview with Mike Hoolboom. In Steve Reinke and Tom Taylor, eds., *Lux: A Decade of Artists' Film and Video,* 227. Toronto: YYZ/Pleasure Dome

Baker, Rob. 1994. *The Art of AIDS.* New York: Continuum.

Baldassarre, Angela. 2003. *Reel Canadians: Interviews from the Canadian Film World.* Toronto: Guernica.

Bataille, Georges. (1957) 1986. *Erotism: Death and Sensuality.* San Francisco: City Lights.

Beard, William, and Jerry White, eds. 2002. *North of Everything: English Canadian Cinema since 1980.* Edmonton: University of Alberta Press.

Bersani, Leo. 1987. "Is the Rectum a Grave?" *October* 43: 197–22.

Bérubé, Allen. 1990. *Coming Out under Fire: The History of Gay Men and Women in World War Two.* New York: Macmillan.

Blackbridge, Persimmon, and Sheila Gilhooly. 1985. *Still Sane.* Vancouver: Press Gang.

Blackbridge, Persimmon, Lizard Jones, and Susan Stewart (Kiss and Tell). 1994. *Her Tongue on My Theory.* Vancouver: Press Gang.

Boullé, Denis-Daniel. 1998. "Rencontre Laurent Gagliardi: Farouchement gai." *Fugues* 15, no. 7 (October): 66.

Bourcier, Marie-Hélène. 2001. *Queer Zones: Politiques des identités sexuelles, des représentations et des savoirs.* Paris: Éditions Balland.

Bradley, Richard. 2004. "La présence québécoise dans les films pornos gais des années 80." *L'Archigai* 14 (October): 4–5.

Britton, Andrew. 1978–79. "For Interpretation: Notes against Camp," *Gay Left* 7 (winter).

Bruce, Jean. 1999. "Querying/Queering the Nation." In Kay Armatage et al., *Gendering the Nation: Canadian Women's Cinema,* 274–90. Toronto: University of Toronto Press.

Burstyn, Varda. 1999. *The Rites of Men: Manhood, Politics and the Culture of Sport.* Toronto, Buffalo, and London: University of Toronto Press.

Butler, Judith. 1990. *Gender Trouble: Feminism and the Subversion of Identity.* New York and London: Routledge.

– 1993. "Imitation and Gender Insubordination." In Henry Abelove, Michèle Aina Barale and David M. Halperin, eds., *The Gay and Lesbian Studies Reader,* 307–20. New York and London: Routledge.

Campbell, Colin. 1979. *Modern Love*. Toronto: Art Metropole.

Carr, C. 2003. "A World of Their Own: General Idea Made Art from Culture's Forgotten Shell." *Village Voice* 18 June 2003.

Castiel, Elie. 2000. "Rodrigue Jean: Retour aux sources (interview)." *Séquences* 206 (January/February): 33–4.

Champagne, John. 1995. *The Ethics of Marginality: A New Approach to Gay Studies*. Minneapolis and London: University of Minnesota Press.

Chopra, Radhika, Caroline Osella, and Filippo Osella, eds. 2004. *South Asian Masculinities: Context of Change, Sites of Continuity*. New Delhi: Women Unlimited and Kali for Women.

Claude Jutra: filmographie et témoignages. 1987. Special issue, *Copie zéro*, no. 33 (September).

Cohan, Steve. 1997. *Masked Men: Masculinity and the Movies in the Fifties*. Bloomington IN: Indiana University Press.

Cole, Stephen. 1995. "Home Ice: A Comparative Guide to Hockey Movies, Theirs and Ours." *Take One* 3, no. 8 (summer): 32–5.

Connolly, Mark, with David Werner. 1990. *The Karate Kids Book: What We Need to Know about AIDS*. Toronto: Street Kids International.

Corber, Robert. 1993. *In the Name of National Security: Hitchcock, Homophobia, and the Political Construction of Gender in Postwar America*. Durham, NC: Duke University Press.

– 1997. *Homosexuality in Cold War America: Resistance and the Crisis of Masculinity*. Durham, NC: Duke University Press.

Cossman, Brenda. 1995. *Censorship and the Arts: Law, Controversy, Debate, Facts*. Toronto: Ontario Association of Art Galleries.

Cossman, Brenda, Sharon Bell, Lise Gotell, and Becki L. Ross. 1997. *Bad Attitude/s on Trial: Pornography, Feminism, and the Butler Decision*. Toronto, Buffalo, and London: University of Toronto Press.

Coulombe, Michel, and Marcel Jean, eds. 1999. *Le Dictionnaire du cinéma québécois*. 3d ed. Montreal: Boréal.

Crimp, Douglas. 1987. "How to Have Promiscuity in an Epidemic." *October* 43: 237–71.

Cutler, May Ebbitt. 1983. "McLaren Perspectives: The Qualities of Tragedy." *Cinema Canada*, no. 99 (September): 22.

Darren, Alison. 2000. *Lesbian Film Guide*. London: Cassell.

de Bruyn, Dirk. 1993. "What he SAID: an interview with Mike Hoolboom." *Workprint* (spring).

Demczuk, Irène, and Frank W. Remiggi. 1998. *Sortir de l'ombre: Histoires des communautés lesbienne et gaie de Montréal*. Montreal: VLB Éditeur.

D'Emilio, John, 1983. *Sexual Politics, Sexual Communities: The Making of a Homosexual Minority in the United States, 1940–1970*. Chicago: University of Chicago Press.

D'Emilio, John, and Estelle Freedman. 1988. *Intimate Matters: A History of Sexuality in America*. New York: Harper & Row.

Diamond, Sara. 1996. "Sex Lies with Videotape: Abbreviated Histories of Canadian Video Sex." In Michael Renov and Erika Suderburg, eds., *Resolutions: Contemporary Video Practices*, 189–206. Minneapolis: University of Minnesota Press.

Dickinson, Peter. 1999. *Here is Queer: Nationalisms, Sexualities, and the Literatures of Canada*. Toronto: University of Toronto Press.

– 2005. "Space, Time, *Auteur*-ity, and the Queer Male Body: The Film Adaptations of Robert Lepage." *Screen* 46, no. 2 (summer): 133–54.

Ditta, Su. 1999. "The Summer of the Suiciding Nuns: Sex, Art and Controversy in Canada's Public Museums." In Sylvie Gilbert, ed., *Arousing Sensation: A Case Study of Controversy Surrounding Art and the Erotic*, 73–115. Banff: Banff Centre Press.

Dorland, Michael. 1998. *So Close to the State/s: The Emergence of Canadian Feature Film Policy*. Toronto: University of Toronto Press.

Dowler, Andrew. 1996. "The Cultural Industries Policy Apparatus." In Michael Dorland, ed., *The Cultural Industries in Canada: Problems, Policies and Prospects*, 347–65. Toronto: Lorimer.

Doyle, Judith, Marc Christian Tremblay, and Scott Treleaven, eds. 1995. *Michael Balser: Positive Practices*. Toronto: Second Decade.

Dyer, Richard. [1977] 1992. "Entertainment and Utopia." Reprint, 17–34.

– 1979. "Out! Out! Out!: A Review of *Outrageous!* and *Word is Out*." *Gay Left: A Gay Socialist Journal* 9: 27–30.

– 1987. *Heavenly Bodies: Film Stars and Society*. London: BFI/Macmillan.

– 1992. *Only Entertainment*. London and New York: Routledge.

– 1997. *White*. London and New York: Routledge.

– 2002. *The Culture of Queers*. London: Routledge.

Dyer, Richard, with Julianne Pidduck. [1990] 2003. *Now You See It: Studies in Lesbian and Gay Film*. 2d ed. London and New York: Routledge.

Earle, Neil. 2002. "Hockey as Canadian Popular Culture: Team Canada 1972, Television and the Canadian Identity." In Sloniowski and Nicks, *Slippery Pastimes*, 321–44.

Ebert, Roger. 2001. "*Lost and Delirious*," *Chicago Sun-Times*, 13 July, 9; http://www.suntimes.com/ebert/ebert_reviews/2001/07/071303.html.

Ehrenreich, Barbara. 1983. *The Hearts of Men: American Dreams and the Flight from Commitment*. Garden City, NJ: Anchor Press/Doubleday.

Ehrenreich, Barbara, Elizabeth Hess, and Gloria Jacobs. 1987. *Remaking Love: The Feminization of Sex*. New York: Anchor Press.

Evans, Gary. 1991. *In the National Interest: A Chronicle of the National Film Board of Canada from 1949 to 1989*. Toronto: University of Toronto Press.

Exposed: Aesthetics of Aboriginal Erotic Art. 1999. Curated by Lee-Ann Martin and Morgan Wood. Published in conjunction with the exhibition "Exposed: Aesthetics of Aboriginal Erotic Art," shown at the Mackenzie Art Gallery in Regina, Saskatchewan.

Feder, Elena. 2003. "Beyond the Homeland: A Comparative Introduction to Latino Film in Canada and the U.S." *Cineaction* 61: 40–51.

Fernie, Lynne, Dinah Forbes, and Joyce Mason, eds. 1988. *Sight Specific: Lesbians and Representation*. Toronto: A Space.

Fetherling, Douglas, ed. 1986. *Documents in Canadian Film*. Peterborough, ON: Broadview.

Folland, Tom. 1995. "Deregulating Identity: Video and AIDS Activism." In *Mirror Machine: Video and Identity*, edited by Janine Marchessault, 227–37. Toronto: YYZ.

Fothergill, Robert. (1973) 1977. "Coward, Bully or Clown: The Dream Life of a Younger Brother." In Seth Feldman and Joyce Nelson, eds., *Take One* 4, no. 3; reprinted in *Canadian Film Reader*, 234–49. Toronto: Peter Martin Associates.

Foucault, Michel. (1976) 1990. *The History of Sexuality.* Vol. 1, *An Introduction*, trans. Robert Hurley. New York: Vintage Books.

– 1980. "Body/Power." In Colin Gordon, ed., *Power/Knowledge: Selected Interviews and Other Writings, 1972–77*, 55–62. New York: Pantheon.

– 1986. 'Text/Context of Other Space." *Diacritics* 16.1 (1986): 22–7.

Fox, Ted. 1977. "Richard Benner's *Outrageous!*" *Cinema Canada* 41 (October): 21.

Fraser, Brad. 1995. *Poor Superman: A Play with Captions.* Edmonton: New West Press.

Fraser, Keath. 1997. *As for Me and My Body: A Memoir of Sinclair Ross.* Toronto: ECW Press.

Fuchs, Cynthia. 2003. *"Lost and Delirious,"* PopMatters (webmagazine), http://popmatters.com/film/reviews/l/lost-and-delirious.html (accessed 29 November).

Fuller, Janine, and Stuart Blackley. 1996. *Restricted Entry: Censorship on Trial.* 2d ed. Vancouver: Press Gang.

Fung, Richard. 1991. "Center the Margins." In Russell Leong, ed., *Moving the Image: Independent Asian Pacific American Media Arts*, 62–7. Los Angeles: UCLA Asian American Studies Center.

– 1991. "Looking for My Penis: The Eroticized Asian in Gay Video Porn." In Bad Object Choice, ed., *How Do I Look: Queer Film and Video*, 145–61. Seattle: Bay Press.

Gagnon, Jean. 1995. *Paul Wong: On Becoming a Man.* National Gallery of Canada.

Gagnon, Jean, and Karen Knights. 1992. *Sara Diamond: Memories Revisited, History Retold.* National Gallery of Canada.

Gaines, Jane M. 1999. *"Lonely Boy* and the *Vérité* of Sex." *Canadian Journal of Film Studies* 8, no. 1 (spring): 102–19.

Gardiner, Judith Kegan. 2002. *Masculinity Studies and Feminist Theory: New Directions.* New York: Columbia University Press.

Gawthrop, Daniel. 1994. *Affirmation: The AIDS Odyssey of Dr. Peter.* Vancouver: New Star.

Gellman, Dara, and Leslie Peters. 1999. "Video as Video." In thematic issue, "Voyeurism." Lisa Steele + Kim Tomczak and Nayan Shah, eds., *Felix: A Journal of Media Arts and Communications* 2, no. 2: 274–78.

Gilbert, Sylvie. 1999. *Arousing Sensation: A Case Study of Controversy Surrounding Art and the Erotic.* Banff: Banff Centre Press.

Gittings, Christopher E. 2002. *Canadian National Cinema: Ideology, Difference and Representation.* London and New York: Routledge.

The Glade: A Performance/Installation by Zachery Longboy. 1996. Curated by Zachery Longboy and published in conjunction with the exhibition The Glade, shown at AKA Artist-Run Centre, Saskatoon.

Glover, Guy. 1967. "How to Make a Canadian Film." In André Pâquet, ed., *How to Make or Not to Make a Canadian Film*, statement 3. Montreal: La cinémathèque canadienne [unpaged].

Goldie, Terry. 2003. *Pink Snow: Homotextual Possibilities in Canadian Fiction.* Toronto: Broadview.

– ed. 2001. *In a Queer Country: Gay and Lesbian Studies in the Canadian Context.* Vancouver: Arsenal Pulp Press.

Gonick, Noam, ed. 1997. *Bruce LaBruce: Ride Queer Ride!* Winnipeg: Plug In Editions.

Grant, Michael, ed. 2000. *The Modern Fantastic: The Films of David Cronenberg.* Westport, CT: Praeger.

Greyson, John. 1990. "Strategic Compromises: AIDS and Alternative Video Practices." In Mark O'Brien and Craig Little, ed., *Reimaging America: The Arts of Social Change*, 60–74. Philadelphia and Santa Cruz: New Society Publishers.

– 1993. *Urinal and Other Stories.* Toronto: Art Metropole and The Power Plant.

– 2002a. "The Autobiography of Alice B. Fungus." In Helen Lee and Kerri Sakamoto, eds., *Like Mangoes in July: The Work of Richard Fung*, 11. Toronto: Insomniac Press/Images Festival.

– 2002b. "The Singing Dunes: Colin Campbell, 1943–2001." *C Magazine* (summer), 29–31.

– 2003. *Fig Trees: A Video Opera.* A multimedia production curated by Marnie Fleming in conjunction with the Oakville Gallerie.

Grube, John. 1997. "'No More Shit': The Struggle for Democratic Gay Space in Toronto." In Brent Ingram et al., eds., *Queers in Space: Communities/Public Places/Sites of Resistance.* Seattle: Bay Press.

Gustav-Wrathall, John Donald. 1998. *Take the Young Stranger by the Hand: Same Sex Relations and the YMCA.* Chicago: University of Chicago Press.

Guttmann, Allen. 1996. *The Erotic in Sports.* New York: Columbia University Press.

Haig, Thomas. 1994. "Not Just Some Sexless Queen: A Note on 'Kids in the Hall' and the Queerness of Canada." In "Canadas," special issue, *Semiotext(e)* no. 17 (vol. 6, no. 2): 227–29.

Handling, Piers, ed. 1983. *The Shape of Rage: The Films of David Cronenberg.* Toronto: General Publishing.

Hannaham, James. 1995. "Reel to Reel: *Super 8½.*" *Village Voice*, 7 May, 60.

Hannon, Gerald. 1977–78. "Men Loving Boys Loving Men." *The Body Politic*, 39 (December–January); reprinted in Jackson and Persky, eds., *Flaunting It*, 147–59.

– 1989. "Comic Relief." *Advocate* 540 (19 December): 41–3.

Hanson, Ellis, ed. 1999. *Out Takes: Essays on Queer Theory and Film.* Durham, NC, and London: Duke University Press.

Hays, Matthew. 1998. "Profile: Thom Fitzgerald." *Advocate* 753 (February 17): 50–1.

– 2004. "Epidemic Amnesia: AIDS Is Curiously Forgotten in Denys Arcand's *Les Invasions barbares.*" *Take One* 12, no. 45 [June], 42–3.

Hébert, Jacques. 1970. *Obscénité et liberté.* Montreal: Éditions du Jour.

Henricks, Nelson, and Steve Reinke, eds. 1997. *By the Skin Of their Tongues.* YYZ Books.

Higgins, Ross. 1995. "Murder Will Out: Gay Identity and Media Discourse in Montreal." In William Leap, ed., *The Lavender Lexicon: Authenticity, Imagination and Appropriation in Lesbian and Gay Languages*, 107–32. Amsterdam: Gordon and Breach.

– 1997. "A Sense of Belonging: Pre-liberation Space, Symbolics, and Leadership in Gay Montreal." PHD diss., McGill University.

– 1999a. "Baths, Bushes, and Belonging: Public Sex and Gay Community in Pre-Stonewall Montreal." In William Leap, ed., *Public Sex/Gay Space*, 187–202. New York: Columbia University Press.

– 1999b. *De la clandestinité à l'affirmation: Pour une histoire de la communauté gaie montrèalaise.* Montreal: Comeau et Nadeau.

Higgins, Ross, and Line Chamberland. 1992. "Mixed Messages: Gays and Lesbians in Montreal Yellow Papers in the 1950s." In Ian McKay, ed., *The Challenge of Modernity: A Reader on Post-Confederation Canada,* 422–31. Toronto: McGraw-Hill Ryerson.

Holland, David. 1977. "Honest, Beguiling, 'Outrageous!' Step Forward," *Gay Community News,* 27 August, 8.

Hoolboom, Mike. 1991. "A History of the Canadian Avant-Garde in Film." In Rose Lowder, ed., *The Visual Aspect: Recent Canadian Experimental Films,* 16–25. Avignon: Éditions des archives du film expérimental d'Avignon.

– 1998. *Plague Years: A Life in Underground Movies,* ed. Steve Reinke. Toronto: YYZ.

– 2001. *Inside the Pleasure Dome: Fringe Film in Canada.* New expanded edition. Toronto: Coach House.

Houle, Michel. 1980. "Some Ideological and Thematic Aspects of the Quebec Cinema." In Pierre Véronneau and Piers Handling, ed., *Self Portraits: Essays on the Canadian and Quebec Cinemas,* 159–82. Ottawa: Canadian Film Institute.

Ibranyi-Kiss, A. 1973. "Film Review, *August and July.*" *Cinema Canada* 6 (February/March): 62.

Imagine Native: Aboriginally Produced Film and Video. 1997. Ed. Cynthia Lickers. VTape, in association with the Aboriginal Film and Video Alliance of Ontario.

Irwin, Nancy. 2002. "*Stand Together*: A History of Ontario's Gay Liberation Movement." *Siren Magazine* (2 April): 1–3.

Jackson, Ed, and Stan Persky, eds. 1982. *Flaunting It: A Decade of Gay Journalism from the Body Politic.* Vancouver and Toronto: New Star Books and Pink Triangle Press.

Jagose, Annamarie. 1996. *Queer Theory: An Introduction.* New York: New York University Press.

James, David E. 1989. *Allegories of Cinema: American Film in the Sixties.* Princeton: Princeton University Press.

Johnson, Lorraine. 1997. *Suggestive Poses: Artists and Critics Respond to Censorship.* Toronto: Toronto Photographers Workshop and the Riverbank Press.

Juhasz, Alexandra. 1995. *AIDS TV.* Durham, NC: Duke University Press.

Katz, Jonathan D. Forthcoming. "The Silent Camp: Queer Resistance and the Rise of Pop Art." In Trish Kelly and Serge Guilbaut, eds., *PLOP! Goes the World.* Durham, NC: Duke University Press.

Kibbins, Gary, and Susan Lord, eds. 2002. "Experimentalism." Special issue, *Public* 25.

Kinsman, Gary. 1995. "Queers in the Streets versus Queen's Park." *Fuse* 18, no. 4 (summer), 40–1.

– 1996. *The Regulation of Desire: Homo and Hetero Sexualities.* Montreal: Black Rose.

Knelman, Martin. 1977. *This Is Where We Came In: The Career and Character of Canadian Film.* Toronto: McClelland and Stewart.

LaBruce, Bruce. 1997. *The Reluctant Pornographer.* Toronto: Gutter Press.

Larkin, Philip. (1988) 1989. "Annus Mirabilis," In *Collected Works,* ed. Anthony Thwaite, 167. London: Marvell Press.

Larouche, Michel, ed. 2003. *Cinéma et littérature au Québec: Rencontres médiatiques*. Montreal: XYZ Éditeur.

Lavoie, André. 1993. "Image et nation – Gaie et lesbienne." *Ciné-bulles* 12, no. 2 (February/March): 23–6.

Leach, Jim. 1999. *Claude Jutra: Filmmaker*. Montreal and Kingston: McGill-Queen's University Press.

Leap, William L., ed. 1995. *Beyond the Lavender Lexicon: Authenticity, Imagination, and Appropriation in Lesbian and Gay Languages*. Australia: Gordon and Breach.

Leduc, Jean. 1974. "*Il était une fois dans l'Est, The Apprenticeship of Duddy Kravitz*: La représentation d'un milieu donné." *Cinéma Québec* 3, nos. 6–7 (April/May): 43–4.

Lee, Helen, and Kerri Sakamoto, eds. 2002. *Like Mangoes in July: The Work of Richard Fung*. Toronto: Images Festival of Independent Film and Video.

Lehman, Peter, ed. 2001. *Masculinity: Bodies, Movies, Culture*. New York and London: Routledge.

Levitin, Jaqueline, Judith Plessis, and Valerie Raoul, eds. 2003. *Women Filmmakers: Refocusing*. Vancouver and Toronto: University of British Columbia Press.

Locke, John W. 1977. "A Healthy Case of Craziness." *Cinema Canada* 41 (October): 17–18, 20–1.

Lockerbie, Ian. 1994. "Le Documentaire autoréflexif au Québec: *L'Émotion dissonante* et *Passiflora*." *Cinémas* 2, no. 2 (spring): 119–32.

Longfellow, Brenda. 1999. "Hyperbolic Masculinity and the Ironic Gaze in Project Grizzly." *Canadian Journal of Film Studies* 8, no. 1 (spring): 87–101.

Lost and Delirious. 2003. Unsigned review accessed 29 November on *The Great Canadian Guide to Movies & TV*, http://www.pulpanddagger.com/movies/13.html/.

Lynch, Michael. 1982. "*Track Two*: Giving Us Back Ourselves." *The Body Politic* 86 (September): 31.

MacDougall, Bruce. 2000. *Queer Judgments: Homosexuality, Expression and the Courts in Canada*. Toronto, Buffalo, and London: University of Toronto Press.

Maddin, Guy. 2003. *From the Atelier Tovar: Selected Writings*. Toronto: Coach House Books.

Marcorelles, Louis. 1966. "La semaine de la critique." *Cahiers du cinéma*, no. 179 (June): 47–8.

Marcuse, Herbert. 1964. *One Dimensional Man; Studies in the Ideology of Advanced Industrial Society*. Boston: Beacon.

Markowitz, Murray. 1973. Interview. *Cinema Canada* 6 (February-March): 54–61.

Marks, Laura U. 1993. "Sexual Hybrids: From Oriental Exotic to Postcolonial Grotesque." *Parachute* 70: 23.

Marshall, Bill. 2001. *Quebec National Cinema*. Montreal and Kingston: McGill-Queen's University Press.

Martin, Robert K. 1991. "Sex and Politics in Wartime Canada: The Attack on Patrick Anderson." *Essays on Canadian Writing* 44.

Martineau, Barbara Halpern. 1981. "Review of *P4W: Prison for Women*." *The Body Politic* 78 (November), 35.

Mauriès, Patrick, ed. 1998. *Les gays savoirs*. Paris: Le Promeneur! and Éditions du Centre Pompidou.

Maynard, Steve. 1994. "Through a Hole in the Lavatory Wall: Homosexual Subcultures, Police Surveillance, and the Dialectics of Discovery: Toronto,
1890–1930." *Journal of the History of Sexuality* 5, no. 2 (October): 207–42.

McGregor, Gaile. 1985. *The Wacousta Syndrome: Explorations in the Canadian
Landscape.* Toronto: University of Toronto Press.

McIntosh, David. 1997. "Engines of Desire, Empire of the Undead: LaBruce, Sex,
Money and Celebrity from *J.D.s* to *Hustler White.*" In Gonick, *Bruce LaBruce,*
142–60.

McKay, John (Canadian Press). 2002. "Gross Gets Swept Away." *Gazette,* 27
February: F5.

McLaren, Norman. "Interview by John Kramer for the documentary *Has Anyone
Here Seen Canada.*" Transcript, 1978. Archives of the National Film Board of
Canada, Montreal.

– 1982. Letter to Robin Hardy, 13 May. Photocopy of handwritten letter
provided by the addressee to the author's personal collection.

McLeod, Donald W. 1996. *Lesbian and Gay Liberation in Canada: A Selected
Annotated Chronology, 1964–1975.* Toronto: ECW.

Medjuck, Joe. 1966. "*Winter Kept Us Warm.*" *Take One* 1, no. 1 (September-
October): 24.

Meigs, Mary. 1991. *In the Company of Strangers.* Vancouver: Talonbooks.

Miller, James, ed. 1992. *Fluid Exchanges: Artists and Critics in the AIDS Crisis.*
Toronto: University of Toronto Press.

Milroy, Sarah. 2002. "Vindication of an Art Pioneer." *Globe and Mail,* 22 October. R1,4,

Monk, Katherine. 2001. *Weird Sex and Snow Shoes and Other Canadian Film
Phenomena.* Vancouver: Raincoast Books.

Morris, Peter. 1993. "In Our Own Eyes: The Canonizing of Canadian Film."
Canadian Journal of Film Studies 3, no. 1 (spring): 27–44.

Morrison, Ken, and Allan Klusacek, eds. 1992. *Leap in the Dark: AIDS, Art and
Contemporary Cultures.* Montreal: Véhicule.

Muñoz, José Esteban. 1999. *Disidentifications: Queers of Color and the Performance of Politics.* Minneapolis: University of Minnesota Press.

Nadeau, Chantal. 1999. "*Barbaras en Québec*: Variations on Identity." In Kay
Armatage, et al., *Gendering the Nation: Canadian Women's Cinema,* 197–211.
Toronto: University of Toronto Press.

– 2000. "Bubbles Galore, Bubbles Money; Canada, the Sexx Nation." Unpublished
paper delivered to the Society for Cinema Studies, Chicago, 9–12 March 2000.

– (2000) 2004. "Copines et compagnes à la campagne: réflexions queer sur *Revoir
Julie.*" *Nouvelles vues sur le cinéma québécois,* no. 2 (summer/fall 2004);
http://www.cinemaquebecois.net/edition2/accueil.htm

– 2001. *Fur Nation: From the Beaver to Brigitte Bardot.* New York and London:
Routledge.

Namaste, Viviane K. 2000. *Invisible Lives: The Erasure of Transsexual and
Transgendered People.* Chicago and London: University of Chicago Press.

– 2005. *C'était du spectacle! L'histoire des artistes transsexuelles à Montréal
1955–1985.* Montreal: McGill-Queen's University Press.

Ndodana, Bongani. 2003. "Thoughts on *Fig Trees.*" In *Fig Trees,* Greyson 2003,
25–34.

Nichols, Bill. 1991. *Representing Reality*. Bloomington and Indianapolis, IN: Indian University Press.

– 1994. *Blurred Boundaries: Questions of Meaning in Contemporary Culture*. Bloomington, IN: Indiana University Press.

Nicks, Joan. 1995. "*Gross Misconduct*: Atom Egoyan's Hulk Skates Figure 8s around the Legacy of the Black Maria." Unpublished paper, annual conference, Film Studies Association of Canada, Université du Québec à Montréal.

Osella, Caroline, and Filippo Osella. 2004. "Young Malayali Men and Their Movie Heroes." In Radhika Chopra, Caroline Osella and Filippo Osella, eds., *South Asian Masculinities: Context of Change, Sites of Continuity*, 224–63. New Delhi: Kali for Women and Women Unlimited.

Pâquet, André, ed. 1967. *How to Make or Not to Make a Canadian Film*. Montreal: La cinémathèque canadienne.

Parpart, Lee. 1997. *Nostalgic Nationalisms and the Spectacle of the Male Body in Canadian and Québécois Cinema*. MA thesis, York University.

– 2001. "The Nation and the Nude: Colonial Masculinity and the Spectacle of the Body in Recent Canadian Cinema(s)." In Peter Lehman, ed., *Masculinity: Bodies, Movies, Cultures*, 167–92. New York and London: Routledge.

– 1999. "Pit(iful) Male Bodies: Colonial Masculinity, Class and Folk Innocence in *Margaret's Museum*." *Canadian Journal of Film Studies* 8, no. 1 (spring): 63–86.

Pasolini, Pier Paolo. (1973) 1994. "Tetis." In Patrick Rumble and Bart Testa, eds., *Pier Paolo Pasolini: Contemporary Perspectives*, 243–49. Toronto: University of Toronto Press.

– (1975) 1982. "Coitus, Abortion, Power's False Tolerance, and the Conformism of Progressives." In Beverly Allen, ed., *Pier Paolo Pasolini: The Poetics of Heresy*, 116–121. Saratoga, CA: Anma Libri.

Perrault, Pierre. 1982. *La Bête lumineuse*. Transcription of commentary and dialogue by Pierre Perrault. Montreal: Éditions Nouvelle Optique.

Pevere, Geoff, and Greig Dymond. 1996. *Mondo Canuck: A Canadian Pop Culture Odyssey*. Scarborough, ON: Prentice Hall.

Pidduck, Julianne. 2004. "New Queer Cinema and Experimental Video." In Michele Aaron, ed., *The New Queer Cinema Reader*, 80–100. Edinburgh: Edinburgh University Press.

Pître, Martin. 1995. *L'Ennemi que je connais*. Moncton: Perce-Neige.

Plummer, Kenneth. 1995. *Telling Sexual Stories: Power, Change and Social Worlds*. New York and London: Routledge.

Pomerance, Murray, ed. 2001. *Ladies and Gentlemen, Boys and Girls: Gender in Film at the End of the Twentieth Century*. Albany, NY: State University of New York Press.

Pronger, Brian. 1992. *The Arena of Masculinity: Sports, Homosexuality and the Meaning of Sex*. New York: St Martin's Press.

Rabinovitz, Lauren, 1991. *Points of Resistance: Women, Power, and Politics in the New York Avant-Garde Cinema, 1943–71*. Urbana, IL: University of Illinois Press.

Ramsay, Christine. 1999. "Dead Queers: One Legacy of the Trope of 'Mind Over Matter.'" *Canadian Journal of Film Studies* 8, no. 1 (spring): 45–62.

Rayns, Tony. 1994. "Everybody Knows." *Sight and Sound*, 5 September, 9.

Redding, Judith M., and Victoria A. Brownsworth. 1997. *Film Fatales: Independent Women Directors*. Seattle: Seal Press.

Refigured Histories, Remembered Pasts. 1997. Curated by Robert W.G. Lee.

Published in conjunction with the exhibibiton Refigured Histories Remembered Pasts shown at the Galerie du Centre des arts Saidye Bronfman in Montreal, Quebec, 1997.

Reinke, Steve and Tom Taylor. 2000. *LUX: A Decade of Artist's Film and Video.* Toronto: YY2 Books and Pleasure Dome.

Renov, Michael, and Erika Suderburg. 1996. *Resolutions: Contemporary Video Practices.* Minneapolis and London: University of Minnesota Press.

Rich, B. Ruby. 1999. "Collision, Catastrophe, Celebration: The Relationship between Gay and Lesbian Film Festivals and Their Publics." *GLQ: A Journal of Lesbian and Gay Studies* 5, no. 1: 79–84.

Riordan, Michael. 1977. "How Can You Argue with Success?" *The Body Politic* 37 (October): 14–15, 23.

Rist, Harry Peter, ed. 2001. *Guide to the Cinema(s) of Canada.* Westport, CT: Greenwood Press.

Ross, Becki L. (1990) 1996. "Having the Last Laugh: The Independent Video Production of Margaret Moores and Almerinda Travassos." *Fuse,* June/July, 26–9. Reprinted in Peggy Gale and Lisa Steele, eds., *Video Re/View: The (Best) Source for Critical Writings on Canadian Artists' Video,* 391–7. Toronto: Art Metropole and VTape.

– 1995. *The House That Jill Built: A Lesbian Nation in Formation.* Toronto: University of Toronto Press.

Ross, Christine. 1995. *"Je vais vous raconter une histoire de fantômes:" Vidéos de Nelson Henricks.* Montreal: Oboro.

Ross, Sinclair. 1968. "Cornet at Night." In *The Lamp at Noon and Other Stories,* 29–45. Toronto: McClelland and Stewart.

Roud, Richard. 1966. "The Cannes Festival." *Sight and Sound* 35, no. 3 (summer): 154.

Rousseau, Bernard. 1999. *La Petite histoire de Priape.* Montreal: Fugues.

Roy, André. 2001. "La dérive des corps et des sentiments." *24 images* 101 (Spring): 41.

Rubin, Gayle S. (1982) 1993. "Thinking Sex: Notes for a Radical Theory of the Politics of Sexuality." In Henry Abelove, Michèle Aina Barale and David M. Halperin, eds., *The Gay and Lesbian Studies Reader,* 3–44. New York and London: Routledge.

Schaefer, Eric. 1999. *"Bold! Daring! Shocking! True!" A History of Exploitation Films, 1919–59.* Durham, NC: Duke University Press.

Schwartzwald, Robert. 1991. "Fear of Federasty: Québec's Inverted Fictions." In Hortense Spillers, ed., *Comparative American Identities: Race, Sex, and Nationality in the Modern Text,* 175–95. New York and London: Routledge.

– 1993. "'Symbolic' Homosexuality, 'False Feminine,' and the Problematics of Identity in Quebec." In Michael Warner, ed., *Fear of a Queer Planet: Queer Politics and Social Theory,* 264–299. Minneapolis: MN.

Scott, Jay. 1985. *Midnight Matinees.* Toronto: Oxford University Press.

– 1994. *Great Scott! The Best of Jay Scott's Movie Reviews.* Ed. Karen York. Toronto: McClelland and Stewart.

Sedgwick, Eve Kosofsky. 1985. *Between Men: English Literature and Male Homosocial Desire.* New York: Columbia University Press.

– 1990. *Epistemology of the Closet.* Berkeley and Los Angeles: University of California Press.

– 1992. "Nationalisms and Sexualities in the Age of Wilde." In Andrew Parker, ed., *Nationalisms and Sexualities*. New York and London: Routledge.

– 1993a. "Queer Performativity: Henry James's *Art of the Novel*." GLQ: *A Journal of Lesbian and Gay Studies* 1, no. 1: 1–18.

– 1993b. *Tendencies*. Durham, NC: Duke University Press, 1993.

Setliff, Eric. 1999. "Sex Fiends or Swish Kids? Gay Men in *Hush Free Press*, 1946–1956." In Kathryn MacPherson, Cecilia Morgan, and Nancy M. Forestell, eds., *Gendered Pasts: Historical Essays in Femininity and Masculinity in Canada*, 158–78. Toronto: Oxford University Press.

Shilts, Randy. 1987. *And the Band Played On: Politics, People, and the AIDS Epidemic*. New York: St Martin's Press.

Simpson, Mark. 1994. *Male Impersonators: Men Performing Masculinity*. New York: Routledge.

Shogan, Debra. 2002–3. "Queering Pervert City." *Torquere: Journal of the Canadian Lesbian and Gay Studies Association* 4–5: 110–24.

Slonowski, Jeanette, and Jean Nicks, eds. 2002. *Slippery Pastimes: Reading the Popular in Canadian Culture*. Waterloo, ON: Wilfrid Laurier University Press.

Smith, Miriam. 1999. *Lesbian and Gay Rights in Canada: Social Movements and Equality-Seeking, 1971–95*. Toronto, Buffalo, and London: University of Toronto Press.

Sobchack, Vivian. 1997. "Baseball in the Post-American Cinema, or Life in the Minor Leagues." In Aron Baker and Todd Boyd, eds., *Out of Bounds: Sports, Media and the Politics of Identity*, 179–90. Bloomington: Indiana University Press.

Steven, Peter. 1996. "The Art of Calculated Risk: Richard Fung's *Dirty Laundry*." POV (Toronto), no. 29 (spring): 30–3.

Stychin, Carl F. 1998. *A Nation by Rights: National Cultures, Sexual Identity Politics, and the Discourse of Rights*. Philadelphia: Temple University Press.

Swan, Susan. 2001. "A New Prologue about the Process of the Novel Becoming a Film." *The Wives of Bath*. Toronto: Vintage. http://www.susanswanonline.com/wives_bath_adaptation.html/.

Thomas, Sheila Marie. 1994. "Speaking the Unspeakable: Annie Sprinkle's Prostitute Performances." MA thesis, University of Colorado.

Tinkcom, Matthew. 2002. *Working like a Homosexual: Camp, Capital, Cinema*. Durham, NC, and London: Duke University Press.

Treichler, Paula A. 1999. *How to Have Theory in an Epidemic: Cultural Chronicles of AIDS*. Durham, NC: Duke University Press.

Troster, Ariel. "Penetrating Power: Queer Women's Porn Plays with the Stereotypes." *The Link* (Concordia University): 1 November 1999.

Véronneau, Pierre, ed. 1991. *À la recherche d'une identité: renaissance du cinéma d'auteur canadien-anglais*. Montreal: Cinémathèque québécoise.

Villarejo, Amy. 1999. "Forbidden Love: Pulp as Lesbian History." In Ellis Hanson, ed., *Out Takes: Essays on Queer Theory and Film*, 316–45. Durham, NC: Duke University Press.

Vogel, Amos. 1974. *Film as a Subversive Art*. New York: Random House.

Walcott, Rinaldo, ed. 2000. *Rude: Contemporary Black Canadian Culture Criticism*. Toronto: Insomniac Press.

– 2003. *Black Like Who? Writing Black Canada*. 2d ed. Toronto: Insomniac Press.

Wall, David. 2003. "Opera Games." In John Greyson, *Fig Trees: A Video Opera*, 17–22. Oakville, ON: Oakville Galleries.

Warner, Tom. 2002. *Never Going Back: A History of Queer Activism in Canada.* Toronto, Buffalo and London: University of Toronto Press.

Waugh, Thomas. 1981. "Nègres blancs, tapettes et butch: Images des lesbiennes et des gais dans le cinéma québécois." *Copie zéro* (October): 12–9.

– (1988a) 2000. "Reclaiming McLaren and Jutra." *Rites* 4, no. 10 (April), 10–11; rpt. Waugh 2000, 195–207.

– 1988b. *Too Outrageous!* [review], *Cinema Canada* 155 (September), 40.

– 1990. "Words of Command': Notes on Cultural and Political Inflections of Direct Cinema in Indian Independent Documentary." *Cineaction!* 23 (winter): 28–39.

– 1992. "Erotic Self-Images in the Gay Male AIDS Melodrama." In James Miller, ed., *Fluid Exchanges: Artists and Critics in the Aids Crisis*, 122–34. Toronto: University of Toronto Press.

– 1993. "Cultivated Colonies: Notes on Queer Nationhood and the Erotic Image." *Canadian Journal of Film Studies* 2, nos. 2–3 (fall): 145–78.

– 1993. "The Third Body: Patterns in the Construction of the Male Body in Homerotic Photography and Film." In John Greyson et al., eds., *Queer Looks: Perspectives on Lesbian and Gay Film and Video*, 149–50. London and New York: Routledge.

– 1996. *Hard to Imagine: Gay Male Eroticism in Photography and Film from Their Beginnings to Stonewall.* New York: Columbia University Press.

– 1998a. "Good Clean Fung." *Wide Angle* 20, no. 2 (April), 164–75. A Festschrift in Honor of Erik Barnouw on the Occasion of his Ninetieth Birthday.

– 1998b. "'Effigies de nos Adonis en quête d'immortalité': La photographie homoérotique à Montréal, 1950–1965." In Frank Remiggi and Irène Demczuk, eds., *Sortir de l'ombre. Histoires des communautés lesbienne et gaie montréalaises depuis les années 1950*, 53–80. Montreal: VLB.

– 1999. "Cinemas, Nations, Masculinities (The Martin Walsh Memorial Lecture, 1998)." *Canadian Journal of Film Studies* 8, no. 1 (spring): 8–44.

– 2000. *The Fruit Machine: Twenty Years of Writings on Queer Cinema.* Durham, NC, and London: Duke University Press.

– 2001. "Queer Film Anthologies." *Sexualities* 4, no. 1 (February): 109–15.

– 2002. *Out/Lines: Underground Gay Graphics from before Stonewall.* Vancouver: Arsenal Pulp Press.

Waugh, Thomas, and Joyce Rock. 1981. "Gays Set the Record Straight (on the CBC's *Sharing the Secret*)." *Cinema Canada*, no. 73 (April), 32–3.

Weeks, Jeffrey. 1985. *Sexuality and Its Discontents: Meanings, Myths and Modern Sexualities.* London: Routledge and Kegan Paul, 1985.

Whitaker, Reg, and Gary Marcuse. 1994. *The Making of a National Insecurity State, 1945–57.* Toronto: University of Toronto Press.

Williams, Linda. (1989) 1999. *Hard Core: Power, Pleasure, and the "Frenzy of the Visible."* Expanded edition. Berkeley: University of California Press.

Wilson, Elizabeth, and Angela Weir. 1992. "The Greyhound Bus Station in the Evolution of Lesbian Popular Culture." In Sally Munt, ed., *New Lesbian Criticism: Literary and Cultural Readings*, 95–114 New York: Columbia University Press.

Wise, Wyndham. 1998. "*Take One*'s Top 20 Canadian Films of All Time." *Take One* 6, no. 19 (spring): 18–24.

– ed. 2001. *Take One's Essential Guide to Canadian Film*. Toronto: University of Toronto Press.

Wong, Paul, cur. and ed. 1990. *Yellow Peril Reconsidered*. Published in conjunction with the exhibition Yellow Peril Reconsidered shown at the Prim Gallery in Montreal and other venues.

Wood, Robin. 1978. "Responsibilities of a Gay Film Critic." *Film Comment* 14, no. 1 (January-February): 12–17.

Wood, Robin, and Richard Lippe. 1979. "Saying Goodbye to John Wayne." *The Body Politic* 52 (May): 30.

Zinovich, Jordan. 1994. "Canadas." Special issue, *Semiotext(e)* 17.

Index